D0742881

The Thirty-Year Genocide

THE THIRTY-YEAR GENOCIDE

Turkey's Destruction of
Its Christian Minorities,
1894–1924

BENNY MORRIS & DROR ZE'EVI

HARVARD UNIVERSITY PRESS

Cambridge, Massachusetts, and London, England

2019

First printing

Library of Congress Cataloging-in-Publication Data

Names: Morris, Benny, 1948– author. | Ze'evi, Dror, 1953– author.

Title: The thirty-year genocide : Turkey's destruction of its Christian
   minorities, 1894–1924 / Benny Morris and Dror Ze'evi.

Description: Cambridge, Massachusetts : Harvard University Press, 2019. |
   Includes bibliographical references and index.

Identifiers: LCCN 2018028342 | ISBN 9780674916456 (alk. paper)

Subjects: LCSH: Religious minorities—Turkey—History—19th century. |
   Religious minorities—Turkey—History—20th century. |
   Genocide—Turkey—Religious aspects—Christianity. |
   Genocide—Turkey—History—19th century. | Genocide—Turkey—History—20th
   century. | Christians—Turkey—History—19th century. |
   Christians—Turkey—History—20th century. |
   Persecution—Turkey—History—19th century. |
   Persecution—Turkey—History—20th century. | Armenian question. |
   Kemalism.

Classification: LCC DR576 .M6725 2019 | DDC 364.15/10956109041—dc23
   LC record available at https://lccn.loc.gov/2018028342

For my grandchildren,
Eliya and Stavi,
Ayala, Zohar, and Matan
Haleli, Eden, Nuri, and Kedem

Benny

And for mine,
Itamar and Roee

Dror

Contents

Glossary

Words in Turkish are rendered in modern Romanized Turkish orthography. In this system *c* is pronounced *j* in English; *ç* is pronounced *ch;* *ğ* is usually unvocalized and lengthens the preceding vowel; and *ı* (undotted) is pronounced as the vowel *u* in the word *turn*. When a non-Turkish version is commonly used, the Turkish version is given in parentheses.

aga (ağa)	(Kurdish) chieftain
amele taburları	labor battalions
amira	an Armenian notable, in the service of the Ottoman state
bashi bazouk (başıbozuk)	irregular soldier, sometimes brigand
cavass (kavas)	ceremonial guard at an embassy or consulate
çete (cheteh)	brigand, guerrilla, gangs
chiftlik (çiftlik, jiftlik)	large farm, estate
Dashnak (Dashnaksutyun)	political party, federation, short for Armenian Revolutionary Federation or ARF
dhimmi	legal system whereby non-Muslims are protected by Muslim states in exchange for undertaking certain obligations
dragoman (tercüman)	embassy translator (and often negotiator on behalf of the embassy with the authorities)
Emniyet / Emniyet-i Umumiye Müdüriyeti	Interior Ministry's Public Security Directorate
emvāl-ı metruke	abandoned property
eşkiya (eshkiya)	rebels, mutineers
esnaf	artisans, or guilds of merchants and artisans

fatwa (fetva)	an opinion on a point of Islamic law given by a recognized authority
ferik	lieutenant general (army rank)
firman (fırman)	sultan's decree
giaour (gavur or kafir)	infidel, heathen (derogatory); in colloquial speech also "infidel dog," merciless, cruel
hafir, ghafir	protection tax paid by Armenian villagers to tribes in their vicinity
hamal	porter, stevedore
Hunchak, Hanchak	Clarion, or Bell; name of an Armenian opposition party
halal	permitted according to sharia law
hodja (hoca)	title for a teacher, Islamic leader
iltizam	tax farm, state lease of taxes
irâde	sultan's command, declaration
İskan-ı Aşayir ve Muhacirin Müdüriyeti	Directorate for Settlement of Tribes and Muhacirs, previously, "muhâcirin komisyonu"
İttihad ve Terakki Cemiyeti	Committee of Union and Progress (the Young Turk party)
kadi (cadi)	religious judge
kaymakam (kaimakam)	town or sub-district governor, acting governor
kaza (caza)	sub-district
khan (han, kervanseray)	inn
komiteci (komiteji)	member of (usually Armenian) revolutionary committee, or rebel group
konak	government house, residence
masbata (mazbata)	record of testimony, or official report
madrassa (medresseh, medrese)	Muslim religious school or seminary
millet	religious community / nation, often referring to Ottoman non-Muslim communities
muavin	aide, assistant
mudir (müdür)	director, commissioner, administrator, sometimes commander
muezzin	a crier who calls Muslims to prayer
mufti (müftü)	Muslim cleric, often a state employee, and issuer of fatwas

muhacir (muhajir)	immigrant, used almost exclusively in reference to Muslim refugees
mullah (mollah)	high-ranking kadi, priest
multazim (mültezim)	one leasing the right to collect taxes in a certain area
muşir (mushir)	general, marshal (army rank)
mutesarrif (mutasarrıf)	district governor
mutesarriflik (mutasarrıflik)	district
padishah	sultan
raya (rayah, reaya)	non-Muslim subjects of the sultan, sheep
sanjak (sancak, liva)	district
sharia	Muslim law
softa	Muslim seminarian
tabur	battalion
Tanzimat	reforms, usually referring to a series of reforms undertaken by the Ottoman state from 1839 to 1876
tekkeh (tekke)	dervish lodge, place of Sufi congregation
teşkilat	organization
Teşkilat-ı mahsusa	Special Organization
tezkereh (tezkere)	travel permit
Turan	the imagined ancient homeland of the Turkic peoples
ulema (ulama)	(council of) Muslim theological experts; Muslim priests or teachers
vali	provincial governor (governor-general)
vilayet	province
zaptiyeh	police force, gendarmerie; also police officer, gendarme

Place Names

Many of the villages mentioned in this study no longer exist; the names of many others have changed (usually from Greek or Armenian to Turkish). The alphabet reform in the 1920s (from Arabic-Ottoman script to an adapted Latin alphabet) affected the transliteration of place names. Wherever we could locate the Turkish name we include it in parentheses. If the current name is well known, we use that instead of an old transliteration.

English common name WWI	Ottoman name (simplified)	Turkish name	Armenian, Arabic, Greek, Syriac, Latin, or Kurdish name	Variations
Ada Bazaar	Adapazarı	Adapazarı		
Adana	Adana	Adana	Arm.: Atana	
Adrianople	Edirne	Edirne	Grk.: Adrianopolis	
Aidin	Aydın	Aydın		
Aintab	Ayntab	Antep, Gaziantep	Arab.: ʿAyntāb	
Alania	Alanya	Alanya		
Al-Bab, El-Bab	Al-Bab	Al-Bab	Arab.: Al-Bāb	
Aleppo	Haleb	Alep	Arab.: Halab	Alep
Alexandretta	Iskenderun	Iskenderun	Grk.: Alexandretta	
Amasia	Amasya	Amasya		
Angora	Ankara	Ankara	Latin: Angora	
Antalya, Attalia, Adalia	Antalya	Antalya	Grk.: Attaleia	
Antioch	Antakya	Antakya	Grk.: Antiocheia	
Arapgir, Arapkir	Arapgir	Arapgir	Arab.: Arabgir	
Bafra	Bafra	Bafra		Baffra
Baiburt	Bayburt		Grk.: Paipert	
Batman	Batman	Batman		
Bilijik, Bilejik	Bilecik	Bilecik		
Birejik, Biregik	Birecik	Birecik	Grk.: Birtha Arab.: Birha	

(Continued)

English common name WWI	Ottoman name (simplified)	Turkish name	Armenian, Arabic, Greek, Syriac, Latin, or Kurdish name	Variations
Bitlis	Bitlis	Bitlis	Syr.: Bet Dlis Arm.: Paghesh	
Bodrum	Bodrum	Bodrum	Latin: Petronium	Bodroum, Boudrum
Bolu, Bolou	Bolu	Bolu		Bolou
Broussa	Bursa	Bursa	Grk.: Prusa	
Caesarea	Kayseri	Kayseri	Grk.: Caesarea	
Chanakkale (Chanak)	Çanakkale	Çanakkale	Grk.: Dardanellia	
Chankiri	Çankiri	Çankiri		
Cheshme	Çeşme	Çeşme	Grk.: Cysus, Kysos	
Constantinople	Istanbul	Istanbul		
Damascus	Şam	Şam	Arab.: Dimashq / Shām	
Deir Zor	Der Zor	Zor	Arab.: Dayr al-Zawr / Deir al-Zor	
Dersim	Dersim	Tunceli	Kurd.: Dersim / Zaza: Desim	
Develi	Develi	Develi	Arm.: Everek / Evereg	
Diarbekir	Diyarbekir	Diyarbakır	Kurd. and Grk.: Amid / Amed	
Dortyeul	Dörtyol	Dörtyol	Arm.: Chorkmarzban	
Elbistan (Albistan)	Elbistan	Elbistan	Grk. and Arm.: Plastha / Ablastha	
Erzinjan	Erzincan	Erzincan	Arm.: Yerznka Grk.: Celtzene	
Erzurum, Erzerum	Erzerum	Erzurum	Arm.: Karin Grk.: Theodosiopolis	
Eski Shehir	Eskişehir	Eskişehir	Grk.: Dorylaeum	
Gallipoli	Gelibolu	Gelibolu	Grk.: Kallipolis	
Gebze	Gebze	Gebze	Grk.: Dakibyssa	
Geuljuk (?)	Gölcük	Gölcük		
Gumushane	Gümüşhane	Gümüşhane		
Hadjin	Hacin	Hacin, Saimbeyli		
Hakkari	Hakkari	Hakkari	Kurd.: Colemêrg	Hakkiari
Hasaka	Hasaka	Hasaka		
Idlib	Idlib	Idlib	Arab.: Idlib	
Ismid, Nicomedia	Izmit	Izmit	Grk.: Nikomedeia	Ismit
Janik	Canik	Canik		
Jizre / Jazira	Cizre	Cizre	Grk.: Gazarta Arab.: Jazirat ibn 'Umar	
Karaman	Karaman	Karaman		

(Continued)

English common name WWI	Ottoman name (simplified)	Turkish name	Armenian, Arabic, Greek, Syriac, Latin, or Kurdish name	Variations
Karesi	Karesi	Karesi		
Kemach / Kamach	Kemah	Kemah	Arm.: Ani-Kamach	
Kerasund (Karsund, Kerasaund)	Giresun	Giresun	Grk.: Kerasund	
Kharpert	Harput	Elazığ	Arm.: Kharpert	
Kilis, Killis	Kilis	Kilis		
Kırklaleli	Kırkkilise	Kırklareli	Grk.: Saranta Ekklisies	
Kirshehir	Kirşehir	Kirşehir		
Konia / Iconium	Konya	Konya	Grk.: Ikonion	
Kutahia	Kütahya	Kütahya	Byz.: Cotyaeum	
Livissi	Livissi	Kayaköy	Grk.: Livissi	
Magnesia, Manissa	Manisa	Manisa	Grk.: Magnesia	
Makri	Fethiye	Fethiye	Grk.: Makri	
Malatia	Malatya	Malatya	Grk.: Malateia	
Mamouretulaziz, Mamuret	Mamuretülaziz	Elazığ		
Marash	Maraş	Kahramanmaraş	Arab.: Mar'ash	
Mardin	Mardin	Mardin	Kurd.: Merdin	
Marsovan	Merzifon	Merzifon	Grk.: Mersyphon Persian: Merzban	Marsuvan Mersivan
Menteshe	Menteşe	Menteşe		
Mersina (Mersine)	Mersin	Mersin	Grk.: Zephyrion Latin: Hadrianopolis	
Mezreh (Mamuret ul Aziz)	Mezre	Mezre		
Midyat	Midyat	Midyat	Kurd.: Medyad	
Mossoul	Mosul	Mosul	Arab.: Al-Mawsil Syr.: Ninwe	
Moush, Mush	Muş	Muş	Kurd.: Mush	
Nicaea	Iznik	Iznik	Grk.: Nicaea	
Nigde	Niğde	Niğde	Grk.: Magida	
Nizip	Nizip	Nizip	Latin(?): Nisibis	Sometimes mistaken for Nusaybin
Ordou	Ordu	Ordu		
Osmaniye	Osmaniye	Osmaniye		
Osmanjik	Osmancık	Osmancık		
Osmanli	Osmanlı	Osmanlı		
Pergamon, Pergama	Bergama	Bergama	Grk.: Pergamon	
Phocia	Foça	Foça		Fogia
Pozanti	Pozantı	Pozantı	Grk.: Pendhosis	Bozantı

(Continued)

English common name WWI	Ottoman name (simplified)	Turkish name	Armenian, Arabic, Greek, Syriac, Latin, or Kurdish name	Variations
Rakka	Rakka	Rakka		
Rasulayn	Re'sülayn	Rasülayin	Arab.: Rās al-'Ayn	
Rize	Rize	Rize		
Rodosto	Tekirdağ Rodosçuk	Tekirdağ	Grk.: Rhaedestus, Biysanthe	
Samsun, Samsoun, Sampsoun	Samsun	Samsun	Grk.: Amisos	
Sassoun	Sasun	Sason	Arm.: Sasun	Sasson, Sasoun
Scutari	Üsküdar	Üsküdar	Grk.: Skoutarion	
Sharkeuy(?)	Şarköy	Şarköy		
Sinope	Sinob	Sinop	Grk.: Sinope	
Sis	Sis	Sis		
Sivas	Sivas	Sivas	Latin: Sebastia	Sebastea, Sebasteia, Sebaste
Smyrna	Izmir	Izmir	Grk.: Smyrna	
Talas	Talas	Talas	Grk.: Dalassa	
Talori	Talori	Talori		
Tarsus	Tarsus	Tarsus	Grk.: Tarsos	
Tirebolu / Tripoli	Tirebolu	Tirebolu	Grk.: Tripoli	
Tokat	Tokat	Tokat	Grk.: Evdokia	
Trebizond	Trabzon	Trabzon	Grk.: Trapezunt / Trapezous	
Urfa, Edessa	Urfa	Şanlıurfa	Grk.: Edessa Kurd.: Riha	
Van	Van	Van	Kurd.: Wan	
Viranshehir	Viranşehir	Viranşehir		
Yalova	Yalova	Yalova	Grk.: Pylae	
Yenikeuy	Yeniköy	Yeniköy		
Yozgat	Yozgat	Yozgat		
Zeitoun	Zeytun	Süleymanlı	Arab.: Zaytūn Arm.: Zeytun	Zeytoun
Zonguldak	Zonguldak	Zonguldak		

Introduction

We embarked on this project in quest of the truth about what happened to the Ottoman Armenians during World War I. Most Western scholarship on the subject has concluded that the Ottoman Empire, exploiting the fog and exigencies of war, carried out a genocidal campaign that resulted in a million or so Armenian dead. Turkish and pro-Turkish scholars have argued that Turkey, embattled by the British and Russian empires, was assailed from within by treacherous Armenians and simply defended itself. On this view, thousands of Armenians died amid deportation from troublesome combat zones, while the Turks suffered significant casualties at Armenian hands. Turning to the available contemporary documentation, we set out to discover for ourselves what had actually happened, and why.

We found the proofs of Turkey's 1915–1916 anti-Armenian genocide to be incontrovertible. The reports by Leslie Davis, the U.S. wartime consul in Harput, in central Turkey, offer a good illustration. Davis was no "Armenian-lover"; in December 1915 he questioned Armenians' moral fiber, writing, "Mothers have given their daughters to the lowest and vilest Turks to save their own lives . . . lying and trickery and an inordinate love of money are besetting sins of almost all. . . . Absolute truthfulness is almost unknown among the members of this race. . . . From every point of view the race is one that cannot be admired."[1] But he did not let his prejudices cloud his eyesight. During the deportations Davis sent home dozens of reports describing the Turkish atrocities, which he summarized in a conclusive memorandum in early 1918. In these reports he recalled observations such as that of September 24, 1915, when he toured the area southeast of Harput, around Lake Gölcük (Hazar Gölü), accompanied by the American missionary Dr. Henry Atkinson:

> We saw [dead bodies] all along the road. They . . . had been partially
> eaten by dogs. . . . There were several hundred bodies scattered over the
> plain . . . [mostly] of women and children. . . . Some of the bodies . . .
> had been burned . . . [by] Kurds . . . in order to find any gold which the
> people may have swallowed. . . . In most of [the lakeside] valleys there
> were dead bodies. . . . In one [valley] . . . there were more than fifteen
> hundred. . . . The stench . . . was . . . great . . . I explored [this valley]
> more carefully a month later. . . . [An old Kurd] . . . told us that the gen-
> darmes had brought a party of about two thousand Armenians . . . and
> had made the Kurds from the neighboring villages come and kill
> them. . . . He acted very indignant . . . as he said the smell of their dead
> bodies was very disagreeable.

The old man also described a "system" whereby Armenians were massacred. They were, he said,

> allowed to camp for a day or two in the valleys. . . . The gendarmes
> summoned the [local] Kurds . . . and ordered them to kill [the Arme-
> nians]. . . . An agreement was then made by which the Kurds were to
> pay the gendarmes a certain fixed sum—a few hundred pounds, or more,
> depending on circumstances—and were to have for themselves whatever
> they found on the bodies . . . in excess of that sum.

Davis learned "that the people were forced to take off their clothes before they were killed, as the Mahommedans consider the clothes taken from a dead body to be defiled." Most of the dead had "bayonet wounds. . . . Few had been shot, as bullets were too precious. . . . Nearly all of the women lay flat on their backs and showed signs of barbarous mutilation."[2]

One of these lakeside massacres was witnessed by three Europeans on September 17, a week before Davis's first trek. They saw Kurds on the hills above the lake shoot up a large Armenian convoy and then, bearing axes, attack the "defenseless flock" like "ferocious animals." Kurdish women ran down the hillside to "strip the bodies."[3]

What happened at Lake Gölcük in August–September 1915 was emblematic of the Armenian Genocide. But we discovered that the Armenian Genocide of 1915–1916 was only part of the story, a story that began decades before and extended for years afterward. The story is both deeper and wider than the Armenian Genocide. It is deeper in the sense that the events of 1915–1916 were part of a protracted history of violence; one has to look at Turkish behavior before and after World War I in order to understand what happened during the war years. And it is wider in the sense that one also has to look at how Turkey dealt with its other Christian minorities, Greeks and various Assyrian (or Syriac or Syrian) communities.[4] This larger story extends from the prewar years under Sultan Abdülhamid II through the wartime dominance of the Committee of Union and Progress (CUP) and the immediate postwar rise of the Turkish Nationalists led by Mustafa Kemal Ataturk. We found that, under each government, Muslim Turks—including the political leaders and everyday citizens—came to see Asia Minor's Christian communities as a danger to their state's survival and resolved to be rid of this danger. In line with changing political, military, and demographic circumstances, the successive regimes dealt with Christian communities somewhat differently, though to the same end. In the course of three campaigns beginning in 1894, the Turks turned variously to tools of steady oppression, mass murder, attrition, expulsion, and forced conversion. By 1924 they had cleansed Asia Minor of its four million–odd Christians.

This book is structured in accordance with the staggered nature of the Turkish campaign. There are chapters on the pre-1894 background; the massacres of 1894–1896; the Armenian Genocide of 1915–1916; and the destruction of the Greeks, Assyrians, and remaining Armenians in 1919–1924. The coverage of 1915–1916 is relatively modest in light of recent, perceptive, and comprehensive scholarship on the Armenian Genocide by Raymond Kevorkian, Donald Bloxham, Taner Akçam, Ronald Grigor Suny, and others.[5] By contrast, historians have devoted little attention to what happened in 1894–1896 and 1919–1924, and almost none to what befell Turkey's Greeks and Assyrians during this thirty-year period. We tackle these subjects in great detail.

If other historians have not treated the entire thirty-year scope of oppression and carnage as one continuous saga, they arguably have good reasons. For one thing, the period spans three very different regimes: that of the last autocratic sultan, until 1909; of the CUP, or Young Turks, who ruled during the Great War after promising equality and supranational constitutionalism; and of Mustafa Kemal, the war hero and founder of modern Turkey during 1919–1924. For another, each regime had different aims and constituencies. The CUP and Ataturk each accused their predecessors of unnecessary cruelty toward non-Muslims. Indeed, Ataturk is famously credited with labeling the mass murder of Armenians during World War I a "shameful act."

The traditional interpretation thus identifies three separate policies carried out according to distinctive logics tailored to their particular circumstances. The massacres of the 1890s are usually understood as Abdülhamid's effort to cow disruptive Christians into submission. The 1915–1916 genocide is depicted as a momentary war-induced aberration. And the ethnic cleansing during 1919–1924, which resulted in hundreds of thousands of deaths, is portrayed as part of a chaotic, multisided bloodletting triggered by foreign invasions and the reactive Turkish war of national liberation.

But from the documentation now available, it is clear that treating the three periods separately obfuscates the reality of what the Turks intended and what transpired. Nor does it make sense to view what happened to each of the victim communities—Armenians, Greeks, and Assyrians—in isolation. To be sure, the Turkish project evolved over time. What appeared to Abdülhamid and his entourage as a vague and disembodied idea in the 1890s crystallized under the Young Turks into a full-fledged genocidal program, with the last nails hammered into the coffin during Kemal's National Struggle. Each regime confronted a different cluster of dangers, acted under different constraints, and imagined a different future. Ultimately, however, all three engaged in a giant and continuous crime against humanity.

The Armenians were the main victims of Turkish atrocity, in terms of the numbers slaughtered in 1894–1896 and 1915–1916. Certainly, the Turks appear to have hated them the most. This is cogently illustrated by events in Smyrna (Izmir) in September 1922. There, conquering Turkish troops murdered thousands of Armenian inhabitants before dealing with the town's Greeks, even though the retreating Greeks had just (unsystematically) massacred hundreds, and perhaps thousands, of Turks on the outskirts of the city. Still, tens of thousands of Greeks would be murdered during the following days. Smyrna would prove to be merely one chapter in the destruction and expulsion of Anatolia's vast Greek minority, which had begun before the Great War, in the first months of 1914.

As we hope to show, the annihilation of the Christian communities was not the product of a single cause. At play were fears of foreign machinations and interference, Turkish nationalism, ethnic rivalries, economic envy, and a desire to maintain political and social dominance. Perpetrators sought power, wealth, and sexual gratification. A combination of these motivations was manifest in each period and location. In the course of our research we have also concluded that these forces were joined by another overarching element: Islam. As an ethos and an ideology, Islam played a cardinal role throughout the process, in each of its stages.

We are not arguing here that Islam is a single dogma, worse than other religious dogmas. Islam has various streams, and individual Muslims feel differently about questions of practice, scriptural interpretation, and moral behavior. Inherent in Islam are humanistic and moderate traditions, and, as we emphasize in our conclusion, Christians lived in relative security under Ottoman rule for centuries. Indeed, their standing was probably more secure than that of Jews or Muslims under Christian governments during the same centuries.

Yet there is compelling evidence showing that Islam was an important driver in the events and processes described in this book. Ottoman authorities invoked jihad to mobilize the Muslim masses to massacre and plunder. Perpetrators cited jihad and Muslim law more generally to explain and justify their actions, even to argue that these actions were obligatory. Moreover, Muslim religious leaders and seminarians were prominent figures in the massacres. Indeed, even during Kemal's ostensibly secularist National Struggle, officials, himself included, frequently referred to Islam as the basis of their actions. These same officials described the massacres of thousands of Christians, and the expulsions of hundreds of thousands more, as jihad. Islam was the glue that bound together perpetrating Turks, Kurds, Circassians, Chechens, and Arabs and was the common marker of identity separating them from their Christian victims. In 1894–1896, 1915–1918, and 1919–1924, conversion to Islam was often the only path to survival for Christians who remained in the empire.

The Sources

This study focuses on what happened in Asia Minor and Constantinople, with more limited treatment of events in eastern Thrace (specifically, the vilayet of Edirne) and in the northwestern corner of Persia. We refrain almost completely from covering events in the Caucasus, despite the fact that this remote mountainous region was periodically engulfed in warfare among Turks, Russians, Azeris, Armenians, Georgians, and other groups, with accompanying large-scale massacres by all who participated. What happened in the Caucasus requires a study of its own, partly because these events were not synchronic with those in Asia Minor, and partly because the relevant archival material is often inaccessible or written in languages with which we are unfamiliar.

Focusing on Asia Minor and Constantinople, one also encounters serious archival problems. To some degree, these affected our research and writing and so need to be described and explained.

The Ottoman Empire, and later Turkey, had large, organized bureaucracies churning out massive amounts of state papers, which eventually made their way to a number of archives. The most important are the Ottoman Archives of the Office of the Prime Minister (Başbakanlık Osmanlı Arşivleri) and the archive of the General Staff Military History and Strategy (Genelkurmay Askeri Tarih ve Stratejik Etüt) Institute in Ankara. The military archive is in effect closed to researchers. And the prime ministry's archives, as well as smaller provincial archives, have undergone several bouts of purging, starting with the weeding out of records by exiting CUP officials at the end of World War I. Since then, Turkish officials have further sanitized the archives so that researchers today will find almost no documentation incriminating Ottoman Turkish leaders in the ethnic cleansings between 1894 and 1924. Similarly, the many volumes of state documents covering these years, which the Turkish government has published over the past few decades, contain almost no direct evidence of Turkish culpability.

While much has been whitewashed, a good deal was never archived in the first place. Knowing that they were ordering or engaged in criminal activity, the political leaders in Constantinople and in the provinces, often in real time, ordered all copies of telegrams destroyed after reading. Sometimes they transmitted instructions orally, to avoid leaving paper trails, or used euphemisms to camouflage their intentions and deeds. The same, apparently, is true of reports going up the chain of command, from local officials and commanders to Constantinople.[6]

A scholar relying only, or principally, on Turkish state archives and published Turkish official volumes will inevitably produce highly distorted history of Turkish-Christian relations from the beginning of the Hamidian period, in 1876, until the end of the ethnic cleansing in 1924. Countless Turkish and "pro-Turkish" historians have done just that.

How do we know that the Ottoman and Turkish archives have been purged of incriminating materials? There are some clear indications. First, hundreds of large-scale massacres were committed throughout the period we have studied. This is no longer a matter of opinion, and even those who claim that there was no deliberate and organized genocide do not question that many massacres took place. Yet in all the accessible archival and published documentation on the events of 1914–1916, there are just a handful of mentions of "improper treatment." In the only such accessible Turkish document openly admitting a massacre by the Ottoman side, a cabinet minister berates a governor for also murdering non-Armenians, in contravention of his orders.

Second, senior officials resisting orders to deport and massacre were recalled, punished, and replaced. Several were executed. There is hardly any mention of this in the accessible correspondence. Occasionally, the archival purge was insufficiently thorough, and one or two letters from recalcitrant governors have surfaced. But the government's responses and reactions are always missing.

Third, there is almost no mention of the actions of the Special Organization (Teşkilat-ı mahsusa), whose operatives played a prominent role in the destruction of the Armenians. Even if, as some critics argue, the Special Organization was not, as a body, part of the extermination process, the absence of Special Organization operatives and activities from the accessible documentation attests to the archival cleansing.

Fourth, according to external materials, CUP stalwarts and Special Organization executives such as Dr. Bahaettin Şakır and Dr. Selanikli Mehmet

Nâzım (Nâzım Bey) orchestrated massacres, and provincial party secretaries played key roles. Their powers often exceeded those of governors and military commanders. The archives and officially published documentation contain almost no correspondence from these CUP members and provincial secretaries.

Fifth, in the brief, largely inconclusive postwar trials conducted by the Ottoman government under Allied tutelage, a substantial number of telegrams were presented as evidence of massacres and murderous intent. Many of these documents have disappeared. Historians who present the official Turkish narrative argue that the documents were fakes.

Finally, the fact that Turkey has always barred researchers from viewing 1914–1924 materials in the Ankara military archive strongly suggests that the state is hiding something.

Akçam offers the most comprehensive description of Turkish archival manipulation and obfuscation.[7] At the end of World War I, Talât Pasha hurriedly gathered and burned every government document related to the Armenian genocide that he could find. So did the new grand vizier, Ahmet İzzet Pasha.[8] Members of the CUP Central Committee, including Nâzım, did the same for relevant CUP documentation. Purges of documentation continued in stages, long after the establishment of the republic. The archives were opened to foreign researchers in the 1980s, but only after government agents would have had a chance to locate any remaining incriminating material and ensure it would not be seen. Even as researchers were first gaining entry, it was well known that a group of retired diplomats and military officers had privileged access, which they could have used to destroy evidence.[9] On the basis of information provided by other researchers, we believe that a final purge was conducted more recently, during the digitization of the archives. Readers today initially have access only to digitized documents.

But the main reason not to trust the Turkish archives is that reliable sources contradict them. Masses of 1894–1924 German, Austro-Hungarian, British, American, and French documents, produced by diplomats and consular officials working in Turkey and available in Western archives, as well as the papers of dozens of Western missionaries who worked in Turkey during those years, tell a completely different story from the one purveyed in official, accessible Turkish papers and in Turkish nationalist narratives.

For decades, Turkish apologists and their supporters have dismissed this Western documentation as tendentious and even specious, the invention of prejudiced Christians aiming to vilify blameless Muslims. As seen from Constantinople, Britain, France, and the United States were allied against the Turks during the First World War, so their official documents must have been anti-Turkish propaganda. The Christian missionaries, most of them Americans, were deemed even worse. They were intimately connected to the Armenians and had themselves fomented anti-Turkish and anti-Muslim sentiment among Christians. How could they be expected to produce unprejudiced accounts of Turkish, Armenian, and Greek actions and thinking during the decades when Turks and Christians were busy "fighting each other"? (Turks have long, and falsely, characterized the events of this thirty-year period as mutual bloodletting and warfare rather than as genocide.)

This dismissal of American, British, and French documentation is highly problematic. For one thing, it wrongly presumes that foreign diplomatic opinion toward Turkey was uniform. There were many foreign diplomats in the Ottoman Empire—in 1905, the British alone had twenty-nine consulates—and they were not all of one mind. Most British, French, and American diplomats and consuls present during 1894–1924 probably did see the local Christians as persecuted underdogs, but others were neutral. Still others—most prominently High Commissioner Mark Bristol, the top U.S. representative in Turkey during August 1919–1927—favored the Turks and dismissed Greeks and Armenians as pusillanimous and inferior races. Bristol was not alone in harboring such sentiments.

Moreover, while many Western diplomats and officers may have shared, and even displayed, pro-Christian sympathies, almost all were professionals. They were trained and expected to report accurately what they saw, while, of course, casting a positive light on their own activities and their governments' policies. British, American, and French reporting was classified and for internal, institutional consumption, not designed to sway public opinion or international mediators. If their reports were "anti-Turkish," this was mainly because they heard about or witnessed behavior and attitudes that were brutal and often criminal.

It is particularly important that French sources corroborate stories of massacres, forced deportation, and, in general, ethnic cleansing. That is because the French were typically less "pro-Christian" than were their Anglo-Saxon allies, certainly before and after 1914–1918. French diplomacy during 1920–1924 tended to be pro-Turkish, and the French military, while fighting the Turks during 1920–1921, tended to have a jaundiced view of the Armenians, Greeks, and even the British. The French army in Turkey was largely composed of Muslim colonial troops, and their superior officers had to take these soldiers' affinity for local Muslim populations into account in their dealings with Turks.

Accusations against Christian, and especially American, missionaries are no more persuasive than those against foreign officials. Most missionaries were well-educated and liberal, albeit deeply Christian, in outlook. Diligently following Ottoman rules, they had come to work only with Christian denominations, not to illegally convert Muslims. They did wish to protect Christians from harm and often supplied them with aid, but they rarely deliberately endeavored to undermine the state. By and large their reports, like those of the diplomats and officers, were intended for internal, not outsiders', perusal. The missionaries were writing to superiors, friends, and family to inform them as accurately as possible of what they saw, heard, and understood. Few of them had great sympathy for Muslim Turks or Kurds but all shared a common fear of divine and collegial reproach and so tried to cleave to the truth.

In addition to reports from missionaries and British, French, and American diplomats, in some chapters we have used extensively reports by German and Austrian diplomats, residents, and travelers in Turkey. German-Ottoman relations began warming a few years before World War I, and Austria-Hungary and Germany were the Ottoman Empire's main allies in the war. Some officers in the higher echelons of the German army condoned the Armenian deportations; many didn't. While Germans and Austrians had nothing to gain from tarnishing the Ottoman reputation, their reports from the provinces during 1914–1918 almost invariably parallel and corroborate the findings of Allied counterparts: Muslim-Turkish genocidal and expulsionist intent and the butchery of masses of unarmed Christians. Reports and diary entries by German and Scandinavian missionaries tell the same story.

The German diplomatic reports, as well as reports by German travelers and German-linked missionaries, were assembled from the German Foreign

Ministry archive by a German scholar, Wolfgang Gust. They are published online at www.armenocide.com and in a densely packed, 786-page English translation. We have also used a similar volume of Austro-Hungarian diplomatic reports emanating from Turkey during the war.

Further corroboration comes from postwar trials of war criminals in Constantinople, memoirs and speeches by Turkish officials, and interviews published in Turkish newspapers and journals. And while, as we have noted, there are serious problems with Turkish state archives and official documentation, these are not totally useless. We have combed them thoroughly and have found documents that help explain what happened. Often they reinforce the evidence in Western sources. We have also relied on secondary literature, which, in the case of Turkish-Armenian relations during World War I, has burgeoned in recent years.

Although we have made every effort to be comprehensive in our use of archival materials, we realize that a great deal is missing. This was, after all, the intention of those covering their tracks. If more Turkish sources were available, we would have included them. We believe, though, that the documentation we have used is a sufficient basis for a credible description and analysis of what happened. The reader will judge.

I

Abdülhamid II

1

Nationalist Awakenings in the Nineteenth-Century Ottoman Empire

For many in the Ottoman Empire, the first months of 1878 were a nightmare come true. Russian artillery batteries pounded the suburbs of Constantinople, and the empire's European provinces were all but lost. Large chunks of the Caucasus and northeast Anatolia, as far as Erzurum, were overrun by the Russian army, the Ottomans' age-old nemesis. The imperial coffers were empty, and a new, authoritarian regime was doing its best to sweep away hard-won civil liberties.[1]

Only a year or so earlier, the situation looked very different. Not only was life relatively peaceful, but it also seemed that a measure of open-mindedness had taken hold. On December 23, 1876, after a century of incremental legal reforms, Turkey adopted a modern constitution. Drawn up mainly by the reformist minister Midhat Pasha and his Armenian companion Krikor Odian, the charter promised a new bill of rights for all and improved status for the empire's non-Muslim subjects. Midhat hoped that by guaranteeing certain freedoms and protections for minorities, including Christians, the empire might stave off threatened European encroachment. The constitution even placed some constraint on the sultan, forcing him to share power with a senate of grandees—albeit, subject to his own appointment—and a chamber of deputies selected by an electoral college directly elected at the provincial level.[2]

Midhat and fellow reformists had taken advantage of a moment of anarchy. In May 1876 the veteran sultan Abdülaziz, under whose reign the pace of westernization had quickened, was deposed in a coup d'état. His opponents accused him of squandering the country's assets on grand homes and grand ships. He was replaced by Murad V, his nephew, but the new sultan was ousted after only three months, when it emerged that he was mentally unstable. He was replaced by his brother, Abdülhamid II, who was believed to be sympathetic to the reformist cause.

But even as the reformists were formulating the constitution and electoral system, the stage was being set for the Russian invasion. The immediate cause was a rebellion in the Ottoman territory of Bulgaria. The empire was already on shaky ground, brought to the edge of bankruptcy by an exceptionally long dry spell and a welter of high-interest loans coming due. The Bulgarian uprising added to these considerable woes. Determined to protect his rule and his empire from existential threats, Abdülhamid responded with a hard line. He moved to crush the Bulgarian rebellion, curtail the new freedoms, reinstate

An Armenian volunteer soldier during the Balkan Wars. Some Armenians fought in the Ottoman army, while others joined Bulgarian and Russian combat units.

his authority, and restore order and discipline. He suspended the constitution; dispersed the parliament; and sent his irregulars, the Başı Bozuks, to quash the Bulgarians.

The Bulgarian suppression triggered outrage in the West, especially in Britain, where former Prime Minister William Gladstone and his opposition Liberal Party decried the cruelty of the "Turkish race" and what soon became known as the "Bulgarian atrocities." Gladstone memorably wrote of the Turks, "They were, upon the whole, from the black day when they first entered Europe, the one great anti-human specimen of humanity. Wherever they went, a broad line of blood marked the track behind them, and as far as their dominion reached, civilisation disappeared from view."[3] Outraged Europeans called for Balkan liberation from Ottoman rule.

This was the opening Russia needed. Exploiting the anti-Turkish fervor and claiming its position as standard-bearer of a new pan-Slavic consciousness, the tsar moved to rescue his Bulgarian protégés and attack a traditional foe. In April 1877 Russian forces passed through Romania and crossed the Danube. Another Russian army invaded eastern Anatolia. By summer, the Ottoman army was in retreat, and the Russians had occupied Edirne (Adrianople) and eastern Thrace. The road to Constantinople was open.

Germany, Britain, and France refused to take sides, leading to condemnation from Abdülhamid. However, notwithstanding the sultan's suspicions of collusion against him, the three powers were not in cahoots with the Russians and had no wish to see the Ottoman Empire dismantled. Britain and Germany sought to preserve the balance of power and avert a new pan-European war. They were therefore loath to get involved with Russia's adventure, which could lead to widening conflict and weaken their own positions. But as the Russians closed in on Constantinople and the Straits, European leaders took fright and successfully forced the Russians and Turks to accept a ceasefire. When that broke down, a Russian fleet descended on the Bosporus for what could have been the death blow. Finally a British squadron made for the Dardanelles. The threat persuaded the Russians to halt at San Stefano (Yeşilköy), a village near Constantinople, where they and the Turks signed the treaty that ended the war on March 3, 1878.

The Ottomans paid a steep price. They were forced to cede most of their Balkan possessions. Romania, Serbia, and Montenegro were declared independent; Bosnia and Herzegovina were to enjoy greater autonomy under Austro-Hungarian tutelage; and the Bulgarians were awarded an enlarged, autonomous principality. Russia entrenched itself in eastern Anatolia and the southern Caucasus, establishing an official presence in Kars, Batumi, and other key sites.

Some Ottoman Armenians, alienated by Abdülhamid's increasingly repressive rule, hoped to make permanent the Russian occupation in eastern Anatolia. During the San Stefano negotiations, the Armenian patriarch in Constantinople attempted to turn these hopes into reality. In a secret note sent via the exilarch, the spiritual head of the Armenian Church at Etchmiadzin, he asked the tsar to hold on to the parts of Anatolia captured in the war. The patriarch also sought Russian protection in case the treaty allowed the Ottomans to retain power over Armenians and asked the Russians to ensure that Armenians would receive the same rights as those granted the Balkan peoples. Russia, the patriarch urged, should insist on supervisory powers and Armenian security against the marauding Circassian and Kurdish tribes of the eastern provinces.[4] The patriarch didn't get everything he wanted, but Clause 16 of the treaty provided for substantive reforms in the Armenian-inhabited areas, including a larger measure of autonomy, representation in provincial governance, and security guarantees.[5]

The treaty almost immediately became a dead letter. Wary of growing Russian influence in the Balkans and eastern Anatolia, the great powers scuttled the accord a few months after it was signed. In Berlin in 1878, British Prime Minister Benjamin Disraeli and German Chancellor Otto von Bismarck agreed on a new settlement, favoring the Ottomans. Macedonia and eastern Thrace were returned, the size of the Bulgarian autonomous zone was reduced, and the Straits were left in Turkish hands, albeit with assurance of unhampered passage for international shipping.

But the Treaty of Berlin failed to mollify the Ottoman leadership or foster reconciliation inside the ethnically diverse empire. Indeed, the effect was the opposite. By preserving a considerable degree of Ottoman rule over the Christian minorities, while also offering those minorities some protections, the outside powers merely reinforced the divisive status quo. The treaty left the Greek situation ambiguous: Greece was awarded Thessaly and parts of Epirus, but Crete and some Greek-speaking regions north of Greece remained under

Ottoman control, ensuring continued tension and grievances among the Ottoman Greek minority.

The Ottomans also had misgivings about the treaty's handling of the Armenians. Article 61, using a common diplomatic term for the Ottoman government, stated:

> The Sublime Porte undertakes to carry out, without further delay, the improvements and reforms . . . in the provinces inhabited by Armenians, and to guarantee their security against the Circassians and Kurds. It will periodically make known the steps taken to this effect to the Powers, who will superintend their application.[6]

Although San Stefano had also included reforms, it had said nothing about external supervision.[7] The Turkish governing elite saw Article 61 as a prelude to Armenian independence, abetted by foreign powers.

Even before Berlin the Turks had regarded "their" Christians with suspicion, which the patriarch's outreach to Russia only confirmed. After Berlin suspicion turned to near-certainty; non-Muslim communities were pegged as traitors collaborating with outside powers to dismember the empire. The cost of keeping Russia at bay was to elevate Ottoman fears of Christian fifth columnists and thereby further isolate and endanger the minorities whose plight had so angered European people and governments.

Over the course of the next fifteen years or so, European ambassadors busied themselves devising mechanisms for reform. They insisted on fair treatment and guarantees of security for Armenians and to some extent for Greeks. But Constantinople was never on board and sought to derail the process, leading to further persecution of minorities who eventually radicalized in response. It was the growing Armenian nationalist ferment that the government sought to crush in 1894.

But it was not Article 61 alone that drove Ottoman anxieties. The tension between the empire's Muslim majority and Christian minorities had been rising for decades. To understand what led the outside powers to advocate Ottoman reform and, ultimately, to the first major outbreak of anti-Christian violence, we need to go back to the first half of the nineteenth century and trace the changing status of the empire's non-Muslim minorities.

Such understanding begins with the recognition that Anatolia's Christian groups were not monolithic; while urban communities flourished for much of the eighteenth and nineteenth centuries, their rural coreligionists suffered both Ottoman attention and neglect. Where there was government, it often behaved harshly. Where there wasn't—for the farther reaches of the vast empire were virtually impossible to control—Kurds, Turkmen, Circassians, and other non-Turkish Muslim tribes filled the void with tacit state approval. They tended to rule for the benefit of their own, with little regard for the welfare of Christian minorities. Sometimes local warlords operated in parallel with the state, piling on additional taxes and supplementing the discriminatory Ottoman justice system with their own mistreatment. While outside influence and foreign events inspired the first stirrings of Greek and Armenian nationalism among prosperous city-dwellers, it was to great extent the plight of rural groups—especially Armenians—that precipitated the growing sense of ethnic unity among the Christian communities.

This complication—acknowledging the distinctive experiences of urban and rural communities, and their coproduction of nationalism—defies conventional historiography. Typically, historians propagate two narratives about the decades leading to the explosion of 1894–1896.[8] One, crudely referred to as the Armenian narrative, describes a worsening saga of Ottoman oppression directed against Armenian and Greek subjects. The other, equally crudely described as the Turkish narrative, tells the story of an enlightened and generous Ottoman state falling prey to nefarious outside imperialist forces conspiring with perfidious Christian minorities. Each account is biased and politically driven. Each breaks along national-ethnic lines. And each relies on verifiable historical sources. The two narratives are so far apart that they seem irreconcilable.

We suggest that both are true—or, more precisely, that solid evidence can be found to buttress both. The real story is one of urban-rural bifurcation, which, amid the peasants' distress, was eventually resolved in the form of emergent proto-national communities. It was these that the Ottoman state found so threatening.

The Rise of the Urban Armenian and Greek Communities

For the major urban Armenian communities of western Anatolia and the Balkans—in Constantinople, Edirne, Smyrna (Izmir), Bursa, and elsewhere—the nineteenth century, until the retrenchment of the late 1870s, was largely a time of progress, prosperity, and growing autonomy. In particular, the second half of the nineteenth century saw a significant increase in commerce with Europe and a concomitant growth of coastal cities such as Smyrna, where Greek communities benefited disproportionately. Greek merchants also had considerable success along the Black Sea littoral. Most trade with Europe and in the interior of Asia Minor was in the hands of Greeks and Armenians. And both groups were prominent in industry, such as goldsmithing, textile production, mining, and shipping. Armenians dominated Bursa's silk manufacture.[9]

Indeed, urban religious minorities had long held important economic roles in the empire. In the eighteenth century, the great majority of bankers who provided loans to Turkish grandees seeking office were Armenian. These bankers, who became the richest in Europe, also lent to local potentates who leased tax farms *(iltizam)* from the government and other wealthy individuals and guaranteed the loans. Jews and Greeks had previously dominated this field.[10] Armenians were further valuable as dragomans, interpreters offering linguistic and cultural guidance. They worked in the newly opened embassies in the fashionable Constantinople quarter of Pera or as local representatives of commercial enterprises, such as the British Levant Company and its French, Dutch, and Italian rivals.[11] Some Armenians prospered by branching out westward: "By the middle of the nineteenth century there were over thirty Armenian commercial firms in London and Manchester with their headquarters located either in Smyrna or Constantinople."[12] Armenians and Greeks also figured significantly in the modern professions. The Armenian Balyan family, for example, provided the palace with its architects.[13] Other Ottoman minorities rose to prominence as royal financial advisors. Many of these professionals were trained abroad, in European universities.

Prosperity earned minorities invitations to join the Ottoman elite. Well-to-do Armenian families were known as *amiras,* from "emir." The title, initially conferred by the palace only on notables in the sultan's service, came to designate all Armenian grandees.[14] For their part, several Greek-Orthodox families traditionally residing in the Phanar quarter of Constantinople, and hence known as Phanariotes (*Fenerliler,* in Turkish), held some of the most influential positions in the empire, including as prince-governors (hospodars) of Wallachia and Moldavia. Greeks had the honor of serving as dragomans of the palace and the imperial navy. However, most of these privileged positions were rescinded after the Greek mainland revolted against Ottoman rule in 1821, a process that culminated in Greek independence in 1830.[15]

At the beginning of the nineteenth century, urban minority communities were well organized and enjoyed a degree of control over their affairs. The major urban Armenian communities were divided into three groups: a religious-clerical hierarchy headed by the patriarch, a notability, and the mass of cityfolk, most of whom were associated with professional guilds known as *esnafs.*[16] While some of the esnafs were ethnically mixed, others, such as the silversmiths, coppersmiths, grocers, and shoemakers, were entirely Greek or Armenian.[17] Though not as rich or powerful as the amiras, the heads of successful esnafs wielded considerable influence. Some guilds accumulated large fortunes, which they used to fund the needs of their communities, such as paying taxes on residents' behalf. Such charity assured guilds sway in the day-to-day running of their respective *millets,* the empire's non-Muslim confessional communities.

Each millet—the main ones being Armenian, Greek Orthodox, and Jewish—was governed by the laws of the *dhimma.* While the patriarchs, chief rabbi, and their organizations possessed some lawful authority, their communities also had to demonstrate obedience to Muslim rule by fulfilling a series of obligations such as paying additional taxes and observing limitations on the construction of churches and synagogues. But marriage, divorce, certain internal disputes, and matters pertaining to religious law were dealt with inside the millet. Each had its own courts with the power to enforce verdicts, including imprisonment and corporal punishment. The mid-nineteenth century Tanzimat reforms—legal changes introduced by Constantinople to modernize the country and relieve pressure from European powers—annulled many of the dhimma laws but essentially left the millet system in place.[18] Minorities were thus granted civil rights that put them almost on a par with their Muslim peers, while retaining a large measure of religious and lay autonomy.

Turkish, Russian, Greek, and Jewish boys in Constantinople. The non-Muslim communities of the Ottoman Empire enjoyed relative toleration for centuries, but tensions grew at the end of the 1800s.

In the early nineteenth century, urban Armenians—traditionally "the most pacific of all the ethnic elements in the empire"—were already doing well and were clearly on an upward trajectory.[19] Greeks and Jews were, too. The size of these minorities is unclear: Constantinople periodically conducted surveys and published estimates, which downplayed the number of non-Muslims; the Armenian and Greek patriarchates, usually with still greater distortion, exaggerated Christian numbers. But what demographic information exists suggests that, by late century, Christians constituted a significant minority. An 1880 survey prepared by the Armenian Patriarchate found that in the six eastern vilayets of Anatolia alone there were 1,561,600 Armenians, outnumbering the 1,054,800 Muslims.[20] These were largely rural regions, but the sizeable number of eastern Armenians was an important basis for their urban brethren's claims to special status. One scholar has estimated that the Ottoman Empire had a population of 38,500,000 in 1876, of which 35 percent were Turks, 6.5 percent Armenians, and 5.5 percent Greeks.[21] But in Anatolia, the proportion of Armenians and Greeks was greater. In 1897, after the massacres of 1894–1896, the Ottoman authorities, who traditionally under-counted the number of Christians, assessed that there were more than a million Greeks and about 1.1 million Armenians in Anatolia, compared with just over 10 million Turks.[22] There were also more than 600,000 Assyrian Christians in the areas of the Ottoman Empire and western Persia, exclusive of Greater Syria, before World War I. Most were rural peasants.[23]

Rural Decline

As urban non-Muslim communities in western Anatolia and the Balkans were growing stronger economically and politically, their rural counterparts faced increasing hardship. In part this was a product of Constantinople's limited reach. In eastern Anatolia, outside the major towns, central-government control was mostly nominal. The countryside was dominated by shifting groups of local notables, insurgents, semi-nomadic Kurdish and Turkmen tribes, and the occasional governor sent from the capital who might "go native" and disregard Constantinople's "instructions" on guidelines.

Political authority was measured mainly by the ability to collect taxes and, relatedly, extort money from the populace. Peasants often ignored government demands, instead paying taxes—in cash or kind—to local warlords and factions. In the areas of Armenian inhabitation, taxes were collected by tribal leaders, ex-governors and army officers who had martial retinues, and other potentates. The experience of rural Turkish, Arab, and Greek communities was much like that of the Armenian peasants: all were fleeced by local bigshots. The absence of central authority was felt everywhere, and the result was a gradual weakening of rural society. Ironically, it was these taxes, often forcibly collected from impoverished peasants, which enriched many Armenian bankers.[24]

Before the rise of Armenian nationalism, very little connected the Armenian notables of Constantinople to their compatriots in the countryside. The two groups may have shared a belief system, a language, and a vague sense of common ethnic origin, but any possibility of unity was undermined by the economic and social chasms that lay between. Granted, the dichotomy was not always sharp; Armenian communities in provincial town centers occupied a middle ground. On the whole, though, the disparate experiences and trajectories of the two groups indicate the preeminence of class over ethnic solidarity.[25]

Reform and Proto-Nationalism in Constantinople's Christian Communities

Ottoman Armenians and Greeks took different paths toward nationalism. While Greeks could seek guidance and a sense of shared peoplehood from a state beyond the empire's shores, Armenians had to find their national bearings within the empire. This resulted in relatively low-intensity agitation on the part of Ottoman Greeks. Until the beginning of the twentieth century, Ottoman Greeks were basically satisfied with the existence, in the distance, of the Balkan Greek polity. They respected that state and were proud of its achievements, but they did not see themselves as belonging to it. From the perspective of the Muslim elite, Greece was a part of the empire that had already been given up.

In the Armenian case, on the other hand, there was no state, not even a lucidly imagined one, and when an Armenian national movement finally materialized, the state it contemplated included heavily Armenian regions of the empire: the six eastern vilayets and Cilicia. Some nationalists extended this vision to encompass all of eastern Anatolia and the Caucasus, stretching from the Mediterranean to the Black Sea. Such a state would dissect the empire, severing Anatolia from the Arab provinces of Greater Syria and Mesopotamia and separating the Ottomans from the Turkic peoples of central Asia. The Ottoman elite thus regarded the Armenian "dream" as far more threatening than anything the Ottoman Greeks might strive for.

The Greek Orthodox Church and faith long served as the glue binding the Ottoman Greeks together. But during the last decades of the nineteenth century, urban Greeks increasingly looked toward Greece itself, which almost none had ever seen, as a cultural beacon and source of pride. Critical to this process was "linguistic rehellenization." Many Greeks, notably in Cappadocia, spoke only Turkish.[26] A vastly expanded Ottoman Greek school system would teach them the Greek language and the culture associated with its speakers.[27]

The Kingdom of Greece was instrumental in this effort. Through its expanding range of consulates, Greece exported cultural and, eventually, political Hellenism to Anatolia.[28] The first consulates were installed in the Ottoman Empire in the 1840s; by 1904, there were twenty-two.[29] Consuls toured the countryside, gave lectures, and dispensed Greek-language publications. They propagated both Greekness and the *Megáli Idéa*—the Great Idea—of Greek geopolitical expansion. Consuls celebrated the ancient Athenian and medieval Byzantine empires as models for the reestablishment of a large Greek polity, perhaps with Constantinople as its capital, on the eventual ruins of the Ottoman Empire. Underlying the Great Idea was also a cultural mission "to civilize the East by rising against Ottoman rule, in the manner of Christ's rising to save the world," as historian John S. Koliopoulos puts it.[30] In 1864 King George I of Greece was crowned king of the Hellenes, hinting at these expansionist dreams and indicating the Greek state's claim to represent Greeks wherever they were. Athenian politicians spoke of saving the "unredeemed portion of the Greek nation."[31] Koliopoulos writes that most mainland Greeks "viewed the territorial settlement of 1830," when the Kingdom of Greece was established, "as nothing more than a temporary arrangement. Successive Greek territorial gains were expected to keep pace with Ottoman decline."[32]

Beyond the official work of the Greek government and its consuls, mainland cultural and linguistic clubs such as the Athens-based Association for the Propagation of Greek Letters fostered the national awakening of the Ottoman Greeks, much as Arab-language groups within the empire were concurrently promoting Arab nationalist movements. In the 1880s the government in Athens officially charged the association with "the supervision of educational and national activities" among the Ottoman Greeks, effectively endorsing irredentism.[33] Teachers were sent from the mainland to the far reaches of Anatolia and Anatolian youngsters were brought to Greece for study. Anatolian teachers returning from Greece nationalized the curriculum of the community's main religious college, the Halki Seminar on Heybeliada, near Constantinople.[34]

Despite these efforts to instruct Ottoman Greeks in the Great Idea, their nationalism was largely cultural rather than political. The expansion of literacy and the spread of nationalism among Ottoman Greeks had the "peasant and merchant . . . say, parrot-wise, 'I am a descendant of Pericles'," in Arnold Toynbee's memorable phrase.[35] But it didn't have them fomenting rebellion.

One moderating factor was the relatively open atmosphere in the Ottoman Empire generated by the Tanzimat and its ideology of Ottomanism. This view facilitated the spread of particularistic identities by holding that one could be Ottoman while celebrating one's Greek, Armenian, or other affiliations.[36] For some, this meant there need be no contradiction between Greek ethnicity and Ottoman nationality. Moreover, in the decades immediately preceding World War I, the focus of official Greek irredentism was on Macedonia, not Asia Minor.[37] The Orthodox clergy also proved a tempering influence. Clerics developed the Greek school system and helped disseminate Greek culture and language, but, until the beginning of the twentieth century, church higher-ups opposed the propagation of pan-Hellenic nationalism as "irresponsible." Joachim III, who served as Greek Orthodox patriarch between 1878 and 1884 and again from 1901 until 1912, feared that the spread of nationalism would undermine the position of the patriarchate and bring catastrophe down on the Ottoman Greeks. But younger members of the fin de siècle Church brass—such as Chrysostomos and Germanos, the future bishops of Smyrna and Amasya, respectively—supported the Great Idea.[38]

Still, the spread of Greek nationalism in Asia Minor was slow and hesitant.[39] As evidence, consider that between the 1820s' Greek War of Independence— which might have provoked strong irredentist tendencies—and the fall of Abdülhamid in 1909, Ottoman Greeks and Turks managed largely to avoid confrontation.[40] In 1863 the British consul in Smyrna predicted as much. "The appeal to arms will not have much impression upon the minds of the [Greek] subjects of the Porte," he anticipated.[41] Greek nationalism in Asia Minor may have appealed to "the most enlightened and liberal . . . the medical, legal and literary" professionals and to the rising middle class, especially in large cities and provincial towns. But it was opposed by the "ancient [Greek] nobility, the superior clergy, the lay dignitaries of the church, and the wealthy merchants."[42] Whatever the extent of nationalism's hold on Ottoman Greeks at the end of the nineteenth century, it failed to stir concrete political activism.

The trajectory of Ottoman Armenians would prove different. Armenian nationalism was in its own way nurtured by outsiders, such as American missionaries. But it was motivated by domestic exigencies, not by a foreign kingdom's yearnings for a lost imperial glory. Whereas Greek nationalism was cultural and intellectual—wistful, even—Armenian nationalism was much

more immediate, galvanized by urban Armenians' growing awareness of the
wretched conditions under which their rural brothers and sisters lived. One
effect was a more conflictual relationship between the Ottoman state and Armenian nationalists than that between the state and Greek nationalists, resulting in the violence of the 1890s, years before the Turks systematically
turned their guns on the Greeks in their midst.

We can trace the initial development of Ottoman Armenian nationalism to
the Greek revolt of 1821. In response to that revolt, Constantinople stripped
Ottoman Greeks of titles and official responsibilities. Much of their influence
passed into the hands of the amiras. The amiras, in turn, used their increasing
wealth and authority to foster partnerships with the Armenian Patriarchate
in Constantinople: rich Ottoman Armenians would pay church expenses and
invest in philanthropy and education, and, in return, the patriarchate would
recognize the civil leadership of the amiras. Thus Pezciyan Amira, the director
of the imperial mint, renovated the patriarchal headquarters; built schools,
churches, and drinking fountains; and in 1833 Constantinople's Holy Savior
Hospital. In recognition, the patriarch gave him the title of *azgapet,* designating the head of the community.[43] A similar situation prevailed in other
cities, such as Smyrna.[44] The fifty or so exclusively Armenian esnafs of
Constantinople also funneled money from guild taxes and donations to the
church and the community, increasing their power and esteem. Amiras and
esnafs competed for community leadership and in 1834 elected a joint
committee for the administration of the schools.[45]

These efforts mark clear steps in the evolution of national consciousness.
By committing their fortunes and influence to the concrete needs of Ottoman
Armenians, amiras and other notables helped to demarcate a distinct civic
community. In doing so, they asserted that Ottoman Armenians did not just
pray to the same God and perform the same religious rites but also constituted a social grouping that cared especially for its own in this life. At the same
time, the imprimatur of the church helped to universalize the elites' appeal,
affirming their roles as leaders not just of particular guilds and geographically
bound populations but of Armenians generally.

At this point, during the first decades of the nineteenth century, there was
still no Armenian independence movement. At most, elites sought a stronger
sense of community and additional civil liberties, perhaps culminating in

equality with their Muslim neighbors. But the growth in civil leadership was the beginning of an important shift in power that facilitated nationalist ideas: away from the patriarchate and toward lay authorities.

This shift was reinforced by the fracturing of the Armenian religious community, which had begun some years before the rise of the amiras. Starting in the late eighteenth century, various Catholic clerics attempted to reunite the Armenian Church—also known as the Apostolic or Gregorian Church—and the Catholic Church, from which it had parted in the fifth century.[46] After a small group of Armenians aligned itself with the Vatican, Pope Benedict XIV formally recognized the Armenian Catholic Church. In 1829 the sultan gave Catholic Armenians permission to form a separate millet and to appoint archbishops of their own in Constantinople and Lebanon. In 1867 the two sees would be united, with a patriarchal residence established in the capital alongside the Gregorian Patriarchate, emphasizing the widening religious divisions within the Ottoman Armenian community.[47]

At about the time the Catholic Armenian millet was formed, Protestant missionaries began making inroads among Gregorian Armenians. The sultan probably would have preferred to keep these outsider missionaries away from his subjects, but there was little he could do to prevent their admission. Caught in a tangle of geopolitical fears, debts, and strategic commitments to European patrons, the Ottoman elite was forced to acquiesce in these foreign inroads. Thus, in the 1774 Treaty of Küçük Kaynarca, the tsar was recognized as the official protector of all Orthodox communities in the Ottoman Empire. Soon afterward France, the Ottomans' main European strategic partner, was allowed to intercede on behalf of the empire's Catholics; the French frequently represented Catholic interests in the Holy Land and Lebanon. The missionary presence would grow substantially, especially after the Crimean War. All the government could do was ban the missionaries from targeting Muslims. As long as the missionaries preached only to Jews and other Christians, the Ottoman authorities regarded them with benevolent disdain.

The first Protestant missionaries were Anglicans admitted in the 1820s as a condition of Britain's agreement to provide Sultan Mahmud military assistance. In the early 1830s, the Anglicans were joined by Americans sent by the American Board of Commissioners for Foreign Missions. The missionaries organized parishes, built churches, and established networks of schools, hospitals, welfare institutions, and small industries throughout the empire, with a focus on the Turkish heartland.[48]

This missionary activity caused a crisis in the Armenian community, as the Gregorian Patriarchate excommunicated the converts to Protestantism. Some of the new Protestants were forced out of their guild jobs or trades. But two Tanzimat edicts, in 1847 and 1850, came to the converts' aid by sanctioning freedom of conscience and recognizing the Armenian Protestants as a new millet, with a status akin to that of the Gregorians. The consequence was continuing growth in the Protestant element and growing divisiveness in the community as a whole. In the eastern provinces, where most Armenians lived, there were about 1,300 Protestants in the 1860s. By 1914 there were some 50,000 Protestant Armenians in the empire, most of them in eastern Anatolia.[49]

The rise of Armenian Catholicism and Protestantism pushed the Gregorian Patriarchate toward reform. The Gregorian Patriarchate had traditionally invested little in education, but as dissentients multiplied, it responded by establishing schools and colleges—with the aid of the amiras. Thus, in the process of asserting itself as spiritual leader, the patriarchate turned to civic institutions, further empowering them. At the same time, Tanzimat reforms were elevating a civic sphere understood as explicitly distinct from religious authority. Some of the new legal structures reduced the autonomy and prerogatives of traditional religious-ethnic leaders. For example, Armenian patriarchs were banned from exiling community members and inflicting corporal punishments. And in 1840 the Armenian millet was required to establish a council comprising four clerics and four amiras to conduct the millet's affairs and represent it in dealings with the government. Although the council was appointed by the patriarch, it formalized power-sharing between religious and lay leaders.[50] This was followed by the 1847 imperial edict, which also ordered the heads of the millets to elect two separate and independent governing bodies, one civil and the other spiritual.

The new civic leadership, referred to as the Armenian National Assembly, took its role seriously. In 1853 it founded the first Armenian Educational Council, administered not by clerics but by fourteen lay graduates of European universities. Directing its efforts toward Armenian language reform, the publication of Armenian literature, and the study of Armenian history, the council contributed perhaps more than any other institution to the growing sense of national identity. In its first year, the council published an Armenian grammar book by Nahapet Rusinian, one of the drafters of the eventual Armenian national constitution. The publication sought to replace the archaic ritual syntax and lexicon with a modernized vernacular. The patriarch tried, and failed, to ban Rusinian's book and to bring the budding printing industry under his control.

While Armenian communal leadership was taken over by the laity, the younger generation increasingly came into contact with Western ideas. This was due in part to interaction with missionaries, who helped to inculcate liberal and democratic values. Exposure to Western ideas was also facilitated by the Ottoman government itself, which, during the reform-minded 1830s, began sending batches of hand-picked students, including Christians, to France for schooling. Two decades later, under Sultan Abdülmecid, an Ottoman school was established in Paris to prepare the future elite to meet the challenges of the modern world. The government also revamped Constantinople's Galatasaray School, which educated the empire's bureaucrats. The curriculum was "modernized" to match European standards, with French installed as the language of instruction.[51] In 1863 a new American missionary institution, Robert College, was established in the heights over the Bosporus. The college soon developed into one of the city's first universities, accepting students of all denominations.[52]

The first Christian students to go west were Catholic Armenians who studied medicine in Italy. Gregorian Armenians preferred France and Switzerland, where many studied science or engineering. Others focused on architecture, banking, and economics. Almost all were influenced by Auguste Comte's new, quasi-scientific ideas of positivism; by the humanistic concepts espoused by Alphonse de Lamartine and Victor Hugo; and by Jules Michelet's history of France, which emphasized nationalism. In the intellectual ferment leading up to the revolution of 1848 in France, the sons of amiras, guild members, and clerics of multiple Christian denominations studied together, breaching traditional social boundaries and creating a new type of bond based on ethnicity and language.[53] Young Armenians—and Greeks—learnt ancient history and debated constitutionalism and popular representation.

On returning home from the Sorbonne, Rusinian sought to spread the idea of nationhood in his own society. Although professionally a medical man—in 1851 he became the personal physician of future-Grand Vizier Mehmed Fuad Pasha—he also published nationalist poems, essays on language, and Armenian translations of European classics.[54] In one poem, paraphrasing Frederic Berat's "My Normandy," Rusinian pined for the ancient Armenian Kingdom of Cilicia, which he equated with a modern homeland:

> When the gates of hope are opened
> And winter takes leave of our homeland,
> When our beauteous land of Armenia
> Beams its euphoric, delightful days;
> When the swallow returns to its nest;
> When the trees are clothed in leaves;
> I yearn to see my Cilicia,
> World that deluged me in eternal sun.[55]

As educated Armenians began to think more in terms of national unity and a national home, they also started taking greater interest in the status of the fellow Armenians who would be their compatriots—in particular, those suffering in rural Anatolia. An important force in this regard was the Araratian Enkerutiun, or Ararat Society, a nonsectarian student organization founded in Paris in April 1849. Calling themselves the Young Armenians, they established the journal *Hayastan*—a medieval name for Armenia—which later became *Masis*, the Armenian name for Mount Ararat. The journal was the main mouthpiece of the Armenian cause from 1852 to 1907. The Ararat Society focused less on independence than on national identity, and much of its energy was spent on pan-Armenian efforts, crossing over urban-rural divides. In particular, the group hoped to bring education to Armenians and modern agricultural techniques to the peasants.[56]

In June 1855 members of the Ararat Society—most had returned from Europe and were employed by the government—proposed that the Armenian assembly formulate a constitution. After debate, the assembly appointed a constitutional committee composed of members of the Young Armenian movement, lay leaders, and clergymen.[57] The first draft, completed in 1857, was rejected by the Ottoman government, which claimed that it set the stage for a state within a state. A final draft, endorsed by the Armenian community and the Ottoman government, was approved in 1860 and ratified in 1863.[58] It provided for a refurbished 140-seat assembly with 80 members from Constantinople and its environs, 20 from the clergy, and 40 from the provinces. Although rural areas were grossly under-represented, they did at least have some presence, demonstrating the growing recognition of their membership alongside urbanites in an Armenian community whose boundaries extended across Anatolia. The patriarch was designated head of the community but in effect stripped of his lay powers, emphasizing the distinctively national, as opposed to religious, quality of the emerging Armenian people.[59] The Jewish and Greek communities also formulated constitutions, but with the chief rabbi left in charge of his people and the Greek clergy retaining many of the sorts of privileges that the Armenian Patriarchate lost.[60]

In Armenian the document was entitled The National Constitution of the Armenians; in Turkish, The Regulations of the Armenian Millet. In the Armenian text, the assembly was referred to as the National General Assembly; the word "National" was omitted from the Turkish version. Nonetheless, as Kamuran Gurun, a Turkish diplomat and historian of the early republic put it, the document was designed to create a "landless autonomy."[61] But the Armenian nation had not yet fully coalesced. For, as we have seen, rural communities, though recognized, were not totally embraced. And while the constitutional system enabled further autonomy and opportunity for minority communities in the capital, it had little impact on the beleaguered peasants.

A Rural Community under Siege

During the 1860s the situation of the peasants in the east deteriorated further. For roughly a century, more and more Muslim groups from outside the empire had settled the region, leading to tensions with Christians. The government established an Immigration Commission *(Muhâcirin Komisyonu)* to try to resolve problems, but to little avail.

Many of the Muslim settlers had been nomads, but during the eighteenth and nineteenth centuries, they gradually became sedentary. Circassians and Chechens arrived from the Caucasus, where they were fleeing Russian armies.

Muhacirs—Muslim refugees—from the Balkans. Thousands flocked to western Anatolia in the wake of the Russo-Turkish war of 1877–1878.

Kurds and Turkmen were driven by political instability and government pressure in northern Iran. It has been estimated that during the "long nineteenth century" (1789–1914), five to seven million people immigrated to the empire and settled mainly in eastern and central Anatolia. They were joined also by thousands of Muslim refugees, known as *muhacirs,* from the Balkan wars.[62]

As the population in the eastern and central regions grew, arable land became scarce, leading to disputes. Powerful clans took over cultivated fields and extorted tribute and bribes from local communities. The Christian peasantry were easy marks because the government had little interest in protecting them.[63] In some cases, clans bought from each other the right to tax Christian villages.[64] In the early 1860s a British consul traveling through eastern Anatolia sent London this grim description:

> The Kochers and Koords are under very imperfect subjection, and it is only by satisfying all demands, however outrageous, that the Christian agriculturists can maintain their position. One unbearable custom, that

of *kishlak,* has done more than anything else to contribute to their present paucity and decay. That custom, originating some years ago in the weakness of the Government and growing power of the Koords, enabled the latter to exercise the extraordinary right of quartering themselves and their flocks during winter in and about the Christian villages, entailing upon the inhabitants large expenses, not only for fodder for their animals, but also food and fuel for themselves, during at least four months.[65]

Clashes erupted. In one instance in 1862, the government suppressed a brief rebellion in the mountainous region of Zeytun, whose Armenian peasants had a reputation for steadfastness.[66]

As word of the injustices in the east flowed into a Constantinople community that increasingly saw itself as not just Gregorian but Armenian, the Ararat Society and its allies were moved to action. In 1870 they convinced the National General Assembly to appoint a commission to investigate the peasants' plight. But the commission would have little impact, as its interim report, submitted two years later to the Ottoman leadership, fell largely on deaf ears. The report mentioned illegal taxes but was carefully worded to overlook other injustices for fear of antagonizing the government, which was already annoyed by European demands to improve conditions in the east.[67]

In 1876, during the government crisis in Constantinople, the assembly submitted a second report. This time, the commission was more thorough, detailing 320 cases of maladministration and oppression in the east. Most cases dealt with land seizures by local strongmen and tribal leaders. Many of the seizures were ascribed to recent Circassian arrivals; others were triggered by Kurdish, Afshar, and Turkmen tribes from Iran and Syria. In almost all instances, local authorities ignored or rejected Armenians' proofs of ownership. Provincial courts, disregarding the legal reforms prescribed by Constantinople, arbitrarily dismissed appeals. Even in cases where Armenian peasants produced solid documentary evidence, courts tended to rule in favor of Muslim expropriators.[68] The report also cited numerous incidents of extortion, theft, cattle rustling, and sexual assault on women. One of Britain's consular representatives in Van, a Mr. Rassam, wrote on October 15, 1877:

After making some allowance for the exaggerated reports regarding the sufferings of the Christian population in the vilayets of Diarbekir and Van, it cannot be denied that a good deal of misery has been caused in these parts from want of proper protection to life and property. The apathy and weakness of the local authorities, and the corruption of the collectors of taxes in the districts, have been the main cause of the present troubles. It seems that the [nomadic] Kurds . . . have never been properly brought under subjection, and as a matter of course, as soon as they found they could exact what they liked with impunity from those Christians who are in their power, they did so. . . . The highland Kurdish tribes from Diarbekir to Solaimania, are more or less unmanageable. They not only refuse to pay any taxes, or conform to the law of conscription, but they plunder and kill at their pleasure, and anyone who dares to deny them anything, he is sure to lose his life and property. . . . In many instances . . . Mahommedans suffered as well as Christians from the ravages of the Kurd.[69]

Abdülhamid, newly installed as sultan, was perturbed by the details emerging from the far-flung provinces, where marauding tribes appeared to threaten his own power. He sent new governors, judges, tax collectors, and troops to reinforce his authority in the eastern vilayets, but not to improve the lot of the Christian peasants. Indeed, the effect was the opposite, as the central government added a new layer of misery. Now peasants would be fleeced three or four times: by the tribal overlords and local officials who "protected" them, mafia-style; by new tribes moving into the area; and by military and civilian agents from the center.

The peasants gained little from their many payments. In the east transportation, communication, agricultural, and security infrastructure all were underdeveloped. What the state did invest in—railways, roads, telegraph technology, and water projects—seldom benefited the peasants directly. To the contrary, peasants were forced to leave their homes unguarded and fields unworked while they were conscripted to take part in construction. In some areas, such as around Lake Van, the situation became so unbearable that thousands of Christian peasants abandoned their lands and migrated to Russia.[70]

Throughout the late 1870s, further appeals forwarded to the government by the patriarchate and assembly were largely ignored.[71] Instead the authorities and banks confiscated land from peasants who failed to pay off debts. These lands were often given to the Circassian and Kurdish immigrants who, being Muslim, were considered more loyal to the state. Kurdish notables, appointed to advisory committees of local and regional councils as part of the Tanzimat reforms, subverted even the few and half-hearted government efforts to improve the Armenians' circumstances.[72]

All this was coupled with a religious awakening among Kurdish and other Sunni tribesmen, inspired by government-backed clerics. As part of its struggle against missionary activity, and in order to strengthen its base in the southeast, Constantinople sent religious scholars to preach "true" Islam to the tribes.[73] The government also increased investments in religious education in primary and secondary schools and established religious schools (madrassa). One result was a new generation of militant Kurdish preachers who saw Christians, at home and abroad, as eternal enemies of Islam. The tribal chiefs thereby gained divine justification for their persecution.[74]

The Sublime Porte, of course, knew what was happening in the East and exploited matters to its own advantage—to impose its authority or at least garner additional taxes for its own coffers. In the pedantic Ottoman bureaucratic tradition, officials, police, and army units in the provinces reported every incident. Abdülhamid's military aides followed the situation closely, the peasants sent countless complaints, and European ambassadors constantly protested. But the sultan was unmoved. From his vantage point, the Armenians were part of a much larger problem: rebellion among subjects throughout the empire, encouraged by foreigners. What began with the Greeks had continued with the Serbs, who sought and won independence between the 1830s and 1860s. Rebellion continued as well in Lebanon in 1860, where agitating Christians won special autonomy, practically detaching their enclave from the empire. The late 1860s saw further uprisings in Herzegovina, Bosnia, and Crete. Revolution was also afoot in Bulgaria. The Armenian provinces to the east seemed no different, especially in light of the patriarch's treasonous outreach to Russia, the reforms promised the Armenian vilayets in the 1878 Berlin Treaty, and an Armenian National General Assembly pleading the peasantry's case.

For the ambitious and somewhat paranoid Abdülhamid, the creeping divisions and revolts proved that the Tanzimat reforms, tilted as they were toward ideas of equality and cultural autonomy, had been misguided. Their consequence was greater Christian influence in the empire and the empowerment of secessionist minorities. Abdülhamid therefore renounced many of the reforms and refused to make good on liberalizing promises to outside powers.

But, to appease the powers, Abdülhamid played the diplomatic game. In 1879, after it became clear that the Ottoman government was not introducing the reforms agreed to in the Treaty of Berlin, the British threatened war and sent a flotilla to the entrance of the Dardanelles. The Porte agreed to dispatch a commission of inquiry to the east. But nothing changed. Constantinople dragged its feet, arguing that, as a minority group, the Christians should not be given special status—and that, in any case, they were a source of instability. The government also contended that it could do little for Christians because Kurdish rights had to be protected.[75]

The Reverend Herbert M. Allen, a missionary in Van vilayet, offers a good snapshot of conditions in the east. By his count, in the districts of Shadakh and Norduz alone, between eighty and one hundred Armenian villagers were murdered by Kurds in the decade preceding the massacres of the mid-1890s. "Hardly one of the murderers has been brought to justice," he added. The Kurdish tribes, he said, "subsist principally by preying on" Christian villages and could "kill and rob with impunity." One favored method was to take on debt with Armenian merchants and then refuse to pay them back. Emin Pasha, a Kurdish chieftain in the nearby Adelcevaz District, ran up a debt of 400 pounds and then forced the lending merchant to write it off without payment. The merchant went to the authorities, to no effect. "These Kurds not only have *carte blanche* as to the property and lives of the Christians, but as to the sanctity of their homes as well," Allen reported. "In many villages no Christian dares refuse his daughter, or wife, to a Kurd. In a village near Arcış, a certain Dervish Bey ravishes women, in open daylight, in the presence of their husbands."

Such brazenness was possible because the vilayet's officials—from the vali, Bahri Pasha, down—allowed it. They were, Allen claimed, leading the province to "the verge of financial and moral ruin" and appeared especially bent on "bringing ruin upon the Armenians as fast as possible." When an honest or efficient official arrived, the vali and his colleagues made sure he was dismissed. Van's courts, Allen wrote, "are places where under a legal name, the most shameless and heartless injustice is perpetrated."

According to Allen's calculations, each of the fifty-one Armenian villages in Shadakh and Norduz was compelled to pay the government, on average, 10,949 piastres per year in taxes "or turn Moslem." In addition, each village paid local Kurdish agas 2,690 piastres and another 1,000 piastres in tribute to "Shakir, the brigand chief." The hundred Kurdish villages paid almost no taxes. Christians provided "five-sixths" of the vilayet's revenues, which paid officials' salaries and for "building Turkish mosques and sustaining Turkish schools." At the same time, basic infrastructure in Armenian areas languished. "The roads are never repaired," Allen wrote. "Is it any wonder that in three years more than two hundred families have moved away?"[76]

The Radicalization of the Armenian National Movement

In 1878 the sultan overturned the reformist constitution enacted just two years before, dissolving the parliament and undermining many of the gains minorities—and even the Sunni majority—had enjoyed. In short order, the Armenian National General Assembly became a hollow edifice without authority even in the Constantinople community. One by one the privileges of the lay leadership were stripped away. They were barred from making autonomous decisions about school curricula and community taxation. The teaching of Armenian history and display of Armenian historical images were banned. Outspoken newspapers were closed, and the General Union of Armenian Schools, established by the National General Assembly several years earlier, was abolished. The sultan was restoring the pre-Tanzimat status quo, in which millet autonomy would be largely spiritual in nature, with civil authority entirely in the hands of the state.

Proving, as ever, that their interest in the Ottoman situation lay in geopolitics rather than protecting the persecuted, the outside powers did little to object. Bismarck, who had been a major player in the Berlin Treaty, congratulated the sultan for dissolving the parliament and advised him to prioritize the survival of the empire.[77] And, as we have seen, the British only made noises about enforcing Article 61. They backed off as soon as the Sultan promised to investigate reports of persecution in the east.

Small wonder, then, that some young Armenians abandoned the idea of autonomy within a reformed empire and looked for more radical solutions. Early stirrings of an organized national movement could be seen in the platforms and manifestoes of groups such as the Black Cross Society and the Armenakan Party, established in Van in 1878 and 1885 respectively, and The Protectors of the Fatherland, formed in Erzurum in 1881.[78] In 1887 a group of Russian-Armenian students in Geneva founded the first nationalist political party, the Social Democrat Hunchakian Party, better known as Hunchak (meaning "bell" or "clarion"). Armenian youths from Constantinople and Anatolia were quick to join and take leadership positions. Although missionaries publicly opposed revolutionary activity, Protestant Armenians teaching at Anatolia College in Merzifon, such as Karabet Tomayan and Ohanes Karayan, also became covert Hunchak leaders.[79] Influenced by Marxism and the populist anti-tsarist group Narodnaya Volya, the Hunchaks adopted violent tactics widespread among the era's Russian movements. The Hunchaks' strategy was to pursue ideological indoctrination and train the masses for revolt whenever an opportune moment, such as a future Ottoman-Russian war, arrived.[80]

Three years later, another group of Armenians, based in Tiflis, founded the Armenian Revolutionary Federation, better known as Dashnaksutyun ("Federation") or simply Dashnak. Their aim was to unite under one roof the various groups of Armenian nationalists and revolutionaries in Russia and the Ottoman Empire. The two parties, Hunchak and Dashnak, tried to work together, but, though the ideological differences between them were slight, they split on tactics. While the Hunchaks had no faith in the possibility of Ottoman reform, the Dashnaks believed that working together with opposition and progressive elements within the empire might lead to better prospects for Armenians. The two movements would become competitors for leadership of the national movement and in resisting the Ottoman authorities.[81]

Soon after they were established, the two parties began to attack Ottoman targets. From bases in the Caucasus and northern Iran, they hit troops, gendarmerie bases, and police posts and assaulted Kurdish bands believed to have perpetrated crimes against Armenian villagers. One of their aims was to provoke the authorities to take harsh countermeasures that would trigger European intervention.[82] These rebels sent operatives into rural Anatolia to indoctrinate Armenians and sow subversion. Armed bands installed themselves in the mountains, close to Armenian villages. Here and there, villagers joined them; others were persuaded to stop paying taxes and confront the authorities. Acts of resistance mounted.[83] Arms were smuggled from Russia into Anatolia, though the number was probably small and vastly inflated in Ottoman propaganda. Revolutionaries extorted from wealthy Armenians and murdered internal enemies. The authorities reacted with a heavy, undiscriminating hand, and "many of the law-abiders were persecuted by the government for [allegedly] conniving at a revolt."[84]

The increasing assertiveness and scope of the Armenian independence movement during the 1870s—embracing both western cities and eastern provinces—frightened not just the Ottoman state but also the rural tribes that enriched themselves at Armenian expense. Following Berlin, Kurdish and Turkmen tribal leaders began to worry that the eastern provinces would ultimately fall under Armenian rule. In 1879 this concern triggered a rebellion along the Ottoman-Persian border. Led by a Kurdish chief, Sheikh Ubeydullah, the rebels believed that the moment was ripe for the Kurds to take control in a region under weak Iranian and Ottoman governance. Mistakenly thinking that the uprising was aimed at Iran only, the Ottomans initially supported Ubeydullah and his band. But the state soon recognized the danger and sent in the army. The Kurds took to the hills, and southeastern Anatolia descended into chaos. Muslim peasants who had only recently come under the government's sway refused to pay taxes, and communications were disrupted. Disarray also plagued the northern frontier, where Russia allowed Cossack militias free rein. The Cossacks frequently mounted cross-border raids against Muslim communities and effectively pushed the international boundary southward.[85]

The sultan realized that the old tactics—sending troops to quash local tax rebellions, delaying reform, installing sham commissions of inquiry, reneging on promises to the powers—were no longer sufficient. A comprehensive solution was needed, one that would respond to the deteriorating situation across the empire.[86] The answer the sultan found was sectarianism, a policy of political Islam that would replace the multiethnic commitments and religious

toleration of Ottomanism. The idea was that, by explicitly and unapologeti-
cally favoring Muslims and elevating their status, the sultan would win the
loyalty of restive Muslim tribes. Ideally, they would stop pressuring the state
and also do the sultan's bidding in the marchlands they shared with the
Armenians.[87]

Thus in 1891 the authorities formed the Hamidiye Light Cavalry Regiments
(Hamidiye hafîf süvari alaylari), composed mainly of Kurds and Turkmen.
They were equipped with guns and horses, given a command structure,
dressed in military-style uniforms, and allotted state salaries.[88] Officially the
cavalry were tasked with defending the border and combating Russian encroachment; their job was "to incorporate or at least to neutralize the non-
state spaces" that the state "could claim, but perhaps not yet govern."[89] But
the sixty-four regiments were deployed mainly in areas of Armenian concentration, suggesting that the government had one particular set of disobedients
in mind.[90]

Regardless of their stated purpose, the Hamidiye would go on to join in
the massacre of Armenians. Kurdish commanders understood that suppressing Armenians was their mission. In his memoirs, Sadettin Pasha, who
was governor of Van vilayet after the Hamidian massacres, recalled a particular conversation. On his way to his new posting, he had reprimanded a group
of Kurdish Hamidiye officers for excessive zeal and disobeying orders. The
Kurds responded that controlling the Armenians was their duty, that Armenian insubordination and insurrections were a blow to their honor as soldiers
of the sultan, and that a *firman* (imperial edict) had made seizure of Armenian property halal, a religiously permissible act. Denying that such a firman
had been issued—indeed, it probably had not—Sadettin Pasha admonished
the Kurds to respect the chain of command.[91]

The establishment of the regiments further radicalized the eastern Armenians.
Although the revolutionaries were still just a tiny fraction of the populace,
many villagers now came to believe that the Hunchak and Dashnak diagnosis
was accurate. The battle lines had been drawn, with the Kurds (briefly) made
favorite sons and Armenians cast as enemies of the state, their oppression
tacitly permitted and sometimes actively encouraged. For the Kurds, this
meant official recognition of their local power, state medals and honors, and a
set of privileges that often entailed *carte blanche* to appropriate land held by

Armenians for centuries. (Ironically, it was also a first step on the road toward the Kurdish independence movement that, to this day, resists the Turkish state.[92])

Abdülhamid was to rule the empire as absolute monarch for thirty-two years, until he was deposed following the Young Turk Revolution of 1908. During his reign, Armenian autonomy all but vanished.[93]

2

The Massacres of 1894–1896

By early 1894 mass murder was in the air, and by mid-1896 at least 100,000 Armenians lay dead—shot, stabbed, and axed to death by Turks and Kurds in a succession of horrific massacres. More died through starvation and exposure in the weeks and months that followed, an indirect result of the destruction of their homes, the confiscation of their property, and the wholesale murder of breadwinners. Some historians put the total death toll as high as 300,000.

The Turks then and later largely blamed so-called Armenian revolutionists for what had happened, even as they denied that it in fact had happened. There were no massacres, the Turks claimed. Only Armenian attacks or "battles" between Armenians and Muslims.

Western observers often criticized the Turks, but they were not uncritical of Armenian behavior. They blamed supposed Armenian revolutionaries, on three counts: they promoted murder—mainly of informers, but also, on occasion, of Turkish police and officials; they provoked Turkish responses, which included mass imprisonment and massacre; and they caused Ottoman antagonism toward Westerners, who were believed to be supporting and inciting the Armenian "cause." In particular, the Ottomans were upset at American missionaries, of whom there were 176 in 1895, working with locals to run 125 churches and 423 schools with more than 20,000 pupils.[1] "The Government did not like to have foreigners going about among the people," one official said.[2]

But foreign influence was only a small factor in the instability in the eastern provinces. It stemmed in large part from the triangular relationship between

Armenians, Kurds and other tribal groups, and Ottoman officials, which admixed economic envy and covetousness, religious antagonism, disputes over disparate traditions, and an Armenian revolutionary frisson that was vastly exaggerated in Muslim minds.

Since 1876 routine depredation had steadily impoverished rural Armenians.[3] The court system, police, and prisons figured large in this system of debasement and exactions. Armenians were punished for resisting Kurdish raiders, parrying extortion, or trying to obtain payment when coerced into lodging Muslims.

The palace was well aware of the Armenians' plight but did very little to alleviate it. The palace received a stream of reports from the provinces about these depredations. Osman Nuri, Sultan Abdülhamid's biographer, later conceded that "there were a few things which caused the conflict between the Armenians and the Muslims. [These included] the aggression of the Kurds and the corruption of the local officials." Disappointed by the state's failure to implement any semblance of reform, some Armenians pinned their hopes on the great empire to the north, but the Russians were reluctant to interfere directly and even quietly supported the formation of a Kurdish confederation, which they hoped eventually to place under their own tutelage.[4]

Van missionary Herbert Allen related an occasion in early 1895 when gendarmes came to the village of Kurubaş to collect taxes: "After gorging themselves with all they could get out of the villagers, they demanded a certain woman. . . . Finally [she was given] up to the lust of these shameless brutes." A few weeks earlier, tax-collecting gendarmes arrived in the district of Müküs. An Armenian who could not pay was shut up in a room full of smoke. He was "told that if he would become a Moslem they would release him." He refused "and before many hours he was dead. Seeing his fate, nine others, including women and children, were frightened into declaring that they would become Moslems."

If the police were bad, the prisons were even worse. In these overcrowded, "vile dens," Christians received "no food except bread from the Government." Food sent by relatives was plundered by the guards. Christians regularly died in the cells from poison, disease ("no medicine allowed"), beatings, and torture. The experience of Mesak Shadvorean, a Van Armenian, is illustrative. In 1893 he was arrested with seven family members for the murder of a policeman. Mesak and a son died from beatings; another son was hanged a year later. Another Armenian, one Yeghiazar Pambagisian, "was kept chained in a dungeon in winter weather till his feet froze, and finally the toes of both dropped off."[5] Muslim prisoners were probably not treated much better.

In early 1895, months before the large wave of massacre swept eastern Anatolia, the local British consul described the situation in one Van district: "The oppressions, murders, and forcible proselytizing in the district of Mukus . . . would fill a volume. . . . This district has been all but emptied of its Christian inhabitants. The taxes of those who have moved away are demanded of those who remain although their fields have been all seized by the Kurds. Those who remain are . . . beaten, imprisoned, and wish to emigrate, but are prevented from doing so and turned back to die in their desolate homes."[6]

Occasional Armenian resistance to raids, or reluctance to pay officials were interpreted, or at least designated, by Ottoman administrators as rebellion. Indeed, these were seen as violations of the natural order and unconscionable lèse-majesté: resisting oppression, passively or actively, however ineffectually and minutely, challenged the political and religious status quo and threatened or seemed to threaten the sultan's primacy, honor, and manliness. Such thinking was linked to religious views and *sharia* law, which, as one Western observer put it, using a term for Christian subjects of the Ottoman regime, "prescribes that if the *'rayah'* Christians attempt . . . to overstep the limits of privileges *(berat)* their lives and property are to be forfeited, and are at the mercy of the Mussulmans. To the Turkish mind the Armenians had tried to overstep those limits by appealing to foreign Powers. They therefore considered it their religious duty and a righteous thing to destroy and seize the lives and property of the Armenians."[7] It appears that in the early 1890s there was a rise in religious tempers, probably generated in part by the Islamist winds blowing from Abdülhamid's Constantinople. In Maraş, for instance, it was reported that "Muslim fanaticism" had grown into a "fierce . . . passion."[8]

There were, by then, Armenian nationalist parties, but most Western observers, and Armenians themselves, attributed their emergence not to a collective revolutionary impulse but rather to despair following the complete failure of the government to implement the Treaty of Berlin reforms.[9] A British diplomat explained that local officials believed that it was in their interest "to maintain the friction [*sic,* fiction] of a perpetual Armenian agitation, which is only prevented from breaking out into open revolt by their zealous efforts." Moreover, these officials understood "that any act of oppression or injustice towards Armenians will be overlooked, if not actually rewarded, by their superiors, an idea which has also taken root and borne fruit among the Kurds of the country districts."[10]

There also were acts of violence by Armenians, but neither Turkish officials nor the masses looked beyond their stereotypes about ethnic-religious collectives: the actions or thinking of a few Armenians in specific places were attributed to all Armenians. As one British diplomat put it, "The Ottoman officials, instead of distinguishing between the guilty and innocent, chose, some from ignorance, many from motives of personal pecuniary gain, to regard all Armenians as traitors, scheming to throw off the Ottoman yoke."[11]

In the story Ottoman officials told themselves, revolutionaries and "agitators" had infiltrated from Russia or Persia and were preparing for "the day." Alternatively, Armenian revolts might coincide with war with Christian powers along Turkey's borders, in the Caucasus or the Balkans. Or a revolt could serve as an excuse for, and trigger of, cross-border offensives by Christian powers bent on aiding Christians. The fear among Turkish officials was very real, even if the potential or reality of Armenian revolution were not.

The Ottomans therefore reacted harshly to even whiffs of sedition, and tended to blame Christians without evidence. For example, when, in 1892 and early 1893, seditious posters appeared on walls in Amasya, Merzifon, Tokat, Yozgat, Ankara, and Diyarbekir, the authorities responded with mass arrests. One poster read, "The last days have approached of Abdül-Hamid, the tyrant, who has soiled the sacred Throne of Osman and rendered the religion of Islam detestable. . . . The moment of vengeance has arrived."[12] Armenians—who would not likely criticize the regime in Islamist terms—said the posters were hung by *softas* (Muslim seminarians), who disliked the regime. Alternatively, discontented local ex-officials may have hung them in order to inflame Turkish sentiment against Christians. Whatever the case, the authorities used the posters to crack down on the Armenians. The British consular agent in Samsun, Alfred Spadaro, spoke in early 1893 of 1,800 Armenians arrested in the eastern and central provinces of Asia Minor. Others thought the real number was about half that.[13]

Although the Ottomans routinely upbraided the outside powers for under-mining their authority, many bought into the idea that Christians were rebel-ling with the aid of foreign powers. After meeting with Ankara Vali Abidin Pasha, Robert Windham Graves, the British "consul for Kurdistan," agreed that "a widespread movement of disaffection existed among the Armenians in this province, and that of Sivas, having its centre in Marsovan." The move-ment was "financed and inspired from abroad" and had recruited "a number of adherents, mostly young and ignorant hotheads of the lower classes." They had been responsible for violence against government informers and other tar-gets. Abidin produced a detained Armenian who said, according to Graves, that "the intention of the movement was . . . to cause such disturbances in the country as should attract attention to the oppressed condition of his fellow-countrymen, and compel the interference of Foreign Powers." Graves praised the vali and noted that Christian prisoners were "treated with humanity."[14]

But within weeks Graves was skeptical about "the genuineness of the sup-posed insurrectionary movement" in the two provinces he had toured. The Armenians, he wrote, "had no special grievances," and "everything points to the fact that an insurrectionary movement was never seriously intended, the design really being to create an appearance of revolt and disorder for the pur-pose of attracting attention and provoking foreign interference." Graves said that a revolutionary committee had put up placards and recruited supporters in the two provinces, but its outreach was largely unsuccessful. The "total number . . . joining the movement can[not] have exceeded a few hundreds," he wrote. The Turks managed quickly to stifle the movement with mass arrests. Graves thought the crackdown and occasional "misconduct" by the authorities partially "justified the complaints of persecution."[15] He would soon become a severe critic of Ottoman behavior.

Most Western observers agreed with Graves's assessments. They recog-nized in Armenian nationalism not some wayward collective revolutionary impulse but an understandable response to oppressive conditions. These were supposed to be ameliorated by reforms. But the Sublime Porte failed to im-plement each of the successive schemes for reform. Instead the government became increasingly paranoid, attributing to all Armenians the rebellious ac-tions of a few in isolated places. When Armenians acted up, they were usu-ally refusing excessive taxation or resisting raiders, not revolting.

"The Quarrelsome European Nursery." Emerging nationalist parties in the Balkans and Anatolia were sometimes seen as proxies of the squabbling European powers.

When considering the Ottoman actions of the mid-1890s, it is important to keep in mind both motivations and realities. Yes, Armenians in eastern Anatolia were buying small arms surreptitiously and by late 1893 there were revolutionary groups at work, with foreign agitators adding fuel to the fire. Christian missionaries sowed discontent merely by invoking and inculcating foreign modes of thought.[16] But, for all that, the Armenian national movement posed no serious threat to Ottoman power—certainly nothing that could warrant the oppression they lived under and the slaughter that was to follow.

The Early Massacres

The underlying hatreds, fears and tensions of the early 1890s came to a head in late 1893 and early 1894 in two episodes that heralded the giant massacres of a few months later. In Yozgat and Sason (Sassoun), local officials and the Constantinople brass perceived a hint of Armenian assertiveness and a wish for equality. This "alarmed the Palace considerably."[17] In both places, but especially Sason, local Muslims and the state responded with unprecedented ferocity, demonstrating the lengths to which they would go to crush what they seemed to view as mortal threats.

Yozgat

The events immediately precipitating the bloodletting in Yozgat, in Ankara vilayet, began in November 1893, when an Armenian activist in the nearby village of Incirli (Indjirli) Keris killed an Armenian police informer.[18] Fearing collective punishment, the villagers handed the killer over to the authorities. But after Armenians accused of involvement in an armed revolutionary committee freed the man from custody, gendarmes responded by ransacking the village. They robbed homes and arrested twenty "of the principal inhabitants." These men, unconnected to the supposed committee, were taken to Yozgat, imprisoned, and tortured to elicit confessions. The gendarmes beat them with chains, cut them with "blunt tin knives," inflated their intestines with bellows inserted a posteriori, and "squeezed" their testicles. An Ottoman commission subsequently freed thirteen of the prisoners, but seven had signed confessions and remained in jail.[19]

Then, in December, gendarmes raided another village, whose name appears in reports as Kara Chair. The gendarmes were looking for "committee men"—or, alternatively, men who had cut telegraph wires nearby—and briefly detained twenty villagers. While the men were in custody, the gendarmes and chief of police went to detainees' homes and there raped six or seven women, "three of whom were virgins." Several other young women also were raped. Although there was no evidence of crimes on the part of the detainees, fifteen of them were taken to jail in Yozgat. On December 12, after officials refused to talk to the villagers about the prisoners, the villagers met in a Yozgat church to decide what to do. During the meeting, the Kara Chair Armenians "excited the Yozgat Armenians to fury."

Muslims, including soldiers, surrounded the church. The district governor called on the crowd to disperse and promised the Armenians redress. When Armenians emerged from the church, a Turkish soldier fired, hitting an Armenian in the leg. Fearing impending massacre, Armenians fired back; three Muslims and an Armenian died, and dozens were injured. Thereafter Yozgat's Christian shopowners defied official "orders and entreaties" by closing down their businesses for two weeks in an effort to secure their goods from possible looting. Some Muslim-owned shops were shuttered as well. The military commandant, Osman Pasha, prevented Turkish "reprisals" against the Armenians. According to the local British consul, Henry Arnold Cumberbatch, these events had "no connection with any 'revolutionary' movement, as was at first suggested in some quarters."[20]

After word of the mayhem reached Constantinople, the government sent a commission of inquiry to investigate. Led by Hilmi Pasha—whom a Protestant cleric described as "mild and civilized" but also a morphine taker, "indolent and addicted to drink"—the commission arrested dozens of Armenians. "The victims [were] apparently selected for their wealth or position or because some official bore them a grudge," a British report stated.[21]

Hilmi's commission never made much progress, in part because its work was soon overtaken by new emergencies. On February 1, 1894, Yozgat gendarmes attempted to arrest a man "for alleged treasonable language." In the course of his flight, he shot and wounded a local police commander. The authorities quickly caught up and arrested him. He was murdered by his jailers that same day. The following day, a crowd of soldiers and locals attacked Christian passersby, their homes, and Christian-owned shops, killing perhaps fifteen and wounding eighty. The majority of injuries were reportedly caused by bayonets, indicating the primary responsibility of soldiers. The riot continued from morning till sunset. Hearing the hubbub in the streets, Hilmi reportedly rushed out "into the snow . . . in a dressing gown and stockings and with a coffee cup in his hand" and asked whether "the Armenians were rising." After soldiers explained what was happening, Hilmi replied, "Thank god, I will finish my coffee" and returned to his rooms. The British ambassador, relating the incident, said that "no Turkish officers took part in the riot, but they did not attempt to restrain the rioters all day." In the course of the pogrom, some 200–300 Armenians were jailed, and several of these were murdered in prison. According to the ambassador, no Muslims were killed, hurt, or imprisoned.[22]

The tumult was brought to an end on orders from Hilmi. The wounded were taken to prison "and kept there till they recovered or died." Armenian civilian doctors were barred from attending; the injured were instead treated by Turkish military doctors. Martial law was proclaimed, and Hilmi left town the next morning without investigating the riot or completing the inquiry into the previous incidents.[23]

That job would be left to a military court headed by Mustafa Pasha, whom British Ambassador Philip Currie described as "an exceedingly fanatical Turk." Mustafa freed a hundred of the prisoners taken during the pogrom, but the court was otherwise hostile to the Armenians, abusing them and ignoring their testimony. While the court addressed the events at Kara Chair, Incirli, and the Yozgat church, it overlooked the pogrom and its perpetrators. The women raped at Incirli were put on the stand, where the commission "spoke to them severely and in very coarse language." The three ex-virgins were "told . . . to describe the exact details. . . . The girls began to cry and said they could not tell a man of their own religion such things, much less Turkish officers, and one of them fainted." The married women "volunteered full details," but the court nonetheless ruled that "as the persons said to have been assaulted refused to confirm the details, there was no case."[24] Although no Turks were brought to justice, several dozen Armenians were tried for crimes related to these events.[25]

The proceeding was a farce. Witnesses present in court later said that the judges intimidated, reprimanded, and harangued Armenian witnesses as infidels. "You see the Islamic nation is great," one judge proclaimed in the midst of the trial. According to Western reports, Muslims were cajoled to "bear false witness," the local mufti having issued a fatwa declaring it "lawful to kill, assault, and falsely accuse" men who oppose the government.[26] Sentences were carried out in April: one Armenian was hanged, fifteen more were condemned to death, and three dozen were given long prison terms.[27]

The incidents in and around Yozgat deepened the conviction among Ottoman officials and the Muslim public that Armenians presented a revolutionary threat. Hearts and minds were conditioned for violence—whether preemptive strikes against Armenians or vengeance following seemingly inevitable rebellion. In February the American consul in Sivas, Dr. Milo A. Jewett, raised the alarm. He warned his superior Alexander Watkins Terrell, the American minister in Constantinople, of "rumors" concerning a "contemplated assassination of the Christians at Sivas."[28] To the British consul in Trabzon, Henry Z. Longworth, Jewett wrote of an impending "massacre": "notables . . . plotting an attack upon Christians." Jewett had obtained the names of the

Sites of Massacre of Armenians, and Resistance, 1894–1896

BULGARIA

Black Sea

RUSSIA

IRAN

Istanbul
✕ 8/95, 10/95

Eskisehir
✕ 10/95

Ankara

Merzifon
✕ 11/95

Amasya
✕ 11/95

Zile
✕ 11/95

Tokat
✕ 3/95

Yozgat
✕ 2/94

Kayseri
✕ 11/95

Sivas
✕ 11/95

Gurun
✕ 11/95

Zeytun
▲ 10–12/95

Maras
✕ 10–11/95

Trabzon
✕ 10/95

Gumushane
✕ 10/95

Bayburt
✕ 10/95

Erzincan
✕ 10/95

Arabkir
✕ 11/95

Egin
✕ 9/96

Erzurum
✕ 10/95

Harput
✕ 11/95

Malatya
✕ 11/95

Adiyaman
✕ 11/95

Severek
✕ 11/95

Diyarbekir
✕ 11/95

Birecik
✕ 1/96

Urfa
✕ 10–12/95

Antep
✕ 11/95

Aleppo

Sason
✕ 8–9/94

Van
• Van ✕ 6/96
▲ 6/96

Lake
Van

Lake
Urmia

Tbilisi

Yerevan

Tigris

Euphrates

Nicosia

Mediterranean Sea

KM

0   100   300   500

✕ Massacre   ▲ Organized resistance

plotters, "fanatical and unprincipled men," including Nuri Bey, the mayor. Jewett further reported that the vali had angrily declared, "I will outrage the mother of these giaours or they will outrage mine." In other words, as Jewett put it, "I will crush and ruin these infidels or be ruined by them." He also reported "a similar plot at Cesarea [Kayseri]." Back in Sivas, Jewett observed Turks walking the streets "heavily armed." The garrison had received "new arms and ammunition," and gendarmes were going about with "two belts full of cartridges," contrary to "the usual custom," apparently of one cartridge belt.[29]

Sason

The injustice in Yozgat had largely been perpetrated by Turkish officials and soldiers; in Sason, in Bitlis vilayet, local tribes joined in. Together these Muslims perpetrated the first large-scale massacre of Anatolian Christians during the 1894–1896 period.

According to Currie, Sason was "wild and mountainous," "poor," and "the worst-governed" independent district in the empire. The Armenians lived under the thumb of a Kurdish majority who "exercise a sort of feudal authority." Armenian villagers, "their vassals," paid an annual tribute to the Kurds, above and beyond the taxes they owed, and often paid, to the government. Though oppressed, the local Armenians were a proud people, "fierce and warlike" and "hardly distinguishable from their Kurdish neighbours."[30] An American missionary considered these Armenians "an exceptionally hardy, brave set."[31]

Armenian-Kurdish relations in the Sason area were often described as amicable.[32] After the massacre in Sason was over, a Kurdish chieftain lamented the loss of "love and perfect confidence" that had prevailed "for hundreds of years between us and the Christians." In a petition to the great powers, he wrote of a kind of paternalistic bond. "Peace and safety existed among us, so that though each one of us owned a Christian, and every year exacted a fixed amount for protection afforded, yet we cared for them more than [for] our own children, and if they suffered oppression and injustice from any one, we would labor for them to the extent of sacrificing our very life for the love of them, and this cannot be denied."[33]

Armenians, however, did not see the situation as idyllic. One testified that Ottoman policy seemed geared toward "extermination, persecuting us in all sorts of ways and continually inciting neighboring Kurdish tribes against us. Taxes were arbitrarily raised to a most exorbitant rate and levied in a most tyrannical fashion." He added, "Besides, we had to pay tribute (in kind) to some seven different Kurd 'Ashirs,' or chieftains . . . and at the same time were continually exposed to their plunder, rape and murder."[34] The levies worsened with the arrival of additional tribes from Persia and Kurdistan. In the early 1890s, some villages, including Talori (Dalvoreeg or Talvori) and its satellites, refused to pay the government taxes, arguing that they could not afford the multiple charges and that the government was failing to carry out the basic task of providing security against marauders. Local officials designated this behavior subversive.[35]

Whatever the historical relations between Sason's Armenians and the local tribes, during the two years leading up to the massacre, matters there had grown worse. Fearful of rebellion, troops and gendarmes had placed the area under a virtual "siege," preventing "intercourse with neighboring towns." An Armenian explained, "Our elders were constantly arrested, imprisoned and tortured and life was made generally unbearable—all under pretense of our being revolutionists." In summer 1893, after a severe two-year famine and after paying tribute to two local tribes and taxes to the government, the situation became "insupportable" when Kurdish tribes from Diyarbekir, the Badikanli and Bekiranli, entered the town and demanded additional tribute. When the Armenians refused, the Kurds raided nearby villages.[36] Armenians then mounted counter-raids.[37] At Talori, villagers fired at a nearby Kurdish encampment; the Kurds responded by sacking the village and driving the villagers to the nearby hills.[38] The government sent reinforcements, ostensibly to protect the villagers, but proceeded to arrest and torture Armenian notables, charging them with sedition. The soldiers' horses ate what little grain was available. In nearby Simal, Turks "hung Azo," a local Armenian notable, "by the feet from the ceiling . . . and literally covered his body, face, forehead and tongue with cruciform scars made with a red-hot iron." The villagers told Tahsin Pasha, the vali, that they could pay no further taxes unless he protected them from the Kurds. He instead demanded that they surrender their weapons. They refused, "having no faith in the promises of the [Otto-mans]."³⁹ Thus matters stood at the end of 1893.⁴⁰

As the state became more suspicious, it turned to arresting alleged rabble rousers who had come to Sason. In 1894 officials detained two outsiders. One, Mihran Daghmatian, called on the villagers to stand up for their rights and demand that Constantinople put an end to local misgovernment and Kurdish depredations. The other, Harmpartsoon Boagian, was a physician trained in Constantinople, Athens, and Geneva, who tried to teach Arme-nian villagers "not to sell their daughters in marriage" and to stand up to the Kurds.

But while outside agitators did play some role in Sason, contemporary re-ports suggest that the "desperate" villagers were poorly armed and had not rebelled.⁴¹ Indeed, it is clear from the evidence that the massacres that took place in Sason in August–September 1894 came in response to Armenian re-sistance to Turkish and Kurdish aggression; they were not a Turkish effort—even an overblown one—to stave off insurrection.⁴²

The immediate prelude to massacre came in July, when officials in nearby Muş, the seat of the district, were said to have "commissioned" a tribal leader, Sheikh Mehemet, to muster near Talori "large numbers" from the Diyarbekir region. A group of Kurds camped near Simal. Then, in August, the vali reportedly urged or ordered the tribesmen to attack.⁴³ The orders likely origi-nated with Süreyya Bey, first secretary to Sultan Abdülhamid II, who sent explicit instructions to the army's commander in chief to "neutralize all ban-dits by force, no quarter to be given." This was interpreted by the Sason au-thorities as a license to kill.⁴⁴ Ottoman Army correspondence clarifies that the orders were to kill the men and spare women and children.⁴⁵ From Erzurum, Graves reported "I learn privately that the Ferik [lieutenant general], Edhem Pasha, while at Muş received telegrams from Zeki Pasha ordering the slaughter of Sason Armenians which he refused to obey. The execution of these orders then devolved upon [Colonel] Tewfik Bey."⁴⁶ Armenian witnesses testified that the Kurds were "saying among themselves" that they had received orders from the Ottoman authorities "to exterminate the Armenians."⁴⁷

In a post-massacre petition to the queen of England, thirty-nine local Kurdish chieftains, including leaders of the principal tribes engaged in the vio-lence, also blamed Turkish officials. The chieftains wrote that Turkish officials "deceived us with fallacious arguments, saying 'The Christians are enemies of our religion. Do not allow their eyes to be opened. Give them no peace. Rob them of their property, seize and abduct their wives and daughters by force. Give false witness against them. For when they are left at ease they will ruin our land and religion.'"[48]

The assaults on the Armenian villagers began on or around August 19 and lasted three weeks. The precipitating incident occurred in Simal, where Bekiranli Kurds raided the herds, killing a shepherd and carrying off a thousand head. Armenians gave chase and, after a firefight, retrieved the stolen animals. Two or three Kurds were killed. The Kurds brought the bodies to the authorities, apparently after mutilating them. The Kurds alleged that "the Armenians were up in arms and that there were foreigners among them instigating . . . revolt." An Ottoman commander backed them up.[49] In response, a missionary wrote, "The government secretly gave the Kurds carte blanche to do what they could to the Armenians."[50] The Kurds then demanded an indemnity in cash, which the Armenians said they could pay but only in kind. The Kurds refused, and attacked the next day.[51]

The first targets were the small villages of Ghelie Genneman and Alliantz. After destroying these, the Kurds moved on to Simal, Senik, and their satellites. These were wealthy, tax-paying villages. Most of the inhabitants fled to Geligüzan or into the hills, where they joined other villagers, who apparently had sought refuge there after local Kurds warned them of impending attacks on their homes.[52]

At Geligüzan the Armenians beat back repeated Kurdish assaults. The Turks responded by sending in regulars and mountain guns from Diyarbekir, Van, Bitlis, and Erzurum to reinforce the Kurds. There may also have been several regiments of Hamidiye cavalry. Some reports say they bivouacked in Muş and never actually reached the killing fields, but instead ravaged nearby Armenian villages. Nominally Zeki Pasha, the *muşir* (general) of the 4th Army Corps, was giving the orders, though command in the field appears to have been exercised by Colonels Ismail Bey and Tevfik Pasha. According to a British diplomat, a Major Salih, of the Muş Battalion, was a prominent participant in the massacre.[53] In an effort to cover their traces, some government troops dressed as Kurds.[54] The Kurds were "constantly in and out of [the soldiers'] camp," one Turkish soldier later testified.[55]

The resisting Armenians, women among them, eventually ran out of ammunition and fled to Mount Andok (Anduk Dağı) with Kurds and Turks on their heels.[56] "That night the sky was red with the flames of our burning homes," an Armenian fighter later recalled.[57] Hundreds, perhaps as many as two thousand, made it up Mount Andok, firing and rolling boulders down the slopes at their pursuers. But Turkish and Kurdish firepower and resolution gradually prevailed.[58] Within days, the Armenians collapsed. Some defenders were killed; some women, with their children, jumped to their deaths from the cliffs.[59] Other Armenians managed to escape and hid for weeks in forests and scrublands. Kurdish and Turkish troops scoured the area for survivors, usually killing them on the spot. One survivor later described her ordeal:

When the Kurds came on us, I . . . tried to escape with 3 other women (two being aunts of my husband) but, there being no time, we hastily hid ourselves amongst some thick bushes, where we were soon discovered by a band of 4 Kurds and 3 soldiers. We begged and implored for mercy. But they knocked us down with the butt-end of their guns and killed my three companions. Then a soldier snatched my three-months-old babe (a boy) from my arms and, in spite of tearful pleadings, threw him against a rock, then pierced him with his fixed bayonet and threw him up in the air. The other soldiers then cut him up into pieces. They then all fell on me, swearing and kicking, and knocking me down with the butt-end of their guns. One of the Kurds then, finding me young, decided to take me with him. But I refused to follow him and become a Mohammedan. They threatened and tortured me and finally decided to kill me, but I was dressed in fine clothes, [so] they undressed me—so as not to soil them with my blood. When, in doing so, they discovered the gold coins in my head-dress and some thirty pounds in my belt, they immediately began to fight amongst themselves. Taking advantage of this opportunity I flew away through the dense brushwood. They fired after me but missed me. I hid myself and remained there all day, all night and all next day—trembling from fright, famished with hunger, and shivering from cold. . . . During the second night I ventured out and putting on some clothes which I got from the dead bodies of some women, I wandered through the forest in search of food and assistance. I then met an Armenian named Kaleh . . . and we managed to reach Khnoos.[60]

Led by a priest, Der Hohanes Mardovan, about 400 men and women who had first fled to Mount Andok surrendered at Geligüzan in exchange for a guarantee of protection. They were "urged to accept Islam" but refused. On Colonel Ismail's orders, a soldier gouged out Mardovan's eyes. The mutilated priest then begged for his own death—"Let me die," he said—and was bayoneted, according to both a survivor and a soldier who witnessed the scene.[61] In the days that followed the troops massacred many of the men who had returned to Geligüzan. Some reports speak of a single mass killing of about 40 villagers. Another describes hundreds systematically killed in batches of ten to twenty over a number of nights. All reports agree that the dead were dumped into one or more pre-dug trenches or pits and covered with earth.[62]

A further massacre, by soldiers, appears to have taken place in the Ghelie San Ravine, five hours walk from Geligüzan. Hundreds of Armenians hid there.[63] Some were burnt to death, others hacked to pieces, still others killed by shrapnel.[64] Armenians, including women, were tied to horses and dragged through fields until they died. Houses crammed with people were set alight. Kurdish chieftains and Ottoman officers abducted women, raped them, and forced them to convert. Some were serially raped at the church in the nearby village of Galin, then murdered.[65] Young boys were abducted into Muslim households.[66] Occasionally, abductors sold the children. For instance, a chief of the Kurdish Rushkotli tribe sold a brother and sister, aged 9 and 11, for 150 piasters.[67] To avoid discovery, mothers suffocated crying children.[68] Fearing what would befall them if they were found, some Armenians jumped into a "raging" river and drowned. "The river is said to have been red with blood for three days," a missionary reported.[69] Several survivors went mad.[70] Priests were subjected to especially vile treatment. One was reportedly "strung to a beam and cut to pieces." Another was chained by the neck, with two soldiers pulling from opposite sides. In the end, bayonets were placed upright in the ground and the priest was thrown on them. All told, six or seven were murdered.[71]

Surviving villagers also told stories about Kurds and soldiers who showed mercy to women and children. But these incidents usually ended with the deaths of those initially reprieved.[72] Soldiers who refused to butcher the innocent were punished and chastened as infidels while their more willing comrades dispatched the victims.[73]

All this murder came at the behest of the sultan himself, in an Islamist message delivered via the vali, Tahsin Pasha, who visited Mount Andok while the Armenians were still on the run. His secretary read the troops a firman from Abdülhamid ordering that "the disaffected villages that were supposed to be in rebellion were to be wiped out." The troops and Kurds were "to spare no one or nothing . . . for their King and Prophet."[74]

After the stand at Mount Andok and the massacre at Ghelie San Ravine, troops moved on to Talori and nearby villages, which they destroyed while carrying off anything valuable they could handle. Cecil Hallward, the British vice-consul in Van, later met survivors. Some told him that while Kurds there had taken cattle and sheep, they had generally refrained from participating in the massacres. One local Kurdish leader, Khishman Aga, was reportedly imprisoned for "befriending the Armenians." That said, Kurds reportedly also kidnapped "a number of [Armenian] girls." One report put the number in the hundreds, with one Kurdish tribe, Bekiranli, taking 400 girls.[75] The soldiers raped "many others."[76] Allen, the Van missionary, reported in 1895 that one local Kurdish chieftain, Hussein Pasha, had twenty Sason girls in his harem. Others were apparently in the hands of a Kurdish chieftain in the Jazira area.[77]

In the second week of September, Zeki Pasha arrived and halted the murders.[78] Altogether, some thirty Armenian villages had been "wholly blotted out." A missionary compared what had happened to the atrocities of 1877, in which Abdülhamid's government was accused of slaughtering thousands of Bulgarian Christians.[79] One estimate places the number of dead at 800 in Geligüzan, 2,200 in and around Talori, and 2,000 on Mt. Andok.[80] In all, between 3,000 and 6,000 Armenians were killed. At the time, Kurdish losses were estimated in the thousands, but the balance of forces suggests this was probably an exaggeration. The government claimed no losses among its troops, though later estimates put the number at 150–200. Hundreds of Kurds, Turks, and Armenians likely succumbed to cholera.[81]

During and immediately after Sason, the authorities tried to prevent word of events there from leaking. The grand vizier told the British ambassador in Constantinople that "the Armenians had attacked Moslems" and "had desecrated their corpses."[82] "No atrocities ever occurred or were ever proved," the grand vizier told the American minister, Terrell. The terrible stories that filled the Western press were the concoctions of "Armenian anarchists"; what occurred was an Armenian "revolution."[83] For months, American diplomats in Turkey were taken in by the deceit. Terrell telegraphed Washington that "reports in Armenian papers of Turkish atrocities at Talori are sensational and exaggerated. The killing was in a conflict between armed Armenians and Turkish soldiers" and was necessitated by Armenian "insurrection."[84] He believed that the clashes were initiated by Armenian revolutionaries. "Public opinion" in Europe was, he wrote, "deceived" by Armenian propaganda.[85]

The Ottomans did their best to prevent Hallward from reaching the area to see for himself, arguing that the roads were unsafe and that the area was beset by cholera. (One missionary suggested that the outbreak was in part due to the "stench of carnage" floating in from the nearby mountains.[86]) Once Hallward reached Muş, policemen were stationed prominently outside his lodgings and "spies" followed him wherever he went.[87] He speculated that the authorities hoped to keep him away from the affected districts until winter, when the roads would be impassable, and that the affair would blow over by the time he could get to the massacre sites. Fearing retribution, Armenians routinely refused to meet him or tell him what had happened. The authorities also arrested leading Armenians, including six monks, and prevented businessmen from other provinces reaching the area.[88]

Ottoman officials pressed local Armenians to sign a *mazbata*, testimony expressing "satisfaction with [Abdülhamid's] rule" and asserting that it was they who had "stirred matters up."[89] Police arrested dozens of Armenians in Muş and Bitlis to intimidate the communities into silence, extort funds, and coerce them to write letters approving the government's conduct and condemning fellow Armenians. At least six prisoners died of torture and other ill treatment. According to a missionary, all, "with hardly a rag on them," had been "put down . . . a damp filthy dungeon, half starved, often cruelly beaten." The missionary suggested that the prisoners had suffered the usual fare of "political prisoners" in Turkey: "flogging . . . the branding iron," being made to "stand for several hours barefoot on the snow." He noted with astonishment, "There are actually those who have had tacks driven into their heads." The

Turks claimed the prisoners died of cholera.[90] By late 1895 twelve other prisoners, from Talori, had died in Muş, and another was at death's door. British representations only resulted in additional abuse of the prisoners.[91]

In the winter of 1895, under pressure by the great powers, the government set up a commission of inquiry to investigate the massacre—or at least pretend to do so. Constantinople also ordered officials in the eastern provinces to restrain soldiers and Kurds: the great powers would be closely monitoring the work of the commission and, in general, goings on in the eastern provinces.[92] One British report said that initially the government ordered Kurds in the Khouit district to resume anti-Armenian activities but then countermanded the order, enjoining them "to keep the peace till the Commission shall get away."[93]

The commission set up shop in Muş.[94] Attached to it, at the great powers' insistence, were three delegates representing Britain, France, and Russia. They watched the proceedings and reported to their ambassadors. Sometimes the delegates, individually or collectively, pressed the commission to take a certain step or summon a particular witness. But the commission was free to reject such suggestions and often did.[95]

Assisted by local officials, the commission spent the winter and spring of 1895 framing the Armenians for their own slaughter by manipulating evidence, intimidating witnesses, and denying and manipulating testimony. In the estimation of Vice-Consul Hammond Smith Shipley, the British delegate, the commission's efforts were "directed towards showing that the Armenians were in a state of revolt and that they were guilty of atrocious outrages upon the Kurds." The commission was intent on showing that Armenians "were in every case the aggressors" and that "they were guilty of acts of revolting barbarity."[96] On rare occasions the commissioners made a show of seeking out "pro-Armenian" witnesses.[97] Meanwhile, in a largely successful effort to expunge physical traces of the massacres, soldiers dug the bodies from the trenches at Geligüzan and dispersed them in the snow.[98] Though one delegate described the "smell" as "overpowering," the commission found just one skeleton and, otherwise, "fragments of human bones."[99]

According to Shipley, the delegates were "closely watched" and hampered. They were subjected to "insulting and violent conduct" by police and were forced to contend with "systematic persecution of their servants, guides and other Christians" who were "brought into any communication with them." Authorities exercised "administrative pressure on an extensive scale" against "all persons suspected of their capacity or intention of giving damaging evidence." The British even got hold of a letter from General Rahmi Pasha ordering Hamidiyes in the Malazgirt district to make sure that "no one is to be allowed to visit Moush during the inquiry, for the purpose of laying complaints before the Commission."[100]

In cases where the murder of Armenians was undeniable, the authorities and commissioners tried to exonerate Turkish officials and soldiers and lay blame exclusively on the Kurds.[101] One Armenian witness, Hebo of Shenik, claimed he had been "threatened with death by the chief of the Gendarmerie if he accused the regular troops and not the Kurds of massacring the Armenians." Cooperation, on the other hand, would be lucrative. In exchange for testifying to the revolutionary commitments of those killed, and attributing "the burning of the villages to the Kurds" rather than Turkish regulars, the mutesarrif of Muş and the secretary of the commission promised to rebuild Hebo's house; provide him "five hundred sheep, ten oxen and one thousand piasters"; and restore to him 160 liras taken from his brother Kriko, who was killed in the massacre.[102]

The thirty-nine Kurdish chieftains who petitioned Queen Victoria were wise to this betrayal. They explained in their letter that the Turks had prodded them to attack and plunder and then blamed them for what had happened, even though much if not most of the killing had been carried out by regular soldiers. It was, the chieftains alleged, soldiers and gendarmes who carried out "the massacres, robberies, burning and other disgusting works that have taken place among the Sassoun Mountains . . . and they have laid everything on the Kurds."[103]

In spite of the cover-up, details of what had happened gradually emerged from the investigations of diplomats and the foreign press.[104] Operating from distant Russian-held Kars, a special correspondent for London's *Daily Telegraph* reported that he "and his assistants" had examined "over 200 persons who saw or took part in the massacre." Among the interviewees were Turkish noncommissioned officers and "wild Kurds." The Turkish witnesses, he wrote, "are often drunk, but the Kurds speak the truth soberly and fearlessly." One Kurd described how "the Turkish soldiers took little children by the feet and dashed them against stones." The Kurd said he saw soldiers torture an Armenian priest, "squeezing his neck, gouging out his eyes, and tearing off his flesh with pincers." The Kurd added, "We hate that; we only stab, or bayonet, or cut off heads. We dislike needless pain." He also claimed he "saw the soldiers . . . joking around" a pregnant woman and making "bets as to the sex of her child. She was then cut open and the money was paid to the scoundrel who had guessed rightly." The report concluded that "the soldiers delighted in torture. They put some to death with scissors, cutting them and opening veins in the neck. Others were sawed, others had the tongues cut out, eyes gouged out, and several fingers removed before death."[105]

The commission's determination was that Sason had been the site of an Armenian rebellion. The Turks' report and the delegates' differed, Shipley said, like "night and day."[106] Graves complained of the commission's bias, its failure to probe the 1893 Kurdish depredations that had led to Armenians' "isolated acts of hostility towards the Kurds and . . . insubordination towards Government officials," which had triggered the "terrible reprisals" of 1894. Graves also decried the lack of Ottoman cooperation, which meant he was unable to assess the precise share of the "regular troops in the massacre."[107] The acting British vice-consul in Diyarbekir, Thomas Boyajian, recognized Kurdish culpability, condemning in particular the "Sheikhs of Zilan and Dudan, Gendjo and Khalil of Sassoun, Eumer the chief of the Bekiran tribe, another chief of the Charabi tribe and the brother of [the Sheikh of Zilan], Molla Djami."[108] And Hallward denounced the Turkish explanations as "an extraordinary tissue of misstatements."[109] Ottoman officials, he said, knew that what had occurred were not "clashes" but massacres by Kurds and Turks. None of the Western diplomats bothered to translate the commission's brief report for their own files.

For their part, the British ruled that there was "reason to believe that the Bitlis Government had secretly encouraged the Kurds to pick a quarrel with the Armenians." The Ottoman authorities "were apparently driven by a desire to destroy the independence of the district" or, in an alternative phrasing, to break "the strength of the Sassoun Armenians." Tahsin, the British concluded, also sought to extract money from Armenians and gain personal prestige as the suppressor of a revolt. Although there was no such revolt, he may have really believed that he was suppressing one.[110]

Western observers initially hoped that the appointment of the commission might "modify" government and popular attitudes toward the Christian communities but were forced to admit that the opposite had happened. "A more than usually fanatical spirit is manifesting itself not only among the soldiers but among the Kurds and other Moslems," Hallward wrote. Soldiers returning to Van from the massacres apparently told Armenian villagers along the way that "their turn would come next if they remained Christian." These soldiers, Hallward thought, seemed "to regard their proceedings at Sassoun in the light of a religious war." The massacre would prove to be merely an "episode" in "the government's general policy of suppressing the Christian element in Kurdistan."[111]

The survivors were still suffering acutely a year after the massacres. One British diplomat believed that the authorities were continuing their effort "to consummate the ruin of the Christians of Sassoun and Talori" under "the guise of superintending" relief for the survivors, who were still living in abject poverty, without housing, food, or clothes.[112] Kurdish nomads had returned to the pasturelands, where they continued "eating up the hay," threatening the harvests, and demanding tribute.[113] A letter from a missionary in Muş described the situation around Talori in 1895:

At the beginning of spring oppression began at the hands of the nomad Kurds and others, and the villagers then decided that it was best to return to their former homes. There are about 860 of these houseless wanderers now living in the woods and mountains, in caves and hollow trees, half naked and some indeed entirely without covering for their nakedness. Bread they have not tasted for months, and curdled milk they only dream of, living, as they do upon grass and the leaves of trees. There are two varieties of grass which are preferred, but these are disappearing. . . . Living on such food, they have become sickly and their skin has turned yellow, their strength is gone, their bodies are swollen and fever is rife among them.

The Kurds would shoot these unfortunates "on sight . . . so . . . they will gradually die out. . . . The authorities do not allow them to wander out and beg."[114]

Survivors largely fled to unaffected villages or to Muş. But some remained in the Sason area, eventually emerging from forests and caves. And some who hid did not emerge. During a snowstorm in mid-March 1895, a *Daily Telegraph* correspondent in Simal visited a house where two girls, aged six and fourteen, had lived on their own since the massacre. He found them "dead, curled up on a wisp of straw, in a corner of the room, with only a skirt apiece for clothing. They were close together. The room was cold as an ice-cellar, and there were no provisions whatsoever."[115]

The massacre—and the failure to punish the perpetrators—persuaded Muslims in the eastern provinces that "the Christians have been delivered into their hands to do with as they please." So in spring 1895, local officials allowed themselves to behave in "the most brutal manner, beating and torturing [Christian] men, and shamefully ill-using the women" while quartering gendarmes for free in the villages as they extracted exorbitant taxes.[116] In Kegi *kaza,* a sub-district jurisdiction, tax farmers reportedly went "so far as to hang up, head downwards, those who, from poverty, cannot pay what is due."[117] The abuses continued through the summer. In villages in the plain around Muş, "men are beaten" by gendarmes, "imprisoned, human excrement rubbed in their faces; women and girls are insulted and dishonoured, dragged naked from their beds at night; children are not spared."[118]

Little aid reached the survivors, in spite of Western missionaries' and consuls' attempts to provide relief. The authorities, who suspected that British diplomats and American missionaries were working to promote Armenian separatism, severely hampered the aid project. Eventually, in what likely was an effort to reduce contact even further, the Ottomans decided that all relief would be handled by themselves rather than by foreigners.[119]

The news from Sason reverberated across the empire. Reporting from Van nine months later, the British vice-consul wrote that "matters have been brought to a crisis by the Sassoun massacre" and that, if nothing would be done, "similar scenes will be repeated in this province, and existence rendered impossible to the Christian population."[120] In the Musa Dağ and Kesab areas, news of the affair gave "great impetus" to recruitment among the Armenian revolutionary movements. "The argument that, unless they armed, their wives and children would be butchered was used with great effect," the local British consul reported, "and men would part with everything they had in order to obtain money enough to buy shot-guns and revolvers."[121] It is not clear how widespread was this galvanizing effect.

Following Sason, the great powers did nothing except renew the diplomatic pressure to implement reforms. Constantinople noted that its massacres had come and gone without Western retribution.

Constantinople: The Turning Point

More than a year passed before the destruction of the Armenians resumed. The second wave began in Constantinople, on September 30, 1895, and continued in a series of massacres around the eastern provinces. Events in the capital, filtered through distorted news reports and official propaganda, enraged Muslims in the provinces and led directly to orders commanding the slaughter of tens of thousands of Armenians.

What happened in Constantinople is fairly clear. On September 30, groups of Armenians, at least partly organized by Hunchaks and numbering between 500 and 2,000, assembled at Kumkapı, near the Armenian Patriarchate, and advanced toward the grand vizier's offices to voice their "grievances."[122] According to Currie, the demonstrators "were armed with pistols and knives of an [*sic*] uniform pattern" implying that organizers had distributed the weapons.[123] The demonstrators, described in one report as "mostly young men of the middle class," carried a petition railing against "the present state of affairs in our country." The petition protested "systematic persecution . . . with the one object of causing the Armenians to disappear from their own country," "innumerable political arrests," "barbarous and inhuman tortures," "and the iniquitous exactions of the officials and tax-gatherers." Citing "the massacre in Sassoun," the Armenians demanded reform in the eastern provinces and a curb on Kurdish brigandage.[124]

Currie was not convinced of the group's civil-minded goals. He believed that the Hunchak aim was to provoke "bloodshed," which would induce foreign intervention. Many of the demonstrators apparently "took the Sacrament in the various Armenian churches on the preceding Sunday in order to be prepared for death," he wrote.[125] The patriarch was also alarmed and tried unsuccessfully to stop the demonstration.

The petition and demonstration plan were submitted to the Sublime Porte two days before the gathering, so no one was caught off guard. But when the day came, the demonstrators were blocked by police near Sultan Mahmud's tomb and told to disperse. After shots rang out—it is unclear who fired first—the demonstrators ran off with police giving chase. According to informants working for the American minister between fifteen and fifty people were killed, "the Turks suffering as much as the Armenians." The Ottoman minister of police said the Armenians initiated the clash when an Armenian drew a knife on a battalion commander "who tried to parlay with them." The French ambassador reported that the Armenians killed a policeman.[126]

Sparked by the clash, Turks swarmed the downtown streets and attacked Armenian passersby. Many of the assaults were carried out by softas armed with clubs. Policemen either looked on or took part. The "repression was merciless," the French ambassador reported. Westerners witnessed gendarmes holding down and then shooting an Armenian, clubbing to death two others, and bayoneting nine prisoners.[127] A Turkish *cavass* (ceremonial guard) assigned to the British consulate saw four Armenians "bayoneted in cold blood" in the courtyard of the Ministry of Police.[128]

Muslim clerics played a prominent role in the assaults. French Ambassador Paul Cambon reported that immediately after the clash at the Sublime Porte, "a multitude of mollahs . . . gathered on the Hagia Sophia square to deliberate the attitude to be taken."[129] At least some of them decided to join in. They went about the streets "arresting people, threatening and mistreating the ones they met."[130] Ginning up their fellow Muslims, they "paraded through the city" a coffin allegedly containing the body of an Ottoman officer slain by Armenians.[131]

The following day several Armenians were killed "with sticks and stones" by "the Turkish rabble."[132] One missionary reported seeing "a number of softas on the streets who looked very savage and who I observed had revolvers under their long gowns." Missionary employees reported witnessing arrested Armenians beaten to death by mobs of softas and other Turks.[133]

On the night of October 1, and into the early morning of October 2, isolated and sporadic attacks gave way to a full-scale pogrom. Cambon spoke of "passions . . . unchained."[134] A number of caravanserai (known in Turkish as hans and in Persian as khans) inhabited by Armenians were attacked, with police connivance or participation.[135] In one case, twenty-five Armenian laborers were "butchered" by assailants carrying "sticks and knives." Fifty more were murdered in another. Two Armenians were killed near a Protestant school. Seven were killed in Scutari (Üsküdar), on the Asian side of the Bosporus. Contemporary reports indicate that a total of about eighty Armenians were killed and 800–1,000 imprisoned. According to Terrell, the mobs were largely composed of armed softas and "fanatical Moslem priests."[136]

Some Armenians fought back: in at least one case, they attacked a police post.[137] Many others preferred to stay away from the melee and took refuge in churches around the city.[138] A missionary remarked that "women have not been molested in any case, even in cases where the mob broke into and robbed houses." As night turned to day, Terrell found the streets empty apart from patrolling soldiers and "turbaned ulemas."[139]

The authorities appear to have paid the rioters, after the event if not before. A softa who murdered an Armenian told a shopkeeper who witnessed the killing that "he used the money received from the imperial bounty on this occasion to complete his theological library." Rewards could be considerable. A Turkish newspaper, *Sabah,* reported on October 5 that the government had just given the madrassas around Sultan Beyezid Mosque "11 sheep and a sufficient amount of the Imperial bounty."[140] An American missionary reported, "Many persons . . . believe" that "police agents disguised as softas" had carried out the pogrom. If true, this would "imply that the authorities had long before prepared the softa garb for hundreds of police agents knowing that the odium of their deeds would thereby fall upon the softa class."[141] But, according to most reports, there were genuine softas among the rioters.

After the two days of unhampered violence, the government, under pressure from the Christian ambassadors, arrested sixty softas and deployed guards around the Armenian quarter.[142] But the tension was only deepening. An October 8 report describes softas patrolling Constantinople's streets "in unusual force."[143] On the 14th a British businessman reported that a number of Armenians were murdered. Hunchaks were forcing Armenians to keep their shops closed—"to prolong the excitement," according to one report.[144] Terrell believed that the Armenians were acting under "orders" from the "revolutionary leaders, whose vengeance they dread if they disobey," while the Muslims, he wrote, "pretend to see in [store closures] a demonstration to arouse sympathy among Christian nations." But Armenian behavior was probably not, or not only, a function of revolutionist pressure. As one observer noted, in Pera, they "sought refuge in the churches, owing to Mussulman threats."[145]

On October 21, to appease the great powers, the government announced a series of reforms. The Constantinople killings provided the urgency, but the sultan's *irâde* (imperial decree) was in fact a belated response to the Sason massacre and the resulting inquiry. The reforms were hammered out in negotiations between the ambassadors of Britain, France, and Russia and the Sublime Porte and were communicated to the valis of Erzerum, Van, Bitlis, Diyarbekir, Mamuret-ül-Aziz, and Sivas—the six eastern provinces, with large concentrations of Armenians. According to the decree, Christian *muavins* (aides) would be appointed to assist local governors. Christians would be allowed to join the police and gendarmes, in proportion to the size of their communities. There were also regulations designed to curb Kurdish depredations.[146]

But the sultan and his bureaucracy had no intention of implementing the reforms. The previous November, the sultan had made his position crystal clear in a talk with the German ambassador, Prince Hugo von Radolin. Abdülhamid "solemnly swore that under no circumstances would he yield to the unjust Armenian pressure, and that he would rather die than introduce far-reaching reforms in Armenia," Radolin reported to Berlin.[147] Terrell considered the irâde largely meaningless: the steps prescribed were not made public, and, in practice, the Ottomans failed "to embrace the radical measures so emphatically demanded by" the great powers. Although the irâde "restored confidence" among some of the Armenians and Western diplomats who knew of it, Terrell's "own conviction is that [calm] will be only temporary. Permanent security and order . . . are made impossible by the rancor of race and religious hatred, now more bitter than ever." He particularly blamed the scheming of "Armenian anarchists, who will never rest while certain of the sympathy of the Christian world" and "will continue to foment strife."[148]

Whatever the culpability of Armenian revolutionaries, the brunt of the damage would be felt in the provinces, where the independence movement was weakest. In Trabzon, the first provincial massacre site in the wake of the riots, "the excitement of the Turks was . . . greatly increased on hearing of matters in Constantinople." They "seemed to infer that all the Armenians were banded together and in armed rebellion against the government," as one missionary put it.[149] Trabzon had long been on tenterhooks; events in the capital merely intensified existing resentments. In December 1894 Longworth, the local British consul, warned vali Kadri Bey of the Muslims' "bitter feeling." Though such sentiments were "dormant," Longworth was concerned by talk of a future "massacre . . . of infidels" as Muslims reacted to "wild and loose reports of Armenian atrocities committed on Muslims in the interior."[150]

The East Ignites

Immediately following the Constantinople pogrom, orders went out to officials in the eastern provinces to organize anti-Armenian massacres. This, at least, was the view of most leading Western diplomats in Turkey. While unable to obtain copies of these orders, the diplomats were convinced by the "uniform methods and system" employed in each outbreak. Such consistency implied that the violence was "directed by some central authority which had powers to enforce its desires." Terrell wasn't sure whether it was the sultan himself who had given the orders or whether the command came from what he called "the Mohammedan priesthood," but he had no doubt that the call had come from on high.[151] Cambon was a rare dissenter, suggesting that there might be a split between the government and the perpetrators. To his mind, the government at least appeared to be trying to stop the killings.[152]

Such confusions are understandable, given how the authorities labored to cover their tracks. Postal and telegraph officials often "lost" telegrams and letters sent by diplomatic agents and missionaries, or else postponed their delivery, the better to muddy the waters of culpability and prevent information from spilling out of affected areas. Henry D. Barnham, a British consul, wrote from Aleppo in November 1895:

> The authorities . . . have withheld the delivery of the post from Urfa, Aintab and Marash. Special messengers bearing letters addressed to myself and to the American Vice-Consul have been arrested and imprisoned, and my letters restored to me after so long a delay, and in such a condition . . . [as to] warrant the belief that they had been opened. Friends at the various Missions, apprised of these facts, and unwilling to expose their messengers to ill-treatment, are deterred from

writing frequently. Telegrams received by private individuals are value-less, as they are subject to the Censure, and nothing [is] allowed to pass which has not the approval of the Government.[153]

For weeks after the massacres, diplomats in Istanbul were at a loss to understand how the orders had been transmitted to the provinces. One British diplomat initially suggested that the "chief instigators of the massacres" were not the Ottoman rulers but rather "spies of the Palace."[154] In time, however, evidence pointed to the Sublime Porte itself: the orders had reached valis, mutesarrifs, and military and gendarmerie commanders from the highest echelons. One British vice-consul, Charles Hampson, quoted a Muş Muslim notable: "After the disorders in Constantinople, instructions were received from above to massacre and to put the blame on the Armenians, and naturally these instructions were followed." Hampson said he could "vouch for the accuracy of the . . . remarks."[155] He subsequently reported hearing from a "generally . . . trustworthy" Armenian that the sultan had sent a circular telegram "to the authorities of the various districts" stating, "The seven Powers are pressing me to execute their wishes in regard to the Arm. question. Such a course would be most prejudicial to our Empire; &, sooner than adopt it, Turkey must shed every drop of the blood of her soldiers. Be ready, therefore, &, on receiving my order, put every Arm. to the sword." Hampson was hesitant to believe that precisely these words had been sent, but he was convinced that "some such order" had been received by the mutesarrif of Muş before the massacres.[156]

In late 1896 another British diplomat, Fitzmaurice, offered a watered-down variant of this explanation: in the wake of the events in Constantinople, the Sublime Porte had triggered the massacres by sending "cypher" telegrams to the provinces. "The Porte . . . , either willingly or unwillingly misinformed, telegraphed the first garbled accounts" of what had happened. "This, becoming known through the officials to the Mussulman population, tends to poison and excite the minds of the latter against the unsuspecting Christians. . . . The telegraphic circular . . . contributed largely to bring about the massacres. . . . The news . . . led to a distinct ebullition of fanatical feeling among the Moslems of [Urfa] while at Birejik they became fiercely excited against the former converts to Islam."[157]

The exact phrasing of these telegrams is unknown; no copies are accessible in Turkish archives. There is clearer evidence regarding the transmission of massacre orders lower down the chain of command. For example, in May 1896 a British diplomat, Raphael Fontana, sent to his embassy the translated text of two signed statements by Kurdish agas from the Harput and Malatya areas. In the first, six agas swore that one Hadji Khalil Aga of Kizil Ushaghi (Kızıl Uşağı) had led 2,000 Kurds in a raid at Harput kaza on "the command of our Padishah"—a term denoting the sultan. In the second, an aga of the Kızılbaşı Kurds from the village of Bekir Uşağı, testified that Herirje Zade Abdüllah Aga, a member of Malatya's administrative council, had "sent us a letter inviting us to attack the Malatia Armenians." The aga and his men refused to participate. Some days after the "disturbances" in the town, Herirje sent another official to the Kızılbaşı Kurds to "take back the letter," which was returned.[158]

Trabzon (Trebizond)

A multiethnic seaside town inhabited by 20,000 Turks, 15,000 Greeks, and 7,000 Armenians, Trabzon in the mid-1890s was ripe for an explosion.[159] Turks in the area claimed they feared large-scale Armenian violence, though as one missionary put it, "it seems incredible that they could have been sincere in this."[160] "Rumors of massacres at Constantinople tended to aggravate matters," Longworth reported.[161] There was considerable homegrown instability, too. On October 2, 1895, Lieutenant General Bahri Pasha, the outgoing vali of Van, was nearly assassinated in Trabzon, on his way to Constantinople. Bahri had been walking with the Trabzon town commandant, Ahmed Hamdi Pasha, when both were lightly wounded by a gunman. The shooter was not caught, but the Turks charged two Armenian "accomplices."[162]

The situation escalated further on the night of October 4, when "large bands of armed Muslims from the neighboring villages," intent on plunder, attacked Christian houses, firing guns and breaking in doors and windows. A rumor then spread that Christians were massacring Turks—or, alternatively, that Armenians had assassinated the vali.[163] A mob of "at least 3,000" mustered, "with knives, pistols and revolvers," and rushed through the streets. Christians fled to consulates and public buildings. But the vali, Kadri Bey, and some Muslim notables intervened and troops were deployed. They arrested the

ring-leaders and "unmercifully beat" many of the "rowdies." The crowd
dispersed before any lives were lost. The next day, the local consuls—
British, Russian, French, Belgian, Austrian, Greek, Persian, and Italian—
ostentatiously rode in procession down the main street to government
house. Their aim, Longworth explained, was to "calm the fears of the Christians and strike fear in the hearts of the Turks!"[164]

The Turks were not impressed. On October 8, at about eleven o'clock in the
morning, the mayhem in Trabzon began "like a clap of thunder in a clear sky."
Turkish authorities later claimed that "it was impossible to determine on which
side the brawl began" and that Armenians "from their shops and bazaars . . .
indeed from anywhere and everywhere . . . fired at random on soldiers, police,
zapties, and citizens alike" such that the "crowd which found itself in the square
and the adjoining streets was obliged to respond."[165] But Western observers—not
to mention Armenian witnesses—offered a different story: the Turks had
initiated the massacre without provocation. According to an unsigned report,
probably by an American missionary, Armenians were shot down in the street
"or sitting quietly at their shop doors. . . ." Some were slashed with swords.
The Turks "passed through the quarters . . . killing the men and large boys,
generally permitting the women and younger children to live. For five hours this
horrid work of human butchery went on." The report continued:

> Every shop of an Armenian in the market was gutted and the victors . . .
> glutted themselves with the spoils. . . . So far as appearances went, the
> police and soldiers distinctly aided in this savage work. They were min-
> gled with the armed men and so far as we could see made not the least
> effort to check them. Apparently they took care to see that the right
> ones—that is, Armenians, were killed; also that an offer of surrender
> might be made to all that were found unarmed. To any found with arms
> no quarter was given, but large numbers were shot down without any
> proffer of this kind.

In the evening, after a full day of murder and plunder, the vali and his troops
stepped in and stopped the massacre.[166]

The violence spilled over into the rural surround. The French consul in
Erzurum noted, "The whole country between Trabzon and Erzerum is

devastated. On the outskirts of Bayburt, he counted one hundred dead bodies lying together near the road. Nearly all the villages are burned and in many cases the male population is entirely wiped out." The consul also reported the "cattle and grain stolen."[167] According to Longworth, the attackers spared only communities that had "dressed as Moslems [and] professed their conversion to Islamism." Much of the area had been "entirely depopulated," at least temporarily.[168]

Most of Trabzon's Armenians escaped death by fleeing to consulates and public buildings guarded by troops. The town's Greek inhabitants by and large refused shelter to the "hunted down" Armenians. Some 2,000 took refuge in the Catholic Freres' Mission house.[169] Several local Muslim officials also tried to help. The following March, the authorities arrested Essad Bey, a judge, apparently because he had assisted Armenians. "Honest, impartial, and tolerant," the French ambassador wrote, "Essad Bey demonstrated the most laudable attitude during the October massacres. . . . Such a judge could not have found grace among the fanatical Muslims of Trabzon. They denounced him to the palace."[170]

The local branch of the Anglo-American Relief Committee carefully tabulated casualty figures: 298 Armenians were killed, along with another 100 or so "wayfarers and strangers," 9 Turks, and 3 Greeks. Another 200 Armenians were killed in the surrounding villages, including 118 in Gümüşhane (Gumush Khaneh). Altogether 1,500 houses were looted and 320 burned. By February 1896, when the body counts were published, some 1,700 Trabzon Armenians and more than 3,000 from the surrounding countryside had fled the empire.[171]

Following the massacre the authorities rounded up some 400 Armenians, though all but 50 were released by early November.[172] The authorities pressured Armenians to sign a declaration blaming the bloodshed on revolutionaries.[173] By early November, "not one Turk" had been arrested. Turks and Greeks—under Muslim pressure—boycotted Armenian shops, adding to Armenian woes. The British consul described the Armenians as "virtually outcasts, bereft of their belongings, reduced to beggary and expelled from their hired houses."[174]

As with other massacres, the government sought to portray Armenians as aggressors who brought violence on themselves. Trabzon authorities claimed the "disturbances" had started when an Armenian fired at soldiers after he had heard that his brother had been killed in Constantinople.[175] They further claimed that, in the days and hours before the outbreak, Armenians had walked about town "armed to the teeth."[176] In late October, Cambon reported, "The Sublime Porte is ... sending [circulars] to its representatives abroad, claiming that ... Armenian armed bands are now burning Muslim villages, invading mosques and slaughtering Muslims."[177]

Yet foreign observers were not taken in; their condemnation of the Turks was swift and definitive. Even the Germans, who at this stage tended to justify Ottoman policy, were appalled. Upon hearing of the events at Trabzon, the kaiser reportedly said, "This surpasses everything before. This is indeed a St. Bartholomew's massacre!"[178] The British consul wrote that the Turkish mob at first shot down every Armenian they encountered; then, joined by soldiers and later "Greeks and Persians," the mob systematically looted Armenian "houses, shops and storerooms throughout the town," killing anyone who resisted.[179] Greeks, "possibly from fear, refused in the majority of cases to shelter the hunted down people in their shops and houses, schools and churches."[180]

Longworth considered the affair "well organized."[181] Although the vali and the president of the criminal court opposed the massacre, the civilian and military authorities had "behaved disgracefully"; Longworth found "serious reasons to suspect that the slaughter was encouraged if not planned and ordered by some officials." As he understood it, between October 2 and 8, the authorities had disarmed Armenians in the streets and in their houses while word of an impending massacre spread. Per the rumors, non-Armenian Christians "were to be spared." Longworth also reported that Bahri Pasha had been overheard on October 7 persuading Hamdi Pasha to allow a massacre. Hamdi then "unaccountably delayed his departure" for Constantinople. Moreover, bands of Muslims appeared to have been "armed and organized" in advance and, on the eighth, the troops were ordered by their officers "to shoot at or towards Armenians in the square and in their houses." The carnage only ceased when the vali himself declared that "the Sultan had pardoned the Armenians." The looters spared Greeks, suggesting that they were instructed to assault only a particular set of Christians—Armenians.[182] Longworth assessed that the "government of the country is entirely to blame" and that the massacre was "more political than fanatical," stemming less from religious fervor than from Turkish fears of Armenian rebelliousness and the possible disintegration of the empire.[183]

Perhaps the strongest evidence of organization came from a Mr. Cypreos, the Greek acting consul. Longworth wrote that Cypreos had witnessed part of the massacre. Based on his observations and information collected by his agents, Cypreos concluded that the violence at Trabzon constituted "a planned attack" on Armenians. He accused the troops of taking "a prominent part in the butchery," which had commenced almost simultaneously in five different parts of town, triggered by a trumpet signal from a mosque minaret.[184]

Maraş

Hard on the heels of Trabzon, Armenians were massacred in some two dozen sites in eastern Anatolia.

The carnage was especially great in Maraş. The town had a population of roughly 50,000, about one-third Armenian. They had long been subject to persecution and ethnic hatred. Sanders, the American missionary, reported in January 1895 that "suspicion and fear reign there supreme" and that the local military force was "more anti-Christian" than the civilian inhabitants. A key figure was the police chief, Shahan (Şahin?) Effendi, "one of the . . . bitterest haters of Christians, and especially Armenians." A major problem, Sanders felt, was "the credulity of the Moslems." They would "act at once on the wildest stories." Maraş was therefore like "a loaded and cocked musket," ready to go off. When it did, Sanders predicted, "not much of the Christian population would be left."[185]

The musket powder was finally lit on October 25. A Muslim had been killed in a fracas with Christians, provoking murderous rage. As news of Constantinople's planned reforms spread, Turks killed dozens of Armenian men—at least twenty-five and as many as fifty—in the streets and surrounding fields.[186] Fearful for their lives, Armenians closed their shops, schools, and churches and "shut themselves up in their houses."[187] Prominent Armenians were arrested.[188]

On November 18 a full-scale massacre erupted. The killing began in the town center and spread outward, as soldiers sealed off the roads into Maraş to prevent escape. They set fires in three or four locations in town. An American missionary reported that, at one of these sites, "the soldiers were drawn up in a line, and the bugle sounded, and they rushed to their work of plundering and murder." Joined by a mob, the soldiers eventually entered the American missionary compound, which was on a hill overlooking the town. The Turks set fire to the theological seminary and looted the buildings. Some soldiers participated in the arson, but others tried to stanch the flames. "Arab soldiers, followed by a rabble of men, women and children" attacked Armenians and looted homes just outside the compound.[189]

Missionaries who treated the wounded reported, "The work was fearful, children were disemboweled, men's heads [were] used as balls by the soldiers, or carried on pikes through the street." Armenians were threatened with death unless they converted. One of the missionary school teachers was "flayed and cut to pieces." "Women and children took refuge in a church which was then burned to the ground."[190] All the Armenian churches were looted and vandalized and a number of priests were tortured and killed. Hundreds who refused to convert were murdered.[191] Dozens of Armenians were imprisoned, many severely tortured. But fifty were released just before a delegation of diplomats was due to arrive.[192] All told, the immediate death toll was around 650, with more subsequently dying of wounds.[193]

Locals and soldiers also attacked Armenian villages around Maraş, causing Armenians to abandon their orchards and vineyards.[194] One missionary was reminded of "the Sioux massacre in Minnesota in 1862."[195] The greatest bloodletting appears to have taken place in Furnuz. The village had become a gathering point for refugees throughout the Maraş area. In mid-November troops surrounded Furnuz and slaughtered the men. One woman said that the soldiers took her two children "and threw them into a river."

Hundreds of survivors, all women and children, reached Maraş, pushed by Turkish troops "like a drove of cattle." They arrived "sick and footsore, weeping and ragged, cold and hungry" and were imprisoned in a Protestant church. The authorities gave them bread rations and eventually allowed the town's Christians also to send food: "Moslem women . . . came to jeer and laugh at the sufferers. . . . One morning such a crowd of Moslems gathered on the balcony of a house overlooking the church, to feast their eyes on the sight of the captives, that suddenly the balcony gave way and some 60 people fell into the street." One died. "We trust," a missionary wrote, "that some at least felt that this was a righteous judgment."[196] Eventually the authorities set the captives in the church free and allowed the Maraş Christians to take them in. But dozens died of dysentery.[197] Some Protestants were spared, but not all; of the Maraş area dead, about 250 were Protestants.[198]

Conversion was one possible means of self-preservation. "In the district of Albistan all the Christians are reported to have saved their lives by embracing Islam," the British consul reported. The story was different at Yenice Kale, where twelve monks and their superior, Padre Salvatore, were forced to leave for Maraş in chains, under Turkish escort. Along the way, they were given the option of converting. They refused and were "massacred, and their bodies burnt."[199]

The killing in and around Maraş proceeded "with all the appearances of a preconceived plan," as one missionary put it.[200] Barnham wrote to Currie that what had happened in Maraş was "evidently with the approval of [the] Government."[201] Barnham later reported that on November 18 the mutesarrif was seen "riding through the streets, urging on the soldiers in their bloody work."[202] "It does look as tho' deliberate extermination was purposed," one missionary wrote.[203] Following the massacre, another missionary argued that "there was no rebellion here and no resistance . . . except in one or two isolated cases when individuals seeing that death was certain tried to sell their life as dearly as they could."[204]

Harput

In the summer of 1895 Harput, in Mamuret-ül-Aziz vilayet, was calm. The vali was "taking good care to preserve order," an Armenian reported. But in the surrounding countryside the situation was "intolerable." Armenian villagers were assaulted, and gendarmes and Kurds were committing "all kinds of exactions and outrages," especially in Palu kaza.[205]

The situation then worsened in response to the demonstration and massacres in Constantinople, with Harput itself gearing up for violence. Dr. Herman Norton Barnum, an American missionary in the town, reported on October 2 that Christians were "almost [in] a panic" as some officials were busily distributing arms in Muslim villages and mending fences with Kurdish agas.[206] Other missionaries reported a measure of Armenian provocation: "Almost every day lads from 15 to 18 years of age gather outside the town singing Armenian national songs, and then parade to the town."[207] On October 24, sensing impending massacre, the Armenians "hastily closed their shops." "Turks were seen to be openly carrying arms, gathering in little knots . . . and some thought they even heard them say that the work was to begin at noon." "The air," one anonymous letter-writer said, "is full of . . . rumors."

At first the vali, the local chief financial officer *(defterdar)*, and Harput's leading Muslim cleric took effective steps to restrain the townspeople, including by bringing in troops.[208] As a signal of goodwill, the Christians gave up their weapons, thereby casting "themselves wholly upon the protection of the government," a missionary noted. The authorities issued reassurances even as "the circle of fire kept on contracting around the city."[209]

The dam broke in the countryside, deluged in what a British consul described as a "religious crusade." Starting on November 2, a Kurdish band and "fanatical Mussulman neighbors" attacked and plundered the village of Shepik. The attackers took everything, including doors and windows, and stripped the women and children of "their shoes and clothing." They burnt houses and murdered two priests who refused to convert. They abducted and then murdered forty young men "who had acquired wisdom"—presumably the best-educated villagers—and also refused conversion. One parent described how, "with . . . feet bare, little clothing upon us, we passed from rock to rock, mountain to mountain, with great wailing and lamentation, to find our children."[210]

The flood reached Harput itself on the morning of November 11. Muslims attacked the town's Christian quarter, killing three. At first they were driven off by soldiers, but the Armenians were soon abandoned by their defenders. Caleb F. Gates, president of the missionary-run Euphrates College, described what happened, as seen from his vantage point up the hill: at noon, a crowd of Kurds and Turks, some 800 strong and armed mainly with "clubs and knives," advanced on a military outpost at the city's entrance, then halted. The crowd's leaders, town notables, and Turkish officers conferred. The soldiers then packed up and "marched leisurely back to the city, dragging their cannon." Then the Kurds advanced, "shouting 'Allah, Allah,'" and stormed into the Christian quarter, supported by soldiers. "The work of plunder was largely done by the Turks of the city," according to Gates, but the soldiers "seemed to superintend" it.[211] Other observers confirm soldiers' participation.[212]

After the pillage, the houses were torched. Most inhabitants fled to the missionary buildings, chased by a "storm of bullets."[213] Some Armenian women were raped, "the foremost ravisher being Said Effendi, the commissary of police."[214] The soldiers made a "sham" of firing at the Kurds, hitting none.[215] As the massacre unfolded, Derviş Effendi, the *kaymakam* (sub-district governor), asked the missionaries to leave the compound, where 450 Armenians were holed up. When the missionaries refused, the mob, joined by soldiers, entered, plundered, and torched homes and school buildings. Colonel Şükrü Bey looked on. One missionary later wrote that "at one time it looked as if we should all go up in a fiery chariot together." Another lamented that "for nearly forty years we have been here and never dreamed that we had such neighbors."[216] Only one Ottoman official, a Circassian regimental commander named Mehmet, came to the missionaries' aid, guarding them and helping to douse the flames. The massacre ended the following day when the soldiers, under orders to shoot offending Muslims, drove back Kurds approaching the city.[217]

The attack on the Christian quarter and the torching of the missionary houses and college all had the appearance of orchestration and premeditation, and evidence points to orders from above. British consul Raphael Fontana, who investigated the massacre, reported that, weeks before, the city's military commander, General Mustafa Pasha, had personally visited "various Kurdish villages" and "sent emissaries" to others "with instructions to invite the tribes to attack the town." The authorities gave the Kurds modern Martini rifles, and one chieftain, Bekir Effendi, was "ordered by letter to bring 500 of his clan to the sack of Harput." According to Fontana, Kurds later told Armenians that government officers had visited "bearing letters authorizing the slaughter of Christians and the pillage of their property" and that a bugle had sounded the beginning of the assault on the missionary quarter.[218]

Barnum found that "the soldiers . . . presided over the affair so as to keep the Kurds and the mass of the Turkish population of the city . . . from going beyond the prescribed limits" and that the authorities intended that Euphrates

College and other missionary schools be torched.[219] One missionary subsequently related that a leading cleric and judge, Deli Haji, blessed the mob as it left a mosque, saying, "May your swords be sharp."[220] Six months later, Turks questioned by a British investigator referred to what had happened as *resmi jinayet*—an official crime.[221]

Gates later learned that a high official in Harput said the attackers had acted "in accordance with a prearranged plan" and that "the raiders"—presumably referring to the 800 who entered the city—"were soldiers of the reserve corps" who had dressed as Kurds. He alleged that the soldiers used artillery to break down the missionary compound's gates. To Terrell, he wrote, "We are confronting a . . . plan . . . to render the reforms useless by destroying the Christian population."[222] In a letter to a fellow missionary, he was more straightforward. "It is perfectly clear," he wrote, "that this whole thing emanated from the Sultan." Gates took the Kurds and the local Turks at their word when they said that "they had orders from the Sultan to kill the Christians." Noting that "simultaneously" with the proclamation of the reforms the Kurdish tribes and Turks, "in localities widely separated, began to move," he again concluded that there was afoot "a deliberate plan to exterminate the Christians so that they might not enjoy the benefits secured to them by the Powers."[223]

According to a British investigation, at the start of the massacre soldiers had opened fire on the Christian quarter while "the Kurds were still outside the city." After the cannonade, some thirty soldiers were seen entering a madrassa and putting on Kurdish costumes. The soldiers and civilians then attacked the Protestant quarter. An officer shouted, "On to the pastors' houses," and the crowd surged in, setting fire to the American missionary compound.[224]

British records of the massacre contain the translation of extracts from a letter by a Turkish soldier, Hafiz Mehmet, of the 25th Regiment, 2nd Battalion, 4th Company. He informed his family, "We have killed 1,200 Armenians, all of them as food for the dogs." He went on, "20 days ago we made war on the Armenian unbelievers . . . I myself fired 47 cartridges." According to Hafiz Mehmet, the massacre was a resounding success: "If you ask after the soldiers and Bashi-Bazouks, not one of their noses had bled"—that is, none of the Turks were hurt. Finally, addressing his parents, he wrote, "There is a rumor that our battalion will be ordered to your part of the world—if so we will kill all the Armenians there."[225]

In the weeks after the Harput massacre, surrounding villages were subjected to consistent depredations. "All the Christian villages and Christian quarters of villages . . . have been burnt so far as I know," a missionary reported.[226] In Husenik, a mile from the city, about 200 Christians were killed. In Choonkoosh (Çüngüş), 600–700 died. Neighboring Adish (Adış?) was "almost exterminated."[227]

Violation of women was the norm. According to Gates's informants, "when zaptiehs come, the Turks give to each an Armenian woman for the night."[228] At Zaremja (Garemja), "few women and girls . . . appear to have escaped dishonor." At Hock (Hockn), "seventeen females . . . were carried off . . . and ravished by Kurds and Turks." These included four girls between the ages of ten and fourteen. At Aivos forty women and girls were "outraged." In Habab, more than a dozen were assaulted. Most of those raped were allowed to stay in their villages or return to them; a few were killed or permanently held captive.[229]

The village raids also saw forced conversions.[230] In İçme, outside Harput, many crowded into the Gregorian church for safety. "They were taken out, one by one, and whoever would not renounce his faith . . . was shot down or butchered. Fifty-two were killed. . . . Pastor Krikor was one of the first. . . . The Gregorian Church is turned into a mosque and the Protestant church is used for a stable." In the village of Oozoonova (Uzun Oba), across the Euphrates, a large number were driven to a Turkish village "to change their faith." "In their desperation," dozens of Armenians "rushed into the river and were drowned rather than deny their faith." Many women were abducted to Muslim homes.[231] "In some places [the converts] are circumcised by force," a Harput missionary reported in December. "To-day word has come from Perching (Perçin?) that this is being done there. . . . The same is being done in Reawan," between Siirt and Mardin, and "a sheikh is teaching the Christians the tenets of Islam." An official telegram from Mamuret-ül-Aziz reported that some Christians circumcised themselves out of desperation. In Çüngüş the pastor's house was torched. When he emerged he was offered the choice to "accept Islam or die." He died.[232] In one Palu-area village, Turks tore down a church "and it is [now] used as a privy."[233]

In December 1895, under great-power pressure, Constantinople sent a commission of inquiry to Harput to investigate. Muslims and Christians were summoned. According to a missionary who observed the proceedings, the Muslims testified first. Then the commissioners "harangued" Armenian witnesses about alleged "seditious practices" and accused them of "sending men to Washington and Chicago to agitate, of publishing secret newspapers, of stirring up strife." One commissioner threatened that the Armenians would be "blotted out" if they renewed their rebelliousness.[234] The Christians in Harput and the countryside were repeatedly pressed to sign statements blaming themselves for what happened.[235]

The death toll in and around Harput was immense. One tabulation, by the local Gregorian bishop, found 4,127 deaths in the episcopate, which included Harput and seventy-three surrounding villages. More than a thousand of these were due to "hunger and cold."[236] In mid-January 1896, a missionary counted 39,000 dead in Mamuret-ül-Aziz vilayet as a whole. The missionary also recorded 8,000 wounded, 28,562 homes burned, 15,179 people forcibly converted to Islam, 5,530 "women and girls outraged," and 1,532 women and girls forcibly married to Muslims. He also claimed that nearly a hundred thousand people, mostly women, children, and the elderly, were left "absolutely destitute."[237]

The Harput mission district now had 4,000–5,000 orphans.[238] Children were left wandering "bare-footed in the snow, great spaces of purple flesh showing through the rags, no bed to lie in at night, no food to eat, the future all dark." In Malatya, orphans wandered in the markets, "where those who had made them orphans broke off scraps of bread and threw at them [sic] as if they were dogs and laughed to see them scramble for the pieces."[239]

American missionaries set up an Armenian Relief Commission to raise funds for the orphans, but the good deed would not go unpunished. The money reaching destitute Armenians "stimulated" the authorities to launch a forceful tax-collection campaign. Villagers would collect funds in Harput, and officials would waylay them on the route home. In the village of Shehaji (Şehaci), for example, tax collectors took "every piaster [of the] 420 piasters" Armenians had received in relief. Harput missionaries warned the relief commission, based in Constantinople, "You must know that some of the money which you send goes into the government treasury."[240]

Urfa

The Armenians of Urfa were subjected to two massacres: one in October 1895, the other, far larger, in December. Much of what is known about the violence in Urfa comes from Fitzmaurice, the British consular official and Turkish speaker who visited the town in mid-March 1896. He found that, despite the authorities' "attempts during the preceding ten weeks to remove the traces," Urfa, and especially its Armenian quarter, had "the aspect of a town which had been . . . laid waste by some scourge more terrible than any war or siege." The scenery was devastating. "The shops with their windows and doors broken in, lay empty and deserted, practically no grown males were visible, and only a few ill-clad and ill-fed children and women, with a scared look on their faces, were to be seen moving about apparently in search of . . . dry bread and scanty bedding."

Fitzmaurice was keen to understand how the massacres came about. On the basis of interviews with dozens of Muslims and Christians, he dismissed the charge of widespread Armenian insurrectionary activity, though he believed that there had been "well-grounded discontent" among Armenians who were treated by the authorities "practically as outlaws." But "the amount of actual disloyalty among them was very restricted," he wrote. Some "revolutionary pamphlets" had reached Urfa but "no rifles or explosives."

Rather, he found that the source of the massacres lay in the events in Constantinople and their aftermath, which inflamed anti-Armenian sentiment. Fitzmaurice discovered that, following the Constantinople demonstration, the government had instructed local authorities to quell any Armenian disturbances that might arise. If there was resistance, the Armenians were to be taught "a terrible lesson" *(terbiyyeh shedideh)*. The locals, who were fed rumors of Armenians slaughtering Muslims across the Empire, interpreted the instructions as an order to "put into execution the prescription of the [sharia], and proceed to take the lives and property of the rebellious Armenian 'rayahs.'" In addition, "the telegraphic news of [Ottoman] acceptance of the reforms was interpreted by the Mussulmans as the granting of autonomy to the Armenians," which had "a disastrous effect on Moslem feeling." The masses were incited to "do their duty by Islam." He concluded that Muslims and non-Muslims agreed that "the Government wished these massacres to take place, and that if it had not so wished, they could not have taken place."[241]

The immediate trigger of the first massacre was the stabbing, on October 27, of an Armenian moneychanger by a Muslim in his debt. The murderer was seized by Armenians and, initially, handed over to gendarmes. But, fearing that the gendarmes would release him, Armenians raided the guardhouse, and the prisoner was killed in the ensuing scuffle. Exactly who killed the man is unclear; an Armenian doctor who insisted that the injuries were caused by bayonets—indicating the responsibility of gendarmes—was later murdered by Turkish troops.

The massacre began the next morning. A Muslim mob attacked merchants in the bazaar and chased the survivors to their homes amid cries of "death to the infidels." Resisters at the entrances to the Armenian quarter drove back the mob, killing four or five Muslims. The mob then plundered hundreds of Armenian shops and homes outside the quarter, killing "all Armenian [males] found" there. Assisted by gendarmes, the mob continued looting throughout the next day, and the quarter would remain under siege for two months.[242] In a letter to friends dated a few days later, Corinna Shattuck, the only Western missionary in town, wrote, "We felt distrust of all but God."[243]

Hassan Pasha, the mutesarrif, had been out of town when the massacre began. When he returned on October 30, he sought to restore order, albeit in a highly repressive fashion. Hassan demanded that the Armenians surrender their weapons, which allegedly included 1,800 modern Martini rifles. He promised also to disarm Muslims. Reserves were deployed in small units inside the Armenian quarter, ostensibly to protect the inhabitants. What followed was extortion and intimidation. Turks were undeterred in their plunder. The soldiers joined in, demanding protection money and robbing passersby of "watches, money and outer clothing in broad daylight." Soldiers were overheard saying that the government had ordered the extermination of the Armenians.[244] Meanwhile, outside Urfa, Arabs attacked and robbed Armenian villagers. So bereft were these country Armenians that they sought shelter in a Kurdish village.[245]

Shattuck recorded that gendarmes were "arresting men . . . and requiring them to declare themselves to be Mohammedans, the penalty for refusal being death." Converts were ordered to don white turbans and raise white flags above their homes. Twenty flags went up on October 30 and many more the following day as gendarmes went from house to house, "axe in hand with their demand for the people to become Mohammedans."[246] Six months later, Fitzmaurice reported that "the Armenians in utter despair turned Moslem en masse." In the surrounding villages, Kurds pressed Armenians to convert, sometimes murdering those who refused. Shattuck doubted that the mutesarrif had a hand in the conversion campaign and asserted that "he stopped the full execution of the plan."[247]

As the weeks ground on, the authorities continued to demand Martini rifles, and the Armenians continued to deny that they had any. But they gave up other weapons to appease the Turks. By mid-December, the discarded arsenal amounted to 1,200 weapons: old rifles, revolvers, daggers, and one Martini. Armenians also handed over "large sums of money to the mutesarrif, the [military] commander Nazif Pasha, and other Moslem" notables. To some extent, the authorities held up their end of the bargain, pushing back a mob that attacked the quarter on December 1. But the siege was unrelenting, and food and water supplies were dwindling.

Throughout December the authorities seemed to be softening up to the Armenians. On December 13 Nazif ordered them to open their shops, presumably to pretend that all was well and perhaps to create targets for looting. Some Armenians complied but were attacked when they left the quarter. Then officials forced twenty-five Armenian notables to telegraph Constantinople that their compatriots had disturbed the peace and that Urfa was now calm. "Friendly Turks" warned Armenians "to be on their guard" and non-Armenian Christians were told to don black turbans so that they could be identified and spared.[248]

The second massacre began on the morning of December 28. Nazif sent word to non-Armenian Christians "to assemble in their churches and not stir out" and to refrain from sheltering Armenians. In a further sign of official complicity, the captain of the gendarmes finally granted Shattuck permission to leave on a long-planned trip to Antep, after weeks of rejections. (She didn't go.) The troops were then drawn up at the entrances to the Armenian quarter. Behind them "an armed Mussulman mob [gathered], while the minarets were crowded with Moslems evidently in expectation of some stirring event. The

Turkish women, too, crowded onto the roofs and the slopes of the fortress, which overlooked the Armenian Quarter." The mob was "cheered on by their women, who kept up the well-known zilghit or peculiar throat noise, used on such occasions by Oriental women to encourage their braves." At around noon a muezzin cried out the midday prayer as "a glittering glass ornament resembling a crescent was seen shining from the top of the fortress" overlooking the town. "A mullah waved a green banner from a tall minaret overhanging the other end" of the town. Shots were fired and a "trumpet sounded the attack." The soldiers opened their ranks so that the mob could pour into the quarter, assaulting "males over a certain age."[249]

According to Fitzmaurice's investigation, Nazif was seen "motioning the crowd on," the mob guided by troops who had familiarized themselves with the quarter during the siege. A "body of wood-cutters," armed with axes, led the way, breaking down doors. Soldiers then rushed inside and shot the men. "A certain sheik," Fitzmaurice wrote, "ordered his followers to bring as many stalwart young Armenians as they could find. To the number of about 100 they were thrown on their backs and held down by their hands and feet, while the sheik, with a combination of fanaticism and cruelty, proceeded, while reciting verses of the Koran, to cut their throats after the Mecca rite of sacrificing sheep." Those hiding were dragged out and butchered—stoned, shot, and set on fire with "matting saturated with petroleum." Women were cut down shielding their husbands and fathers. More Armenians were shot as they scampered along rooftops trying to escape. When the killing subsided, the houses were looted and torched. As sunset approached, the trumpet sounded again, calling the troops and the mob to withdraw.[250] Soldiers specifically forbade the mob to "touch" Shattuck's house, "the residence of a foreigner." The missionary, who witnessed a portion of the massacre from her window, reported that "Syrians and Catholics were also spared."[251]

The atrocities resumed the following day, December 29, with a trumpet sound at dawn. The largest number were killed at the Armenian cathedral, where thousands had gathered for sanctuary. The attackers first fired through windows into the church, then smashed in the doors and killed the men clustered on the ground floor. Fitzmaurice relates that, as the mob plundered the church, they "mockingly call[ed] on Christ . . . to prove himself a greater prophet than Mohammed." The Turks then shot at the "shrieking and terrified mass of women, children and some men" in the second-floor gallery. But gunning the Armenians down one-by-one was "too tedious," so the mob brought in more petroleum-soaked bedding and set fire to the woodwork and the staircases leading up to the galleries. For several hours "the sickening odour of roasting flesh pervaded the town." Writing the following March, Fitzmaurice noted, "Even today, the smell of putrescent and charred remains in the church is unbearable."[252] Shattuck described the horror as "a grand holocaust" and for days afterward watched "men lugging sacks filled with bones, ashes" from the cathedral.[253]

The trumpet again sounded at 3:30 p.m., the time of the Muslim afternoon prayer, and the mob withdrew from the Armenian quarter. "Shortly afterwards," Fitzmaurice wrote, "the mufti, Ali Effendi, Hussein Pasha, and other notables, preceded by a band of musicians, went round the quarter, announcing that the massacre was at an end . . . , and that there would be no more killing of Christians."[254] For the next three days, the authorities employed "Jews and donkeys" to remove the dead.[255] The soldiers clearing the church reportedly collected "large quantities of melted gold" that Armenians had hidden on their persons."[256]

Before the massacres, Urfa was home to about 20,000 Armenians. All told, "close on 8,000," perhaps as many as 10,000, died over the course of the two days, 2,500–3,000 of them at the cathedral. Forty Assyrians and one Greek Catholic also died. Three months on, according to Fitzmaurice, the condition of the survivors, who included many widows and orphans, was "wretched in the extreme," and mortality was high. The majority had lost all "except the clothes on their backs." The authorities announced that there would be a restitution of plundered property, but it was a "sham."[257] For months, Shattuck wrote, stolen goods were openly sold in the marketplace.[258] Armenian financial losses also included a large number of debts Muslims refused to honor.

The government failed to punish the murderers but took care quickly to remove to distant provinces officials linked to the massacres. These included Hassan Bey, the major of gendarmes, who was sent to Yanina (Ioannina), Greece, and Nazif Pasha, who was transferred to Kornah (Al-Qurnah), at the confluence of the Tigris and Euphrates. But Hussein Pasha, a "local magnate . . . prominently connected with the massacres," apparently was allowed to return to Urfa in summer 1896 after a brief exile, none the worse for wear.[259]

Between October and December, hundreds of Christians converted.[260] In the weeks following the December massacre, another 600 converted "in the hope of saving their lives." But most reverted over time to Christianity, some after leaving Urfa. In September 1896, Fitzmaurice wrote that two hundred Muslim converts remained in the town.[261] Some Gregorian Armenians turned Catholic or Syrian, a lesser apostasy also designed to save life and limb. Indeed, turning Muslim hadn't necessarily been of much use in December; Shattuck observed that many, after declaring themselves, were "quickly murdered."[262]

The Sublime Porte denied that any massacre had occurred. As the sultan told Currie, the British ambassador, in January 1896, "there had been an affray . . . and some lives had been lost on both sides." The ambassador pretended that the sultan was unaware of the true facts and played along, telling him he was being "willfully deceived" and "hoodwinked" by his agents.[263]

Diyarbekir

After the 1894 massacre at Sason and subsequent appointment under European pressure of a commission of inquiry, Thomas Boyajian noted rising anti-Christian sentiment in Diyarbekir, where he was vice-consul for Her Majesty's Government. He felt the "lower classes" were especially afflicted.

Such hard feelings were routinely reinforced, as in spring, during a visit by Kurdish chieftains on their way to Mecca. One, the sheikh of Zilan (Zeylan), was "deeply implicated" in the Sason Massacres, according to Boyajian. He was also outspoken, warning the townspeople that Armenians were "in revolt and doing their utmost to undermine the Empire." He questioned the locals' patriotism, asserting that the "Kurds appear more religious and patriotic in defending the authority of the Sovereign than the Turks." Boyajian blamed such inflammatory rhetoric for the hardship of Diyarbekir's Christians. They were, he observed, "treated very shamefully in the bazaars, being assailed, insulted and threatened with extermination." The situation in the neighboring districts of Palu and Silvan appeared even worse.[264]

The pent-up rage in and around Diyarbekir exploded on November 1. Turks and Kurds rioted for three days, "absolutely unchecked by the authorities." Armenians were killed in the bazaars, the streets, and their homes. About 1,000 Armenians and 160 Assyrians died, and some 2,500 shops and 1,700 homes were pillaged or burnt.[265]

About 700 Christians found refuge in the French consulate, which successfully repulsed an attack. The Turks claimed that Armenians had provoked the "clashes," but Hallward concluded that the "authors of the disturbance were well under Government control." Soldiers and gendarmes "took an active part" in the violence, and the rioting ended immediately upon the arrival of an order from the Porte. It was generally believed, Hallward wrote, that the violence was organized by the vali of Sivas, Ennis Pasha, and leading local Muslims.[266] Another example of orderly planning came immediately after the massacre. Just as the violence was ending, local Muslims already had their story straight; hundreds sent a telegram to the sultan justifying what had happened. They bemoaned the reforms as harbingers of Armenian independence and blamed Armenian "intrigue" for the outbreak of violence.[267]

The massacre was followed by Kurdish attacks on nearby Armenian and Assyrian villages and towns, including Nisibin, Midyat, and Siirt, and on two Yezidi villages. In most, churches were burned and priests murdered.[268] Mardin was assaulted by Kurds on the ninth, eleventh, and sixteenth of November, but each time the town's Muslims and Christians made common cause to drive them back. Muslim leaders feared that the Kurds would also sack Muslim homes, and some Muslims came from Assyrian stock, fostering bonds of sympathy. Assyrian villages around Mardin were raided, and some, such as Tell Armen and Al Kulye, completely destroyed. The Syriac inhabitants of Qalaat Mara fled to the nearby Za'faran Monastery (Deyrulzafaran), which they successfully defended against a Kurdish force, perhaps with the assistance of soldiers.[269]

Hallward estimated that 800 or 900 Christians were murdered in the villages around Diyarbekir, and 155 women and girls were carried off by Kurds.[270] By mid-March 1896, "perhaps twenty" girls had been recovered, some having "declared themselves Moslem." This may have been a smart move, for themselves and their families. After an abducted Assyrian from the Silvan district was "restored to her husband" unconverted, Kurds proceeded to kill "both her husband and father-in-law." In many of the region's villages, massacre survivors were forced to convert, and churches were converted to mosques. In Lice all of the men were circumcised.[271]

Silvan and Palu suffered especially. According to Hallward, of the estimated 20,000 Armenians residing in Silvan before the disturbances, 7,500 were "reduced to destitution," 7,000 were "forcibly made Moslem," and 4,000 had "disappeared." Twenty-three villages were entirely burned. Palu, home to an estimated 15,000 Armenians, saw 900 deaths. Six villages were razed and seven "half-burned." Hallward counted 195 women and girls abducted and "a large majority" of the Christian females aged 12–40 "violated." In one village, Yeniköy, Christians took refuge "with a certain Shukri Bey who, with his servants, [then] violated all the young women and girls." The "worst man" in Palu district, according to Hallward, was the mufti, who "was very active in the massacre and killed the principal Protestant, Manoog Aga, with his own hand."

Altogether, in Diyarbekir vilayet, some "8,000 appear to have been killed," Hallward wrote. He put the number of those converted at 25,000. "Upward of 500 women and girls" were abducted. "One of the principal elements of disorder here is the so-called 'Young Turkey,'" Hallward added, referring to the party that, in 1908, would topple Abdülhamid's rule. Among them were "some four of the worst characters in the place." Hallward said they regarded the situation as "revolutionary" and had sought to provoke disorder in order to topple the sultan.[272]

The French ambassador reported that the 400 Armenian families still living in the Diyarbekir area after the massacres were in dire need, but the authorities were withholding aid. The local priest had refused to sign a telegram to the sultan blaming the Armenians for inciting the violence they had suffered. Until he did so, the government wouldn't help.[273]

Antep (Aintab)

In the fall of 1895, Antep, in Aleppo vilayet, was experiencing a by-now-familiar tension between Armenians struggling under Turkish oppression, and Turkish authorities perceiving in that struggle only insurrectionary activity. On October 9, under authority of Constantinople, officials there arrested "the Protestant Pastor and a College professor" considered "guilty of sedition and the organization of [revolutionary] societies."[274] Barnham, the British consul in Aleppo, complained of revolutionaries stirring up "younger

Armenians." Led by a Hunchak called Aghasse, they were, Barnham thought, trying to provoke Turkish "retaliation."[275] But he offered no concrete illustration, and missionaries in Antep interpreted the situation differently. They felt, quite to the contrary, that local Christians had behaved with the "greatest forbearance" in the face of the "grossest and most wanton insult, abuse and violence" from their Muslim neighbors.[276] Barnham saw it himself. Shortly after the October 9 arrests, he watched troops pass through the town "followed by crowds of Mussulman women weeping and cursing the infidels."[277]

Fear gripped local Christians, who worried that the fate of Trabzon and Sason would soon befall them. They shut themselves in their homes. Unable to work out of doors and shop in town, "thousands are without food," a missionary reported. "Over 1,000 men" had fled to "mosques and khans and houses of powerful Moslems" where they obtained shelter but lived as virtual prisoners.[278]

Americus Fuller, a missionary and president of the town's Central Turkey College, believed—or hoped—that Antep would escape the suffering endured by Armenians elsewhere. Circumstances in the town were different: the Christians were "exceptionally intelligent and influential" and "the leading Moslems . . . able men" who "have shown themselves to a degree tolerant of and even friendly to Christians." Furthermore, "the Governor has seemed disposed beyond most Turkish officials to respect the rights of Christians," the town had a relatively large contingent of foreigners "sure to be witnesses of any violence done to Christians," and the missionary hospital and college had generated "good will" among "all classes." Moreover, the town's Christians had "given very little countenance to the ultra-revolutionists."[279] Still, there was no mistaking the repeated threats of anti-Christian violence, and the local government largely disarmed Christians while arming Muslims, allegedly to put down a possible Armenian uprising.[280]

The violence caught up with Antep on November 16, when the missionaries, at breakfast, heard "a great noise of shouting and firing of guns . . . telling us that the work of blood and plunder had begun." Crowds ran to and fro, and the roofs were covered with "excited men, women and children." Missionary physician Fred Douglas Shepard rode his horse through the town and heard, "most terrible of all, the shrill, exultant lu-lu-lu of Kurdish and Turkish women cheering on their men to the attack." Fuller too remarked on the "loud shrill Zullghat . . . raised by Turkish women crowded on their roofs and cheering on their men to attack." He likened the sound to that "of our northern loons, prolonged and sharpened." Shepard and Fuller saw Armenians assaulted and their homes looted. Armenians, "women . . . often foremost," defended their homes from the rooftops with "stones and firearms."[281]

Some mobs were beaten back, but where Armenian houses were isolated, the rioters broke through, plundering and torching. In certain areas, the "uproar went on till near midnight." Hamidiyes took part in the massacre, while other troops protected the missionary schools and hospital from the mob but made no attempt to stop the violence. Indeed, they took part in the looting. Missionaries watched villagers leave the city loaded down with stolen goods.[282] Weeks later army deserters were seen in the streets of Aleppo selling their loot.[283] A Franciscan priest who witnessed the massacre later told Barnham that "butchers and tanners . . . armed with clubs and cleavers" were prominent among the killers. They screamed "Allahu Akbar" as they broke down doors "with pickaxes and levers or scaled the walls with ladders" and then cut down the Armenians they encountered. "When mid-day came they knelt down and said their prayers, and then jumped up and resumed the dreadful work. . . . Whenever they were unable to break down the doors they fired the houses with petroleum."[284]

The plunder and massacre continued the next day, after Turkish villagers entered the town, brushing past a cordon of soldiers. Kurds, "waving a green flag and beating tomtoms," tried to join the villagers but were blocked by the mufti and soldiers "because it was feared that they would plunder Moslems as well as Christians."[285] This time the Christians were prepared and repulsed their assailants. "At one point on the line of defense were a few Muslim houses and we were delighted to learn that the men heartily and bravely joined in the defense with their neighbors," Fuller recorded. But "the gallantry of this act was somewhat marred . . . by the demand which they made the next day for a large sum of money for this service." The men received "about five dollars apiece for this neighborly help."[286] Some Muslims "behaved with great humanity" and protected Armenians.[287] Even so, "not less than 400" Armenians were killed, according to Shepard.[288] Fuller reported that Muslim casualties amounted to no more than twenty-five killed or seriously wounded.[289]

Following the massacre, Antep's prisons were crammed with Armenians.[290] In January 1896 some 750 were still "shut up in the Armenian church," and all Armenian shops remained closed.[291] Four thousand people depended on charity "for daily bread."[292] Barnham suggested that the continuing, wholesale arrest of wealthy Armenians was in large measure designed to enable expropriation.[293] The arrests may also have been used to press for conversion. As Antep's leading Muslim notables, including the new kaymakam, told the Armenians after the massacres, there was now "no hope of their living in security unless they will become Mohammedans."[294] By March, it was reported that at nearby Cibin all but one of the 500 or so Christians were forced to profess Islam. The exception was a "lady over 110 years of age" who told her tormentors, "I am too old to change my faith. I know no one but Christ." Many converts were robbed.[295] Christian graveyards were desecrated, the bones carried off and scattered, and Christian-owned trees were destroyed.[296]

No Antep Muslims were punished, and the authorities systematically portrayed the Christians "as the aggressors."[297] In June 1896 Lutfi Pasha, the newly appointed commander of the reserve troops at Aleppo, tried to restore Christian property and bring the plunderers to justice. But his efforts came to naught after arrests of robbers led to a mass demonstration of Muslims in Antep. The detainees were soon released. Some threw stolen property into the street or burned it to protest Lutfi Pasha's offenses against impunity.[298]

In the aftermath, Fuller was sure that the local government was "wholly in sympathy with the rioters." Indeed, there could "be no doubt that it has incited and directed nearly all the disturbances."[299] A few weeks after the killings, an American missionary described a firman ordering the massacre. Alternatively, he suggested that there had been "a wink from Constantinople." More concretely, "the Mufti and Cadi [kadi, religious judge], together, issued a Fetva [or fatwa] the evening before the massacre to the effect that the lives and property of the Christians were lawful prey."[300] Barnham was later told that "a number of persons from Constantinople dressed as dervishes" had arrived shortly before the massacre and "were received with extraordinary honor" by the authorities, who then spent hours closeted with them.[301] Even if it could not be proven that orders had come from on high, at the very least, the arrival in town of crowds of villagers at the start of the massacre suggested that the disturbances "had been planned beforehand."[302]

Additional Massacres

There were hundreds, perhaps thousands, more attacks on Armenian communities during 1895–1896. More, certainly, than we are able to discuss in detail. What follow are brief summaries of some incidents about which documentation is available.

In the town of Tokat, in central Anatolia, a pogrom broke out on March 19, 1895, triggered by a brawl in the marketplace. Between five and ten Armenians were killed, and about a hundred were wounded.[303]

Merzifon was the site of a massacre on November 14, 1895. Around noon, a rumor spread that Armenians had attacked a mosque. Villagers swarmed into the city, and the mob descended on the market, goaded by cries from the minarets. The troops, according to all accounts, did not participate in the massacre but were "tardy" in protecting Armenians. An estimated 150 died.[304]

Gurun, in Sivas vilayet, was bathed in blood in November 1895. Replaying a standard pattern, the Armenians there were duped into defenselessness by official lies. The Armenians handed over their guns to the vali in exchange for a promise of state protection. When the mob attacked, its members had no trouble breaking into homes, where reports indicate that they killed the men "and outraged the young women and girls; they cut open mothers with child, and tossed little children from knife to knife." Then they torched the houses, burning to death anyone hiding inside.[305] Estimates of the death toll range from 400 to as many as 2,000.[306] The French ambassador sent home word that "more than a thousand bodies lay on the ground for ten days."[307]

The massacre in Kayseri began on November 30. A rumor spread that "the Christians are killing the Mussulmans," provoking violence. Rioters rushed the markets and broke into houses.[308] Women were murdered in a public bath and men in a local factory. "There is ample evidence," wrote a Western correspondent and witness, "that the Government deliberately gave permission for plunder and murder to continue for four hours. Soldiers said so plainly."[309] The number of dead was estimated at 500.[310]

On January 1, 1896, the Christian quarter of Birecik, in Aleppo vilayet, was attacked by local Muslims, apparently with some soldiers participating and others observing from the sidelines. According to Fitzmaurice, who investigated these assaults as well, Birecik's Armenians were "poor and hard-working" and had little "connection with political agitation" save "one or two so-called seditious documents" that had been "found among them." The mob invaded Armenian homes and demanded "money, trinkets and other valuables on the promise of sparing their lives." After valuables were handed over, many adult males were killed "with ruthless savagery" and the houses and churches pillaged. Armenian girls were taken "and much dispute and quarrelling occurred in dividing them among the captors." The authorities subsequently restored almost all to their families.[311]

Altogether, about 150 Armenians were murdered, and one Muslim was wounded "in a brawl over the plunder."[312] The dead were thrown into the Euphrates. Armenians attempted to secure their lives by converting to Islam, but even some converts were killed. About 1,600 Gregorian, Protestant, and Catholic Armenians turned Muslim; the Gregorian church was converted into a mosque; and some converts were circumcised. All "now wear turbans and are apparently most zealous in their attendance at the mosque," Fitzmaurice reported.[313]

But, under Western pressure, the sultan in effect refused to recognize the Birecik mass conversion. For months the local authorities, Western diplomats, and the Sublime Porte waged a struggle over the converts' souls. "My task has been a melancholy one," Fitzmaurice wrote, "for the fanatical outburst, which had at first some political colouring, gradually . . . degenerated here into a fierce crusade against Christianity. It was conducted with . . . thoroughness [and was] carefully planned."[314]

Urban pogroms, some substantial, occurred throughout the period of October 1895–June 1896. On October 8, 31 Armenians were killed in Akhisar, Izmit sanjak, and 55–60 went missing.[315] "Nearly 800" were killed in Bitlis on October 25–26.[316] Gümüşhane, in Trabzon vilayet, lost between ten and thirty Armenians to violence on October 25.[317] Bayburt, Erzurum vilayet, was the site of 650–900 killings on October 26 or 27.[318] Erzincan (Erzingan) and Erzurum, both in Erzurum vilayet, witnessed mass killings: 200 or more dead on October 21 and 350 on October 30–31, respectively.[319] Eight hundred were killed in Severek, Diyarbekir vilayet, on November 2.[320] Estimates of the number killed in Arabkir, Harput vilayet, on November 1–5 range from 1,171[321] to 2,800.[322] The Armenians of Malatya, Harput vilayet, suffered massacres on November 4–7; between 1,580 and 3,000 were killed.[323] In the

Harput town of Adıyaman, 410 were killed between November 7–9.[324] Sivas vilayet saw several massacres. On November 12, 1,200–1,500 were killed in the town of Sivas.[325] On November 15, forty were killed in Amasya;[326] on November 26 or 28, perhaps 300 in Zile (Zela);[327] and on June 20, 1896, 400–500 in Niksar.[328]

Armenian Rebellion?

As the killing unfolded, Constantinople repeatedly offered the same justification: Armenians were not the victims of massacre, because they were engaged in a rebellion that the state had a right and duty to suppress. Yet at only two sites, Zeytun (Süleymanlı) and Van, did Armenians even arguably rebel. Indeed, it might be more accurate to say that Armenians in these locations did not rebel but only attempted to preempt massacres they sensed were coming.

Zeytun

The Armenians of Zeytun took up arms around October 20, 1895, in response to the news of massacres elsewhere. During the following weeks, the Zeytunlis killed dozens of Turkish prisoners and burnt a handful of Muslim villages before being overwhelmed by Turkish troops.[329]

Built on a remote mountainside, Zeytun had a population of 8,000–9,000, overwhelmingly Armenians, plus 400 troops garrisoned in a fort overlooking the town. For centuries the residents had managed to preserve a measure of autonomy.[330] Zeytunlis were known as a hardy people and, in the parlance of colonial times, backward. In 1881 a British diplomat wrote, "I find them to be a semi-barbarous and depraved community, little better than savages . . . ignorant, self-opinionated and conceited."[331] Barnham was more generous; yes, they were "poor", because "ignorant and lazy," but they also were "brave and independent."[332]

Turkish ill-treatment primed the Zeytunlis for action. In 1894 a newly appointed kaymakam seized the possessions of local Armenians—whom he dubbed "dogs"—in lieu of unpaid taxes. A handful of Hunchak agents arrived from outside and exploited the discontent. According to Barnham, the rebel leader here, too, was Aghasse, "who won over the villagers by presents of money, and by telling them fairy tales about the English. They were made to believe that the movement had the support of the British Government, which was sending troops to Alexandretta."[333]

On October 25 the kaymakam asked the Zeytunlis to lay down their arms, arguing that the sultan had agreed to reforms. Aghasse was distrustful, and the following day four gendarmes were killed near Fernuz, probably by armed rebels. On the 27th the rebels attacked Muslim villagers. A company of soldiers from Maraş then arrived in the area. The rebels laid siege to the Zeytun garrison fort and cut its main water supply. They also surrounded the eighty-man contingent at the *konak* (government building) inside the town and demanded its surrender. On October 30 Colonel Iffet Bey surrendered the fort, his battalion's two mountain guns, and 370 Martini rifles, actions for which he was later tried on charges of treason.[334] The rebels freed many prisoners, including Muslims. But the revolt, Barnham wrote, "had developed into a racial war." From nearby villages, Muslims fled to Maraş and Armenians to Zeytun, which filled with 14,000 Christians fearing reprisal.[335]

The Turks reported the rebels were "8,000 strong."[336] In response the Turks mobilized 15,000–20,000 troops, who were ordered to "utterly destroy the city and raze it to the ground."[337] As they approached Zeytun, they attacked Armenian villages along the way.[338] One of these, Fernuz, was the main rebel stronghold outside Zeytun. Eight hundred men died there, while the women and children were driven off to Maraş.

The fall of Fernuz and the influx of Christian refugees carrying tales of Muslim atrocity provoked the Zeytunlis, who massacred the prisoners remaining in the konak. The killers, reportedly including "many women," carried out the slaughter with "hatchets, butchers' knives and pickaxes." A priest on hand to witness testified that the killing lasted two hours; he said the victims' "shrieks were appalling." An Ottoman source indicates that 350 prisoners, many of them Arab conscripts from Palestine, died. But fifty-seven were saved when other Armenians intervened.[339] Ulema and Muslim notables in Maraş urged the sultan to punish the Zeytunlis, while a petition from Muslim women alleged that Zeytunlis had "outraged" Muslim girls.[340]

Meanwhile, the Turkish columns, under the command of Mustafa Remzi Pasha, the ferik of Acre, closed in. A tight siege began on December 18, and the army recaptured the garrison fort on the 23rd. At first the Zeytunlis were ready to parlay, but after a deputation of townspeople was "roughly handled" by the army, robbed and briefly imprisoned, the Zeytunlis decided to fight on. The Turkish forces, plagued by dysentery, failed to crush the rebels. But they kept up the siege.[341]

At this point the great powers intervened. The consuls in Aleppo mediated a truce, which took hold January 7, 1896, and sent a delegation later that month to negotiate a more lasting accord. In the course of the talks, the Turks demanded the surrender of weapons and rebel leaders. The Zeytunlis called for "the constitution of an [autonomous] Armenian province" in the region of what had been Cilicia, which would include their town. Barnham, who was on hand for the negotiations, called the Armenian demands "extravagant pretensions."[342] Through it all, food shortages, disease, and winter were taking a toll on both sides.[343] Barnham reported that "at least 140" Armenians were dying daily.[344]

Barnham feared Turkish deceit: the consuls would engineer an Armenian surrender and then the Zeytunlis would be massacred, "whatever the Turkish authorities may promise."[345] Nonetheless, on February 11, the parties reached agreement. The Zeytunlis freed the remaining Turkish prisoners and gave up their rifles, while the Hunchak leaders were promised safe passage out of the country and the refugees in Zeytun were allowed to move to Maraş. When the consuls eventually entered Zeytun, they were met "with every expression of delight and gratitude." But, despite these celebrations and the agreement's "liberal" terms, Barnham worried about what would come next "The future of Zeytun is likely to be a very stormy one," he wrote after the conclusion of the negotiations, "owing to the acute hostility of the Moslem population."[346]

Barnham's fears proved well-founded. During February and March, thousands of refugees streamed out of Zeytun. One group, upon arriving in Maraş "in great destitution," was stoned and then beaten by a mob of townspeople and soldiers. Girls were taken and raped. The authorities prevented missionaries from providing bedding and food.[347] Owing to their poor treatment in majority-Turkish towns, many of the refugees eventually returned to their devastated villages.[348]

The Zeytunlis themselves suffered tragic consequences. Under the watchful eyes of the consuls, the authorities more or less adhered to the terms of agreement, which allowed the imprisoning of about seventy-five of the rebels but otherwise barred retribution.[349] But little was done to improve conditions for the sick and hungry townspeople. A missionary noted at the end of March that 3,000–4,000 Zeytunlis were ill, chiefly with typhus and dysentery, and thousands could barely walk. The town had just one doctor.[350] Barnham concluded that the residents "should be allowed to emigrate, . . . or they will be gradually exterminated."[351] Of course, this would not have been easy, either. Barnham reported in March 1896 that a group of Zeytunlis travelling to Albistan with an escort of gendarmes had been set upon by a mob. Nine were killed.[352]

Van

In the town of Van, there was "no special ill-feeling between the local Turks and Armenians," Hallward wrote in late 1894. But it served the administration's interest "to maintain the fiction of a perpetual Armenian agitation." Locals took "their cue" from officials who used "every means to show that agitation and disorder reign among the Armenians." He quoted the commander of a gendarmerie unit telling a "friendly" village priest that "he deserved death like all other Armenians of this district as they were rebels against the Sultan." In Hallward's estimation, though, "the Armenians of this province are and have been for a long time past absolutely impassive in spite of the gross injustice which they suffer at the hands of the vali and his subordinates." The Armenians could do nothing else, he concluded, as they were virtually unarmed. Yet "upwards of fifty Armenians" were in prison "on absolutely unfounded charges," kept in jails that Hallward described as "a scandal to civilization." He concluded that "the spirit of the administration . . . is fanatical and hostile to all Christians."[353]

Conditions outside the town, in the rest of Van vilayet, were no better. Armenian lives and property in the Shattakh (Çatak) and Norduz districts, south of Lake Van, were completely at the mercy of Kurdish brigands, who were "actively encouraged by the vali."[354] Amid the prevailing atmosphere of rapine and massacre in November 1895, raids grew more frequent and brutal. The Kurds abducted children and stole "everything down to the outer garments of the men [and] women."[355] Robbery was often accompanied by cold-blooded murder as well as the killing of any who resisted.[356] Thousands fled to Van town or took refuge in caves. Hallward related how one woman "started for Van from a village about two and a half hours away with 3 small children. Finding that they could not keep up with her, she took one in her arms and one on her back and left the third in hiding in a cave." After reaching Van with two of her children, she went back to the cave to fetch the third but found him dead.[357]

Amid the despair, there were a few efforts to improve circumstances in Van vilayet. After a new vali, Şemseddin Pasha, defended coerced mass conversions with the paradoxical argument that Armenians were "incline[d] . . . naturally to convert," Constantinople ordered him to desist. "Group conversions will lead our enemies to claim that the Muslims are converting the Christians by force," the Sublime Porte explained.[358] And in the summer of 1895, following complaints by diplomats, many political prisoners were released.[359]

But nothing really changed. Already in summer 1895 Graves was warning of massacre. Kurdish raids on the villages augured gradual "starvation."[360] In the town of Van, Armenian schools and shops were shuttered.[361] The town was "full of village women and children going about bare-footed in the snow with the scantiest rags to cover them." Zeki Pasha, commanding the 4th Army Corps, gave "ambiguous orders" that seemed designed to ensure violence against Armenians. For example, he ordered his troops to fire on Kurds when attacked, though he knew full well that the real problem was army behavior when Kurds attacked Armenians—not Turkish soldiers.[362] Armenians began smuggling in arms from Persia and perhaps Russia in order, they said, to defend themselves.[363] Yet another new vali, Nazim Pasha, threw up his hands, telling Hallward he could "do nothing against the Kurds" and that Constantinople needed to instruct the military commanders directly if it wanted the Kurds curbed.[364]

Van town saw no massacre during the murderous days of October–December 1895, probably because it was home to a relatively large number of armed revolutionists and because of its relatively benign vali.[365] But tensions increased in the spring of 1896. According to British Vice-Consul Major W. H. Williams, this was due "principally . . . to the succession of outrages committed by the [Armenian] revolutionary party." Revolutionaries walked about Van "always armed and covered with belts of cartridges." Naturally, Williams wrote, "the Moslem population became excited."[366] Revolutionary "outrages" included an assault in late May, in which five or six Kurds were killed.[367]

Another source of friction was the rural refugee population in Van town, which fled there to escape Kurdish marauders. The authorities, townspeople, and missionaries all wanted the refugees to return to their villages, and eventually "over 500 persons . . . were sent on their way, on the express assurance of safety." But safety was more easily promised than procured. A missionary stationed outside Van described a scene in which "three of these villages were surrounded, sacked . . . and the men shot down like partridges. Twenty-five . . . were killed and many wounded." She described a "poor terrified remnant" brought to her office: "One little boy of ten was standing before me, his clothes drenched with blood. I asked if he was wounded, and they told me: 'No, it was his father's blood.' The father and son fled to a heap of straw and covered themselves. But the father, who was lying over the boy, was discovered and killed, the boy lay there with his dead father on him until the Kurds withdrew."[368] Troops sent to the area apparently halted the Kurdish depredations but made no arrests. The troops then settled down in the villages "until they had eaten all the stray fowls and other scanty edibles the Kurds had left."[369]

In the town of Van, matters escalated on June 14, 1896, when a patrol exchanged fire with a group of men—either Muslim smugglers or Armenian revolutionists—and two soldiers were wounded. The following day a column of 200 well-armed Hunchaks, led by one Martick, marched into town singing the Armenian song "Our Country."[370] Anti-Armenian "disturbances" followed, launched by "a mob of Turks, gypsies, and gendarmes." Revolutionaries later alleged that soldiers murdered a group of Armenian workmen in the street.[371] But most sources agree that the soldiers generally refrained from attacking Armenians at the start of the affair.

The next day, June 16, Hunchaks clashed with Muslims and fired on troops. Williams argued that the Hunchaks "were no patriots trying to defend their wives and children, but pure and simple rebels." There were "600 or 700" Armenian fighters, armed with Russian rifles and led by a "Russian," a "Bulgarian," and a dozen or so "naturalized" Russians and Americans. "I have ample proof that they murdered in cold blood unarmed and inoffensive Mahommedans," he wrote. During the fighting, Armenian townspeople fled their homes. Some holed up in the American mission compound, others in various locations around town. About 1,500 were initially saved by a Muslim, Omar Aga, and his friends.[372]

Turks and Armenians traded shot and shell for a week, and Kurds from outside joined the fray. On June 18 and 19, the army stepped up its involvement, letting loose with artillery from the heights of Akerbok. About 15,000 Armenians fled to the missionary area. The revolutionaries beat back repeated assaults, killing some 250 Muslims. Eventually local Armenian leaders and missionaries persuaded the Hunchaks to leave town and head to Persia. On the evening of June 21 they complied, after Mayor Galip Pasha turned out of his house several hundred Armenians to whom he had given shelter, and "more than a hundred men and boys" were slaughtered. Thereafter, troops and townspeople poured into Armenian neighborhoods, looting, torching, and, here and there, killing. Meanwhile, the army gave chase and "cut to pieces" the withdrawing revolutionaries. Of the hundreds of fighters who fled, only thirty-eight managed to make it to Persia.[373] According to Père Defrance, a French missionary, the revolutionaries massacred Kurdish villagers as they made their way through the countryside.[374]

The following day soldiers restored order after Constantinople publicly pardoned the Armenians. The Kurdish bands left town, here and there causing havoc in the countryside, most prominently torching a large monastery. The Armenians left the missionary buildings, which had come to resemble "pig sties," and dispersed to their homes. "Naked, starving and wounded" Armenians straggled into town from the surrounding villages.[375]

In the course of the week-long hostilities, 547 Armenians died in Van, hundreds more in the flight to Persia, and thousands in the surrounding villages.[376] It was subsequently estimated that, altogether, 5,522 Armenians lost their lives in Van and its villages. The following year, at least 5,000 more died from disease and starvation, and 10,000 emigrated. In the kaza of Agants alone, some 5,000 children were left without fathers, and about half that number lost their mothers as well. At least 6,771, and perhaps as many as 10,000, converted.[377]

The Last Wave: The Ottoman Bank Affair and the Massacre at Eğin

On August 26, 1896, Armenian revolutionaries attacked the Imperial Ottoman Bank in Galata, a neighborhood of downtown Constantinople. Two dozen fighters, led by the revolutionaries Papken Siuni and Armen Garo, rushed into the bank, killed guards, and took about a hundred hostages, many of them British, Greek, and French nationals.[378] Several Turks were killed in exchanges of fire.

The plotters apparently aimed to seize several key institutions besides the bank. They attempted but failed to take the Armenian Patriarchate and the Credit Lyonnais bank. They did, for a time, occupy a number of buildings near Hagia Sofia and in Galata, from which they threw bombs onto the streets below.

The purpose of the raid, as Terrell put it, was "to attract the attention of Europe, and force intervention for the Armenian race." The Armenians hoped "to rouse the Powers to secure . . . better government" by reviving the mooted reforms or by securing Armenian "autonomy."[379] More broadly, the raiders appear to have been motivated by a desire "to save their fellow countrymen from oppression and wrong" and to stir rebelliousness among "lower class" Armenians who, until then, "were . . . holding aloof" from the struggle. After interviewing the raiders, a British diplomat described them as filled with "hatred" for the Turks "beyond all description."[380]

The Ottoman leadership responded harshly to this deliberate challenge in the very heart of imperial power. The public did too. Muslim mobs, sometimes assisted or incited by soldiers, reacted with both spontaneous and organized mass killings of Armenian men in Constantinople and nearby villages including Bebek, Rumeli Hisar, and Hasköy. According to Michael Herbert, the British chargé d'affaires, the Turks had been vaguely aware of the impending bank raid and, once the slaughter began, ordered troops and police not to interfere, giving the "fury of the Turkish mob" free rein. "A large number of Softas and other fanatics, were encouraged to come over from the Asiatic side and there is nothing improbable in the stories current that the clubs and iron bars with which they were armed were furnished by the municipal authorities," Herbert reported. Some Turks later told their European employers that they had "been enrolled by the police as special constables, provided with knives, and told to kill Armenians during 36 hours."[381]

Armenians were shot, knifed, and clubbed in the streets, and mobs broke into houses, including those of Europeans.[382] Warehouses, shops, and homes were pillaged. One British diplomat reported two Armenians killed by soldiers "under my own eyes" in a house next to the embassy.[383] Here and there policemen handed Armenians over to the mob.[384] The killing went on for two days. On the evening of August 27, under Western and Russian pressure, the government began to restore order, but clashes continued for several days.[385] On the 29th, sixty Armenians holed up in a building threw grenades and fired shots at soldiers, killing a captain and wounding several before the building was stormed.[386]

As the mayhem unfolded, Western diplomats mediated an agreement between the bank raiders and the government: the raiders would be allowed free passage out of the country in exchange for release of the hostages. Early on August 27, the surviving raiders were conveyed to a French merchant vessel, the *Gironde*, which took them to Marseille.[387]

Many were not so lucky. According to Terrell, 4,000–6,000 Armenians were killed during the rampage.[388] The British reported some 200 Turkish soldiers killed or wounded.[389] Terrell told an eerie story of massacre characterized by "little noise. No shouting by the Turks and no loud pleadings for help or mercy by the victims. They were slaughtered and seemed to consent to their sacrifice like sheep." At one graveyard he counted seven hundred bodies. Criticizing the ineffectuality of the powers—including his fellow Americans—Terrell described the victims as "mute witnesses against timid and blundering diplomacy." As to the "better class of Turks," during the days of massacre they sat around in the coffee shops "solemnly smoking or sipping their coffee in dignified silence." At one point during the massacres, Terrell was struck by the sight of "a solemn-looking old Ulama." He trod the streets "with white turban, flowing white robe and staff in hand" and "stop[ped] by the body of a dead Armenian. He struck the body with his staff, kicked it three times and then resumed his deliberate walk." Terrell was not blind to what had occurred at the bank—"the atrocious scheme of desperate men to . . . deliberately and wantonly provoke a massacre of their own race"—but he believed this could neither "excuse nor palliate the crime of the Turks in butchering the innocent." He predicted that "Asiatic Turkey will be again the scene of massacres."[390]

After the killings Herbert concluded, "There is evidence that the authorities organised and armed the mob which committed all the massacres on Wednesday and Thursday. It was only on Thursday evening that the Sultan sent orders to stop the mob, when they were instantly obeyed." The sultan subsequently sent Herbert a message explaining the delay: supposedly the court had not at first realized "how grave the situation was." But Herbert knew this was a lie because the government had informed him early on Wednesday, during the bank raid, that "all the necessary orders were given for the preservation of order."[391] "The Mohammedan mob is always entirely under the Sultan's control," Herbert wrote.[392]

In the weeks after the massacre, the authorities rounded up and imprisoned hundreds of Constantinople Armenians. Thousands in the city and its outskirts holed up in churches, which afforded relative safety.[393] Thousands more were exiled to distant parts of the empire; about three thousand reached Trabzon, Giresun, and Samsun by boat.[394] The exiles arriving in Erzurum were "cruelly treated and half starved," Graves reported.[395] The massacre also triggered a nationwide wave of Armenian emigration. On September 11 Shipley, the British consul in Trabzon, reported that some 1,400 Armenians, mostly "small traders, silversmiths, and artisans," had boarded steamships bound for Russia.[396]

Fearing further anti-Christian outbreaks, some diplomats suggested that a combined ground and sea campaign by Russia and the Western powers might keep the Turks in check. In the absence of such intervention, Terrell wrote, Ottoman Christians were at the mercy of the soldiers and "twenty thousand Ulama and Softas and a fanatical mob" that could spring into action at an hour's notice.[397] But the Christian powers declined to intervene. Instead, they lodged a few protests and dispatched small detachments of marines to protect their own legations.[398]

Eğin

Unlike the Constantinople demonstration of September 1895, the attack on the Ottoman Bank did not trigger widespread massacres. Rather, the effects were localized and constrained. That the response was so limited is further proof of the central government's firm control over anti-Christian violence throughout the country: following the bank takeover, the relative quiet in the provinces came at the Porte's command, with local officials nipping potential massacres in the bud.[399] Most likely the central government had determined that it needed to quell anti-Christian violence in order to appease outside powers and prevent possible foreign intervention.

There was, however, one significant massacre following the bank raid, possibly authorized by the Sublime Porte. The killings occurred at Eğin, in Mamuret-ül-Aziz vilayet. Eğin was a mixed Christian-Muslim town, with a population of 12,000. It was noted for its wealth and refined inhabitants. In autumn 1895 the town's Armenians had "purchased exemption from massacre and plunder" by paying the surrounding Kurdish tribes 1,500 lira and handing over their weapons to the authorities. The Eğin Armenians understood their peril. A good number of family members lived in Constantinople, where they suffered after the bank raid. Some seventy were killed in the massacre in the capital; others abandoned their businesses and fled.[400]

In Eğin itself the violence broke out in mid-September. On the fourteenth, Kurdish tribesmen gathered on a slope overlooking the town, unquestionably a menacing sign. Initially soldiers held the tribesmen back, while the Armenians closed their shops. The next day the governor ordered the Armenians to reopen their shops, assuring them of "perfect safety." The Armenians complied. The slaughter began with the firing of a gun by an unknown shooter at about noon.

The killings lasted three days. According to one report, 857 of the town's 5,000–6,000 Christians were killed; 50 of the dead were women.[401] Another report put the death toll at 2,000.[402] Evidently many ran to the konak seeking refuge but were cut down nearby.[403] Most of the killing appears to have been done by soldiers, who also guarded the marketplace, to prevent its destruction.[404] Armenians "fled hither and thither" and hid in basements, caves, drains, and gardens. They were hunted methodically. "Every male above 12 years of age who could be found was slain," Fontana reported. Muslims were forbidden to shelter Christians.[405]

The murders were accompanied by widespread arson and rape. Most of the town's 1,100 Christian homes were put to the torch.[406] Two Armenian churches also went up in flames. Thirty women were abducted; a missionary reported that "many women and girls threw themselves into the Euphrates."[407] The vali's aide-de-camp apparently described the massacre as "enough to break a heart of stone." A missionary reported the feeling among many survivors, who had lost their homes and bread-winners: "there is nothing left . . . but emigration."[408]

As with other massacres, the damage wasn't limited to the town itself. In the days after Eğin burned, Turkish soldiers and Kurdish tribesmen attacked nearby villages, killing hundreds of Armenians.[409] One soldier, a Lieutenant Kiamil, later wrote that a hundred Armenians and eight Kurds were killed in the village of Pingan. "I myself killed nine of the biggest swine," he boasted. "These blasphemed our lord and prophet."[410]

Muslims did at times come to the Armenians' aid. Fontana wrote that Kyamal (Kemal) Bey, the "most influential Turk" in Çemişgezek, went out of his way to protect Armenians, earning the wrath of local Kurds, who attacked his farm and granaries. Another Turk, Mustapha Bey of Khoshgeree (Hoşgeri?), reportedly sheltered and protected about 1,000 Armenians. In Eğin itself a retired colonel, Hussein Effendi saved Armenians. Fontana also reported that the acting kaymakam of Çemişgezek "acquired the respect and gratitude of the Armenians" and Hassan Bey, the *mudir* (administrator) of Eğin, was even more averse to "injustice and outrage, displaying real heroism."[411]

After Eğin settled down, its Armenian bishop was forced to send Constantinople a cable asserting that the "massacre originated with the revolutionary Armenians" and that the Turks merely defended themselves.[412] But there is solid evidence to support an American missionary's conclusion that the attack "was carefully planned with intent to exterminate the Armenians."[413]

Fontana pointed out that Haji Muhammed of Saracık, who reportedly played a "prominent part" in a massacre in and around the town of Arapgir a year earlier, arrived in Eğin three or four days before the killings. He may have had a hand in organizing the violence. Fontana also found that, just before the massacre, the municipal authorities had ordered from Christian artisans a hundred axes that were later used to break down doors. Drawing on the testimony of what he described as eight or nine prominent Eğin Turks, including "an officer of rank" and "a corporal of gendarmes," Fontana determined that the mob and soldiers must have coordinated, as they used primarily "bayonet, dagger, club and axe" in preference to firearms, which were "more noisy." These sources also told Fontana that Eğin officials had conspired for weeks and that, days before the massacre, had gone to the countryside and informed Kurdish chieftains and Muslim villagers to prepare themselves, for "Eghin would burn."[414]

While there can be little doubt that the killings were planned, the question of local versus central-government culpability is harder to answer. Constantinople denied ordering the massacre and insisted, to the contrary, that it had given "stringent instructions . . . to prevent an outbreak." The government maintained that "the whole blame for the disturbance rests with the acting Kaymakam and the local functionaries."[415] But the government had reason to target Eğin, the hometown of Siuni, the bank-raid leader. And a Turk who worked for the telegraph system told Fontana that "the Palace" sent Eğin officials a telegram warning that Armenians there were about to cause trouble. The message did not explicitly order massacre, but local authorities knew what to do when instructed to "take the necessary action." At the very least, it seems that the army was involved in the planning. On the first day of the massacre, September 15, Mustapha Pasha, the military commandant at Harput, wired instructions to Eğin officials—including acting kaymakam Zade Hakki Effendi—to arm themselves and muster Muslims.[416]

An American missionary, basing his views largely on the testimony of "two candid Turks," was convinced that "the massacre was official"—the effort of local and central-government authorities working in concert. The Armenians, he claimed, had offered "no resistance whatever"; the killings were unprovoked. "There was no disturbing element, except in the imagination of a few officials."[417] Yet, during the weeks leading up to the massacre, local officials had complained to Constantinople that there were "seditious characters" in the town. The government "was persuaded . . . and orders were sent to eliminate" the disloyal element.[418]

Halting Massacres

The waves of violence ended in autumn 1896, when the Sublime Porte sent the provinces "the most stringent orders" and "every possible instruction" to "prevent fresh disturbances." Officials who disobeyed would be "held responsible," the grand vizier warned.[419] Provincial officials followed through. In Erzurum, for instance, the vali separately called in the town's Armenian and Muslim notables and read them the "telegram of the Grand Vizier." All disturbers of the peace, he said, would be dealt with on the basis of "impartial severity." The vali also ordered Muslim clerics "to preach peace and denounce . . . violence."[420]

Even before receiving the cessation order, some local officials did what they could to resist violence. This was possible because the central government's orders concerning Christian minorities were often inexplicit, which meant local officials were allowed a measure of discretion. To be sure, many local officials interpreted "do-what-needs-to-be-done" orders as authorizations for mass murder. But such phraseology also allowed for less lethal interpretation. Some officials exploited this opening to act humanely, stymieing massacres before or just after they got under way and thereby preventing bloodshed.

One such case occurred in November 1895, when an "infuriated mob" of Arabs gathered in Aleppo. Reportedly, "women [took] the leading part in the demonstration . . . shouting out curses on the ghiaours." But the ferik quickly dispersed the mob.[421] In Ankara, similarly, Vali Mamduh Pasha stopped would-be rioters in their tracks after Muslims began purchasing arms and threatening "to exterminate . . . every Christian." A clandestine committee reportedly was "arrang[ing] for a sudden and simultaneous attack," but the vali dispatched patrols with strict orders to arrest "any disorderly Christian or Turk," enjoined café proprietors to prohibit political discussion, and exiled six Turkish conspirators.[422]

That same month, officials prevented major violence in Muş. Taking note of the massacres elsewhere, Muslims there paraded "the streets fully armed, declaring that Muş must not be the only exception in the good work of exterminating the Christians."[423] Several Armenians were killed or wounded, including one by a softa who, according to multiple reports, "drank [the victim's] blood afterwards." But "the better class Mussulmans," as Vice-Consul Hampson put it, saved Armenians. The mutesarrif himself rode "into a crowd of softas and dispers[ed] them with blows of his whip."[424]

Local officials of outstanding character and energy again came to the rescue of Armenians during the second, smaller bout of massacres, in summer-autumn 1896. For instance, in Ankara Vali Tevfik Pasha and a number of senior military commanders were unwilling to massacre Christians or see them massacred. In September, after Turks attacked Armenian passersby "with bludgeons and knives," Tevfik ordered his troops to take a hard line. They killed a Turk and arrested between fifteen and thirty more. One day that month, the vali made official resolve clear by patrolling "the streets personally" for "six hours."[425]

Explaining the Massacres

The questions of who instigated the massacres and for what reasons are not just matters of historical interest. They were critical at the time, for the European powers were watching, and the Ottomans feared they might intervene. In their reports the mutesarrifs, valis, and Sublime Porte tended to follow a consistent script intended to protect the state against accusations of premeditation and orchestration. The massacres, these officials alleged, were triggered by specific incidents involving Christians and Muslims: a quarrel in a shop, a murder in an alleyway. In some cases, these "events" were probably fictions. In others, they were post facto rationalizations. They implied that assailants' actions were spontaneous and, where reactive, justified. Somehow, these one-off matters ended up producing large numbers of Armenian dead and wounded, so officials routinely took care to deflate the number of Christian casualties.[426]

Yet, in spite of Ottoman and Turkish archival purges, a substantial body of available evidence makes clear that almost all the massacres of 1894–1896 were organized by the state. Either they were unambiguously directed by Constantinople, or they were ordered by local authorities executing what they understood to be the government's desires and intentions.[427]

In the wake of the September 1895 Armenian demonstration and pogrom in Constantinople, diplomats were convinced that the government had ordered massacres. At the very least, the government had instructed local officials to be mindful of potential Armenian rebellion and "do what needed to be done" in their areas, but it is probable that some governors were explicitly instructed—by telegram or in person by agents of the sultan or grand vizier—to kill the members of vaguely defined rebel groups. Given Ottoman norms, it is inconceivable that these officials would have unleashed such attacks unless they believed they were carrying out the will of the Sublime Porte. Further down the food chain, mobs confirmed official sanction by chanting "the state is with us." Whatever is known about orders, official permission is obvious in the fact that, almost invariably, perpetrators went unpunished. The blind eye of the authorities could be as deadly as a massacre order.[428]

One source of ambiguity concerning responsibility for massacres lies in the long history of Kurdish violence toward eastern Armenians. Were the Kurdish depredations of 1894–1896 simply a continuation of earlier practices, or did they reflect a state-directed campaign of terror? The pattern points to the second explanation. For one thing, there is evidence that the state ordered Kurds to pillage. Speaking of the Van vilayet countryside, Hallward pointed out, "Many Kurds have declared that they had distinct orders to plunder the Christian villagers."[429]

Furthermore, Kurds did not previously behave so lethally or plunder to the extent that they did in the mid-1890s. Raiding Christian villages and extracting tribute from them was an important part of many Kurds' livelihoods. To kill large numbers of Armenians and take everything they had was tantamount to killing the goose that lays the golden egg. Devastating Armenians meant harming Kurds, too. Something else must have instigated their irrational choices. (For Turks, the economic motivations were more straightforward. In July 1894, just before the first major massacres, Terrell wrote of the "unpaid and poorly fed" Ottoman army as a factor in potential anti-Christian disturbances that might break out.[430] Recall as well the supposed firman authorizing looting of Armenian property.[431])

Foreign observers believed that in certain towns so-called Turkish Secret Defense Committees—composed of officials and notables and "created under the auspices of the central authorities"—had been formed to combat prospective Armenian insurrection. There can be little doubt that such committees were active, and they may have played a part in fomenting massacres.[432]

Finally, government instigation and organization are clear from the uniformity of the massacre process and the consistent presence of state agents. Soldiers and gendarmes took an active part in pillage and killing across eastern Anatolia. Consuls and missionaries called out many a vali, mutesarrif, kaymakam, and military commander for ordering and organizing massacres. Even where we don't know who exactly took the reins, the presence of a bugle call or shot signaling troops and mobs demonstrates the organized nature of their bloody work. Foreign observers remarked on the preparedness of the mobs. Attacks on Armenian quarters were sometimes unleashed simultaneously from several directions, indicating that the killers had strategized beforehand. In certain places, Kurdish tribesmen were summoned from the countryside or ordered by local officials to move into position in preparation for massacre.[433] On multiple occasions soldiers and Kurdish tribesmen were seen coordinating their actions. Soldiers told missionaries, or were overheard saying, that they had been assigned particular hours in which they were free to slaughter or pillage. And in almost all sites, an order by a civil or military official brought about an immediate cessation of the slaughter, indicating effective control from above.

The Role of Political Fear

In some measure, the massacres were inspired by Ottoman fears of potential Armenian rebellion. Such fears were understandable. Turks and Muslim tribes had oppressed and despoiled the Armenians of eastern and central Turkey for decades, helping to foment a nationalist movement that sometimes spoke angrily and acted violently. It was only natural that Constantinople and provincial officials were beset by concerns—concerns they disseminated widely in official pronouncements and the press. In 1894–1896 some Turks may have genuinely believed that they were preempting Armenian violence.

As reports of real and imagined Armenian violence ran up and down Ottoman chains of command, they were amplified and aggravated. Skirmishes were turned into battles; hesitant, dissenting pastors became Svengalis of propaganda and subversion. Recall British Consul Longworth's account of "wild and loose reports of Armenian atrocities committed on Moslems in the interior."[434] In truth the overwhelming majority of Armenians—urban and rural, lower class and better off—refrained from challenging the state and sought only amelioration of their condition through reform, an idea that achieved "centre stage in 1895."[435]

Reform itself engendered fear among the Turkish masses, who worried that Armenians and other Christians in the empire would attain political, social, and legal equality, eating away at formal and informal Muslim control and superiority. American diplomats later drew comparisons to the Reconstruction-era United States, in which many whites feared that former slaves were attaining equality with, or even dominance over, the white population.[436] In the Ottoman Empire in the 1890s, the threat to the Muslim majority's centuries'-old supremacy seemed very real.

This perceived danger extended to the integrity and very existence of the body-politic. Armenian activism might not end at the point of equality within a multiethnic state; it portended autonomy in the eastern provinces followed by independence. This would in turn mean dissolution of the empire's Anatolian core. It is hardly surprising, then, that it was precisely in the six provinces named in the 1895 reform scheme that the bulk of the massacres occurred.[437]

Prominent in these nightmares of imperial dismemberment were the western, especially American, missionaries. Missionaries were accused of fomenting ideas of equality and independence that threatened to tear the state apart. As one missionary reported from Sivas in early 1895,

> The ever increasing discomfort, hardship, poverty and despair of the [Muslim] people are attributed to Christian and foreign influence. The great decline of business, and the loss of friendly commercial and social relations between Mohammedans and Armenians is attributed to the revolutionary spirit of the Armenians, fostered by foreign influence. The Governors have publicly told the people that all the troubles of the Empire are due to the foreigners. . . . The missionaries . . . have come to be feared and hated for the disturbing influence it is seen education and Western ideas introduce.[438]

However, it is worth noting that Turkish officials, soldiers, and mobs took great care during the massacres to avoid harming missionaries. It is likely that orders to this effect emanated from Constantinople. True, the Turks suspected that missionaries routinely appealed to the powers, usually through their embassies, to intercede on behalf of Armenians. But if the missionaries themselves were assaulted, the great powers might well intervene with force to protect their nationals. In particular, the United States was viewed as an unknown, but powerful, quantity, having previously demonstrated its naval strength against Barbary Coast pirates in Ottoman territory.

The Role of Islam

In January 1896 Ambassador Currie met with the sultan to complain about the massacres. He was at pains to avoid asserting religious motivations, saying, "The religion of Mohammed was highly respected in England and that no one attributed the crimes that had been committed to its teachings."[439]

This was hogwash. British diplomats, like most Western observers, understood that what had happened was closely bound up with the Islamic fervor projected from the Porte and embraced by many Turks. According to Fitzmaurice, Abdülhamid's predecessors, Abdülmecid and Abdülaziz, had "recognized" the "political danger" of "fanaticism" and had in great measure "rendered [it] dormant." But Abdülhamid "has reawakened and fomented that fanaticism," spending "large sums" on "Moslem schools, medressehs, mosques and tekkehs [dervish lodges]." Abdülhamid's "whole administration" was directed, in Fitzmaurice's view, toward "strengthening the Moslem elements . . . to the prejudice of non-Muslims." This was obvious in the company the sultan kept: "fanatics" from "Arabia, India, Afghanistan, Egypt . . . upon whom he lavishes large sums of money" and whom "he uses as his emissaries in furtherance of his Pan-Islamic" goals.[440]

Strident religiosity spread across Ottoman lands and expressed itself in the 1890s as a visceral hatred of Christians. British Vice-Consul P. J. C. McGregor, writing from Beirut, recounted the testimony of a Christian travelling from Damascus to Jerusalem. Along the way, "he and his wife were constantly stoned and insulted by the Moslem peasantry, who also made free use of blasphemous and obscene expressions." The British cemetery in Nablus had been "laid waste by the Mohammedans" and used as a refuse dump. In Palestine more generally, "The Ottoman authorities, and, at their instigation, the Mollahs, were doing their utmost to foster the growing animosity against everything Christian and European."[441]

The situation in Asia Minor was no different. As a British diplomat put it in 1896, Turkish Muslims were "animated with the old spirit of meting out Islam on the sword to their Christian subjects. They believe that rayahs, whom they have allowed to exist in their territory, are traitorously conspiring against Islam and the State and that it is their duty to their religion to extirpate them."[442] Mullahs and hajjis—Muslims who had made pilgrimage to Mecca—were prominent in disseminating this hatred. In late October 1895, Fontana reported that, in Yozgat, twenty-eight Muslims who had returned from pilgrimage the previous year were "the chief cause for anxiety to the local Christians owing to their fanaticism and to influence they possess over their Mahometan fellow townsmen."[443]

Muslim holy days and observances tended to heighten anti-Christian sentiment; often, Friday prayers were followed by acts of violence. For instance, on Friday January 18, 1895, when a group of hajjis returned to Yozgat, "a Turkish rabble" marked the occasion by stoning houses belonging to Armenians and Greeks, breaking "several hundred panes." A handful of people were injured. The crowd comprised 200–300 softas attached to the town's madrassas and was led by two hajjis.[444]

During the massacres, the power of religious enmity was manifest in the desecration of Christian sites and symbols, which were particular objects of the mobs' wrath. There was widespread and deliberate destruction of churches and monasteries; some were converted into mosques. Christian clergymen were singled out for torture, before being dispatched often by beheading, the Koran-sanctioned method for killing infidels. Here and there, clerics were crucified. In Aivose (Ayvos), a village in the Harput area, the priest "was made to mount the roof of his church and give the Mussulman call to prayer" before being murdered.[445]

The memoir of Abraham Hartunian, an Armenian survivor, provides a good illustration of the nexus between Islam and massacre from the victims' perspective. Hartunian was in Severek, his hometown, on November 2, 1895, the day of the massacre. "The mob had plundered the Gregorian church, desecrated it, murdered all who had sought shelter there, and as a sacrifice, beheaded the sexton on the stone threshold," he wrote. Then rioters filled the courtyard of the Protestant church.

> The blows of an axe crashed in the church doors. The attackers rushed in, tore the Bibles and hymnbooks to pieces, broke and shattered whatever they could, blasphemed the cross and, as a sign of victory, chanted the Mohammedan prayer 'La ilaha ill-Allah, Mohammedin Rasul-Ilah' (There is no other God but God, and Mohammed is his prophet). We could see and hear all these things from the room in which we huddled. . . . They were coming up the stairs . . . now butchers and victims were face to face. The leader of the mob cried: 'Muhammede salavat' (believe in Mohammed and deny your religion). . . . Squinting horribly, he repeated his words in a terrifying voice.

Then the leader "gave the order to massacre."

> The first attack was on our pastor [Mardiros Bozyakalian]. The blow of
> an axe decapitated him. His blood, spurting in all directions, spattered
> the walls and ceiling with red. Then I was in the midst of the butchers.
> One of them drew his dagger and stabbed my left arm. . . . I lost con-
> sciousness. . . . What happened to me some women who had remained
> alive told me later. . . . Three blows fell on my head. My blood began to
> flow like a fountain. . . . The attackers [were] sure that I was dead. . . .
> Then they slaughtered the other men in the room, took the prettier
> women with them for rape, and left the other women and children there,
> conforming to the command that in this massacre only men were to be
> exterminated.[446]

Another revealing incident, unconnected to massacre, occurred at Misis
(Yakapınar), in Adana vilayet, on November 9, 1895. An Ottoman army
reserves commander brought his men into the Armenian church during services, "tore the vestments from the priest's back, desecrated the sanctuary,
poured out the holy oil and the sacred wafers, tore up the Bible and prayer
books, beat the priest and outraged his wife, who lived in rooms adjoining
the church. The priest afterwards sought to make complaint to the civil
authorities, but was imprisoned for slander."[447] And Barnham wrote on
August 2, 1895, of an episode that appeared to mock Christ's entry to Jerusalem on a donkey. An Armenian farmer, Aghdaz Oghlon Ibrahim, was set
upon by Muslim neighbors, who beat him, "smeared his face with filth,
placed him on a donkey facing the tail, which they made fast around his
waist with the aid of a cord." Then "he was driven along the high road into
the town of Killis, while his tormentors ran alongside, shouting 'This is the
respect due to Giaours!'"[448]

  Perhaps the most obvious indication of the religious character of the Muslim
violence in 1894–1896 was widespread forced conversion. Tens of thousands
of Armenians were converted during the massacres, fulfilling a doctrinal demand of jihad.[449] Mass conversion affected almost every area seared by massacre. The documentation is incomplete; most conversions in rural areas, like
most massacres, went unrecorded. But here and there we catch glimpses. For

instance, Hampson reported that in the last months of 1895, 19,000 villagers converted in the sanjak of Siirt alone.[450] Seven thousand were forced to convert in Silvan sanjak and 3,000 more in Palu kaza. These districts were far from alone.[451]

The process was systematic. In December 1895 Currie, quoting one of his subordinates, reported that without effective foreign intervention, the Turks would "probably continue until all the surviving Armenians become Mussulmen."[452] Several months later, an American missionary from Antep wrote, "The demand that Christians become Moslems is being relentlessly pressed in all the region east and north of here." He went on, "Our Governor and other prominent Moslems have told several Christians . . . that the only security for life and property now is by becoming Moslem."[453]

Already in the last months of 1894, Armenians were under pressure to convert. In January 1895, Graves reported that a family in Van vilayet had converted to Islam in order to avoid paying oppressive taxes levied only against Christians. Graves added that word of conversions had grown "more frequent of late." He was also aware of cases in which officials refused Armenian requests to "embrace Islam . . . on the very practical ground that if the Armenians all turned Mussulmans, there would be no one left for [them] to squeeze."[454] Some officials tried to restrain their subordinates, as in the case of the vali of Erzurum, who instructed two of his mutesarrifs "not to admit the validity of these conversions."[455] Curiously, other officials, including the vali of Sivas, encouraged the conversion of Gregorian Armenians to Catholicism.[456]

In many cases converts were forced not only to accept and practice Muslim rituals and take Muslim names but also to undergo painful and dangerous circumcision. In November 1895 Harput missionaries reported that "some six hundred have been circumcised" in two villages.[457] At Garmuri, a village in Harput sanjak, a seventy-year-old priest was "tied to a post and circumcised in public."[458] In other places, circumcision was waived.[459]

Often during the massacres, Armenians were presented by Turkish mobs, Kurdish tribesmen, and troops with the simple option of conversion or death. The latter fate befell the Armenians of Tehmeh, Uzunova, Hoh, and other villages where they refused to convert. Here and there, Armenians committed suicide to avoid conversion. At Khizan, converts were forced to kill relatives who refused to convert.[460] Sometimes, after converting, Armenians were prohibited from speaking their language.[461]

It is unclear whether authorities carrying out mass conversions were acting on specific instructions from Constantinople or on the basis of hints. Publicly, the sultan accepted individual conversion but refused to recognize mass conversions. When presented with the facts, he either denied that conversions were coerced—"calumnies invented by ill-disposed persons"—denied all knowledge of what had happened, or denied responsibility.[462] Unrecognized converts found themselves in a dangerous limbo, with local Muslims threatening their lives even after they had undertaken the humiliation that supposedly could save them.[463]

For months after forced conversions, holdouts might be threatened with fresh massacres. Christian missionaries unfavorably compared what was happening to the seventh-century Muslim conquests in the Middle East, when Christians could avoid conversion by paying tribute. During the "crusade" of the mid-1890s, Christians first offered up tribute in the form of valuables but were then told that "the only condition upon which they would be spared was to accept Mohammedanism."[464]

The conversions were widely reported and caused outrage in the West. Christian diplomats complained vociferously, leading to the sultan's declaration that his government discouraged conversion "when there was reason to believe it was not prompted by religious conviction." He added, though, that "it was difficult for him to discourage persons sincerely desirous of embracing the faith of Islam."[465] Abdülhamid was eventually persuaded to agree to the dispatch of a "delegate," Fitzmaurice, to investigate one of the largest mass conversions, at Birecik.[466]

In April 1896 Fitzmaurice reported that in the area he had toured, 5,900 Christians had been forcibly converted to Islam, 4,300 of them in Birecik itself. More had been converted in the adjacent Maraş and Albistan areas. He worried that, whatever the pronouncements against forced conversion emanating from Constantinople, the local authorities had made no effort to enable the converts to revert to Christianity, and the local populations intimidated them into continuing to adhere to the new faith. They were obliged "to wear turbans, to attend mosques, and learn the Koran, to be circumcised, not to speak Armenian, and to be known officially and privately under the Mussulman names." Some converts abandoned their property and fled to other towns where, unknown, they might renew their Christian worship. But these were hunted down and dragged back to their hometowns where they were obliged to continue living as Muslims.

Fitzmaurice qualified his report by pointing out that much depended on the characteristics of each town. In Adıyaman, where some 400 Christians had been massacred, there did not seem to be "intense religious fanaticism," and the majority of local converts had been allowed to revert to Christianity. Similar stories emerged from Maraş and Antep. But in Birecik and Albistan, reversion had been more difficult. Reversion, Fitzmaurice worried, would be regarded as treachery and "punishable by death, according to the precepts of the Koran," so he advised against immediate reversion, lest it trigger a new wave of killing.[467] Instead, he hoped time would cool tempers and that an Ottoman commission would be sent to the eastern provinces to endorse and safeguard reversion.[468] Some local officials used incentives to prevent reversion. In March 1897 a British consul wrote that authorities in the Khizan area, in Bitlis vilayet, were "secretly offering charity" to the converts "if they would finally embrace Mohammedanism."[469]

Constantinople's orders to refuse recognition of forced conversions, which arrived in late 1895 and early 1896, occasionally triggered fresh atrocities. In March 1896 Hampson reported that fifteen Armenian families had been massacred by Kurds in Çapakçur (Chabakchur) kaza after reverting to Christianity following the sultan's orders. The leading Armenian in the kaza, Serkis Agha, was dragged out of the government house and murdered "before the eyes of the kaimakam." Troops restored order, but no Kurds were arrested, and a number of Armenians were detained.[470]

The fate of converts was mixed. Writing from Diyarbekir in spring 1896, Hallward claimed, "The majority of the forced converts . . . have now returned to Christianity." But in the Silvan area, he added, "a good many . . . remain Turk through fear."[471] Still others may have felt that, in the long term, even after anti-Christian passions abated, wisdom dictated continued adherence to Islam. To be sure, the vast majority of Christians in the eastern provinces, despite the turbulence and threats, never converted.

Rape and Abduction

Mass rape was part and parcel of the massacres. Thousands of young women were carried off and enslaved or forced to marry Muslims. In some cases, Armenians committed suicide rather than be raped or carried off.[472] Most of the abductees were never returned. They remained, for the rest of their lives, in Muslim households as servants, wives, or concubines.[473]

Such behavior reflected an escalation of earlier practice. In the years before 1894, rapes and abductions of Armenian women were fairly common in the eastern provinces, but on the scale of individuals and small groups. After a tour of Erzurum vilayet in the late 1880s, one American correspondent reported, "There were no general atrocities. . . . But the system of abduction of Armenian women by Kurdish agas and landlords was going on, and the violation of women in Armenian villages by bands of Kurds was almost general." He provided a concrete example. Traveling from Erzurum to "the Russian frontier" in 1889, "I happened to arrive soon after daybreak at an Armenian village in the plain of Passim, named Keuprukioi [Köprüköy]. I found it in possession of a band of Kurds, who had come in during the night, had turned the unarmed men out of their houses onto the roads, and were indulging in an orgy of outrage among the women."[474] In July 1894 Armenians from Karahisar complained of a recent series of rapes carried out by Kurds and Turkish soldiers.[475]

Women abducted during the massacres might find themselves far from home, making escape nigh impossible. Vice-Consul Hallward, writing from distant Van in March 1895, reported that nine girls had been brought there from Sason, two of them ending up with Nuri Effendi, Van's chief of police, and another two with the vali's aides. Abductees from Sason were given out as presents by Kurdish agas.[476] The Armenian bishop of Van sent the vali a list of "twenty-six women and young girls forcibly abducted by Kurds and made Muslim."[477] The missionary Thomas Christie wrote in July 1896 that a fourteen-year-old Armenian girl from the village of Kans Bazan was being held in an imam's home in Tarsus, some 125 kilometers away. Her father was imprisoned for complaining of the abduction, and "her ravisher" was allowed "free access" to her at the imam's home. The imam persistently tried to persuade her to convert.[478]

Much as rape and abduction preceded the massacres, they continued afterward. In Harput, the killings and arson occurred in November 1895, but Gates complained in January 1896 that "the Palu Turks still continue to carry off girls and women, keeping them a few days and then returning them with their lives blasted."[479] In April 1897 Fontana reported testimony from an Eğin *hodja* (professor or teacher), who said that "outraging of [Armenian] women still continues" there "and that 80 girls are with child" by their rapists.[480]

Raped women were damned by the conservatism of their abusers and their communities alike. Either they were imprisoned in Muslim households or, if abandoned, unable easily to reintegrate in Armenian society. As one missionary wrote:

> In our going about among the villages we saw girls not a few who returned from the hands of their captors, weeping bitterly, shrieking and crying: 'We are defiled, defiled! No one will take us in marriage, for not only are we defiled but those who would notwithstanding that take us, dare not for fear of our captors, and also the young men are few, most of them having been slain by the sword. Our fathers and mothers have been killed and we are become vagrants. What shall we do! Whither shall we go! . . .' How pitiable, how hard and bitter such a lot.[481]

In some cases Muslims who initially protected fleeing Armenians went on to rape and domesticate them. For instance, as anti-Christian violence raged in the village of Tadem, near Harput, a hundred people, mostly women and children, took refuge in the house of a Kurdish aga, Haji Beygo. According to one Western report, "The younger and more attractive were outraged the same evening and subsequently by the Aga, his son Hafiz, and their Kurdish friends. Many of the victims were afterwards given as presents to *Bekjis* (guards) and to Kurdish visitors from the surrounding country. Several women were led away from the Aga's house in a state of complete nudity." An Armenian official estimated that out of Tadem's thousand women, "not more than 350" had been "ravished."[482]

Western diplomats and missionaries tried to retrieve abductees, and occasionally Ottoman officials lent them a hand. In early 1896 British Vice-Consul Philip Bulman managed to get the vali of Sivas to restore to their families "fourteen Armenian girls detained in Turkish houses at Kangal."[483] In general, however, officials denied that women had been abducted or, at best, allowed that one or two cases had occurred. Typical was the response by the vali of Diyarbekir, who would allow only that "Christian women and children took refuge in Mussulman houses" and were subsequently returned to their homes.

Nonetheless, following French and British complaints, Ottoman commissioners "were sent to all the villages in the vilayet, but, notwithstanding searching inquiries, they were only able to discover one [Armenian] woman, one girl, and two [male] children," who were all restored to their community.[484] Hallward was unimpressed by the commissioners' findings, reporting that they had allowed few suspected abductees to meet with their Armenian relatives and, in the end, left large numbers of abductees in Kurdish hands.[485] Herbert experienced similar frustration. The authorities' response to his inquiries concerning abductions in Diyarbekir "only supplies another instance of the uselessness of all similar representations to the Sublime Porte and the impossibility of obtaining an impartial investigation into the outrages," he lamented.[486]

There can be little doubt that the government intended to impede the return of abductees. Fontana obtained an official circular demonstrating as much. The document enjoined provincial officials to take "precautionary measures" against consular investigations because these could result in "dishonor . . . to the State and to Islamism." Referring to an "Imperial order and Firman," of September 1, 1897, the aim of the circular, according to Fontana, was "the obstruction, by all possible means, of any effort made by consular officers to obtain the surrender of Armenian women and children."[487]

Officials were shrewd in carrying out the order. Consider the behavior of the vali of Mamuret-ül-Aziz, Rauf Bey. On Rauf's instructions, a group of girls abducted from Hekim-Han was hauled before the authorities in Malatya, including the Gregorian Catholic bishop, but not until long after they had been kidnapped. It is no wonder that, at this point, all except one refused "to abandon their Moslem husbands and the Mussulman creed." Fontana noted that, given the lapse of time since their abduction, it was likely that all or most had been impregnated by their new husbands or had given birth: "in that case their unwillingness to re-enter the Armenian community (among whom their chance of marriage would henceforward be very slight) and to face possible destitution accentuated by the care and support of an illegitimate child, would appear far from unnatural or unjustified."[488]

Indeed, almost invariably, alleged abductees subject to investigation refused to be separated from their Muslim husbands. Some feared Muslim retribution if they announced Armenian origin or a desire to re-convert.[489] But, in many cases, no threat was needed. By the time consuls or reluctant officials began to examine cases, unmarried Armenian girls probably understood that they had nowhere to return to. Given the vulnerability they would face in their destroyed villages, abducted women were better off staying in the homes of their Muslim husbands. One also cannot rule out the possibility that some fell in love with their new spouses or genuinely wished to be with their new families. When in 1897 Telford Waugh, the British vice-consul in Diyarbekir, bemoaned the Turkish administration's "failure to recover any of the Xian women carried off by the Kurds nearly two years ago," he may not have grasped the unfeasibility of the goal.[490]

Imprisonment and Torture

As with rape and abduction, the arbitrary imprisonment accompanying the massacres was not a novel practice. What changed were the scale and motivations. In the early 1890s, before the massacres, many hundreds of Armenians—routinely including prominent businessmen, priests, teachers, and lawyers—were jailed on flimsy allegations of sedition or rebellion. But often the real motive was pecuniary: officials could extort bribes in exchange for release or better prison conditions.

During the massacres, thousands were arrested for political crimes and for allegedly initiating violence or planning to kill Muslims. Prominent among the detainees were those who tried to fight off Muslim mobs. Mass imprisonment was a logical corollary to the dominant Ottoman narrative that Armenian rebellion and outrages had triggered the disturbances. In the minds of the credulous, incarcerations proved Armenian guilt and justified retaliatory violence against them. At the same time, the authorities almost uniformly refrained from arresting or charging Muslims, as doing so would have strengthened allegations of Muslim responsibility. Moreover,

Muslims were carrying out the official will; their arrest might lead to embarrassing revelations.

Armenian prisoners were held in the same horrendous conditions that Muslim criminals were familiar with. Many were tortured in order to elicit information, confessions, and the names of supposed accomplices. Professor Artin Thoumaian of Merzifon, who was tried in Ankara for sedition, recounted "that he was beaten" on the order of the kaymakam of Çorum, "until three strong sticks were broken over his back." That was only the beginning. "A round hole" was made in his head "into which a nut-shell, half-filled with lice, was pressed down by means of a heavy stone until it stuck there by itself. He fainted several times, and each time he was restored to consciousness . . . only to have the nut-shell pressed into his head again. . . . For a whole night he was hung up by the head and legs between two suspended chains. In addition, hot iron rings were applied to his ankles, which were severely burnt." When confronted by Cumberbatch, the British consul, the local vali denied the prisoner's allegations. The vali also asserted that "many Armenians have been known to purposely inflict injuries on their persons in order to create an ill-feeling against the authorities." Cumberbatch demanded that the vali investigate the allegations. He declined.[491]

Sometimes the Turks dispensed with torturing prisoners and went straight to murder. On June 26, 1894, between the massacres at Yozgat and Sason, six Armenians escaped from prison, were almost instantly recaptured, and executed at a police station.[492] Another especially cruel form of punishment was internal exile. The Turks often sentenced political prisoners to serve time in distant parts of the empire, far from home, family, and workplace. Prisoners incarcerated near home at least enjoyed visits and food sent by their families and friends. There is no way of calculating the number of Armenians thus exiled. In July 1895, before the big wave of massacres, a list of Armenians exiled to the fortress-prison of Acre contained seventy-seven names, including Petros Marimian, a thirty-five-year-old painter from Trabzon; Aristakes Adjemian, forty-seven, a priest from Constantinople; and Gaspar Gulbenkian, a fifty-year-old "advocate" also from Constantinople.[493]

Emigration

The massacres resulted in large-scale emigration of Armenians as well as temporary internal migration. The trend was visible even before Sason. In early 1894 some 20,000 Armenians reportedly emigrated from Erzurum province to Russia, about 3,500 with passports and the rest clandestinely.[494] After the Yozgat affair, one observer wrote that "every Armenian who can manage it has made up his mind to abandon the place as soon as possible."[495] The pressure mounted especially after the massacres of late 1895. Often men would leave first, expecting to establish themselves abroad and then bring their families.

One American missionary wrote of the would-be émigrés, "They generally seem to feel that whatever may be the outcome of the present situation it will be quite impossible for them to remain in this country and large numbers seem . . . determined at every cost to get away somewhere. Cyprus, Egypt, England, America, anywhere out of Turkey."[496] In the Alexandretta area, Armenian clergymen banded together to petition the British consul "to help us in quitting this country for the safety of our lives for we feel certain we shall be killed one after the other in a short time."[497] Bulman wrote from Sivas that, where emigration was permitted, "a very large number would avail themselves of it."[498] British Consul William Shortland Richards, writing from Ankara, made a similar observation. Noting that Armenian families from Kayseri were passing through on their way to Constantinople, presumably headed for parts abroad, he pointed out that only "comparatively well-to-do" families could afford to emigrate; travel was expensive, and obtaining *tezkereh* (travel permission) often required large bribes. But if a "general permission" to emigrate were issued, "half, if not more, of the Christian population would leave . . . at once."[499]

Even with the impediments, Armenians departed in large numbers. In February 1896 the British consul in Trabzon reported that 1,725 had emigrated from the town and altogether 4,797 from the vilayet since the previous October.[500] The following September Graves reported from Erzurum—whence 20,000 had already departed—that since October, 566 families and 507 single men, amounting altogether to "3,000–4,000 souls," had their passports "viseed" for emigration to Russia. A "much larger number . . . probably" crossed the frontier without permission.[501] In February 1896 the French vice-consul in Erzurum, one M. Roqueferrier, transmitted the request of a thousand rural Armenian Catholics to emigrate to Algeria. He estimated that 50,000 more might follow.[502]

The massacres seem to have precipitated emigration among other minority communities, who feared that their day would come once the Turks were finished with the Armenians. Fitzmaurice wrote, "The Jewish population of Urfa is leaving the town. They have a presentiment that the next 'incident' here will be directed not solely against the Christians. . . . In fact, the exodus of the Children of Israel possibly reminds one of the action of certain small animals when the ship is about to sink."[503]

Sometimes authorities allowed emigration where it offered financial benefits: officials would withhold permission to leave until tax arrears and bribes were paid.[504] When permission to leave the country could not be obtained locally, Armenians might instead bribe their way to permits for internal travel and then leave via Constantinople, Smyrna, or Samsun.[505]

Another sort of self-interested response came from Raouf Pasha, the vali of Erzurum. Cumberbatch reported that the administration placed "no obstacles in [emigrating Armenians'] way" because "Raouf Pasha . . . tacitly approved of their departure." Whatever the vali thought of Armenians and their plight, he had at least two reasons for wanting them gone. First, he lacked the means to care for the destitute thousands left in the wash of the massacres. Second, he had to take account of "the animosity of the Mussulman population" toward the Armenians. Muslims wanted Armenians gone, and Raouf was willing to give them what they wanted.[506]

Missionaries were ambivalent about emigration. Some, including Americus Fuller of Antep and F. W. Macallum of Maraş, busily arranged departures, especially of widows and orphans. Others, including Corinna Shattuck, opposed the idea. She argued that the émigrés would suffer from adjustment problems and that emigration would engender Turkish hostility toward those Armenians left behind. But if the Armenians stayed, they could take part in what she hoped would be Turkey's "new future."[507] Perhaps she also worried that if the Armenians moved away, the missionaries, herself included, would lose their raison d'etre.

American missionary F. W. Macallum. After the massacres of 1894–1896, some American missionaries argued that the Armenians should immigrate to the West, as they would never be safe among Turkey's Muslims.

In October 1896 the central government stepped in. Embarrassed by the wave of emigration, which showed that "there is no security for life and property in Turkey," or perhaps concerned by the economic damage caused by the departure of the highly productive Armenians, the government announced a new policy intended to curb Armenian emigration.[508] Now Armenians wishing to emigrate would have to face a "Special Commission," which stripped them of citizenship and made them sign guarantees that "they will not return to Turkey." Armenians who had already left clandestinely would be given six weeks to apply to return, and Ottoman consular officials would decide whether to allow it. Failure to return would mean forfeiture of citizenship.[509]

The new policy had some effect on the behavior of Armenians, who feared that departure would lead to loss of property and, should they return, imprisonment. Before the new policy was in effect, the Russian consulate in Erzurum was approving forty to fifty passports daily, for "entire families." The day after the new rules were in place, Graves observed that "not more than half a dozen single men, with no property to lose, have presented themselves."[510]

Local exercise of discretion ensured that the situation remained confused. In some locations, officials were still allowing Armenians, albeit in small numbers, to leave without going through the prescribed procedures.[511] In November 1896 a group of fifty Armenian widows and orphans was denied permission to leave for Cyprus; that same month a different group of orphans and widows, from Trabzon vilayet, was permitted to emigrate to the same destination.[512] (In general Ottoman authorities opposed the emigration of orphans. Missionaries put this down to the authorities' desire to lay hold of and "educate" them "as Mohammedans, and so to bring a welcome reinforcement of intelligent minds."[513])

It is unclear how many Armenians emigrated during and immediately after 1894–1896; perhaps tens of thousands left, but they were not always welcome elsewhere. British officials discussed a variety of possible settlement locations, ranging from Cyprus to northwestern Canada.[514] Some felt Cyprus was appropriate because of "its proximity to Asia Minor and its climate and other features to which the Armenian agriculturists might [readily] adapt."[515] But the island's British high commissioner ruled against.[516] Canada also refused to accept Armenian refugees.[517]

Casualties

There is radical disagreement among historians about the casualty figures for the massacres of 1894–1896. Armenian historian Vahakn Dadrian cites Ernst Jäckh, a German Foreign Ministry operative, who said 200,000 were killed and one million "pillaged and plundered." Taner Akçam, a Turkish historian living in the United States, has compiled estimates ranging from 88,000 to 300,000 killed.[518]

The contemporary documentation is unreliable. Ottoman figures were invariably on the low side, while official Armenian figures—tabulated by, say, the patriarchate—may have been inflated. It appears that, in 1896–1897, no one tried to compile accurate casualty figures for the whole 1894–1896 period in all of Asia Minor. The best figures exist for individual sites, sanjaks, and vilayets during the October–December 1895 period. In general, figures from the cities are more reliable than those from the countryside, about which there is little detailed documentation. The missionaries and consuls, who did much of the counting, tended to focus on the towns where they lived. They rarely went into the villages, which could be distant or otherwise inaccessible. Moreover, casualty figures in contemporary documents usually refer to those killed on the day of massacres, not to those who died later of injuries, exposure, starvation, or disease.

Missionaries tended to rely on Armenian body counts, often provided by priests. In some localities, these were highly accurate because each victim was named. But even these counts would have omitted the deaths of Christian wayfarers caught up in a massacre in a specific site. Missionaries and consuls also might come to incompatible conclusions, as the former usually compiled figures relating to their stations' areas of operation, while the consuls hewed to Ottoman administrative districts or their own areas of jurisdiction, which usually were larger than Ottoman districts. The counters then tried to extrapolate more general estimates or simply passed on the figures they had been given.

The examples below provide a sense of the partiality of the contemporary tabulations, but also a window on the magnitude of what transpired.

In January 1896 Cumberbatch provided estimates for the massacres of the previous October–November in Erzurum vilayet. He conceded that the figures, compiled by "Armenian sources," were probably exaggerated, but added that this was offset by the fact that they did not include input from "various places" in the province, so the provincial total is probably "near to the truth." He wrote that, all told, 2,855 people had been killed and 11,173 homes and shops pillaged.[519] The American mission station in Harput estimated that 15,834 people had been killed in its area and 8,049 houses and shops burnt, but added that details from 130 villages were unavailable.[520] The Anglo-American Relief Committee at Trabzon provided harrowing figures for the Karahisar-Şarki sanjak of Sivas vilayet: 21,034 killed and 2,444 houses looted and 168 destroyed.[521] The relief committee also supplied figures for Trabzon and Gümüşhane sanjaks: 507 Armenians killed and 5,197 emigrated, 1,510 houses and shops looted and 320 burnt.[522] A table of depredations in Sivas vilayet during 1895–1896, based on Armenian sources and possibly compiled by missionaries, gives a village-by-village breakdown totaling 5,263 Armenians and 241 Turks killed, as well as over 2,000 houses "burnt or ruined."[523]

Terrell sent Currie a tabulation of Armenian losses in Harput vilayet provided by a local "Turkish official . . . whose nature revolted at the barbarities around him." According to the official, 29,544 Armenians were killed throughout the vilayet, 5,523 dead in Harput town and its immediate surroundings; 7,550 in Arapgir and its villages; 2,670 in Eğin and nearby villages; 6,540 in Malatya; and so on. But the official also provided a table listing 39,234 "total deaths." This figure included those "burned" (1,380), those who "died from hunger and cold" (3,266), those who "died in fields and on the road" (4,330), and those who "died from fear" (760). It is not clear exactly what this final category refers to. The official also counted separately fifty-one "ecclesiastics and teachers killed."[524]

The German pastor Johannes Lepsius counted a wide range of outcomes, in addition to Christian dead. He estimated that 1,300 Muslims had died in the massacres, "645 churches and monasteries had been destroyed, about 560 villages had converted to Islam, about 330 churches had been converted into mosques, and more than half a million destitute people had been left behind."[525]

Altogether, it appears that about 100,000 Christians, almost all of them Armenians, were murdered by Muslims during 1894–1896. In addition, between 100,000 and 200,000 more died of causes related to the massacres.

The Aftermath

By autumn 1897 the eastern provinces had returned to a state of near-normalcy. "The people appear to be taking heart again," Vice-Consul Waugh wrote from Diyarbekir. "In some cases I found them rebuilding their homes . . . the progress towards recovery appears to me as quick as could be expected."[526] Reporting from Bitlis in October, British Vice-Consul Francis Crow wrote, "The harvest is generally good" in the Muş and Bitlis sanjaks. The Sason area had achieved a condition "bordering on prosperity." Muş Plain, though, remained in "a lamentable condition," still bedeviled by "outrages" and 4,000 refugees who needed substantial relief.[527] In Trabzon vilayet the state of public security was more than "satisfactory." "Incredible though it may be," Longworth wrote, "such safety to life and property as at the present exists has not been known for many a year. It is an agreeable surprise. . . . Acts of lawlessness and violence indeed have been remarkably few. . . . Brigandage in particular seems to have died out."[528]

But there had been no progress in the implementation of the reforms agreed to in 1895 or, for that matter, some twenty years earlier. In particular, unequal and oppressive taxation continued. Following the massacres tax farmers in much of the countryside demanded—and sometimes got—sums determined in the pre-massacre days. For example, Fontana reported in early 1897 that the taxmen were demanding "the ordinary yearly tax" from the largely Armenian village of Tadem, Mamuret-ül-Aziz vilayet, where 200-odd homes had been plundered and razed. The villagers had managed to pay 32,000 of the required 40,000 piastres and were hoping to scrounge up the rest, but the tax collector then demanded a further "30,000 piastres owing for last year." The inhabitants of Mismishan were also hit hard. Almost all the houses there had been destroyed; the village was "a shapeless pile of ruins among which the inhabitants burrow under brushwood roofing constructed over such walls as have not wholly subsided." Yet even after extracting 23,000 piastres, tax collectors were demanding a further 20,700 in arrears. Fontana complained to the vali, who eventually ordered arrears waived for Tadem and Mismishan. Fontana called the effort to levy the arrears "monstrous."[529]

Elsewhere, while there were occasional murders, robberies, rapes, and threats of massacre, a general quiet was maintained—clearly the product of orders from Constantinople. The exception appears to have been the series of massacres at Tokat and surrounding areas of Sivas vilayet, on March 19, 1897. The assault was carried out by locals and villagers who arrived in town "the day before." The killings went on for hours, while the 500-strong military garrison did nothing. The commander, Mustafa Bey, reportedly was "unable to get the men to obey orders and disperse the crowd."[530] Some of the violence was of "exceptional brutality," Bulman reported. He pointed to the case of two Armenians "whose legs were cut off." The men were then "thrown into the street."[531] Altogether about ninety Armenians were murdered in Tokat.[532]

Sixteen more were killed during the plunder of the nearby village of Bizeri and an adjacent monastery, another nine in the village of Biskunjik, and another seven in a third village whose name is unrecorded.[533]

According to Bulman, the perpetrators—many from surrounding villages, and some of them Circassian tribesmen—were invited by letter to "to come and pillage and massacre." The letters, stating "that there was an order from the Sultan for a massacre at Tokat," were reportedly signed by two Tokat Turkish notables, Hajji Sali and Ali Bey. In another version of the story, the letters were signed by one Rezi Effendi. The signatories appear to have been fronting for senior officials, including the Tokat town commandant, Hasan Fehmi Pasha, and the mutesarrif, Mahmud Nazim Pasha. On the day of the outbreak, the mutesarrif was reported to have seated himself near the Pasha Han, a prominent building, and given the order for the massacre to begin. Yet another explanation emerged from the subsequent trial of the perpetrators: that "a committee of about 20 men, notables and others," secretly organized the massacre.[534] Bulman, however, believed that "the government itself ordered the massacre."[535]

A handful of Muslims were put on trial, following the work of a commission of inquiry, which made its way swiftly to Tokat on orders from Constantinople. Twelve perpetrators were sentenced to death and dozens to prison terms. According to Bulman, the Tokat massacre had had one "good result": it persuaded those who could emigrate to do so, for they now realized they could never be sure the massacres were over.[536]

Tokat did prove to be the last ember in the conflagration that engulfed Asia Minor in 1894–1896. Throughout eastern Anatolia, Armenian survivors—the tens of thousands of widows and orphans, the newly homeless and impoverished—spent the next several years, if not the rest of their lives, trying to hold body and soul together.[537] They were assisted by large injections of Western relief and grudging, minimal aid from the Ottoman government.

II

The Young Turks

3

A More Turkish Empire

The sultan's absolute rule came to an end in 1908. Under pressure from the Committee of Union and Progress (CUP), also known as the Young Turks, Abdülhamid II restored the Constitution of 1876, ushering in a new era of multiparty parliamentary politics.

Over the ensuing decade, the Young Turks' vision of the Ottoman state became ascendant. At least initially, it encompassed a complex set of ideas. As the leaders of an avowedly multinational empire, the Young Turks made some efforts to protect and advance the political rights of minorities. At the same time, the Unionists were driven by their commitment to what they understood as the Turkish race. Consistent with the guiding notion of pan-Turkism (Turanianism), the CUP sought the political union of all ethnic groups speaking Turkic languages, from China's Uyghurs to Eastern Europe's Tatars and Turks.[1] Cemal Pasha, one of the three leaders of the CUP during World War I, synthesized these opposites—imperial cosmopolitanism and Turkish nationalism—eloquently. "Speaking for myself," he wrote in his memoirs, "I am primarily an Ottoman, but I do not forget that I am a Turk, and nothing can shake my belief that the Turkish race is the foundation stone of the Ottoman Empire."[2]

This attitude was clear, for example, in the Unionists approach to the vast Muslim, Arabic-speaking areas of the empire. The CUP had no intention of jettisoning these regions. Instead, they hoped to "Turkify" them. "Increasingly after 1909," Eugene Rogan writes, Turkish "displaced Arabic in schools, courtrooms and government offices in the provinces of Greater Syria and Iraq. Senior government appointments went to Turkish officials, while experienced

Arab civil servants were left to fill lower-level jobs."[3] Although widely considered secularists, the CUP embraced Hamidian pan-Islamic ideas, which may have helped to keep Arab regions comfortable in the imperial fold.

Ultimately the CUP's goal was to foster a strong Ottoman state, which, in the view of the party's leaders, demanded a population wholly loyal to it. In 1910 the CUP congress at Salonica resolved to Ottomanize "all Turkish subjects," even if this "could never be achieved by persuasion, and recourse must be had to force of arms."[4] Such stridency further alienated minorities in the Balkans and North Africa, whose own efforts to escape imperial control strengthened the Young Turks' attachment to their historic heartland, Anatolia. This was especially the case as the disaster of the First Balkan War sunk in. In 1912 the Ottomans were defeated by a coalition of Bulgaria, Serbia, Greece, and Montenegro. Describing the political impact within the empire, Erik-Jan Zürcher writes, "After the loss of the Balkans in 1912, Mehmet Ziya Gökalp," the leading Young Turk ideologue, "propagated the idea that the peasants of Anatolia represent 'true' Turkish culture and values as opposed to the 'Byzantine' and 'Arab' high culture of the Ottomans."[5]

The debacle of the First Balkan War provided the Young Turks an opportunity to wrest full control of the state. On January 23, 1913, after almost five years of sharing power with the weakening sultanate, a group of CUP activists led by Mehmed Talât and Ismail Enver carried out a coup against the government of Kâmil Pasha, whom they blamed for the Balkan disaster. Nominally Sultan Mehmed V was head of state, but, while he was not an irrelevant figure, the Young Turks were firmly in command. From there they increasingly ignored the opposition—indeed, abandoned the very idea of multiparty government they had once fought for. They also shed any commitment to a supranational state.

This reversion to the exclusivist politics of Abdülhamid, we believe, was most clearly manifest in the subsequent deportation and murder of the empire's Armenians. In the midst of World War I, the CUP initiated what has become known as the Armenian Genocide: the forced march of Anatolian Armenians south, to Syria and Mesopotamia, and the slaughter that accompanied it. The CUP government's methods differed from Abdülhamid's, but the aim was much the same: to de-Christianize the empire. Whereas Abdülhamid used winks, nods, and informal allies among eastern Anatolia's Muslim tribes to carry out his campaign of massacre, the CUP adopted a more systematic approach, issuing direct orders, overseeing the process, and tallying up the results with bureaucratic precision.

The government would turn to a shadowy construct, the Special Organization *(Teşkilat-ı Mahsusa),* to aid in its policy of Armenian removal. Born during another Ottoman defeat—at Italy's hands, in 1911–1912—the Special Organization was refashioned during the Great War to wreak havoc in the Russian Caucasus. But as the policy of genocide moved to the fore after May 1915, the Special Organization's focus changed, and its original cadres of Circassians, Kurds, and former soldiers were reinforced by more than 10,000 criminals—including murderers and rapists—freshly released from prisons. They were deployed mainly in the eastern vilayets, home to the densest populations of Armenians: "Enver relied on his Special Organization . . . to carry out the dirty jobs of assassination or terror against gavurs."[6] That is, against infidels. Even when the Special Organization itself was not directly involved in massacres, its members handled their logistics, led gangs of brigands *(çetes),* and arranged death marches.

That the Ottomans forcibly and methodically deported Armenians between 1914 and 1916 is beyond dispute. Nor can there be any doubt that hundreds of thousands died in the process. What remains controversial are questions of justification and intent. Why did the Ottoman government remove the Armenians? Did the state intend from the first to kill them off, or were the killings a side-effect of barbarous wartime conditions? Was deportation the nasty, if understandable, business of war—an effort to neutralize dangerous revolutionaries and Russian-sympathizing Armenians by removing them from conflict zones? Or was the mass deportation a novel means toward fulfilling a longstanding goal of ethnic cleansing?

In Chapter 6 we will argue that, in spite of Turkish efforts to cover their tracks, there exists abundant evidence to support the charge of genocide. It is our contention that resettlement was never the intended outcome of deportation; the ethnic cleansing of the Ottoman Armenians was the goal throughout the planning and execution of the process. Between 1915 and 1918, the CUP-dominated government deliberately marched Armenians to their deaths, or hastened the process using bayonets and bullets, advancing the same agenda Abdülhamid had begun before them.

The Main Sites of Massacre and Rebellion, 1914–1915

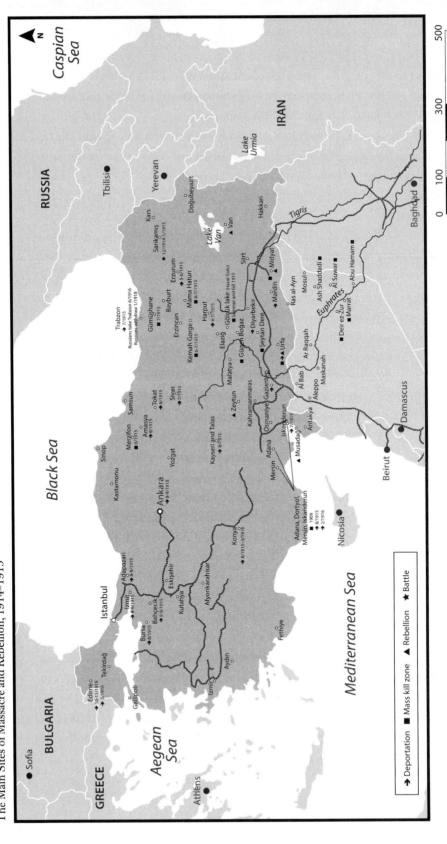

For now, we turn to the origins of the crisis. The genocide plan, also discussed in Chapter 6, was hatched between December 1914—just after the empire signed on with the Central Powers fighting in Europe—and May 1915, when the first deportation orders were sent from Constantinople to the provinces. During that half-year period, several events deepened the CUP's conviction that the Armenian problem required an immediate, radical solution.

Planning was already underway in February 1915, when the Ottoman army was decimated by the Russians at the Battle of Sarıkamış. But the embarrassing defeat was blamed on disloyal Armenians and became a pretext for killing them in large numbers. Fierce fighting between Armenians and Ottomans in Van and Zeytun in early 1915 had a similar effect. In March Zeytun became the first site of mass deportation. While the wider policy was still being designed, the central government ordered Zeytunlis removed southward in an augury of what was to come.

All of this came hard on the heels of the CUP government's first foray into ethnic cleansing: the expulsion in 1914 of tens of thousands of Ottoman Greeks. The government did not apply the Greek policy to Armenians; what began in 1915 was far more vicious. But the Greek removal does demonstrate that Armenian deportation was not sui generis. The campaign against the Greeks is further evidence, albeit circumstantial, that the CUP had the motivation and capacity to commit premeditated ethnic cleansing—that political will, not the exigencies of the Great War, underlay mass murder.

Radicalizing the CUP: The Eve of World War I and Greek Removal

For the European powers, the outbreak of world war in the summer of 1914 shattered a long era of relative peace. But for the Ottomans, who secretly joined the Central Powers in August and entered the fray at the end of October, the Great War was just one more round in a long stretch of continuous bloodletting.

Tensions had been simmering with European powers for a century, occasionally flaring into armed conflicts with Balkan peoples and the great powers of Russia, France, and the United Kingdom. In the years immediately preceding World War I, the Ottomans suffered two serious defeats. First, in 1911–1912, they fought a brave but unsuccessful war with Italy over Tripolitania (Trablus-garp) vilayet, encompassing much of present-day Libya. An estimated 14,000 Ottoman soldiers died. Then, emboldened by the Italians' success, the Balkan League of Bulgaria, Greece, Serbia, and Montenegro attacked the Ottoman Empire in October 1912.

The First Balkan War was replete with massacres and ethnic cleansing by both sides. Christian and Muslim villages were razed, their inhabitants murdered or deported. By the time a ceasefire was announced in May 1913, the League had pushed the Ottomans out of almost all their remaining European territories.[7] But matters did not end there. Unsatisfied with the division of the spoils, Bulgaria then attacked its former allies, Serbia and Greece, and was in turn attacked by the Ottomans and Romanians, who saw an opportunity to recoup losses. By the end of the Second Balkan War in August 1913, the Ottomans had retaken Edirne, their Thracian capital.

More than 200,000 people died in the Balkan wars, and millions lost their homes. For the Turks, the most dramatic outcome was the influx of one and a half million destitute Muslims. These muhacirs joined the thousands who had arrived during the Russo-Turkish war of 1877–1878. Many came with harrowing stories about murderous Christians.[8] Crammed into towns around Anatolia, the muhacirs were a constant reminder of humiliation and defeat. The population balance further shifted toward Muslims as Constantinople encouraged Bulgarian and Greek subjects to leave and thereby create space for muhacirs. The state facilitated the departure of Christians by easing bureaucratic requirements and simplifying the visa-application process.[9]

CUP leaders viewed the Balkan fiasco as part of a conspiracy led by the Christian powers, above all Russia. Using the fledgling Balkan states, which they helped create through constant pressure on Constantinople, the Christian powers aimed to destroy their empire and replace it with servile Christian statelets. This theory prevailed despite the fact that, in the years immediately preceding the war, Armenian nationalists sought to maintain peace and the empire itself. In 1909 the Dashnaks signed an agreement of cooperation with the CUP to preserve "the sacred Ottoman fatherland from separation and division." The Hunchaks, in a similar move, affirmed that they would act exclusively within the law.[10]

Muslim refugees in a mosque in Salonica. During and after the Balkan wars (1912–1913), a new wave poured into Turkey, among them relatives of the Young Turk leadership.

For Armenians, these agreements were major concessions, indicating their willingness to cooperate despite enduring Muslim-Christian inequality. In heavily Armenian Erzurum vilayet in 1913, only 18 of 2,193 officials were Christians.[11] During the run-up to the world war, the Kurds and the authorities in the eastern provinces continued to harass Armenians. The Armenian assembly detailed 7,000 cases of illegal land seizures between 1890 and 1910.[12]

The CUP may have earned some Armenian good will with its handling of a massacre against Christians in Adana vilayet, in Cilicia, in 1909. Crucially, the CUP was not in power during the two-week period when the killing occurred. It came in April, less than a year after the Young Turk revolution, in the midst of a counter-coup staged by disgruntled soldiers. Ministers who had just taken office fled Constantinople. Just a fortnight later, with the aid of army commanders, the CUP launched a successful counteroffensive and was back in control. But during the short spell of anarchy, the vilayet was the scene of a large-scale pogrom.[13]

Tensions had been building in the area ever since Armenian refugees flocked in after the 1894–1896 massacres. Many Cilician Muslims felt that the newcomers were taking over agriculture and commerce, pushing them out. The strain was greatest in springtime, when tens of thousands of migrant workers arrived for the harvest from other parts of eastern Anatolia.[14] Around the turn of the century, mechanization of agriculture was also reducing the number of jobs available, intensifying the rivalry between Muslim and Armenian seasonal workers and shaking social and political stability as a result.

It was under such circumstances that the Young Turks set up shop in 1908. When the government dismantled Abdülhamid's extensive monitoring and censorship structure, it left a void in the public arena that was filled by hotheads on both sides. For some of Adana's Armenians, hopes of autonomy and independence were rekindled. For many local Muslims, including CUP delegates, this Armenian resurgence was seen as a threat and an affront to Muslim primacy.

A series of mishandled incidents between Armenians and Muslims during the counter-coup evolved into a full-blown clash in Adana city and its suburbs from April 14 to 27, 1909. The disturbances culminated in a massacre, with mobs attacking the Armenian neighborhoods. Army units sent to restore order joined the fray on the Muslim side. On April 25, after shots were fired at a military encampment, "a battalion attacked the Armenian school that housed the injured from the first wave of the massacres. Soldiers poured kerosene on the school and set it on fire with people inside. Regular soldiers, reserve soldiers, and mobs, along with Başıbozuks, attacked the Armenian Quarter. They burned down churches and schools."[15] The army's rampage continued through April 27. When the soldiers and the mob were finally restrained, the Armenian quarter lay in ruins, as did houses elsewhere in the city. By most accounts, more than 20,000 Armenians and 1,270 Assyrians were murdered, leaving traumatized, impoverished communities.[16]

Although CUP representatives took part in the incitement and violence, when the party regained power in Constantinople, it denied involvement and saddled reactionary Hamidian elements with responsibility. Investigations and trials followed; 124 Muslims and 7 Armenians were convicted and hanged.[17]

The international community was reminded, just a decade after the massacres of the 1890s, of Turkish "barbarism." But the events and their aftermath also strengthened the belief that the CUP's hands were clean, that in contrast to Abdülhamid its politics were liberal and pluralistic—that its attitude towards the Armenians would be different. Of course, the reinstated CUP leaders would draw their own conclusions about the dangers of Armenian nationalism, the zeal with which Muslims attacked their Christian neighbors, and perhaps also their own ability to carry out such a large-scale massacre without serious consequences. In this sense the massacre should be seen as an important milestone on the road to the genocide of the Great War years. But in the moment, the Young Turks appeared to be striking a new political tone. If they did not recognize Armenian equality, then at least they seemed to recognize a right to exist in security. Hence the government's acknowledgement of the massacre and willingness to punish Muslim wrongdoers.

In early 1912, with the CUP now solidly in command, the Hunchaks and Dashnaks reaffirmed their commitment to the empire's territorial integrity.[18] In return the CUP promised to promote reform in the east, the urgency of which only increased with defeat in the Balkan Wars, renewing Christian fears

An Adana street after the 1909 massacre. The Armenian neighborhoods were almost completely destroyed by a mob of Turkish civilians and soldiers.

of massacre and elevating Kurdish-Armenian tensions.[19] But the Ottoman authorities were not mollified by Armenian assurances and, as usual, reneged on their reform proposals. By December 1913 Cemal Pasha was warning Dashnak leader Vartkes Serengulian against pushing for European supervision of the proposed reforms, which was tantamount to rejecting them altogether. Insisting on European intervention could result in the massacre of hundreds of thousands of Armenians, Cemal reportedly said.[20] The German ambassador, Hans Freiherr von Wangenheim, took such threats seriously. In a letter to Chancellor Theobald von Bethmann-Hollweg, Wangenheim wrote that, under the Young Turks, "any previous inhibitions about harming the empire's Christians were finally gone."[21]

Russian and German pressure eventually prevailed, and on February 8, 1914, the Ottomans assented to reforms. By agreement with European powers, foreign inspectors would be on hand to oversee the implementation. The Young Turks were not happy. In his memoirs Cemal claimed the empire went to war later that year in part to bury the agreement.[22] At the very least, the agreement contributed to Turkish resentment toward Christians. The missionary Ralph Harlow could hardly escape it during his visit to the Ionian coast that year. In one especially disconcerting passage, he describes depictions of Christian atrocities on classroom walls in Turkish schools:

> These pictures are often in brilliant colors and exhibit bloody and awful massacres and outrage in which helpless Moslem women and children and old men are being done to death and outraged by CHRISTIANS. On the walls of a school for little girls for instance there hangs a lurid scene in blood-red and white. Headless bodies lie around; hands, arms, feet, from all of which blood streams. In the center stands a Christian hacking an old man to death. On all of these pictures are words certain to arouse bitter fanaticism. . . . I pleaded with the hoja to remove these pictures but he stamped his foot and said, "We will grind these enemies under our feet." Another scene is of an expectant mother stripped naked and her unborn child being torn from her side. . . . The hojas told me that these damnable pictures were SENT THEM BY THE GOVERNMENT TO PUT UP. Along with such pictures the children

are being taught the most fanatical poems . . . , all written to inspire . . . hatred. It is well . . . and timely to ask what will the harvest be?[23]

The CUP leadership may have felt especially aggrieved, admixing guilt and humiliation. Not only had the empire lost almost all of its remaining European domains on their watch, dashing hopes of revitalization, but many CUP men themselves hailed from the Balkans and the Aegean and so took the conflict with Christian minorities personally. Some CUP leaders were recent refugees and many had lost family in the Balkan Wars. Almost all had lost property and the landscapes of their youth.[24] Talât Pasha, the powerful interior minister from 1913 and chief architect of the 1915–1918 bout of genocide, was a scion of a Bulgarian Muslim family from Thrace. War Minister Enver Pasha's father was Macedonian and his mother Albanian. Cemal Pasha, the third member of the CUP triumvirate during World War I, was born in Mitylene, Lesbos. The Balkan hurt counterbalanced the appeal of imperial cosmopolitanism. "A casualty of the Balkan Wars," Ronald Suny writes, "was the ecumenical vision of the Ottomanists, the idea of a multinational, religiously diverse empire of equal subjects. Even other Muslims, like the Arabs, were not trustworthy."[25]

But while not all Muslims were trustworthy in the eyes of the CUP, just about anyone who was trustworthy was Muslim. Among top CUP officials, Islam defined the boundaries of the nation. In this respect, they were Islamists like Abdülhamid, not the secularists assumed in conventional history. Bahaettin Şakır—a CUP founder, a member of its powerful central committee, and a Special Organization chief during the Great War—saw the theological stakes clearly: the strength of the Ottoman state was the "starting point for the salvation of all Muslims," he said. "If the poor Muslim nation does not awake and care about its salvation, it will lose its reputation in this world. . . . Possession and nation, religion and state are perishing. . . . Hurry up, O Muslims, hurry up, heroes, sons of heroes; this is the day."[26]

To men such as Şakır, the defense of the Muslim nation was ordained by God a bloody affair. His colleague Gökalp welcomed the outbreak of World War I in verse: "God's will / sprang from the people / We proclaimed the jihad / God is great." Şakır specified one target of the holy war in 1906, describing Armenians as "infidels who are enemies of Islam." Their defeat would bring God's glory to all Muslims. "In the name of God, the Most Merciful, the Most Compassionate! . . . Let us make our nation prosperous by taking our revenge! God is the Speaker of the Truth," he wrote in a 1907 pamphlet.[27]

In November 1914, when the empire went to battle with the Great Powers, it did so with the blessing of the Şeyhülislam, the chief Ottoman cleric. Mustafa Hayri, who happened to be a member of the CUP central committee, issued a fatwa proclaiming jihad against the Allies with the aim of persuading Muslims worldwide that the war threatened the survival of Islam itself. The call for holy war also reinforced religious fervor against Ottoman Christians. Though the fatwa did not name internal Christian minorities, many Muslims mentally lumped them together with Russia, Britain, and France. Wilfred Post, a missionary and physician born and raised in Turkey, observed, "The proclamation of the holy war, which failed to unite all Islam against the Entente, nevertheless had the effect of arousing the old fanatical spirit of the Turks themselves and they prosecuted the holy war within their own Empire with a zeal exceeding that of their forefathers."[28]

Did Turks detect the irony of allying with Christian powers—Germany and Austria-Hungary—for the preservation of Islam? We are not privy to the CUP leadership's secret discussions, so we cannot say. But their strategy is easily enough understood when considering Russia's support for the Christian minorities, whose presence so threatened the CUP's Islamist conception of the nation. High on the party's list of worries was the potential nexus of Russia, the perennial enemy, and the Armenian revolutionaries who looked to it for succor. The Young Turks fought both in the name of their religion.

Greek Removal

The Turkish government's radicalism was evident in the statements of its leaders and its rejection of Armenians' gestures of good will. But it took time to boil over into mass murder. Along the way, officials—including CUP leaders and members of the sultan's court—exercised their anti-Christian agenda through the expulsion of Greek communities. During the bout of ethnic cleansing between January and June 1914, between 100,000 and 200,000

Greeks from coastal areas were uprooted. Most fled to Greece in order to escape the Turks' coordinated campaign of harassment. A small number were forcibly transferred to other parts of the empire.

It is unclear whether the CUP viewed Greek removal as a trial run for the subsequent destruction of the Armenians. But, in pushing out Greeks, the Turkish authorities probably learned techniques of abuse that proved useful when the Armenians' time came. The government also learned that the Western powers would look on without physically intervening to save fellow Christians.

Still the processes of Greek removal and Armenian destruction were quite different. While Armenians were subject to a carefully planned and brutally executed campaign of extermination, the Greek removal was, at least early on, carried out by the relatively benign means of boycott and intimidation. Officials sought to pressure Greeks to leave "voluntarily," by making their lives miserable. But if the means differed, the goal in each case was ethnic cleansing.

The Greek policy was an outgrowth of the political situation in the Balkans, but not a necessary one: Turkish authorities took advantage of the influx of muhacirs displaced from the Balkan Wars in order to justify expelling Greeks and at times used these muhacirs as the agents of expulsion. In the wake of the Balkan Wars, the Ottomans resettled about 500,000–600,000 Muslim refugees in their diminished domains.[29] This included "very considerable" numbers from Salonica, which had been annexed by Greece. "They arrive in Turkey with the memory of their slaughtered friends and relations fresh in their minds," the British consul in Salonica wrote. "They remember their own sufferings" and find "themselves without means or resources." The Ottomans placed many of these refugees in the homes Greeks left behind. Notably, these Muslims had not been expelled; their emigration, according to Western diplomats, was not "actively support[ed]" by the Greek authorities.[30]

The muhacirs saw "no wrong in falling on the Greek Christians of Turkey and meting out to them the same treatment that they themselves have received from the Greek Christians of Macedonia," and in this they enjoyed the backing of the CUP. From its first days in power, the party had resolved to rid the empire of its Greek problem. As Hakki Bey, a CUP man and Ottoman

Ambassador to Rome, put it in 1909, compared to the Turk, "the Greek belonged to a totally different order of morality. . . . Anything which promoted the ambitions and interests of his country down to the assassination of those who stood in his way, partook of the nature of virtue. . . . The new regime in Turkey was determined to stamp out this internal cancer."[31] The Turks were particularly annoyed by the economic and demographic flourishing of Greeks in Aydın vilayet, centered on Smyrna.

To the British consul in Edirne, the goal of Ottoman policy was unambiguous: to make the vilayet's population "as far as possible purely Moslem." Underlying that goal, he recognized a twofold purpose: to nullify "on ethnological grounds" neighboring states' potential claims to the territory of the vilayet and to secure "lines of communication" in any future military operations by substituting "friendly" Muslims for "hostile" Christians. Thus, beginning early 1914, the government carried out an insidious program of intimidation aimed at many aspects of daily life. For instance, authorities gave Turks seed and agricultural implements, while denying them to Greeks. The government also demanded that Greeks billet muhacirs in their homes. The authorities ramped up the pressure by levying special taxes against Greeks and forcing them to pay extra fees in support of the Ottoman Fleet Fund, a CUP-founded organization that raised money to buy and build new warships for the imperial navy. The campaign paid immediate dividends. By March 1914 the consul estimated the number of Greek emigrants "considerably exceeds" 20,000.[32]

Greek removal was both a government effort and a popular affair; ordinary Ottoman Muslims joined in. Harassment was systematic, carried out in large part by gangs of Rumelian and Caucasian refugees "financed and run by the state."[33] The authorities designed their campaign to appear locally authored, relying on regional governors and CUP secretaries, and the Special Organization, to do much of the on-the-ground planning and preparation.[34] But Celâl Bayar—who in 1914 was CUP secretary in Smyrna and later the third president of Turkey—confirmed in his memoirs that the central CUP and the Ministry of War jointly planned to displace non-Muslims in the Aegean region and developed together the methods used "to 'encourage' them to emigrate."[35] He recalled the motives behind the campaign: "a war of salvation to liberate the Turkish nation," to "Turkify the gavur," and "to free Izmir's economy from the anational, treacherous, and malicious heads and hands."[36]

Numerous Ottoman officials are known to have taken part in the campaign of harassment, starting at the very top. "The Greeks . . . must go," Talât told Aydın vali Rahmi Bey at the beginning of the process, according to the Russian consul-general in Smyrna.[37] Rahmi then instructed his sub-governors "to force [out] the Greek population."[38] W.H. van der Zee, the dutch-born Danish consul, reported more such instructions from Rahmi in March— "semi-official orders to the sub-governors" of several small towns on the coast "to force the Greek population . . . resident therein to evacuate." As with the Armenian massacres of the mid-1890s, the orders were phrased vaguely, to allow official deniability. "No order of expulsion was decreed, but the Turkish officials were to make use of tortuous and vexatious measures so well-known to them," van der Zee wrote. "Similar instructions were, I understand, given by the Governors of the other maritime provinces."[39]

Talât followed up in a May 14 cable to Rahmi, which is notable for its Islamist appeal to underlings and its dissimulation with respect to motivations—both common rhetorical tactics in the mass deportations to come. "It is urgent for political reasons that the Greek residents of the Asia Minor coast be forced to evacuate their villages and be settled in the vilayets of Erzurum and Chaldea," Talât wrote. "Should they refuse . . . please give oral instructions to brother Muslims, for the purpose of forcing the Greeks, by every kind of actions, to be voluntarily expatriated."[40] The Porte—not just the CUP—was on board. According to Wangenheim, Grand Vizier Said Halim Pasha told him that month that "he intends the cleansing of the entire Asia Minor littoral from the Greeks, in order to replace them."[41] The partnership between the sultan and the CUP was sometimes ambiguous; in discussions with the sultan and parliament, Talât brazenly denied the existence of the campaign and its orchestration by the government.[42]

As George Horton, the American consul-general in Smyrna, explained, the government and the press worked together to make the campaign a success by "appealing to fanaticism and race hatred, and calling the Turks to rise against the Greeks."[43] Newspapers harped on Greek atrocities in Thrace, Thessaly, Crete, and the Peloponnese. Typical was the article "Greek Savagery," which appeared in *Tanin,* the semi-official CUP mouthpiece, on

March 9, 1914. "God knows what these poor [Muslim] people have suffered since the Greek invasion" of Salonica, the paper intoned, referring to those who stayed behind when the territory entered Greek hands. "Greek immigrants from the Caucasus and Western Thrace . . . have been invading the houses of Mussulmans at night, and attacking their wives and daughters. . . . Not a night passes on which their wives and daughters are not outraged and their property is plundered. . . . The savagery of the Greeks . . . will not be forgotten . . . throughout the world of Islam." An editorial in *Tasvir-i-Efkâr* on March 11 scolded Ottoman Greeks for complaining in parliament about the boycott of Greek-owned businesses.[44]

The boycott was a major element of the campaign and one of its first manifestations, encompassing Trabzon and Samsun as early as January 1914. Although the boycott had relatively little impact in Constantinople, it otherwise spread widely.[45] Greeks were considered a dominant, alien presence in the Ottoman economy, which made Greek-owned businesses a ripe target. As the popular Turkish writer Ibrahim Hilmi warned after the Balkan Wars, "The Greeks aim at their own lives. They pretend to be friends but actually they are our most awful enemies. They are cunning, tricksters and hypocrites in order to find their way in their commerce."[46]

In Ionia the boycott was strictly enforced. Muslim-owned restaurants were prevented from buying meat from Greek butchers. Muslims picketed Greek-owned shops, occasionally using violence to prevent customers entering. In Manisa, the chief of police threatened "every Mussulman dealing with Christians." In Aydın town, the mutesarrif told Muslim olive growers not to sell to Christians. In mosques posters went up denouncing Greek traders by name.[47]

In the interior east of Smyrna, Barnham found that "all semblance of free commerce or equality is at an end." Greeks were even prohibited from wearing clothes with colors considered non-Ottoman.[48] In late May G. Henry Wright, a British businessman operating in Asia Minor, worried that Greeks in the interior were "pressed and suffering, and they will be obliged at the end to expatriate as they are doing in Thracia."[49] In Bursa, the Greek Patriarchate reported, "Turks armed with clubs, and paid for the purpose, scoured the marketplace, threatening and ordering the [Greek] shopkeepers to close. . . . Peasants on their way to Broussa, for the sale of their products there, were daily arrested and plundered."[50]

The boycott exemplified the cooperation between the Turkish public and political elites in carrying out the campaign. Barnham concluded that CUP "emissaries are everywhere instigating the people."[51] Horton believed the CUP was using the boycott not only to express "race hatred" and "religious prejudice" but also to "cement its power."[52] It was clear to Wright that the boycott was "the initiative of the Young Turkish Government."[53] When British ambassador Louis du Pan Mallet wrote to the grand vizier that Turks, persuaded by CUP agents, were working "to ruin and supplant Greek traders, etc. by starting 'Moslem' shops and companies to which all true Mohammedans should give their custom," the grand vizier replied that "he was not encouraging the boycott" but also "could not force Mussulmen to buy from Greeks, who were thoroughly disliked throughout the Empire."[54]

Alongside the boycott, the authorities employed stronger measures. Muslims received arms, while Greeks were disarmed; Greek officials were dismissed from their posts, while key appointments were given to "fanatical" Muslims.[55] Volunteers armed by the government engaged in "a system of terrorization" orchestrated by the vali, Haci Adil Bey, a friend of Talât's. By April the Greek Patriarchate was reporting that Greeks were being forcibly deported from villages in Karası sanjak and from Balia, along the southern shore of the Sea of Marmara.[56] The decision to turn to outright violence may have been taken in a series of secret meetings in May and June in which Talât, Enver, and Celal participated.[57]

In some places the Turks dispensed entirely with the fiction of voluntary emigration. The kaymakam of Ayvalık, an overwhelmingly Christian town of 30,000, was not asking for anyone's cooperation when he told the inhabitants, "This is no longer your country; if you don't go today you will be compelled to go tomorrow."[58] In late May, when villagers from Yakaköy, Gümeç, Kemerköy, Yenitsarohori, and Ayazmati fled to Ayvalık, they were attacked on the way by "wild gangs of armed Turks, who stripped them of their money and clothes, beat them, and violated four girls."[59] The Greeks of Kato-Panaya ran for Chios, gunfire at their heels. Villages in the Çeşme district, west of Smyrna, were almost entirely evacuated; Horton reported some 23,000 Greeks "expelled." Many Greeks, he wrote, were now living "in the open air." An agent of Singer Manufacturing Company reported, "The villagers of Christianochori were driven out at night, escaping in their night apparel, leaving everything behind." In Zaganos the mudir directed an assault against Christians. Muhacirs were often accompanied by soldiers and policemen, and some boats carrying escapees foundered at sea.[60]

Resistance met with a firm hand. When a Greek assassinated the mayor of Sevdiköy, soldiers responded with collective punishment. The wife of John Malamatinis, an American citizen of Greek origin living in the town, described soldiers with long whips riding "at breakneck speed through the village . . . lash[ing] out right and left every time they spied a Greek." The soldiers "inflicted painful injuries . . . on many women and girls" and "knock[ed] to the ground little children whom they pass[ed]." Horton recognized the authorities' signature on the violence. "It is only when the Mussulmans are officially incited against the Christians that they resort to brutality," he wrote.[61]

The most serious outbreak of violence occurred at Foça (Phocia or Focateyn), a fishing town of 8,000–9,000 Greeks and 400 Turks, just north of Smyrna. There Turks murdered between fifty and a hundred townspeople, raped women, and drove out the Greek population.[62] According to a Greek source, the attack was organized by Turkish notables, including Talât Bey, head of the gendarmerie in nearby Menemen. Foça's mayor Hassan Bey allegedly participated in the killing.[63]

After Foça the Greek government threatened to intervene, and Western diplomats lodged complaints.[64] Constantinople took fright and made a series of conciliatory gestures, such as inviting diplomats on placatory tours of the coasts, chaperoned by Talât and Enver.[65] Then, with the pan-European crisis of July 1914, the spark that inflamed the Great War, the campaign was abruptly ended. Perhaps the CUP no longer considered it effective, and no doubt the government worried that Greece would join the Allied cause.[66] After the war the British Foreign Office estimated that, all told, 250,000 Greeks had been uprooted before Turkey entered the conflict.[67]

The consequences of Greek removal extended beyond the lives disrupted and destroyed. In November 1915, when the deportation and murder of the Armenians was in full swing, Morgenthau wrote that Turkish "success in deporting . . . about 100,000–150,000 Greeks without any of the big nations . . . then still at peace with them, seriously objecting, led them to the conclusion that now, while four of the great Powers were fighting them . . . and the two other great Powers were their allies, it was a great opportunity . . . to put into effect their long cherished plan of exterminating the Armenian race."[68] In May

U.S. Ambassador in Constantinople Henry Morgenthau,
who during World War I
tried to persuade Turkey's
leaders to halt the massacre
of the Armenians. His
reports provide valuable
documentation of genocide.

of that year, when the Armenian campaign was just beginning, another senior American diplomat glossed over any distinction between the Greek and Armenian cases, anticipating our own contention that both were part of a larger project of genocide. Of the CUP he wrote, "They have crushed the Turkish opposition, they expelled the Greeks, and now is the Armenians' turn."[69]

Blaming Armenians: War Losses, Disarmament, and the Van "Rebellion"

At the end of October 1914, the Ottomans entered the war by bombarding Russian targets in the Black Sea. Russia responded by deploying to the Caucasus a large army, which included two battalions of Armenian volunteers.[70] Thus, just as its most hated foreign adversary had returned for another fight, Constantinople's gaze returned to its most hated internal one. In November and December, the Special Organization massacred thousands of Armenians along the front lines, ostensibly on suspicion of collaborating with the enemy. The Russians took similar actions against their Muslim border communities. Soldiers on both sides deserted. Some Ottoman Armenian deserters joined the tsar's battalions, triggering Ottoman revenge attacks. Armenian civilians on the frontier, and Armenian soldiers in the Ottoman army, were both subject to assaults.[71]

The Russians believed that the Ottomans would not be foolhardy enough to attack during winter, but Enver Pasha had other ideas. Taking personal charge of the 120,000-man-strong Ottoman Third Army, he prepared to attack Russians encamped in the Caucasian town of Sarıkamış. He aimed to envelope the Russian army, take the town, and cut the enemy off from his bases. The maneuver, which would push two corps around the Russians' right flank, was modeled on German operations in August 1914's Battle of Tannenberg, in which the Russian Second Army was almost entirely destroyed.[72] Enver's plan demanded perfect timing and the element of surprise. Otto Liman von Sanders, a German general who advised the Ottomans, described the operation as "extremely difficult, if not altogether impossible."[73]

Adding to the difficulty was a lack of supplies. To preserve mobility and prevent a drawn-out and highly visible buildup of forces, Enver ordered his soldiers to leave behind much of their baggage, including tents, blankets, rations, and munitions.[74] This proved fatal. "Carrying only flat bread for rations, dressed in light uniforms without proper coats . . . , and shod with inadequate footwear," the troops pushed off on December 22 in the midst of a blizzard.[75] Snow and freezing temperatures slowed the advance and caused many casualties, helping to level the playing field with the smaller but better-equipped Russian army.

It took the Russians just a few weeks to drive back Enver's offensive. Retreat turned into near-rout as the Ottomans, riddled with disease and frostbite, made their way through the snow-covered Allahuekber Mountains.[76] By battle's end, in mid-January of 1915, less than a third of Enver's troops were still standing. His huge ambitions—dealing a decisive blow, stabilizing the eastern front, freeing the Third Army to reinforce other theaters of operation, and, perhaps, opening the way for a pan-Turanian union across the Caucasus—had "burst like a soap-bubble."[77] He never again commanded an army in the field.

The debacle would have a severe impact on Turkey's Armenians. The Ottoman leadership viewed Sarıkamış as proof of Armenian perfidy and said so publicly. Although at Sarıkamış a wearied Enver was himself saved by an Armenian officer who carried him back to Ottoman lines, the pasha and his colleagues "framed the story of the battle in their own way, and the prevailing view placed Armenian treachery at the center of the narrative," Ronald Grigor Suny writes.[78] "Given the attitudes and sentiments that many Muslims had toward Armenians, they became a convenient . . . scapegoat."[79] As for the thousands of Ottoman Armenian troops taken prisoner by the Russians and sent to Siberia, the Ottoman army listed them as deserters.[80] In general, the ease of the subsequent Russian advance into Anatolia was blamed on supposed Armenian fifth columnists.

In March Şakır, arriving from the eastern front, presented the government with documents supposedly proving Armenian coordination with Russia to undermine Ottoman forces. The evidence was thin. Exhibit A, found in an Armenian village during the fighting at Sarikamiş, was a seditious booklet written more than a decade earlier. But it dovetailed with the accusations Enver and his staff were making.[81] The government hardly needed persuasion: it had already decided to punish the Armenians, starting with those in Ottoman military service.

Disarmament and Massacre in the Ranks

Christians were first conscripted into the Ottoman Army in 1909, during the more liberal early days of the Young Turk revolution.[82] The decision was controversial, and all the more so after the Balkan Wars, as Ottoman Muslims came to believe that non-Muslim recruits had "made common cause with their co-nationals," weakening the imperial army.[83] The government was wary about drafting Christians for the Great War, too. But, facing the realistic prospect of a multi-front conflict, the Ottomans needed a large army; able-bodied Christian men aged twenty to forty-five were called up, while teenagers and older men were mobilized in labor battalions or as munitions carriers.

If the government was ambivalent about drafting Christians, draftees were no happier about being forced to serve. Indeed, desertion was rampant among all ethnic groups. After the war, General Liman claimed there were more

Turkish deserters than soldiers in service.[84] Just a few weeks after the initial mobilization announcement, bands of deserters were already roaming the countryside, hiding from police and gendarmes. "It was not unusual for units— even as large as divisions—to lose up to half their strength on their way to the front," Zürcher writes. "The problem was especially great with Arab units." There are "reports describing how Arab recruits were being taken to their frontline units under escort—and in chains."[85] Still, many Armenians showed up for service, enough to impress the German ambassador and leave him fearful for the communities they left behind: "Their villages have been left defenseless before the excesses and attacks of military deserters," Wangenheim observed.[86]

The problem ran deeper, though. As Zürcher points out, "Drafting the Armenian male adults" not only deprived their hometowns of defenders but also placed the soldiers themselves "in a vulnerable position within the army."[87] That vulnerability was heightened in the wake of Sarıkamış and the opening of the Gallipoli campaign—the Allied naval attack in the Dardanelles, which began on February 17. On the 25th Enver instructed the army to disarm all Armenian soldiers and ordered that "Armenian individuals are absolutely not to be employed in armed service, either in the mobile armies or in the mobile and permanently deployed gendarmerie, nor in service in the retinue or offices of the army headquarters." By March most Armenian soldiers had been disarmed, and many had been moved to labor battalions.[88]

Enver justified his orders with the usual allegations of treason. In particular he alleged that secret codes in French and Russian were discovered in the hands of Armenian spies. He also pointed to a report stating that the Armenian Patriarchate was transmitting military secrets to the Russians. But history vindicates the observations of Captain Sarkis Torosyan, an Armenian artillery officer who served at Gallipoli. In his memoirs he wrote that disarmament was linked to "plans for large-scale massacres and wiping out the Armenian population, or deporting it from the interior of the country . . . and reducing it to slavery."[89] For, as Zürcher writes, "The unarmed recruits in the labour battalions were sitting ducks. . . . Here there were tens of thousands of Armenian men, who were already assembled and under guard of armed soldiers. They did not stand a chance."[90] They were also weakened by harsh conditions: even in the best of times, men in the labor battalions "were underfed, exhausted, suffering from disease. Their officers beat them mercilessly."[91]

In one case, in Harput in November 1915, disarmed soldiers were assembled and detained in a large building called the Red Konak, where they were kept for two days without food or water.[92] After their brief incarceration, they were joined by able-bodied Armenian civilians, and the whole group was divided into labor units. Initially they were sent to pave the road to Malatya; many died from the cruel work regimen.[93] A month later the Harput town commandant, Süleyman Faik, reconvened the remaining laborers, declared himself "the friend of the Armenians," and announced that he was "sending them to a good place."[94] They were divided again, and the sub-groups sent piecemeal on the road to Diyarbekir. En route, they were slaughtered by their escorts, assisted by local gangs, at a mountain pass called Deve Boynu (Gugen Boğaz).[95]

Faik duly informed Third Army Commander General Kâmil of what had happened, but with his own spin. "Armenian brigands attacked the caravan," he claimed, "and the Armenian *Ameles* [laborers] began to desert. The escort opened fire and killed a great part of the battalion and the brigands. . . . In the affray one of our soldiers disappeared."[96] After the war, Faik was court-martialed; Mustafa Pasha, a judge in the case, rejected this story as nonsense.[97]

The numbers killed were massive. When General Vehib Pasha took command of the Third Army in February 1916, he learned that an entire labor battalion, some 2,000 men, had gone missing. They had been stationed in Aleppo vilayet, far from any battlefield. He sent investigators to find out what happened. He discovered that the whole battalion had been executed.[98] A year later he arrested Kör Nuri, the gendarmerie commander in charge of the labor battalions, and Çerkes Kadir, head of the gang who operated under his instructions. Both were hanged. During the postwar court-martial, General Vehib also accused the vali of Sivas of responsibility. "Vehib's December 5, 1918 deposition for the court-martial," Vahakn Dadrian writes, "is the most explicit and unequivocal confirmation of the premeditated and organized nature of the Armenian genocide."[99]

The massacre of labor battalions—which is also recalled in the memoirs of Jakob Kunzler, a Swiss missionary who worked at Urfa's missionary hospital—testifies to the government's overarching interest in Armenian eradication.[100] Armenians' work building roads and shuttling supplies should have been seen as crucial to the war effort. From the standpoint of the Ottoman authorities, though, Armenian men were better off dead than helpful. Many laborers were executed by their supposed comrades in arms. American Ambassador Henry Morgenthau wrote that laborers were taken away in groups of fifty or a hundred to a secluded spot, stripped naked, and shot by fellow soldiers or gendarmes.[101]

Van, Crushed

Van in the spring of 1915 was home to the Armenian eruption that the CUP, and Abdülhamid before, both feared and cultivated through their repressive measures. In April and May, Armenians in the town fought off an Ottoman siege, and did so with the enemy's help. Here was the proof. Armenians, taking up arms en masse against the state, and joined by the Russian army. By the time the dust settled, those Russians estimated that, all told, as many as 55,000 corpses were scattered across Van vilayet.[102] The government's May deportation orders reached a cadre of eastern authorities very much primed for action.

To say that Van's Armenians were provoked would be an understatement, but clearly their grievances bred anti-Ottoman subversion. Life in Van had never been easy. The Armenians had been hard hit in the massacres twenty years earlier, and the effects lingered amid new depredations. While missionaries strained to provide housing and education, tribesmen raided Christian villages in the surrounding countryside.[103] In November 1914, with preparations for Sarıkamış in full swing, the government diverted troops from Van and undertook large-scale requisitions of the region's munitions, wagons, and beasts of burden. Both orders heightened the Christians' vulnerability, depriving them of both the means to protect themselves and potential protectors against Kurdish marauders.[104] Alienated and threatened, many Armenians evaded the call-up. Some draft dodgers joined robber bands, whom the authorities quickly labeled "revolutionary."[105] Others really did have foreign allegiances, though. Some Armenians joined a Russian-backed Christian mi-

litia in the nearby Urmia district of Persia, to defend against possible attack
by Muslims. And occasionally Christian clerics, including a Nestorian bishop,
even converted to Orthodoxy to prove their loyalty to the Russians.[106] Turks
suspected that the Russian government was supplying the Armenians with
arms.[107]

It was amid these tensions that, on March 15, a new vali took over. Cevdet
Bey, Enver's brother-in-law, arrived with thousands of fresh troops, most of
them Circassians and Kurds with a reputation for brutality. Cordial at first,
he promised to compensate Armenians for losses due to Kurdish predation.
But he soon changed his tune. Like other governors in the east, Cevdet sent
most of the Armenian police officers in his jurisdiction to distant Mosul. He
also demanded that Van's Armenians supply 4,000 able-bodied men for the
labor corps. Fearing execution, the Armenians refused, deepening tensions
and elevating Ottoman concerns about rebellion. In April, on instructions
from Constantinople, Cevdet arrested several leading Van Armenians, some
of whom were murdered in jail. In surrounding villages, his irregulars killed
hundreds of Armenians. The townspeople called these troops *Kasap Taburu*,
the Butcher Battalion.[108]

Inside Van, Armenians made a fateful choice. Rather than hunker down and
absorb punishment, they barricaded their quarters and appealed for the release of their surviving leaders. To Cevdet, this was rebellion, and he was in
no mood to back down. On April 17 he summoned two American missionaries, Ernest Yarrow and Elizabeth Ussher, to relay a message to the Armenian community. "He was determined," he said, "to crush the rebellion [even]
if it involved the extermination of the whole Armenian population, but that
he would prefer not to injure the women and children."[109]

The confrontation escalated. On April 20 Cevdet's artillery began shelling
the Armenian quarters from the citadel above the town. The Armenians
responded by attacking the Muslim quarters. The Ottomans then sent reinforcements from Erzurum, Bitlis, and Başkale and laid siege to the Armenian
quarters.[110]

With so little documentation available, it is impossible to say whether
Cevdet truly believed the Armenians were a threat when he ordered the
shelling, or whether he was trying to trigger resistance that could justify massacre and deportation. It also is not clear whether Cevdet's actions were

coordinated with Constantinople, though he did inform the government of the supposed rebellion before unleashing the batteries.[111] We can be confident, though, that he would have disagreed with the assessment of Max Erwin von Scheubner-Richter, the German vice-consul in Erzurum. The Armenians fighting in Van, he wrote Ambassador Wangenheim, were not traitors. The trigger for their resistance had been the Turks' "arrest and murder" of the Armenian dignitaries.[112]

As the siege set in, missionaries opened their compound to noncombatants, including refugees from the countryside. At the end of April, the town's post office burned down, largely preventing uncensored news from Van reaching the outside world.[113] The telegraph wires, which were less accessible than postal mail, still worked, though. On April 26 local officials sent the Interior Ministry an incendiary note claiming that many of the Armenians killed in the old city wore Russian-made clothes or uniforms, which the Turks took as evidence of collusion with the enemy.[114]

In early May Morgenthau reported wide-ranging massacres in the Van countryside, where government forces had complete control. From her window in Van, Ussher saw surrounding villages going up in smoke. In some cases, she wrote, villagers fought until their ammunition was spent and then fled with the women who could follow, "leaving the women with little children to be killed or insulted by the Turks." Kurds joined the fray; Cevdet, Ussher explained, had promised them "plunder and glory." Thousands of Armenians were killed and others fled.[115]

Many Turkish soldiers were averse to the killing but carried it out anyway, on orders from CUP-aligned officers.[116] One of these officers was Halil Pasha, Enver's uncle. After an expeditionary force under his command was driven back from Iran, he blamed his defeat on local Christians and ordered his troops to exact revenge on villages in the Van countryside. Enver justified Halil's actions by claiming that "Russian Armenians were responsible for destroying with bombs public buildings."[117]

Van's Armenians pressed on. Some 10,000 villagers eventually battled their way into the city to join the rebels. Many died en route. Rafael de Nogales, a Venezuelan soldier who fought for the Ottomans during World War I, recalled in his memoirs, "To right and left of the road, circled screaming flocks of black vultures, disputing with the dogs the putrefied Armenian corpses thrown about on every side."

To deplete the Armenians' food and medical stocks, Cevdet ordered that Armenian women and children scattered in the villages be escorted "to the trenches of the besieged, in the belief that the latter would admit them to the city." De Nogales was astonished to see the Armenian defenders, aware of the ploy, fire on the approaching survivors, who turned and fled. In the town, the siege was characterized by "furious fighting," de Nogales wrote. "It was an uninterrupted combat, sometimes hand to hand or with only a wall between. Nobody gave quarter nor asked it. The Christian or the Moor who fell into the enemy's hands was a dead man. To try to save a prisoner during those days would have been almost as difficult as to try to snatch the prey from a starving tiger."[118]

With the noose tightening, the Armenians appealed for the intervention of Russian troops stationed a few miles to the northeast. In mid-May, they began to close in.[119] On May 17 the vali and his troops fled and joined forces with Halil's column. They wreaked havoc on Armenians in the Van countryside, around Siirt, and in Bitlis and Diyarbekir vilayets.[120]

On May 22 the Russians, with some Armenians, reached Van's outskirts and unleashed an intense barrage on the town's Muslim quarters. Within days most of the Muslim population fled along with the remaining Ottoman troops. After the siege was lifted, some 20,000 Armenians from the surrounding hinterland arrived in the city. They burned homes and massacred Turks left behind. Missionaries took in, and saved, more than a thousand Muslim women and children. "The Armenians seem perfectly debauched," Mattie Raynolds, a missionary, wrote her husband. "Plundering and revenge the only thought of the day, and we might as well talk to the wall. The Armenians have suffered awfully and the [Turkish] massacring was done so cruelly it is no wonder perhaps that they are swept away." But they were not driven only by revenge, Raynolds believed. "I think too . . . the Armenians [wish] to make this a purely Armenian province."[121]

The withdrawing Ottoman forces continued to massacre Christians. In mid-June, in the mountains south of Van, de Nogales saw thousands of "half-nude and still bleeding corpses, lying in heaps." He was told that Cevdet had ordered massacres around Van and in Bitlis to avenge Armenian collaboration with the Russians.[122]

In Van town, conditions were dim in the wake of the siege. No food arrived from the devastated countryside. Many died of hunger, untended wounds, and typhus. Almost all the missionaries working in the hospital were infected; Ussher died from the disease. To make matters worse, Ottoman troops were gathering to retake the city and areas of the province that had been conquered by the Russians, who were now outnumbered. In mid-July they were routed by Cevdet's forces and began withdrawing to Tiflis, modern-day Tbilisi. Armenians joined them in great numbers. Missionaries such as Yarrow, whom the Turks accused of colluding with the Russians, also fled. Through the long trek, Turkish villagers and Kurdish tribesmen attacked the evacuees. Many died on the way to Tiflis, and many others—including Raynolds, who was injured during the flight—died soon after arriving.[123]

In December 1916, after the Russians had reoccupied the Van area, Yarrow returned to survey the damage. The town was in ruins. Once the thriving center of the province, now it was practically uninhabited. Of the missionary schools and orphanages, only ashes remained. The Armenian church was a black husk. "There is not much that I can say," he wrote. "It was a doleful time . . . like being in a city of the dead."[124] The "black book," a meticulous province-by-province survey of the Armenian population prepared by Talât's assistants, estimated that in 1914 Van was home to 67,792 Armenians. Yarrow encountered not one during his return visit.

Zeytun: The Beginning of Systematic Deportation

In April 1915 the isolated, mountainous region of Zeytun became both a makeshift lab and a model for the campaign of deportation-cum-genocide that would begin a month later. In Zeytun neither deportations nor massacres were planned ahead of time; the national-scale preparation was still underway in Constantinople as events in Zeytun unfolded. Nor were Zeytunlis the first Armenians deported. In October 1914 Talât, fearful of Christian-Russian collaboration, had ordered the deportation of small numbers of Armenians and Assyrians from borderlands to inland areas.[125] But the symbolism and timing of the Zeytun deportation were important to the process of genocide.

In 1895 the Zeytunlis had put up strong resistance to Turkish repression. Crushing a perceived rebellion there twenty years later dampened Armenian morale and reinforced Muslims' distrust, just in time for the state campaign of terror. Zeytun also served, like Van and Sarıkamış, as a potent propaganda tool, helping to justify a more general Armenian repression in the eyes of Ottoman Muslims. When large-scale deportations began in May 1915, the government could point to Zeytun. There, according to the official narrative, deportation cut away the cancer of Armenian insurrection before it could metastasize. Who could object if the Turkish remedy were applied, again and again, elsewhere?

Zeytun had done its best to rebound from 1895, and some Armenian and Turkish leaders had tried to foster a spirit of reconciliation. In a January 1914 letter, the Western traveler Philip Price described a church mass attended by the Turkish kaymakam and the region's mufti. There were skirmishes from time to time in the nearby countryside, though, as Kurdish tribes and government troops continued to assail Armenians. The town of 10,000, nearly all

The formerly Armenian town of Zeytun, in the mountains above Maraş. One of the few Armenian communities that fought back against Turkish oppression, the Zeytunlis were massacred and deported en masse on three separate occasions.

Armenians, also experienced tension with its small muhacir population. Some Zeytunlis joined revolutionary bands, which occasionally attacked tax collectors and police officers.[126]

In Zeytun, as in Van, the government's mobilization orders were greeted with suspicion. Many believed that Constantinople was keen on payback for the 1895 resistance, and adult men feared being sent away while their loved ones were left without protection. Rather than the army, some Zeytunlis joined resisters in the mountains. In response to the defiant draftees, the authorities arrested several dozen Zeytun notables and dragged them to Maraş in chains. Most were executed or tortured to death.[127] When Armenians complained that gendarmes were molesting women and otherwise harassing townspeople and residents of surrounding villages, the kaymakam and gendarmerie chief turned a deaf ear.

As the war dragged on, more Armenians evaded the draft or deserted. Tensions rose yet further on March 9, when, as Walter Rössler, the German consul in Aleppo, reported, "Armenian deserters . . . shot a couple of Turkish gendarmes." The true number may have been greater. Zeytun's leaders condemned the attack, and, at first, Ottoman officials managed to avoid bloodletting. Taking note of the situation throughout the kaza, Rössler explained, "The Islamic population of Marash clearly was going to use this incident as a reason to start a massacre but remained calm since the set-up of a court-martial was announced." The possibility of killings remained, though. "If the inhabitants do not hand over the ring leaders," Rössler feared, "military intervention will be used."[128]

On March 13 government troops arrested a handful of notables, despite their opposition to the deserters' attack. Soon after, the army sent in troops to ferret out deserters and draft dodgers holed up in the St. Astvatsatsin Monastery, above the town. On March 25–26, the Ottomans razed the monastery to the ground.[129] In response the townspeople "hoisted a white flag."[130] At this point the potential for further violence was extreme; to their credit, diplomats, clerics, civic leaders, and local Ottoman officials sought to prevent a repeat of 1894–1896. On March 30 the American consul in Aleppo, Jesse B. Jackson, telegraphed Wangenheim, asking that he press the Porte to send Vali Celal Bey of Aleppo, "a very able man and knowing Armenians thoroughly," to Zeytun to prevent disaster. But before anything could be done, the government flooded the town with troops "to bring the rebels to justice." Troops arrested and tortured dozens of leading citizens "and declared victory."[131]

As in so many cases, Turkish complaints of violent insurrection read as post-hoc justification. No doubt many Zeytunlis were sympathetic to the Armenian national cause. In March 1915 Allied intelligence sources estimated the number of activists ("Hunchakists") in the Zeytun area at about 3,000, with revolutionary committees active in all the province's towns. But they could not have rebelled had they wished to: the government had disarmed them well before any putative rebellion, even taking away their knives.[132] When, on March 12, Wangenheim informed his government that Zeytun had "risen," he was merely repeating what Ottoman sources had told him. In that same dispatch, he referred to his consul in Adana, who was close to the scene and denied that there was a rebellion. Rather, the consul described the incidents in Zeytun as "isolated expressions in reaction to recruitment procedures."[133]

For his part, when Consul Rössler visited the area, he found no evidence of Russian or other foreign influence. Though he didn't ignore the killing of the gendarmes, he blamed the government for escalating the situation. The Ottomans were arresting and prosecuting "rich and respected Armenians" who had nothing to do with the violence. Indeed, these prominent Armenians wanted the "robbers removed." Rössler believed that events in Zeytun reflected not just countermeasures in the face of rebellion but the will of a government faction "inclined to consider all Armenians as suspicious, even hostile."[134]

In this he was correct, for the fate of Zeytun was decided long before any revolutionary event could be construed there. As early as February Cemal had proposed deporting Armenian families from the Zeytun area, and Talât had agreed.[135] The deportations began about a week after the Ottoman army declared victory in Zeytun. On April 8 a batch of notables were sent to Osmaniye with their wives.[136] Cemal cabled Talât the following day, widening the scope of deportation to include all "of those whose residence in Zeytun and Maraş is deemed to be harmful"—which is to say, every Armenian.

The first group of deportees arrived in Tarsus a week after setting out, not much worse for wear but anxious about the children they had left behind in Zeytun.[137] They were then sent northwest by train to Konya but were stopped on the way and separated.[138] The women were dispatched to Ankara-area villages and the men to Deir Zor and the desert to the southeast.[139] Cemal also requested that muhacirs waiting in Antep be settled in Zeytun "for political reasons."[140]

In this moment before widespread deportation, a missionary who came upon the Armenians passing through Maraş found the process incomprehensible. His only explanation was greed. "When I heard exactly who had arrived today, it hurt me, because they included people who had done everything to fulfil the wishes of the government, and still they had to be deported. But why? Because they are wealthy! I am convinced of it." He added that "among them there were no Eshkians," meaning *eşkiya*—rebels.[141] Dr. John Merrill, another missionary, lamented the future awaiting the deportees. They were being sent "to the Irak" where they would be "Christian emigrants among an Arabic-speaking population of strong Mohammedans, branded at the same time as having been disloyal to the government." They were, Merrill realized, suffering for their willingness to work with the authorities. "They never would have trusted the government and surrendered to it, if they had dreamed that the result was to be this."[142]

In the weeks after the initial deportation of notables, Zeytun was emptied of Armenians. Celal Bey, the vali of Aleppo who was never given the chance to mediate in Zeytun, wrote in his memoirs, "Without any justification, the military was sent in, and the people were deported, along with their families."[143] The exiles were sent to Maraş and then southward. According to Rössler, the Turks employed deceit to eject the Zeytunlis from their homes:

> It appears that those who have been led away from Zeitun were not told the truth but, as I have heard from the people themselves, they were told that they would be brought to Marash, and in the hope that they will be able to stay here, they accepted it all in silence. Once they were here, they were simply put in a khan and transported on after only one day of rest.[144]

An American witness reported what happened to the Zeytunlis along the roads east:

> Hundreds of them have been dragged through [Urfa] on their way to the desert whither they have been exiled. These poor exiles were mostly

women, children and old men, and they were clubbed and beaten and lashed along as though they had been wild animals. Their women and girls were daily criminally outraged, both by their guards and the ruffians of every village through which they passed, as the former allowed the latter to enter the camp of the exiles at night and even distributed the girls among the villagers for the night. . . . About two thousand of them have passed through [Urfa], all more dead than alive.[145]

In early May Talât confirmed his plans, ordering that Zeytun be completely emptied of Armenians and muhacirs settled in their homes.[146] On May 12 the Interior Ministry completed the erasure of Zeytun, changing its name to Yenişehir, meaning Newtown.[147] By mid-May there were no Armenians there or in nearly all of the forty-five adjacent villages.[148] According to Raymond Kevorkian, 18,000 Armenians were deported from the Zeytun district in the spring of 1915, 6,000 to Konya and the rest to Aleppo, Rakka, Deir Zor, Mosul, and Baghdad.[149] The Interior Ministry created a special commission to apportion the property left behind.[150]

On the heels of Zeytun, and still in advance of the May general deportation order, a string of nearby areas was cleared of Armenians. In mid-April the authorities called up the adult males of Maraş; after Armenian men registered and were taken away, their families were rounded up and marched off. The inhabitants of the villages of Furnuz and Gehen had sworn allegiance to the government and resisted demands to join the rebels. They were nonetheless deported. On April 20 Constantinople inquired as to whether their lands were fertile enough to maintain Balkan muhacirs.[151] In May U.S. Consul Jackson summarized the Zeytun and Maraş deportations:

Between 4,300 and 4,500 families, about 26,000 persons, are being removed by order of the government from the districts of Zeytun and Marash to distant places where they are unknown, and in distinctly non-Christian communities. Thousands have already been sent to the northwest into the provinces of Konia, Cesarea, Castamouni, etc., while others have been taken southeasterly as far as Dier-el-Zor, and reports say to the vicinity of Baghdad. The misery these people are suffering is terrible to imagine. . . . Rich and poor alike, Protestant, Gregorian,

Orthodox, and Catholic, are all subject to the same order. . . . The sick drop by the wayside, women in critical condition giving birth to children that, according to reports, many mothers strangle or drown because of lack of means to care for. Fathers exiled in one direction, mothers in another, and young girls and small children in still another. According to reports from reliable sources the accompanying gendarmes are told they may do as they wish with the women and girls.[152]

On April 19, after the start of the Zeytun and Maraş deportations, the Dashnak leadership wrote to the American Embassy in Constantinople, "The government has decided to evacuate by force all the other Armenian regions."[153] At the time, this was only a suspicion. It proved alarmingly accurate.

4

The Eastern River

In the earliest days of the mass deportation, it was still possible to believe that the government had no overarching design against Anatolia's Armenians, to believe that Turkey, however ham-fistedly, was defending itself from its wartime enemies. "I have to admit," Celal Bey wrote after the war, "I was not convinced that these orders and actions were meant to destroy the Armenians, because I believed it was improbable that a government would destroy its own subjects in such a way, and in particular the human treasure that had given it such riches. I believed these were merely steps stemming from the necessities of war, meant to remove the Armenians temporarily from the campaign arena."[1] Merrill, one of the missionaries stationed in Zeytun during the first deportation, for his part thought he had witnessed the unfolding of "a plan for the breaking down of the Christian population without bloodshed and with the color of legality."[2]

While deportations from Zeytun and some frontier areas began in April, formal orders to deport Armenians began reaching the provinces only on May 23. On May 27 an act of parliament made of the orders a comprehensive law. The *Tehcir* (Deportation) Law made no direct mention of Armenians, instead using neutral-sounding terms and a series of exemptions to ensure that Armenians would bear the brunt of the damage. The law specified military action against rebels and resisters, for the purpose of maintaining peace and security. It also provided for mass displacement from communities whose residents, in any number, were suspected of treason or sedition. Turks readily understood these terms as legalizing and therefore encouraging the mass arrest, exile, and killing of Armenians. The law's explicit exemption of Catholics and Protestants reinforced the point, although, in practice, Catholics and Protestants would be deported and violated routinely. (The same was true of Armenian soldiers' families. Though technically exempt, they were also subjected to deportation and massacre.)

A July 12 cable from Talât, one of the few accessible official documents admitting to massacres, confirms that the government selected Armenians for eradication. Talât was writing to Dr. Çerkes Reşid (Cherkes Reshid), a CUP founding father, graduate of Constantinople's Military Medical School, and vali of Diyarbekir. Reşid was such an energetic and indiscriminate murderer of Christians that Talât had to remind him he was only allowed to kill one specific group.

> Lately it has been reported that massacres were organized against the Armenians of the province and Christians without distinction of religion, and that recently for example people deported from Diyarbekir, together with the Armenians and the Bishop of Mardin and seven hundred persons from other Christian communities, were taken out of town at night and slaughtered like sheep, and that an estimated two thousand people have been massacred until now, and if this is not ended immediately and unconditionally, it has been reported that it is feared the Muslim population of the neighboring provinces will rise and massacre all Christians. It is absolutely unacceptable for the disciplinary measures and policies destined for the Armenians to include other Christians as this would leave a very bad impression upon public opinion, and therefore these types of incidents . . . need to be ended immediately.[3]

Consistent with the CUP's Islamist and secular goals, the purpose of the massacres was not to quell rebellious Christians: it was to replace them with Muslims on whose loyalty the state could rely. The deportation law permitted the resettlement of muhacirs in former Armenian lands, and it was Talât's intention to see that the law was followed. On July 13 he wrote to the commission of abandoned properties in Aleppo and Maraş, "The definitive solution of the Armenian question" (Ermeni meselesinin suret-i katiyede hall-i keyfiyeti) was the "transfer and deportation of Armenians" coupled with "increasing the Muslim population by settling refugees and tribes in their place." If these refugees were reluctant to settle in the homes of the dispossessed—were they to "flee or hide"—officials were instructed to herd them into the abandoned villages.[4]

The dilution of the Armenian population and its replacement by muhacirs was rigorously enforced on the basis of a demographic formula promulgated by the central government. Shortly after the first deportation orders were issued in late May, "The Ottoman General Staff determined three conditions for the re-settlement of Armenians. First, the ratio of Armenians to be settled 'should not be more than 10 percent of tribal and Muslim inhabitants.' Second, newly-established Armenian villages should not contain more than '50 households.' Third, once resettled, they would at no time be permitted to change their location."[5] The orders evolved to encompass more and more Armenians. The first order was quickly followed by another endorsing the deportation of all Armenians from the "war zone."[6] Then Talât and his team decided that the six eastern provinces were to be emptied of Armenians entirely. Armenians could be resettled in other provinces of Anatolia and in Deir Zor, but at a ratio of no more than 5 percent of the Muslim population. In Aleppo the figure was 2 percent. In practice, the ratio was usually 5 percent, rarely 10 percent. "Each new decision to deport was taken only after the ratio of Armenians (including Catholics and Protestants) to the Muslim population was calculated," Turkish historian Fuat Dündar writes.[7]

There is evidence of direct orders to kill off Turkey's entire Armenian population. After the war Ahmed Moukhtar Baas, an Ottoman army lieutenant who took part in the ethnic cleansing of Trabzon, told his British interrogators that he and his troops had received two instructions. One was the Interior Ministry's official deportation order of June 21, calling for the expulsion of "all Armenians, without exception," from the vilayets of Trabzon, Diyarbekir, Sivas, and Mamuret-ül-Aziz and from Canik sanjak. The other was an irâde, an imperial directive from the sultan himself. The deportation order specified that "deserters" were to be shot without trial. In the irâde, the word "Armenians" was substituted for deserters.[8] Reşid Akif Pasha, who served briefly in the Ottoman cabinet immediately after the war ended, told a similar story. Speaking to the Ottoman Chamber of Deputies on November 21, 1918, he announced that he had found several hidden documents. After the initial order of deportation was sent to the provinces, he said, "The inauspicious order was circulated by the Central Committee to all parties so that the armed gangs could hastily complete their cursed task. With that, the armed gangs then took over and the barbaric massacres began to take place."[9]

But the record of what actually happened on the ground testifies more persuasively than any order or irâde. Armenians throughout Asia Minor were funneled southward in convoys toward Syria. In the east, able-bodied men were rounded up, separated from their families, and massacred immediately after departing in convoys, if not before. In the west, where the risk of organized Armenian resistance was lower, men were typically allowed to join the convoys. Anyone on the road—men, women, children, the sick or elderly—might be massacred, or else die of disease, starvation, injuries, exposure, and exhaustion. Throughout the journey, the deportees were robbed, raped, and forced to convert to Islam. Those who reached the Syrian and Iraqi deserts around Deir Zor were subsequently butchered in the tens of thousands.

The Eastern River of Deportation and Massacre, 1915

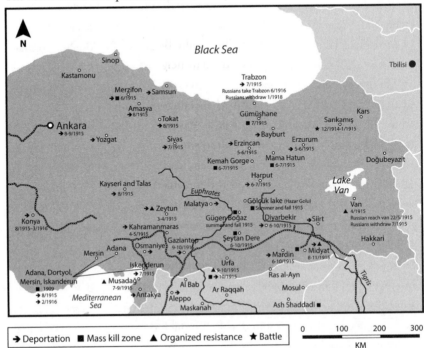

In his memoirs, Celal Bey recalled what it felt like to witness what were, in effect, death marches. "I was like a person sitting beside a river," he wrote, but "with no means of rescuing anyone from it":

Instead of water, blood was flowing down the river. Thousands of innocent children, blameless old men, helpless women and strong youngsters were streaming downriver towards oblivion, straight to dust and ashes. Anyone I could hold onto with my bare hands, with my fingernails, I saved. The rest, I believe, went down the river, never to return.[10]

Erzurum

The vilayet of Erzurum had one of the largest Armenian populations in eastern Anatolia, roughly 125,000 in 1914. As such, it had been a focus of massacre in 1895. Thousands lost their lives, and many emigrated. But the rise of the CUP seemed to portend fundamental change. In a signal of reconciliation, the CUP and the Dashnaks signed their 1909 cooperation agreement in Erzurum. Intellectuals, journalists, and political leaders celebrated the accord and dreamed of a rosy future.[11]

Nothing came of these hopes. During the Balkan Wars, a wave of nationalist fervor swept the region, leading to heightened Armenian demands for equality and autonomy, which angered officials. In January 1914 Russian intelligence sources described meetings among Erzurum's Muslim notables, which featured "open talk of massacres." Some Muslims donned white turbans, indicating their readiness to die as jihadi martyrs whenever Constantinople gave the sign.[12] In December, after the Ottomans joined the world war, Wangenheim reported routine attacks on Erzurum's Armenian villages and priests. Locals ascribed the attacks to CUP instigation.[13] By early 1915, with genocide planning underway in Constantinople, Erzurum officials were seeking guidance on which of the city's Armenians to eradicate. On February 17 local officials sent the central government lists of Armenians whose professional expertise was essential, the implication being that they should be exempted from harm.[14]

At the end of the month, Şakır, the Special Organization chief, arrived in the city. At first, not much happened. All eyes were on Van, and Şakır laid low, maintaining his official front as a representative of the Red Crescent.[15] Then, on April 5, the Directorate of Muhacir Affairs urgently requested housing in the Erzurum area for 20,000 refugees. The Interior Ministry replied that Şakır would handle the matter.[16] Soon after, Şakır and Nâzım, the other Special Organization chief, met with Mahmud Kâmil Pasha, the commander of the Third Army, and Tahsin Bey, the vali of Erzurum recently transferred from Van. Although there is no documentation from the meeting, postwar testimony indicates that Şakır and Nâzım relayed Constantinople's as-yet-unannounced decision to deport large numbers of Armenians, and probably to murder them as well. The group then developed procedures to carry out the removal and to resettle muhacirs.[17]

The decisions taken at this meeting likely affected areas beyond Erzurum. Testimony indicates that the plans hatched there were coordinated with valis Muammer of Sivas, Cevdet of Van, and Mustafa Abdülhalik of Bitlis. At about the same time, Sivas and a number of other eastern vilayets were instructed to search Armenian homes and businesses for weapons and ammunition.[18]

After Şakır's arrival in Erzurum, Scheubner-Richter wrote to Wangenheim predicting that life would soon get much harder for the Armenians. But the ambassador told his consul not to interfere. Scheubner-Richter could try to provide aid, but, Wangenheim warned, "It is important to avoid appearing as if we have a right to protect the Armenians and intervene in the activities of the authorities."[19] On May 20 Scheubner-Richter reported that the authorities had ordered the deportation of all Armenian villagers from the plain of Passin, north of Erzurum, southward to the area of Mama Hatun (Tercan), midway between Erzurum and Erzincan. According to the consul, they were given two hours' notice, and as they left, their houses were plundered by soldiers and neighbors.[20] The Dashnaks made similar reports. In one they identified Şakır, Hilmi Bey, and former CUP deputy Seyfullah Effendi as prominent culprits. Their plan, the report claimed, was to provoke the Armenians into acts of resistance that would justify massacre.[21] But there was no resistance.

Tahsin told Scheubner-Richter that he opposed the measures but had to follow orders from Constantinople. Next in line, he said, would be the inhabitants of Erzurum city itself. The consul opined that there seemed to be no reason for the deportation, as the Armenians were not seditious and were unarmed. Moreover, many of the young men had already been drafted, and those who sympathized with Russia had crossed the border long ago. Deportations would mainly affect women and children. On May 22 the consul reported his astonishment at the speed with which muhacirs were replacing the deportees. "These people are also plundering the Armenians' property. There are grounds for the assumption that possibly even from the very beginning the purpose of the relocation was to make room for the immigrants." He suspected that the measures were being taken on German advice. On the margins of the consul's letter, Fritz Bronsart von Schellendorf, the German Chief of Staff of the Ottoman Army, noted that he thought the Armenians were in rebellion and the Turks were the ones deserving sympathy.[22]

As in Zeytun, when the rural Erzurum deportations began, the destination was not yet clear. The first convoys made their way to Erzincan, a six-day walk due east, and continued to Sivas and Kastamonu in central Anatolia. But soon the accompanying troops were told that these areas were "unsuitable," and the Public Security Directorate of the Interior Ministry *(Emniyet-i Umumiye Müdüriyeti)* instructed the valis to redirect convoys southward through Urfa and Mosul to Deir Zor.[23] To most of the deportees, the never-ending trudge must have seemed aimless, designed to kill them off through exhaustion, hunger, and thirst.

On June 13 deportations began from Erzurum city itself. The first to go were members of the Armenian business community. The initial caravan—consisting of some forty notable families from the city and from nearby Bayburt—was at first allowed to travel in relative comfort, perhaps to mislead those who would follow. In Kığı sanjak, about sixty miles southwest of Erzurum, roughly a hundred of the notables were murdered and some of the women and children abducted. Two men disguised as women survived the massacre.[24]

Victoria Barutjibashian, another survivor, described the departure from Erzurum city. Her family had packed what provisions it could on three horses, but, two hours after starting out, the convoy was robbed by brigands and villagers. In the following days, the accompanying gendarmes "separated the men, one by one, and shot them . . . every male above fifteen years old. By my side were killed two priests, one of them over ninety years of age." She testified that brigands "took all the good-looking women and carried them off on their horses . . . among them my sister, whose one-year-old baby they threw away; a Turk picked it up and carried it off. . . . My mother walked till she could walk no farther, and dropped by the roadside on a mountain top."[25] At some point Barutjibashian gave up and agreed to convert and join a convoy of wagons taking widows to Constantinople. Along the way, she passed many corpses, mainly of women and girls.[26]

At the end of July, reports of a massacre at Kemah Gorge began leaking out of the empire. Lepsius, the German missionary, informed Morgenthau that the deportees from Erzurum had been taken to the gorge, between Erzincan and Harput, and were slaughtered there: gendarmes, assisted by some 250 brigands, killed about 7,000 people. Lepsius's report was corroborated by Scheubner-Richter and a year later by Lieutenant Baas, who told a British officer:

> The Armenians deported from Erzeroum started with their cattle and whatever possessions they could carry. . . . The vali of Erzeroum . . . assured them most solemnly that no harm would befall them. . . . Word came that the first batch had arrived safely at Kamach, which was true enough. But the men were kept at Kamach and shot, and the women and children were massacred by the shotas [brigands] after leaving that town.[27]

Another large Erzurum convoy, escorted by gendarmes under the command of Major Adil Bey, was attacked nearby in the area of Mama Hatun. Among the witnesses were survivors, such as Missak Vartanian, a former cavass at the British consulate, who was left for dead. According to the testimony of brigands later arrested by the British, those spared in the initial killings were led the next day to the banks of the Tuzla Su River and murdered by soldiers and brigands on Adil's orders.[28] Garabeth Hadji Oglu Georgian, a farmer from the village of Irdazur, told Scheubner-Richter that his column of thousands of villagers was attacked repeatedly by Kurds, and many jumped into the Euphrates to save themselves. Some, who escaped to a nearby village, were pursued by guards and shot down. Georgian himself was shot in the arm.[29]

Further testimony makes clear that representatives of the CUP and Special Organization participated in the killing. Kourkin Kellerian, an Armenian who in summer 1915 served in the army as an orderly, testified on September 2, 1920, that Majid Bey, a CUP representative at Erzincan, took part in the Kemah Gorge atrocities along with the local mutesarrif, Memduh Bey. Both were dressed as brigands.[30] Binganoush Bogosian of Erzincan claimed to have seen Memduh Bey with CUP member Eczacı Mehmet Efendi during a massacre on the road between Erzincan and Kemah. Bogosian survived by feigning death, and a few months later became a servant in Memduh's house, where he heard discussions about further killings.[31] Another eyewitness, a Mr. Saprastian, claimed that thousands, mostly peasants from Erzurum villages, were massacred in Kemah by brigands working for the Special Organization. This despite the fact that the vali, Tahsin, had accepted a bribe of a thousand Turkish Lira to keep the Armenians safe.[32]

Gradually restored to strength after Sarıkamiş, the Third Army, commanded by General Kâmil Pasha, also played a role in the Erzurum massacres. The exact extent is unclear, but reports indicate that its officers were

Thousands of Armenians were murdered, in batches, at Kemah Gorge in 1915. Today the spot is marked with a monument, constructed in 2001, commemorating fourteen Turkish soldiers who died there when their truck fell into the ravine.

aware of what was happening and cooperated with the Special Organization. An Armenian doctor serving in the military accused the general of organizing massacres in the region. During the postwar investigations, General Süleyman Faik Pasha, commander of the garrison in Mamuret-ül-Aziz, claimed that Kâmil sent "many cables ordering that the Armenians be exterminated."[33] Colonel Stange, a German officer in the Third Army during the deportations, also pointed the finger at his commander who, "besides the Director of Police, had proven to be the most brutal in executing the orders."[34] He added, "It is definitely a fact that these Armenians, almost without exception, were murdered in the region of Mama Hatun by so-called 'chetes,' Ashirets [tribes], and similar scum. These acts were, in fact, tolerated by the military escort cadres, were even accomplished through their assistance."[35] According to Kevorkian, Kâmil was incensed to discover that Muslims had sheltered Armenians during the massacres. He warned that any subordinates caught doing so would be hanged and their houses burned down.[36]

Not all of the Armenians marched out of Erzurum died in the area of Mama Hatun and Kemah Gorge. At about the same time reports of these massacres were reaching Western observers, Leslie Davis, the American consul in Harput, informed Morgenthau that several thousand Erzurum area Armenians had just arrived in his town. "A more pitiable sight cannot be imagined," he wrote. "They are, almost without exception, ragged, filthy, hungry and sick. This is not surprising since they have been on the road for almost two months":

> As one walks through the camp mothers offer their children and beg one to take them. In fact, the Turks have been taking their choice of these children and girls for slaves, or worse. In fact, they have even had their doctors there to examine the more likely girls and thus secure the best ones.

> There are very few men among them, as most of them have been killed on the road. All tell the same story of having been attacked over and over again. . . . Women and children were also killed. Many died, of course, from sickness and exhaustion on the way, and there have been deaths each day that they have been here. Several different parties have arrived and, after remaining a day or two, have been pushed on with no apparent

destination. Those who have reached here are only a small portion, however, of those who started. By continuing to drive these people on in this way it will be possible to dispose of all of them in a comparatively short time.

In a follow-up letter, Davis recounted that a few hundred people, who were too weak or sick to continue, remained in Harput.

Their camp is a scene from the Inferno. . . . It was bad enough before when there were several thousand all in a most wretched condition. Now, when only the worst of them are left behind, the scene beggars all description. The dead and dying are everywhere. . . . I presume a little food is brought to these people, but most of them are too far gone to need food.

Refusing to be deceived that the authorities simply wished to relocate Armenians to less combustible parts of the empire, Davis concluded, "The entire movement seems to be the most thoroughly organized and effective massacre this country has ever seen."[37]

Trabzon

When the deportation order reached Trabzon in late June 1915, it probably surprised no one. The Tehcir law had been in force for a few weeks, and horror stories had been emerging from Erzurum for more than a month. Many of Trabzon's Muslims opposed the deportations, especially of women and children, but officials were determined.

On June 16, after meeting with local CUP Branch Secretary *(Kâtib-i Mesul)* Nail Bey, Trabzon Vali Cemal Azmi Bey posted an official proclamation intended to allay Armenians' fears and avert possible resistance.[38] According to the vali, deportation was necessary and justified because Armenians had collaborated with the enemy "to destroy the peace and security of the Ottoman state." The government was therefore "compelled to adopt extraordinary measures and sacrifices both for the preservation of the order and security of the country, and for the welfare of the Armenian societies."[39] But the deportees, the vali promised, would be treated decently. When the time came, they would be given five days to prepare. They would be allowed to carry some movables and livestock but would be strictly forbidden to sell the rest of their possessions or even to give them to neighbors and friends for safekeeping. Muslims would also be forbidden from helping, on pain of court-martial. Instead, all property left behind would be registered with authorities, who would store it and return it to the deportees after the war. Convoys leaving Trabzon would be guarded by gendarmes, who would protect the deportees from attack or affront.[40]

The Armenians had to settle for such mollifying words, for, unarmed and disorganized, they were in no position to defy anyone. In the weeks before the deportation announcement, the authorities had done the grisly work of eliminating the community's leaders. The bishop of Trabzon was sent south for interrogation and, along with the bishop of Erzurum, murdered by the governor of Gümüşhane sanjak.[41] Others, including Dashnak leaders, teachers, businessmen, and Armenians with Russian passports, were dispatched by boat to Samsun, but "met with an accident at sea" and were never seen again.[42] A survivor called Vartan managed to return to Trabzon a few days later, severely wounded and incoherent. He died shortly thereafter. A local Turk later told the American consul, "This boat was met not far from Trebizond by another boat containing gendarmes. They proceeded to kill all the men and throw them overboard."[43] The vali of Trabzon confirmed that seventy-four people were arrested, "accused of spreading evil and intrigue of the first degree, [and] were sent on their way by land and sea."[44]

The Interior Ministry's deportation guidelines arrived five days after the vali's announcement, but it took another few days before the deportation order was made public. "Several witnesses, both Turkish and Armenian, affirm that the course of events was accelerated after Bahaeddin Şakır paid a visit to Trabzon around 22 / 23 June," Kevorkian writes.[45] On the 24th, after meeting with Şakır, the vali gave his staff official word of the coming deportation. The following day Trabzon's remaining Armenian notables were rounded up. And the day after that, the deportation date was announced publicly: July 1.

Şakır may have imparted lessons learned from the previous expulsions, but just as officials became skilled in the art of lethal removal—how to keep deportees docile while extracting their riches and deluding them about their fate—the Armenians became shrewder. Albeit, their methods were tragic. "I have seen strong, proud, wealthy men weep like children while they told me that they had given their boys and girls to Persian and Turkish neighbors," the American consul, Oscar Heizer, reported. "Many are providing themselves with poison which they will take in case the [deportation] order is not rescinded."[46]

Even the Ottomans' allies were shocked by the looming deportation at Trabzon and by what had happened in Erzurum. "Heartbreaking" was the word Ernst von Kwiatkowski, Trabzon's Austro-Hungarian consul, used. "Considering the great distance, and lack of food and shelter along the infested route, banishment to Mosul is the equivalent of a death sentence." His report emphasized that Armenian removal would have negative political and economic consequences; his boss, Ambassador Johann von Pallavicini, probably the European ambassador best connected to the Ottoman court, forwarded the report to Vienna with an additional comment on the humanitarian situation: "I hear that the Armenian population expelled from its homeland has not only been consigned to the greatest of misery, but is also doomed to complete eradication at the hands of the Kurdish bands lying in wait for them."[47]

As the deportation deadline approached, panic took hold in Trabzon. Witnesses described "horrific scenes" in the streets, as well as frantic efforts to hide women and children.[48] To reduce tensions, the vali promised exemptions for the elderly, widows, women in late pregnancy, and government employees. German, Austrian, and American consular officials did their best to rescue children. They took pupils from an American missionary school as well as others left behind and enrolled them in a new Muslim school. They even invited the vali to be the school's honorary president and the Greek metropolitan its vice president. Nail Bey caught on to the ploy, but he didn't shut down the school. Instead, he found a way to turn the situation to Muslim advantage. He rescinded the blanket ban on aiding Armenians and called on Muslims to take in children. Many did, including Nail Bey himself. According to Heizer, he "chose ten of the best-looking girls and kept them in a house for his own pleasure, and the amusement of his friends." Later, the Turks would remove some of the children from the makeshift school and add them to convoys heading south. Others were disposed of more abruptly. "Many of the children were loaded into boats and taken out to sea and thrown overboard,"

Heizer wrote. "I myself saw where 16 bodies were washed ashore and buried by a Greek woman near the Italian monastery."[49] According to Lieutenant Baas, the children "were taken out to sea in little boats. At some distance out, they were stabbed to death, put in sacks and thrown into the sea."[50]

Mass deportation began on the designated date of July 1. That day gendarmes deployed around town and corralled Armenians into the main squares. From there they were pushed in droves to a clearing just outside the city. Some brought along carts and carriages but were ordered to send them back. The first 2,000 were assembled in three convoys and launched southward, to Gümüşhane and Erzincan. An additional 4,000 would be dispatched a few days later, and more from the vilayet as a whole.[51] Heinrich Bergfeld, the German consul in Trabzon, estimated at the end of July that 30,000 people had been deported from the vilayet through Typhus-infested countryside. Even without deliberate murder, he wrote, the journey would claim an enormous number of victims.[52]

Trabzon's Armenian men were massacred at Gümüşhane. According to Baas's testimony,

When the first batches of deported Armenians arrived at Gumush-Khana, all the able-bodied men were sorted out with the excuse that

Armenians assembling for deportation in the main square of an Anatolian town, 1915.

they were going to be given work. The women and children were sent ahead under escort with the assurance . . . that their final destination was Mosul and that no harm will befall them. The men kept behind were taken out . . . in batches of 15 or 20, lined up on the edge of ditches prepared beforehand, shot and thrown into the ditches. Hundreds . . . were shot every day.

The procession of old men, women, and children faced a similarly grim fate at the hands of brigands, with whom "the military escorts had strict orders not to interfere."[53] Many deportees were thrown into the Değirmendere River, polluting the water and air for miles around.[54] Bergfeld wrote that the riverbanks were "filled with piles of corpses."[55] Others were loaded on boats, ostensibly headed for Samsun, but which usually returned empty after just a few hours. "It is generally believed," Heizer wrote to Morgenthau, "that such persons were drowned."[56] It was not just men. Kwiatkowski noted, "Others (women, children) have been put on boats and sunk in the sea. This has been confirmed by several reports."[57] Nail Bey, Vali Cemal Azmi Bey, and Mehmet Ali Bey, a battalion commander, later ordered the removal of Armenian Catholics and anyone ambulatory, even if they were pregnant or infirm.[58]

In the last stages of the Trabzon deportation, Lieutenant Baas was ordered to take a convoy southward. Setting out with a group of 120 men, 200 women, and 700 children, he reached Gümüşhane, where the men were taken away and killed. Continuing on the road to Erzincan with the rest, Baas passed "thousands of bodies of Armenians unburied." The convoy was periodically halted by gangs demanding the women and children. Lieutenant Baas refused, but he did hand over some 200 children to Muslims willing to adopt them, whom he must have considered decent people. At Kemah, according to his statement, he fell ill and asked to be relieved, but was ordered to keep going, moving his charges from place to place as long as they were still alive. Finally, he managed to foist his deportees onto another convoy, from Erzurum, led by an acquaintance, a gendarmerie officer named Mehmet Effendi. The group apparently did not survive long. Mehmet later told Baas that, upon reaching the Euphrates, south of Kemah, the convoy was attacked by brigands. The gendarmes kept clear, and the gangs shot the remaining Armenians and threw them into the river. Baas explained that Kemah was the brigands' regional headquarters; their commander, a Kurd named Murzabey, boasted that he alone had killed 70,000 Armenians. Even the Turks considered him dangerous. He was later charged with assaulting a gendarme and executed.[59]

According to a non-Armenian soldier, an Armenian construction battalion working on the road between Trabzon and Gümüşhane was massacred along with Trabzon deportees. The witness told Heizer that he did not observe the killing, but he heard rifle fire and shortly thereafter took part in the burial detail. The bodies, he said, "were all naked, having been stripped of clothing."[60]

With Trabzon's Armenians gone, the authorities began emptying their houses and shops. Furniture, bedding, and other valuables were put in storage. No attempt was made to record ownership of the belongings. "The idea of 'keeping the property in bales under the protection of the government, to be returned to the owners upon their return,' is simply ridiculous," Heizer wrote. "The goods are piled without any attempt at labeling or systematic storage."[61]

About a year later, in June 1916, the Russians captured Trabzon. Dr. Lyndon Crawford, principal of the American school, wrote that as the Russians entered, about five hundred Armenians suddenly emerged from caves in the mountains. Others, mainly young children taken by Greek and Turkish families, were handed over to the Russians.[62] Little by little, other Armenians who had survived the ordeal returned and reestablished a community. Some avenged themselves by committing atrocities against Turks. But in early 1918, after the Bolshevik Revolution, the Russians hastily departed, and the Ottoman forces returned. The subsequent atrocities rivaled "those of 1915," according to one report. "Wholesale drowning in the Black Sea is said to have been resorted to on this occasion, as it was three years ago. Male children especially have been thus disposed of, while women and girls have been handed over, even more extensively than before, to Moslem families."[63]

Sivas

In early 1915 Fazıl Berki toured Anatolia preparing hearts and minds for the deportations. An army physician and a rising star in the CUP, Berki was an able orator, well suited to what the Armenian Patriarchate dubbed an "anti-Christian propaganda tour." Speaking in March at the central mosque of Sivas city, he labeled Armenians "enemies of the Turkish nation" and declared that the empire would have to get rid of them. He also conveyed the party's latest thinking to Vali Muammer and the local CUP branch secretary, Gani. According to a special report by the Armenian Patriarchate, the three men organized a secret committee to oversee the coming deportations and massacres in Sivas vilayet. A few weeks after Berki's visit, Gani traveled to Constantinople to confer with CUP chiefs and coordinate the campaign.[64] By May 19, before deportations from Sivas began, the government had plans to replace the vilayet's Armenians with tens of thousands of Balkan muhacirs, many of whom were already in the province waiting for housing.[65]

Throughout the spring, local Turkish newspapers fanned the flames, helping to impress on Turks the justification for deportation. Early 1915 had seen small clashes between Armenian militants and government forces outside the town of Sivas, with both sides suffering casualties. The newspapers *Kızıl Irmak* and *Sivas* reported sensationalized versions of the events, exaggerating the Armenians' crimes and claiming that Armenian conspirators were caught planning to stab the empire in the back.[66] In response about eighty gendarmes "of notoriously evil reputation" were brought in to bolster the local garrison.[67]

Massive roundups began in mid-June, with about 2,000 middle-class Armenians arrested in Sivas town.[68] The detainees were routinely tortured, and most were never released. Under torture, some detainees disclosed old weapons caches, where a few Hamidian-era bombs were found.[69]

The deportation was announced on July 2, and removal began three days later. Large groups were marshalled to a staging area outside the city and sent away in caravans, each accompanied by four or five gendarmes. The deportees left behind most of their property, but many rented ox carts and piled them high with household items. Some took donkeys, cows, and chickens. In less than a month, some 25,000 Armenians were deported. About a thousand, most of them new converts, stayed in Sivas.[70] Surrounding villages and towns were also depopulated.[71] Deportees from throughout the vilayet were sent to Aleppo and Mosul. The missionary and educator George E. White described the sad squeaking of the ox carts passing by his college night after night, for weeks.[72] He recounted, that, "in all about 1,200 persons, mostly women and girls" converted, after the men had been removed.[73]

In late July Sivas' small population of Protestant Armenians was also deported. Unusually, Mary Graffam, a Protestant school principal, was allowed to accompany her students and the rest of the deportees, 2,000 in total. She provides a rare firsthand description of a convoy's arduous trek. On the second day, the routine began: "The gendarmes would go ahead and have long conversations with the villagers and then stand back and let them rob and trouble the people until we all began to scream, and then [the gendarmes] would come and drive [the villagers] away." On the third day, the men were separated from the women. The convoy commander claimed that they had gone back to Sivas, but villagers told them that the men had been executed.

> When we approached the bridge over [the stream of] Tokma Su it was a certainly fearful sight. As far as the eye could see over the plain was this real slow moving line of oxcarts. For hours not a drop of water on the road and the sun pouring down its very hottest. As we went on we began to see the dead from yesterday's company and the weak began to fall by the way. . . . I piled as many as I could on our wagons and our pupils both boys and girls worked like heroes.[74]

When the convoy reached Malatya, the authorities ordered Graffam to return to Sivas. The deportees trudged on. U.S. Consul Jesse B. Jackson, who witnessed the convoy's arrival at Aleppo, provides an epilogue:

> One of the most terrible sights ever seen in Aleppo was the arrival, early in August 1915, of some 5,000 terribly emaciated, dirty, ragged and sick women and children, 3,000 in one day and 2,000 the following day. These people were the only survivors of the thrifty and well to do Armenian population of the province of Sivas.[75]

Similar stories piled up around Sivas vilayet. In the city of Merzifon, "gendarmes went through the town gathering up all the Armenian men they could find, old and young; rich and poor; sick and well." All were detained and supposedly moved to Sivas city, the provincial capital. The first group dispatched sent messages to their homes indicating that they were safe. Their survival may have been a ruse concocted by the Turks to mislead others or allay their fears, because subsequent groups of men sent to Sivas were never heard from again. Wagon drivers and officials told missionaries that they had been killed on the road.[76] J. K. Marsden, a Merzifon missionary, described the process:

> They were in groups of four with their arms tied behind them and their deportation began with perhaps one-hundred or two-hundred in a batch. As we afterward learned, they were taken about twelve miles across the plains to the foothills, stripped of their clothing and in front of a ditch previously prepared, were compelled to kneel down while a group of villagers with knives and axes quickly disposed of them. For a week, every night, this was repeated until twelve hundred and thirty of the leading Armenian men had been disposed of.[77]

White, the missionary, later claimed that officials had "supervised the whole [process], under tents that were erected close at hand, and an official named Husseyin Effendi was said to have supervised the excavating of the trenches before the deportations from the city."[78]

When the killing was done, only a few hundred of Merzifon's 12,000 Armenians were left alive.[79] The kaymakam, a Dr. Faik, openly boasted about killing thousands of Armenians. Faik, who was also the CUP branch secretary, was too cruel—or, perhaps, too honest about his cruelty—even considering his party's standards; he was soon dismissed and investigated.[80]

Similar atrocities took place in the large provincial towns of Amasya and Tokat. In Amasya, out of 9,598 Armenians, 1,454 converted, most of them women who married Muslims. About half of the male population was drafted for the labor battalions. The rest were deported. The figures from Tokat look much the same.[81] In August 1915 an American consular agent in Samsun wrote Morgenthau that the men of these towns had been taken away and had not been heard from since.[82] Exactly what happened to them is not clear. While many Armenian prisoners in Sivas vilayet were killed, a substantial number were spared. Some were even allowed to join their families on the trek south, probably thanks to lobbying by missionaries.[83]

According to Talât's interim calculations of 1917, of the 141,592 Armenians who had lived in Sivas vilayet before the war, about 8,000 remained after deportation. Another 4,000 were dispersed in other provinces.[84] That leaves almost 130,000 dead, missing, exiled from the empire, or, owing to conversion, no longer counted as Armenian. When the deportations were over, the authorities plowed up the Armenian cemetery in Merzifon and put the land to agricultural use.[85]

Mamuret-ül-Aziz

In February 1913 the president of Harput's Euphrates College, Ernest Riggs, sent a cheerful letter to James Barton, the foreign secretary of the American Board of Commissioners for Foreign Missions. Riggs described a city looking toward a harmonious future. He believed that the Armenians' neutrality in the Balkan Wars would "tend to make the Turks more tolerant toward them and their religion." He also had considerable faith in the moderating power of secular governance. "The divisions between the parties of Turks tend to the obliteration of the old great division between Christian and Moslem," he explained. "Just now, we are basking in the unusual sunshine of good government and all looks rosy."[86]

The Armenians seemed to be thriving. Even some of those who had emigrated in the 1890s to the United States and Europe had felt safe enough to return. There were about 120,000 Armenians in Mamuret-ül-Aziz vilayet, centered on Harput. Armenians in the province were leaders and innovators in industry, especially the silk business.[87]

But the situation worsened in 1914. The mountains and crags of Mamuret-ül-Aziz were natural hiding places for deserters, who formed small gangs with Kurdish tribesmen in the wild Dersim region. A March telegram from the Interior Ministry instructs the vali and other local governors to deal with these outlaws.[88] Once the war began, reports of banditry became more frequent; in May 1915 tribal chiefs were given an ultimatum to hand over the deserters.[89]

These steps appear to have originated with CUP orders. The local CUP secretary, Mehmet Nuri Bey, helped to install a new vali, Sabit Cemal Sağırzade, a hardliner who at one point told Scheubner-Richter that "the Armenians in Turkey must and were going to be killed." Promoted from his former position as mutesarrif of Dersim, Sabit was indebted to the CUP and eager to help

Senior American missionaries, including Ernest Riggs, president of Harput's Euphrates College. Riggs and his wife Mary witnessed the destruction of Harput's Armenians, as well as the condition of deportees passing through on their way to the killing fields of the Syrian Desert.

carry out its plans. When Nâzım Bey arrived in late spring to organize the deportations and killings, he found an energetic partner in government house.[90] Sabit seemed in fact to relish the job, sending out joking, sarcastic telegrams about his victims. In one, from late July, he assured Talât that all the deportees were being treated with dignity.[91]

In early May Sabit ordered the local chief of police, Mehmet Namık, to collect Armenians' weapons and arrest revolutionaries. The police found only twenty-nine Dashnaks and few weapons.[92] Namık urged Sabit to punish only those against whom there was proof of revolutionary activity, but the vali "refused to listen, replying that orders had come from the central government, signed by Bahaeddin Şakır, that the whole Armenian population had to be deported and annihilated." Namık was hastily dismissed and dispatched elsewhere.[93]

In mid-May, Johannes Ehmann, Germany's consular agent in Harput, alerted his embassy to a wave of arrests of alleged Dashnaks and Hunchaks, including members of parliament.[94] Many prominent Christians were also detained and tortured. "Practically every male Armenian of any consequence at all here has been arrested," Davis reported in late June. "A great many of them were subjected to the most cruel tortures under which some of them died."[95] Maria Jacobsen, a Danish missionary, wrote in her diary:

> The Turks . . . at night . . . go into the prison. The prisoners are sent for, especially the well-known men, and made to run around on the wet floor until their feet become sodden. Then they have to lie on their backs with men sitting on their chests, while others flog their sodden feet until they are swollen and bleeding. They rip out their fingernails and the hairs from their beards one by one. They put their hands and heads in a sort of pinching machine until bones crack and break.[96]

When nothing more could be gleaned by torture, the detainees were murdered. "Several hundred of the leading Armenians were sent away at night and it seems to be clearly established that most, if not all, of them were killed," Riggs wrote.[97] One of his Armenian colleagues—Tenekejian, a professor of Turkish and history who had worked in the college for thirty-five years—was "arrested May 1st without charge." In clipped sentences, Riggs described what befell this poor man: "Hair of head, mustache and beard pulled out in vain effort to secure damaging confessions. Starved and hung by arms for a day and a night and severely beaten several times. Taken out towards Diyarbekir about June 20th and murdered in general massacre on the road."[98] Those who remained in prison were dealt with later, when the wing where they were kept burned down and those trying to escape were shot.[99]

As to the mass of Harput's Armenians, events followed the usual pattern. Before the deportations began, the Directorate of Muhacir Affairs asked the vali to keep an eye on money, movable property, and real estate that the deportees would be leaving behind.[100] The Armenians were hard-pressed to sell their belongings and wound up having to take virtually nothing for them.

"Sewing machines which had cost twenty-five dollars were sold for fifty cents. Valuable rugs were sold for less than a dollar." The scene reminded Davis of "vultures sweeping on their prey."[101] Officials, gendarmes, villagers, tribesmen, and brigands all stole from the meager cash proceeds deportees earned from the forced sales. Money they deposited in banks or sent to relatives was seized. Then, after the arrest, torture, and murder of the community leaders, came the announcement of an imminent, phased deportation.[102]

On June 28 Harput town criers proclaimed that all Armenians and Assyrians were to be deported. Dates and assembly points were soon published. "The full meaning of such an order can scarcely be imagined," Davis wrote. "A massacre, however horrible . . . would be humane in comparison . . . . In a massacre, many escape, but a wholesale deportation of this kind in this country means a lingering and perhaps even more dreadful death for nearly everyone."[103]

As in Trabzon and Erzurum, the Armenians complied. Davis was shocked by their passivity:

The most remarkable feature of the situation is the helplessness of the Armenians and the total lack of resistance on their part. With two or three insignificant exceptions, there has not been a blow struck by any of them. . . . One would think that some would have chosen death here, knowing that it awaited them a few hours after their departure, and many talked that way, but when the time has come all have started [on the trek] without making any resistance.[104]

During the first days of July, Harput, and Mamuret-ül-Aziz generally, were emptied of Armenians. Most of the men were herded out of town in groups, tied up, and killed. Women and children were sent on.[105] "The women and girls were dressed in very strange ways as they started out," Mary Riggs, a missionary educator and wife of Ernest Riggs, wrote. "So much so that I did not recognize some of my own pupils until they spoke to me and told me their names. They had disfigured their faces, marking them with charcoal and coloring them so as to make themselves look hideous. I could understand without asking them what the purpose was. . . . The people wore old clothes for fear of having good clothes taken from them."[106]

On July 10 the authorities ordered that all those remaining in Harput must leave town. "Not one single sparrow must be left," the instruction read.[107] A week later, soldiers and gendarmes rounded up everyone left, including the sick and the elderly. Some women gave away their children to Turks. A number of Armenians found refuge in mission buildings. Talât agreed they should be allowed to stay, for a time, lest upsetting the missionaries damage relations with the United States.[108]

According to Davis, the Harput deportees were to be sent to Urfa, but they were transported via Malatya, hinting at the government's intentions. If the authorities had wanted the deportees to reach Urfa or the Syrian Desert beyond, the convoys should have proceeded along the much shorter route through Diyarbekir.[109] The circuitous path through Malatya meant the deportees would march endlessly—either until they dropped or into remote valleys where they could be killed more easily and without witnesses.

Over the course of the summer, Mamuret-ül-Aziz was not only a site of deportations but also a transit point for deportees arriving from the north. Missionary Tacy Atkinson saw them at Mezre, near Harput:

> At this time, thousands were coming to us from . . . Erzroom, Erzingan, Ordou, Trebizond and many other places. In the second company that came there were about eight thousand. They said they were about thirty thousand when they started. They had been attacked seven times by Kurds, robbed and the men killed, but it had been impossible to kill all the men as the company was so large.

Atkinson described a heroic Turkish doctor who aided the transiting Armenians and whom she hoped to meet one day "in the Kingdom of Heaven." The man, in charge of the Red Crescent hospital, "sent away all his sick soldiers and kept a horse and wagon busy all the time going between his hospital and the camp, bringing in the sick. He rented other buildings and filled them all. . . . Many died, but he had done what he could."[110]

Seeing these convoys, the Harput Armenians could imagine their own fate. Davis detailed what happened to them on Monday, July 7. "Many men were arrested both at Harput and Mezreh and put in prison," he wrote. The next day, they were taken out and made to march towards an almost uninhabited mountain. There were about eight hundred in all and they were tied together in groups of fourteen each. . . . On Wednesday morning they were taken to a valley a few hours distant. . . . Then the gendarmes began shooting them until they had killed nearly all of them. Some . . . were then disposed of with knives and bayonets. A few succeeded in breaking the rope with which they were tied . . . and running away, but most of these were pursued and killed. A few succeeded in getting away, probably not more than two or three.[111]

Those who survived continued on their way south. Jackson saw the few who reached Aleppo. One of the survivors from Harput described the end of the trek:

On the 60th day when we reached Viran Shehir [Viranşehir], only 300 had remained from the 18,000 exiles. On the 64th day they gathered all the men and the sick women and children and burnt and killed them all. The remaining were ordered to continue their way. In one day they arrived at Rasoulain [Rās al-'Ayn], where for two days, for the first time, the Government gave them bread.[112]

Arrival in Mamuret-ül-Aziz did not necessarily mean transit from there. The vilayet was also a killing field. Most of the roads connecting the northern vilayets of Trabzon, Erzurum, and Sivas with the Syrian Desert passed through Mamuret-ül-Aziz. As the convoys—consisting mostly of women, children and the elderly—pushed southward into the few arteries cutting across the mountains, they gradually merged near Harput and turned into one endless stream.[113] Riggs later wrote, "The number of survivors passing through Harpoot from the north was very great, but comparatively few were known to have passed on beyond the vilayet."[114] Swedish missionary Alma Johansson noted, "Mamouret-ul-Aziz has become the cemetery of all the Armenians; all the Armenians from the various vilayets were sent there, and those that had not died on the way, came there simply to find their graves."[115] "The whole country is one vast charnel house, or, more correctly speaking, slaughterhouse," Davis wrote.[116]

The source caption reads: "A common sight among the Armenian refugees in Syria.
An Armenian child dead in the fields within sight of help and safety at Aleppo."

Davis made it his mission to trace and document the mass murder. He journeyed on horseback and, once back in the United States, wrote up what he
had seen. Just south of Harput, on the way to Lake Gölcük, he had encountered infernal scenes, hundreds of women's and children's bodies scattered
across the plain, and thousands lying on rocks at the bottom of narrow valleys and canyons, especially around the lake.[117] The descriptions fill fifty pages
of his report:

> Few localities could be better suited to the fiendish purposes of the Turks
> in their plan to exterminate the Armenian population than this peaceful
> lake in the interior of Asiatic Turkey, with its precipitous banks and
> pocket-like valleys, surrounded by villages of savage Kurds and far re-
> moved from the sight of civilized men. This, perhaps, was the reason
> why so many exiles from distant vilayets were brought in safety as far
> as Mamouret-ul-Aziz and then massacred in the "Slaughterhouse
> Vilayet." . . . That which took place around Lake Gooljik in the summer
> of 1915 is almost inconceivable. Thousands and thousands of Arme-
> nians, mostly innocent and helpless women and children, were butch-
> ered on its shores and barbarously mutilated.[118]

Since 1915, a series of dams, artificial lakes, and canals have been constructed around the lake, now known as Lake Hazar. The land is so altered that whatever Davis found probably is no longer accessible.

Davis performed his investigation in spite of considerable official obstruction. From Constantinople on down, the order was sent to cover up the killing in Mamuret-ül-Aziz and beyond. In September 1915 Sabit rebuked his subordinates:

> It has come to my attention that in contravention of my repeated messages, one may still find a great number of bodies along the roads. Needless to talk here about the many inconveniencies that this state of affairs presents, and the Interior Minister has once again demanded that functionaries who are proved negligent in this matter be punished. I repeat [my demand] to send to all corners of the vilayet gendarmes in sufficient numbers . . . charged with carefully burying the bodies that are found.[119]

Sabit persisted. A few months later, after Talât angrily cabled the valis that he "was informed that in certain areas one can see unburied bodies" and demanded the names of those "in whose territories such bodies will be found," Sabit acted immediately to carry out orders—and protect himself.[120] He wrote to subordinates: "Above I have transcribed a coded telegram from the Interior Minister. As soon as these types of corpses are discovered in your kaza, the kaymakam, mudir, and commanders of gendarmerie will have to be immediately suspended and referred to a law-court."[121]

Perhaps Sabit worried he would be held accountable for what the Allies had defined in May 1915 as "crimes against humanity."[122] This is corroborated by his strenuous efforts to obtain personal exoneration. In summer 1915, as the river of blood was flowing through his vilayet, he arranged a meeting with the American, German, and Italian consuls and told them he was touched by the suffering of the people. He promised to end it, if only the consuls would send him formal letters asking to spare the lives of the remaining Armenians. He said "he should like to have as many details in the letters as possible, so that it would appear that all those [Armenians] who were guilty of anything had been sent away and all those who remained were innocent." The consuls understood that this meant selling out the deportees as criminals and refused to provide the requested letters.

Sabit tried again later, sending to Davis his chief of police, Reşid Bey, to make the same entreaty on his behalf. Reşid asserted that three gendarmes had been shot by Armenians in one of the vilayet's villages. He insisted that the deportees had been guilty of similar crimes, while Armenians who remained were innocent. He then demanded a letter from Davis affirming the same narrative. Reşid "argued and argued and argued that I make some kind of statement," Davis recounted. "I don't know that I ever saw a more persistent man in my life. . . . He said orders had already been issued for more severe measures than ever on the morrow, but he might delay their enforcement a little if I would make a statement." Davis declined.[123]

In 1917 Talât affirmed that no Armenians remained in Mamuret-ül-Aziz.[124]

Diyarbekir

Under Vali Çerkes Reşid, Diyarbekir vilayet became one of the bloodiest Christian killing fields of 1914–1916. Reşid murdered Armenians, Greeks, and Assyrians without discrimination. He also executed subordinates who opposed or evaded his directives. These included the kaymakams of several provincial towns, Derik, Lice, and Beşiri, and possibly the mutesarrif of another, Mardin.[125] The vilayet's health inspector, Dr. Ismail Bey, openly opposed killings of Christians and especially the murder of babies and children; he was dismissed and packed off to Constantinople.[126] Unlike many officials who protested innocence or justification, it appears Reşid knew what he was doing and made no excuses. At the end of the war, he committed suicide rather than submit to Ottoman and British intelligence agents hard on his heels.[127] By that point more than 100,000 Armenians and some 60,000 Assyrians from Diyarbekir vilayet were dead. These numbers do not include thousands of unfortunate nonresidents who happened to be in the vilayet at the wrong time.

What happened in Diyarbekir was especially jarring in light of the progress the vilayet had made after the violence of 1894–1896. Not only had trade picked up in the following decades, but the quality of administration had also improved. "The police seemed more efficient and fair," the British acting vice consul wrote in May 1914. "The best branch of the administration appears to be that of the police." This was the result of serious reforms by a succession of honest and hard-working valis, including Ismail Hakki Bey, Celal Bey, and Hamid Bey.[128] Hamid, the last of the valis before the new outbreak of violence, was known for imprisoning Kurdish chiefs who allowed brigandage in their areas. An outlier in so many ways, Hamid was also pro-British and was shocked by Turkey's alliance with Germany. He even offered assistance to the British consul when he was ordered to pack up and leave.[129]

Conditions in the vilayet rapidly deteriorated after the start of World War I. On August 19, 1914, Diyarbekir city's bazaar, whose proprietors were mainly Armenians and Assyrians, burned to the ground. Thomas Mugerditchian, the British pro-consul in Diyarbekir, claimed that the fire was an arson proposed by the city's CUP parliamentary deputy, Feyzi Bey Pirinççioğlu, and carried out by police officers after Muslim shop-owners had been warned to stay away and clear out their merchandise.[130] Hamid Bey had Gevranlizâde Memduh Bey, the chief of police, arrested and banished for his suspected role. Crusading against an official conspiracy only made CUP officials more wary of Hamid. Not long after the fire, he was removed from office, and, on March 28, 1915, replaced by Reşid.[131]

As an arch-nationalist with military training, Reşid was well suited to enact the CUP plan for Armenian destruction. Indeed, historians have long assumed that these qualities made him an attractive choice for vali in the eyes of party bosses.[132] Recently, however, historian Hilmar Kaiser has argued on the basis of Ottoman documents that Reşid was transferred to Diyarbekir in order to defuse a personal feud with authorities in Baghdad and Mosul, where he had previously been vali.[133]

Whatever the reason for Reşid's reassignment, he was an energetic agent of the government's will. He brought to Diyarbekir dozens of shady characters, whom he immediately placed in charge of the local gendarmerie. He also immediately joined forces with Pirinççioğlu to coordinate the massacres. Testimony from an Ottoman official indicates that Feyzi had attended secret CUP Central Committee meetings in Constantinople in which the annihilationist policy was discussed and was then sent back to Diyarbekir to help orchestrate the campaign.[134] He also recruited Kurdish and Circassian chieftains to the cause and offered to pardon perpetrators.[135]

Along with the new police chiefs, Ruşdi and Veli Necdet (Nejdet), Feyzi set up a local branch of the Special Organization.[136] According to a detailed report by one eyewitness, the three men gathered the "worst specimens of thieves, brigands, murderers, deserters," fashioned them into eleven battalions, and appointed themselves commanders. With Reşid, the group established a Superior Council, which met regularly to discuss operational details.[137]

Weeks before the national deportation plan was set in motion, Reşid and the council had produced their own, approved tacitly by Talât.[138] The strategy was set in motion on April 16, when local units of the Special Organization surrounded the Armenian quarters in Diyarbekir, searched for arms, and arrested 300 young men.[139] Three days later most of the community's notables, including religious leaders and directors of financial institutions, were under lock and key. Party leaders came next. At the beginning of May, government employees, lawyers, intellectuals, educators, and many of the more established artisans were jailed. Altogether 900 were imprisoned in just a few weeks. The city's remaining Armenians called a general meeting. Some proposed resistance, even rebellion; others advocated passive defiance. But any idea of opposition was dropped when Hachadoor (Khatchadur) Digranian, a member of the provincial council, warned that he would support the exile or imprisonment of resistance advocates.[140]

The detainees were tortured to extract confessions.[141] Reportedly, one of these detainees was the Armenian bishop, Chilgadian, who was dragged through the city to the entrance of the main mosque, where he was doused in petroleum and burned nearly to death. He was then thrown into the stables of the municipal hospital, where he died in agony.[142] According to the Armenian assistant of Britain's consular agent in Diyarbekir, the American missionary Floyd Smith was the only doctor who dared treat Bishop Chilgadian. Apparently, when the vali heard of this, he warned Smith to keep away. Smith and his family were later banished from the city.[143]

After a sham trial on May 30, 636 Armenian notables were found guilty of various crimes and sent down the Tigris on rafts, toward Mosul. Ten days later they came ashore at the village of Shkifta, where a Kurdish brigand called Amero (or Ömer)—apparently in cahoots with Reşid—lured the Armenians into a trap and had them shot in a nearby valley. In the days that followed, more Armenians were sent down the river and disposed of in a similar fashion. The German vice-consul in Mosul, Walter Holstein, protested after body parts and abandoned rafts floated through his city.[144] A few weeks later, Reşid invited Amero to Diyarbekir to receive a medal. The brigand set out but never arrived. It was rumored that he was assassinated by his Circassian escorts, provided by Reşid, so that no one would be left to testify about the authorities' role in the mass murder.[145]

While Diyarbekir's Armenian notables were being disposed of, Reşid set his sights on Mardin, the province's picturesque second city and a center of multisectarian Christian life. But Mardin's mutesarrif, Hilmi Bey, refused to take part in the extermination. Mardin Armenians, he argued, were loyal citizens. Most were Catholic and spoke Arabic rather than Armenian; they had little in common with rebels in other regions. In spite of Hilmi's guardianship, Mardin's Christians sensed the coming storm. On May 1 the Armenian Catholic archbishop, Ignatius Maloyan, sent a letter to his congregation naming his successor and proclaiming, "I have never broken any of the laws of the Sublime Porte. . . . I urge all of you to follow my example. . . . Pray to [God] to give me the power and courage . . . to carry me through this final time and the trials of martyrdom."[146]

Starting on June 3, Reşid's men began rounding up Mardin's Christian leaders. Hundreds of Armenian, Assyrian, and Greek notables, including Maloyan, were interned in the citadel or in underground dungeons outside the city. A week later, after torture and forced confessions, the notables were dispatched on the road to Diyarbekir. Muslim townspeople "jeered and children threw stones" at the men as they were paraded out of Mardin, chained or roped together in batches of forty. Last in the procession was Maloyan, bareheaded and barefooted.[147] On the road, Gevranlizâde Memduh Bey—the former chief of police, set free by Feyzi Bey after the bazaar fire and rehired by Reşid—read out what he claimed was an imperial edict condemning the detainees to death. Maloyan apparently improvised a religious service and then was marched off alone and executed. The rest followed.[148]

More convoys left Mardin on June 14; July 2, 17, and 27; and August 10. Almost all of the deportees were Armenians. Most were stripped naked and murdered soon after leaving town, although some apparently reached the Syrian Desert. The caravan of June 14 included Assyrians, but, soon after setting out, many of them were returned to Mardin unharmed, probably on instructions from Talât.[149]

In general, the reprieve of non-Armenian Christians was an illusion. Clemency was short-lived, and, even while the order was supposedly in force, local officials regularly ignored it without penalty. One need look no farther than Tur Abdin, an area east of Mardin including the heavily Christian kazas of Midyat, Beşiri, Cizre, and Nisibin (Nusaybin).[150] On June 15 the Gregorian, Armenian Protestant, and Syrian Chaldean males of Nisibin were rounded up and executed. A few days later, the women were slaughtered, some in a stone quarry. The Syrian Orthodox community was left untouched until August, when they, too, along with their bishop, were murdered. Only a few Assyrians managed to escape to Mount Sinjar.[151] On August 24 Muslim militiamen dealt with Cizre's 2,000 Christian inhabitants, most of them Assyrians. Before then, the Christian communities had managed to buy off local powerbrokers. But, when the time came, the adult males were taken and murdered on the banks of the Tigris. The women and children were taken to a Dominican monastery and an Assyrian church, where they were robbed and raped. Some were then taken away by Muslims; the rest were murdered.[152]

The Syrian Christians of Diyarbekir did offer significant resistance. Their strongest stand came in July, at the villages of Azakh (Hazik, Azik), Ayn Wardo, and Basibrin. For months, Kurdish tribes and Turkish soldiers commanded by Inspector-General Ömer Naci Bey—apparently a Special Organization operative—were unable to subdue the mostly Syrian Orthodox and Syrian Catholic villagers, who were joined by Armenian and Assyrian refugees from surrounding villages. The state even had at its disposal Christian collaborators from Cizre, who hoped to save their own skins. But the Azakh leaders reportedly swore, "We all have to die sometime, do not die in shame and humiliation" and lived up to their fighting words. In mid-November the rebels even managed to raid and put to flight a large Turkish military encampment, killing hundreds. The Ottomans eventually pulled back, leaving the Assyrians in possession of their villages and weapons.[153]

This was a rare event in the maelstrom of Christian destruction. By October virtually the entire Armenian population of Diyarbekir had been either murdered or deported, and, in total, Christian communities lost between 70 and 80 percent of their members. Most of the deportees were killed in valleys around Diyarbekir city—24,000 in Devil's Valley (Şeytan Dere), between Diyarbekir and Urfa, alone. Occasionally, the wealthiest bought their survival. Morgenthau wrote, "I was told that Kazazian, perhaps the richest Armenian at Diarbekir . . . paid a large sum of money to the governor general . . . for the privilege (!) of being imprisoned in order to avoid deportation and certain death. This was arranged and Kazazian and the Armenian Catholic Bishop were imprisoned on a political charge." Others managed to survive by converting, but many converts were also deported and killed.[154]

In late June, when the massacres were in full swing, the Venezuelan mercenary de Nogales arrived in Diyarbekir and met with Reşid, whom he described as "a hyena who kills without ever risking his own life."[155] Reşid did not try to hide the fact that he and his men were committing mass murder. Indeed, he told de Nogales that they had been ordered to do so in a pithy circular telegram from Talât "containing a scant three words: 'Yak—vur—Oldur!' meaning, 'Burn, demolish, kill.'" Although de Nogales was fighting with the Ottomans, he could not help mourning. "As a result of the extermination of the Armenians who were the nucleus of [the vilayet's] artisan and merchant classes," de Nogales recounted, "the bazaars of Djarbekir were almost deserted at the time of my visit; and the city's rich industries of tapestries, Moorish leather, silks and woolens were practically paralyzed."[156]

After the war the British high commissioner in Constantinople, Admiral Somerset Gough-Calthorpe, estimated that the Armenian population of the vilayet had been reduced from 120,000 to 20,000 and the Assyrian population from 81,000 to 23,000. The admiral's goal was not to determine the extent of the injustice committed against the Christians; it was, amid conflicting claims for self-determination, to demonstrate that the existence of such a small Armenian population could not justify demands for Armenian autonomy, much less independence. Still, his report—which was based on Turkish records, an extended tour by British officers, and meetings with the heads of Diyarbekir communities—is revealing.[157]

Other numbers differ in absolute terms but tell the same story. According to Talât's calculations, there were 56,000 Armenians in the vilayet before the war and fewer than 2,000 in 1917. Yet in a telegram sent on September 15, 1915, Reşid claimed to have deported 120,000 Armenians.[158] Historian Uğur Ümit Üngör suggests that altogether some 150,000 Christians were murdered

Ethnic composition of Diyarbekir, according to British calculations, July 1919

Ethnic group	Prewar population	1919 population
Kurds	750,000	600,000
Chaldeans and Assyrians	81,000	23,000
Armenians	120,000	20,000
Turks	3,000	2,500
Yezidis, Greeks, and Circassians	10,000	8,000

in the summer of 1915 in Diyarbekir vilayet, more than half of them, and perhaps as many as two-thirds, belonging to various Assyrian sects.[159]

In late 1915 Reşid was summoned to Constantinople to explain his actions. In doing so, he stated the very position from which the CUP, for public-relations purposes, was trying to distance itself:

> If you, like me in Diyarbekir, had had the opportunity to see at close quarters with what kind of secret plans the Armenians let themselves be possessed, in what prosperity they lived, what an awful animosity they felt toward the state, then you would not today be making any admonitions. The Armenians in the Eastern Provinces were so aggressive . . . if they were allowed to remain in place, not a single Turk or Muslim would be left alive.

It was, he concluded "either them or us."[160]

What happened in Diyarbekir was so grotesque that even high-ranking Ottoman officials could deny neither their horror nor the lawlessness of the perpetrators. In testimony before a postwar court martial in Constantinople, General Vehib Pasha admitted that the treatment of Christians in Diyarbekir constituted "crimes" of incomparable "magnitude and tragic character." In "number and nature," they "went beyond all the crimes" he otherwise described to the court martial. Accompanying the supposedly protected classes of Greeks and Assyrians, "Families who had been known for centuries for their loyalty to the state and the services they rendered it, were killed, along with their children."[161]

Urfa

After the massacres of 1895, Urfa was left with a relatively small Armenian population. According to Francis H. Leslie, a U.S. consular agent and head of the local American mission, there were only four Christian villages and about ten of mixed population within a day's journey.[162] Lacking Christians to teach and proselytize, Leslie and his fellow missionaries busied themselves with humanitarian work among Muslims and ran a handkerchief factory. By October 1914 Leslie, like many foreigners elsewhere in Anatolia, did not feel any special tension around him: "We cannot see . . . that the Moslems are in any respect less friendly, at least not in our city. . . . There seems to be no cause for alarm."[163]

His mind would soon change. From late May 1915, long columns of deportees began passing through the city on their way to the desert. In Urfa's old town—according to local lore, a holy site where the prophet Abraham was born and persecuted by Nimrod, the king—people thronged the dusty pavements to watch the ragged survivors from Zeytun, Trabzon, Erzurum, Erzincan, Harput, and Diyarbekir slog through.[164] In August Leslie reported that for weeks he had "witnessed the most terrible cruelties inflicted upon the thousands of Christian exiles who have daily been passing through our city from the northern cities. All tell the same story and bear the same scars: their men were all killed on the first day's march from their cities, after which the women and girls were constantly robbed of their money, bedding, and clothing, and beaten, criminally abused and abducted along the way." Upon arrival in Urfa, some women were taken by local Muslim men. Many others, and children, died in an encampment outside the city.[165]

In the suffering of the arrivals, Urfa's Armenians could picture their own future. Some responded by stockpiling weapons and ammunition, and, as summer wore on, they would dig tunnels and erect barricades.[166] But little happened. In mid-May, when deportees were first coming through, a few prominent Urfan Armenians were sent off to Rakka and probably killed on the way. Otherwise, the central government's repeated orders to deport and destroy had no effect on the Armenians of Urfa.[167] As late as September 18, after all other eastern regions had been cleansed, the mutessarif, Haydar Bey, was able to report that, with a few exceptions, "no Armenians were deported from this district."[168]

Several factors explain the slow pace of persecution in Urfa. One was Haydar himself. In May and June, he had received the same instructions as other governors, and, to some extent, he did Constantinople's bidding. He ordered searches, arrested and tortured notables, and sent a few suspected rabble-rousers to Rakka. He also brandished constantly the threat of mass deportation if Armenians did not hand over rebels or weapons. Yet, while other governors were busy organizing convoys and executions, Haydar dilly-dallied, quietly resisting the Interior Ministry's orders, though never confronting Constantinople head on. How did he get away with it? Perhaps, from the central government's perspective, the relatively small number of Armenians in the sanjak meant it was pointless to quarrel with the mutessarif. Urfa's population numbers put it close to the 5–10 percent Armenian target anyway; further culling was not critical.

Another moderating influence was the presence in Urfa of hundreds of French and English nationals, as well as citizens of other enemy states. Stranded in the city at the start of the war—or relocated there amid the hostilities, from Damascus, Beirut, Aleppo, and elsewhere—these "belligerents" were dispersed in Christians' homes—known addresses, where the authorities could keep tabs on them. This complicated life for Armenians, who had to care for the foreigners and report their activities to the police. But the foreigners may also have saved their Armenian hosts, at least for a time. Officials had to assume that any offenses against Armenians would be reported abroad, so they could not act with impunity.[169]

In nearby Diyarbekir Vali Reşid was unhappy with the tarrying in Urfa. Although he had no formal authority there—Urfa was in Aleppo vilayet—he sent two CUP men and their helpers from his local Special Organization battalion, to "assist" Haydar. In late July the team began to arrest leaders of Urfa's Armenian community and deport them to "that death-trap" Diyarbekir.[170] According to Jakob Künzler, a Swiss deacon and surgeon then in Urfa, it was generally believed that none of the detainees—including fifty imprisoned Armenian notables plus the Armenian bishop and a pharmacist working in Künzler's hospital—"will ever reach Diyarbekir."[171]

August 19 brought Urfa still closer to the brink. In a search of Urfa's Christian quarter, police encountered several deserters, who opened fire, killing two officers. Locals, mostly Kurds, retaliated by slaughtering Christians and looting their houses. An estimated 250 or more were killed before Haydar stopped the massacre, following appeals by missionaries and an American envoy.[172] The city and district were teetering on a precipice when, two days later, Talât telegraphed Haydar to remind him of the deportation order.[173] The elusive mutessarif gave instructions to prepare for removals but did not carry them out.

Urfa finally exploded on September 16, when Armenians ambushed and killed two gendarmes and wounded eight. Police and soldiers then surrounded the Armenian quarter and opened fire. Some Armenians took refuge in missionary compounds. Others took Leslie and seven other Westerners hostage.[174] They also killed some Muslim neighbors. Consul Jackson reported that "the authorities urged" local Kurds to attack the Armenians in response. "This they did willingly in the expectancy of rich loot." But the Armenians,

Armenian militiamen in Urfa 1915, some in Arab dress. The fighters finally surrendered when promised they would not be harmed by their captors, but all were killed by Ottoman troops.

who "had a goodly supply of arms and ammunition," held out and inflicted heavy losses on the Kurds.[175]

At the beginning of October, the Fourth Army arrived to finish the job. One of its commanders, Fakhri Pasha, demanded that Urfa's kadi, Mustafa Şevket Bey, issue a fatwa approving bombardment of the Armenian quarter. The kadi refused, but the army went ahead anyway. Before the attack, a large poster went up warning missionaries not to shelter Armenians and to abandon their buildings, a message that was useless to the hostages. The next day 6,000 troops attacked the Armenians, bombarding the quarter and the mission compound.[176] The Armenians, Jackson recounted, "were literally blown from their homes.[177] In four weeks of fighting, the army lost dozens but crushed what Enver called the "rebellion."[178]

The Armenian fighters were promised that they would be allowed to leave town unharmed if they laid down their arms. But after surrendering, they were shackled and executed—hanged, shot, or pushed from a cliff. Şevket Bey later claimed that Fakhri had ordered Ali Galip (Ghalib), the commander of the 132nd and 133rd infantry regiments, to carry out the executions.[179] As for women, children, and old men, they were corralled into khans inside Urfa, where many died of diseases. "Gendarmes, soldiers, officers and civilians came to these khans and picked out the girls they wanted and carried them away," Elvesta Leslie, a missionary and wife of Francis Leslie, recalled.[180] The survivors were deported to Rakka and Deir Zor, but apparently not directly. Elvesta Leslie later learned that the women and children were turned around again and again. "In this way they were obliged to travel over the same road five or six times."[181]

Distraught by the carnage, Francis Leslie committed suicide on October 30.[182] The American Embassy pressed for an explanation. Talât apparently responded that he would look into the matter, then cabled Haydar, seeking scapegoats. Talât decided that "the escort accompanying the first convoy from Urfa to Rakka witnessed improper behavior on the part of negligent gendarmes, which included the abduction of women." Supposedly it was this that resulted in Francis Leslie's suicide. "Investigations should be made and the culprit gendarmes . . . punished," Talât added.[183]

Haydar's efforts notwithstanding, the Urfa of 1916 was much like the rest of eastern Anatolia: essentially devoid of Armenians. In February 1917, Talât's people estimated that, of 15,000 prewar Armenian residents, 14,000 were un-accounted for.[184] At the beginning of 1916, members of the Commission for Disposition of Abandoned Property *(Emvāl-I Metruke Tevsiye Komisyonu)* ar-rived in Urfa to take charge of Armenian homes and belongings. They broke into Armenians' stores and sold the wares, pocketing some of the receipts and delivering the rest to the government. Some of the money was used to fix Muslim-owned houses burned in the fighting; Muslims were also resettled in former Armenian homes. Some Armenians had entrusted property to the German missionary Franz Eckart, but he betrayed them and sold the prop-erty to the government.[185]

Urfa's Muslims soon realized they needed the Christians. "Finding them-selves without pharmacists, millers, bakers, tanners, shoemakers, dyers, weavers, tailors, or other artisans or tradesmen," Muslims petitioned Cemal Pasha in December 1916 to return tradesmen who had been exiled to Rakka. By May 1917 about 6,000 Armenian deportees were resettled in Urfa. They worked "in perfect harmony with the ferocious characters that only one year before had fanatically destroyed 14,000 Christians," Jackson wrote.[186]

Musadağ

The story of Musadağ, immortalized in Franz Werfel's novel *Forty Days of Musa Dag,* stands out as a symbol of Armenian resistance in the bloody summer and fall of 1915.[187] A few thousand Armenians lived in villages in the rugged foothills of Musadağ (Mt. Moses), which looms over the Mediterranean near the westernmost part of the present-day Turkish-Syrian border. Com-munications between the villages and the regional capital, Antakya (Antioch), were maintained only by "narrow mule paths."[188]

Initially the area was exempted from deportations, but in late July, Constan-tinople ordered the governor to expel the Armenians.[189] By then Reverend Dikran Andreasian, a Protestant pastor who had worked in Zeytun and wit-nessed the destruction of the community, managed to return to his native Musadağ-area village, Yoğunoluk, and helped convince the locals to resist.

On July 31 4,000–5,000 villagers climbed up the mountain and fortified positions around its summit. They had just 120 modern rifles and a cache of shotguns. A Turkish detachment was sent to demand their surrender. The

Armenians refused, and, on August 8, repelled a Turkish assault. The Turks then sent in reinforcements, but their plans were foiled by a daring raid. In the middle of the night, Armenians snuck into the Turkish camp and stole guns, explosives, and ammunition.[190]

In an August 19 cable, Jackson described the actions as "the most effective resistance so far offered by the Armenians."[191] The Turkish army apparently concurred and brought in local Muslim villagers to mount fresh assaults, shelling the defenders and laying siege. But an Armenian messenger slipped through and reached Aleppo, a hundred miles away, with a letter from Andreasian describing their predicament. Jackson then tried to contact the French fleet patrolling the littoral to let them know of the siege and its proximity to the Mediterranean shore.[192] It is unclear whether the message got through, or whether French sailors simply noticed the giant flags hoisted on the mountaintop. In any event the French sent a shore party to make contact with the Armenians and provide them munitions and provisions.[193]

The French then asked the British to assist in the "removal of 5,000 old men, women and children to Cyprus."[194] The British were reluctant, but on

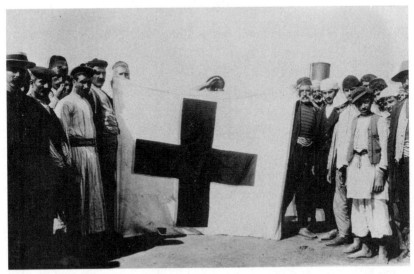

The Armenian defenders of Musadağ, with their flag. U.S. diplomat Jesse B. Jackson described their stand against the Turks as "the most effective resistance so far offered by the Armenians."

September 12, after fifty-three days on the mountaintop, the Armenians trekked down, boarded French warships, and from there were transferred to British custody.[195] The refugees were taken to Port Said, where most remained until war's end.

After the war, most of the refugees were shipped back to Musadağ, which was placed under French rule as part of the Hatay area of the Syrian Mandate. But in 1939 the French transferred the Hatay to Turkey, and most of the Armenians left again. A few remained, though. Today one can visit their descendants at Vakifli, on the slopes of Musadağ. It is the only Armenian village in Turkey.

5

The Western River, and Downstream

For the architects of genocide, the western part of the empire was less challenging than the east. There were fewer Armenians in the metropolitan heartland and on the coasts. Urbane, comparatively well-off, and better integrated in Ottoman life, westerners were also less militant than their more downtrodden eastern cousins. While western Armenians were subject to the same deportation law as easterners, their removal was treated with less urgency and attended by less immediate violence. But Constantinople was only delaying the inevitable, giving the Special Organization time to soften up the easterners before the westerners, too, were deported into their clutches.

Those clutches were tightest in the area of Deir Zor, in Aleppo vilayet. From all points across Anatolia, the rural east and the cosmopolitan west, Armenians trudged through the vilayet on their way to the Deir Zor camps. The arrivals were mostly women, children, elderly people, and the ill or otherwise nonthreatening. All had suffered months of acute hardship. But, unlike countless loved ones, they still had their lives. For a time, they entertained the possibility that they would start over there. Instead they were taken into the desert in groups, shot or stabbed to death, and dumped into unmarked graves.

The West

The deportations in the West were preceded by arrests of Armenian leaders at the local and national levels. During the first two weeks of April 1915, politicians, professionals, and intellectuals were rounded up in Maraş, Hacin

(Saimbeyli), and other central Anatolian towns. The decapitation effort reached peak intensity on the night of April 24, when several hundred leading Armenians, including members of parliament and party leaders, were arrested in Constantinople on charges of assisting the enemy.[1] The detainees included major figures in the national movement identifiable to Armenians throughout the empire.[2] All were deported to the villages of Ayaş and Çankırı in central Anatolia; most were later murdered.[3]

With the elite out of the way—an elite that could influence outsiders and organize Armenians in the east—the west could be left alone for a while. Only in August–October, when the deportation and massacres in the east were drawing down, were orders issued to start deporting large groups of Armenians from the west.

Most western communities were denuded of Armenians, but Constantinople and Smyrna were important exceptions. In both cases, elites were deported, but quietly, without fanfare, and the masses never joined them on the journey southward. This may reflect an effort to avoid outside scrutiny. As coastal centers of political and commercial life, both cities were home to large foreign communities, including diplomats. Large-scale deportations would be closely observed and could trigger international repercussions. Turkey's German allies would have been embarrassed, and the Americans alienated.

In Smyrna other reasons were also at play. The vali, Rahmi Bey, appears to have opposed the policy. And there were only 13,000 Armenians in the city itself and a few thousand in outlying towns and villages—clearly less than 5 percent of the vilayet's population. Another obstacle was General Liman von Sanders, the German commander of the Ottoman Fifth Army, deployed in Ionia and Gallipoli. He was chiefly worried about potential Ottoman Greek disloyalty but saw little point in persecuting the barely felt Armenians.

When the western deportations began in earnest in the fall, the pattern differed from that in the east. Although murders and arrests occurred, wholesale massacres were few, and men were at times allowed to accompany their families into exile. Where able-bodied men were separated, they might not face immediate execution but instead be forced to march.

Another major difference was the use of rail. By 1915 a rail network connected western and central Anatolia to Baghdad, with the Syrian Desert in between. In some cases western deportees were allowed to buy train tickets to their designated destinations, perhaps because the thousand-mile treks would have been a logistical and security challenge, taxing escorts and affording many opportunities for escape. This dispensation might have made the journey appreciably easier, but instead it created a new hardship. With troops and supplies needed on multiple fronts, the rail system was usually monopolized by the military. Deportees were often barred from boarding trains, and thousands found themselves huddled under guard in railway stations for weeks or months, rain or shine. They lacked food, and disease abounded. A Palestinian-Jewish traveler who passed through such a station in Osmaniye or Gülek, in December 1915, reported, "They were lying about . . . on the sidings and some on the track itself. Some were jostled on to the line when the train arrived, and the engine ran over them, to the joy of the engine driver, who shouted to his friends: 'Did you see how I smashed about 50 of these Armenian swine?'"[4] In November, seeking to speed up removals, Talât ordered that Armenians be allowed only to carry hand luggage onto trains. Officials along the route were ordered to confiscate any other items with promises that they would be returned once the Armenians were settled in their new homes.[5]

Onboard, the deportees were packed tight in small, two-tiered livestock cars. Up to eighty might be crammed in a single car. No food or drink was supplied during the entire journey, which went slowly thanks to the limited rail infrastructure: the lone track carried many trains travelling in both directions, so cars were forced to sidetrack for hours at a time. Many died in the cars. Escape was virtually impossible, as "all along the railway line from Konia to Karaman, Eregli and Bozanti . . . hundreds of thousands of Armenians were pursued by the gendarmes."[6] When the surviving exiles finally disembarked, usually in the town of Pozantı, they still had to march hundreds of miles through arid countryside to reach the deserts of Syria and Iraq.

Edirne

Located in the far northwest, on the European side of the empire, the vilayet of Edirne had no significant "Armenian problem" at the start of the Great War. The Armenian population was small, just 20,000. Attempts by the Balkan states to recruit them in 1912–1913 had gotten nowhere. The few Armenians suspected of disloyalty had been expelled to Bulgaria.[7] Local authorities were more worried about the larger and more threatening Greek and Bulgarian communities.[8] Almost 30,000 Greeks had crossed the border to join the Greek army during the Balkan wars. Many of these volunteers also fought against the Ottomans during the world war.[9]

Thus when Britain and France began bombarding Gallipoli in late February 1915, General Liman ordered the deportation of the region's Greek inhabitants. Greeks were gradually driven from their homes, transferred to Edirne city, and then nudged across the border into neighboring countries.[10] Whereas Armenians were routinely prevented from leaving the empire, forced to stay and be killed, Greeks were encouraged to go. The government furnished travel documents with alacrity, and in short order some 40,000 Greeks emigrated. Their properties were seized, in most cases turned over to muhacirs.[11]

Edirne's governors received the Armenian deportation order in May, but they at first believed, or were given to understand, that they were not expected to comply. Edirne was regarded as marginal, as indicated by its absence from Talât's pedantic deportation summaries of 1917.[12] Adil Bey, the vali in the first half of 1915, welcomed the government's indifference. According to Dashnak sources, he was far from keen on deportations. He did, on orders from the Interior Ministry, have some leading Armenians arrested in late April. But he refrained from torture, trials, and executions.[13] However, later in 1915 he was replaced by Zekeriya Zihni Bey, a CUP stalwart.[14]

On the night of October 27, most of Edirne city's Armenian community was rounded up, and the deportation began. The authorities put on a show of civility. Each of the 500 or so families was provided a carriage; gendarmes helped load the vehicles and direct traffic. But "a few kilometers in[to] the interior," the American consular agent in Edirne, Charles Allen, reported, "the people are compelled to descend from the carriages and proceed on foot, the carriages returning to the city."[15] Many were murdered or died during the initial journey. The rest were put on boats, two of which sank under mysterious circumstances near Tekirdağ (Rodosto), in the Sea of Marmara.[16] The other boats anchored in Izmit, where the deportees disembarked and continued on foot toward the Syrian Desert. In the postwar trials, Edirne's

CUP representative, Abdülgani, "whose power matched that of the vali," was convicted of having planned the murders.[17]

In the wake of the deportation and killings, Austro-Hungarian Consul Arthur Nadamlenzki lamented that "all city life has ceased" in Edirne. "The shops are closed at 3 in the afternoon. Armenians and Greeks do not dare to leave their houses: the entire Christian population is passing anguished hours and living in constant fear."[18] Houses were confiscated and looted. The authorities invited muhacirs and locals, presumably Muslims, to rent them.[19]

Halil Bey, the Ottoman foreign minister, told Morgenthau that the Edirne deportation was a mistake, the personal initiative of Zihni Bey, the zealous new vali. By the middle of November, Talât had ordered Zihni to halt the deportation.[20] But in early March 1916, the rest of Edirne's Armenians were deported, including the chief cleric, Archimandrite Arsen, who was dragged

The Western River of Armenian Deportation and Murder

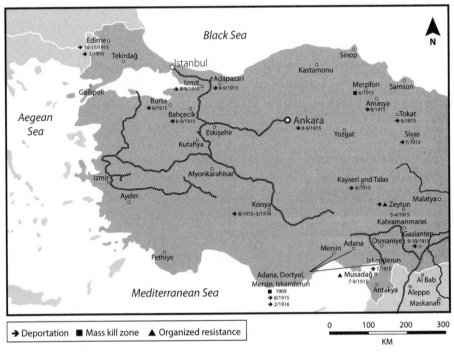

through the streets and beaten. "Only conversion to Islam can save the unfortunate victims," Nadamlenzki reported. "Forty families have already submitted requests for conversion."[21] Permission was granted, but a few days later several converts were caught trying to cross the border to Bulgaria. The authorities then revoked the entire group's conversion, declaring, "They have not become Muslims in their hearts."[22]

Izmit

Since the sixteenth century, Izmit, the city and mutasarriflik (a kind of sanjak), had been major Armenian centers. The absence of major Muslim religious sites meant that more ardent believers tended to spend their time elsewhere, making Izmit a relatively welcoming place for Christians. And Armenians there took advantage of proximity to Constantinople and the ports of the Marmara to develop a thriving silk industry.

But no region was immune to the crackdown. At the beginning of the war, the authorities carried out systematic searches and discovered guns and bomb caches in Armenian homes in towns and villages around Izmit, including Bahçecik (Bardizag), Arslanbey, Döngel, and Yuvacık. The German consul-general in Constantinople later claimed that most of the bombs were antiques, made, ironically, by Armenians collaborating with the Young Turks against Abdülhamid's regime years before.[23] Around the same time, a number of Izmit inhabitants were arrested on suspicion of contacting a French spy ring. Then, in April 1915, many local leaders were arrested. Abuse and torture seem to have been minimal, and most were released. In May police began patrolling Izmit's Armenian quarters, looking for deserters. In one incident, shots were fired and a deserter wounded. Emboldened by what they had found, police then undertook more searches and arrests.[24]

On July 20 official notices went up around town, instructing the Armenians to prepare to leave. People packed suitcases and sold belongings, but the deportation was delayed, perhaps at foreign insistence. Morgenthau had, after all, secured from Enver a promise that these deportations "would be done with moderation and decency."[25] But Talât was insistent. On August 9 he cabled Izmit's mutesarrif to ask why the deportation was being delayed.[26] At this point, Morgenthau wrote, the government's "decision was definitely rendered."

Supposedly the authorities "had found 100 bombs at Adabazar [Adapazarı] and were afraid that the Russians might come . . . and the Armenians in that region might assist them!" Morgenthau was incredulous, given the distance to the Russian front.[27]

A few days after Talât's cable, thousands of families and soldiers were deported from Izmit and surrounding towns and villages. Armenian properties were looted. A range of officials took part, from the mayors of Bahçecik and Derbend to the local prison warden and the CUP secretaries for Adapazarı and Izmit mutesarriflik. The Armenians either were dispatched southeastward or scattered among larger neighboring Turkish villages, in line with the 5 percent rule.[28]

While the women, children, elderly, and infirm traveled by train, some men were sent out on foot. Dr. William Dodd of the American hospital in Konya encountered Izmit deportees as they entered the town's train station:

> They came by hundreds on train after train. They had been compelled to pay the railway fare, 180 piasters for each person, and then were packed into box-cars forty to forty-five in the car, men women and children, sick and well, for the journey that took four or five days. There were deaths on the cars, there were babies born in the midst of this crowd, there were those who threw themselves into the lake on the way. Of the beatings and treatment received before starting I have heard much.[29]

The deportees were led to believe that Konya would be their destination, where they would be reunited with the men sent on foot. But, for many, the stay in Konya proved as temporary as it was hazardous. For months, while the rails were devoted to military usage, deportees were stuck in the city. Those who could afford to rented rooms; others camped in the open or in makeshift tents near the station.[30] Eventually many of the deportees were put on trains to Pozantı, from which they continued to the desert on foot, still without their husbands and fathers.[31] At one point that summer, a group of Izmit Armenian Protestants and state employees whose expertise was thought indispensable received special permission to return with their families. They made their way home, only to have their permits torn up by the vali. They were sent back to Konya.[32]

Some Izmit-area Armenians, mainly from Bahçecik, were massacred as they left town.[33] This seems to be what an Austrian diplomat had in mind when he reported to his foreign office, "A specialist for the slaughter of Armenians whom I personally know, ex-vali of Adana Emin Buad, . . . was sent to Ismid on a secret mission to organize a small, condensed version of his work in Adana."[34] The diplomat was referring to the killing of thousands in that city in 1909, amid an attempted coup against the new CUP-led government.

Those who survived the journey to the desert reached their destination more than seven months after setting out.[35] At the end of the war, a British officer, Lieutenant C. E. S. Palmer, estimated that, in total, about 120,000 Armenians had been deported from Izmit mutesarriflik. About 30,000 were accounted for, living in other regions of the empire; only 4,000 remained in the mutesarriflik.[36] Talât's 1917 numbers were considerably lower, but the ratio was similar. According to his black book, there were just over 56,000 Armenians in the mutesarriflik before the deportation, of whom slightly more than 13,000 were alive afterward, mostly living elsewhere.[37]

Bursa

Both the governor and CUP responsible secretary in Bursa pushed for deportations from an early date, but higher-ups apparently held them back. Deportation from the vilayet was finally announced on August 14.[38] Armenians were essential to the international silk trade centered on Bursa, but, as elsewhere, their economic clout could not protect them. "All Armenians must be deported," the vali declared, "without regard for gender, age and health." During the postwar trials, a prosecutor accused the secretary, Midhat, of going out of his way to ensure immediate removal of the sick, who were usually exempted from initial deportation orders. Per local directives, Armenians' property would be used to pay their debts to merchants and suppliers and otherwise would be sealed away. Their houses would be rented out. The deportees were given three days to prepare for departure. They sold what they could; heirlooms went for a pittance. Officials told the deportees that they would be settled in Konya, but at this point well-founded rumors held that, from there, they would continue on foot to Deir Zor.[39] The expulsions kicked off on August 18, with about 1,800 Armenians loaded onto 500 ox carts. More would be dispatched in the days that followed.[40]

At the beginning of September Dr. Wilfred Post, another American physician working at the hospital in Konya, encountered "perhaps 5,000 exiles" from Bursa. They camped in fields near the rail station, begged in the streets, and waited for a train. The deportees told Post that the authorities seemed intent on starving them to death: "Within two weeks the Government had made two distributions of bread, neither of them sufficient for more than one day, and had given nothing else." The deportees met further abuse on arrival in Konya, according to Post. "I myself saw police beating the people with whips and sticks when a few of them in a perfectly orderly way attempted to talk to some of their fellow-exiles on the train, and they were in general treated as though they were criminals." At Çay, sixty miles northwest of Konya, Post observed "perhaps a couple of thousand" en route. "Here the men and women were together, and the Turks had not succeeded in carrying off more than two girls. By keeping constant guard the Armenians, although unarmed, had been able to frighten the assailants away." Still, there was "great suffering, followed by sickness and some deaths, especially among the children. A good many of the people had gone insane."[41]

After the deportations, Bursa's authorities, like similarly thorough officials elsewhere, discovered that they had exiled most of their region's skilled mechanics, artisans, and bankers. In September the officials pleaded with the central government to permit some Armenians to return.[42] A few were allowed back, but their homecoming was fraught. In October, perhaps in order to justify persecution of the returnees, the vali informed Talât that "Armenian gangs" had resurfaced and renewed sabotage operations in the area.[43] Several alleged saboteurs were eventually caught, tried, and sentenced to death.[44] The evidence supporting the allegations was questionable at best. During the postwar tribunals, Turkish prosecutors argued there were no such gangs.[45]

According to Talât's summaries, 66,413 people were deported from Bursa vilayet during the war, and fewer than 3,000 Armenians remained afterward. Only about 10,000 of the deportees were alive in 1917.[46]

Ankara

Hasan Mazhar Bey, the vali of Ankara, was one of several in western Anatolia who opposed the CUP's campaign. The party suspected as much. Considered a sentimental relic of the ancien regime, Mazhar was kept out of Constantinople's decision-making. He had his first inkling of the deportation plan on April 25, 1915, when he was informed that 180 alleged Armenian *komitecis*—members of revolutionary committees—would be passing through and that another hundred had been sent to the nearby town of Çankiri. He was ordered to provide men to assist the guard detail.[47]

Mazhar stalled. "I pretended not to understand," he testified several years later. "As you know, other provinces were done with the deportations before I had even started."[48] Rather than begin deportations, he decided to investigate the government's allegation that Ankara's Armenians were engaged in mass treason. Finding no evidence, he asked Muslim notables to sign a petition to this effect and sent it to the Interior Ministry.[49]

By July the government had lost patience with Mazhar's delays. Talât sent to Ankara a new police chief and deputy governor, Atif Bey, a young and zealous CUP apparatchik. His job was to carry out the deportation, no matter Mazhar's wishes. Mazhar later recounted, "One day Atif Bey came to me and orally conveyed the interior minister's orders that the Armenians were to be murdered during the deportation. 'No, Atif Bey,' I said, 'I am a governor, not a bandit, I cannot do this, I will leave this post and you can come and do it.'"[50] Mazhar resigned on July 25, and Atif was named acting vali. To remain in step with the eastern provinces, Atif and his men had to move fast. In a matter of days they carried out the preliminaries: they searched for arms, arrested Armenian leaders, and formed a local branch of the Special Organization comprising gangs of volunteers and ex-prisoners.

On August 11 Ankara's entire Armenian population was rounded up and concentrated in a number of buildings. The first removed were the notables, herded in step to the rhythm of marching bands and murdered in a forest a few hours outside town. Next were convoys of able-bodied men; they were also murdered. Among them were many of the politicians and party figures expelled from Constantinople in April.[51] Lieutenant Palmer would later report that the massacre "was committed at Hassan Oglu Ashi Yozgat, a village

4 hours east" of Ankara. He alleged that "55 troops of a Turkish battalion helped in the massacre."[52]

As in other vilayets, Armenian Catholics and Protestants were initially spared on orders from the central government. But this exemption, requested by foreign ambassadors, was rapidly discarded in secret.[53] Most of Ankara's Catholics and Protestants were eventually deported, and many were killed along the route. According to Richard Lichtheim, *Die Welt*'s correspondent in Constantinople, among Catholic and Protestant males, "only boys under five were permitted to live and all of them were circumcised. Women and girls were made Moslems and distributed."[54]

A Catholic priest from Ankara later told British officials:

After our departure, all our churches, convents, schools, houses and shops were first pillaged and afterwards, burnt down; so that, of a Christian community dating back to the time of St. Paul, there remains not a trace save heaps of cinders. . . . Of 18 Priests who left with me only seven are left, all the others died on the road either of hardship or by violent death.[55]

On September 17, with a final batch of 550 Armenians awaiting departure in Ankara's train station, Atif reported his mission accomplished.[56] "Angora now is a dead town," Stepan Semoukhine—a steward of the Russian Embassy, who had been exiled to Ankara with 129 other Russian Armenians—observed in November. "All goods belonging to Armenians are sold at auction. At six o'clock in the evening everything is dreary and mournful and even the Turkish families are grasped by fear."[57] According to Talât's bookkeeping, before the war there were 44,661 Armenians in the vilayet. After, there were 12,766, with 4,560 of Ankara's Armenians living in other vilayets.[58]

Konya

Konya was chosen as an initial destination of deportees because of its small Armenian population: it could absorb more without compromising its Muslim majority.[59] The number of Armenians there grew quickly, though. According to Dodd, "there were, at one time, 45,000 lying out in the fields with no provision for their food or shelter." Conditions were grotesque. "I saw men and women lying in ditches half-filled with mud and water gasping out their last breath, some conscious and some unconscious," Dodd reported. "The scantiness of the water supply added to their sufferings."[60] He tried to feed them but was overwhelmed by the size of the problem.[61]

The relatively few Armenians native to Konya were deported and killed alongside Armenians sent there from elsewhere. Plans were handled by local CUP agents, whom missionaries referred to as "the Salonika clique."[62] Their greatest obstacle was the clogged railway lines. As Dodd put it, "Emptying out the population is so out of proportion to the executive ability to keep the channels of travel open, that the result is this great damming."[63] Konya's Ereğli station, where lines converged, was a major bottleneck. Deportees had to leave the trains, wait for convoys to form, and then trudge down to Adana and Aleppo.[64] Some managed to escape the forced marches and returned to Konya, but they were usually rounded up, placed in new convoys, and re-deported.[65]

Various ostensibly exempt groups were deported to and from Konya. These included not only Catholics and Protestants but also soldiers' families. Even when soldiers and officers were left in the service—usually because their skills were indispensable—the authorities made their wives' efforts to obtain exemption so difficult that one can hardly imagine the policy was more than a fig leaf. When soldiers' wives asked for exemption, they were required to pay for and prepare a special petition, which then had to be stamped by three different agencies, including, absurdly, the Hejaz railway. If the petition was accepted, the wife had to pay another fee to telegram her husband's unit and verify the request. Navigating this bureaucratic thicket was not only expensive but also time-consuming. In many cases, verification did not arrive when needed, and ostensibly exempt families were deported along with everyone else.[66]

In Konya the perpetrators moved quickly in order to avoid obstruction by an incoming vali—Celal Bey, the deportation opponent previously stationed in Aleppo. Transferring Celal to Konya allowed the government to kill two birds with one stone. The previous vali, Samih, had also been recalcitrant. Though in May 1915 he banished Konya's leading Armenians to the remote town of Sultaniye, he allowed them to take money and receive remittances.[67] Just as the insubordinate Samih had to be removed from Konya, Celal had to be removed from Syria, where deportation survivors would congregate and eventually be annihilated. In Konya, Celal could apply his skills in a location of negligible Armenian population—negligible because the government hoped to carry out the cleansing of Konya during the gap between Samih's and Celal's tenures.[68] Indeed, no deportations were scheduled for the period after Celal's arrival; the Salonika clique was confident it could finish the job before he took his post.[69]

But when Celal finally came in late August, there were still tens of thousands of Armenians stranded in Konya. He refused to continue their deportation. The Special Organization's Nâzım Bey sent CUP Deputy Ali Rıza Efendi to persuade Celal that Armenian removal was crucial for the state's survival and should not be resisted. In any case, Ali Riza claimed, the central government had made its decision.[70] Unconvinced, Celal traveled to Constantinople to argue his case, but, Post later testified, "with diabolical cleverness the officials in Konia plotted in his absence and one day the larger part of that great crowd of 50,000 was driven off on foot with whip and cudgel."[71]

Still, Celal's efforts were not entirely wasted. He probably saved some lives, as reflected in the relatively small percentage of Konya Armenians who were killed. In mid-October, Konya's CUP responsible secretary, Ferid, reported that some 9,600 of its Armenians had been deported, yet Post noted that many thousands still roamed the streets and surrounding fields.[72] Talât was surely disappointed to discover that, according to his calculations, 56 percent of Konya Armenians were accounted for in 1917. That still meant that about 5,700 had disappeared.[73]

Kayseri

In February 1915, after a bomb exploded at the home of an Armenian activist in Kayseri, police conducted searches across the province. Scores of homemade bombs were found. As elsewhere, some were of recent manufacture or were freshly filled with explosives, but most were relics. The usual script then played out to its awful conclusion.

First the government ordered Armenians to surrender their arms. But, recalling 1895–1896, when disarmament preceded slaughter, the Armenians hesitated. In response, there were further searches and more weapons found, most of them old guns.[74] In late April Ottoman officials claimed to have found more bombs and some Martini rifles in an Armenian church.[75] Armenian notables and activists were then rounded up. Under torture, a few admitted to collaborating with the Russians or to heading sabotage cells, but most of the detainees had nothing to do with revolutionary operations.[76] The police then ordered the prisoners, and a few notables still walking free, to prepare for deportation to Diyarbekir. None finished the journey. Within three days of departure, the wagons returned empty, and word spread that they had been murdered.[77] In August dozens of other notables—including a former parliamentary deputy, Hampartsoun Boyadjian—were tried for treason and hanged.[78]

A few days later, fresh orders arrived instructing Kayseri officials to deport the province's entire Armenian community.[79] They were given three days' notice, then dispatched. Along the route they were joined by deportees from neighboring Talas and subjected routinely to robbery, abduction, and other abuses. In many cases, the men were first weeded out and murdered. Clara Richmond, a missionary in Talas, recounted that men and boys from a nearby village were locked in a church, bound in groups of five, taken out, and shot.[80] Some villagers, who had heard of the massacres, resisted the gendarmes. "Most were slaughtered . . . by their Moslem neighbors," an unnamed missionary wrote.[81] In one Kayseri village, Boğazlıyan, the kaymakam ordered 3,160 Armenians massacred. Most of the men were lined up and killed, while women and children were taken to Muslim houses.[82]

On September 5 Vali Zekai reported to the Interior Ministry that "a total of 49,947 Armenians, including Catholics and Protestants, were deported to Aleppo, Sham [Damascus] and Mosul" from Kayseri. The vali and his men were exceedingly diligent: "Seven hundred and sixty . . . who were deported earlier but managed to escape and return and lived in hiding were also captured and sent back to exile," he told his superiors. The deportees included members of supposedly protected classes: some were "families of soldiers and others . . . Catholics and Protestants. These were dispersed in the villages at a ratio of 5% of the population."[83] In November Armenian teachers in the American mission schools—a group that generally managed to pull strings and stay behind for a while—were deported.[84]

Some Kayseri Armenians were initially saved by conversion.[85] "We were told that it was in accordance with the principle that in the new Turkey, no

Christian must be found," a local missionary explained.[86] But the Security
Directorate later decided that the option of lifesaving conversion had been
granted too liberally. The Directorate warned Zekai that Armenians tended
to convert only to save themselves and instructed him not to hesitate to deport converts.[87] The situation was different for younger converts, who could
be forcibly integrated in Muslim communities. Many children in Kayseri were
taken to government orphanages and circumcised.[88]

In March 1916 the surviving leaders of Constantinople's exiled Armenian
community were sent to the Syrian Desert via Kayseri. One of them, a priest
named Grigoris Balakian, wrote in his memoir of entering Talas:

> When our caravan was passing through the streets . . . , we saw in the
> windows of the two-story stone houses women clutching handker-
> chiefs, apparently crying. Subsequently we heard that these were
> Islamized Armenian families who had been moved at the sight of
> new caravans of exiled compatriots. No doubt they thought that we
> too were being taken to Der Zor, that Armenian graveyard without
> tombstones.[89]

According to Ottoman reports and Talât's calculations, there were 47,974
Armenians in Kayseri at the beginning of the twentieth century. By 1917 6,650
lived in the vilayet and 6,979 were living in other parts of the empire. Altogether 71 percent of Kayseri's Armenians had disappeared.[90]

Adana

As mentioned in Chapter 3, in April 1909, during the brief spell of anarchy
following the pro-Hamidian coup d'état, Adana vilayet was the scene of a
large-scale massacre of Christians.[91] By most accounts, more than 20,000
Armenians and Assyrians were murdered by Muslim mobs in Adana city and
throughout the province, leaving behind traumatized, impoverished communities.[92] Although CUP representatives took part in the incitement and
violence, the party denied involvement and saddled reactionary Hamidian
elements with responsibility. Investigations and trials followed; 7 Armenians
and 124 Muslims were convicted and hanged.[93]

By 1915, though, the CUP was little interested even in the appearance of clean hands. Party leaders probably did worry that finishing the job in Adana would constitute proof of its responsibility for the 1909 massacre, but if the Armenian problem was ever to be solved, the region could not be ignored. There were more than 200,000 Armenians in the vilayet, probably the largest concentration in Anatolia. Towns such as Dörtyol were almost entirely Armenian, and Armenians were prominent throughout the area's economy and civic life. The CUP was also keenly aware that, as the capital of the Medieval Armenian kingdom of Cilicia, Adana was seen by many Armenians as the core of a future state. If the vilayet achieved independence alongside the six in the east, Anatolia would be cut off from the Russian border and a wedge driven between the Turkic brothers on either side.[94] What is more, Adana had a particularly large concentration of Protestants and Catholics as well as a dense network of German, American, and British missionary activity. These strong links to the Great Powers made Adana's Armenians appear especially threatening. The CUP would therefore have to be doubly careful: cautious not to provoke its Christian allies and neutral powers, yet also exhaustive in eliminating the danger.

Another aggravating factor was Adana's strategic location. Straddling the country's main route southeastward, Adana served as the gateway for military forces and supplies to Syria and Iraq. The British and French knew it, too. In 1914–1915 their military planners discussed landings near Adana, to sever the Arab provinces from Anatolia, and on December 18, 1914, a landing party from *HMS Doris* destroyed telegraph lines in Adana and sabotaged a nearby railway, causing a train crash. *Doris* then shelled the coast and destroyed railway bridges at Dörtyol and Payas. The gunboat also hosted several Armenian visitors on board.[95] Thereafter, in preparation for a possible large-scale landing, British intelligence sent expatriate Armenian agents into the area to promote dissent. But their attempts to recruit locals were largely unsuccessful. These overtures may have prompted hopes of deliverance, but actual cooperation was rare.[96]

Still, the possibility of Allied-Armenian collusion weighed on the minds of Turkish officials, prompting home searches. In April 1915 a few pistols and hunting rifles were found in Adana city, precipitating the arrest and torture of notables.[97] Later that month Cemal Pasha, the 4th Army commander, ordered the deportation of some Armenians from Adana city and Hacin and all the Armenians of Dörtyol and the port city of Mersin.[98] Cemal's reasoning was probably based on military concerns, but his orders were incompatible with the plan taking shape in Constantinople: the deported Armenians were to be sent to unspecified locations in the Anatolian interior, not to the desert. The timeline probably also differed from that taking shape in the CUP's discussions. Talât rescinded the order.[99]

Unaware of the bigger picture, the American consul in Mersin ascribed the vacillation to tension between local CUP leaders and Adana's vali, Hakki Bey. Hakki's attitude upset CUP stalwarts, who reported him to Constantinople.[100] Yet it seems that, at this stage, the source of indecision was the government itself. Even when the general deportation order arrived in May 1915, Adana city and a few surrounding towns were exempted.[101]

The rest of the vilayet, however, was not. Thousands were directed to railway stations, but the trains going south were already filled to capacity with soldiers and supplies bound for the front. As in Konya, Armenians camped outside the stations for weeks.[102] Then, on August 4, Talât ordered the deportation of Adana city's Armenians, as well as those of Mersin and Sis. As usual, the government took measures to prevent the Armenians from profitably selling their property and to assure that it fell into Muslim hands.[103] Thousands more joined the camps around the stations.[104] Catholics and Protestants were uprooted with the rest. Eugen Büge, the local German consul, thought that the order to spare Catholics and Protestants was a deliberate deception, with secret orders to do otherwise delivered to the vali by a special envoy, CUP Secretary Ali Munif Bey.[105]

By late August, as its own Armenians were leaving, Adana was flooded by thousands of deportees from central Anatolia. They filled the encampments, many dying of disease and malnutrition. Some were executed. Taking stock of the crowd passing through the city and the many dying there and en route, Büge surmised that "the number of Armenians ordered to be murdered probably already exceeds the amount of victims in the Young Turkish massacre of 1909."[106] William Nesbitt Chambers, an Adana-based Canadian missionary, felt similarly. "We thought that the massacres [in 1909] were the acme of ruthless cruelty," he wrote. "But they were humane as compared to this."[107]

The deportations were briefly halted in October. There is reason to believe that Cemal was responsible—that he tried to prevent ethnic cleansing in Adana, an area under his jurisdiction, though he did not directly challenge the policy elsewhere.[108] Kevorkian suggests that "his opposition" was "rooted in a certain military rationale that consisted in profiting from the Armenian deportees' labor power before liquidating them." Yet Cemal worked, sometimes with foreign consuls, to assist the refugees created by the deportation process; quite a few were spared.[109]

Cemal's exact motivations are hard to pin down. Aaron Aaronsohn, a Palestinian-Jewish agronomist and British spy, who had worked closely with Cemal in the eradication of Palestine's 1915 locust plague, provides insight into the general's thinking. On the one hand, Aaronsohn told his British handlers that at one point Cemal went to Constantinople and "insisted that the massacres should cease, urging that it was not only a crime but a mistake." Those killed and deported were, he said, needed for "public works in Syria and Palestine." Aaronsohn reported that, in appreciation, 40,000 Armenians paraded past Cemal's house in Constantinople as he stood on the balcony "with his arms folded like Napoleon the Great."

But Aaronsohn concluded that Cemal was no great humanitarian. Rather, his "actions [were] a mere farce to impress the outside world, and to increase [his own] importance." In other circumstances, he had sent off the Armenians in "his clutches . . . to remote parts of Syria and Palestine" to prevent them infecting the Turkish population with diseases. Upon visiting Cemal's refugee camps, Aaronsohn discovered a deep vein of exploitation and sadism:

> They were made to live in the desert. Men, women and children were put to hard labour, and each working man and woman received 2 pence a day. . . . In some cases, there was no water nearer than 6 miles. . . . The writer has seen an overdue train, carrying water, arrive. The Armenians, parched with thirst, rushed to the halting place, each carrying an earthen jar or a tin. As soon as the train stopped it was besieged by the mob, which was beaten back by the Turkish guard. . . . All the taps of the tanks were then turned on and the water allowed to run to waste in full view of the hundreds who were dying for want of it. The administration duly

despatched water to the desert, and that was enough as far as Djemal
Pasha and his friends were concerned. . . . Hunger and thirst swept away
half the numbers in these camps in a few weeks. . . . In the meantime,
Djemal loudly proclaimed that he was colonizing waste lands with thrifty
Armenians, which was enough for the inspired press and the Central
Powers to give out to the world that in the last two years Syria and Pal-
estine under Djemal's administration had flourished.[110]

Whatever Cemal believed and sought to achieve, in February 1916 the government launched another wave of deportations in the vilayet, mostly of aged
and handicapped Armenians from Adana city.[111] And some evidence indicates
that earlier deportees were being massacred. A group had managed to sneak
back and find work on the Baghdad railway under German supervision. But
when the government discovered the breach, the workers, numbering between
9,000 and 11,000, were rounded up and sent away once more. Unconfirmed
reports allege that the majority were killed.[112]

Downstream: The Syrian Desert

The architects of genocide envisioned a site of exile simultaneously within and
without. It had to be a place deep in the empire, where Armenians who survived the massacres and marches would be far from the battlefield and the foreign powers arrayed there. But it also had to be far from home and from other
Ottoman Christians who might rally to their side. The sort of place where they
could be lost and forgotten.

That place was the Syrian Desert, in particular the area encompassed by
Aleppo and Deir Zor vilayets. The city of Aleppo became a critical transit
point for Armenians from eastern and western Anatolia alike. Some, after
an arduous stay in the Aleppo camps, were settled for a time in Mosul. But
in the course of 1916–1917, the second stage of the Armenian Genocide,
most of those who had reached Aleppo—along with the estimated 37,000
Armenians native to it—were dispatched to Rās al-'Ayn or Deir Zor for
extermination.[113]

Aleppo

When Celal Bey, Aleppo's vali, learned in April 1915 that deportees from Zeytun and Maraş were heading his way, he asked Constantinople for funds to prepare lodgings. The request revealed his naiveté. A moderate, relative pluralist, and outsider in CUP circles, Celal was not privy to the government's plan for the Armenians. He later recalled that, in response to his request, the government "sent a functionary, whose official title was 'Head of the Muhacirs Section at the Directorate for Tribes and Muhacir Settlement,' but in reality was charged with deporting the Armenians."[114]

The convoys began arriving in early summer. Celal was told that Aleppo would be their ultimate destination, but he was also ordered to deport all his vilayet's Armenians to Deir Zor. He refused on the grounds that doing so would be criminal. It was then that Talat ordered Celal moved to Konya and replaced him with Bekir Bey. But Bekir, it turned out, was also no genocide enthusiast, and he made excuses to avoid deporting Aleppo's Armenians. He also asked Talât to send deportees to vilayets other than Aleppo.[115]

In late October Talât solved this critical vilayet's administrative problem by installing as vali one of his own relatives, Mustafa Abdülhalik Bey. Abdülhalik and his aides immediately started deporting Armenians from the coastal areas of Alexandretta, Antakya, and Harem. He also ordered the deportation of Armenians from Antep and Kilis, but effective intervention by Consul-General Jackson, backed by Morgenthau, delayed implementation.[116] However, the Americans were unable to prevent another round of deportations beginning in August.[117]

Abdülhalik was assisted by likeminded local officials such as Ahmet Bey, the newly appointed mutesarrif of Antep. After the war, the British occupying Aleppo laid hold of a batch of telegrams containing correspondence between Abdülhalik and Ahmet. In one, dated November 7, 1915, Ahmet requested female deportees be sent to his district, probably for use as servants and concubines.[118] On January 11, 1916, after Antep had been emptied of its own Armenians, Abdülhalik wrote Ahmet, "We hear that there are Armenians from Sivas and Kharput in your vicinity. Do not give them any opportunity of settling there, and, by the methods you are acquainted with, which have already been communicated to you, do what is necessary and report the results."[119] A week later Ahmet replied,

> It has been ascertained that there are about five hundred people from the said provinces in the vicinity of Roum Kale, which is under our jurisdiction. The Kaimakam of Roum Kale reports that most of them are women and children, and that, in accordance with the methods, with which the Turkish officials were acquainted . . . these women and children have been sent under Kurdish guards with the understanding that they are never to return.[120]

We do not know why it was deemed necessary to promptly drive off the surviving women and children from Sivas and Harput, rather than allow them to continue south and expire slowly like many others. But Ahmet was not about to question orders.

As for the many thousands of deportees who filled Aleppo, they had survived massacre, abduction, rape, robbery, disease, exposure, and starvation, yet the last leg of their journey may have been the most agonizing.[121] Rössler, the German consul in Aleppo, provides a glimpse into the particular horrors of a forced march coming to its conclusion. On September 12, 1915, he witnessed the arrival of 2,000 battered Armenians. "Using whips, the gendarmes drove the wretched, emaciated creatures, many of whom had a death-look about them, through the streets of Aleppo to the train station, without permitting them to drink a drop of water or to receive a piece of bread," he wrote. "Two women fell down to give birth and were only protected from being whipped by the gendarmes by town dwellers, who rushed to help them."[122]

The refugees faced horrific living conditions. Crowded into empty buildings, khans, and churches, hundreds died in their own excrement each day.[123] The arrivals of early 1916 carried a strain of typhus that killed hundreds more, including soldiers.[124] "On some days the funeral carts were insufficient to carry the dead to the cemeteries," de Nogales observed.[125] Some of the survivors were sent to makeshift camps erected in barren fields north of the city. But the camps could only house a fraction of the deportees, so the rest hunkered down on their fringes. The camp-dwellers were easy prey for gendarmes.

Armenian doctors hanged in Aleppo, 1916, with Turkish officers standing in the foreground.

Each day they collected groups of women, children, and old people—there were almost no able-bodied men—from the camps and drove them toward Deir Zor.[126]

Jackson and his assistants were energetic in helping Armenians deported to and from Aleppo. For instance, American diplomats collected valuables from deportees at their places of origin and worked hard to locate the owners downstream. When the authorities told Jackson to stop, he ignored them. When his consular resources were depleted, he sought and received additional funds from the U.S. State Department. "Very soon the consulate was the Mecca for the deported Armenians that were lucky enough to arrive with sufficient strength to carry them hither," he wrote.[127]

The consulate tried to get the deportees off the streets, where they were targets for deportation sweeps and slavers; women were sold for a pittance in the markets of Aleppo. Fortunately diplomats found Muslims, Christians, and Jews willing to take in deportees. For the people of Aleppo, it was not easy to absorb deportees, who were mostly weak and unhealthy and spoke little Arabic. Still the consulate managed to place some 40,000 women and children in homes as servants, where presumably they were better off than in the homes of Turks to the north and certainly better off than massacre victims.[128]

Saving men was more difficult, but Jackson and his contacts managed to persuade Cemal to place them in factories producing uniforms and other items. The authorities set up six textile factories in Aleppo vilayet employing 10,000 men and women. They worked for virtually nothing—a bowl of soup and a loaf of bread a day, per the terms Jackson had arranged with Cemal. But they did receive something of priceless value: documents assuring their status as workers in war industries, which saved them from deportation and almost-certain death.[129]

Orphans constituted another major humanitarian challenge. Many were sent to the camps, but thousands still thronged Aleppo's streets. The authorities opened an orphanage, but it was badly managed and children died there in droves. When local Armenians came to donate blankets, the Turks sent them away, saying that the government could take care of them. In November, Rössler reported the anguished findings of Baron von Kress, Cemal's German chief of staff, who had inspected the orphanage:

> When the Turks have the men killed during the processions, they can use the excuse that they must defend themselves against rebellion; when women and children are raped and kidnapped, the Turks can use the excuse that they do not have the Kurds and gendarmes under control; when they let those in the processions starve, they can use the excuse that the difficulties of feeding people on the march are so great that they cannot master them; but when they let the children in the middle of the town of Aleppo become run-down from hunger and dirt, then that is inexcusable.[130]

American missionaries responded to the situation by inviting the experienced Swiss missionary Beatrice Rohner to Aleppo to take charge of the orphanage. Cemal assented, and, on December 29, 1915, she was appointed director. Taking charge of more than a thousand orphans, she rented new premises; hired employees, including Armenians who thus acquired protection; and obtained food and clothing from all possible sources, including the reluctant government.[131]

In addition to running the orphanage, Rohner worked with Jackson to establish an underground network of communication and support with the outlying deportation camps. Older kids in the orphanage and other young Armenians would smuggle letters between the deportees and the townspeople and bring the deportees money. The network proved a crucial source of witness and, as long as the deportees were still alive, humanitarian aid: the smuggled letters informed aid workers and diplomats of camp conditions and of the fate that befell residents there, and some deportees were able to use the money to live another day or bribe officials to set them free.[132] The operation ground to a halt in September 1916, when the Turks caught one of the messengers, who, under torture, revealed the system's workings. After the network was exposed, Rohner concentrated exclusively on the orphanage. Eventually the authorities shut that down, too, and transferred the wards to a facility in Lebanon run by Halide Edip, who later became a well-known Turkish nationalist politician and women's rights activist. In the Lebanese orphanage, the children were

Armenian refugee children in Aleppo. Many were later transferred to Turkish orphanages in Lebanon and brought up as Muslims.

circumcised and indoctrinated in Turkish nationalism.[133] Her work subverted, Rohner suffered a nervous breakdown in March 1917 and left Aleppo.[134]

On April 20, 1917, when the United States entered the war, there were still some 50,000 Armenians in Aleppo and almost twice that number in surrounding villages and towns. This despite the removal over the previous months of countless locals and northern deportees to the camps and the desert beyond. Forced to depart, Jackson entrusted refugee relief to Emil Zollinger, a Swiss businessman and philanthropist.[135]

Because Aleppo's native Armenians lived relatively close to the Syrian Desert, and so did not have far to march, and because some of the vilayet's governors and consuls were active in protecting them, they fared well compared to Armenians from other vilayets. Of 37,000 prewar Armenians, almost 14,000 survived in the vilayet itself and almost 20,000 elsewhere in Syria, according to Talât's 1917 estimates. Moreover, another 24,000 Armenians from other vilayets managed to endure in Aleppo vilayet.[136] However, many of them were later sent to Deir Zor, where they may have perished after Talât's staff assembled these statistics.

Deir Zor and Rās al-'Ayn

From the start of mass deportations in 1915, Deir Zor was a major refugee destination. By August 1915, 15,000 Armenians had reached the town, and thousands more were living in makeshift camps nearby.[137]

We do not know if the architects of the second phase of the Armenian Genocide also designated Deir Zor from the beginning as the final site of liquidation, but they clearly did not intend that deportees who reached the town should form a community there. Little preparation had been made for their arrival; the situation was so desperate that, according to Jackson, parents sometimes had to sell children to keep their siblings alive.[138] Indeed, the central government took active measures to prevent any sort of regrouping at Deir Zor. For instance, on July 24, the Security Directorate warned the mutessarif, Ali Suat Bey, that Armenian Catholicos Sahag and his companion Eczaci (Ejzaji) Serkis were on the way to the region: under no circumstances should they be allowed to make contact with the deportees. Instead these clerics were to be ordered to return to Aleppo.[139]

After the war, Jackson summed up the situation in late summer 1915: "The daily departure of convoys of Armenians, re-deported from the encampments at Aleppo, as well as many thousands that were sent direct from the interior, finally numbered about 60,000 collected at Deir el-Zor." There, "for about a year they were as well taken care of as possible with the limited means" at Suat's disposal. He did what he could to settle deportees on farmland, build makeshift homes, and provide food, clothing, and medical assistance. Constantinople asked him repeatedly "to make other disposition of them," Jackson wrote, referring to the deportees. But Suat pretended not to understand the government's intentions.[140] He probably was also aware of the Jackson-Rohner network supplying the Deir Zor deportees and may have secretly supported it.[141]

Suat was also in charge of the camp in Rās al-'Ayn, more than a hundred miles to the north, where he allowed some of the deportees to move into town and open small businesses. For a while, some Armenians believed they would be able to build new lives under Suat's protection.[142] Even Morgenthau, who always suspected that the purpose of the deportations was annihilation, had momentary pangs of optimism. In a letter to his wife, he wrote that he "was surprised to hear that the Armenians at Zor were fairly well satisfied; that they had already settled down there and were earning their living."[143]

But even under Suat's relatively benign rule, the death rate was appalling. A German officer who visited Deir Zor in what was most likely late October 1915 learned from a local doctor that, with mounting hunger and plague, 150 to 200 people were dying each day. "No linguistic expression of thought can even come close to describing the reality of this human misery," the officer wrote. "And this tragic heap is continually building up. . . . Hundreds of unburied corpses, dragged off, then lie further away!"[144] There was only so much a conscientious local official could do, given the state of the arrivals. In a September letter, a German railway engineer described seeing in Rās al-'Ayn "a transport of 200 girls and women" who "arrived . . . completely naked: Shoes, shirts, in short: everything had been taken from them and they were left to travel naked for four days under the burning sun—40 degrees [Centigrade] in the shade—mocked at and derided by the soldiers accompanying them . . . . 'We have been given strict orders by the government to treat you in this manner," officials back home had told them.[145]

As bad as things had gotten in late summer, in early November, the flow of arrivals increased further. The government realized that some of the deportees sent to Aleppo, perhaps emboldened by Cemal Pasha's relatively lenient treatment, had found ways to continue to Damascus and other Syrian towns. So the Interior Ministry ordered that deportations to Aleppo cease.[146] Instead convoys were to be sent eastward using two direct routes: one, along the Euphrates, to Deir Zor, the other to Rās al-'Ayn and Mosul, via the Baghdad Railway.[147]

As the pressure on Deir Zor increased, Suat Bey could no longer avoid acknowledging instructions. The postwar court-martials reveal that Talât eventually had enough, sending Suat a destroy-after-reading telegram demanding that he comply with orders.[148] Suat then sought to placate Constantinople by adhering to its overt instruction to ensure that Armenians did not comprise more than 10 percent of the Deir Zor area's population.[149] When, in early 1916, this proportion was exceeded, he sent two large convoys to Mosul. He still did not take deportation to mean massacre. According to the German consul in Mosul, the convoys reached the town. Jackson, who was sure the convoys would not make Mosul, was pleasantly surprised by the survival rate.[150]

Later convoys would not be so lucky. In June 1916 the Interior Ministry, tired of Suat's guileful resistance, sent him packing to Baghdad, an area almost uninvolved in the genocide. His replacement was Salih Zeki, who as kaymakam of Everek, in Kayseri vilayet, had efficiently and brutally rid his territory of Armenians. This was likely one outcome of February 1916 discussions in Constantinople. At the time Talât estimated that more than 200,000 Armenians were still alive in northern Syria, a number that worried him greatly and led to redoubled extermination efforts.[151] But the CUP leadership feared that a heightened project of murder in Aleppo vilayet would leak out via the American consulate. Enver and Talât knew that Jackson was keeping tabs and reporting to the State Department. Hence another probable outcome of the meetings: that same month, Enver ordered Jackson to deliver all the consulate's mail "unsealed to the post office authorities, to be read and censored by the Turkish military officials."[152]

The final chapter of this stage of the genocide, marked by mass murder along the Euphrates, began shortly after the February discussions. In March the government officially announced an end to deportations, no doubt to re-

A pile of bodies in the desert. In spring and summer 1916, the Turks and their helpers—Kurds, Circassians, Chechens, and Arabs—systematically murdered many of the Armenian deportees who had reached the Deir Zor area of northeastern Syria.

lieve American, and possibly German, pressure.[153] But immediately afterward, secret instructions went out rescinding that announcement.[154] By April 6 Rössler was reporting that, in just a few days, Circassians and others had massacred most of "the unarmed 14,000 inmates" of the Armenian camp in Rās al-'Ayn.[155] Each day 300–500 inmates were taken out and killed six miles from the camp and their bodies thrown into the Euphrates. The kaymakam in charge calmly told a querying Turkish officer that he was "acting on orders."[156] After the killings, a group of Circassians plaited a rope twenty-five yards long from the hair of young women they had killed and sent it as a present to their commander, Pirinççioğlu Feyzi, the parliamentary deputy of Diyarbekir.[157]

So committed was Zeki to the annihilation plan that he carried it out even over the objections of army commanders. In June 1916 the Turkish military was planning Operation Yıldırım, an effort to block the British advance in Iraq. The army recruited several thousand Armenians to help build rafts for use on the Euphrates, a critical component of the operation. But Zeki refused to allow the recruits to join the troops. Instead he sent the recruits off with their families to be murdered on the way to Marrat, a few hours walk south. Unable to rely on the army, Zeki remobilized bands of brigands and organized new ones, comprising Circassians, Kurds, and Chechens from the Rās al-'Ayn area and some local Bedouin Arabs. They did their dirty work in sparsely populated areas at the confluence of the Khabour and Euphrates rivers.[158]

At the beginning of July, the government began concentrating survivors in Deir Zor. Talât instructed Aleppo to send any remaining deportees there.[159] In addition, all deportees previously resettled in Muslim areas of Mosul were ordered back to Deir Zor.[160] From there they were rounded up in groups of thousands and sent across the river southward, with no water or provisions, to expire from thirst and illness.[161] "A hopeless wandering took place," Rohner wrote.[162]

Most of them suffered a fate similar to the Armenian recruits assigned to support Operation Yıldırım. They were told that they were being sent for resettlement at Mosul or to the camp at Marrat. But at Marrat, or at the Khabour River crossing, gendarmes broke the big convoys into smaller groups and handed the refugees over to brigands, who separated the men, robbed those who still carried money or valuables, and killed them.[163] Twenty such

The Syrian Desert, Where the Deportees Were Murdered En Masse, in 1916

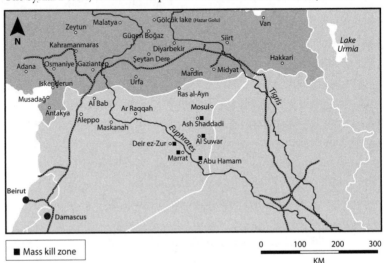

convoys were dispatched from Deir Zor, the first leaving the town on July 15. In the final stage of the killing, later in 1916, those remaining were mostly women and children; they were starved for a while and then handed over to Bedouin tribesmen to finish the job. Often they were killed near Suvar (al-Suwwar).[164] Sometimes, though, they were taken down the Euphrates as far as Abu Hamam, more than fifty miles south of Deir Zor. One eyewitness described the scene at the Abu Hamam camp:

> The people fight for the blood of slaughtered animals which is poured out onto the ground, they nibble at bones they find on manure heaps, they search through horse manure in the hope of finding a few grains of barley and devour them ravenously. They eat the flesh of animals and humans who have died by the wayside. Many of them who cannot stand it any longer throw themselves in the Euphrates, taking their children with them.[165]

Those who managed to survive were driven deeper into the Khabour valley, toward the village of Sheddadiye (al-Shaddadi), "where they were, as a rule, killed behind the hill that looked down on this Arab village."[166]

While more and more Armenians were dispatched from Deir Zor to their deaths, still others were left in the camps awaiting their fates. They left few testimonies on which to draw, but witnesses pass down to us the trauma experienced merely observing their plight. One of these witnesses was August Bernau, a German employee of the American Vacuum Oil company, who lived in Syria and took over Rohner's Aleppo-based clandestine operation after it was compromised. In August, under the pretext of collecting debts, he distributed financial aid to deportees at Deir Zor. "What I have seen surpasses all imagination," he wrote. "To speak of 'a thousand horrors' is too little. . . . I believed I was passing through a corner of hell." He predicted that all the Armenians in the region would soon be dead.[167] At Meskene (Maskanah), another area along the river, one of Jackson's aides reported seeing more than 150 long mounds, in each of which 100 to 300 bodies were buried, and that similar evidence of killing could be found at other points along the river route.[168]

Occasionally Zeki was spotted watching and encouraging killings.[169] He worked diligently to clear Deir Zor. Each day, criers announced that new places of settlement had been found for deportees still in town, and that they should leave when called. As they assembled on one side of the Euphrates Bridge, brigands gathered on the other. Only Armenian women taken as wives or domestics by local Arabs—one per family—were allowed to stay in the city.[170] In September Jackson reported, "The Mutessarif of Der-el-Zor has arranged and carried out the massacre of all the remaining Armenians that were there, some 12,000 in all, having gone personally to superintend the work." Jackson added, "Before the end, all the presentable women and girls were outraged" by men "whose participation was at the invitation or command of the Mutessarif."[171]

According to Talât's statistics, there were 63,000 Armenians in Deir Zor in 1914. In 1917 he found that there were 1,771, a figure later amended, with no explanation, to 6,778.[172] In this case, perhaps more than in any other, the numbers do not tell the story. Between 1915 and 1917, hundreds of thousands were marched to this forlorn destination and vanished in the sand. Yves Ternon suggests that from summer 1915 to the end of the war, about 350,000 people perished in the area.[173] Aram Andonian puts the number of murders during just the five worst months of 1916 at 192,750. The indictment of the Young Turk leadership at the postwar court-martial spoke of 195,750 killed.[174]

At the end of 1916, with his work done, Salih Zeki was recalled to Constantinople. Apparently he arrived at the capital with coin-filled coffers. Immediately after the Ottomans signed the Armistice of Mudros, which ended hostilities with the Allies on October 30, 1918, he went into hiding. He was tried in absentia at the court-martial, convicted, and on April 28, 1920, sentenced to death. The judgment held that Zeki

Organized mounted and marching gangs from among those who had brought over the deported Armenians from various parts of the realm. In his presence, they pounced on the victims who were once again forced to march under the pretext of further deportations, and robbed. . . . Many were murdered and massacred along the Habur basin. . . . Many witnesses, Muslims and non-Muslims, testified [to this] under oath. Based on the evidence in (descending) order of gravity: the testimonies; the contents of investigation reports; the fact that the defendant is on the run; and [other] legal clues, we have concluded, with a clear conscience, that the charges have been sufficiently proven. We have therefore found Zeki Bey guilty of . . . robbing and looting and murdering, and . . . he is to be executed and his property seized.

The punishment was never carried out. Instead Zeki continued to enjoy a life of influence in Turkish politics, later resurfacing as a founder of the country's Communist Party.[175]

6

A Policy of Genocide

There is no question that the deportation of the Armenians was planned and initiated from the political center. Hundreds of documents published by the Ottoman and later Turkish governments make clear that removal was a state project; it was not the incidental result of wartime hardships and local clashes. The deportation was a premeditated, calculated, and pedantically implemented operation.

Two matters, however, are still in dispute. First, the exact timeline of deportation. Did planning begin after the outbreak of violence in Van and Zeytun in March 1915? If so, one could conceivably argue that deportation was a response, wise or unwise, just or unjust, to perceived Armenian treachery in these conflicts. But perhaps there was already a plan in the making in the weeks before Zeytun, and Van, not to mention the Entente landings at Gallipoli, another event that historians have viewed as encouraging CUP fears and the solution of deportation. If planning began before these events, there can be no defense on the basis of paranoid miscalculation.

The second, more crucial, matter is whether the deportation was planned as a genocide. That is, were the deaths—not just the deportations—of between one and two million Armenians, Greeks, and Assyrians during Word War I part of the plan? (We cover Assyrians and Greeks more thoroughly in Chapters 8 and 9.) Or did these deaths result from a combination of war conditions and local initiatives taken by governors, gangsters, and tribesmen driven by ideology, fear, greed, sexual appetite, and religious fervor? If the latter was the case, then was the state ignorant of the killing, or was it just too weak to intervene?

These issues remain controversial in part because there is no smoking gun: no accessible Ottoman master plan or general order of extermination, no protocols of the CUP meetings in which this genocide was discussed and agreed upon. Certainly no policy of genocide was publicly announced.[1] Indeed, at times Ottoman behavior seems inconsistent with such a blanket policy. In key places, notably Constantinople and Izmir, there were almost no deportations during the war and no mass killings. And where Armenians were deported in large numbers, they were not always massacred, at least not at first. This was the case especially in the early phases of deportation. If the leadership had planned throughout to kill off the Armenians wholesale, wouldn't the pattern of action have been uniform around the empire and throughout the deportations? Even if one agrees that the government was responsible for mass killings, one might argue that official behavior was not inconsistent with a process of gradual radicalization during the deportation campaign itself.

The controversy over exactly what the Ottomans planned and when echoes that surrounding the genesis of the World War II Holocaust. In both cases uncertainty has generated debate between so-called intentionalists and functionalists. With respect to the Holocaust, intentionalists argue that the destruction of European Jewry was planned well before it started. The seeds and blueprint of the Holocaust are found in Hitler's *Mein Kampf* and other writings of the 1920s and 1930s, which demonstrate that comprehensive ethnic cleansing of the Jews was a Nazi goal from the first. The Final Solution—the killing of six million Jews and millions of others in death camps and elsewhere—may have begun years later, in 1941, but only because that was when opportunity knocked following the start of Operation Barbarossa, the German invasion of Russia.

Functionalist historians do not disagree that ideological underpinnings of the Holocaust can be found in the earlier writings and speeches of the Nazi elite, among other sources. But these historians argue that the extermination project began in an ad-hoc manner, spurred by *Einsatzgruppen* killings carried out at Babi Yar and elsewhere, amid the fog of Barbarossa. Like the perpetrators of the Final Solution, the Einsatzgruppen and others in the SS and Wehrmacht enjoyed the backing and direction of the state. But unlike the perpetrators of the Final Solution, the early Nazi murder squads claimed that their killings were improvised responses to war circumstances, whether retaliatory or prophylactic. These first massacres and the mass murder of prisoners of war initiated a process of brutalization, whereby respect for life is thrown out the window by the act of killing, spurring more killings. On this view, it was only after the first stages of mass killing that the predicates were in place for an orchestrated effort to exterminate the Jews, which was then planned in Berlin and implemented at the death camps.

Today's consensus synthesizes the intentionalist and functionalist perspectives: bottom-up pressures from the field combined with top-down pressures from the Nazi elite to create the Final Solution. On this understanding Hitler was indeed determined to annihilate world Jewry and was the main driving force behind the Holocaust, but he had had no master plan until well into the war. The Holocaust was therefore a result of "cumulative radicalization" inside Germany and at the front, inflamed by a genocidal ideology that preceded the mass murder.[2]

The same cumulative-radicalization approach has been applied to the Armenian case in 1914–1916, most notably by Donald Bloxham. He suggests that CUP leaders opted for war partly in the vague hope that the conflict would provide an opportunity to solve the Armenian problem once and for all. But, according to Bloxham, evidence does not sustain the argument that solving the problem meant physically destroying the Armenians. Rather, the idea of mass murder, and even deportation on a grand scale, evolved gradually as the war progressed. Killings may have begun already in January 1915 along the Russian frontier, but these were local initiatives, not the initial episodes in a general campaign of genocide. "Only by the summer of 1915 may we speak of a crystallized policy of empire-wide killing and death-by-attrition," Bloxham writes.[3]

In an important 2003 article, Bloxham presents a point-by-point argument against the intentionalist position. He begins by noting that the restructuring of the Special Organization in 1914 does not constitute proof of genocidal intent. The Special Organization did become a kind of death squad, but, Bloxham suggests, we need not question its initial redesign as a covert, anti-Russian military unit on the eastern front. After all, the original Special Organization had been deployed for special operations in the Libyan War. It stands to reason that, with a new war on, it was resurrected for military, not genocidal, purposes.

Bloxham also notes that, until the war, there was no enmity between the CUP and the Dashnaks. In fact, the parties had a strong relationship prior to the hostilities. This may indicate that the CUP entered the war believing the solution to the Armenian problem lay in some sort of cooperation with Armenian nationalists. Only during the fever of war did that position change.

This shift, Bloxham argues, was conceivably a product of Ottoman fears, legitimate or overblown. The disarming of Armenian soldiers and civilians, the formation of the labor battalions, and the mass arrest of notables need not be understood as preliminary stages in the implementation of a planned genocide. Instead the arrests could be seen as a reaction to the anticipated Gallipoli landings and to the uprising in Van; the disarmament motivated by genuine fear that Armenians, if armed, would assist the invaders. There was of course serious concern surrounding a possible Armenian-Russian alliance, given that Armenian volunteers had joined the Russian army and fought the Ottomans at Sarıkamış.

Bloxham further questions whether the earliest massacres and deportations should be seen as evidence of an unfolding, top-down plan for ethnic cleansing. It is true that in late 1914 and early 1915 the Special Organization perpetrated massacres in the northeast and in eastern Van vilayet, on the border with Iran. But this was in line with a known CUP policy of punishing recalcitrant villages and therefore not necessarily a signal of an overarching plan to totally destroy the Armenians.

As to the deportations from Cilicia in January and February 1915, these were isolated events, born of the fear of Armenian collusion with Entente forces planning landings in the eastern Mediterranean. Furthermore, the Armenians from this region were deported to the interior, not on death marches southward, suggesting that there was no annihilation plan at this stage. Morgenthau may have reported that Talât told him there was a "decision" to deal with the Armenians, but a decision is not a plan. At this point there was only an "ongoing search for a solution."

Bloxham also notes that, during the course of April, committees were formed in each province to suggest solutions for the Armenian problem. CUP representatives in these committees insisted on massacre, but were instructed by the governors to hold off. This suggests that, whatever ideas were brewing in the CUP leaders' minds, they had not yet settled on a course of action.

If they had, they wouldn't have been seeking input from the provinces on how to proceed.

Finally, Bloxham sees the timing of the first large-scale atrocities as evidence that genocidal ideas did not become a plan of action until late May. On May 24, 1915, the Entente announced that it would hold Ottoman officials accountable for "crimes against humanity." Thereafter the atrocities intensified. Talât admitted his fear of international condemnation, but once it came, there was no longer reason to hold back the Turks' most vicious tendencies. They had already been damned for smaller-scale affronts to justice and decency; refraining further would have no effect on their international reputation.[4]

In his attempt to prove the case for cumulative radicalization, Bloxham blurs two distinct questions. First, was there systematic, state-organized killing of Armenians in the first months of 1915? Second, did a plan of physical extermination take shape in the first months of 1915? Bloxham's study offers convincing evidence that there were no systematic, state-organized mass killings in January and February of 1915. But he doesn't achieve his goal of demonstrating that no genocidal plan emerged in this period. We agree that mass killings of Armenians at this time, mainly along the Russian border, were in all probability initiated by local commanders and governors, not by Constantinople. Yet this does not preclude the possibility that a detailed plan for mass killings was taking shape at the time and was kept secret until after the events at Van and Zeytun.

As we outline below, we believe that such a plan existed already in the early days of 1915. Indeed, there is reason to believe that, even before the plan came together during winter, the highest ranks of the CUP were preparing the ground for annihilation of the Armenians. After the war, many officials testified that as early as September 1914, Talât had instructed the provinces to start monitoring the local Armenian leaderships and their communications. A short time later, Armenian police officers on active duty were dismissed. Both of these moves would, at the very least, have been useful in preventing organized Armenian resistance.

The design was then finalized over some additional months, and implementation began in spring 1915 after the bloodshed at Van and Zeytun. Though these events were not part of that plan, they did shape it, elevating

CUP fears and demonstrating the viability of deportation as a mechanism for killing Armenians.

The 1915 plan would finish the job begun in 1894–1896. Massacring Armenians in large numbers more or less openly had proven only partially successful, as Western diplomatic intervention had helped stay the killing. Perhaps there was a better way. War and its exigencies made mass deportation opportune. Under the cover of war and deportation, Turks would have a chance to carry out their annihilationist campaign.

Many officials viewed the destruction of the Armenians as a sacred mission on behalf of the nation and their religion, some as a strategic necessity, and still others as a financial opportunity. And there were decent and courageous Ottoman officials who defied the central government and refused to carry out the policy of genocide. But there was such a policy and, as we have shown, it was implemented.

Preparation for Genocide

Although there is no documentation of the planning preceding the deportation decree of late May 1915, there are strong indications that the CUP leadership discussed the coming effort and concluded in the early months of 1915 that it would perpetrate genocide. Evidence shows a small circle of CUP activists began the planning in the wake of the debacle at Sarıkamış. The discussions were underway before the Allied naval attempts to break through the Dardanelles in February and weeks before the uprising in Van and the alleged rebellion in Zeytun. When Bahaettin Şakır arrived in Constantinople in March, early talks solidified into a set of guidelines for action. In turn, these led to a concrete plan, which was consolidated in April. Fuat Dündar captures the atmosphere:

> Following these military defeats [Sarıkamış, Van], Unionists, who in parallel with German military war strategy had dreamt of destroying the Russian and British armies with lightning strikes and of reaching Egypt and the quasi-imaginary Turan, suddenly panicked about the security of Anatolia. This led to the conclusion that the only possible way of saving Anatolia . . . was to change its ethnic composition.[5]

There is testimony to the effect that the Turks had by February developed, at the very least, a plan to deport Armenians en masse. In his memoirs the Armenian bishop Grigoris Balakian recalled a revealing conversation with an Armenian acquaintance in Adana. This man told Balakian that in February a Turkish official urged him to save himself because calamity would soon strike. "Go to Mersin, get on a steamship and escape to Europe," the Turk had enjoined him. "I say little; you must understand a lot. Do what you have to do and get away from here as soon as possible so that you also will not drown in the coming storm." When Balakian reported this to the Catholicos of Cilicia, Sahag II, the latter asked to speak to Cemal Pasha, who was then passing through Adana on his way to the Syrian front. Sahag then relayed the contents of the conversation to Balakian. According to Balakian, Cemal told Sahag, "During the deliberations over this matter in the council of ministers, I tried very hard to argue that instead of deporting and exiling the entire Armenian population, only the writers, intellectuals and Armenian political party leaders—say fifteen or twenty people from each town—should be exiled. I felt that the helpless common people should be spared, but I am sorry to say that I was not able to make my voice heard."[6]

Also in February, the military command ordered the disarmament of the Armenian soldiers and their transfer to labor battalions. There are, of course, multiple interpretations of this decision. Like Bloxham, Zürcher and Akçam believe that disarmament was a product of the government's genuine distrust of Armenian soldiers. In view of the expected landing at Gallipoli, Enver and Talât, who took the decision, felt the urgent need to remove Armenians from combat ranks.[7] But, in light of other evidence, the move is highly suspicious. Depriving the Armenians of their status as soldiers not only undermined their ability to defend themselves and their communities but it also denied them legal protection. Technically, the deportation orders exempted soldiers and their families—but what if the soldiers were no longer soldiers? Enlisted men went missing all the time—died in battles, were taken prisoner, or deserted. There was no real need to explain their disappearance. Recall the case of the former soldiers massacred on their way from Harput to Diyarbekir in 1915. Prior to disarmament, Commandant Süleyman Faik erased the names of all Armenian soldiers from the rolls. From this point on, he had no need to account for their whereabouts or condition.[8]

According to the testimony of CUP officials at the postwar trials, the pivotal planning meetings occurred in March and April, as CUP leaders summoned provincial administrators and CUP representatives to Constantinople. In addition to Talât, Enver, Şakır, Nâzım, and other members of the Central Committee, attendees included several of the provincial responsible secretaries and senior army officers deemed loyal to the party.[9] Evidently the cabinet was never informed of these meetings, and even Cemal Pasha claimed he was not privy to decisions taken in them.[10] One of the most important gatherings, apparently on March 22–23, featured Şakır. He presented the CUP Central Committee with documents from the eastern provinces, which supposedly proved Armenians were preparing to betray their homeland and attack the Ottoman army in the rear.[11] This was probably the moment when the Special Organization was converted from a military combat unit to a domestic death squad.[12] We know from postwar trials that Şakır insisted on being given authority over all Special Organization operations and on moving its headquarters to Erzurum.[13] Some of his requests were denied; the Special Organization was subordinated to the Third Army. But Şakır was given authority to requisition Special Organization men and was moved to Erzurum. At the same time, according to a series of telegrams exchanged between the Interior Ministry and some of the eastern vilayets, another large group of convicts was released from prison to participate as "volunteers" and gang members in the forthcoming campaign.[14]

After these meetings, a pattern of identical actions played out across the empire, offering crucial proof of centralized, state planning. Among these were the clearing from the police force of suspect elements; staffing of telegraph stations and other vital government services with individuals selected for their loyalty to the empire and the CUP; preparation of lists of Armenian leaders who would be capable of organizing resistance or pulling strings; decisions on deportation routes and destinations; preparation of gendarmerie and Special Organization units to lead the hundreds of thousands of deportees to their destination; and coordination of movements between districts and provinces. The first fruit of these preparations came in April 1915, when leaders of Armenian communities across the country, from Edirne to Van, were arrested and imprisoned.[15] Could far-flung officials calling upon dodgy, early electronic communication networks have effected virtually simultaneous mass arrests of a consistently defined population group—Armenian notables—without the benefit of advanced planning? Perhaps, but such a contention strains credulity.

Conclusive Evidence

The most compelling evidence for prior top-down planning and for the true genocidal intentions of the CUP leadership is the way the deportation and mass murder actually unfolded. The initial moves were perfectly designed to soften up the broader civilian population. First came the disarming of the soldiers, then the beheading of the Armenian communities via the April mass arrests of notables. Most of the notables and soldiers were soon murdered. By removing the prominent Armenians and disarming the soldiers, the government rendered the community unable effectively to resist.

As well, the timing and scope of the April mass arrests is telling. Arresting community leaders in Constantinople, and perhaps even Izmir, on the eve of the Gallipoli landings could be seen as a logical precaution against collusion with the enemy. Perhaps the same could be said if the mass arrests in the east had occurred immediately after the defeat at Sarıkamış. But the arrests came months later. Similarly, Armenians were arrested in places far from any war zone, such as Konya, Kütahiya, and Bursa. And in Thrace, the Black Sea littoral, and parts of the Aegean coast, where Armenians were greatly outnumbered by Greek Orthodox—who had demonstrated their sympathy with the enemy in the recent Balkan wars—the Greeks were left untouched and the Armenians persecuted. Another point to bear in mind is that spies and possible collaborators need not necessarily be notables. If the authorities' goal had been to contain a real or perceived immediate threat, they targeted the wrong people. One can only reasonably conclude that that was not the goal—that the government wasn't engaged in prudential war planning but instead was systematically ridding the country of the Armenian leadership.

Even more striking is that individual instances of deportation followed a clear playbook. They would begin with the arrest of the remaining community leaders, who were held in local prisons and usually subjected to torture. After securing a few minor confessions, some of which may be have been true, the authorities escorted the community leaders out of prison and sent them away under guard to an announced destination. They were then, routinely, murdered, after which the mass deportations began. This is precisely how events unfolded in Erzurum, Diyarbekir, Harput, Sivas, and Trabzon.

Lastly, consider the formulaic nature of the mass killings, as the convoys set out and along the road. True, there was variation as far as the perpetrators: sometimes it was soldiers and gendarmes; sometimes Kurdish, Turkmen, or Circassian tribesmen or criminal gangs or villagers. But the process itself was more-or-less uniform. Men were almost always separated from their families at the beginning of the journey, taken to remote locations, and systematically slaughtered. Afterward, according to the testimony of survivors from across the empire, the bodies would be looted, suggesting that organizers routinely brandished the prospect of ill-gotten riches in order to recruit killers. Then, as the remaining deportees made their way south, they were subject to periodic ambushes and harassment. Those not killed or abducted by marauders and gendarmes might gradually succumb along the roads to starvation, illness, exhaustion, and the elements. In 1915–1916 anyone who had survived this standardized program of killing and predictable course of attrition was "settled" in camps and villages in the Syrian Desert and subsequently dispatched from there to the killing fields around Deir Zor.

Such uniformity is unthinkable in the absence of guidance from Constantinople. That guidance evidently was broad enough to admit some variation at the local level by governors, CUP apparatchiks, and military and Special Organization commanders. But they knew their jobs and took similar approaches, working with Turks and other Muslims on the ground to achieve the same outcomes.

But what, one might ask, of western Anatolia? There notables were less likely to be killed in advance of the removals, and able-bodied men were usually marched with their families rather than murdered before the marches got underway. That these cases defied the eastern pattern only demonstrates how carefully the authorities had crafted their blueprint. Captivated as they were by the emerging sciences of demography and statistics—including ideas about population engineering—CUP leaders differentiated between the eastern and western provinces, developing separate formulas tailored to each area.

Another indicator of centralized planning is the secretiveness with which the genocide was carried out, which also attests to the perpetrators' recognition of their criminality. Killings did not take place in the middle of towns where Western diplomats and missionaries might see them, but rather far from prying eyes. Organizers also used elaborate methods to obfuscate their identities. Recall that Diyarbekir's Reşid Bey hired the Kurdish brigand Amero to kill Armenians for him, and then most likely had Amero assassinated in order to cover up his own responsibility. Hence as well the elusiveness of the Special Organization at Kemah Gorge and elsewhere, the use of misleading uniforms, and the shadowy participation of military units. Secrecy also necessitated the urgent burial of the dead, such as of the thousands killed at Lake Gölcük.

One reason the premeditated and carefully planned nature of the killings and deportations is sometimes questioned is that inefficiency, sometimes bordering on chaos, accompanied the entire process. Decisions not to deport a certain segment of the Christian population might be rescinded the next day. Conversion to Islam was encouraged and then rejected. Convoys to the south "leaked," with some deportees taking to the hills. There was also disagreement between leaders about the right course of action. Such inefficiency had many causes, the most obvious of which may be the need to keep the entire operation under wraps. Decisions were made by a small group of party leaders and kept secret even from other committee members. Killing orders were relayed by coded telegram or orally from messenger to governor. Most provincial- and district-level officials received no orders at all, instead obtaining their instructions secondhand. If the reports we have are reliable, the orders themselves were vague, in the style of "burn, demolish, kill," and probably made sense only in light of earlier verbal exchanges. It should also be borne in mind that the entire concept of killing-by-deportation was new, and many of the problems that emerged—shortage of qualified gendarmes, difficult terrain, kindhearted people along the way, nosy American consuls and missionaries in remote provinces—were not foreseen. Finally, there was much room for horse-trading, ensuring frequent corruption.

After all this, it remains true that direct evidence of a genocide plan is impossible to come by. Maybe that will change someday, if Turkey opens its archives. But the available combination of direct and circumstantial evidence concerning genocide itself weighs strongly in favor of a planning process occurring in the winter and spring of 1915. The consistent character of the deportations and massacres that followed suggests that these instructions specified not only removing Armenians but also, at least in the east, killing them en masse with as much secrecy as possible. We do not know if the second stage—mass murder along the Euphrates in 1916—was included in the planning during spring 1915. Perhaps the organizers did not believe that substantial numbers would survive to reach the Syrian Desert, so they arranged for the slaughter of Deir Zor only when it became necessary. One way or another, that final and most extreme spasm of violence proves that the CUP-led government's intention and policy was genocide, not relocation.

The Problems of Conversion and Assimilation

As in the previous bout of genocide, between 1914 and 1916, Armenians throughout Anatolia and Syria converted to Islam. Some grasped the opportunity, knowing that it was the surest way to stay alive. "During this reign of terror," an Armenian from Merzifon recounted at the height of the deportations in July 1915, "notice was given . . . that anyone who accepted Islam would be allowed to remain safely at home. The offices of the lawyers who recorded applications were crowded with people petitioning to become Mohammedans. Many did it for the sake of their women and children."[16]

Others did not so much convert as discover all of a sudden that they were Muslim. They were women taken by and then married to Muslim men, their children adopted and raised Muslim. This process, too, was at least partially systematic. One Armenian deportee reported seeing sixty wagons carrying Turkish women to Constantinople, each having "five or six Armenian girls of 10 or under with her."[17] Thousands were placed in Muslim-run orphanages to be reeducated. On the whole, converts tended to be women, children, the elderly, and men only in the western provinces. Their eastern brothers were rarely given the option.

As for the Turks who brought Armenians into the fold of Islam, they had numerous methods and motivations. Sometimes local governors and religious leaders encouraged conversion out of compassion, in order to spare people deportation and massacre. Occasionally they would convert Armenians en masse. In June 1915, for instance, the German consul in Samsun reported that "the government sent fanatical, strictly religious Muslim men and women, to

spread propaganda for conversion to Islam, of course with the threat of serious consequences for those who remain true to their beliefs." The consul
estimated that many had already converted and the numbers were increasing.
In Merzifon it was publicly announced that people could save themselves by
conversion.[18] Some governors encouraged this by inviting Armenians to fill
out official conversion applications, which were presented as name-change
forms so they would be easier to swallow.

Often, though, the aims of facilitators were venal. Officials sought to impress their superiors or enhance their standing in their communities by winning trophies in the form of converts.[19] Or they directed conversion appeals
to members of essential professions, people whose removal would do economic damage.[20] Officials and other Muslim men of standing also targeted
the daughters and sons of rich Armenians for abduction, adoption, and marriage. Then, taking advantage of an Interior Ministry decree allowing recognized Armenian converts to inherit family wealth and property, their new
Muslim families laid claim to their inheritances.[21] Sophia Tahargian, an Armenian who was abducted while her prominent family was deported, testified, "In order further to facilitate stealing of my trousseau and my husband's
property, [Mehmet Ali] adopted me as his daughter. All my property and my
deported husband's thus became his and the vali could not claim it."[22]

Children were taken to shore up household staff or to serve as field workers.
For instance, "Children and young people arriving in Aleppo told of deportations, separations, mass extrajudicial killings and repeated rape, followed by
years of unpaid servitude as agricultural workers or domestic servants,
servile concubines, unconsenting wives, and involuntary mothers." After the
war, at an Aleppo rescue home, Lütfiyye Bilemjian, a young woman from
Antep, recounted that at six years of age she was deported with her family,
her parents and brother were killed by gang members, and she was seized
and sold. She was then resold several times until she reached the household
of one Mahmud Pasha, where she remained, presumably as a servant, for
eleven years.[23]

Conversion might happen, as well, at the behest of an opportunistic lover,
a Turk or tribesman infatuated with an Armenian woman suddenly available
for the taking. She might be plucked from a convoy. One missionary told of a
Professor Vorperian from Harput who "has a daughter fourteen years old

which a lieutenant noticed on the way and began to beg the parents to give her to him as his wife. They . . . were finally forced to give her by the threats of . . . higher officers. Now she has gone back to be his wife, with her parents' consent."[24]

Children were sometimes entrusted by their parents to Muslim neighbors, friends, or business acquaintances, for good and ill. Some proved conscientious guardians, even trying after the war to return foster children to their parents. But in many cases, adoptive families assumed that Armenian parents had died, or tried to keep the children anyway.[25] Other children ended up in overflowing orphanages or else, having escaped convoys and dragnets, roamed the towns and countryside.[26]

It can never be far from our minds that a great many of the Armenian women placed in the households of Muslim men during 1914–1916 were abducted for the purpose of rape. Officials, gendarmes, soldiers, and the general population treated women on convoys as prey, to be consumed and disposed of.[27] Prepubescent girls and boys were raped and abused, sometimes for many days, and then killed or sent on their way. Lieutenant Ahmed Moukhtar Baas testified that "government officials at Trebizond picked up some of the prettiest Armenian women of the best families. After committing the worst outrages on them, they had them killed."[28] Shefik Bey, kaymakam of Bulanik in Bitlis vilayet, told his interrogators that Hodja Ilias, a deputy for the Maraş region, "was addicted to the raping of Christian girls; it was so well known that it became a scandal among the Muslims, more especially as he wore a turban"—a sign of religious office.[29]

Witnesses have testified of women taken to the makeshift harems of local functionaries, where they would be raped by their abductors and possibly their abductors' guests.[30] A patriarchate report alleged that a customs director, Hadji Bekir Mehmed Ali Bey, "retained at Trebizond young Armenian girls and . . . kept a number of these girls at the Red Crescent hospital while he distributed the rest among the important persons of the Ittihat [CUP] at Trebizond."

Armenian women were also sold for sex. According to the same patriarchate report, authorities in Mosul set up brothels *(lupanara)* stocked with good-looking deportee girls for the military's use. "The opening of the lupanara was announced in official communication from the military government of the town."[31] Swedish missionary Alma Johansson reported that in Mezre, "a public house was erected for the Turks—and all the beautiful Armenian girls were put in it."[32] In Constantinople, "hundreds of young Armenian girls" were driven by destitution into prostitution.[33]

Some of these prostituted women may have been brokered on slave markets. Although slavery was abolished in the Ottoman Empire at the beginning of the twentieth century, markets sprung up in Aleppo, Damascus, and elsewhere. The cost of a slave girl was extremely low. A British intelligence report from December 1915 states that, in Damascus, "the price of an Armenian girl from 12 to 14 years of age was from 2 mejidiehs to 1 Turkish Lira."[34] (In 1914 one Turkish lira—five mecidiyes—was worth about 0.9 British pounds sterling, or slightly more than four U.S. dollars.[35]) Dashnaks in Bucharest reported the average price of an Armenian women was sixty piasters, or 0.6 Turkish Lira.[36] Fellow activists reported that "all Armenian women and girls from 7 to 40 years of age" at Vazir Keupru in Merzifon sanjak, "have been sold at auction."[37] As a rule, only Muslims were allowed to participate in the auctions.[38]

This trade occurred with the complicity of state security personnel. A British agent stationed at a hotel near the barracks in Damascus reported seeing Ottoman soldiers pushing in front of them hundreds of naked Armenian girls and women. "These were put up for auction and the whole lot disposed of, some for 2, 3, and 4 francs," the agent wrote.[39] From the American Hospital in Konya, Dodd wrote, "I myself noticed that in several places large groups of young women and girls were being kept separate from the rest and guarded by the police, and was told that in several instances the police had allowed them to be outraged."[40] In another letter, Dodd reported that Protestant and Catholic women and girls were distributed among Turkish villages, "the Turks . . . choosing what they wanted."[41]

Collectively, practices of abduction, prostitution, family separation, adoption, and marriage between Armenian women and Muslim men resulted in masses of converts and dependents for whom the state was not prepared. This is telling: it appears that when CUP leaders drew up their plans, they did not have survivors in mind. While the procedures surrounding deportation and massacre were routinized from the start, those concerning conversion, adoption, and the fostering of orphans evolved haphazardly throughout

1914–1916. The central government was placed in a reactive position, issuing contradictory directives as it sought to keep up with facts on the ground.

Thus, at times during the deportations, the government encouraged Muslim men to take Armenian wives. The Directorate for Tribes and Refugees Settlement repeatedly instructed officials in the provinces that "the marriage of young [Armenian] girls and widows to Muslim men" was "suitable." In December 1915 the directorate urged that it was not just suitable but in fact "necessary for young [Armenian] girls to be married with Muslims." A few months later, in April 1916 all the provinces were notified that "young [Armenian] women and widows [should be] married."[42]

Yet top officials also showed great skepticism toward such marriages and conversions. On June 22, 1915, after it had become clear to Constantinople that converts were multiplying, Talât ordered that those already converted be "dispersed in Muslim villages around the province." At this stage, he tolerated the act of conversion but did not trust the sincerity of the converts; they could not be treated like any other Muslim, but instead were objects of suspicion.[43]

About a week later, he hardened his instructions to provincial authorities:

Some of the Deported Armenians have petitioned to convert to Islam, either collectively or individually, in the hope of remaining in their original places. . . . It is to be expected that such acts do not arise from true conviction but from a will to save themselves from danger, and therefore should not be trusted. From now on, you should not accept the conversion of those who are doing so for their own interests . . . and you should keep sending them to the designated places.[44]

Even then, officials were left some discretion, but orders soon changed again. Talât apparently concluded that there was no such thing as genuine Armenian conversion, so converts would receive no protection. "Since the conversion of Armenians is merely an excuse to serve their interest, do not tarry in deporting them," he instructed the mutessarif of Kayseri in mid-August.[45] In September Talât reiterated the point, writing one vali, "We hear that some of the people and officials are marrying Armenian women. We strictly prohibit this, and urgently recommend that these women be . . . sent away."[46]

Yet this was not the final word, for in the midst of issuing a blanket ban, Talât made an exception for young women, whose offspring almost certainly would be raised as Muslims. A few days after the admonition to the mutessarif of Kayseri, he wrote an official in Niğde, "Armenian girls who have been converted must not be abused, and it would be appropriate to marry them off to Muslims."[47]

The authorities also vacillated on the care for and integration of orphans. Days before deportation began in Mamuret-ül-Aziz vilayet, the Interior Ministry asked about Harput buildings suitable as orphanages for Armenians younger than fifteen.[48] But the government was sufficiently reluctant to house orphans that thousands were left to Christian-run services established on local initiative to pick up the slack. Such was the case in Trabzon, where Christians tried to mobilize the authorities' support for an asylum run by the Greek Orthodox community. The asylum functioned for a short while under the auspices of the vali, until the local CUP secretary caught on. Something similar happened in Aleppo, where Sister Rohner took over a shelter for more than a thousand children and ran it for several months as an independent semi-missionary institution.[49]

At times Talât endorsed placing orphans in government-operated facilities, but at other times he said children should be sent to Muslim villages.[50] In September 1916 he instructed the mutesarrif of Kayseri to remove girls from an orphanage and "settle them in appropriate places."[51] Then, in November, Talât instructed the mutesarrif of Canik to care for the needs of orphans in his area, whether or not they had converted.[52] At about this time, the government set up its own orphanages in Lebanon, Konya, Balıkesir, Izmit, and Adapazarı. The government insisted that all orphans be transferred to its own institutions, which would promote Islamic learning and the Unionist party line.[53]

By the end of the deportation and annihilation process, Talât had finally made up his mind about the genocide's unexpected remainders. In December 1917 he cabled Sivas vilayet, warning against "those who have converted in areas close to the front" who might act as spies. He asked Sivas officials to respond with confirmation of the converts' deportation. He even advised the officials against showing mercy to orphans. "There is no need for an orphanage," he wrote. "It is not the time to give way to sentiment and feed the orphans, prolonging their lives. Send them away and inform me."[54]

During the war, the inconsistent conversion rules left thousands in limbo. Some women taken by Muslims were registered as converts, but not all. Adopters of Armenian children may have received official guarantees or letters of permission to keep them, or they may have received no authorization of any kind. After the war, the government that replaced the CUP issued large batches of identity cards making marriages and adoptions official and registering women and children as *muhtedi*—converts.[55] (The formation of that government, led by Mustafa Kemal Ataturk, is discussed in the next chapter.)

Constantinople's evolving positions on conversion and integration were outgrowths of its initial silence on the matter. CUP leadership had no assimilation policy because it had no interest in assimilation; its goal and expectation lay in deportation and annihilation.[56] The CUP was trying to restore the lost grandeur of an empire led by and encompassing all Turkic peoples. Doing so required the defeat of enemies, traitors, and those who might upset the pan-Turanian ambit of the empire by challenging its Turkish leaders. Though CUP leaders were no doubt Muslims, and though faith often factored in their decisions, their goals did not require demographically enhancing the sphere of Islam.[57]

To do so was not unacceptable: unlike the Nazis, the Turks did not believe in an insurmountable racial difference; a Jew could not become Aryan, but an Armenian could become Muslim. That made conversion a vehicle for the erasure of Armenians, and, indeed, millions of today's Turkish Muslims have at least one ancestor who began life Armenian.[58] But to the degree that conversion complicated their goals of preserving and uplifting the state, CUP leaders were wary of it.[59] They would have felt justified in their skepticism, given memories of the recent past. In 1894–1896 some Armenians opted for conversion to escape death, but when the clouds lifted the majority returned to Christianity. Assisted by European diplomats and missionaries, Armenian leaders located stray sheep—children in orphanages, abducted women, even communities that had converted en bloc—and convinced them to return to the fold.[60] There is no reason to believe that these reverse converts were actually a threat to the empire, but, filtered through the CUP's paranoia, relapse would have looked much like treason.

Ultimately, the confusion surrounding conversion reflected the priorities of the particular ethnic-cleansing program the CUP designed. The first priorities clearly were the elimination of Armenian notables throughout the empire and men in the eastern provinces. Women and children were less concerning and therefore more of an afterthought. Their fates would be dealt with as exigencies arose.

What was not left to ad-hoc determination was the genocide itself. It was protean, its terms changing as the months went on and official focus shifted to whichever Armenian groups had not yet been destroyed. But the preponderance of the evidence indicates that nationwide destruction was the goal all along.

III

Mustafa Kemal and the Nationalists

7

Historical Background, 1918–1924

Between the armistice ending World War I and 1924, hundreds of thousands of Greeks, Armenians, and Assyrians were murdered in new waves of massacre and deportation. Countless others were exiled, some of them redeportees. And, in 1923–1925 tens of thousands of Greeks were officially exchanged for Muslims from the Balkans. At the end of this process Anatolia was almost completely cleansed of its Christian populations. This chapter describes the historical context in which this last, five-year bout of ethnic cleansing and genocide took place.

On October 30, 1918, Ottoman Navy Minister Rauf Bey and Admiral Somerset Arthur Gough-Calthorpe, commander of the British Eastern Mediterranean Fleet, met aboard HMS *Agamemnon* in Mudros (Mondros) harbor, on the Greek island of Lemnos, to sign an armistice ending the Great War in the Middle East the following day. The terms of the armistice amounted to a Turkish surrender, though Turkish officials at the time claimed that the agreement was not "concluded between victor and vanquished; rather it is more a situation in which two equal powers . . . cease hostilities."[1] Two weeks before, on October 14, the wartime CUP and Special Organization leaders—including Enver, Talât, Cemal, Şakır, and Nâzım—had fled Turkey in a German vessel, fearing punishment for war crimes.[2] In the following months, the Ottoman parliament annulled the deportation decree, of May 27, 1915, and the confiscation law of September 27, 1915, which had sanctioned the appropriation of Armenian property. (These decrees would be reinstated, as law, on September 14, 1922.[3])

The Mudros agreement provided, among other things, for Allied occupation of the Dardanelles and Bosphorus forts (the "Straits"), "the withdrawal of [Turkish] troops from Cilicia with the exception of those necessary to maintain order," Allied occupation of the Taurus tunnel system and the installation of "control officers" along Turkish railway routes, and the demobilization of the Turkish army except for troops needed for "surveillance of the frontiers" and "maintaining internal order." The numbers and dispositions of these troops were to be determined later by the Allies "after consultation with the Turkish Government." All Allied prisoners of war and "interned" Armenians were to be handed over unconditionally, and it was stipulated that the Allies had the "right to occupy any strategical points in the event of any situation arising which threatens" Allied security. Clause 24 stated that "in case of disorder in the six Armenian vilayets, the Allies reserve the right to occupy any part of these."[4]

As it turned out, Allied troops only minimally occupied Turkish soil, the Ottoman Army was only partially demobilized, and the great bulk of the Turkish people never knew that they had been defeated or else never accepted defeat.[5] This posture of denial was to underlie Turkish attitudes and policies toward both the Christian minorities and the Great Powers in the years to come. As one British officer put it, "The Turk in Anatolia still feels himself to be a member of the ruling nation. Defeat has not been brought home to him. [He has never heard the truth about] the disasters in Palestine and Mesopotamia. . . . He has seen no Allied troops and his towns and villages have not suffered."[6]

During November–December 1918, British, French, and Italian troops occupied Constantinople and strongpoints along the Dardanelles, including parts of Thrace. The British also occupied a string of towns in northern Aleppo vilayet and Cilicia, and installed control officers, with small military detachments, in towns along the Black Sea coast and at principal rail junctions. In February 1919 a small group of French officers, led by Colonel Edouard Brémond, deployed in Adana. They were to be the area's future "military governors," under overarching British control.[7] Greek troops occupied points along the southern shore of the Sea of Marmara and, from March 1919 until July 1921, Italian contingents lightly occupied the southwestern segment of Anatolia as far inland as Konia; the Italians argued that

British Indian troops taking part in the occupation of Constantinople.

the area had been ruled by Rome 2,000 years before.[8] Russian and Russian-backed Armenian troops controlled areas of northeastern Turkey. And, east of the border, in May 1918, Armenian nationalists established an Armenian republic with Yerevan as its capital.

In May 1919, with authorization from the Allied Supreme Council, the Greek Army occupied Smyrna and the contiguous coastline. Turkish nationalist groups—which would later unify under a single flag and take control of the country under the leadership of Mustafa Kemal—responded with a ferocious guerrilla war. As early as January 1915, the British had tried to persuade the Greeks to join the Allied cause with the vague promise of territorial compensation in Asia Minor.[9] But the Greeks had declined, and the Allies promised the Ionian coast to Italy.[10] But then, in June 1917, the Greeks (reluctantly) joined the Allies, leaving the British and French prime ministers, David Lloyd George and Georges Clemenceau, in a quandary. The situation came to a head in spring 1919. The Italians landed troops in Antalya, and appeared to be inching toward Smyrna. Meanwhile, Turkish anti-Christian terrorism was on the rise, with massacre threatened. On May 5–6, the principal Allied leaders—Lloyd George, Clemenceau, and U.S. President Wilson—decided to let the Greeks have Smyrna. The British foreign secretary, Arthur Balfour, immortally described their meeting: "These three all-powerful, all-ignorant men [are] sitting there and carving up continents with only a child to lead them."[11] (The "child" in question may have been forty-one-year-old Maurice Hankey, secretary of Britain's War Cabinet.) Lloyd George then summoned Eleftherios Venizelos, the Greek statesman, and asked, "Do you have troops available?" Venizelos replied, "We do. For what purpose?" Lloyd George responded that the Allies had "decided today that you should occupy Smyrna." Venizelos: "We are ready."[12] Ten days later the Greeks landed.

In June–July 1920, with Allied authorization and after Nationalist troops attacked British positions in Izmit, the Greek Army pushed inland, occupying Bursa and other parts of the western Anatolian highlands as far as the Sakarya River. They also occupied Eastern Thrace (Edirne vilayet).[13] In doing so, the Greeks bit off more than they could chew: their aims were monumental, but they had relatively meager resources. With the defeat of the Ottoman Empire in World War I, some Ottoman Greeks began pushing for unification with mainland Greece, their desires dovetailing with those of many mainland politicians. On March 16, 1919, for example, the Greek Orthodox Patriarchal Council of Constantinople endorsed "Union with Greece" and distributed to the city's churches a declaration: "The Greeks of Constantinople . . . regard Union with the mother country Greece as the only firm basis for natural development in the future." Here and there Ottoman Greek schools and homes raised Greek flags.[14] On the mainland Venizelos and many others, driven by the Megali Idea, sought to incorporate the lost Aegean islands, the western Anatolian coastline, Constantinople, and perhaps even the Pontus in a reborn Greek Empire.

The Turkish Nationalist war against the Greek Army following the landing in Smyrna was soon accompanied by a campaign of ethnic cleansing against the Ottoman Greek communities, which had in some measure rooted for Greece during the Balkan and Great wars. The Nationalists' campaign against the Greeks expanded during 1919–1920 into a simultaneous confrontation with the Russians and Armenians in the eastern marchlands and with the

French, who at the end of 1919 had taken over from the British in Cilicia and Aleppo vilayet.

It looked as if the Turks faced an insuperable challenge. But during 1920 the tide began to turn. Though thrice embattled, the Turks drove the Russian-backed Armenians out of Kars and Alexandropol in the east and in 1921 forced the French out of Cilicia and northern Aleppo vilayet. The following year they swept the Greeks into the Aegean.

At the base of what the Turks were to call their War of Independence was a deep sense that they had been wronged—in the Balkan wars, during the world war, and by the foreign occupations that followed. Xenophobia burgeoned, mixing hatred for the Allied Powers with hatred for Christians in general. Among most Turks there was no "spirit of regret, much less of repentance at what had taken place, . . . The spirit of race hatred . . . is everywhere dominant," the American missionary James Barton observed after a 5,000-mile trek through Asia Minor. He concluded that the Christian inhabitants were "in danger of extermination."[15]

But the picture was a little more nuanced, and some Turkish leading figures publicly opposed the continued persecution of Christians. When the war ended and the Ottoman parliament reconvened, there were stormy debates about the anti-Christian atrocities. Some deputies blamed the CUP and absolved the rest of the Turkish political establishment.[16] Many demanded that the wartime ministers be tried. When three Greek Orthodox parliamentarians proposed that the state acknowledge the atrocities, some of their Muslim colleagues concurred.[17] But the new government's interior minister, Fethi Bey, finessed the question of blame, while seemingly conceding that "injustice" had occurred and promising that the new regime would make concrete amends:

> The approach of the government will be to grant freedom and perfect equality to all segments of society. . . . Apart from this, it is the intention of the government to cure every single injustice done up until now, as far as the means allow, to make possible the return to their homes of those sent into exile, and to compensate for their material loss as far as possible. . . . It is also our common duty to make sure that such an event does not recur.[18]

Even those who pressed for individual blame tended to hew to the overall tenor of the debates, which held that the Turkish nation as a whole bore no responsibility for what had happened.[19]

Events conspired to harden the Turkish position, and Allied actions exacerbated Turkish xenophobia. During 1919 the Allies—principally Britain—tried to redress some of the wrongs committed. They helped Armenian deportees return to their homes and regain their property, incarcerated in British-ruled Malta hundreds of Turkish officers and officials implicated in the massacres and the abuse of Allied prisoners of war, and extricated women and children abducted to Muslim homes. According to one possibly exaggerated calculation, by September 1919 some 90,000 women and orphans—out of a total of 170,000 wartime abductees—were recovered.[20] Armenians were also freed from prisons.[21]

But by 1920 these reparative efforts were largely ended, and Turkey slipped out of Allied control. Horace Rumbold, Britain's perspicacious high commissioner in Constantinople, put it this way a year later: "The history of the armistice has been the history of the gradual decline of Allied influence and

Armenian survivors on a train back to Anatolia.

authority in Turkey. . . . Allied influence counts for nothing at all in the bulk of Asia Minor."[22]

During the first months of the armistice, the Ottoman government, under the guns of Allied warships in the Sea of Marmara, played along with Allied wishes, or at least pretended to. But the government quickly lost legitimacy and power, partly because of this appearance of subservience. It was gradually replaced by a new, uncowed Turkish force, independent of Constantinople. These were the Nationalists, based in Ankara and led by Mustafa Kemal, the Salonica-born general who projected a "marble like coldness."[23]

The surge of Turkish nationalism—and of the Nationalist movement that gave it expression and came to govern the country from Ankara—were products of the defeat and the attendant humiliation of the officer class and political nation. But the chief immediate trigger of these surges was the Greek occupation of Smyrna. Defeat at the hands of the Great Powers was one thing; conquest and occupation by a formerly subject, contemned people, the Christian Greeks, auguring the permanent dismemberment of Turkey, was quite another. Fuel was added to the fire when the French took over from the British in Cilicia and northern Aleppo vilayet at the end of 1919. The French were overbearing and more intrusive than the British and appeared to have a long-term imperialist agenda vis-à-vis Turkey. The Turks were particularly fearful of the establishment of a Western- and Russian-backed Armenian state comprehending the six eastern provinces and possibly also parts of Cilicia, and of the emergence of a Greek mini-state in the Pontus, whether aligned with, or independent of, Greece.[24]

Days after the Smyrna landing, Rear Admiral Mark Bristol—the commander of American naval forces in Turkish waters who, from August 1919, doubled as the U.S. high commissioner in Constantinople—pointed out the danger of the Greek invasion. It "will have a very bad effect," he began. "Such occupation without the complete military occupation of Turkey is very apt to cause disorders in the interior."[25] "Disorders" was to prove a gross understatement. The gradual replacement, in terms of sway, of Constantinople by a Nationalist government, and simultaneous wars by the Nationalists against the clutch of foreign occupiers, accompanied by the destruction of the remaining Christian communities of Asia Minor, were to be the chief "disorders" that ensued.

Turkish recovery from the shock of defeat and the rise of the militant nationalist spirit were already apparent before the Greek landing. The recovery was spearheaded mainly by the CUP-dominated officer corps. Already in October–November 1918, CUP veterans were preparing for a protracted guerrilla struggle against possible Allied occupation. They resurrected the Special Organization, under the label of the General Revolutionary Organization of the Islamic World *(Umum Alem-i Islam Ihtilal Teşkilatı)*, amassed weapons and ammunition around Anatolia, and reconstructed the armed bands that had been active against the Armenian and Greek communities during the war. Their ranks were filled by "men of bad character, released convicts, etc."[26] The budding Nationalist movement also set up a new organization, the Karakol, to protect and empower Unionist officials in the interior.[27] Karakol—meaning 'guard' or, literally, 'black arm'—was a direct continuation of the Special Organization, and many of its founding members were SO veterans.[28]

Nationalists set up regional organizations—"national defense" or "national rights" committees—comprising CUP branch secretaries, mutessarifs, gendarmes, army officers, and educators, among others. During the spring of 1919 these committees—The Erzurum Association for the Defense of the Fatherland, The Cilicia Association for the Defense of the National Rights, and so on—loosely joined together under the banner of the Society for the Defense of National Rights. Kemal, appointed commander of the Yıldırım Army Group on October 30, 1918, and enraged by the Mudros terms, began clandestinely stockpiling arms and organizing cadres for The Day, as did generals Nihat Pasha in Adana and Ali Ihsan north of Mosul.[29]

Already in March 1919, two months before the Greek landing, there was a sense of impending insurrection, "to be accompanied by slaughter of Christians." Anti-Christian and Nationalist revolutionary propaganda were rampant, and CUP veterans mobilized manpower and amassed weapons.[30] The Allies were stymied in their efforts to collect guns and ammunition that the Turks were obliged to surrender.[31] A British control officer at Izmit reported that CUP agitators "poison[ed] the minds of a considerable portion of the common people."[32] "The country was full of combustible material, and it needed only a torch to set it aflame," Rumbold wrote later. The Greeks' arrival in Smyrna and their misbehavior during their first days ashore—including several massacres of Turkish civilians—provided that torch.[33]

Actual violence against Allied troops and local Christians was rare between the signing of the armistice and the Smyrna landing.[34] But Turkish intentions were clear. The resurrected brigand "bands will do as they did during the war" one British observer predicted. The Turks threatened "that the Greeks and Armenians will, this time, be wiped out to a man."[35] The bands were led by regular Turkish army officers: "practically the whole of the military seem to be implicated," as were the preachers in the mosques.[36]

Some historians see the Nationalist movement as a thinly veiled resurrection of the CUP. Indeed, the emergent struggle against Turkey's invaders is sometimes considered merely a second, Anatolian stage of the Great War, based on a secret plan drawn up by Enver and Talât as early as spring 1915, when, between Sarıkamış and Gallipoli, the Ottoman Empire appeared to face defeat.[37] Indeed, many leaders of the budding Turkish nationalist movement were former members and adherents of the CUP. During 1919–1920 Kemal made a point of publicly distancing himself from the CUP, but Turkey's "alarmed" Christian communities, as well as some Muslim dissenters, viewed Kemal's movement as "a regeneration of the [CUP] spirit which triumphed in 1908 . . . [and which bred] the Adana massacres of the year 1909, and which, again triumphing in January 1913, worked steadily up to the 'boycott', deportations and massacres of the years 1914–1916."[38] Ideologically the connection between the CUP and the Nationalists was clear. After Talât was assassinated in 1922, *Yeni Gün,* an official publication of the Nationalist Ankara Government, declared: "Our great patriot has died for his country. We salute his fresh tomb . . . Talaat was a political giant. Talaat was a genius. History will prove his immense stature and will make of him a martyr. . . . Talaat . . . was . . . the greatest man Turkey has produced." On another occasion, *Yeni-Gun* stated, "We, the heirs of the great patriots of 1908, shall continue their work."[39]

The Nationalist movement came together around the figure of Mustafa Kemal, the hero of Gallipoli, who, as commander of the 19th Division, had helped turn the tide against the Allied invaders in the grueling, protracted battle. By May 1919 the government was sending him to Samsun as inspector general. Ostensibly he was in charge of the military in eastern Anatolia and was to report on the situation and on "Greek complaints of harassment."[40] But the purpose of his assignment may have been different: to thwart the emergence of a Pontic Greek polity.[41] His arrival could not have been more timely.

As the British high commissioner put it, the Smyrna landing had "stimulated a Turkish patriotism probably more real than any which the [Great] War was able to evoke."[42]

Kemal had been an early CUP member, and, before leaving for Samsun, had frequently visited party stalwarts incarcerated in Constantinople.[43] But from 1919 through the early 1920s, he made a point of dissociating himself from the CUP old guard. Indeed, eventually he even tried and executed a few.[44] At times, Kemal distanced himself from the Armenian massacres as well; occasionally, he condemned them. He was also critical, or at least ambiguous in his appreciation of, the CUP's expansionist tendencies, embodied in both its pan-Turanian and pan-Islamic ideological strains. But during 1919–1923 he made use of both to mobilize the masses and to frighten the British and French. This wasn't just a utilitarian calculation. As Akçam puts it, the Nationalist movement was "fundamentally defined by [its Muslim] religion . . . [and] character."[45]

Kemal may have occasionally entertained wide territorial ambitions. But his pragmatism won out. He understood that expansion beyond Asia Minor would lead to war with Britain over Mosul, with France over Aleppo, and with Russia over the Caucasus. Still, he was not, in principle, opposed to expansionism, instead leaving decision on such matters to evolving conditions on the ground. Hence the National Pact of 1920, the Nationalist movement's "constitution," announced, "We shall establish the borders [of the Turkish Republic] according to the degree of our power and our strength."[46]

When Kemal arrived in Samsun, hundreds of officers gathered around him. Within months, regular army units rallied to his cause. Almost from the first, he dominated the movement, as he was to dominate Turkey for the next two decades. An American intelligence officer in summer 1921 described him, after a meeting, as "a clever, ugly customer" who looked like "a very superior waiter."[47]

In late July 1919, Kemal summoned some 200 nationalists to the abandoned Armenian Sanasarian High School in Erzurum. At that point the pan-Turanian dream was still very much alive: in addition to the Anatolians there were also a few delegates from Afghanistan, Turkestan, Daghestan, Mesopotamia, Azerbaijan, and Georgia. Yet the attendees mostly hailed from the eastern and southern provinces claimed by the Armenians for future Armenian sovereignty. These areas were flooded with muhacirs from Russian-occupied territory and with recently demobilized or still-serving Turkish troops who found available housing and uncultivated lands, formerly owned by Christians. The Turks living in these regions were not only "instinctively anti-Armenian," according to British Colonel Alfred Rawlinson, but they also had a vested interest in blocking Christian repatriation. They constituted manpower at the ready for refashioned Turkish army units and brigand bands.[48]

The stated aim of the Erzurum gathering was to unite Nationalist forces and organize the defense of the fatherland against the invaders, though there were some, outside the gathering, who charged that the movement's aim was "to arm the people for a massacre of the subjugated races and make a clean job of what was started in 1915."[49]

The Erzurum Congress was informed with jihadi rhetoric. A few days before Erzurum, Kemal had resigned from the army, saying that the affiliation would hamper "the national holy war now commencing to save our sacred race and fatherland from the danger of dismemberment." Now he was a simple "crusader *(mudjahid)* fighting for the glory of his race." Others at the gathering echoed him. Former Constantinople minister Rauf Bey proclaimed, "I have joined in the sacred war" for "the independence and liberation of our land and race."[50]

On August 7, the congress issued a manifesto. It avoided the word "jihad" but declared that "the sacred fatherland" was threatened with partition and dissolution thanks to the Allied occupation, which was charged with the "stamping out of Islam." The manifesto also claimed that the Turks were being massacred by Greeks and Armenians and declared the congress's opposition to the formation of Greek Pontine and Armenian states. "All Moslem elements" in eastern Anatolia would fight for the "integrity of Turkey . . . and . . . the Sultanate and Caliphate." The manifesto pointed out that in the eastern vilayets, as throughout Turkey, there was an overwhelming "Moslem majority," precluding severance of the vilayets from the Turkish body politic. Still undecided about the measure of commitment the new organization should exhibit to the sultan's government in Constantinople, the manifesto settled for a vague title. It declared the establishment, on the basis of the local defense committees, of The League of Eastern Anatolia for the Defense of Our Rights. Finally, the manifesto warned against "the grant of a new series of privileges to the Christian elements" while vaguely averring "respect" for the "acquired rights" of non-Muslims.[51]

The Erzurum congress was followed, on September 4, by a second gathering, in Sivas, of representatives of the movement's branches in western Anatolia and Western Thrace (Rumelia). At the conference they united as The League for the Defense of the Rights of Anatolia and Rumelia. At Sivas Kemal advanced the narrative at the heart of the Nationalist struggle: "The non-Moslem elements with which we have led a joint existence *ab antique,* encouraged by the favor shown them by the Entente Powers, broke into open attacks on the dignity and rights of the Nation and State." He accused the Greek army and Ottoman Greeks of a "general massacre of the Moslem population" and charged the Armenian Republic at Yerevan with carrying out a "policy of extermination" against that region's Muslims.[52] On September 11 the Sivas meeting declared that no Armenian or Greek sovereignty would be countenanced in the territory of Turkey.[53]

Three months later, after moving his headquarters to Ankara, Kemal made his clearest statement regarding the wartime massacres and deportations. He blamed the Armenians and Greeks for what had happened, while never actually defining what had happened: "Whatever has befallen the non-Muslim elements living in our country is the result of the policies of separatism they pursued in a savage manner, when they allowed themselves to be made tools of foreign intrigues and abused their privileges."[54]

At the end of 1919 the Nationalists won a majority in the Ottoman parliament. Thereafter, in January 1920, they promulgated the National Pact, which stated that the territories inhabited by a Muslim Turkish majority were an indivisible whole. The vilayets to the south, with a largely Arab population, would be allowed to determine their own future—whether to remain part of Turkey, achieve independence, or follow some middle course. The same right was granted the inhabitants of the three eastern sanjaks occupied by the Russians—Batumi, Kars and Ardahan—and of Western Thrace, occupied by Greece. The rights of Turkey's Christian minorities would, it stated, be determined in conformity with past Ottoman-European treaties.[55]

Assessing the National Pact, Rumbold saw the Nationalists as duplicitous: they actually aimed at the "complete subordination, if not extinction, of non-Moslem communities."[56] In time he grew increasingly anti-Turk. In 1923 he wrote, they are "so shameless. . . . I have never met such people and . . . I never wish to see any of them again. I am convinced that they are heading straight for ruin and the sooner they get there, the better I shall be pleased."[57]

The Nationalist government controlling Anatolia in 1920 had in effect supplanted Constantinople's rule in Asia Minor the previous autumn. The October 3 takeover of Bursa, one of the Constantinople government's last footholds, sealed the Nationalists' victory over its domestic rivals and the movement of the seat of real power from Constantinople to Ankara. The government of Sultan Mehmet VI Vahdettin, the last of the Ottoman monarchs, nominally remained in existence until 1923, when the Nationalists dissolved it. But while the Sultanate spent the transitional years officially opposing the Nationalists, Constantinople's War Ministry secretly funneled supplies, manpower, and intelligence to Nationalist military campaigns.[58]

In Britain, the leading Western power in the Middle East, councils were divided on what to do about a resurgent Turkey. The dominant view was that Britain should hold on in Turkey until a peace treaty ended World War I in the Middle East. More vaguely, policymakers sought to contain the Nationalists. But there was also dissent. The secretary of state for war, Winston Churchill, favored avoiding a clash with Kemal. The failure at Gallipoli—Kemal's triumphal moment—hung over Churchill's head. And Churchill was more interested in cutting military expenditure and containing or defeating Soviet Russia, his biggest bugbear. He hoped that the Turks, traditional enemies of Russia, could yet be harnessed for this purpose.[59] And there were other considerations:

The [Nationalist] movement grows daily in strength, and if we show ourselves as definitely opposed to [its ends, "to prevent the partition of Turkish territory amongst the Greeks, Italians and Armenians"], we must be prepared for the following consequences: (a) A spread of Pan-Islamic feeling allied, perhaps, to Bolshevism, to Trans-Caspia, Persia, Afghanistan and India. (b) Fresh disturbances in Egypt. . . . (c) Increased unrest amongst the Arabs. (d) A greater likelihood of a massacre of the Armenians.

Churchill therefore advised revising

> our present attitude. . . . If we reinforce our troops on the Anatolian
> Railway, we must be prepared to find ourselves committed to operations
> on an indefinite scale against the Turkish Nationalists . . . solely for the
> benefit of alien and predatory races [i.e., the Greeks and Italians]. . . .
> The possibility of [saving money by] reducing our garrisons in Egypt,
> Palestine and Mesopotamia turns directly on [this].[60]

Of course, Churchill and likeminded officials were keenly aware of the
damage Britain's standing would suffer should it withdraw hastily from Turkey.
But they also worried that hanging tough with the Nationalists might trigger
rebellions in Britain's heavily Muslim colonial possessions. Opinion in India,
Iraq, Egypt, and other lands had to be placated.[61] Moreover, during 1919–
1921 it was not always clear to what frontiers the Kemalists aspired—Turkey
as configured then or Turkey plus Thrace, Syria, Mesopotamia, and the
Caucasus. If the Nationalists were prepared to restrict themselves to Asia
Minor, then perhaps Britain need not oppose them. Kemal kept everyone on
tenterhooks in this respect. On March 19, 1920, a year into the Nationalist
resurgence, he defined "all Mesopotamia and Syria" as part of the patrimony
that he intended to restore to "Ottoman" rule.[62] And during the following
years, he tried to use proxy forces to disrupt Western rule in these lost
Ottoman territories.[63] But it is unclear whether Kemal really sought to incorporate them in the newborn Turkey or merely brandished the threat as a
means to subvert the French in Cilicia and Western resolve generally. He refrained from sending Turkish troops to Syria or Mesopotamia and vaguely
endorsed a "plebiscite" to determine their future.[64] Indeed, some Turks were
averse to reincorporating the Arab lands, as the Arabs were viewed as having
betrayed the empire during the world war.[65]

Almost from his arrival in Anatolia, Kemal was seen as a problem. By January 1921 Rumbold was writing to Foreign Secretary Lord George Curzon:
"It is useless to regard Mustapha Kemal any longer as a brigand chief. [The]
Angora Government has [a] tight grip on the whole of Asia Minor not in
effective foreign occupation. . . . Bulk of population, sheep-like as always,
recognized its authority without demur, and majority of the Moslem element

support it strongly, as standing for best interests of Turkey and individual Turks."[66] Already by spring 1920 a knowledgeable Italian observer thought the Kemalists the "only party in Turkey to which any importance should be attached."[67]

Nonetheless, during 1919–1922 the British had not yet thrown in the towel and often displayed true grit in face of Kemalist challenges. Britain must not "allow the Kemalists to kick us when and where they like," as John de Robeck, commander-in-chief of the Mediterranean Fleet, put it in November 1921.[68]

But, following the vast expenditure of blood and treasure in the world war, the British ultimately were unwilling to commit the resources necessary to defeat Kemal or protect Turkey's Christian minorities. Neither was seen as a vital national interest. As a result, sympathy for downtrodden Christians failed to translate into concrete support. During 1920–1923 Britain walked a fine line between confronting the Kemalists and capitulating to their demands.

France, the second important Western imperial power in the Middle East, took a clearer tack. After 1918, the French sought reconciliation with Turkey. True, the French initially were guided by colonial hands such as François Georges Picot, who hoped to expand and consolidate imperial holdings in the Levant and southern Turkey. In November 1918 the French landed in the northeastern Mediterranean and, during 1919, took over most of Cilicia from the British in the hope of establishing long-term rule and realizing commercial opportunities. But war-weary France was not inclined to battle a resolute Nationalist movement. The French quickly lost their taste for combat and sought to extricate themselves from Cilicia while holding on to as much as they could of Syria and preserving as much face as possible. Already in 1919 the French High Commission in Constantinople had apparently sent emissaries to Kemal offering him Cilicia and support in future international conferences. The High Commission even proposed abandoning the alliance with Britain.[69]

Something of a split developed between French officials in Constantinople and Beirut. In Constantinople successive French high commissioners pursued a pro-Turkish stance, to the great annoyance of the British. In Beirut, by contrast, military commanders were at least initially steadfast in their resolve to hold Syria-Lebanon, including Aleppo vilayet. But, perennially short of money and manpower, they eventually were persuaded to abandon Cilicia and northern Aleppo vilayet, the heavily Armenian region where the Nationalists fought the Allied occupation hardest.

In France the debate raged largely out of the public eye. On one side were the anti-imperialist left and the Quai d'Orsay, which generally supported reduced commitments and withdrawal. On the other was the colonialist right, which advocated retaining as much of Cilicia and northern Aleppo vilayet as possible. But the Turco-French warfare of 1919–1921 and budgetary problems gradually persuaded middle-of-the-roaders such as Clemenceau to give up Cilicia and northern Aleppo vilayet. In June 1920 the many-time Prime Minister Aristide Briand captured the sentiment of a nation tired of expending itself in Turkey, describing the Kemalists in Cilicia as "patriots merely defending their homeland," even as they fought his own troops.[70]

The Turkish Nationalists came quickly to understand that the Allied coalition was rickety. Turkey and its Christians were not a vital Western interest, and the French could be pushed out. Kemal was shrewd in handling the minorities issue, crafting different messages for his international and domestic audiences. His official statements avowed Nationalist support for equality and maintained that Ottoman rulers had always been tolerant toward their non-Muslim subjects. But he was careful to avoid specific policy guarantees.[71] All the while he never stopped telling Muslims that Turkey's existence was imperiled by Christians abroad and at home, the great powers and the domestic subversives who constantly invited their intervention. As Kemal told the Erzurum assembly in 1920, the Greeks aimed at nothing less than "the enslavement of the Turks."[72] He beat the same drum for years, reflecting in 1927 that, after the Great War, Greeks and Armenians had worked "to hasten the break-down of the state."[73]

In spite of Kemal's double-talk, the Nationalists' take on the Christian minorities was clear to most foreign observers. In June 1920 even Bristol, who was generally pro-Turkish, or more sympathetic to the Turkish predicament, wrote, "The Turks, undoubtedly, want to get rid of the Armenians and will probably exterminate them if they cannot find another means."[74] The Armenian Patriarchate shared this assessment. The Kemalists, the patriarchate observed, followed the CUP policy of solving "the Armenian question by exterminating the nation. The only deviation from this common policy . . . lay in the methods of promoting it. So, the Kemalists did not resort to massacre or looting [in] those places where their influence is absolute." In these locations, "the Armenians . . . are condemned to annihilation . . . by starvation and poverty. . . . In the Armenian vilayets . . . the Kemalists have absolutely and irrevocably forbidden the Armenians to make a residence there. Their return to these vilayets has not been allowed." In places where the Nationalists faced resistance or did not wield exclusive control, they were more aggressive. In the few spots where Muslims resisted Ankara's takeover, the Kemalists found pretexts to massacre Christians. There were also anti-Christian massacres in places "in the direct path of the advance of the Greek" Army. And in regions "under foreign administration as in Cilicia, the Kemalists never restrained themselves from massacring."[75]

While the Nationalists were growing in strength and fighting the foreign occupiers, the government in Constantinople made a show of conciliation, kowtowing to the Allies in the hope of extracting favorable peace terms. But the Allies came to understand they had no real partner in the increasingly irrelevant Porte. With a possible Nationalist takeover in Constantinople looming, the British, on March 16, 1920, sent in troops to occupy important areas of the city. They took over key buildings and cracked down on the local Nationalists. One hundred and fifty were arrested, including members of parliament.[76] There was almost no Turkish resistance. The French were careful not to take part in the operation; their high commissioner, Albert Defrance, left town the day before. Kemal denounced the occupation of the "seat of the caliphate" as a "new crusade" against "the whole Mohammedan world."[77]

In occupying the city, the British were partly driven by a desire to force the Turkish government into at last signing a war-ending treaty. The tussle continued through spring and early summer, as the remains of the Constantinople government, under pressure from the Nationalists and the occupiers, dragged their feet and eked out a few more Allied concessions. The treaty would finally be signed at Sèvres, in the suburbs of Paris, on August 10. The agreement—between the Allies and representatives from Constantinople, but not Ankara—provided for severing extensive areas from the prewar empire. Alexandretta (the Hatay) and an east-west strip of northern Aleppo vilayet including Urfa, Mardin, and Cezire were consigned to French rule. In the south, portions of Mosul, Mesopotamia, Syria, Lebanon, and Palestine were to become either British or French mandates. Most of the Arabian Peninsula became sovereign Arab territory. Eastern Thrace, including Edirne, was slated for Greek sovereignty. The bulk of Trabzon, Erzurum, Van, and Bitlis vilayets were to be added to the Republic of Armenia. A chunk of eastern Anatolia south of the Armenian areas, including Harput and Diyarbekir, was to become an autonomous Kurdish area, which could apply to the League of Nations for independence. Smyrna and the surrounding district were to remain under Greek control, the area's fate eventually to be decided by plebiscite. France and Italy were to enjoy spheres of influence in Cilicia and southwestern Anatolia respectively. Constantinople was to remain sovereign Turkish territory and the capital of Turkey. But the Straits Zone, the shoreline north and south of the Dardanelles and the Sea of Marmara, would be under international control.

Sèvres also imposed substantial constraints on key Turkish institutions. With respect to the military, Sèvres echoed the severe limits Versailles had placed on Germany. Turkey's armed forces, including gendarmerie, would have to be cut to 50,700 men, and the country was prohibited from maintaining an air force. Its navy was reduced to a handful of small vessels. In addition Turkey's economy and finances were placed under Allied supervision and, to a degree, regulation. Finally, Turkey was enjoined to ensure Christians equal rights, facilitate the return of deportees to their homes, and work to restore plundered Christian property. All conversions to Islam since November 1, 1914, were to be annulled.[78]

Aware of the treaty's extreme unpopularity at home, Constantinople refused to ratify. Even senior Allied officials had "grave misgivings." Bristol, naturally, thought the terms "absolutely unjust."[79] De Robeck, then the British high commissioner, wrote that he had no problem with Allies financial controls and the internationalization of the Straits, but the forced cession to Greece of Eastern Thrace and Smyrna were in "flagrant violation of the principle of self-determination." Their transfer would, he predicted, lead to endless warfare and expulsions. "I am amazed at the lightheartedness with which the [Allied] Supreme Council seem to contemplate another war," he wrote. The Turkish public would reject the treaty, he wrote.[80] Others forecast that Sèvres would lead to a surge in violence against the Christian minorities.[81]

The Ankara government denounced the terms as harsh and humiliating. The treaty boosted their motivation to drive out the foreigners and immediately triggered an increase in anti-French and anti-Greek violence around Anatolia. Following Sèvres and the British occupation of Constantinople, the new political landscape solidified. The Allies governed Constantinople and the parts of Cilicia and Ionia under their direct control, while the rest of Turkey was governed by the Nationalists, who had further consolidated power after the occupation of the capital. Many deputies moved to Ankara and, in April, reconstituted themselves, with additional activists, in a new parliament: the Grand National Assembly of Turkey. The rift between the two Turkish regimes was thus complete. The old government condemned Kemal to death in absentia, and the Şeyhülislam issued a fatwa designating the Nationalists "rebels" whom believers were authorized to kill. The Sultanate even tried—briefly and ineffectually—to challenge the Nationalists in skirmishes in Izmit, Balikesir, and several other towns.

On June 14 and 15, the Nationalists attacked British troops for the first time, in Izmit. The Allies immediately lifted their ban on an eastward Greek advance from Smyrna, believing it would improve their own threatened positions in Izmit. The Greeks made their move on the 22nd, occupying Bursa and Panderma (Bandırma). In July they occupied Edirne and in August the heights of Uşak on the Anatolian plateau. The Nationalists, meanwhile, gained the upper hand in Turkey's eastern marches, decisively beating the ragtag Armenian republican forces in November–December. In March 1921, after the Bolshevik takeover of Yerevan, the Turks and Soviets signed a treaty of friendship. The Turks ceded Nakhichivan and Batumi, and the Soviets began to arm the Nationalists. With the eastern frontier out of the picture, Nationalist troops were free to turn and face their other enemies, the Greeks and the French.[82]

At this point the French tried to reach an accommodation with the Nationalists. In March 1921 they signed an accord with Kemal, agreeing to withdraw from Cilicia in exchange for a handful of largely symbolic concessions. But Ankara scrapped the pact, confident that they would achieve better terms after further fighting.[83] That improved deal came in October. Represented by the right-wing parliamentarian Henry Franklin-Bouillon—whom Rumbold described as "a perfect curse"—the French reached an accord with the Nationalists "behind the back" of the other Allies. Rumbold thought the Allies' position "gravely compromised."[84] The French withdrew completely from Cilicia and northern Aleppo vilayet. No provision was made to protect the Christian minorities left behind, the French being "quite indifferent to their fate."[85]

The Greeks were more committed. But the Nationalists blocked their last offensive fifty miles short of Ankara. The Greek leadership—including Venizelos, who was ousted from the premiership in the general elections of November 1920, and the reinstalled sovereign, King Constantine—then sought a dignified way out of the quagmire. "Something must be done quickly to remove us from the nightmare of Asia Minor," Prince Andrew, a Greek commander, wrote.[86]

The British gradually abandoned the Greek military effort, reducing and eventually cutting off loans and arms. But Britain continued to supply diplomatic support. In March 1922, with the Greeks flailing, the British proposed the complete evacuation of the Greek Army from Anatolia, but with certain safeguards relating to the evacuation and Ottoman Greek civilians.[87] The Nationalists rejected the terms.[88] Athens contemplated seizing Constantinople but was warned off by united Allied opposition.[89] The British representative in Smyrna predicted that the demoralized Greek Army would "crumple up and run for their ships. . . . There is going to be the father and the mother of a mess!"[90]

At the last minute, in spring 1922, the Greeks turned to a new commander: General George Hatzianestis, "a well-trimmed and well-dressed Don Quixote," according to Lloyd George, as well as a "mental case."[91] It was of no avail. By summer the Greek army "was like an apple eaten out inside by insects or disease, superficially whole and apparently firm, but ready to disintegrate at the first sharp blow."[92] It fell on August 26, in the form of a surprise Nationalist offensive. After months of preparation, the Nationalists took only hours to breach the Greek lines. Defeat turned to rout. In their daily communiqués to the press, the Turkish high command downplayed their success for tactical reasons, but the victory was decisive.[93] The Greek Army fled to the coast and took ship for the mainland. Smyrna and the rest of the Ionian coast fell. Within days thousands of Greek and Armenian civilians were massacred, much of Smyrna was in ashes, and more than a quarter of a million Ottoman Greeks fled Anatolia.

The ejection of the Greek Army and a further Nationalist advance northward brought the Kemalists and the British troops into direct contact along the Neutral Zone on the southern shore of the Straits. Kemal demanded right of passage to cross to Europe. Rumbold's fears were coming true. He had predicted back in March that "if the Greeks crack we may expect to have to eat dirt to an unlimited extent and this is not a form of diet that has ever agreed with me"—though the French and Italian high commissioners "Pelle and Carroni may flourish on it."[94] The French and Italians folded, withdrawing their troops from the Straits and southwestern Turkey. But the British, too, ultimately were forced to beat a humiliating strategic retreat.

True, they blocked Kemal from crossing to Thrace, primarily to maintain their temporary hold on the Straits and Constantinople. Kemal tried brinkmanship, inching his cavalry into the Neutral Zone on September 23. The British feared that Kemal would march on Constantinople.[95] Rumbold quoted Franklin-Bouillon to the effect that there were "150,000 Turkish troops who wanted to advance" and "no victorious army had ever stopped and waited before its own capital."[96]

But this one did. Though effectively alone, the British stood firm. Honor was at stake: Lloyd George argued that abandoning Chanak (Canakkale), the town on the Anatolian side of the Dardanelles where Allied troops were centered, would lead to "the greatest loss of prestige."[97] The Cabinet authorized General Charles Harington, the British officer in command in Constantinople, to issue an ultimatum demanding the Nationalists withdraw. He was ordered to fight if necessary.[98] But Kemal then halted his cavalry's advance and agreed to talks.[99] Negotiations began on October 2, at Mudanya. The British hoped to achieve an armistice between the Greeks and Turks, fix the Thracian line to which the Greeks would withdraw, and calm the Straits.

At the Mudanya talks, the French and Italians were ready to bow to Turkish demands, including an immediate Greek handover of Eastern Thrace. Rumbold characterized the French position as "a treacherous surrender."[100] In Constantinople, it was reported, the Christians were "gibbering with terror"—and some were already fleeing the city.[101] Residents understood that the days of Allied occupation were numbered. Most observers expected all the city's Christians—400,000 Greeks and 130,000 Armenians—to leave, as the Armenians fled Cilicia when the French withdrew (see below).[102]

In the midst of the talks, Britain substantially reinforced its troops along the Straits, and the Turks did not renew their probes into the Neutral Zone. But this was a minor victory. In the larger scheme of things, the Turks had won. In the Mudanya Armistice signed on October 11, Britain conceded eventual Greek and Allied withdrawal from Eastern Thrace and Constantinople.[103] The city and the Neutral Zone remained temporarily under British control, but the Greek military would have to begin retreating from Eastern Thrace on the fifteenth. The territory they left would be occupied by Allied contingents for up to thirty days. Turkish gendarmes would then move in.[104]

Within a fortnight, the Christians of Eastern Thrace, numbering between 300,000 and 400,000, had trekked westward out of the country under Allied supervision. The Turks subsequently charged that "the Hellenic authorities" had provoked and encouraged the migration.[105] Venizelos worried that the Turkish gendarmes moving into Eastern Thrace would harass the evacuees, but almost no incidents were reported.[106] The last to leave were the remaining Christian villagers of Gallipoli.[107]

For Rumbold, it was all very humiliating. The Nationalists had "secured Eastern Thrace without striking a blow" and had made no real concessions.[108] When it came time for a peace conference, slated for Lausanne in late November, the Turks would arrive "with the National Pact in one hand and a drawn sabre in the other."[109] Admittedly "gloomy," Rumbold feared for the Christians still left in Anatolia, Western Thrace, and Mosul vilayet.[110]

Between Kemal's conquest of Smyrna and the Lausanne talks, Turkish politics underwent an earthquake. In November 1922, the Grand National Assembly dissolved the Sultanate and declared the establishment of the Turkish Republic. Ahmet Tevfik Pasha, the last Ottoman grand vizier, handed over his seal of office to the Nationalists, and on the 17th Sultan Mehmed VI fled to Malta on a British warship.[111] (The Grand National Assembly then elected the crown prince, Abdülmecid, caliph, a religious figurehead. But the caliphate would also be abolished the following year.)

On November 20 the Nationalists and the Allies convened in Lausanne to hammer out the postwar settlement that would replace Sèvres. An American delegation also attended, mainly to look out for U.S. commercial interests. It did not participate in the formal negotiations, but on one issue appear to have made a real effort: promoting the establishment of an Armenian "national home" in the eastern vilayets. (The term may have been borrowed from the Balfour Declaration, Britain's 1917 promise to support a Jewish "national home" in Palestine.) The Americans saw the minuscule postwar state that had emerged around Yerevan, ultimately to fall under Soviet rule, as insufficient. The Armenians did not disagree: at the Paris Peace Conference back in February 1919, the Armenian delegation had called for a "greater" Armenia, consisting of the Yerevan republic, the "six vilayets," Alexandretta, Adana, Trabzon, Kars, and Alexandropol.[112] During the war Western statesmen had at least hinted at support for Armenian self-determination, as on January 5, 1918, when Lloyd George stated, "Arabia, Armenia, Mesopotamia, Syria and Palestine are in our judgment entitled to a recognition of their separate national conditions."[113] But there were two large problems: most of the Armenians had been murdered and the Turks opposed the proposed national home.

A further problem was that the Americans, on an isolationist trajectory since Versailles, were not a reliable patron. In September 1919 Washington had sent

The Turkish delegation at Lausanne. The style of kalpak favored by Mustafa Kemal was newly in fashion.

a "military mission" under Major General James Harbord to "investigate" a possible postwar territorial reshuffling. After a month touring the region, the mission failed to recommend Armenian independence outside Yerevan. Instead it suggested that Constantinople, Anatolia, and Transcaucasia be placed under a single mandatory power. Harbord was not especially taken with the Turks—"never . . . has the Turk done other than destroy wherever he has conquered"—but he also did not seem eager to help the Armenians. "The Armenian does not generally endear himself to those of other races with whom he comes in contact," he wrote. "The Armenian stands among his neighbors very much as the Jew stands in Russia and Poland. . . . He incurs the penalty which attaches among backward races to the banker, the middleman and the creditor."[114]

Still, at San Remo in April 1920, the Allied Supreme Council asked the United States to assume a mandate over Armenia, an option supported by many of the American missionaries. The Council also asked President Woodrow Wilson to set the borders for the expanded Armenian national home. Wilson acted swiftly—and blunderingly. On May 24 he asked Congress to approve the mandate; a week later the Senate turned him down.[115] Nonetheless, in fulfilment of his commission, on November 22 Wilson issued his territorial determination, allocating the bulk of Trabzon, Erzurum, Bitlis, and Van vilayets to "Armenia." But the determination was not only superfluous—Sèvres had already demarcated Armenia's borders—it was also meaningless. By this point the Nationalists had occupied most of the region Wilson had apportioned the Armenians, and Kemal was resolved to hold on to it. The Americans, meanwhile, were unwilling to invest more than words in the Armenian cause. As Kemal put it, "Poor Wilson did not understand that a frontier which is not defended with bayonets, force and honor cannot be secured by another principle."[116]

Sèvres unraveled during late 1920 and 1921 under the Nationalist hammer blows on the ground, and the life went out of foreign support for Armenian sovereignty west of Yerevan. France showed the way: in March 1920, while fighting Kemal in Cilicia, it was busy running guns to the Kemalists through the Black Sea ports, and in April, France secretly offered to assist the Turks in fighting the Greeks in Thrace.[117] The French were partly driven by economic considerations—the future of their business interests in Turkey—and by a fear that isolating the Nationalists might lead to a Bolshevik-Kemalist alliance which would subvert French interests far beyond Turkey. In June the Bolsheviks began massively arming the Nationalists. But the Armenians' main problem was that the Allies were too busy demobilizing and licking their Great War wounds to contemplate a new war, with a doubtful outcome, in the east.

Pretty soon, the Armenians themselves gave up hope of achieving self-determination beyond the Yerevan Republic. Indeed, in April 1923, while the Lausanne talks were ongoing, the Armenian Patriarch Kevork Arslanian went so far as to say that "the Armenian nation has completely lost interest in the 'Armenian [National] Home' . . . . Armenians living in Turkey have understood the truth. They are animated by the desire to live in brotherhood with the Turkish element."[118]

For years, indeed decades, the Turks were to remain ambivalent about the Yerevan Republic. On the one hand, they feared that it would serve as a beacon for Armenian irredentists. On the other hand, since the Armenians had a state, there was less international pressure on Turkey to shed territory for Armenian sovereignty, and the Armenians' lost some of their motivation to carry on the fight with Turkey. Yerevan also provided Turkey a resettlement venue, a place it could settle Armenians it sought to expel or already had expelled. Thus, prominent Nationalists, such as Ismet Bey, Kemal's envoy to Turkestan, affirmed that Turkey had no "desire to crush [the Republic of] Armenia. On the contrary, it very much desired to see the establishment of a free and independent Armenia as its neighbor. . . . Let Armenia keep to the territories she controlled now . . . and Turkey would have no quarrel with her."[119]

The outcome of the Turkish War of Independence with respect to the Armenian question was formalized at Lausanne. Curzon and others indulged in rhetorical flourishes in support of the Armenian cause, but that was all. The Allies abandoned both the goal of a greater Armenia encompassing the Yerevan republic and the eastern Anatolian vilayets and the hope of providing effective protection for Turkey's remaining Christians.

What had happened to the Christians and what awaited those still in Turkey was clear to all. Officially Ankara may have been cagey, but the chatter in diplomatic salons made clear the thrust of Nationalist thinking. Bristol described one such conversation, over lunch in 1922, with Sabiha Djennani Hanoum, a recent graduate of Constantinople College and daughter of a

Turkish parliamentarian. "Like most Turks that one talks with nowadays," he said, she "is very much in favor of getting rid of the Christian races. They state that the Christian races have been the source of their misfortunes. . . . These Christian races have for many years been absolutely disloyal. . . . The Turks wanted to get rid of the Christian races once and for all." Djennani granted that Turkish behavior toward the Christians during World War I may have been "wrong." But, she added, "It was a pity all of them hadn't been killed at that time."[120]

When discussions began at Lausanne, the Turks believed that "the only party . . . that really counts is England . . . Italy can be bought and . . . France won't fight." Rumbold's deputy, Nevile Henderson, thought "the Turks are still afraid of us," but London had a weak hand.[121] The wartime army had been demobilized, the public was sick of fighting, and the country was in financial straits even as the spoils of war had added substantially to British commitments around the globe. The Turks, on the other hand, while sapped by a decade of continuous warfare, were confident and ready for further sacrifice in a struggle they saw as existential. They were in high spirits at Lausanne, thanks to their recent victories over the French and Greeks.

The Turkish representatives displayed inflexibility.[122] Across the table, the French were willing to "give way at every point," as Curzon put it.[123] The French said they were simply being realistic. Britain's position was undermined from within "by a combination of forces represented by Labour, the *Daily Mail* and the politicians who imagine that the way to placate Islam is to yield on every point to a militant Turkey."[124] Again, these politicians were mindful of how developments in Turkey might affect the Muslim-populated regions of the empire. The attitude of the new British Prime Minister, Andrew Bonar Law, was particularly concerning to officials wary of Turkey. Rumbold wrote, "The mere thought of hostilities is repugnant to [his] mind."[125] The British military was also keen on avoiding trouble, though it insisted on retaining Mosul for the new British mandate of Iraq.[126]

The Turks, ever suspicious of Allied intentions, implicitly and sometimes explicitly threatened war if their terms were not met. The British disdained them. While Bristol complained that the British treated the Turkish delegates "as if they were schoolboys" to be "scold[ed]" and "preach[ed] at," Curzon believed that Turkish truculence had a different source.[127] The Turkish delegates received an "exorbitant entertainment allowance" and were interested in drawing out the talks because they "greatly prefer the fleshpots of Lausanne to the austerities of Angora," he said.[128]

At the end of January 1923, the Allies handed the Turks a draft treaty.[129] The Turks refused to sign. The conference adjourned with no agreement on economic matters or the minorities question. Rumbold believed that Ankara had been presented with "a wonderful treaty," but the "fanatics," "wildmen" and "ignorant back-woodsmen" in Ankara didn't see it that way.[130] The Turks argued that the January terms placed their country in "economic slavery."[131] The British suspected that the Americans, for commercial reasons, were egging on Turkish obduracy.[132]

The conference reconvened three months later. By then the Turks were "keen to get a settlement." According to Rumbold, now head of the British delegation, their army had deteriorated, and they were "stony broke."[133] Still, several more months were to elapse before the Turks were ready to sign.

The Treaty of Lausanne, which was finalized on July 24, 1923, differed radically from Sèvres. In almost all provisions, Turkey emerged triumphant. There was to be no Western "tutelage" of the new republic and no Allied control of the Straits. The Armenians gained nothing, and the Turks enjoyed far more territory than Sèvres had allowed.[134] Lloyd George, the former British Prime Minister, put it graphically, "The Turk may be a bad ruler, but he is the prince of anglers. The cunning and the patience with which he lands the most refractory fish once he has hooked it is beyond compare. . . . The wily oriental was giving out plenty of line. . . . [But] at last the huge tarpon are all lying beached on the banks—Britain, France, Italy, the United States of America— high and dry, landed and helpless, without a swish left in their tails, glistening and gasping in the summer sun."[135]

The Turks did make some concessions. The sanjak of Alexandretta went to French-ruled Syria (it was transferred to Turkey in 1939), while the fate of Mosul vilayet and the demarcation of the Turkish-Iraqi border was left to future British-Turkish negotiations or, if unsuccessful, to the Council of the League of Nations. Turkey also renounced claims to Cyprus, Libya, Egypt, and Sudan, lands lost by the Ottomans in previous decades. And Greece and Italy retained almost all the Aegean islands. But Turkey received Eastern Thrace and the eastern vilayets of Anatolia as well as Adana. The Straits were formally internationalized but were to be governed by a Turkish-chaired commission, and Turkey was allowed to garrison the zone with 12,000 troops.

The capitulations annulled by Turkey at the start of the war—extraterritorial judicial and economic rights granted over the centuries to Western countries and Russia and their citizens visiting or living in the Ottoman Empire— remained a dead letter, but Turkey had to abide by existing foreign economic concessions. Greece and Turkey agreed on bilateral peace and an exchange of their remaining minority populations. There was no requirement that Turkey pay war reparations. Turkey did commit to honoring the rights of all its citizens, but, as there was to be no foreign supervision, the commitment was meaningless. Indeed, even during the conference, Ankara ordered the expulsion of the remaining Armenians from Maraş.[136] Subsequently the Allies ruled that Turkey had substantially violated its commitments regarding the minorities.[137]

Kemal hailed the agreement. It had, he said, "broken the judicial, political, economic and financial chains which kept us behind other civilized nations."[138] Within weeks, the British evacuated the Straits and Constantinople. The last soldiers departed the city on October 2, 1923, and Turkish troops marched in four days later. An American intelligence officer was impressed by their "ruggedness and hardened physiques."[139] Non-Turkish signs were immediately pulled down: "Chauvinism is rampant, and its object is to Turkify everything," a British observer commented. But there was almost no anti-Christian violence, and the police maintained a tight grip. Anxious to show their allegiance to the new regime, Christians had started wearing fezzes a few days before.[140] Turkey was now "mistress in her own house."[141]

World War I and the subsequent War of Independence had ravaged Turkey and radically changed its demography. Yet, despite the death of some 2.5 million Muslims due to famine, war, and disease, the Muslim proportion of the population rose from 80 to 98 percent, largely as a result of the deportation and massacre of Christians during 1914–1924. The deportations and massacres of 1919–1924 are described in the next two chapters. By 1924 only 65,000 Armenians and 120,000 Greeks remained, almost all in Constantinople.[142] The country had lost most of its merchant class and a large percentage of its skilled workers and craftsmen. A great deal of housing had been destroyed, especially in eastern Anatolia and Izmir. In other ways, too, the economy had been ravaged, with international trade harmed dramatically. But Turkey was free of foreign armies and Christians, and it was independent.

8

Turks and Armenians, 1919–1924

The chapter of Armenian history that is being enacted in Cilicia now is as tragic and pathetic as the great Deportation. Returning from that exile and beginning with energy to live once more and hope once more, they find themselves betrayed, and that by their allies, massacred by their conquered enemy, and stripped barer than they were in 1915. The Turks are warring against the French and make an excuse of that to annihilate the Armenians. The French are toadying to the Turks . . . and are sacrificing the Armenians. . . . The Armenians . . . are doomed.

William Dodd to Mark Bristol, 9 April 1920

According to the Armenians, the population of Cilicia in 1914 totaled 490,000, of whom 286,000 were Christians, 205,000 of them Armenians. Official Turkish figures for 1914, came to a similar total—442,000—but 366,000 of them Muslim and 61,500 Armenian.[1] Whatever the truth, the wartime massacres and deportations drastically reduced the Armenian population, though tens of thousands remained, mostly in Muslim households or orphanages. During 1918–1921, they were joined by over 100,000 more, most of them returnees from the Syrian and Iraqis deserts who had somehow survived and believed that they would benefit from Anglo-French protection. Yet two years later, almost no Armenians remained in Cilicia, or in neighboring northern Aleppo vilayet.

Britain's Year

At the end of World War I, on paper, Allied control of Turkey appeared almost total and discretionary; in practice, a lack of Allied resources and will resulted in gradual, then rapid, loss of dominion. The attenuation of Allied power had already begun when the British were in the saddle. It sped up after the French took over in Cilicia and northern Aleppo vilayet.

Over November 1918–February 1919, British troops of the Egyptian Expeditionary Force, commanded by General Edmund Allenby, fanned out across northern Syria and south-central Turkey.[2] The British remained in control there until November 1919, when governance passed to the French.

The British-occupied area initially had a small Armenian population—survivors of deportation columns, converts, and privileged families and workers. But the number swelled as tens of thousands of deportees made their way home, many under British escort.

The British encountered Armenian deportees in the dying months of the war. Perhaps the first group they met was in Wadi Musa in southern Trans-jordan in November 1917. Hundreds more were found, in ill health and sometimes stripped naked, in the ruins of Petra and in Tafile near the Dead Sea and in the old city of Jerusalem.[3] A few weeks later, a British agent counted 253 freshly minted Armenian corpses, "men, women and children," between Salt and Amman. They all "had had their throats cut, except some babies who had been stamped on. The men were apart, and tied together." They had just been rounded up and butchered by Circassian irregulars. Nearby, some forty-five deportees who had lived in Madaba reached British lines—in the nude. Their clothes had been stripped by Bedouin.[4] The British encountered their first large group of deportees, some 30,000 strong, when they entered Damascus in October 1918.

The subsequent year of British rule was generally characterized by calm. As Irish-American missionary Thomas D. Christie, the president of St. Paul's Collegiate Institute at Tarsus, put it: "Under British control the entire vilayet of Adana . . . was perfectly quiet."[5] "This was the year of freedom, happiness, enlightenment, and reward for the Armenians," Abraham Hartunian, the memoirist, wrote.[6]

But from the first there were also signs of trouble for the British occupation and for the Christian minorities. In November 1918 the British trouble-shooter Mark Sykes, while touring northern Aleppo vilayet, predicted the friction ahead: "Obstruction, stimulation of [Muslim] fanaticism, local propaganda among the Muslims, spread of dissension among Arabs and reestablishment of Turkish prestige by demonstration of Turkey's power to challenge our decisions."[7] A month later, he noted that the Turks were distributing arms to villagers, preparing for resistance to the occupation, and readying massacres of Christians. Discussing the situation, he thought the Entente must "show [it] means business by immediate removal of all Turkish authority in Adana, Marash, Shekere, Aintab. . . . Unless such action is taken I respectfully warn HMG whole future of Cilicia, Syria and Mesopotamia is endangered." Specifically, he cautioned that, with the aid of Arabs and Kurds, "Turkish ascendancy [would] be established and last remnants of Armenians destroyed."[8]

On December 28, 1918, Allenby informed the War Office that a Turkish general, Nihad Pasha, was busy organizing and arming the populace. Large quantities of weapons were available, left in the villages when Ottoman Army units demobilized or withdrew from Cilicia. Soldiers and deserters were "wandering about . . . seizing goods and houses of exiled inhabitants." Nihad was said to be "exhorting Turks" to organize for resistance.[9] Demobilized soldiers were joining the gendarmerie.[10]

Within weeks, a large number of Muslim brigand bands formed and began operating in the countryside, mainly outside areas of British control. At first, they appeared lawless, in the manner of the prewar marauders who persecuted Armenians throughout the east for their own reasons. But soon the bands coalesced into more organized bodies and were said to have "enlisted in a Crusade nominally for the defense of Turkish independence" from Western occupiers.[11] Andrew Ryan, the British number-two in Constantinople, reported that "common brigandage" was transforming into "political brigandage," with former CUP agents guiding the process.[12] By August 1919, with the Nationalists having taken over much of Anatolia, regional governors had largely shifted allegiance from Constantinople to Ankara and began ignoring or even countermanding British instructions. They did not fight the British, though. Instead they directed their efforts at attacking Turks who refused to accept Nationalist authority and toward creating armed groups to persecute Christians. A Turkish gendarmerie officer, one M. Sherif, reported from Gebze, near Izmit, that "bands are being organized . . . under the knowledge of the authorities. Their intention is . . . to attack the Christian villages. . . . The initiator of all this is the kaymakam of Gebze. . . . The authorities are nothing but the accomplices of the brigands."[13]

Accompanying and compounding the chaos engendered by disintegrating governance were dramatic demographic shifts. The country was being swamped by "a migration of peoples which reminds one of the migrations of the Middle Ages," observed British Deputy High commissioner Admiral Richard Webb. He was referring to the influx of Armenian returnees but even more so to the "million Mussulmans—Bosnians, Pomaks, Macedonians, Kurds, Lazes, etc." and Muslims from "east of Erzingan" who flooded into central and western Anatolia.[14] There were also intimidated Christians fleeing their homes and large numbers of demobilized Muslims returning to theirs. All these people in motion faced considerable pressure from bad weather and the Spanish flu, not to mention the destruction wrought by the Russian and Turkish militaries in eastern Anatolia. Large areas had turned into wasteland.[15] By summer 1919, as kaymakam Zia Bey of Michalıç put it, "C'est une anarchie complète."[16]

From the first, Turkish officers and officials were determined to reassert their authority, especially in unoccupied areas of Anatolia and the Caucasus. Local CUP cadres enlisted Kurdish support.[17] Kurds were easily persuaded, seeing in the Western powers interlopers and in the Armenians their traditional, contemptible vassals. "A watery chestnut, a mongrel and an Armenian—don't trust any of them," ran a Kurdish proverb.[18]

Turkish views of the Cilicia Armenians were not much different. In the prewar years, their disdain had also been flavored by envy and resentment due to Armenian prosperity and, here and there, the transfer of Muslim-owned property into the hands of Christian creditors.[19] On top of this, by late 1918–1919, fears of Armenian sovereignty were elevated, and Turks had to worry about Armenian revenge for the wartime massacres. Already in December 1918 Turks complained that Muslims were being robbed by Armenian members of the French occupying force that had come ashore in Alexandretta. Yet few Armenians did exact revenge, and the occupying powers generally were able to curb depredations against Muslims.

In some Cilician towns old CUP hands organized meetings to plan resistance against the occupiers and "to provoke the Muslims into continuing the struggle."[20] British troops were rushed to Antep, Kilis, and Islamiye, "quelling any idea of disorder." But apparently they reached Antep only after Muslims

The Franco-Turkish War, 1920–1921, Sieges and Battles

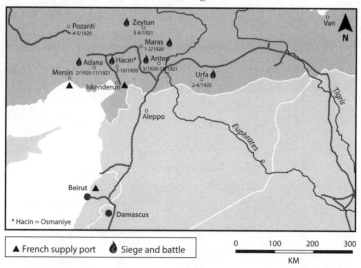

* Hacin = Osmaniye

▲ French supply port   ◉ Siege and battle

0   100   200   300
KM

had "systematically destroyed" houses in the Armenian quarter and "defiled" churches.[21] Sykes wrote of Turkish "impertinence," citing the desecration of an Antep convent the night the commander of the British 5th Cavalry Division was to visit the city.[22] CUP officials in the town declared that "their intention" was "to massacre all Armenians, drive out the British garrison" and declare a "small Turkish republic." They openly discussed attacking the British military, but they took no action. The British warned Turkish officials that, if their people failed to keep the peace, they would be held to account. Entente troops would occupy the region's towns in force, mutesariffs would be replaced with British governors, "rabid 'Young Turks' [would] be deported," and the number of Armenians in the gendarmerie would be increased.[23] Early Turkish violations of the armistice included the occasional sabotage of railway lines.[24]

Muslim anger mounted in the first months of 1919, as the Allied-controlled government in Constantinople issued a stream of directives to local officials to restore Christian orphans and women to their communities, assist refugee return, and return stolen property.[25] British troops managed to nip in the bud massacres planned in Antep and Maraş and at least partially disarmed the Antep Turks. The British punitively closed cafes, shops, and markets.[26] They also exiled to Aleppo six of the town's notables.[27] But in

Armenian returnees in Merzifon—all women and children—collect wool to weave into clothing for orphans. The covered women may be converts to Islam.

Aleppo a massacre took place on February 28, at "Turkish instigation." Between forty-eight and eighty-three Armenian refugees were murdered and more than a hundred wounded. The attack was carried out "principally by Arab police and gendarmes." Intervention by British troops prevented higher casualties. The British later hanged three assailants, jailed others, and exiled fifteen to Sudan.[28]

On March 24 British troops occupied Urfa "to preserve order and protect the Armenian population."[29] Thereafter the British reacted to depredations with firmness and lethality, even resorting to the aerial bombardment and strafing of local tribesmen who had defied their authority. The British also curbed Armenian nationalist demonstrations that might anger the Turks, though the latter were not satisfied.[30] Although in July the troops in Urfa instructed local Armenian leaders to cease "provocative" behavior, Ottoman officials remained convinced that the British favored the Christians.[31]

Muslim depredations against Christians increased in late 1919 throughout Anatolia. Armenian girls were abducted and merchants were robbed. Local authorities jailed Armenians on trumped up charges.[32] Constantinople, citing attacks by Armenian gangs, turned a blind eye.[33] Over a year later, Bristol was to write, perhaps with a dash of exaggeration, "Even when the British were in occupation [of Cilicia] they allowed Christians to be persecuted, intimidated, robbed and killed." The British, like the French who succeeded them, were reluctant to "antagonize the [majority] Moslem element" or use "force to protect the Christian races."[34]

Senior British officials were aware of the situation. In November 1919 Gough-Calthorpe's successor as high commissioner, Admiral de Robeck, reported, "The most flagrant cases of injustice to Christians have to be left unredressed. . . . The Christians are now bewildered and terrified." Brigands "posing as patriots," were regularly robbing Christians and "taking possession of property restored to their Christian owners." Supported by the authorities, Muslims were boycotting Christians and preventing them from earning a livelihood. Indeed, some Christians were terrorized into fleeing their homes. "Behind all these elements of disorder," de Robeck said, "stands Mustapha Kemal."[35] American diplomats agreed. Captured documents signed by Kemal proved "beyond all doubt his responsibility for [the] disorder . . . by inciting to holy war."[36]

But not all British officials were clear about Kemal's personal responsibility. De Robeck's successor, Rumbold, as late as February 1921, opined that Kemal "does not himself encourage or countenance the massacre of Christians, but rather . . . he is powerless . . . to protect from massacre the Christian population of the areas in which military operations are in progress."[37] Rumbold was soon to change his tune.

Early on, the Armenian Patriarchate understood what Rumbold did not. It reported in summer 1919 that Kemal had "issued telegraphic orders everywhere" for the formation of bands and that the Turks were preparing for a "big insurrection." The Patriarchate also found that "many Turkish officers" had moved to Cilicia, where they were going about in civilian dress to "direct the movement" and whip up the Muslim population.[38] And soon the British discovered that elements in the Constantinople government were in cahoots with Kemal. In March 1920 de Robeck reported that the War Ministry had ordered the 15th Corps, in Erzurum, "to distribute to the neighboring army corps and to the Nationalists . . . arms and ammunition." The 13th Corps, at Diyarbekir, was also ordered "to comply" and duly distributed arms at Maraş and Urfa.[39]

By autumn 1919 there were murderous raids on Christian villages in "different parts of Cilicia." In the area of Cihan (Djihan), bands raided Papakhli, Hamdili, Kerune, Köprü, Yenice, and Merdjin (Mercin?). In Küçük Mangheri, Turkish raiders murdered three men and a woman. Eleven Armenians, including women and children, were killed in Sheikh Mourad (Şeyh Murat), near Adana. Many of the perpetrators wore gendarmerie uniforms.[40]

Return

In the months after the armistice, the British and French encouraged and in part orchestrated a mass return of Armenian and Greek deportees, particularly to Cilicia. The British recognized a moral obligation to redress wartime wrongs, and the French believed that the presence of a large Christian population would make it easier to administer the region, which they hoped to add to their imperial holdings.[41] By late December 1918 more than 40,000 Armenian and Greek deportees had returned, according to the Constantinople government.[42] All were destitute and many in ill health. Indeed, "some . . . were quite insane."[43] The numbers grew. According to a possibly exaggerated analysis by the Turkish Foreign Ministry, 138,070 Christians—62,721 Greeks and 75,349 Armenians—had returned by February 1919 and 276,000 by June 1919.[44]

A measure of repatriation had begun already during the Great War. In winter 1915–1916, there was a largescale return of Armenian refugees in the Caucasus to Russian-occupied areas in Van, Bitlis, Erzurum, and Trabzon vilayets.[45] As many as 35,000 reached Van. But a new Turkish push sent them scuttling back to the Caucasus in 1917.[46] Talât and Enver may have told a visiting German Reichstag deputy that "urban Armenians" were allowed to return to their cities, assuming these were not in "war zones."[47] But this was hogwash. The CUP leaders remained dead set against a return of deportees, aside from a few exceptions at select sites, such as Tekirdağ and Adana.[48]

The real return began at war's end, when the Turks were no longer capable, at least for a time, of preventing it. The British authorities had a natural desire to be rid of the burden of refugee care in greater Syria and Iraq, and they sought to do the humanitarian thing by facilitating repatriation.[49] The challenge was enormous. In December 1918 Sykes estimated that there were 80,000 Armenian deportees in Aleppo and Damascus vilayets. Some 4,000–5,000 children of both sexes had been sold to Arabs—bedouin, villagers, and townspeople— "along the road" between the two towns. In Aleppo, he wrote, 200 girls were being "reared as prostitutes." The repatriation of these deportees needed "careful organization." "Indications show that unless steps are taken by Entente to supervise repatriation, Turks will grow more obstructive as they know that while Armenians remain exiled birthrate is diminished and death rate increased," he noted. He also anticipated that the Turks would "flood" Antep and Maraş with demobilized soldiers, then "begin killing [Armenians] on a small scale."[50] He urged Her Majesty's Government to send "permanent military forces" into the six vilayets and to Adana to ensure that the return was peaceful. He also recommended setting up "repatriation commissions . . . to organize the reception of repatriated people when spring comes." Meanwhile, camps had to be established in Aleppo, Homs, Hama, Damascus, Adana, Urfa, and Antep, where the deportees could be temporarily housed. He added that unorganized "individual trekking home should be stopped," again for the protection of the returnees. To encourage the return of Armenian children, he recommended paying rewards to Muslim families that gave them up and punishing those concealing them. He also suggested examining Muslim-Armenian marriages from the war period.[51]

Britain's director of military intelligence felt that Sykes did not "fully appreciate" the manpower problem involved in such an effort.[52] But British officials—as well as American offcials and Armenian leaders—did generally agree in winter 1918–1919 that the deportees should stay put at least until spring.[53] The War Office thought "premature" repatriation would trigger "incidents." It was better to temporarily maintain Armenians in Syrian and Mesopotamian camps where they could be efficiently fed or else, the diplomat Thomas Hohler suggested, "in the town[s] where they have taken refuge."[54] Without delay until spring, the American consul in Salonica wrote, "the remnant of the [Armenian] nation stands a fair chance of perishing on the return trip." Over it all hovered a larger, political question: Should the Armenians be returned to "their former homes or perhaps the new Armenia that may be formed?"[55]

But that winter, no matter the weather, Turkish obstructionism, and the hesitancy or contrariness of Western diplomats, large groups of deportees voted with their feet. The trickle turned into a "stream . . . and it is now very hard to check it," Webb reported in December 1918.[56] "Apparently the desire to return to their former homes has been much stronger than the logic" of sitting out the winter, the U.S. diplomat Lewis Heck explained. By early January 1919, Heck reported, some 800 of Izmit's prewar Armenians had returned; in Bardizag, of 10,000 prewar Armenians, some 1,500 had returned.[57] By February about 2,000 returnees had reached Maraş.[58] In early April 2,761 reportedly had returned to Adapazarı and its surrounding villages, out of the original Armenian population of 26,000.

Armenians came home to insecurity. Most Christian houses had been demolished or were still occupied, churches and cemeteries had been devastated, and Armenians feared tilling their fields outside town, where they would be vulnerable to assault by Muslims. They also feared being conscripted into the Turkish army.[59] This despite official Ottoman policy during November 1918–March 1919, which was to enable Christian return, restore their property, and free abductees from Muslim homes. Even before the armistice was signed,

the Constantinople government asked provincial officials for details about returnees and their properties, apparently with returnees' welfare in mind. In
October 1918 national officials instructed governors to assist the return to
their homes of "people who have been . . . deported during the war by military decisions," and even to support them financially. Governors were also ordered to evict Muslims from Armenian houses, protect empty homes, and
allow converts to revert to Christianity.[60]

Constantinople's early willingness to alleviate Armenian misery probably
reflected Turkish fear of retribution. And the government was certainly under
pressure from the British. On February 7–8, 1919, the redoubtable General
Allenby, who had thrashed the Ottomans in Palestine and Syria, visited the
capital and told the Turkish ministers, "Armenians will be repatriated by me
when this is desirable. Their houses, lands and property are to be restored
now."[61] The officials promised to enact appropriate legislation but never did.[62]
This undercut Allied efforts at the local level to get Turks to give up confiscated property. Provincial officials were under another kind of pressure: from
Muslims who occupied Christians' houses and cultivated their fields, held captive women and children, and opposed Christian repatriation on ideological
grounds.[63] Indeed, many officials were among the appropriators resisting the
restoration of Armenian lives. At least one British officer suggested that hostile
Turkish officials—inspired not only by nationalism and "pan-Islamic doc-
trines" but also by "the desire to keep" what they had "stolen"—would have
to be purged before a general repatriation could be considered.[64]

This is not to suggest that every local official opposed return. In Muratça
and Çalkara, in Eskişehir sanjak, the authorities helped returning Armenians
and even expelled squatting muhacirs.[65] Officials also expelled muhacirs in
Erzurum and Kayseri, and houses were restored to returnees in Akşehir and
Antep.[66] Occasionally, the Turks even covered returnees' rail fares.[67] But more
commonplace was the attitude, if not the behavior, of the mutesarrif of Amasya,
who imprisoned returnees and then forced them to go back to "their places
of deportation."[68]

Even if Constantinople had wished to impose a serious return policy, it held
little sway in the localities or over the muhacirs. Central-government policy
quickly fell into step with local Muslims' wishes. Just a few months after the
end of the war, Constantinople switched formally to obstructionism, for

Armenian survivors of deportation and massacre, mostly women and children. The majority wished to return to their places of origin after the war.

example forbidding refugees returning "in groups" and preventing them set-tling in cities other than their places of origin.[69]

Returnees also suffered from widespread brigandage. A group of returning Armenians were reportedly murdered by Kurds near Birecjik; others were killed in Mardin. The Mardin brigands exploited the survivors, forcing Chris-tian girls to "cut and carry wood in the forests."[70] Initially the Christian re-turnees put their faith in Allied protection, especially in Cilicia, northern Aleppo vilayet, and Ionia. But such protection often proved feeble. Near Samsun in early summer 1919, brigands robbed a column of returnees—after first disarming their Indian Army escort and relieving the British commander of his shoes.[71]

While some of the brigands attacking returnees sought only profit and plunder, others were politically motivated and received assistance from the Nationalists and local officials. This was probably true of the men who mur-dered a dozen Armenians near Catalcham (Çatalçam), a village on the Tokat road, on July 7, 1919. A British "control," or repatriation, officer, John Shays Perring, reported that three of them, girls, were raped "and their bodies cut up." The party had consisted mostly of women and children "reclaimed from Moslem houses." A Turkish investigation found that the killers were led by "Suleyman Ismail Bey, an ex-Turkish officer" and were "part of the Mustafa Kemal organization." Directing this band from behind the scenes was Rifat Bey, Kemal's agent in Sivas.[72] Perring also reported that "this state of affairs is encouraged by the local Turks, both civil and military, . . . a complete working arrangement is in existence for the supply of arms and ammunition to the Turkish brigand bands by the local military authorities."[73]

Given the hazards along the roads, the breadth of destruction in former Armenian communities, and the pervasiveness of Muslim expropriation, returnees often made stops along the way before returning to their home towns. When they did reach home, they sometimes used threats or force to regain properties, often assisted by Allied troops or control officers. More frequently, Muslims employed threats or force to prevent restoration of property.[74] Already by mid-December 1918, violence between locals and returning Armenians was reported from Tekirdağ, Bahçecik, Bey Yayla, Karaağaç, and Yalova.[75] (According to Ottoman reports, some incidents were instigated by Armenians who, protected by the Russians, wreaked vengeance upon Muslim villagers in the foothills of Mt. Ararat.[76]) In Samsun and elsewhere, Muslims torched the homes of newly returned Christians. Fearing for their safety, large numbers of Armenians were induced to leave yet again. In the first year of the return, almost all rural Armenians in the interior fled their farms and villages and concentrated in towns and cities where they were better protected.[77] Many returnees to the interior, if they had the means, drifted off toward Constantinople and Smyrna.[78]

An American missionary defined the core problem facing Christian repatriation. As the war was winding down, he wrote, "The Turk has become drunk with blood and rapine, and plunder and power, and he will be a different man from what he was before the [1915] atrocities." The missionary spoke of minds "obsessed with Moslem fanaticism seven times heated."[79] Thus were returnees, mostly women and children, to be found along the roads north from Mosul and Aleppo "without money, food, shelter, or clothing . . . victims to death and disease" and with so little to go home to.[80]

At the end of 1919, the French governor of Cilicia, Colonel Edouard Brémond, put the number of returnees who had reached the region at

120,000.[81] Some of the return had been facilitated by the British and French. But "many more," according to Jackson, had repatriated themselves, especially from territories outside Jackson's ken, such as Russia and the Balkans.[82]

By summer 1919 restitution of Christian property had more or less ground to a halt, save for exceptional cases where British officers intervened directly.[83] Indeed, local Turkish "administrative or judicial action" led to the reversal of restitutions that had already been made.[84] In some places, Turks demolished empty Armenian buildings rather than see them reoccupied by Christians.[85] By September 1919, the Allied high commissioners had concluded that "it was imprudent to press, in present circumstances, for the restitution of property."[86]

By mid-1920, 12,000 deportees had arrived in Adana town, an American missionary reported; to its 36 surrounding villages some 30,000 had returned; to Hacin, 10,500; to Maraş, 8,000 and less than 3,000 to its surrounding villages. Zeytun now had 1,200 returnees, and its surrounding villages, 1,000. Altogether, the missionary calculated, of Cilicia's prewar 200,000 Armenians, about a third had returned.[87]

Serious aid for returnees came from American missionary institutions—after January 1919, mostly from Near East Relief, which emerged as the chief foreign aid agency in Turkey. Many of NER's officers were former missionaries in Turkey, including its chairman, James Barton, and its general secretary, Charles Vickery. Originally called the American Committee for Armenian and Syrian Relief, NER had been set up at the urging of Morgenthau in September–October 1915 to aid Armenians during the deportations.[88] In August 1919 it was incorporated by act of Congress and changed its name.[89] In late 1922 much of its work was transferred to Greece, where it operated alongside the American Red Cross aiding Greek refugees. The officers and their help saved countless lives. But, in Turkey, one missionary put it like this, referring to the Armenians: "It seems to me that the relief work is a good deal like fattening sheep for the slaughter." Rather, he favored promoting emigration. "I can see no hope for them in this country."[90]

NER and other relief organizations provided food, shelter, and medical services. They also ran orphanages, refugee camps, and rescue or "neutral" houses for recovered abductees.[91] The agencies also offered a small measure of relief to destitute Turks, whether for humanitarian reasons or in an effort to appease the authorities and persuade them to allow continued aid for the Christians. But as the Christians were gradually cleansed during 1919–1923, relief operations tapered off. The missionary and educator Cass Arthur Reed wrote from Smyrna in October 1922, "Relief for Christians is finishing because there are no Christians [left]."[92]

In March 1919 the British set up within their high commission a special Armenian and Greek Section (AGS) to monitor what was happening to these communities, including with respect to repatriation and relief.[93] That month the British also installed repatriation officers in a number of towns. The first two, Captain L. J. Hurst and Lieutenant Perring, went to Samsun; others were stationed in Smyrna, Aydın, Ayvalı, the Dardanelles, Bandırma, Izmit, Tekirdağ, Ankara, Konya, Sivas, and Edirne.[94] Their task was to facilitate return. In many localities, the British set up commissions to adjudicate property claims. The commissions consisted of a British chairman, a representative of the Constantinople government, and local Turkish officials and Armenian or Greek representatives. The British thought it would be easier to repatriate Armenians than Greeks, who "seek inspiration and obtain moral and material support from Greece," making their future "a national question." Moreover many Anatolian Greek expatriates had joined the Greek army and "fought against Turkey."[95]

A March 1919 report by one repatriation officer in Beylik, near Constantinople, illustrates their modus operandi. The officer observed that muhacirs, now "wealthy beys" thanks to their expropriated property, had sown Christians' fields. "We brought the Greek owners and the Muslim squatters face to face," the officer wrote. The Muslims promised to give up the fields the following autumn, after they had reaped them and received "compensation for the ploughing and other expenses incurred." But the British officer demanded that they hand the fields over at once, "unconditionally. . . . Unless pushed to it by force repeatedly, the Turks will stop restoring property as soon as they feel that they are no more watched."[96]

The arrival of spring, with improved weather, facilitated return. But Turkish obstructionism increased apace. It was most pronounced concerning real estate and the rescue of women and children, and paralleled, and was in part due to, the growth of the Nationalist movement.[97] The Turks petitioned the British to halt return. They also threatened renewed massacre, actually killed and robbed returnees, and were unwilling to give up expropriated property.[98] One knowledgeable missionary, C. F. Gates, the President of Constantinople's Robert College, estimated in early 1921 that "not more than one third of the real estate of the Armenians who have returned has been regained."[99] The Greek ecclesiastical authorities reported that in the first quarter of 1919 in the Trabzon and Samsun districts alone, Muslims had murdered sixty-eight Greeks and eleven Armenians and raped ten Greek and Armenian women. No one had been "brought to book." The British high commissioner commented that "while such conditions prevail, it is inadvisable to proceed with repatriation on a large scale."[100] In Trabzon, the condition of both Muslims and Christians was one of "practically complete destitution." "The whole atmosphere of the vilayet breeds decay, misery, starvation and fear," a British officer reported.[101] The Turks were busy demolishing Christian houses, and returnee families, usually missing their breadwinners, who had been murdered, were hungry.[102] The Christians' fields were in Turkish hands and Turks boycotted Christian shops and wares.[103] Muslim clerics promoted the boycotts. In Everek, the Armenian Patriarchate reported, "the motto of the Mufti is that the laws of the [sharia] forbid trading with the Mourtad, which means religious turncoat." Local shopkeepers, too, promoted boycotts, out of concern about competition from returnees.[104] Here and there, returnees were arrested and charged with crimes against Turks during the war; others were conscripted into the army.[105]

In the east, along the borders with the Caucasus and Persia, Turkish obstructionism was expressed in a consistent effort to bar Armenian refugees in Yerevan from returning to homes in Kars and Nakhchivan.[106] Talk during April–May 1919 of an Armenian return to Van caused "great consternation" among local Muslims.[107] At first, according to the Armenian Patriarchate, the Constantinople Government was responsible for the obstruction, but eventually the Nationalists took the reins.[108] They systematically prevented the return of Armenians hailing from Van, Erzurum, and Bitlis vilayets. These refugees either stayed put in the Caucasus or somehow reached Cilicia. By 1921 it was reported that these three vilayets were effectively free of Armenians. According to the Patriarchate, any found there "are persecuted to annihilation."[109]

In spring 1919, general political questions to do with the future of Turkey also acted as a break on return, or at least on Western enthusiasm for an

Armenian return. American diplomats thought that a return needed to be linked to the "fate of Armenia," meaning to the provinces in part or whole earmarked for Armenian sovereignty. If a future Armenia—independent, autonomous, or under a Western mandate—would include some combination of Adana and the six vilayets, then the Allies should direct the returnees from Syria, Mesopotamia, and the Caucasus to these areas rather than to their native sites. And perhaps the returnees should wait in their places of exile until the fate of these territories was determined.[110] Bristol suggested delaying repatriation until either all of Turkey was occupied by Allied troops or the Peace Conference placed all of Turkey under a mandatory regime (he supported an American mandate).[111]

The Armenian Patriarchate and community leaders in Constantinople also favored delaying repatriation. So did British diplomats, who soon suggested that the repatriation officers limit themselves to recovering women and children and property. "The repatriation in Anatolia at this juncture of Christian deportees and refugees might dangerously increase the present tension between Christians and Moslems, and might prove in the end a doubtful blessing to the Christians themselves," one wrote.[112] The British army in Mesopotamia, for its part, recommended holding off on repatriation of exiled Assyrians until political conditions became clearer.[113] The Greek Government chimed in that, due to the "steadily worse" situation in Asia Minor, they too opposed repatriating refugees "before the military occupation of these regions is affected." The Greeks were thinking of Smyrna and its environs.[114] Another factor inhibiting return were the stories circulating about contemporary massacres, as of 600 Armenians allegedly murdered in Karabagh by Azeris.[115] And there were economic considerations. By March 1919 it was clear that the mass of Armenian deportees could not be properly resettled in time for sowing that year's crops.[116]

For their part, Armenian nationalists calculated in summer 1919 that mass repatriation should be hurried. The swifter and larger the repatriation, especially to the six vilayets, the easier it would be to sustain their claim to those territories, where Armenian numbers had been vastly reduced by the wartime deportations. For them, repatriation served a clear political purpose.

Deportees, both Armenian and Greek, steadily trickled back to their villages and towns over the spring and summer of 1919. In September, the British high commissioner wrote that "the people have solved the question" of delaying a return until a "new Armenia" is created "in large part of themselves by returning . . . to the places where they used to live."[117]

For the Allies, the costs and difficulties of maintaining deportees in place, and the bleak choices available, are illustrated by the case of the Ba'quba camp, near Baghdad, in British-occupied Mesopotamia. Set up in August 1918, by summer 1919 Ba'qubah held some 50,000 Christian survivors—40,000 Assyrians, mainly from the Urmia area, and more than 10,000 Armenians, mainly from the Van area. The camp operated for three years. It apparently cost the British taxpayer £6,500 pounds a day (close to half a million current U.S. dollars). The British wanted to send the refugees home, but conditions in Urmia, from which the Assyrians had fled in summer 1918, were dicey, and the Assyrians refused to move back without adequate British protection and arms. (Persia objected to arming them.) And the Armenians could not be repatriated to Van, because the route ran through hostile Kurdish territory.

Armenians from Mesopotamia, Syria, and Kurdistan steadily drifted into the camp, while some Assyrians left, heading north. By January 1920 the camp held 16,000 Armenians and 23,500 Assyrians. A handful of Armenians left for South Africa and the United States, but most had nowhere to go.[118] Some British officials thought that most could be permanently settled in Mesopotamia itself.[119] Curzon preferred Yerevan.[120] No one spoke any more of Asia Minor. In summer 1920 the Armenians were moved to Basra vilayet, and were apparently later shipped to Yerevan. The Assyrians were sent to a new camp at Mindan, in Mosul vilayet, in readiness for transfer to Urmia.[121] The Assyrian men, at last armed by the British, proceeded northward over snow-covered mountain passes, battling Kurdish tribesmen along the way. But they failed to reach Urmia.[122] Eventually they resettled in Mosul vilayet, where their descendants have continued to suffer persecution, most recently at the hands of the Islamic State.

By the end of 1919 the rush of Christian return to Asia Minor had become a trickle. The British even halted Armenian repatriation to Cilicia, now largely under French control. Cilician Muslims, incited by Kemalist agents, were "in a state of excitement." Security was poor. Tens of thousands of returnees hunkered down in Adana. Overall, the tide had turned; more Christians, many recent returnees, were leaving Anatolia than were returning. De Robeck listed the methods the Turks were "employing to render [Christian] life unendurable": "The Greek or Armenian is no longer systematically massacred; he is prevented from making a livelihood. . . . His business is boycotted, his nut crops made dangerous of access and farmed out to Moslems, who repudiate their engagements, and his houses and property retained."[123]

Perring, who was stationed on the Black Sea Coast, reported, "I found everywhere that Greek refugees who had returned to Turkey since the armistice have either left the country again or are on the point of doing so, in many cases accompanied by Greeks who had remained in Turkey throughout the war." Armenians were leaving for Russia. In one village near Giresun, a party of Greek returnees was "met by the Turkish occupiers of their homes, beaten, and robbed . . . and forced to return to Kerasun." The local Turkish authorities did nothing. But when Turkish villagers complained of Christian attack, gendarmes were promptly dispatched. "In many cases" they went on to pillage the Christians.[124] In Platina, outside Trabzon, "the only Armenians to return . . . were assassinated shortly after their arrival."[125]

The situation around Adana was not much better. "Gangs, . . . undoubtedly under the instigation of Nationalist leaders, have appeared simultaneously in several areas . . . and the blood of Armenians flows once again," a report from a Paris-based Armenian information bureau explained.[126] Still, many returnees stayed put; they had nowhere else to go. Bristol had it right. He wrote, "The Turks, undoubtedly, want to get rid of the Armenians and will probably exterminate them if they cannot find another means . . . . A large percentage of the Turks are murderous fanatics."[127] The Armenian Patriarchate reported that some Kemalists "officially" declared that they had decided "to annihilate the Armenians . . . settling definitely the question of Cilicia."[128]

Recovering Christian Women and Children

During their occupation, the British tried to recover, or help missionaries and clerics recover, Christian women and children from Muslim homes and orphanages. Most of the abductees were Armenian. Rumbold thought he understood why Turks abducted girls and women during the Great War. Some were moved by "humanity"—the desire to save helpless people from death or destitution. But others were inspired by "the wish to acquire merit by turning Christians into Moslems, or to reduce the relative proportion of Christians to Moslems in the Empire, a desire to obtain cheap domestic labour, and more ignoble intentions which can easily be imagined."[129]

In 1922 the League of Nations issued its own report on why and how so many Armenian women and children ended up in Muslim homes during the war. Of course, some were abducted. Others were "bought for a trifle." Some joined Muslim households "of their own free will, seeking protection." There were also children given up by their mothers, who could carry them no longer or could not bear to see them die of hunger. And "some were picked up half dead from the roads out of mere charity." The treatment of these Armenians varied. "Some women became the beloved wives of the Moslems and honoured mistresses of the harem; some children were adopted and treated as well as any child could be. But the great number of them were but slaves, given entirely into the hands of their masters without any rights or protection at all, ill-treated and misused."[130] For the same reasons, Turks continued to abduct Greek and Armenian women and girls during 1919–1923, though in much smaller numbers.[131]

Some girls had "changed owners (masters) 5 or 6 times."[132] Many girls were sold by their captors. Kevorkian writes that in this "lucrative trade," Armenian girls sometimes ended up as far afield as "the slave markets in Arabia" and "Tunisia or Algeria, where they were taken by pilgrims returning from Mecca."[133]

The recovery efforts had begun already in spring 1917, when the British reported rescuing "about 80 Armenian girls" from "Mohammedan families" after the conquest of Baghdad.[134] (Two years later, a British officer reported that there were about 1,000 Armenians in Baghdad, a number "daily increasing as girls and children are rescued from [nearby] Arab households."[135]) The British occupation of Aleppo vilayet, Deir Zor, and Cilicia in late 1918 led to a massive expansion of the recovery campaign. Sometimes Muslims handed over Christians voluntarily; others were rescued by force. Occasionally, they were bought back, as happened with Eftimia Topalian, an eleven-year-old Armenian girl who was recovered from Mamdouch (Mamduh) Bey "for 46 pounds." Most of her family had been murdered in Diyarbekir during the war.[136]

Fairly often women and children refused to leave Muslim homes, even of those who had murdered their families.[137] Their recalcitrance had numerous causes. For some women, "it [was] a choice of staying with the Turks or starvation."[138] Sometimes women had formed "a certain attachment for the man" or felt "a certain amount of fear" at the prospect of leaving.[139] Some were branded or tattooed by their Muslim masters on the "forehead, both cheeks and point of the chin"; they had nowhere or no one to return to.[140] For many, leaving a Muslim husband meant having "to leave behind children."[141] Western officials found recovery of Christians from Muslim households easier in Constantinople, where aid agencies and Christian churches were headquartered and where there were still large Christian communities.[142]

After the armistice, the Constantinople government instructed provincial officials to locate Christian women and orphans and hand them over to Christian bodies.[143] At the same time, Faisal, the Hashemite de facto ruler of Damascus and British ally, issued a proclamation ordering Arabs harboring Armenian women and children to return them to "their people."[144] Egyptian Armenians organized squads to recover women in Mesopotamia and Syria from Bedouin. A squad headed by one Rupen Herian reportedly retrieved 533 women and children during June–August 1919.[145] In the Constantinople area, a team led by Arakel Chakrian recovered 750 orphans held in Muslim orphanages and homes.[146] NER's John Dunaway and Stanley Kerr, working out of Aleppo, in early 1919 recovered several hundred Armenian women and children from the Bab area.[147] Caris Mills, an American social worker, ran a rescue house in Constantinople tending to hundreds of children, some of whom were eventually shipped out and adopted in the United States.[148] Thousands were recovered in Cilicia.

Rumbold estimated that, during November 1918–December 1920, 30,000 Armenian orphans and 24,000 women were recovered, 10,000 of the children and 2,000 of the women by the British.[149] How many remained in Muslim hands is unclear. In February 1920, Gates estimated that more than 60,000 Armenian "young girls and orphans" were in Muslim households; in mid-1919, the Armenian Patriarchate had spoken of 70,000 orphans and 50,000 women in Muslim households, and of 87,000 Armenians in orphanages in Turkey, Armenia, and Georgia.[150] All these numbers seem to exclude Greeks. In May 1923 the British Foreign Office maintained that "more than one hundred thousand Christian women and children" had been reclaimed from Muslim homes, but a year later, it stated that "not less than 80,000" Christians, half of them Armenian "and probably more," were still "forcibly detained in Turkish houses," many in "slavery."[151]

In early 1921 the newly created League of Nations appointed a commission to investigate the problem.[152] The following year, the League reported that some freed Christian women later returned to Muslim homes, finding no way to maintain themselves, and "really became Moslems." The report suggested that "more than 50%" of the adult Christian women in Muslim households were afraid to leave. But there were also hundreds of women who "sigh for liberation." Many twelve-to-twenty-year-olds were afraid to flee, dreading savage beatings; some were inculcated with a false picture of life "outside."[153]

In the course of 1919, the Turkish authorities increasingly obstructed British, Armenian, and Greek efforts to recover abductees. In May the interior minister announced that it was illegal to press women to leave a Muslim husband to whom they wished to stay married. The women should remain with their new families, the minister felt.[154] By summer, the government was backing local officials and the public in refusing to give up abductees.[155]

The longer abductees lived in Muslim households, the less they wanted to leave. Most had nowhere to go; their families were dead, their homes destroyed or confiscated, their communities shattered. As with the abductees of 1894–1896, many, now "sullied," feared that they would not be welcomed back by their families or communities. By war's end, many were with bastard Muslim children. And many children recovered from Muslim households, it was found, "want[ed] to go back."[156] An American officer reported that a group of Armenian orphans aged ten to thirteen, who had been "forcibly removed from their Turkish home[s]," had run away from their escort and "returned" to their Turkish families.[157]

The recovery efforts generated extreme tensions. Already in 1919 Allied officers were often persuaded that recovery "entailed so much difficulty that the advantages attained were sometimes outweighed by the resentment aroused and the consequent danger to which the relics of the Armenian community were exposed."[158]

There was violent Muslim resistance. In many towns, local gangs protected the "honor" of those who took Armenian women or children.[159] Bristol reported that "in some cases the Kurds and Arabs will murder the women rather than give them up," and Turkish gendarmes sent to fetch such women and children "often commit assault upon them."[160] Occasionally, "aggrieved" Muslim husbands harassed missionaries at rescue homes and tried to retrieve their lost "property." An American missionary in Harput, Henry Riggs, reported that one husband came to the local rescue home repeatedly and shot up the neighborhood. Riggs, who had personally rescued Armenian women, said his life was threatened separately by four Muslim husbands. He began to carry "a revolver in [his] hip pocket, ready for business." Riggs was eventually expelled by order of Mustafa Kemal.[161]

Sometimes Turks seeking to get back recovered women brandished a more general threat. In early 1920 a missionary in Sivas reported that Ala Olu (Alaoğlu) Ali, the *müdür* (an administrator) of Oulash (Ulaş) came to the rescue home and spoke privately to an Armenian girl who had been a servant in his house during the war. He told her to "accompany him home in order to save her[self] from the massacre of the Armenians that was shortly to take place and from which no one was to escape." She refused.[162] Such threats were not idle; rescued Armenians were sometimes subjected to fresh atrocities. In May 1920 sixty-seven young girls were reported kidnapped from a rescue home by Muslims who "used them for the appeasing of their basest appetites."[163]

By late summer–autumn 1919, the recovery efforts had begun to stall. Western diplomats came to realize that, in the circumstances, the status quo was preferable to the alternative. The British high commissioner wrote, "It frequently happens that Islamized women and children are . . . better off in their present condition than if they were . . . restored to the care of their communities. . . . I am driven to the conclusion that, from the point of view of humanity as distinct from that of religious feeling, our best course is to leave them as they are for the present."[164] By 1922 Bristol was writing that it was "unfortunate" that the American missionaries "ever became involved in this practice of trying to get Christian women out of Muslim homes. . . . I recommended against this practice from the very beginning."[165] At that point recovery efforts in Nationalist-controlled Asia Minor had virtually ceased. "One of the first effects of the Nationalist movement was to bring such work to an end," the Foreign Office concluded.[166]

But in Syria, under French rule since July 1920, one notable recovery effort was ongoing, albeit in a manner "quiet and unobtrusive." The French authorities were wary if not downright opposed to it, fearing possible Muslim reactions. But Karen Jeppe, a Danish missionary who headed the Aleppo branch of the League of Nations Commission for the Protection of Women and Children in the Near East, started a neutral house in 1921. For three years she clandestinely ran agents in the greater Aleppo area, where 30,000 Christians were said to be living in Muslim households. She reported rescuing hundreds.[167]

Some of the sorriest tales to emerge concerned orphans. After years in Turkish hands, some didn't even know their real names. According to Emma Cushman, the American member of the League of Nations commission on abductees, the Turks not only contrived to conceal the children's identities but also turned the children's minds "so far as to revile the Christians as infidels."[168] In 1920 a British officer discovered this for himself on a visit to a Turkish orphanage near Constantinople. Twelve girls there were said to be Armenian. When approached, three wept "bitterly" and said they were Muslim. A nine-year-old said her name was Djelile and that her parents had been murdered by Armenians.

"Who told you that . . . ?" the officer asked.

"I was told so in the orphanage."

He asked her name. The girl responded with a question of her own: "Do you want to know the whole truth?"

"Yes."

"Would you consent to adopt me as your child? Swear in the name of your parents and God."

"I swear."

With this, the girl opened up. She was from Zeytun; the adults, including her mother, had been driven from their homes. She was taken to Aleppo "where the Turks changed my name 'Siranush' to Djelile." She was compelled to pray in Turkish. All twelve girls, Djelile confirmed, were Armenian. Then, the officer reported, she "threw herself into my arms."[169]

Armenian orphans boarding barges at Constantinople. Many were saved by the American Near East Relief organization.

The formal end to the recoveries came at Lausanne, where the Turks refused to include in the peace treaty any provision concerning the rights of abductees.[170] The Armenian Red Cross estimated that "about 60,000" Christians remained in "Turkish harems" at this time.[171] During 1922–1923, the Nationalists closed all Christian orphanages in Anatolia and ordered the removal from them of girls rescued from Turkish harems.[172] In some areas, the Turks ordered Christian orphanages to send away all girls and boys older than fifteen. The girls were forced to find employment in Muslim homes or "starve."[173]

Arresting and Prosecuting Perpetrators

At the end of World War I, Curzon described Turkey as "a culprit waiting to hear the sentence."[174] The Allies sought to punish Turkey—for launching the war in the Middle East and for its war crimes, including maltreatment of Allied war prisoners—and theoretically had two means at their disposal. One was territorial dismemberment. The other was to penalize individual war criminals. The British were the most resolute of the Allies in this regard—partly out of a moral sense and partly out of a sense of guilt. Britain had, after all, prevented Russia's annexation in 1878 of Turkey's eastern provinces, where the Turks later massacred the Armenians. "History will always hold us culpable," Lloyd George declared.[175]

On May 24, 1915, a few days after the start of the Armenian deportations and massacres, the governments of France, Britain, and Russia sent a joint letter to the Sublime Porte warning the Turks against committing "crimes against humanity."[176] After the war, Gough-Calthorpe, then the British high commissioner, cabled the Turkish government, "His Majesty's Government is resolved to have proper punishment inflicted on those responsible for Armenian massacres."[177] He also called for the "arrest and exemplary punishment" of Enver, Talât, Şakır, and their like.[178] On January 23, 1919, British leaders decided on the prosecution of war criminals and demanded that the Turks arrest those deemed responsible. The British handed over lists of suspects. But the Turks balked: they reluctantly arrested a handful and refused to hand them over. Instead they produced a lengthy folder containing documents proving that the Armenians had been at fault and that their "deportation" had been justified.[179] The British reacted by themselves rounding up suspects and shipping them to a detention center in Malta.[180]

But who would try them? Allied jurists spent months mulling over the matter. London proposed setting up Allied military courts but dropped the idea after France and Turkey objected. The possibility of establishing an international criminal court also fell through.

The buck thus passed to the Constantinople government. In November 1918 the Turks convened a special court martial, and Enver and Cemal were tried in absentia—but not for massacring Christians. The following month, they began arresting war crimes suspects and trying them at regular military tribunals. Altogether several hundred were taken in, most on the basis of the British lists. Some were identified by Christian survivors. In January 1919 travelling commissions of inquiry were sent to the provinces, and in February extraordinary military tribunals were established in Constantinople and the provinces to try a portion of the suspects.[181]

The first trial with the accused present took place in Constantinople in February 1919. The defendants were charged with persecuting Armenians in Yozgat. Sixty-two further trials followed. In one, CUP Central Committee members and Special Organization officials were tried. In two others, cabinet ministers and CUP responsible secretaries and delegates appeared in the dock. But the courts, especially those in the vilayets, handed down few guilty verdicts. Indeed, investigating magistrates were either remiss in pursuing evidence and suspects or found it impossible to overcome the recalcitrance of local officials and police and actually bring suspects to book. For example, Setrag Karageuzian, an Armenian investigating magistrate in Trabzon, proved unable to bring any suspects to trial despite three and a half months of work during winter-spring 1919.[182]

The Turks had initially agreed to hold the trials in the hope of softening Allied punishment of Turkey itself. But within months they stopped the proceedings. In Paris the Allies had ruled that the Turkish people were "guilty of murdering Armenians without justification."[183] But the Turkish authorities, both in Constantinople and Ankara, rejected the notion of collective guilt. The first postwar grand vizier, Ahmet Izzet Pasha, a Talât appointee, during his three weeks in office destroyed incriminating documents, helped suspects flee, and blocked arrests.[184] Izzet's successors, Tevfik Pasha and Prince Damat Ferid Pasha, agreed under pressure from the Allies, the press, and a renascent political opposition to the principle of punishing war criminals. But these officials thought that Talât, Enver, and Cemal should be punished rather than "the innocent Turkish nation free of the stain of injustice."[185]

The Yozgat trial ended with the conviction and execution in Constantinople's Beyazit Square on April 10, 1919, of Kemal Bey, the onetime mutesarrif of Boğazlıyan. His funeral the next day, which turned into an anti-Allied demonstration, was conducted with great "pomp and ceremony." "Numerous Young Turks [were] present," as well as "many officers and soldiers" and medical students. One of the students, "holding a bunch of flowers," eulogized: "Hark oh people. . . . Hark oh Mussulmen! He whom we leave lying here is the hero Kemal Bey. The English have been ejected from Odessa, let us drive them out of Constantinople. What are you waiting for? . . . With the help of God we will soon be able to crush their heads." Gough-Calthorpe observed that Kemal Bey "was treated as a hero and martyr."[186] The popular mood no doubt dampened the government's interest in punishing additional perpetrators. "Not one Turk in a thousand can conceive that there might be a Turk who deserves to be hanged for the killing of Christians," the Foreign Office commented.[187]

The Greek invasion of Smyrna, and the nationwide protests that followed, served to reinforce Turkish recalcitrance. On May 17, just after the Smyrna landing, the Turks stopped the trials and arrests of suspects. Some were freed. In the interior perpetrators who had gone to ground were emboldened; they "walked about fearlessly."[188] In June the Turks officially reconvened the Constantinople trials, but the British dismissed this as a deception.[189] Webb concluded, "There are . . . many thousands of Mussulmen in this country who deserve to be treated with the most extreme penalties of the law, but, to my everlasting regret, it appears impracticable."[190] In October the Nationalists and Constantinople secretly agreed that British investigation of Turkish military commanders must cease, Turks exiled by Britain be repatriated, and Armenians be prosecuted for *their* war crimes.[191] After the Allies occupied Constantinople in March 1920, arrested, and exiled to Malta dozens of Nationalist figures, including some implicated in war crimes, the Nationalists responded by arresting dozens of Britons in Anatolia.

One more Turk was to be tried, convicted, and executed for war crimes—Nusret Bey, a subdistrict governor in Urfa, hanged on August 5, 1920. His punishment caused widespread revulsion in Turkey. In 1921 a military court of appeals overturned the verdict and put on trial those who had tried him. General Nemrud Kurd Mustafa Pasha, the chief judge of the Turkish court-martial and one of the judges in the Nusret proceedings, was dismissed, charged with mishandling the war-crimes proceedings, and sentenced to three months in prison.[192] At his trial, the general denounced his accusers—in effect, the wartime CUP establishment, which was by then back in the saddle under the Nationalist label. He blamed them for abominable crimes:

> The pashas who have carried out unprecedented and inconceivable crimes and who, in service of their personal interests, have thus reduced the country to its present straits, continue to cause mischief. They have produced various kinds of tyranny, organized deportations and massacres, burnt breast-feeding infants with petrol, raped women and young girls in the presence of their garroted or wounded parents, separated young girls from their fathers and mothers, confiscated their movable and immovable properties, and exiled them as far as Mosul in a lamentable state. . . .

They have thrown thousands of innocents from boats into the sea. They have had town criers call upon non-Muslims loyal to the government to deny their religion and embrace Islam. . . . They have marched famished elders for entire months; they have sent them to forced labor. They have had young women thrown into houses of ill repute . . . without precedent in the history of nations.[193]

Nusret's successful, albeit posthumous, appeal and the indictment of Nemrud delegitimized the whole war crimes process and, by implication, helped subvert the notion that the Turks had massacred the Armenians.[194] There were no further prosecutions. That same year, 1921, the British freed all the Malta prisoners in exchange for the Britons the Nationalists had taken hostage.[195]

The French Arrive

Most of the postwar deportation, flight, and murder of Armenians in Anatolia occurred in Cilicia and northern Aleppo vilayet, under nominal French control between late 1919 and 1921. These territories had been part of the Blue Area, earmarked for French rule under the secret Sykes-Picot agreement of 1916. The British handover of these territories to French control three years later was, in effect, a fulfillment of the agreement's provisions.

Already in December 1918, four battalions of the French Army—the 4,000-strong Legion d'Orient, later renamed the Legion Armenienne and consisting mainly of Armenian volunteers—landed at Mersin and Alexandretta, serving as part of Allenby's occupation force. Thousands more reached the two ports in June–July 1919, as British units were pulled out to contend with anti-British unrest in Egypt.[196]

The core of the Legion consisted of young Armenians who had been rescued from Musadağ in September 1915 and temporarily housed in a refugee camp in Port Said. Already in early 1915 Armenian nationalists had asked the British to help set up an Armenian volunteer corps to serve in British ranks or, alternatively, raise insurrection in Cilicia. The War Office dismissed both ideas.[197] But in 1916 the French pressed the British to establish a volunteer corps, specifically to help in the liberation and occupation of Cilicia, destined for French rule.[198] At the end of the year, hundreds of volunteers began training in Egypt and then Cyprus. The Legion, three battalions of Armenian volunteers from the Middle East and United States, and a battalion of Syrian Arab exiles, was incorporated in January 1917 into the French Army's Detachment français de Palestine-Syrie, under Lieutenant-Colonel Philipin de Piepape.[199] The Legion saw action in September–October 1918 in northern Palestine and Syria.[200] After landing in Mersin and Alexandretta, the battalions fanned out to Dörtyol, Toprakkale, Islahiye, Pozantı, Tarsus, Adana, Misis, and Cihan.[201] They hoisted the Armenian flag over the government building in Adana and ordered the kaymakams of Payas and Dörtyol to expel the Turkish gendarmes from their towns.[202] The legionnaires liberated women from Turkish homes and may have murdered a Turk outside Alexandretta.[203] A few months later, Armenians—apparently local irregulars—murdered an Armenian "traitor" and spiked a Ramadan gun in Tarsus.[204] In February 1919 tension between the Armenians and companies of (Muslim) Algerian French troops in Alexandretta led the French to disband several of the Armenian companies.

Throughout, the French had discriminated against the legionnaires in pay and equipment. Under local Turkish pressure and inducements—apparently including financial and sexual bribes of French officers—the French command gradually sidelined and replaced the Armenian soldiers with North African colonials. The Legion withered away. By mid-1919 only five hundred Armenians remained in the Legion, and in August 1920 it was officially disbanded.[205] Most of the ex-troopers joined local Armenian militias.

In March–April 1919 Gates toured central and southern Anatolia. He reported worsening political conditions. The Turks feared Armenian revenge. In Adana there was violence. Turks sniped at Armenian soldiers; here and there, Armenians killed Turks. And the Turks feared the creation of an independent Armenian "kingdom" in which they would fare badly.[206] Armenian deportees were streaming into the city. The French pressed the British to disarm the Turks and themselves armed Armenians and helped set up militias in outlying Armenian villages. The Turks resented the prohibition on flying Turkish flags and the installation of Armenians as gendarmes and administrators. The Turks also complained of arbitrary arrests and financial extortion by Armenian troops.[207]

The British, bombarded with these Turkish complaints, grew unhappy with the deployment of the legionnaires. Allenby wrote that "the excesses committed by the Armenian troops" had created "general insecurity" in Cilicia.[208] Curzon told the French that "the sooner" the legionnaires "disappeared from the scene the better."[209]

But there also was pushback in the other direction. In May the French began to press the British to allow them to take over the whole Beirut-Mersin coastline and Cilicia, per Sykes-Picot.[210] On September 13, Clemenceau and Lloyd George reached agreement.[211] The changing of the guard took place in late October and November, the British withdrawing to Palestine, Mosul, and Mesopotamia.[212] In Damascus, Homs, Hama, and Aleppo, the British were replaced by Arab forces loyal to Faisal, who had been ensconced by Allenby in Damascus in October 1918. The French occupied Cilicia and northern Aleppo vilayet.

The British were moderately sanguine about the future of the Mediterranean littoral. But they were less hopeful about the interior, to the east and north. Allenby cabled the War Office, "Disorders will arise in the area north and east of Aleppo." He feared an anti-Western juncture of "extreme Arab Nationalists" and "Mustapha Kemal," and he predicted that "the chief sufferers will be the Armenians. . . . The commencement of our withdrawal will probably start a panic and result in large numbers of repatriated Armenians again streaming south." He proposed that Armenian refugees in Syria be moved to Cilicia, where he assumed they would enjoy French protection.[213] The Foreign Office endorsed concentrating the Armenians in Cilicia.[214] Transports of deportees left Damascus and Aleppo for Cilicia and Antep.[215]

But some British officials were deeply suspicious of French intentions. Allenby's chief political officer, Colonel Richard Meinertzhagen, warned that "any French failure to substitute good French troops for ours will encourage Extremists, and first to suffer will be thousands of defenseless Armenians whom we have collected and distributed in Cilicia and Aleppo."[216] His suspicion that France intended to man Cilicia with low-grade colonial troops was accurate. In 1919, the French had only 20,000 troops in Syria and Cilicia. Most were poorly trained Senegalese and North Africans. The French armed thousands of local Armenians as militiamen and gendarmes. The prevailing assessment, expressed by NER's William Peet, was that "the

French took upon themselves the occupation of Cilicia without counting the cost or making any adequate military preparation." Moreover, the mere presence of the colonial and Armenian troops "excited great [Muslim] opposition." This was compounded by French behavior: "They seem to have succeeded in making themselves cordially hated by all classes of the people," an American missionary wrote.[217] The local Turks feared that the French takeover augured permanent occupation, the dismemberment of Turkey, and preferential treatment for Christians.

French troops reached Antep around October 25, 1919.[218] Almost immediately, Turkish officials protested against unspecified "breaches of the peace" by Armenian soldiers. The British handed over control of Antep on November 4 and Kilis on the 7th, and left.[219] French units occupied Urfa and Maraş on November 1.[220] The troops were Armenian, Algerian, and Senegalese, the officers French.[221] According to a Turkish source, in Maraş the Armenians welcomed the incoming troops "with a band and bouquet of flowers. 'Damn the Sultan! Damn the Turks! Long live the French and the Armenians', they were yelling."[222]

By November 23, the French were "responsible for [the] whole of Cilicia."[223] Here and there Turks nibbled at the withdrawing British columns, as at Katma where, on November 4, three Indian troopers were killed.[224] Acting swiftly, the French executed a number of Turks.[225]

Wishing to avoid overextension, the French desisted from deploying troops as far east as Diyarbekir and as far north as Sivas and Harput, though these towns were earmarked for French rule under Sykes-Picot.[226] The forces that fanned out between Mersin, Islahiye, and Urfa were thin on the ground and insufficient to control both the towns and their access routes. From early 1920, almost all the garrisons were effectively besieged by the Nationalists. French supply lines, stretching from the ports of Mersin and Alexandretta, were periodically blocked. The French frantically shipped in reinforcements and by May 1920 had 40,000 troops in Cilicia.[227] In the towns there was anti-French and anti-Armenian terrorism, and in the countryside irregulars raided Christian villages and ambushed French convoys and patrols.[228]

To some degree the opposition to the occupation was a byproduct of French conduct. Bristol left a graphic description—originating with an American missionary, Francis Kelsey—of the French takeover of Tarsus, the birthplace of

Paul the Apostle and the site of Antony and Cleopatra's first meeting. Tarsus had 15,000 inhabitants, 9,000 of them non-Christians. Entering the town, the French, headed by Major Coustilliers, staged an "imposing ceremony." The Christians and the town's schoolchildren were assembled in front of the barracks. The children were taught the "Marseillaise." "Speeches of felicitation" followed. "All glorified the French valour and civilization. . . . '*Nous sommes ici et nous resterons ici*' (we are here and we are here to stay)," Coustilliers announced.[229] The French hoped to garner Armenian backing for their rule in Cilicia, but the Armenian leadership, aware of French imperial ambitions, preferred an American or British mandate if outright Armenian independence was impossible. From the first, the French were seen as opponents of Armenian nationalist aspirations.

Initially the French told Turkish officials that their occupation would be "provisional and purely military." But within weeks the French began to interfere with local government. They notified the Turks that they would "participate in the administration of the districts of Urfa, Marash and Aintab, that the gendarmerie would be placed under the control of the [French] military . . . and that an officer would . . . control . . . finances." They proceeded to remove Turkish officials, including the mutesarrif of Maraş, from their posts. The Turks complained that the French occupation extended to territory beyond what the British had controlled.[230]

From Alexandretta the British vice-consul, Joseph Catoni, reported that the French were "very unpopular, neither the men nor the officers were respectful to women, native or European. . . . The French officers were a bad class and corruption was rife. . . . The officers filled their pockets with bribes." They also slighted the foreign consuls. A local lady put it this way: "*Les Anglais ont envoyés les fils de leurs 'Lords', mais les Français ont envoyés leurs valets.*" ("The English have sent the sons of their 'lords', but the French have sent their valets.")[231]

Before taking over, the French had been unhappy about the transfer of masses of Armenians to Cilicia. Surely Faisal's Arabs, once in charge in Aleppo, would protect "their" Armenians? As to the "Mesopotamian" Armenians, the French argued, they were best not moved to Cilicia, as they would not be self-supporting. But the real French fear lay elsewhere. "Objections," the French argued, might arise "to grouping Armenians in Cilicia where there would be a risk of their forming an artificial majority of which the Mohammedans might complain and where their presence might later be taken as a reason to justify the creation of a great Armenia from the Black Sea to the Mediterranean which would be in opposition to . . . the economic and political connection between [French-ruled] Cilicia and Syria."[232] In short, even before taking over, the French worried about the Muslim reaction to an Armenian Cilicia and, in any case, wanted Cilicia for themselves, not as part of an Armenian state. And the French almost immediately were put off by the Armenians they came in contact with. As Clemenceau put it, "the Armenians were a dangerous lot to get mixed up with. They required a great deal of money, and gave very little satisfaction."[233]

But maintaining their hold on Cilicia and northern Aleppo vilayet posed a considerable military problem. Allenby wrote, "I do not think that French can occupy Urfa and places to the east of Aleppo in view of difficulty of communications, roads being impossible during winter and railway being outside blue area."[234] The problem wasn't restricted to points east of Aleppo. Logistics and communications between the ports—Mersin, Alexandretta, and Beirut, through which French supplies and reinforcements arrived—and the urban centers of Cilicia as well as northern Aleppo vilayet were to be the Achilles heel of the French position.

As the British withdrew, Armenians were still pouring into Cilicia and northern Aleppo vilayet. They were coming not only from the deportation sites to the east but also from Sivas, Kayseri, Niğde, and Konya vilayets. The Turks believed that the Allies were engaged in a deliberate effort to bolster Armenian numbers in Cilicia to reinforce their territorial claim; Armenians were even arriving from the United States and Europe. Constantinople acted swiftly. The government's Security Directorate and the Ministry's Special Bureau ordered local governors to prevent Armenians from reaching Cilicia.[235] At the same time, the Turks complained that Armenian gendarmes in Adana were committing "all kinds of cruelties."[236] The Sublime Porte claimed falsely that most of the troops occupying Maraş, Urfa, and Antep were Armenian, and that they were animated by "racial hatred" of Muslims.[237] At the end of November the Turks alleged that in Maraş Armenian troops had "insulted and beaten . . . Mohammedan inhabitants," Muslim women had been "obliged to uncover their faces," and a Muslim had been murdered outside town.[238]

Yet the Turks understood that the French Army, though "interfer[ing] in . . . the civil administration" and coming "as conquerors and" being "annexationist," was protecting the Muslim population from Armenian depredations.[239]

For the Armenians, the switch from British to French occupation had drastic consequences. Take Kilis. The British had overseen the repatriation of its deportees, who had found their "houses in great part destroyed, the gardens devastated, the trees uprooted and their property occupied." The British granted "pecuniary assistance," "founded institutions" for widows and orphans, reclaimed women and girls from "distant towns," restored real estate to its owners, and planned reconstruction. (The focus was on rebuilding; the perpetrators of the genocide remained "at large.") With the arrival of the French, almost all financial assistance ceased, as did efforts to restore property or indemnify Armenians for losses. Indeed, the French appeared to accept that property restoration should be contingent on Muslim agreement, in line with the guidelines from Constantinople.[240] Moreover, the French ignored Turkish attacks, even when Armenians were murdered. Meanwhile their officers "entertain[ed] Turkish officials and brigand chiefs" and allowed Muslims to publicly carry arms while denying the privilege to Christians.[241]

This behavior triggered Armenian despair, then animosity. In Adana, the Turkish vali, Celal, asserted that "three-fourths of the inhabitants . . . including Armenians . . . hate" the new administration. He even added, absurdly, that "the Armenians would prefer to live as before with the Turks [in control] rather than to see the prolongation . . . of the French Administration."[242]

The Turks inundated the British and French high commissions with protests against the French. On November 12, 1919, even before the French had properly settled in, Kemal condemned the French for "dismembering" Turkey and "depriving our nation" of its "most beautiful parts": "Aintab, Marash, and Ourfa." He further accused them of perpetrating "massacres, oppression, and atrocities and [a] policy of extermination." French behavior was "identical" to the Greeks' behavior in Smyrna, he concluded. The British considered this a particularly "violent pronouncement."[243]

The French occupiers faced an impossible task: to take over territory inhabited and claimed by both Turks and Armenians, and maintain law, order, and peace, while trying to placate both populations. But meeting Muslim demands took priority, as they formed a majority in almost every site, many were armed and, to a man, they resented the occupation. This ultimately resulted in a "Turkophil policy," as the British called it. The policy had numerous manifestations.[244] In most towns, the Turkish administration, however hobbled, was left in place. The French also ignored Turkish misbehavior toward Christians in order, one Armenian lobbyist concluded, to "ingratiate themselves with the Turks."[245] Indeed, paradoxically, some senior French officials signaled from the start their willingness to leave. According to Kemal, at a secret meeting around December 6, 1919, Picot gave him his "private opinion" that "in exchange for securing economical advantages in Adana, the French might probably evacuate Maraş, Antep, Urfa, and their vicinity, and also Cilicia." Picot apparently also told Kemal he had "order[ed]" the withdrawal of the Armenian Legion and suggested that the Nationalists continue to organize themselves in Adana, Maraş, and Antep. But Picot asked that the Nationalists refrain from an actual "rising."[246] Clearly there were important Frenchmen who supported "the main plank of the Nationalists' programme, namely the maintenance of an undivided Turkey."[247]

As it turned out, two years were to pass before France and Kemal finally reached an understanding. Meanwhile, the Turks unleashed a gradually expanding guerrilla war against the occupiers—and what they saw as their Armenian allies—that was to result in a complete French withdrawal at the end of 1921. The Turkish campaign also led to the death of thousands of Armenians and their wholesale evacuation from Cilicia and northern Aleppo vilayet.

But the Turks' postwar anti-Armenian campaign had begun already in early 1919, well before the French occupation, and was a natural follow-up to the wartime persecutions. It had the same end in mind—to cleanse Asia Minor of Armenians. It seems to have sprung up spontaneously in different locations within weeks of the signing of the armistice and, at least initially, lacked central organization. It was especially pronounced in sites to which deportees were returning.

Western missionaries and Armenians referred to the anti-Armenian campaign of early 1919 as a "white massacre." The goal was to impoverish and dishearten the survivors of the wartime genocide by boycotting their businesses in the towns and preventing them from farming in the countryside. According to the Armenian Patriarchate, the Kemalists were also robbing

Armenians and conscripting them for "heavy labor." But they were not massacring: "this is the only favor they grant them."[248] In October 1919, the Armenian and Greek patriarchs quoted Kemal as asking, "Why massacre when it was so easy to eliminate by steady merciless pressure?"[249]

To be sure, Kemal also understood the utility of straightforward, old-fashioned massacre, at least to complement the white variety. Massacre would trigger immediate mass flight and could bring strategic benefits. According to an intercepted letter, Kemal ordered Şakır Nimet—a Nationalist agent in Aleppo and former staff officer of Enver's—to "organize massacres of Christians in Aleppo, Homs, Damascus and Beirut." The aim was not just to kill Christians but also to persuade the French to shift troops from Cilicia, Kemal's immediate objective, to Syria.[250]

The start of the Nationalist guerrilla campaign in Cilicia and northern Aleppo vilayet in January–February 1920 was accompanied by large-scale massacres. The Turks claimed that their assault on the French-occupied areas was in part a reaction to Armenian and French depredations against Muslims. The charge was largely a Nationalist invention, though it is probable that many Turks believed it. Armenians were enraged by their suffering, and Turks expected them to take revenge. As the Armenian archbishop of Bursa told a French officer, he "would like to see as many Turks killed by Armenians as he had seen Armenians killed by Turks during the war." (The Frenchman retorted: "I don't think that sentiment is very Christian.")[251]

This thinking, however prevalent, rarely inspired action. Armenians were almost everywhere a minority—demoralized, mostly unarmed, and restrained by Allied supervision. Moreover, as the Allies' promises of Armenian independence evaporated and their forces came under guerrilla attack, many Armenians came to understand that the future of those remaining in the country was under Turkish rule. It was therefore best to keep a low and subservient profile. Perhaps Christian values also acted as a brake.

But some atrocities did occur. In summer 1920, Armenians raided and looted Turkish homes in Adana and several villages, precipitating flight. According to French reports, the assailants were bent on torpedoing a Franco-Nationalist agreement. The worst of this violence occurred in Adana itself, on July 10, when police opened fire, killing fifteen Turks. The person responsible, allegedly, was an Armenian police officer, Lieutenant Azzadian,

Massacred Armenians. The Turks claimed that mass killing was a reaction to Armenian and French murder of Turks.

"who seeks an opportunity to kill the Turks and pillage their houses."[252] Reporting the same incident, Bristol wrote of "about fifty Mohammedans" "murdered."[253] The Armenians denied Bristol's report.[254]

But, en fin, while the Turks complained incessantly, Western observers—diplomats, officers, and missionaries—recorded very few Armenian atrocities during 1918–1923. Many detailed Turkish complaints referred to minor Christian misdeeds when compared to ongoing Turkish atrocities (not to mention their crimes during 1914–1918). For example a list of Turkish complaints from Cilicia and Adana between December 29, 1918, and February 15, 1919, speaks of four Muslim merchants killed in a robbery, one woman raped, and the repeated theft of money and jewelry from Muslims.[255] In early 1919 the Turks alleged that Armenians had murdered a handful of villagers at Azairlou, near Dörtyol.[256] The Turks widely disseminated such stories in newspapers, triggering Muslim anger—and anti-Christian atrocities.[257]

The most horrific Turkish allegations came during the war, in the Caucasus (where, of course, Armenians regularly alleged Muslim atrocities). Russian-Armenian soldiers reportedly committed massacres in the Rowanduz and Neri districts in spring–summer 1916.[258] In February 1918 the Turks alleged that

Armenians had massacred Muslims in the Caucasus and Russian-occupied eastern Turkey. Historian Arnold Toynbee, then in the British Foreign Office Information Department's Intelligence Bureau, ruled that the allegations were "for the greater part . . . no doubt misrepresentations." But he conceded that "the turn of the wheel" of fortune, with the Armenians on top, "may be accompanied by certain acts of violence or injustice."[259] In July 1918 British diplomats in Moscow reported a massacre of 800 Muslims, including women and children, in Erzincan before the Russian evacuation of the town.[260] A British officer reported that in the area near Lake Balık, where Russian Armenian and Muslim Kurdish units were at loggerheads, the "entire Moslem population is seeking refuge from Armenian robbery and violence."[261] Armenian troops also appear to have massacred Tatar villagers.[262] Armenian spokesmen routinely denied such allegations.[263]

In January 1919 Muslims from Yerevan and surrounding villages complained of Armenian depredations after the Turkish withdrawal. At Kerni Yassar, they charged, Armenians arrested and killed "the rich and educated," then killed other inhabitants and looted homes. Elsewhere in the area, Armenians allegedly separated men from women and massacred the men. Then "the Armenians carried away with them all the girls and women."[264] A Turkish official claimed that Armenian regulars massacred the inhabitants of Vedi and Sadank, southeast of Yerevan, and that in other areas they killed some 20,000 people, burning women and children.[265] Turks alleged that in six villages near Sarıkamış, the whole population was "burnt alive."[266] A report from the Ankara government even spoke of an "extermination policy" in Kars, with 800 murdered and 900 deported. Altogether the Nationalist report charged that 135,000 Turks were massacred or driven out of 199 villages by the end of 1919.[267] Almost none of these allegations were confirmed by Western observers, and the stories clearly aped Armenian charges against Turks—which, by contrast, were routinely confirmed by outsiders.

There were more reports of massacres in summer 1921, committed by Armenian brigands in western Anatolia as Greek forces retreated from the Izmit area. Bristol wrote of "several hundred Turks" killed, apparently basing himself on a report by an American missionary who had heard from British officials that Armenians had "murdered 200" Turks in Izmit town on June 25.[268] Rosalind Toynbee, a prolific author and Arnold Toynbee's wife, wrote of meeting a little Turkish girl whose lower jaw had been blown off. The girl somehow related that an Armenian band had pillaged her village, driven the inhabitants into a house, and thrown bombs inside. Her mother died in the house, along with nineteen others. Another ten villagers were killed in the street, she said.[269]

Without doubt, there were Armenian depredations in the eastern vilayets and in the Caucasus, where mutual massacre was a norm in the wartime and postwar ethnic clashes. But in central, western, and southern Anatolia, including Cilicia, Armenian criminality was normally limited to theft, including robbery. Murders were rare, and multiple murder was almost unheard of. The July 1920 massacre in Adana and the summer 1921 Izmit-area massacres seem to have been the only ones of their kind. The only Western diplomat who accepted Turkish allegations at face value, and always highlighted them, was Bristol.[270] In general Western observers—diplomats, officers, and missionaries—recorded very few atrocities committed by Armenians during 1918–1923. Even the Turks, though they provided many detailed complaints, produced a catalog of only minor misdeeds when compared to their ongoing crimes.

Maraş

The French takeover in Cilicia and northern Aleppo vilayet "stirred up almost as much feeling as the Greek entrance into the Smyrna district," Bristol wrote.[271] Within weeks, the French garrisons were effectively under siege. Turks severed roads and rail lines and assailed relief columns and the garrisons themselves. Maraş was the first major flashpoint.

Maraş was in difficult straits before the French arrived, at least from the perspective of the Armenians. In late December 1918 Sykes visited and discovered "one of Turkey's most charming spots, a city of trees and running water" surrounded on all sides by the foothills of the Taurus Mountains.[272] But the roughly 6,000 Armenians who had returned—from a prewar population of 20,000—found their homes "demolished, their shops ruined and their churches used as latrines." He noted, "The children are naked in the streets and the Turks still threaten [them]." Thousands more Armenians resettled there during the following months.[273]

The British oversaw law and order with a small garrison but left day-to-day governance to the Turkish administration. Incidents between Turks and Britons and Turks and Armenians were rare, the Turks cowed by the British military presence. The British withdrawal and the arrival of the French in November 1919 appear to have passed smoothly. On the face of it, Turkish-Armenian relations appeared tranquil.

But tensions rose during December 1919–January 1920. It is unclear whether the Nationalists deliberately selected Maraş—the isolated, northernmost French garrison—as the first site of their campaign against the occupation, or whether Nationalist violence there was precipitated by local incidents. A leading American missionary seemed to think Maraş was handpicked, later writing that the Turks "appear to have been moving in this direction for some time prior to the beginning of hostilities. It looks as [though] there was a deliberate intention to make an attack [on Maraş] and as if preparations had been made for it."[274] Indeed, there were standing orders to this effect, albeit not only regarding Maraş. On October 26, 1919, Kemal instructed his army corps commanders "to fight against the French occupation of Marash, Aintab and Urfa."[275]

A chain of incidents began just after this order was received. On October 31 a Turk killed an Armenian legionnaire after he allegedly tore off a Muslim woman's veil.[276] A few days later, Kemal sent four lieutenants to the area to organize irregulars for an attack on the French. Then, on November 16–18, Kemal convened his army's corps commanders in Sivas to discuss ways to limit French "encroachments on Turkish authority."[277] This was followed on the 24th by the arrival in Maraş of the military governor of Osmaniye, Captain Pierre André, at the head of a small troop of gendarmes—Turks, Armenians, and Kurds—and French soldiers. André apparently ordered the removal of the Ottoman flag over the citadel and its replacement with the tricolor. A mob of Muslims, including gendarmes, removed the tricolor and restored the Ottoman flag. Preferring to avoid a fight, André withdrew, leaving the citadel and local government in Turkish hands.[278]

To reassert their rule, the French beefed up their military in and around Maraş and replaced André with a governor they thought would be more steadfast, General Querette. The general was taking over a city on the brink. In January 1920 a missionary reported that, in Maraş, "the Turks are bolder and

more threatening than I have ever seen." Anti-Armenian violence surged on
the town's outskirts; Armenians were murdered almost daily. Two were shot
dead by the son of a wealthy Muslim, and the bodies of four more were found
outside a gendarmerie post after disappearing on the road to Zeytun. Armenian villagers abandoned their fields. The Turks, the missionary reported,
were blaming "bandits," but the Armenians believed their "neighbors" were
responsible.[279] Inside the town, too, the situation grew darker. "Sister E.," apparently a nun, wrote that the local Armenian Catholic school closed frequently "owing to the terror which the Turks spread around."[280] Armenian
villagers fled into town. By late January, the Armenian population of Maraş
had swelled to 22,000.[281]

On January 18 the Turks charged that the French were interfering with their
administration and demanded that they send away the Armenian legionnaires.
Anticipating violence, Armenians and Turks closed their shops, and Armenians
moved into churches for safety. "Armed Turks . . . in considerable numbers"
poured into the city.[282] The French agreed to send away 500 legionnaires, but
the legionnaires were ambushed on the Maraş-Antep road on January 20–21.[283]
The survivors left the dead behind and returned to Maraş.[284] The Turks
had their own complaints, alleging that a 3,000-man French relief column
with cannon and machine guns was advancing toward the town from Islahiye
and had destroyed Muslim villages en route.[285]

On January 21 the French made their move. "They had determined to
strike and strike hard," an American missionary was told.[286] It began when
Querette summoned the Turkish notables and issued an "ultimatum" demanding that they turn over the governance of the town.[287] The Turks refused. Apparently they told him that he was "obliged to wait until the [Paris]
peace conference is finished" because it was not yet clear "to whom Marash
will belong."[288] The French then arrested six of the notables, including the
deputy mutesarrif, and threatened to hang them and "burn" down the town.
The Turks responded by deploying armed men and fortifying key buildings.
At one o'clock in the afternoon, following one or two isolated shots, they
opened fire from the citadel and cut down French sentries and patrols around
town.[289]

It is not clear whether the local Turkish militiamen were following Kemal's
instructions or were acting on their own, though undoubtedly Kemal was

supportive. A few days later, on the 24th, he instructed commanders in the areas bordering Cilicia to back the guerrilla war against the French and to interdict French reinforcements moving northward from Homs.[290] The following day he underlined his approval, cabling his commanders, "There is both harm and disadvantage in delaying operations by the Kuvâ-yi Milliye [National Forces] against the French any longer. . . . We must respond to French actions at Marash everywhere throughout the nation."[291] Kemal's only relevant public statement also hints at his probable approval of the January 21 action: "At first there were British units at Maraş, Urfa and Antep. French troops replaced them. We tried to prevent this occupation. After it became fact, we resorted to political efforts, then to more active ones."[292] But without access to Turkish documents, the only direct evidence of orders concerning the opening of hostilities comes from a Turkish source who claimed the Maraş police commissioner Arslan Bey, "encouraged by orders of Mustafa Kemal Pasha" proclaimed on the afternoon of the 21st, "Comrades, war has begun. With the grace of God, in the spirit of the Prophet, and with the self-sacrifice of believers, be resigned to everything! . . . From us, perseverance; from God, help."[293]

The French answered the Turkish salvos of January 21 with a cannonade from positions on the hills above. A missionary in the American compound outside the city recorded, "The children began to cry and the grown-ups to get panicky. . . . Thru my interpreter I told the children that we had gathered to celebrate the birthday of the Prince of Peace, who had come to teach us how to live, that instead of war, Love and Peace and Goodwill to Men might prevail. . . . It was the first real Christmas for many of the children as they have been in exile for five years."[294]

For two days, the sides traded shot and shell. Here and there Turkish militiamen torched Armenian homes, but the irregulars' initial focus was the French. That changed on the 23rd. The Turks may have noted that the French were busy defending only their own positions, several large buildings in the town center, so they began to "kill the Armenians."[295] Missionaries heard a Turk shouting, "Has the slaughter of the [infidels] begun?"[296] In an attempt to stop the killing and appease the population, the French released the deputy mutesarrif. It made no difference.[297]

During the following fortnight, the Turks systematically murdered Armenians and torched their homes, as the French, besieged in their positions, stood by largely "powerless."[298] The local YMCA secretary, C. F. H. Crathern, had a bird's eye view of the battle from the hospital verandah in the missionary compound on a slope north of the city: "Through our glasses we could see Armenians escaping from their houses and fleeing before the Turks, who were shooting them down like jack rabbits. Other Turks were hiding in the fields behind rocks, trees and manure heaps, and shooting at those who had escaped . . . some dropping wounded . . . and others staggering into the mission grounds with wild eyes . . . and purple faces, telling of an awful massacre."[299] Here and there the Armenians, ensconced in large buildings, fought back, as did pockets of French troops.[300] Most of the Armenians who survived the massacre holed up in walled churches and in Beitschallum, a German orphanage.[301] A few apparently were protected by Turkish officials in the local prison.[302]

The siege lasted almost three weeks. "Hundreds of men, women and children [were] massacred daily," a missionary in the city cabled.[303] The Turks "set fire to the various buildings where Armenians had taken refuge and in one place"—apparently the Armenian church of St. George—"about 800 were burned."[304] Those reaching the missionary compound told harrowing tales. "Mothers had children taken out of their arms and ripped up with knives," Crathern wrote. "The shrieks of the tortured we could hear a mile across the ravine."[305] Another missionary observed, "The Turk, it seems, wastes little ammunition on these helpless people" and often uses "the knife." The Turks were said to be burning some of the bodies in a lime kiln to prevent recognition. "They do this to hide the fact that they have stolen [i.e., raped] the young girls."[306] The town was completely isolated. "If we were in the jungles of Africa we would not be more cut off from the outside world than here in the interior of Turkey . . . the auto road infested with bandits and all telegraph and telephone wires cut," a local American missionary wrote.[307] The first contact between Maraş and the outside world was on day eighteen of the siege, when a French airplane overflew the town.

In the missionary compound, some 2,000 "orphans and refugees" were gathered for safety and sustenance. The missionaries raised the American flag, in an effort to deter the Turks from attacking. Women were "going crazy with fear," Crathern wrote. Down in Maraş French "soldiers are creeping stealthily forth with benzine torches and hand grenades to set fire[s]. . . . It is sometimes like Dante's Inferno."[308] On the 25th he wrote, "News came today that scores of women and children huddled in one house were butchered with knives and hatchets after the men had been taken out and shot." The men had "surrendered on the promise of protection."[309] On February 4th he recorded a story related by one survivor: "Deep pits were dug, and men tied in bunches of three, and led to the edge of it, and then shot and dumped into it, dead or alive."[310]

Crathern's diary contains telling detail. "Little girls, 8 and 10 years old, and wrinkled women of 70 years were agonizing with pain from dum-dum bullet wounds which tore great pieces of flesh from arms and legs."[311] On January 28 the wife of an Armenian protestant pastor, Reverend Solakian, reached the hospital: "She was . . . bleeding from three bullet and three dagger or knife wounds while a child of 18 months had been taken from her breast and slain with a knife, and an older girl killed with an axe. To add to the sorrow of it, this woman was pregnant and had a miscarriage as soon as she reached the hospital." She died the next day.[312]

There were about 2,200 French troops in and around the town, mostly Senegalese and Armenians.[313] They had no communications equipment and lacked food, ammunition, and adequate clothing. Soldiers reached the hospital with frostbite; arms and legs were amputated.[314] Crathern reported that by early February the French were killing their horses and mules. "We had mule roast today and we like it fine," a missionary recorded. "We like it better than horse meat."[315]

Violence occurred outside Maraş as well. While Turkish forces fought in the town, their comrades overran a cluster of villages to the southwest, killing as many as 1,500 Armenians.[316] At Djamostil all the males were reportedly "annihilated."[317] On February 1 two American missionaries, James Perry, the general secretary of the International YMCA, and Frank Johnson were murdered by Turks on a road near Antep.[318]

The siege of Maraş quickly became a rallying cry. In the days after the start of the battle, as we already know, Kemal urged Nationalists elsewhere to join. In particular, he ordered the 3rd Army Corps to help "in every way." "It is very important that the fight commenced at Marash should end to our advantage," he wrote. He ordered other units to prepare to "create strong armed organizations" elsewhere and to force the French to "return to [their] country."[319]

Irregulars from as far afield as Elbistan joined the fight.[320] Turkish forces in Cilicia were apparently commanded by General Polad (Polat) Pasha, also known as "Captain Shukri," a Circassian from Yenibahçe. He had served as Enver's adjutant during the Great War.[321]

On the political side, the Nationalist defense committees around Anatolia bombarded the foreign legations in Constantinople with telegrams alleging Armenian atrocities in Maraş. "The French and Armenian soldiers . . . tie up the limbs of the Mohammedans and then strike them to death with axes," one writer claimed. "They put the men together and burn them, while the women and children are having their limbs cut off one by one."[322] There is no corroboration for this in any Western documentation.

Events were portrayed similarly in messages from Maraş Turks to compatriots elsewhere in Anatolia. "We Turks have protected and respected [the Armenians] . . . in spite of their aggressions," one telegram asserts. Muslims were engaged in "self-defense."[323] Perhaps prompted by what they heard about Maraş, on January 31 a Turkish mob killed or wounded a total of ten Armenians in Antep. The outbreak was promptly quashed by the town's police and gendarmes.[324]

By early February General Henri Gouraud, the commander of the French Army of the Levant, was forced to admit that there was "no longer [an] armistice" in Cilicia; a "state of hostilities" prevailed between the French and the Turks.[325] On February 7 the 3,000-strong French rescue column reached the outskirts of Maraş and the following day the main French redoubt, a position on the slope next to the American missionary compound. Emboldened by the reinforcements' arrival, Armenians downtown emerged from hiding and set alight mosques and Turkish homes.[326] The Turks, exhausted and dispirited, streamed out of town in large numbers.[327] But instead of assaulting and occupying the town, Querette decided—or was ordered—to evacuate his forces and withdraw to Islahiye.[328] The Turks apparently were on the verge of surrender—or so, at least, the missionaries, who were in contact with them, believed. They told Querette but failed to persuade him.[329] Evidently the French command concluded that the garrison in Maraş was untenable or that the prize wasn't worth the fight.

News of the impending French evacuation alarmed the Armenians and the missionaries, who were afraid to stay behind unguarded. "The Armenians . . .

are frantic and desperate. They are determined to leave . . . with the French as they fear massacre," Crathern wrote. The missionaries pleaded with the French for time to prepare an orderly evacuation of Christians. Querette gave them twenty-four hours.[330]

Most Armenians in the compound decided to leave. But most of the missionaries elected to stay and care for the orphans and wounded. During the daylong reprieve, they prepared food and clothing for those leaving on the prospective three-day trek, "75 miles through mountain and plain," to Islahiye. "I fear that many of them will not be equal to it," Crathern wrote. "It is winter and God help them if the weather should be severe." Crathern may also have been thinking about himself—he was seventy years old.

The column of 10,000 French troops and Armenian civilians, along with a handful of missionaries, left Maraş in the dead of night on February 10–11.[331] "It was . . . bitterly" cold, Crathern recorded. "The city was in flames. Guns were booming from the hills covering our retreat."[332] Nationalist soldiers, who knew nothing of the evacuation, continued their withdrawal from Maraş.[333] The French refrained from notifying the Armenians holding out inside the town, but many got wind of what was happening and desperately tried to join the evacuating column.[334] Many apparently were killed by Turkish fighters in the attempt.[335]

February 12 was a "severely cold day." Trudging through deep snow, "Many of the weak ones dropped by the wayside to freeze or to starve."[336] There was little accommodation, so the travelers camped in the open, hungry and exposed.[337] Most of those who walked were able to keep warm enough to survive, but infants and children carried by their mothers or riding in carts or on animals froze to death.[338] "Turkish villages were burnt by the soldiers after the column had passed through," and troops ate cows and oxen the fleeing villagers left behind.[339] Come dawn February 13, a blizzard "raged"; a missionary reported that it was the worst storm the area had experienced in seventeen years.[340] At noon, the sun came out. An Armenian pastor, Pascal Maljian, recorded: "We climbed the mountains, descended, only to climb again and descend. It was a new Israel searching for the Promised Land of Cilicia."[341] Some 1,000–1,200 refugees and dozens of soldiers died before the column reached Islahiye later that day. "The Islahiye road," a missionary later observed, "is bordered with the skeletons of those who perished. In one defile are hundreds still unburied, lying where they fell."[342] More Armenians died at Islahiye, which offered little food and no accommodation. The Turkish governor, French command, and American missionaries did their best to tend to the refugees, who eventually were transported to Adana.[343]

One source speaks of 6,000 Maraş Armenians who died between January 21 and February 10, mostly unarmed civilians.[344] Another speaks of 20,000 deaths in and around Maraş during the whole period, covering the siege, battle, and evacuation.[345] Curzon said that "in all probability, as many as 15,000 had perished."[346] But the French military—assailed by charges of incompetence and of abandoning the Armenians—rejected British and Armenian figures and questioned whether "there had been massacres of Armenians anywhere." The French also doubted that their policies, conceived by Kemal's troops as pro-Armenian, were responsible for the Turks' belligerent attitude toward the Armenians.[347] According to R. A. Lambert—the NER director at Aleppo, who visited Maraş in March—the Turks claimed they had lost 4,500 killed in the battle.[348] The French had suffered 800 casualties.[349]

Back in Maraş, Armenian and Turkish representatives, with American missionaries mediating, reached an accord on February 11 or 12. The town's remaining Armenians—8,500–10,000, "almost all women"—agreed to give up their arms and leave their downtown redoubts, and the Turkish authorities promised them protection.[350] A few days later, James Lyman and Dr. Marion Wilson, two of the American missionaries who had stayed behind, telegraphed Constantinople that the Armenians were safe under Turkish guard. "No more Armenians were killed after that," and Armenians who had fled to Mersin were returning.[351]

There was not much to come back for. It was estimated that about 40 percent of Maraş's houses, most of them belonging to Armenians, were destroyed during the violence. The Turks also renewed the boycott and robbed Armenians as they made their way back to their looted, ruined homes.[352] "Every" Armenian was "grimy with dirt and lice, and half-starved," Wilson wrote.[353]

The protection granted in the immediate aftermath of the January–February battle and massacre was short-lived. An April report from Armenian lobbyists claims that "over fifty" men disappeared from Maraş without a trace.[354] At the same time, Jackson noted that thirty-four prominent Maraş Armenians were in jail, and the Nationalists were "preparing to deport the survivors" of the massacre. He also pointed to its lingering effects: ten to fifteen were dying daily from hunger and illness.[355]

In July an American missionary wrote that Armenians weren't allowed to leave the city and had "few houses, no money, no work, and are in constant fear."[356] The Turks confiscated absent Armenians' homes and closed missionary institutions serving orphans and refugees, though American relief workers were able to feed them through 1920. Armenian women were said to be "knitting socks" for Kemal's army.[357] In summer 1921 the Turks deported hundreds of Zeytunli refugees from Maraş; stragglers were murdered outside the town. James Lyman, an American missionary, said in 1922 that there had been a "good deal of promiscuous killing of Armenians" in and around the town after the French departure, with as many as 2,000 murdered.[358]

The battle and massacre in Maraş proved to be the key event in the Franco-Turkish war. The French did not give up immediately. Amid recurrent policy debates in Paris, they massively reinforced their units in the Levant and had occasional tactical successes. But the strategic outcome of the Maraş retreat was clear: Cilicia was lost. Instead the French focused on the area to the south, encompassing Damascus, Aleppo, and Beirut. With Cilicia off the table, the real battle would be over the borderlands along the Alexandretta-Antep-Urfa-Mardin axis.

London, too, understood that Cilicia was lost; British policy would have to be adjusted accordingly. At the highest level of strategic consideration, de Robeck advised restraint in the peace process. Imposing a "drastic peace," as the Allies had done with Germany, would only stoke the anger the Turks had shown at Maraş.[359] Henceforward the British quietly regarded the French as inept at best. Bristol was of similar mind. Putting the French in charge in Cilicia amounted to sending "a boy to do a man's job."[360] The Armenians were outspoken on the matter. The French, as one notable put it, were "mean, treacherous, cowards and dishonest."[361]

The Turks understandably lost their fear of the French.[362] More widely, after Maraş, the Turks understood that no Western power would intervene on the Armenians' behalf. This meant the Turks could do as they pleased with the Armenians under their control. The Turks probably also noticed that a well-placed, well-timed massacre would expedite and escalate Armenian flight.

Historically, Maraş proved to be a milestone in the last stage of the destruction of the Armenians of Asia Minor.

But in the short term, Maraş had contradictory, consequences. In mid-March, the Allies occupied Constantinople, taking over key government buildings and arresting dozens of Nationalists.[363] The "main object" of the occupation was "to impress on all Turks," especially the Nationalists in the provinces, the need for "good conduct." The "high commissioners were unable to devise any better means of minimizing [the] danger of massacres," de Robeck wrote.[364] On the other hand, the British left the Turkish civil administration intact and withdrew their troops stationed along the railway lines leading from the interior to Constantinople. The French and Italians also withdrew units, from railway lines and from Konya, respectively.[365]

Among Anatolian Muslims, Maraş caused "great excitement." "The vali of Sivas describes the feeling in his district as 'an extraordinary national and religious ferment,'" British intelligence observed. The Nationalist leadership deliberately promoted the furor. Kemal launched a mobilization drive, and "preachers [were] reported to have been sent to work up the Kurdish and Arab tribes" around Antep and elsewhere.[366] In Samsun Nationalist speakers called on the people to be ready to shed their "last drop of blood" in defense of the empire. "The Christians whom we have defended and protected up to the present like beloved beings . . . have thrown off the mask and have revealed themselves to us like vipers," one Nationalist thundered to the Samsun crowd. Get "ready," he said, "to crush the heads of these vipers."[367] On the Armenian side, Maraş triggered revenge attacks against Muslims around Zeytun and in a few other locations.[368]

After Maraş and the Allied occupation of Constantinople, Kemal stepped up the rhetoric of jihad. "We are obliged to continue our holy struggle until the impure feet of these men are removed from our national soil," he declared in an official May 1 message to the British government.[369] Dozens of Anatolian muftis issued a fatwa authorizing jihad against the infidels.[370] Ahmad Sharif as-Sanussi, an exiled Libyan chieftain and militant preacher, toured Anatolia and drummed up support for holy war. In Sivas he declared, "War for religion and for Allah is a treasure which Heaven bestows on its beloved. . . . It is you who have made the Koran live again."[371] In summer 1920 the American consul in Samsun noted that the Nationalists are trying to inflame the population "by preaching a Holy War. Of late the literature . . . emanating from Ankara has become particularly violent and great stress is placed on the religious side of the question."[372]

Such appeals worked, according to the American consul-general in Izmir, because "the common Turk is intensely religious. At the base of his psychology is religious fanaticism, founded on genuine and sincere beliefs. No Methodist deacon in Central Michigan can have the pity and contempt for Mohammedans or Buddhists that the Hodja of a Turkish village and his flock feel for . . . unbelievers." The consul drew an illustrative analogy to his own land, suggesting that a Turk would feel being governed by Christians as "an American of the Southern States of the United States would were he put under negro rule."[373]

The British concluded that Kemal was personally responsible for Maraş; Curzon said that "there was . . . reason to think that he had inspired or instigated . . . [the] terrible atrocities" there.[374] But Bristol blamed the French and Armenians. "The French used black colonial troops and Armenians and at the same time bombarded a defenseless city," he wrote, reflecting the view that Turks naturally would object to military control by Christians and racial others. "That the Turks have ruthlessly . . . massacred Armenians . . . seems true," Bristol allowed, but he thought the killing in Maraş "was all brought about by the French occupation of Cilicia." Indeed, he believed "the Turks do not intend to massacre non-Moslem races at the present time, and they are doing everything in their power to prevent massacres."[375] Bristol informed Washington that "the French destroyed villages, outraged women and killed the natives."[376] As was often the case, Bristol's fairly uncritical acceptance of the Kemalist narrative placed him in the minority among Western diplomats.

In the wake of Maraş the French adopted a schizophrenic strategy. On the face of it, they sent in reinforcements in order to hold the line against the Nationalists. By March 1920 they had deployed two divisions in their embattled areas of occupation. In Cilicia the troops were under the command of General Julien Dufieux, headquartered in Adana; in northern Aleppo vilayet, they were initially headquartered in Katma, and later Kilis, under the command of General Marie C. M. de Lamothe. Another brigade was deployed along the coast south of Alexandretta. But the forces were ill-equipped and unsuitable. Most of the troops were Algerians and Senegalese, who were reputed to be poorly trained. Among them were also 2,000 Armenians, whose presence could only reinforce anti-French sentiment. These forces had almost no aircraft, tanks, or armored cars. An American diplomat, taking note of the poorly armed and largely colonial force, thought that the French generals were pessimistic about their "prospects" of beating back the Nationalists "and frankly look forward to complete withdrawal."[377] "Many French officers," he wrote, are "sick of the whole expedition which they consider work of politicians at home who believed that French would be received with open arms."[378]

Kemal apparently was at least marginally impressed by the French military build-up, but the Nationalists' actions demonstrated their continuing confidence.[379] Just a few weeks after the close of hostilities in Maraş, the Turks were challenging the French throughout Cilicia and northern Aleppo vilayet. On February 29–March 1, Turks, including uniformed gendarmes, raided the Armenian village of Keones (Kunez), near Islahiye. They separated men from women, and killed six men. Then they bayoneted and shot fourteen of the women and girls, one of whom they first raped. Three women survived. Dr. William Dodd, the Near East Relief director at Adana, who interviewed the survivors, remarked that Turkish gendarmes in Cilicia generally crossed over to the Nationalists "whenever they came in contact with them."[380] Dodd reported another massacre in late March, at Kizli Aghaj (Kızlı Ağaç), where eighty-three Armenians were alleged to have been killed.[381] Around April 6 Turkish bands attacked Hach Kiri (Haçkiri?) and Gelebek (Kelebek), villages just south of the Taurus Mountain tunnels. Several hundred Armenians as well as Greeks and Frenchmen were reportedly slaughtered.[382] "Everywhere the bands are supported by regular troops, well-commanded, well-armed, fighting 'European style,'" French intelligence reported. "It is thus no longer a matter of guerrilla [fighting] on a grand scale, but of real battle operations against well-organized and numerous forces." These troops would "not flinch at anything to force the population to do their bidding."[383]

In much of Cilicia and northern Aleppo vilayet, and especially in the countryside, the French proved too weak to protect the Armenians, even had they wanted to.[384] Armenian and French-held towns, including Hacin and Hasanbeyli, were besieged. Hacin appealed to the French for help. Colonel

Brémond replied that "after thinking long and hard," the French had decided not to send troops. But he offered to send a thousand rifles and suggested that women and children be evacuated.[385]

Antep, Urfa, and Adana

After winning Maraş and consolidating their dominance in Cilicia, the Nationalists shifted focus to the eastern extremities of the French zone: Antep, Urfa, and their access roads. The French had a small presence in Antep. In January 1920 the garrison numbered 1,500–1,700, in a town with 16,000–30,000 Armenians.[386] Most, with artillery, were positioned next to the American missionary college, in a compound overlooking the town center.

As the battle for Maraş progressed, tensions built in Antep. On January 22 a jittery French soldier killed a Turk. Turks closed their shops and Armenians began to evacuate the Turkish quarters. On the 31st several Armenians were wounded and one killed in the market. Turks in turn began evacuating Christian areas and boycotted Christian shops.[387] The Turkish authorities were playing "a double game," publicly calling for quiet while distributing arms and organizing Muslims in surrounding villages for action.[388] On the approach roads, Turkish forces ambushed French patrols and supply convoys and attacked Christians. Jackson wrote of "complete brigandage."[389] According to the Turks, the local French commander aggravated the situation by demanding control over the local police and gendarmerie.[390]

By late March the Christians were holed up in their homes and churches, suffering "all sorts of privations and menaces." The food situation was "critical." The Armenians had much to be afraid of: one of the leaders of the Maraş massacres, Kılıç Ali Pasha, was occupying two khans outside Antep with 1,500 men. He apparently commanded the Turkish forces in the region.[391] The Turks were demanding that the Armenians surrender their arms.[392] Turks, too, were on edge. On March 28 a French column, with 400 wagonloads of provisions, reached the town after fighting its way from Kilis.[393] The Turks completed the evacuation of the Christian quarters.

But at dawn on April 1, the French convoy, along with hundreds of garrison troops and their heavy artillery, withdrew. "Much to the surprise and consternation of the [Antep] Christians," they headed back to Kilis. They left behind "only 1,200 Senegalese troops." A few hours later, a shot rang out in the marketplace, followed by two shots from the surrounding hills. The Turks began shooting Armenians. They also detained Armenians and thirty French soldiers. The battle for Antep had begun.[394]

American missionaries later claimed that they had "convincing evidence that a general massacre had been planned by Nationalist forces, with the . . . consent of the government."[395] About 2,000 Armenians rushed to the missionary compound while the bulk of the Armenians stayed put and fortified their positions in town.[396] The Turks demanded that the Armenians raise Turkish flags. The Armenians refused. In the ensuing battle, they would be largely on their own. The French grudgingly sent soldiers to protect the compound while complaining that they had barely enough troops to defend their own strongpoints. They supplied the Armenians with some rifles and machine guns, but otherwise stayed out of the fight, leaving the Armenians to their own devices.[397] "French indifferent, refuse interfere," one Armenian cabled weeks after the fighting had begun.[398]

During the following weeks the Armenians showed "praiseworthy courage" and organization in defending themselves; the Turks repeatedly broke promises and ceasefire agreements. "We have come to know the Turks so well," one missionary wrote, "that the anger is not mingled with surprise."[399]

The French refused to send reinforcements. Two French columns did reach the town's outskirts on April 16 and 17; they shelled the Turkish quarters, Turks fled, and the French pursued them with machine gun fire.[400] But the French intended only "the revictualling of the Christians" and to obtain the release of Christian prisoners, not to crush the Turks.[401] The senior French officer, General de Lamothe, told the missionaries that entering town would "stir the Turks up to fury." He seemed to believe that "a siege would be enough to bring them to terms." The missionaries found French behavior "puzzling and disturbing."[402] The French, who deployed two tanks, apparently killed hundreds of Turks, but they also urged the Armenians to reach "some sort of compact with the Turks."[403] It was reported that Muslim French troops "refused to fire on the Turks."[404] The Nationalists were also confounded by the ambiguous French behavior but accused them of backing the Armenians.[405] The French somewhat confusingly argued that if they lost troops in Antep, "the Armenians would be left at the mercy of the Turks."[406]

On the political level, the French believed that perfidious Albion—and the Germans and Americans—were "encouraging the general hostility" toward them, under the guise of "assisting the [Armenian] refugees."[407] The British even wanted to move orphans to Cyprus "to demonstrate the incapacity of the French."[408]

As the fighting raged in Antep, the French sent mixed signals about the future of Cilicia. According to the British ambassador in Paris, the French in late April denied that they "intended to retire from Cilicia."[409] Yet by early May, Prime Minister Alexandre Millerand said France would leave most of Cilicia to "the Sovereignty of Turkey" while retaining a mandate over a "small part" consisting of Alexandretta and Payas as well as Syria. But what of the Armenian population who had "collected [in Cilicia], trusting to the French protection?" Boghos Nubar, the Paris-based head of the Armenian Delegation to the peace conference, and Armenian Patriarch Zevan asked. "Unfortunately, I cannot send [one] hundred thousand soldiers," Millerand replied. He agreed only to secure the departure of Armenians who had "taken part in [the] fighting."[410]

It is not clear why the French announced contradictory positions. The purpose may have been tactical deception. Or maybe there was no purpose. Individual representatives of the government were at loggerheads, a symptom of real indecision; or those who wished to soldier on in Cilicia were in denial. Certainly the political winds were blowing against them. The political and military elites were clearly losing their will to fight. Given that French forces were also skirmishing with Arab guerrillas in Syria, many in Paris—and Beirut—believed that Cilicia should be sacrificed so that Syria and Lebanon could be held. And many French leaders did not believe the Armenians were worth the expenditure of French blood. During early 1920 French officials steadily grew disenchanted with the Armenians and began voicing "accusations of treachery, cowardice, barbarity, and ingratitude against them," as one historian put it. First, they were disenchanted with the Armenian Legion, then, with "all Armenians."[411]

By spring the Nationalists were certain of the French lack of resolve. In both Cilicia and Syria, Bristol wrote, "French soldiers inspire[d] the Turks and Arabs . . . with no respect or fear."[412] "The Nationalists thought the French "inferior . . . fighters" and demonstrated as much by attacking them directly.[413]

Kemal's regulars and irregulars besieged French garrisons in northern Aleppo vilayet and areas to the west, along the coast.[414] French columns were regularly ambushed. Kemal sent a letter congratulating Kılıç Ali on his "successes" and urged him to further efforts.[415]

An important source of Nationalist confidence was the fight in Urfa, which raged as the battles for Antep and Maraş unfolded. Urfa was France's easternmost position. The French had turned it into "a French city," removing Ottoman flags and "trampl[ing] upon the imperial rights of our Sultan," a local cleric complained. The French, he said, claimed that "the place had belonged to France 800 years ago"—referring to nearby Edessa, which had been a Crusader state during the twelfth century.[416] On February 7, 1920, the Turks presented the French with an ultimatum: evacuate Urfa within twenty-four hours or face battle.[417]

Two days later the Turks, joined by local Kurds and Arabs, attacked the 450–700-strong French garrison comprising mainly Algerian and Senegalese troops—"heroes of Verdun," an American missionary called them.[418] What followed was a two-month siege. The French responded by intermittently shelling the Turkish parts of town and provided local Armenians with some arms.[419] But, despite Turkish sniping, the Armenians stayed neutral.[420] The French lived on "short rations, horse meat and black bread, [and] beans."[421]

The French "have blundered and blundered," an American missionary later wrote. But no blunder was worse than that of April 8 in Urfa.[422] That day the French commander, Major G. Hauger, agreed to withdraw. In exchange the Turks guaranteed the safety of the town's Christians and promised to provide the French with pack animals and an escort of gendarmes to aid their withdrawal. It would be "a withdrawal with honor and safety," Mutesarrif Ali Rıza Bey said.[423] But Ali Rıza knew what was coming. He told a westerner who planned to accompany the column that it was unsafe to go, as the route was surrounded by tribes "in a state of agitation."[424]

The French left early on April 11, with sixty camels and thirty horses. They met their fate nine miles out, at Sebeke Pass.[425] According to Ali Rıza, "tribesmen" and "some of the population of the city . . . without the knowledge of the government and of the commander of the Nationalist forces" ambushed the column. The fight lasted over two hours. Rıza claimed the French feigned surrender and then "treacherously" opened fire, so the ambushers cut them down.[426] Garnet Woodward, a British NER worker who accompanied the column, had witnessed something different. He reported that the French attempted to surrender but were shot down by Kurds and Turks, who proceeded to finish off the wounded. Gendarmes sent from Urfa eventually ended the killing and saved some of the soldiers.[427] Between 50 and 161 troopers, most of them Muslim Algerians and Tunisians, survived and were brought back to Urfa.[428] Three hundred or more soldiers died.

For weeks thereafter Urfa's Turks lived in fear that the French would take revenge. The Turks thus behaved well toward the town's Armenians, at least for a while. The Armenians were even allowed to retain arms.[429] Some time later Sheikh Sanussi used Urfa as a base, from which he delivered sermons inciting against the Christians.[430] The French blamed the Armenians for the debacle at Urfa, aggravating Franco-Armenian relations.[431]

A few days before Urfa's fall, Turkish villagers massacred the Armenian inhabitants of nearby Ehneche. At first local gendarmes intervened. But they were soon supplanted by a new troop, which arrived with the kaymakam of Kheldedi. The kaymakam and his twenty men tied up the villagers and marched them down the road to Kamışlı (Qamishli). According to the Armenian Patriarchate, the Turks "then cut up the small children to pieces, next they led the men to the banks of the Euphrates and massacred them there . . . crushing . . . heads under large stones, skinning, dismembering them alive and so forth. Finally came the women's turn; they were placed on the sand by the side of the river, and burnt alive." Two men and three women escaped; one hundred and sixty-four were murdered.[432]

At Antep the Armenians and the French held on from the slopes outside the city. Armenian artisans and jewelers manufactured ammunition.[433] The Turks periodically bombarded the Christian quarters, and the Armenians responded with what they had. On April 28 Kılıç Ali—signing as Sayf Ullah, "the sword of God"—gave the Armenians an ultimatum: they had twenty-four hours to turn over their arms or else "be considered rebels." In that case the Turks would "resort to violence." "Marash should give you an indication" of what might happen, Kılıç Ali said.[434] But the Armenians kept fighting.

On May 23 a strong French column under Colonel Debieuvre reached Antep, reportedly killing 1,200 and capturing "thousands" of Turks along the way.[435] The Turks also suffered severe losses inside the town: one report spoke of 400 dead. But they, too, kept fighting.[436] On May 27 the Turks ambushed a French garrison at Pozantı. Many were killed or taken prisoner.[437] According to one report, the garrison's 450 Algerians were spared but 120 Frenchmen were executed.[438]

On May 29 Robert de Caix, secretary general of the French high commission in Constantinople, met Kemal in Ankara and signed a limited, twenty-day armistice. The accord provided for French evacuation of Sis, Pozantı, and Antep within ten days, while the Turks were not to attack Antep's Armenians.[439] The agreement represented a partial French capitulation.[440] As one British naval officer observed, the French position in Cilicia was, at this point, "extremely critical," and they needed a breather. The garrisons were too weak to successfully withdraw and were "likely to be exterminated" unless considerably reinforced.[441]

Missionaries called the armistice "a farce," partly because it made no provision for important Armenian sites under siege, principally Hacin, Dörtyol, and Hasanbeyli.[442] The French maintained that their aims in Cilicia included protecting the Christians, but they quietly urged Armenians to move to areas closer to the coast where such protection could be effectively exercised. "Several thousand" Armenians accordingly trekked from Antep to Kilis.[443]

Emir Faisal, in Damascus, while himself at loggerheads with the French, regarded the armistice with misgivings. It would mark "the commencement of a series of defeats in Near East in which not only French but all of [our] Allies will be involved and will shortly menace peace of Mesopotamia, Mosul and other places." The armistice, he warned, opened the way for the Turks to extend their "domination" southward.[444]

Despite Turkish violations of the ceasefire during the first week of June, the French duly evacuated Sis. The town's 6,000–8,000 Armenians, locals and rural refugees who had clustered in the town, were "ordered" by the French "to leave within 24 hours" for Adana. "The Armenians begged to be allowed to remain . . . rather than go out to become beggars," but they were refused. "If they stayed behind, the French guns would be turned on them," an American missionary reported. So they left, abandoning their property.[445]

Kemal "refused to extend [the] armistice," and hostilities resumed after June 20.[446] The Turks shelled the French outposts at Mersin and almost surrounded the Adana plain, which was dotted with Armenian refugee camps.[447]

In August the French abandoned Hasanbeyli; its 1,500 Armenians, under French escort, trekked to Dörtyol. "They were 32 days on the road," arriving at their destination "with only their clothes on their back."[448]

At Antep, the French proposed that all the Armenians leave and promised to provide transport. But the Armenians there felt much like their compatriots in Sis, responding that "instead of going out to die as tramps and beggars, they will stick to their arms and defend themselves, their families and property, as long as they have left a piece of bread and a single cartridge." The missionaries worried that, if the Armenians stayed, "Fifteen thousand souls will surely perish."[449] The French relented, withdrawing from the town center and urging the Armenians to negotiate with the Nationalists.[450]

The resulting ceasefire had unusually good terms, from the Armenians' standpoint. Antep was to be policed by a thousand Turkish regulars. The Turks offered amnesty to the Armenian fighters and agreed to pull all the brigands out of town and allow the Armenians to retain their arms.[451] But 3,500 Armenians, "consisting of elderly people, paupers and non-combatants," left in early June.[452] The town calmed down during the following weeks, though the Turks continued nonviolent forms of persecution, boycotting Armenian traders and refusing to sell to Armenians. The Armenians received substantial missionary aid.[453]

By July the Cilician countryside, ravaged by Kemal's irregulars, had emptied of Armenian villagers. All had fled to the towns. There were reportedly 80,000 Armenians in Adana and its environs.[454] Many, perhaps most, of Adana's Turks had fled, either under Armenian duress or in fear of massacre.[455] Because Armenians were unable to cultivate their fields, there was widespread hunger. In Adana alone 20,000 women and children reportedly were begging in the streets.[456] Here too, Western aid agencies helped stave off famine and epidemics.

In July the French won a victory over the Arabs in Maysalun and ousted Faisal from Damascus, leading some Armenians to believe that the French would go on to reassert control in Cilicia. But nothing changed.[457] Adana's Christians decided to act. On August 4 representatives of the town's Christian communities, with the Armenians in the lead, issued a "declaration of [Cilician] autonomy," albeit under French Mandate. Some called the new polity the Republic of Amanus. The next day the representatives elected an

Armenian prime minister and a cabinet consisting of six Armenians, a Greek, a Turk, an Assyrian, and an Arab. The cabinet took over the konak and expelled the Turkish gendarmes and officials. The vali and others were placed under house arrest.[458]

Brémond reacted swiftly. His soldiers stormed the konak "with fixed bayonets" threw out the cabinet, and declared martial law. General Dufieux proclaimed, "Enough masquerades, fiery speeches and comedies!"[459] A series of pro-Turkish steps followed. The French removed Brémond, who, despite crushing the short-lived "republic," was regarded as pro-Armenian. On September 18 Gouraud ordered his commanders in Adana to "[re]establish a Turkish government," in conformity with the just-concluded provisions of the Treaty of Sèvres.[460] The thousands of Armenian refugees camped around the city were ordered to leave for "Smyrna, Constantinople, Erivan, Marseilles or America" or to French-governed Alexandretta and Beirut.[461] But they refused to budge.[462] The French surrounded the camps and threatened to deport "women, children and old men" and cut off the refugees' rations.[463] The large camp near the new railway station was eventually cleared, but many refugees responded by moving into empty houses in town.[464] Some were sent to Mersin.[465] The French disarmed the local Armenian militia and jailed its commander. They also disarmed a volunteer column that had set out to relieve the besieged town of Hacin, shut down Adana's Armenian newspapers, and arrested journalists and members of the Armenian National Council. All were deported to Alexandretta.[466] The Armenians said that the deportations came at Turkish request.[467] The French invited Muslims who had fled Adana to return.[468]

The French later described the trajectory of their actions. At first "arms were distributed to the Armenians for the purposes of defending their villages and forming auxiliary contingents [for] . . . the French forces." But "the Armenians, profiting by the acquisition of arms, conducted a campaign of revenge against the Turkish inhabitants in the form of massacres, pillage and incendiarism. When an appeal was made to them to rally to the relief of Tarsus, out of the two thousand volunteers promised, seventeen joined the French troops. . . . Eventually it was found necessary to disarm the Armenians." As for the volunteers heading for Hacin, they were disarmed "upon an attempt by the Armenians of Adana to proclaim an Armenian republic in Cilicia to the exclusion of the Turks."[469]

Back in Antep, battle—this time strictly between the Turks and the French—was resumed on July 29.[470] It began with a bombardment of the American missionary compound after the French refused to vacate the buildings.[471] An infantry assault failed, and the French responded by bombarding the town's Turkish quarters with artillery and aircraft. Two-thirds of the Turkish homes were reported destroyed. The Armenians, of whom there were 8,000–9,000 left, remained neutral. They refused to allow the Turks to use their quarter to launch attacks. A joint Armenian-Turkish company patrolled the Armenian quarter. Nonetheless, six Armenians were reportedly killed in a firefight with the Turks. Turkish-Armenian relations deteriorated.[472]

On August 10 a 5,000-strong French column broke through the siege, surrounded Antep, and delivered an ultimatum. The Turks were called to surrender the town.[473] As far as the French were concerned, Antep was theirs, awarded to them that very day at Sèvres. Already in May the Allies had published a draft summary of the provisions. The draft augured the partition of Cilicia into French- and Turkish-ruled zones, in effect awarding France only a small part of the area designated in Sykes-Picot. The Armenians protested, demanding that Cilicia, together with Antep, be left intact as a political-administrative Armenian entity, under Western mandate.[474] The publication of the draft affected French decision-making. In May Gouraud argued that under the treaty, Cilicia, including Adana, Mersin, Tarsus, Maraş, and Hacin was to be returned to the Turks but not "Killis, Aintab, Biredjik and Urfa," which were to be incorporated in French-ruled Syria.[475] But a month later, the French told the British that Sèvres was no longer the guideline, and that they intended to withdraw from "Bozanti, Urfa, Biridjik and Marash," as these were "dangerously exposed." But they had "no intention" of evacuating "Mersina, Tarsus, Adana, Osmanie and Aintab."[476] Clearly, there was confusion in French ranks.

They appeared to want to hold Antep. But the Turks refused to surrender, and the French renewed their bombardment.[477] Thousands of Turks fled to the countryside. The French hoped the blockade and shelling would elicit surrender, but the siege was not tight enough; supplies came in at night from

Malatya.[478] Moreover, the French were still getting no help from the Armenians, who remained neutral despite the horrific effects the siege was having on them. A desperate food shortage led to Armenian riots in August.[479] Only in September, caught between hammer and anvil, did the Armenians at last join the fight. They won French admiration for their bravery and skill.[480]

Nonetheless, the Armenians were sure the French wanted them to leave. The meager rations the French provided seemed to demonstrate as much, but matters were not that straightforward. In Paris there was a serious policy struggle that summer. Some senators called for "peace with Mustafa Kemal," others for a new offensive to cow the Nationalists. For a brief moment, the latter prevailed. But all agreed that to hold the core of Syria, additional troops were needed. A further division was shipped to Alexandretta.[481] Meanwhile, thousands of Armenians left Antep while the French bombarded the Turks. The casualties included the mutesarrif and his son.[482]

In mid-September Gouraud reportedly told his chief aides, Brémond and Dufieux, that he intended "to evacuate Cilicia forthwith."[483] He could not hold both Syria and Cilicia. Even so, after the arrival of the reinforcements, he launched a major push to clear the roads and countryside between Alexandretta, Kilis, and Antep.[484] The French commanders promised that northern Aleppo vilayet would be "calm within eight months." They wanted to incorporate Antep, Urfa, Mardin, Rakka, and Deir Zor in their Syrian mandate while abandoning the core of Cilicia.[485] The new push was to be the last French effort to achieve victory, albeit a limited one.

Meanwhile France sought to clarify its policy vis-à-vis the Armenians. "The French government is committed not to evacuate Cilicia without insuring the protection of Christian minorities and receiving from the Turks all necessary guaranties," an internal memorandum read. "Three quarters of French manpower in the Levant, which has been reinforced, are engaged in northern Syria. They guarantee the defense of [Christian] populations. . . . This protection has brought about the death of many thousands of French soldiers, and many hundreds of millions in expenses." The French claimed they had fed, clothed, repatriated, and armed the Armenians. "All these . . . sacrifices taken . . . have not put an end to the complaints of one section of the Armenian element."[486]

The onset of winter 1921, which rendered roads and mountains impassable, changed the military landscape. The French push came to a halt; the roads to Antep were closed.[487] In Adana a "quiet resignation" took hold. The Armenians "feel their cause is lost . . . and as a people . . . they are doomed. The fever of emigration is again seizing upon them." But funds were unavailable and passports difficult to procure. Many looked to heaven. The pastor of the Armenian Protestant church said that "often the meetings continue so long that he is obliged to go home without dismissing the congregation."[488]

But winter also hurt the Nationalists. In Adana groups of brigands reportedly surrendered.[489] And in Antep, they were overwhelmed. On February 8 the Turkish civil authorities, on orders from Ankara, surrendered to the besieging French, who then occupied the town.[490] But the Turkish military refused to sign the instrument of surrender and continued the fight in the surrounding countryside.[491] Indeed, within weeks the Nationalists issued a proclamation stating "that the mosques and minarets destroyed in the conflicts with the French will [be rebuilt] with the skulls of Armenians."[492] In the following months, NER diverted much of its relief work in Antep to the surviving Turkish population, which had been battered physically and economically. The missionaries offered this as proof of their even-handed humanitarianism.[493] The Turks were unconvinced.

The Kemalists renewed hostilities in spring 1921. The masses of Armenians crowding Adana lived on tenterhooks, panicked by every rumor of French evacuation. "The spectacles of Marash, Aintab, Sis and Hadjin present a sad outlook for Adana," a missionary reported. The Armenians' "spirits are . . . crushed as I have never seen before."[494]

Armenian suspicion of the French had solidified around the fate of Hacin, which the French had not garrisoned. The town, at the edge of the French zone, had an almost completely Armenian population of 6,000–7,000. Eight hundred were armed.[495] In March 1919 the French, then under British jurisdiction, replaced the town's kaymakam and the commander of gendarmerie with Armenians and armed the population. But during the following months, "the Kemalist spirit rolled down like a small stone from a snowy mountain . . . the rolling stone got bigger and bigger. The avalanche was approaching," an Armenian wrote.[496]

At some point the Armenians, led by kaymakam Armenag Keregian, took twelve Turkish village elders as "hostages of peace." The French disapproved. They replaced Keregian and released the hostages. The locals then appointed Sarkis Jebejian, a veteran from the wars in the Caucasus, as overall commander. He organized defenses.[497] On February 3, 1920, Turkish irregulars laid siege.[498] Friendly Kurds warned the Armenians that, as soon as the snows melted, they would come under attack.[499] Reports reached the Security Directorate in Constantinople that Hacin's Turkish inhabitants were terrified.[500] By early March Hacin was entirely cut off, but it held out for another half a year. The Christians took the town's 300 Turks and 150 Kurds hostage.[501] The Armenians were reinforced by villagers who poured in from the countryside. The Armenians appealed for help. The Adana Armenian council demanded that the French send a relief column or arm local militiamen.[502]

In early April the Nationalists tightened the siege by occupying the American missionary compound on the edge of town.[503] In late May they threatened the inhabitants with annihilation, boasting that they had slaughtered the inhabitants of two nearby villages. Armenian gunmen responded by killing as many as 200 of the hostages. Other Armenians condemned this as a "sin and a stain on their reputation."[504] The Turks pillaged the missionary compound and deported the missionaries to Talas.[505]

Brémond refused to send a relief column but offered to help evacuate Hacin. The inhabitants declined. One wrote, "The Armenians of Cilicia are determined . . . to resist and die like heroes. . . . They are inspired by the law of Moses."[506] In Adana the Armenians mobilized a 500-man relief force. The French intercepted and disarmed part of the force when it reached Sis. Turks ambushed a third relief company, and a fourth, sent to save the third, was turned back and imprisoned in Mersin by the French.[507]

In mid-July 1920 the Turks systematically bombarded Hacin. The Armenians held on. The population reached "a point of famine. People ate horses and donkeys and cats" as well as "the leaves . . . and bark . . . of the trees. . . . Bones were powdered to be mixed with a handful of flour" to make bread. "The price of a cat was a gold pound. Dogs, rats, animals of any kind, even the skin of sheep and oxen were eaten after being broiled."[508] "The people had become walking skeletons," a missionary wrote.[509] In August and

September the Hacin defenders mounted sorties against the Turks, capturing cannon, ammunition, and food. In October, the Turks sent reinforcements. The town was subjected to a new bombardment.[510] "The last days of Hadjin were days of hell. Men were struggling with empty stomachs to defend the city. The women were screaming and fainting, the children were crying. . . . The orphans were busy . . . carrying ammunition from ditch to ditch," one chronicler recorded. Two men reportedly killed "their families" before committing suicide; others fled to the mountains, abandoning their "loved one[s]."[511] Hacin fell on October 17. The Turks systematically torched the town, shooting those fleeing the flames. There was little left to loot.[512]

After stamping out the last pockets of resistance and hunting down refugees in the mountains, the Turks "gathered the living relics . . . into the monastery and separated the men, women and children." The women were ordered to take off their clothes and were shot or stabbed. The men were then taken in batches of five or ten "God knows where." Eleven wounded women were said to have crawled out from under the bodies and were later recaptured and murdered, but only after telling their story to other survivors, who eventually reached Adana.[513] About 450 men managed to reach a nearby Turkish village, where the local aga, Hasan Kâhya, "was like an oasis in the desert of the Turks" and helped them; some 350 eventually reached safety in Cihan.[514] "Thirty children" were said to have reached Guelisan (Gürleşen?).[515] These were the survivors of Hacin's population.[516]

Armenian suffering was not limited to the extremities of the French zone. The situation on the Cilician coast in July 1920 was pithily described by a visiting American officer: "[Mersin] closely besieged. . . . Tarsus: Closely besieged and liable to fall by September 1 of starvation. . . . Alexandretta: . . . measles and malaria prevalent."[517]

In Adana there was "famine. . . . Mothers abandon their children in the streets. The surrounding vineyards and crops have been destroyed. . . . Hungry young men go out of the city to try, at the risk of their lives, to find a possible handful of wheat. Few of them return."[518] The Turks intermittently shelled the city and the vast refugee camps outside.[519] The French fortified the towns; beyond the trenches, the Nationalists wrought havoc. Bristol described the area after a visit in March 1921: "The country[side] looks absolutely desolate, and the rich fields that ordinarily would be cultivated have no sign of life."[520]

By January 1921 the French had 80,000 troops in Syria and Cilicia, with several companies of light tanks and four squadrons of aircraft.[521] But they knew Cilicia was lost. Syria could be held if Cilicia was abandoned. The French were "only waiting for someone to whom they can turn it over."[522]

Nonetheless, the Franco-Turkish struggle, and minor Turkish-Armenian clashes, continued for months. Everywhere the Nationalists carried out a campaign of persecution, intimidation, and expulsion.[523] A messenger from Mardin who reached Mosul reported that forty boys were taken forcibly, possibly to be slaughtered, from a missionary orphanage. Girls recovered from Muslim homes were carried off for a night from mission quarters and returned the next day. One night, Muslims robbed the American missionary Agnes Fenanga of her gold, which had been used to aid refugees and orphans.[524]

As in 1920 French efforts to supply and reinforce the garrisons met with ambushes and, often, disaster. In many sites, Armenians were involved. Noteworthy was the Turko-Armenian battle for Zeytun, the mountain redoubt. Like Hacin, it was not garrisoned by the French. In early 1921 Zeytun had about 1,500 Armenians inhabitants, survivors of the 1915 deportations.[525] The houses were in ruins and many inhabitants lived in the empty barracks.

In May 1921 the Turks demanded that the Zeytunlis give up their arms and agree to serve in labor battalions. The Zeytunlis, who knew what that meant, refused.[526] A siege ensued. The Armenians subsisted "mainly . . . [on] grass and herbs." About 300 elderly people, women, and children surrendered and were shipped to Maraş. The Turks bombarded the barracks. On June 27 the remaining Zeytunlis, mostly able-bodied men, decided to fight their way out. Irregulars and soldiers gave chase. Dozens were killed. On July 3 the fighters were cornered with their backs to the Cihan River. Many threw themselves in. Three survived and reached Adana, where they told their tale.[527] Zeytun was left empty and in ruins. In September some 600 Armenians, mostly women and children from surrounding villages, were deported to Maraş. Some died during the trek.[528] In early November the Turks deported the remaining Zeytunlis from Maraş to villages around Chermoug. Many died of starvation and typhus.[529]

On October 19 the French and Nationalist governments, represented by Henry Franklin-Bouillon—designated by Rumbold "the Prince of Levantines"— and Foreign Minister Youssouf Kemal, signed the agreement that brought the Franco-Turkish war to an end.[530] The accord capped the first French defeat in a colonial war since 1763.[531] Franklin-Bouillon accurately represented the wishes of the Quai d'Orsay and the French high commissioners in Constantinople. The accord vindicated the words of Jean Amet, the first French high commissioner, uttered in November 1918: "the traditional friendship for Turkey remains a pillar of French policy."[532]

The agreement provided for immediate cessation of hostilities, exchange of prisoners, and French withdrawal to a line representing the new border between Turkey and French-ruled Syria. Contrary to the Sèvres treaty, Payas, Dörtyol, Osmaniye, Islahiye, Antep, Urfa, and Mardin were to be on the Turkish side. The French were awarded railroad and mining concessions, and the Turks committed to protecting their Christian minorities.[533] Secret annexes provided for the sale of arms and other materiel to the Nationalists and French support for Turkey's territorial claims in Eastern Thrace.[534]

The agreement was subsequently described by a French diplomat as "unsound in principle and derogatory to the dignity and prestige of France."[535] From Beirut, the British consul general reported that General Dufieux, in protest, requested to be allowed immediate retirement. In Beirut Muslims saw the agreement as "a triumph for Islam"; there was "a more ostentatious celebration" than usual of the Prophet's birthday.[536] Franklin-Bouillon told American missionaries the truth: the French were leaving because they feared defeat "and also for financial reasons."[537] France, he said, was spending 500,000,000 Francs a year in Cilicia—between 1 and 2 billion current U.S. dollars in adjusted value, depending on calculation method—and there were "already 5,000 French graves" there. He claimed that France had incurred these losses "in defense of the Armenians," making it the only Allied power to have sacrificed troops for their cause. It was therefore "monstrous . . . to charge France with having abandoned the Armenians."[538]

But that was how Armenian spokesmen saw it. They were stunned, or pretended to be. The Armenians knew they would have to evacuate the areas awarded to the Turks, or face "certain extermination."[539] A French intelligence officer reported, "Armenian population and other Christians say they do not trust any obligation undertaken by Turks and wish to leave the country."[540] An American missionary wrote that Adana "is panic-stricken, and the only business going on is securing passports."[541] Another missionary

reported, "A little Turkish girl in the Seminary told her Armenian companions that they were all going to be killed soon." Within days of the signing of
the accord, Adana's "wealthy and intelligent" began leaving.[542] Chambers
reported that the Armenians' trepidation was shared by the other Christian
communities and by "many Moslems . . . who have been loyal to the French
administration."[543] Christians began selling their property "at wretched
prices," but there were few buyers.[544] Muslims understood that the properties
would shortly fall into their hands like ripe plums.[545]

In follow-up talks with the French, the Nationalists promised that the Christians in Cilicia would enjoy "full security" and be free to decide whether to
stay or leave.[546] But they made their real intentions clear in party newspapers.
Yeni Adana, the Kemalist newspaper that appeared in Pozantı, warned, in bold
"crimson" lettering, "We hear of [Armenian] preparations . . . to emigrate.
Have patience. When we come we will have accounts to settle, after which you
may think of emigration." Turks visiting Adana spoke openly of *Der Tag*—the
coming "Day" of vengeance.[547]

Britain regarded France's conduct as "most reprehensible." The Cabinet
proposed an Allied-Kemalist conference in an effort to modify the accord.[548]
But the agreement, Rumbold wrote, had put the Nationalists in an "unyielding
and intractable frame of mind."[549] They would not be conciliatory.

On November 22, to allay Armenians' concerns, Franklin-Bouillon and two
Nationalist officials jointly declared that "the enemies of peace"—perhaps Armenian politicians or American missionaries—had initiated a campaign to
sow panic in the Armenian population.[550] In other words, there was nothing
to fear. But the Turks were exultant, with a hint of menace, a missionary wrote.
Christians continued to worry about the prospect of massacre or coerced national service.[551]

The Evacuation

The Franco-Turkish agreement ushered in the final stage of the Armenian
departure from Anatolia. In late 1918–1919, tens of thousands of deportees
had returned to Turkey. The start of the Turco-French and Turco-Armenian
hostilities in Cilicia in January 1920 sparked a reversal of the process.
The Franklin Bouillon–Kemal agreement and its implementation dramati-

cally speeded up the exodus. Within months, Anatolia was emptied of Armenians.

In spring 1920 Jackson, looking at what had just happened in Maraş, Antep, and Urfa, concluded that the Turks aimed "to exterminate the Armenians."[552] Certainly, from 1920 on, Turkish policy was at least to finally clear the Armenians out of the country. The Franco-Turkish war in southern Turkey and to a lesser extent, the parallel Greco-Turkish war to the north and west (see Chapter 9), acted as a major spur to, and as cover for, Armenian flight. From early 1920 there was to be a steady Armenian evacuation, southward to Syria-Lebanon; eastward, to Russian-held territories; and westward, to Constantinople and beyond. In April 1920 the Armenian Archbishop of Smyrna, Hovhan Vartabed, basing himself on reports from the field, noted that the Nationalist campaign in Cilicia and northern Aleppo vilayet was causing a "general exodus" of Armenians.[553]

This exodus more or less paralleled the gradual shrinkage of the French zone of control. Sometimes the Armenians joined withdrawing French columns; sometimes they preceded or followed the French. Occasionally, for a time, the French impeded evacuation. But, more often, they ordered or advised Armenians to evacuate. So it was with the orphanage in Haruniye, with 200 children, and the rest of the town's Armenians, who were ordered to leave for Adana at the end of March 1920.[554] So it was with the Armenians of Sis and Chara-Bazar.[555] So it was with the large village of Ekbez, whose inhabitants had, for a time, taken refuge in a monastery from which they fought off the Turks.[556] Many Armenians, such as those who fled Kayseri, were not prodded by immediate threat but still feared for their ultimate safety.[557] Each mass uprooting from one place triggered departure from neighboring sites.[558]

The first wave of departures followed the massacre at Maraş. The French understood that leaving behind defenseless Armenian communities would result in massacre, so the French sought Armenian evacuations, sometimes even from areas they had not yet left themselves. It was the humanitarian thing to do and might also protect France's reputation—they did not want to be blamed for abandoning Christians to massacre. By the end of March, the French were talking of facilitating the "transfer of [the] Armenian population [of Cilicia] to Erevan."[559] By early April the "congestion of refugees in Adana" was so great that refugees were being "pushed" toward Mersin, Adana's Mediterranean port. The French told the Armenians that they would not be afforded protection if they stayed. Brémond recommended that the missionaries move their orphans to Mersin, "pending a possible removal to [British-ruled] Cyprus."

From the missionaries' perspective, the French were no humanitarians. "The French are using the Turks as a whip to drive the Armenians out of the country," an American missionary explained.[560] Another wrote that "the deportation" of the Armenians was "being carried out by the French and Turks combined."[561] This "seems to be a system of deportation carried out by the French in a [covert] manner, that is, they are allowing the Turks to drive out the Armenians . . . while the French appear to protect them. . . . The net result . . . is that the country is being absolutely cleared of them."[562] At Antep, U.S. vice-consul in Aleppo Digby Willson wrote, "the starving of the people . . . is only part of a plan to force the Armenians to leave." It seemed to him "difficult to credit the French military with such inhuman policies" and with such behavior "towards another Christian people."[563]

The March–April 1920 arrival in the Adana plain of masses of refugees triggered a British relocation effort. On April 7 the Lord Mayor's Fund in London asked the government to facilitate the transfer of 2,000–3,000 orphans to Cyprus.[564] In June, after the start of the twenty-day Franco-Turkish ceasefire, 700 orphans were shipped from Mersin to Limassol.[565] There were also appeals for Armenian relocation to the United States. The secretary of the Armenian Red Cross and Refugee Fund in London, Emily Robinson, complained that the Turks were barring Armenians from leaving for America. She asked the Foreign Office to ask the Americans to allow Armenians in.[566] By the end of May, Armenian emigration was reaching "alarming proportions." Most were heading for South America, but substantial numbers were going to the United States.[567] Jackson anticipated increased emigration after the spring harvest.[568]

Many Armenians were driven out of western Anatolia. An Armenian named Garabed Djordian reported that the entire male population of his town, Eskişehir, was deported eastward in May 1921 along with the Armenian men of Kütahiya and Konya. With a group of 380 men, he was first sent to Kayseri, then to Sivas. Gendarmes escorted the party. Ten days later they continued to Malatya and then Harput. From there most were dispersed in Kurdish

Armenians evacuating during the French withdrawal from Cilicia.

"Like little French Soldiers." Armenian orphans evacuating during the French withdrawal from Cilicia.

villages. Djordian finally made it to Aleppo. There were no killings along the way, but many died of hunger, illness, or exhaustion. "The Armenian women that one meets in the towns lead a life of slavery," he said.[569]

As late as the end of 1921, after the signing of the Franklin Bouillon–Kemal agreement, Bristol opposed Armenian emigration and tried to prevent missionaries encouraging it. He even changed his tune on repatriation of World

War I deportees, arguing for the first time that their return home from Syria should be promoted.[570] But the French in Cilicia were "most anxious to get rid of as many as possible."[571] In October about 900 Armenians, 200 of them ex-legionnaires, were shipped to Constantinople.[572] On the way 150 of them disembarked at Smyrna, possibly to offer their services to the Greek Army.[573]

The signing of the accord induced "a state of panic" in all the Christian communities.[574] During the resulting rush to trains and ports, a few people were reportedly trampled to death.[575] All feared massacre, and with good reason. In Sis, according to an Armenian prelate, six old-timers who had stayed behind after the community's departure "were soaked in petroleum and burnt alive."[576] By mid-November Christians were leaving by the thousands.[577] The exodus was like "flight from a plague or escape from a burning house."[578]

The Nationalist takeover of the civil administration in Adana and Mersin likely reinforced the process.[579] "In a hundred little ways the Turks are showing themselves to be very arrogant," a visiting British diplomat reported. Initially the French barred Armenian departure. They feared being encumbered in Lebanon-Syria by a new wave of refugees. But under Armenian pressure, they gradually relented. At first they allowed those they had repatriated from Syria to return to Syria. Then others were allowed out. The exodus was swift. During November–December, some 40,000 Armenians left by boat for Smyrna or points farther afield, including Port Said and Constantinople. Mersin, the main port of exit, was awash with "thousands" of destitute refugees who lacked visas.[580]

The refugees sold what they could for a pittance. Real estate, of course, proved impossible to sell at any price.[581] Pianos went for "one pound gold."[582] Many burnt "all they cannot take with them rather than leave [it] to the Turks."[583] "Cilicia is terror-stricken from end to end," a missionary wrote.[584]

The guerrilla war and the Franco-Kemalist accord also affected sites to the east. In late 1921 there was "indescribable consternation" among Antep's remaining 8,000 Armenians.[585] The French governors at Antep and Kilis at first refused permission to leave.[586] But soon the French were no longer in control. The Turks took over the administration of Antep on December 4, and the French evacuated on December 25. Many Armenians left with the French, though about 3,000 remained.[587] The British consul in Aleppo wrote optimistically, "It is probable that they will not be molested for some time."[588] But during the following months they were subjected to a quiet, and then very public, boycott, and a few were charged with pillaging or other offenses.[589] In June 1922 Turkish ruffians raided the "shops of packsaddlers, farriers, and Koshker [slipper-makers] in the Odoun Bazaar" and threatened customers.[590] The French military cemetery was desecrated. The town's officials, headed by mutesarrif Munir Bey, were actually well-disposed toward Armenians, but "a secret clique of extremists," an Armenian notable complained, "really ruled the roost."[591]

The majority of Christians in Cilicia and northern Aleppo vilayet left the country, mainly through Mersin and Alexandretta, in the last months of 1921. Others trekked by land to Syria. At the two ports, the refugees camped in churches and other public buildings. In Mersin the altar of the Armenian church served as "home for three families"; a field next to the Greek church was "dotted with tents. . . . On rainy days, which meant practically all the time, the field was literally a mud swamp. . . . The basement of the Mission School had over 300 people." There was hunger and disease, including smallpox. As the Christians left each town, Turkish refugees poured in. At a train station outside Adana, an American missionary noted two lines of refugees heading in opposite directions. Adana transformed, almost overnight, from an Armenian to a Turkish town.[592]

In Adana, the largest Armenian concentration in Asia Minor in 1920–1921, flight was propelled by the fact that many Christians were squatting in Turkish homes. In addition, many had served the French in one capacity or another. The local Christian leadership issued instructions to emigrate.[593]

All the Western powers, whether or not they supported the Armenians, regarded the mass evacuation as a disaster. None had a solution to the problem of resettlement. None—Britain, France, Italy, the United States—wanted the Armenians in their countries, and France and Britain also didn't want them in their Middle Eastern protectorates and mandates, as local officials made all too clear.[594] Only the Greeks were willing to take in large numbers of refugees, including Armenians.[595]

The Americans spoke with the clearest voice. Bristol opposed the evacuation of the "Christian races from Cilicia." Where would they go and who would provide for them?[596] He spent long hours trying to order or persuade the missionaries to cajole Christians to stay. If they had already left, he wanted them to return.[597] He even opposed shipping out the Armenian orphans because this would "stampede" the rest of the Christians—better to "sacrifice these orphans," that is, consign them to Turkish hands, so that the bulk of the Christians might stay.[598] In December 1921 he instructed his agents in Mersin to stop relief in the hope that this might induce Christians to "return to their homes."[599]

The French, most directly responsible for and affected by the evacuation, broadcast contradictory messages. In early November their officials in Mersin ordered "all Christians to leave," giving them a fortnight's grace.[600] But the official line, as enunciated by Paris, was that Christians, principally Armenians, should stay put.[601] France's good name was at stake; Christian flight blackened France's image. And there were good concrete reasons to keep the Armenians at home. The French didn't want the area's estimated 100,000–150,000 Armenians.[602] On November 14 the French ordered a stop to the exodus toward Aleppo-Damascus-Beirut and ceased issuing the necessary passes.[603] They even prohibited Armenians from boarding Greek steamers, though an exception was made for Armenians who had served with the French military or administration.[604] But the policy swiftly changed. In the second half of December, accepting the impossibility of stemming the floodtide, the French permitted, encouraged, and even organized the departure of Adana's remaining Christians.[605]

However, even at this stage the French made problems for refugees. Those without tickets had difficulty boarding steamers headed for Syrian-Lebanese ports.[606] Some ex-deportees returned from Cilicia to Syrian "villages where they took shelter during the Great War" in the areas of Jerablus, Manbij, Rakka, Deir Zor, Hama, Homs, and Antakya.[607]

In Aleppo both Christians and Muslims resented the Armenian refugees. Preachers railed against them in the mosques, and homeowners refused to rent them quarters. According to an American consul the hard feelings were a residue of World War I, when the first wave of deportees drove up the cost of living and created a housing shortage. In addition the Armenians' "industry and alleged unscrupulousness," enabling them "to turn their exile to profit," resulted in hostility. There were also terrible sanitation problems in the sites where they were temporarily resettled. Typhus was the major source of concern.[608]

By April 1923 Aleppo's 50,000-odd Armenian refugees, with NER help, had adequately organized their living spaces. The same could not be said for the ten-thousand "indescribably wretched" Greek refugees in and around town. Many lived in caves.[609] It was a similar story in Alexandretta. In late April 1922 there were some 17,000 refugees there, living in a veritable swamp. A local doctor feared "a massacre by mosquitoes." Christian women were reportedly prostituting themselves to French soldiers.[610]

Some Turkish officials were unhappy with the spectacle of the mass evacuation, as it seemed to cast the Turks as villains. They also worried that the Armenians' departure would denude the territory of professionals, craftsmen, and artisans. In Mersin and Adana, reportedly, not one dentist remained. But the "mass of unreasoning, uneducated Turks" was happy with the exodus.[611] One prominent Nationalist, Turkish Red Crescent Director Hamid Bey, believed the "excitement and anxiety" of the Armenians "is due to the fact that they are aiming at covering up the atrocities they committed there and appear as innocent."[612]

By January 1922 the Armenian evacuation of Cilicia and northern Aleppo vilayet was "more than 90%" complete, according to Rumbold. The lot of those who had stayed behind, many of them infirm or old, was not always happy. In August Rumbold wrote that he did not see what advice he could offer the remaining Cilician Armenians. To leave meant dispossession and a life of exile; to stay meant suffering the "bitterly and actively" hostile attitude of the Turks.[613]

In early 1922, after most of the dust had settled, there were still 4,000 Armenians left in Antep, 8,000 in Maraş, 4,000–5,000 in Urfa, 400 in Adana, and 2,000 in Mersin.[614] In April Ankara issued a law effectively confiscating all "abandoned" Armenian property in Asia Minor.[615]

During November–December 1921 Kemalist officers, gendarmes and administrators moved into the Cilician and northern Aleppo vilayet towns. Military units followed. On January 4, 1922, the last French troops withdrew. The handover proceeded without a hitch. However, within days Turks desecrated the French and Armenian cemeteries in Mersin, Tartus, Cihan, and Antep. "In Dörtyol they have even opened the tombs on the pretext of searching for bombs," an Armenian reported. "As they cannot attack the living, they attack the dead."[616]

But Turkish passions were directed primarily against the quick rather than the dead; they wanted every last Christian out of Asia Minor. Events in Izmir in September–October 1922, discussed below, served as an augury and catalyst for what the Kemalists had in mind. The press conveyed Nationalist orders to evacuate all Christians from Antalya, Makri, and southern Anatolia.[617] And Nationalist leaders spoke clearly. The day after he occupied Izmir, General Nureddin, commander of the 1st Army Corps, said that "the Greeks and Armenians must leave Asia Minor," and Kemal himself said "the situation now demands that the Greeks and the Armenians leave Anatolia."[618] Ankara informed NER that Christian orphans in their care "should leave Anatolia immediately" along with NER's native Christian employees.[619] There were even rumors that the "government are . . . preparing to expel entire Christian population of Constantinople."[620] Apparently, the Nationalists were eager to complete the expulsion or "at least [have it] well under way" before the minorities question came up in Lausanne.[621] At Lausanne, the secretary of the Turkish delegation, Celaleddin Bey, said "that Armenians and Greeks were no longer wanted. They were always like [an] open wound not only painful in itself but inviting infection from foreign contacts."[622]

The Nationalists initiated a countrywide push to expel the last of the Armenians (alongside the Greeks), but without explicitly enunciating the policy. In October 1922 some 350 Armenians, mainly from Malatya but some from Harput and Palu, were effectively deported to Aleppo. Malatya Armenians reported that Turkish officials were

"making life intolerable . . . by instigating systematically the ransacking of their houses, taking possession of the women and girls by force . . . and shipping [out] and killing the men if they dare to oppose them. The government have posted up notices on Armenian houses that they will continue to inflict such outrages on them until they leave Turkish territory, and if they do not go of their own free will they will be forcibly deported in winter."[623]

That fall NER removed all Armenian orphans from Harput, Malatya, and Mezre. They traveled in fifteen caravans to French-held Syria. The Turks generally afforded every help.[624] But the deportations were occasionally accompanied by murder. Near Bursa, the Turks arrested and shot dead eight or nine Armenians from Samsun.[625]

In early November the Nationalist government announced that all non-Muslims had a month in which to leave the country. The implication was that if they failed to leave in time, they would be prevented thereafter from leaving or would be deported to the interior. A British consul commented, "This is done in pursuance of the policy that no Christians are to be allowed to stay in Turkey."[626] In Samsun, Trabzon, and some other places, the Christians were explicitly told that they would be deported to the interior if they failed to leave.[627] Some local authorities issued expulsion orders to bring about departure from specific sites: in January 1923 it was reported that such orders were issued to the remaining Armenians of Maraş.[628]

Sometime in November 1922, Antep Armenian representatives went to the mutesarrif, who told them that they were now free to leave. In the event of a new war, he said, "those who remained might be deported." During the following days, an Armenian night watchman was murdered, and a wealthy Armenian was badly wounded and robbed. Others were attacked and threatened with massacre.[629] "If anyone doubts the reality of Satan, he has only to come out here and see and hear what we witness," a missionary wrote.[630] The Armenians took the hint. The government cared for the Armenians' safety until departure, secured the roads out, and enabled them to sell their chattels. The exodus involved "less . . . hardship, loss and danger" than the Armenians had feared.[631] Nonetheless, it proved an uneasy passage. There were "annoyances, extortions, robberies, and even loss of life" along the route.[632]

Having abolished the sultanate, Kemal's directives were now those of the head of state. In 1923 he told a Muslim audience in Adana, "The country is yours, the country belongs to the Turks. . . . The country has finally been returned to its rightful owners. The Armenians and the others have no rights at all here. These fertile regions are the country of the real Turks."[633] The authorities prodded the exodus along by shutting down the Christian schools and cultural institutions. In Adana the YMCA was closed; in Mardin, the American schools.[634] By early December 1922 there were only about a hundred Armenians left in Antep. The government shut the Armenian schools and took over the cathedral. The missionary college and girls' seminary closed. The last services in the Protestant church were held on November 26, 1922,

"Dr. Hamilton leading in the morning and Dr. Shepard in the afternoon." But the missionary hospital, which mainly served the Turks, stayed open.[635]

The convoys southward in 1923–1924 were subjected to a variety of depredations. The authorities stripped all the exiles of gold and silver, expatriation of which was officially forbidden. On the roads the Armenians were robbed by Muslim brigands.[636] An American consul described the robbery as "systematic." One convoy between Maraş and Antep, with 2,000 refugees, was "robbed of everything, even all their outer garments, and left freezing in the sleet and rain." Jackson reported that the caravans were even attacked after they had entered French-held Syria. In one caravan, near Katma, the three daughters of Protestant pastor Assadoor Yeghoyian were raped by robbers and gendarmes.[637]

In dribs and drabs, the Armenians streamed southward from across Anatolia, though there was a brief let-up after the Lausanne Treaty was signed. Letters from émigrés describing poor conditions in Aleppo may also, for a time, have stalled new departures from Anatolia to northern Syria.[638] Nonetheless 800 reached Aleppo in August 1923, mainly from Malatya, Arapgir, and Harput. Another 600 arrived in November, mainly from Malatya, Harput, Arapgir, Eğin, and Palu. Hundreds more arrived in January 1924, 160 of them from Garmouj, near Urfa.[639]

At the end of November 1922 there were 55,000 Armenians in Aleppo—20,000 "old residents" and 35,000 recently arrived refugees. More were arriving every day. They all told the "same tale—that they have been threatened by the Turkish authorities and Moslem population for many months . . . and told frankly that they are not wanted in the country, and to get out."[640]

By spring 1923 the Armenians living in and around Turkey were dispersed as follows: 180,000 in Constantinople (of whom 30,000 were refugees); 120,000 in Syria (100,000 refugees); 107,000 in Greece (77,000 refugees); 60,000 in Bulgaria (40,000 refugees); 100,000 in Anatolia; 37,000 in Rumania (7,000 refugees); 900,000 in Russian Armenia; and 300,000 in the Caucasus (100,000 refugees).[641] Many of the refugees were in a desperate condition. Those in Syria were "scattered over the country extending from Aleppo to Sidon, and herded in graveyards, marshes, caves and noisome places which are shunned by all others, with little or no shelter from sun, rain or snow." Many, were like "scantily clad corpses," disease-ridden and in bad mental health.[642] Meanwhile Kemal's aides complained of French atrocities and of Armenian bands operating around Antioch—"citing details and names of officers that," according to French intelligence, "do not correspond to anything."[643]

The following months saw haphazard efforts to uproot the remaining Christians from Asia Minor. An American consul in Aleppo wrote that "the much-discussed policy of the nationalist[s] of 'Turkey for the Turks' (only) appear [*sic*] to be much in evidence. . . . It is reported here that the nationalist party contemplates not only the exclusion of the Armenian, Greek and Assyrian nationalities but also the Circassians and Kurds."[644]

By early 1924 life for the handful of Christians who still held on had become unbearable. Many, apparently, wanted to stay, but conditions had become too trying.[645] The Turks were employing "secret terrorism and victimization" and unleashing "the last clean sweep of Christians from the Ottoman dominions."[646] Though "no definite" expulsion order had been issued, "various forms of persecution" had made their "life . . . intolerable."[647] Christians were selling their properties for a song: "A fine fertile little garden valued at 500 Turkish gold pounds went for 30 gold pounds." In the south, the Armenians and Assyrians were heading for Aleppo; in the north, they were leaving via Samsun. With the economy depressed, even the Jews were leaving.[648]

Urfa's 4,500 remaining Assyrians were subjected over January–February 1924 to a fresh bout of persecution. The mutesarrif reportedly told them that "all Christians must eventually leave Turkey." There was molestation and robbery. A handful of prominent Assyrians were murdered or arrested. Those leaving were, initially, prohibited from taking anything with them and forbidden to "sell their lands." They left with "two days rations and one blanket."[649] But after it became apparent that Assyrians were leaving, the Turks "relaxed" the orders and allowed them to take some property, including money. Many were required to sign statements to the effect that they were not being forced out. Leading the campaign locally was an Arab named Ajami Pasha, a friend of Kemal's, who had previously been awarded deported Armenians' houses and lands.[650] On March 9 General İsmet Pasha (later İnönü), one of Kemal's aides, wrote that reports about attacks on Christians and desecration of their churches were unfounded, but the "forced deportation of 4,000 Christians from Urfa to Aleppo has already begun."[651] Days later the Americans reported that 1,250 Urfa Assyrians and 750 of its Armenians had reached Aleppo.[652]

Weeks later it was the turn of Mardin and Diyarbekir. In Mardin there was "a systematic campaign against the Christians," who were required to "step aside, stand still and salute" Muslims as they passed in the street. They were forbidden even to ride horses.[653] Though some wealthy families were ordered to leave, there were no general expulsion orders. Rather, there was "clandestine persecution."[654] The Christians, mainly Assyrian, were "forced to work on Sundays" and barred from working on Fridays. They could not pray in churches, celebrate "marriage festivities," or ring church bells. If the head of a family embraced Islam, the rest had to follow suit. Christians were not allowed to "wear any luxurious clothes," sell household furniture, or trade with "firms abroad." If a Christian left the country, he forfeited his property.[655] Many of these anti-Christian measures were based on the so-called Pact of Omar from the early Middle Ages, which defined how Muslims were to treat the "other."

In April the Turkish Interior Ministry announced that no Armenian would be allowed to reside anywhere east of the Samsun-Selevke line.[656] A handful of Christians nonetheless remained in southeastern Turkey. During the following years they were periodically persecuted; some were deported, others massacred. In October 1925 as many as 8,000 Assyrians were deported to the interior by Turkish troops from the strip of territory along the Iraqi-Turkish border near Zakhko. According to escapees the Turks murdered as many as 300 and raped or sold into concubinage some 200 women. The survivors described how Turkish soldiers murdered old men, women who had just given birth, and orphans who could not keep up. At night, the soldiers raped Assyrian girls in the fields. According to the survivors, during one stop, Turkish officers sold ten girls to Muslim villagers.[657]

In early 1926 there was a Kurdish and Yezidi rebellion against the central government. The authorities charged the handful of remaining Christians with complicity. Deportation to Iraq of Assyrians—many of them Kurdish serfs—and Armenians followed. According to reports reaching the American consulate in Baghdad, the deportations were accompanied by mass killing and mass rape. The village of Azakh was singled out for mention.[658]

By the Turkish government's count, in 1927 there were only 25,000–30,000 Armenians left in the eastern provinces and about 100,000 in Constantinople. In 2014 it was estimated that in Turkey as a whole, there were fewer than 80,000 Armenians, almost all in Istanbul.[659]

The Assyrians

There are 15,000–20,000 Assyrians in present-day Turkey, most of them in Istanbul, with about 2,000 in eastern Anatolia.[660] They are the remainder of a community of more than half a million who had inhabited the Ottoman Empire before World War I. Almost all were slaughtered or expelled between 1914 and 1924.

Some 250,000, perhaps more, were killed by Muslims between 1914 and 1919, most in massacres, some in battle.[661] Assyrians and others today refer to what happened as the Assyrian Genocide. But because the Assyrians inhabited remote corners of Turkey and Persia, where there were no Western consuls and few missionaries or travelers, primary sources attesting to their destruction are scarce, and the picture that emerges is patchy and somewhat confused. As well, the picture is complicated by the fact that there were several, separate Assyrian concentrations, which were dealt with by the Ottomans at different times and in different ways.

Before World War I there was no Assyrian national movement, no demand for independence or even "autonomy." There also was no anti-Ottoman political or military activism. But, inspired by the model of other national claimants and provoked by Turkish massacres, an Assyrian-Chaldean delegation at the 1919 Paris Peace Conference called for the creation of an Assyrian state comprising Mosul vilayet, part of Diyarbekir vilayet, Urfa, Deir Zor, and the area immediately west of Lake Urmia.[662] The Assyrians pointedly did not wish to be included in an Armenian state, which, according to the British, they felt would be "scarcely less distasteful" than Turkish domination.[663] But though Britain expressed sympathy for their plight, the Assyrians failed to achieve statehood and remain dispersed in Turkey, Iran, northern Iraq, and

Syria.[664] Their descendants—along with the Yazidis, another "infidel" minority—recently suffered severe persecution by the Islamic State and other Muslims.

Mass murder of Assyrians predated World War I. During the nineteenth century, when Assyrians overwhelmingly lived within the Ottoman Empire, they, like other Christians, suffered from state discrimination and Kurdish brigandage. In the 1840s thousands were massacred by Kurds in the Hakkari area. In 1894–1896, as we have seen, Assyrians were massacred in small numbers in Diyarbekir vilayet alongside Armenians. More died during the Adana Massacre of 1909.[665]

According to one British officer, in the years immediately before the outbreak of World War I, unruly and warlike Kurdish and Assyrian mountain tribesmen raided one another. The Russians came to dominate the Urmia plain in 1912 after the Turks, who had previously occupied the border area, withdrew. The Persian province of Urmia had a population, according to the Russians, of 300,000, 40 percent of them Christian. Of these, 75,000 were Assyrian—mostly Nestorian—and 50,000 Armenian.[666] The Russians established and armed local Christian militias. According to a British report, the Christians of Urmia then "lorded it over, and made themselves generally unpleasant toward the Muslim population."[667] In the mountains to the west, there were sporadic Assyrian-Turkish clashes.

The Ottoman sultans had long sought to incorporate Urmia in their empire, and the CUP were no different. In October 1914 Talât and Enver said as much to the Iranian ambassador in Constantinople. The year before, a team of Turkish military and Special Organization operatives, including Halil Bey, Enver's uncle, had gone to Urmia to scout the region and forge alliances with local tribal leaders in preparation for eventual annexation.[668]

Then the Ottomans entered World War I. Iran announced that it was neutral. But Talât wanted the area, which bordered on Russia, cleared of Christians. According to one report, with the onset of war, the Assyrian Patriarch, Mar Shimun Benyamin, and an assembly of leaders of the mountain Assyrians in Kurdistan, voiced support for the Allies.[669] Assyrian youths refused the Ottoman mobilization en masse, leading at least to one Assyrian-Turkish firefight and then large-scale repression.[670] Some Assyrians fled to Iran; others resisted Turkish and Kurdish raids. Later, in April 1915, Ottoman officers referred to Assyrian resistance as the "Nestorian revolt."[671] Assyrian leaders were arrested and some deported to Persia.

Earlier, in September–October 1914, Turkish troops, supported by Kurdish tribesmen, invaded Azerbaijan and the Persian borderlands. They plundered and burned Christian villages in the Urmia Plain, destroyed churches, and slaughtered inhabitants. Local Kurdish leaders later referred to this as the "great jihad."[672] It is possible that the Turks unleashed the violence in the hope of persuading the Assyrians to join them, or at least to remain neutral, in the war. If that was the intention, it failed.[673]

On October 26, 1914, Talât ordered the vali of Van vilayet to deport to the interior the Assyrians in the Hakkari area, the vilayet's southeastern corner, because of their "predisposition to be influenced by foreigners and become" their "instrument." By foreigners, he meant Russians, and Talât of course knew that Turkey was about to attack Russia.[674] According to Russian intelligence, a "reign of terror" was unleashed in the Hakkari, where Assyrians comprised 37 percent of the population.[675] Some were deported inland and dispersed in villages in Konya and Ankara vilayets. Others were caught up in the general Turkish assault on the Christians communities of Van vilayet.[676] The Turks accused them of collaborating with the Russians, who periodically occupied and abandoned Christian villages in the Hakkari.

Already in November–December 1914, well before the outbreak of Armenian rebelliousness in Van town, Hamidiye troops massacred Christian villagers in the Başkale area of the Hakkari—"pillaged and burned Armenian houses, killed all the men and . . . captured the beautiful girls, and abandoned the women and children without food or shelter."[677] Judad Abdarova, the wife of the headman of the Assyrian village of Ardshi, later testified that the Muslims "tortured" her husband and sons "to death."

> They were beaten from all sides and ordered to become Muslims, but they refused. Before my eyes Hurshid Bey [a Turkish or Kurdish commander] shot my sons with a pistol. . . . I tried to protect my husband, but Hurshid Bey kicked me in the face, knocking out two teeth. Then he shot my husband with six bullets. . . . Hurshid Bey ordered that the corpses be smeared with excrement. Over the following four days the

dogs ate the corpses. Then Hurshid ordered that the corpses be thrown in the latrine. . . . Hurshid had the whole village burned and twelve people killed. . . . All the women, virgins, and children were taken captive and brought to the village of Atis. There they had to choose: Islam or death. 150 women and girls were forced to become the wives of Hurshid Bey's relatives. Of all the prisoners, only I remained, because Hurshid Bey knew that I was the cousin of the patriarch. . . . I was on the road for two days. I was so tired that I had to leave two of my small children under a tree. . . . I know nothing of their fate. My small daughter died of hunger on the way."[678]

In January 1915 several dozen Başkale notables were arrested and used by the Turks to carry equipment—perhaps barbed wire—to Urmia. Most were then executed, but three survived to tell the tale. In November a missionary, Dr. E. T. Allen, went looking for the corpses, to give them a Christian burial. "There were seventy-one or two bodies; we could not tell exactly, because of the conditions. . . . Some were . . . dried like a mummy. Others were torn to pieces by the wild animals. . . . The majority . . . had been shot.[679]

In May, after the Turkish-Kurdish forces under Khalil retreated from Urmia back to Turkey, there was renewed slaughter in the Hakkari. That month the patriarch, Shimun, formally pledged Assyrian loyalty to the Allied cause, effectively "declaring war" on the Ottomans. In Başkale 300–400 women and children, and some Armenian artisans, reportedly were massacred.[680] Another massacre occurred in Siirt. A full-scale Turkish campaign, designed to finally cleanse the Hakkari, was unleashed the following month. It was led by the vali of Mosul, Haydar Bey, joined by what remained of Halil's corps. It was to be an unequal struggle, the Assyrians armed with their antique guns and the Turks and Kurds with modern rifles, machine guns, and artillery. The Turks conquered the key village of Qodshan and by September some 15,000–25,000 Assyrians, along with Shimun, fled to Urmia. Many others remained in the mountains, hunted by the Turks or under siege.[681]

In the course of 1915 the anti-Assyrian operations in the southeast turned genocidal. As Talât informed the German Embassy shortly after Turkey became a belligerent, the country intended "to use the opportunity of the World War thoroughly to eliminate their internal enemies—the indigenous Christians of all denominations."[682] The Turks may not have identified the Assyrians explicitly or publicly as an enemy, as they did the Armenians, but in the Turkish mindset the Assyrians, too, were consigned to eventual oblivion. It is not clear whether the CUP Central Committee, during its secret February–March 1915 meetings, decided to target the Assyrians alongside the Armenians.[683] However, when the campaign against the eastern Armenians began in late spring, the local authorities butchered Assyrians, too.[684] By contrast, urban Assyrians, principally in Diyarbekir and Mardin, were initially left in peace, though in Mardin dozens of notables were eventually arrested, tortured, and murdered.[685] But due to foreign pressure—most of the Syriacs were Catholics—Constantinople apparently ordered local authorities to refrain from mass deportation of Assyrians.[686]

During March–June 1915 Turkish regulars and Kurdish tribesmen massacred rural Christians, including Syriacs, in Bitlis and Van vilayets. Cevdet Bey, the vali of Van and military commander in the area (and Enver's brother-in-law), was heard saying, "I have cleansed the Christians from the country of Bashkale and Saray. I would like to cleanse them from Van and its surroundings."[687] In and around Siirt, in Bitlis vilayet, local Muslims and Cevdet's troops murdered 5,000 Assyrians and razed their villages.[688] Cevdet came to be known as "the horseshoer of Bashkale": he had invented, or resurrected, a torture involving hammering horseshoes into Christians' feet.[689]

Kevorkian suggests that the slaughter of Assyrians (and Greeks) in Diyarbekir vilayet, as elsewhere, may have been a local initiative, but it was consistent with central government policy. However, in the case of the Assyrians, the authorities could not make use of the justificatory excuses of "subversion" and "rebellion," as they did when it came to the Armenians. The Assyrians were not politically organized and had no "national" ambitions.[690]

In Diyarbekir vilayet the Assyrian communities were largely dealt with as an appendage of the larger Christian communities and were swept up in the slaughter of the Armenians. In Urmia the reverse happened: it was the minority Armenian community that was devastated when the Turks and Kurdish troops assailed the far larger Assyrian population. With a Turkish army threatening their lines of communication northward, Russians troops evacuated the Urmia plain and the town itself on January 2, 1915, and the Turkish-Kurdish force swept forward, advancing to a line just beyond Tabriz. The "cry of Jihad" was in the air, and the invaders made a point of distributing jihadi fatwas among Persian Shi'ites. The Turks hoped to mobilize them in the unfolding campaign.[691] Thousands of panicked Assyrians fled in the Russians' wake. It was the heart of winter, and many perished during the weeklong trek to the Russian border.[692] More died after crossing the frontier.[693]

But most of Urmia's Christians stayed put.[694] Some "found refuge with friendly Mohammedans," while others converted to Islam. Still others fought the invaders. The Turks occupied the region until May 24. The January–May period was marked by massacre and rape. At Ardishai seventy-five women and girls reportedly ran into the lake to escape the Turks and were shot in the water.[695] In February the Turks reportedly executed more than 700 Assyrian and Armenian men at Haftevan and dumped the bodies in wells and cisterns.[696] Women were carried off to harems. Elsewhere, villagers were burnt alive.[697] The Persian government complained, while noting that here and there, Christian villagers had massacred Muslims.[698]

In March the men of Gulpashan village were executed in the local cemetery, and the women and children were "treated barbarously."[699] A missionary described what happened in nearby Tchargousha: "In the yard, [Lucy, who related this to the missionary,] saw her younger sister Sherin, a pretty girl of about fifteen, being dragged away by a Kurd. She was imploring Lucy to save her, but Lucy was helpless. . . . [Sherin] tried to conceal her face, and daubed it with mud, but she has such beautiful dark eyes and rosy cheeks! The Kurds grabbed the young women and girls, peering into their faces, till each one found a pretty one for himself, then dragged her away."[700] A Russian official, who later inspected twenty Urmia sites, found widespread vandalism against churches. "The villages are full of . . . victims of massacres," the Russian found. "The corpses bear the marks of cruel killing with axes, daggers, and blunt objects." In the large village of Dilman, an American missionary reported that 1,000 had been massacred and 2,000 had died of hunger and disease.[701] The Turkish Fifth Expeditionary Force, under Khalil, was responsible for much of the slaughter. Among the victims were the force's own Armenian and Assyrian soldiers, who were taken out and executed alongside the Urmia Christians.[702]

Some 20,000 villagers fled to Urmia town and took refuge in the American Presbyterian and French Catholic mission compounds.[703] Between January and May the Turks and Kurds murdered and raped hundreds who had strayed from the compounds—even children as young as seven. The Turks took fifty young men from the French compound and demanded a ransom for their release. When payment proved insufficient, the men were executed. More than 200 women were abducted to harems. Inside and outside the compounds, "not less than four thousand" died of malnutrition and diseases. Kurdish and Turkish irregulars and Turkish regulars, and Persian and Azeri locals, all participated in the killings. A missionary wrote, "Jealousy of the greater prosperity of the Christian population . . . political animosity, race hatred and religious fanaticism all had a part."[704] Many women were liberated from Muslim households when the Russians reoccupied Urmia on May 24.

In Anatolia, while thousands of Assyrians were murdered or deported, a good number were left alive and at home, by specific order from Constantinople.[705] But for many local administrators killing Assyrians came under the broad ideologically driven rubric of eradicating "the Christians," and so went ahead regardless.

After May 24 the Russians held sway in the plain of Urmia for two years. But the successive revolutions of 1917 resulted in a general disintegration of their army, "and many oppressive acts against the Muslims" again took place in and around Urmia.[706] The Persians sought to reassert control. The Assyrians, who were armed, assured the Persians that they intended only to defend themselves. But the Persians didn't trust them. In February 1918 a Persian-Assyrian clash ended in Persian defeat. But Turkish-Christian hostilities were renewed after Kurdish tribesmen, led by Aga Ismael Shasheknaya (aka Simko), murdered the Patriarch Shimun and dozens of his supporters following a peace parlay on March 16 or 17. Seeking revenge, Assyrians massacred Kurds in Urmia, and as many as 200 in the nearby Muslim village of Karasanlui. The Turkish Sixth Army, exploiting Russian weakness, then invaded the area. In June it captured Salmas and Khoi, at the latter massacring Assyrians and Armenians. Thousands fled to Urmia, to which the Turks then laid siege. On July 31 the Turkish army entered the town, and tens of thousands of Christians, mainly Assyrians, fled toward British lines in Mesopotamia. The thousand-odd Christians left behind took shelter in the foreign missions, but 600, mostly Syriacs, were eventually murdered.[707]

During the mass trek southward, to Mesopotamia, many were lost in ambushes, and women and children were carried off. "Hunger, weariness,

sickness and fear reduced our people to bones and skin. . . . Dead and
dying [were] left heedlessly on the road side. . . . Little infants forsaken or
lost were seen walking up and down the hills . . . as in a trance." As many as
30,000 died, or were "lost or captured." Some 35,000 Assyrians and 10,000
Armenians eventually reached British lines near Hamadan. Most were temporarily settled in the Ba'quba camp, though thousands stayed on in
Hamadan.[708] In 1920 the Assyrian and Armenian refugees at Ba'quba beat off
a strong Kurdish-Arab attack during the Mesopotamian uprising against the
British.[709]

In autumn 1920 Ba'quba was closed and the Assyrians transferred to
Mindan, near Mosul, with the aim of eventual repatriation. The following
year, the ex-Urmia Assyrians, "moved by a national homesickness," set out
northwards. Several thousand crossed into Persia. Teheran decided against
their return to Urmia and, eventually, they were allowed to resettle near
Tabriz and Kermanshah, while others resettled in Baghdad and Hamadan.
In late 1922–1923 several thousand Iraqi Assyrians trekked to Urmia, and
some of the original Hakkari exiles eventually ended up in the Tel Tamer
area in northern Syria.

The Turkish government, however, was not done with the Assyrians.
During 1924 the Turkish army attacked the remaining Assyrian monasteries
and villages in the southeast. Kemal obliquely referred to this when he stated,
in 1927, that a plot had been discovered against his government "whilst our
army was occupied with the punishment of the Nestorians."[710]

As to the exiled mountain Assyrians, they were moved from Mindan to
empty villages on the Zakhko-Duhuk-Akra line, at the northern edge of
British-ruled Iraq, many serving the British as native levies or border guards.
A few thousand eventually returned to their homes in Turkish Kurdistan.[711]
Most stayed on in Iraq, where, in July–August 1933, as many as 3,000 were
massacred by Iraqi troops and Arab and Kurdish tribesmen, prompting
many to move to Syria.

9

Turks and Greeks, 1919–1924

[It was] an irrevocable decision of the Committee of Union and Progress. After finishing the Armenians, we shall begin with the mass expulsion of the Greeks.

Johann von Pallavicini, quoting Abdullah Nuri Bey, 31 November 1915

En large, after the Armenians came the Greeks. But, in fact, there was a great deal of overlap in the destruction of Anatolia's two largest Christian communities.

The deportation and murder of the Greeks during 1919–1923 was a direct continuation of the effort to expel them that began in late 1913–1914 and continued periodically through World War I. But in 1919–1923 there was a radical shifting of gears. As a representative of the Greek Patriarchate in Constantinople put it in 1922, what was happening was "on a scale greater than any experienced during the [Great] War. Thousands of Greeks had been, and were being hanged, burned, and massacred, thousands were being deported and exterminated."[1]

In the weeks after the Ottoman surrender ended the world war in the east, the Turks were in a state of shock and largely quiescent. But, as we have seen, circumstances changed dramatically by May 1919, when the Greeks landed in Smyrna. The Turks were jolted into frenetic political and military activism. They feared the permanent occupation and Hellenization of parts of Anatolia, with Ionia falling under direct Athenian governance, and separatism and revolt by the Ottoman Greeks resulting in the establishment of a Pontine state on the Black Sea. During the ensuing Greco-Turkish war, the Turks regarded the Greeks throughout Anatolia—but especially those in the Pontus and near the shifting front lines—as potential fifth columnists who would aid the Greek army thrusting eastward from Smyrna.

Greeks had lived along the northern shore of Asia Minor, or Pont-Euxin, "from the time of the Argonauts, Herodotus, and Xenophon and the Ten Thousand."[2] They claimed that, between Rize, or even Batumi, and a point west of Sinop, they numbered some two million. Western diplomats thought the real number was more like 450,000.[3] The Turks feared, or said they feared, that the Pontic Greeks would attack their armies in the rear, even as they engaged in the west and east with a variety of Christian enemies. The Turks also spoke of a possible amphibious landing by the army of the Kingdom of Greece on the shores of the Black Sea, which the local Greeks would assist.[4] But these well-publicized fears were either highly inflated or entirely manufactured. Even Justin McCarthy, a historian sympathetic to the Turkish narrative, writes, "With . . . the benefit of hindsight . . . there was no real danger of local Greeks participating in a Greek invasion." Not only were the Greeks "incapable of landing in force on the Black Sea coast," but "the 'Pontus Republic' revolutionaries were never a potent political or military force and would have been better dealt with by police than by deportation."[5]

The official Turkish narrative sounds very different. In a 1927 speech, Mustafa Kemal explained what had transpired, in terms that exonerated the Turks without admitting what they had done:

> Prepared morally by the propaganda of the [nationalist society] "Ethniki Hetairia" and the American institutions at Mersifun, and encouraged materially by the foreign countries who supplied them with arms, the mass of the Greeks . . . began to cast amorous glances in the direction of an independent Pontic State. Led by this idea, the Greeks organized a general revolt, seized the mountain heights and began to carry on a regular programme under the leadership of Yermanos [Germanos Karavangelis], the Greek Metropolitan of Amasia, Samsoon and the surrounding country.[6]

Kapancızade Hamit Bey, a mutesarrif of Samsun, later wrote that Greek ships had moved into the Black Sea, Greek brigands were busy preparing for an amphibious landing, and the Greek population, more impertinent with every passing day, was looking forward to a new, Smyrna-like assault.[7] Bristol concurred: "The Greek Government endeavored to organize a political movement among the [Ottoman] Greeks . . . with the hope of eventually establishing Greek sovereignty in a so-called Pontic state."[8]

But the reality was different. The Pontic movement seems to have had little traction before 1919 and not much afterward. A minuscule Pontus Society was founded in 1904 at the American College in Merzifon, and some Orthodox priests, such Damianos and Germanos in Samsun, supported separatism.[9] A British officer later described Germanos as "quite intolerant," with unlimited "ambitions as a Hellenist."[10] In his 1927 speech, Kemal said that new Greek associations, such as Mawrimira, were "forming bands, organizing meetings and making propaganda." Another organization, called Pontus, "worked openly and successfully" toward Greek independence, Kemal asserted.[11] Ali Fuat Cebesoy, Kemal's chief of staff, recounted in his memoirs that some of the Greek returnees, assisted by the British, had even established a "deportation court" *(tehcir mahkemesi)*, presumably to try Turks involved in the wartime deportations, suggesting Greek intent to take over the Pontus.[12]

During World War I, Greek armed bands—composed chiefly of youngsters avoiding the draft—occasionally attacked Turkish villagers and gendarmes. The Turks charged that they were being armed and reinforced from Russia.[13] And in December 1918 it was reported that some Greeks in Batumi had announced the formation of a Pontic government in exile. If true, nothing came of it.

The perceptive British Foreign Office official George Rendel, no friend of the Turks, wrote in 1922 that "there is no doubt that the Greek ecclesiastical authorities in Constantinople had fostered a Greek national movement in [the Pontus], and that the hope of liberation from Turkish rule . . . encouraged the ill-informed Greek population . . . to take a renewed and dangerous interest in politics."[14] But, in fact, all this separatist hubbub had resulted, after the war, in "almost no acts of overt rebellion" and very little anti-Turk terrorism.[15] In reality, most Ottoman Greeks, in the Pontus as elsewhere in Anatolia, remained unmoved by ethnic-nationalist appeals. Or, as an American diplomat who toured the major Pontic cities in summer 1919 reported, "many of the most influential and rational Greeks . . . in Trebizond view this policy [of separatism] with disfavor." The local Greek Archbishop, Chrysanthonos, was also opposed.[16]

Why the Ottoman Greeks by and large distanced themselves from the pan-Hellenic national message, and certainly failed to act on it, is unclear. Perhaps it was a matter of poorly developed political consciousness; perhaps it was due to the centuries-long tradition of submissiveness to Islamic hegemony. In the immediate postwar years, many Ottoman Greeks also feared massacre—as had just befallen the Armenians—or economic harm, should they choose the path of rebellion. And demographic realities assuredly contributed: the Turks predominated in the Pontus, as in Anatolia in general—and the Pontic Greeks knew it, whatever their spokesmen sometimes said.

To be sure, the Greek landing at Smyrna gave supporters of Pontic separatism a boost. In late May 1919, Kemal, having just arrived in Samsun, informed Constantinople that since the Armistice "forty guerrilla" bands, "in an organized program," were killing Turks in order to "establish a Pontus state." The Greek bands were allegedly trying to massacre and drive out the Muslim population and recruit Greeks in Russia in order to create a Greek majority in the Pontus.[17] It is possible that many Turks believed these allegations.

The Greco-Turkish War, 1919–1922

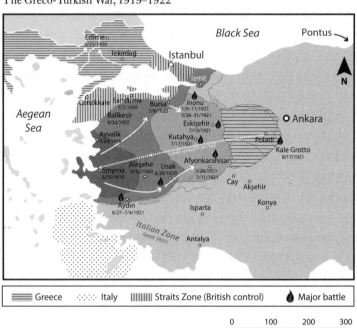

The alleged threat of Pontine separatism was only one factor affecting Turkish policy toward Anatolian Greeks in 1919–1923. Another was actual Greek behavior. Here and there Ottoman Greeks joined the invading army at Smyrna, and some, under army auspices or independently, formed brigand bands that harassed Turkish peasants in the Greek zone of occupation. In the background, looming above all, was the invasion itself and the Greek army's eastward thrusts, which seemingly threatened Ankara. The Greek army also occasionally threatened to turn northward and take Constantinople, a move the British repeatedly vetoed.

These elements all coalesced in Turkish justifications for the ethnic-religious cleansing of the Ottoman Greeks that unfolded.

Prelude: The War (1914–1918)

As we have seen, the Turks had already ethnically cleansed much of the Ionian coast in the months before World War I, and during the war itself uprooted as many as 550,000 Greeks. One observer commented that "comparatively few of [them] survived."[18] Most were deported inland, for what the Turks called "military reasons"; some were expelled or fled to Greece or Russia.[19] But the CUP leadership never adopted a policy of genocide or even of comprehensive ethnic cleansing vis-à-vis the Ottoman Greeks. Certainly the Young Turk brass wanted, under cover of the fog of war, to cleanse Asia Minor of all its Christians. But considerations of public opinion, abroad and possibly also at home, weighed against. While it had been possible to portray the Armenians as rebels, the Greeks clearly were not rising up. And there were practical problems: an Anatolian Greek genocide might trigger intervention by the Kingdom of Greece in the war. (The Greeks only entered the war, on the Allied side, in summer 1917.) The Turks may also have feared that killing Greeks would result in tit-for-tat violence against Muslims in Greece.[20] Thus the war was characterized by a telling dichotomy: while Armenians were forbidden to leave the country—and thereby effectively consigned to death—Greeks were encouraged to depart, with state assistance.

But alongside was real persecution of the Ottoman Greeks, orchestrated by Constantinople. In areas where there were Ottoman Greek concentrations, government officials went from mosque to mosque stirring up the Muslims.

For example, Yusuf Ziya Effendi and Talât Bey of Makri, in southwestern Asia Minor, toured seventy-odd nearby villages announcing, "The hour of the liberation of the sacred soil of our country from the unbelievers has arrived." The authorities enjoined villagers neither to repay debts to unbelievers nor to buy from or sell to Christians. "Chase away from the villages all the unbelievers [but] without massacring them," Yusuf Ziya and Talât Bey declared. "Their property and . . . houses . . . belong to you, and you may divide them among yourselves."[21]

Locals responded by carrying out orders "in the most horrible way." The villagers fled to Makri and Livissi (Kayaköy). On the way they were robbed, and some were murdered. "Women were violated, and their underclothes and shoes were taken away." The two heavily Greek towns were then blockaded. People died for lack of food. Some tried to flee. Two brothers were caught, tied together, and thrown into a fire. The younger resisted and broke his bonds, but "the rascals" cut off his hands and feet and threw him back into the flames. The brothers' fingers were brought to Makri for identification. "Their poor mother lost her senses and is now wandering in the mountains in search of her sons," it was reported. In the village of Trimil, Turkish troops raped six women in a night-long "orgy." When one of their husbands complained, "he was submitted to sodomy—by order of the superior officer." In another incident, near Kestop, villagers raped two women for eight days. One of them later died.[22] Procope, the Greek Orthodox metropolitan of Konya, wrote in February 1915, "It is no exaggeration to say that the sufferings of the Christians here surpass those of the Hebrews in Egypt."[23]

After Turkey entered the war, Constantinople's policy toward its Greeks remained ambivalent. On the one hand, the government feared fifth columnists and consistently deported Greeks from the coastal areas inland or expelled them from the country altogether. Here and there, the authorities also uprooted Greeks from inland towns and villages. Community leaders were imprisoned or exiled. But generally the Turks refrained from massacre, partly because they feared Ottoman Greek rebellion and potential persecution by Greece of its Muslim inhabitants.[24] The Turks insisted that "there was no persecution of Greeks" but admitted that villagers had been removed inland for "military reasons."[25]

Many of the Greek deportations involved chiefly women and children as, by early 1915, most army-age Greek men had been mobilized in Ottoman labor battalions or had fled their homes to avoid conscription. Indeed, an Ottoman law from summer 1915 provided for the exile of "families of deserters." Draft dodging and desertion were widespread. In Edirne vilayet, with 60,000 Greeks in September 1915, there was hardly a family without members who had fled the country.

The deserters, of course, had a case. In the labor battalions Greeks suffered severe, routinely lethal, privations. The Greek consul-general in Konya observed the "unhappy men . . . sent . . . into the interior" to build roads, maintain tunnels, and till fields. "Unpaid, badly nourished and ill-clad, exposed . . . to the burning sun of Baghdad or the intense cold of the Caucasus, struck down by disease . . . they die in the thousands," he wrote. "I have seen these wretched men in the hospitals of Konia stretched upon their beds or on the ground, living skeletons, longing for death." Most got what they desired. "The cemetery," the consul-general found, "is already filled with the tombs of men serving in the labor battalions. . . . In[to] each grave not a single body, but four, five, and sometimes six corpses have been flung, like so many dogs."[26] According to a postwar Greek report, out of some 3,000 labor conscripts from Ayvalık, only twenty-three survived. Another report noted a death toll of 80 percent among conscripted laborers at Islahiye.[27] "The life of a Greek in a labor gang is generally about two months," a British intelligence officer held hostage by the Turks in the eastern vilayets estimated.[28]

Depredation was not restricted to the labor battalions. On March 8, 1915, Turkish police in Constantinople deported some 200 Greek community leaders, intellectuals, clergy, and businessmen, foreshadowing the next month's roundup of the capital's Armenian elite. Both episodes had the same purpose: to decapitate a community.[29]

The eviction of Greeks from the Dardanelles had already begun in October 1914, before Turkey entered the war. It started with the inhabitants of Krithia. The deportation moved into full gear after the Allies began their naval push into the Dardanelles in February 1915. Greek villagers from both sides of the Dardanelles and the Bosporus were driven inland. The Turks apparently also expelled as many as 5,000 Jews living along the Straits.[30] In some sites the empty houses were quickly filled with Bosnian muhacirs.[31] Military concerns, without doubt, played a part. But hovering in the background were nationalism and religion, which explains why many deportees were scattered among inland Turkish Muslim, rather than Greek, villages. In the villages, they were pressed to convert.

By the summer the Turks had cleared the Greeks (and Armenians) from most of the islands of the Sea of Marmara and its coasts. The Austro-Hungarian ambassador in Constantinople, Johann von Pallavicini, believed the removals stemmed from a desire to annihilate the empire's Christians.[32] Many of the deportations were ordered by General Liman von Sanders, who orchestrated the defense of the Gallipoli peninsula.[33] His orders were carried out with excessive zeal and came to include much of the Ionian coastline. "More compassion is shown here to dogs than to the Christian refugees," the Metropolitan of Gallipoli, Constantinos, wrote. Some, deported via Bandırma, were "kicked into the [train] wagons in asphyxiating numbers." In many cases, the deportees were shifted "from place to place" a number of times.[34] Many were given two hours' notice to leave and were dispersed in "groups of five, ten or twenty families" in Turkish villages, where they lived in poverty among hostile inhabitants.[35] Muhacirs sometimes appeared in the villages before their Greek inhabitants were even deported. The muhacirs were known to stone houses while shouting "be gone, or we shall kill you, you swine of infidels."[36] The deportations were often carried out with brutality, and deportees died of hunger and exposure.[37] In June–September the deportations were extended to western Bursa vilayet.[38] There were also deportations from the Ephesus area and from eastern Trabzon vilayet.[39] Thousands found refuge in the forests of Arghyropolis and near Ardache, in the diocese of Chaldi.[40]

The government countered Western protests by claiming that the deportations were "from military zones" and undertaken for "military reasons."[41] Diplomats were fobbed off with promises of amelioration and investigation. The Turks also complained that outside protests constituted meddling in their internal affairs. Even allies were castigated for "interference." "You ought to know that the Germans have no right to interfere in . . . our internal affairs," Enver told the Greek Patriarch in July 1915 after he sought German intercession.[42]

The harsh nature of the deportations inland persuaded Morgenthau that they were not governed only, or even primarily, by military considerations. "The Turks want to wipe [the Greeks] out partly from envy and partly from fear of their superior talents," he wrote.[43] But he added that these deportations were "on a lesser scale" than those of the Armenians and had "stopped short at direct loss of life."[44]

The deportations continued through 1915, affecting areas far from strategic coastlines. In August–October 1915, much of Edirne vilayet was cleared of Greeks, even if they lived far from the straits in places such as Kırklareli and Uzunköprü. The Greeks and Armenians of Eskişehir were deported, most likely in August.[45] Occasional killings were a routine part of the process but there were also full-scale massacres.[46] At Demotika (Dimoteicho), near Edirne city, Turks and Bulgarians killed some 400 Greeks.[47] Some Greek deportees were sent to Malgara and resettled in the homes of deported Armenians.[48] Villagers in the Ünye (Ounia) area, along the southern shore of the Black Sea, were deported in December. According to the Greek Patriarchate, Turkish troops murdered batches of Greek men, and "the nice-looking women and girls . . . were raped and dishonored." In spring 1916 the Turks deported more than 3,000 Greeks from the Alexandretta-Antakya area eastward to Idlib, Manbij, and Al-Bab.[49]

Some deportations were linked to the shifting tides of war. On January 10, 1916, the Russians launched a major offensive in eastern Anatolia. They captured Erzurum and Muş on February 16, Bitlis on March 3, and Trabzon on April 18. Each time the front receded, the regional Ottoman commander, Kamil Pasha, ordered the deportation of Greek villagers immediately behind his lines. They were ejected into midwinter temperatures around zero centigrade and some froze along the road. "We must suffer, so must you," Kamil said.[50]

That spring and summer, the Turks deported the inhabitants of dozens of Trabzon vilayet villages. Hundreds fled to surrounding forests and mountains. A Greek report tells of twenty-six women and girls who, "to avoid dishonor," threw themselves into a river near the village of Gephira. Elsewhere in Trabzon vilayet, the Turks rounded up Greek women and took them to Vazelon Monastery, where they "first violated them, and then put them to death. Many men were also murdered."[51] The Greek population of Inebolu (Ineboli) and its surrounding villages—Cide, Patheri, Atsidono, Karaca, Askordassi—was deported in June.[52]

Most Trabzon Christians were deported inland. But some—from the village of Ardache, for example—were pushed toward newly occupied Russian areas. As the Ottoman army withdrew, Turkish villagers fell back with them. They behaved, the Greek Patriarchate said, "like locusts" destroying "everything" in their path. A Greek metropolitan described a raid by Osman Aga—an agent of Trabzon vali Cemal Azmi, and himself destined for infamy—on the village of Prossori as the army was in its retreat. "They plundered the houses, raped the women, murdered four young Greeks, and beat the parish priest to death. [Osman] then forced the peasants to sign a document certifying that the murderers were Armenians."[53]

Deportations from Trabzon to the Anatolian interior often resulted in rape and death. Metropolitan Germanos later said, "A large number of women and children were killed, the young girls outraged and immediately driven into the interior. . . . These girls had to march thirty or forty days across snow-covered mountains and sleep by night in the open. . . . The majority, of course, died on the road."[54]

The Turks maintained the pretext of military justification even when they were winning. When the tide of battle changed, and they reconquered Trabzon vilayet, they continued expelling Greeks systematically.[55] Greek witnesses alleged that Refet Pasha, the military governor of the Samsun district, burnt and depopulated dozens of villages between November 1916 and May 1917. During December 1916, the Turks deported notables from Samsun, Bafra, Ordu, Tirebolu, Amasya, and Çarşamba and apparently hanged 200 Greeks on charges of desertion.[56] The villagers of the Bafra hinterland were sent "to wander from one village to another." An American naval officer noted that these deportees "were not massacred [like] . . . the Armenians" had been. Instead, the "killing of the Greeks was accomplished" through subterfuge. Pursuant to the deportation order, Greeks were "undressed and placed in Turkish baths for several hours, presumably to cleanse them so as to prevent any spread of disease. They were taken from these hot baths and [marched] . . . in the dead of winter, with very little clothing and generally without food." Naked and freezing, they died of "exposure, sickness or starvation."[57]

In Samsun, deportation of notables was followed by mass removal on January 10, 11, and 13, 1917. The columns consisted mostly of women and children, whose houses were subsequently plundered and torched or occupied by muhacirs. Deportees who survived the journey were dispersed in Turkish villages. But large numbers were not so lucky. A Greek diplomat described the suffering that claimed their lives:

> During the night, pregnant women, youths and old men seek refuge in hovels so confined that they run the risk of suffocation. They have no bread and no water. . . . They lie on the ground in the midst of unutterable filth. Many die on the road from chills. . . . All have to keep up the march, in spite of everything, at all cost; their warders see to this with infinite zeal, cruel traces of which are left upon the shoulders of their victims. The dead are seldom buried.[58]

A postwar investigation by an American consul suggests that about 5,000 Greeks and a similar number of Armenians were eliminated from Samsun by massacre, expulsion, and flight to the hills. Samsun Turks also endured heavy losses during the war, in combat and from disease.[59] There were also Greek deportations from the Fatsa, Nikassar, and Çarşamba areas.[60]

In all, in late 1916–early 1917, tens of thousands of Greeks were marched inland from the Pontus coastline along with a sprinkling of Armenians not deported in 1915.[61] Speaking of Bafra-area villages in particular, Metropolitan Germanos told American officers that "the greatest cause" of the deportations was "religion."[62]

Western Anatolia also witnessed deportations, beginning in spring 1917, mostly from the Ionian coast. (The delay apparently was due to intercession by General Liman and the German Foreign Ministry.) In March–April, weeks before the Greeks entered the war, Ayvalık was emptied of Greeks. It had been a major population center, home to 12,000–30,000 Greeks, according to various estimates. Convoys of 500 and 600 families departed daily for inland Turkish villages. General Liman himself gave the order, though it may have originated with Talât.[63] A Greek official described one of the convoys: "The sight is ghastly. Large and small living skeletons roam through the town, begging. The convoy, after marching for 42 days, is condemned to pursue its journey for a long time yet. Its destination is Jeni-Sehir [Yenişehir] and Biledjik [Bilecik]. . . . More than 180 died on the way . . . the women dropped their newborn babes to keep up." The Greeks struggled with more than the conditions. "Nothing can move" the Turkish escort, the official wrote. "Their hearts are of iron."[64]

To the south, in the Aydın vilayet towns of Makri and Livissi, the Turks conscripted some 3,000 Greeks for forced labor. Reportedly, just 500 survived the war. The Turks also periodically arrested notables, exacted large sums for their release, and then failed to keep up their end of the deal. In July 1916 many of the communities' notables were imprisoned—"weeping and wailing from pain and grief, beaten and blasphemed." Some were deported to Denizli, and some of them died on the way. There were recurrent bouts of arrest and deportation over the next two years. The prisoners were often given the choice of conversion, but most refused. One of the refusers, a John Agioriti, was beaten and tortured. "Nails were thrust into his body, his nails were pulled off, his nose and ears cut off, and finally his eyes were taken off."

Persecution ratcheted up after the June 1917 Greek declaration of war. Though Ottoman Greek communities at this point were effectively unarmed and shorn of fighting-age men, they still were depicted as a current rather than potential threat. Thus between November 1917 and April 1918, 1,300 Makri and Livissi families were exiled to the interior. Boycotts prevented them selling much of anything before leaving, and they left behind their property to be confiscated. They were robbed along the way, and their dead and dying were left by the wayside. The second batch, of 900 families, was treated even "worse," according to Gough-Calthorpe. Some women were taken by Turks. One Pelagia Geron, it was reported, was "violated at the beginning [and] is at present living with the mudir" of Livissi, Hassan Bey. Some converted, including "the daughter of Stefanos Kourti and Katina Voulgarou."[65] Toward the end of the war, in May–June 1918, the Turks deported inland the remaining inhabitants of the Sea of Marmara islands. Many died on the roads. Their houses were filled with Pomak muhacirs.[66]

One British estimate, from December 1917, held that 100,000 Ottoman Greeks had been killed since the start of August.[67] In late 1917 Talât estimated that more than 93,000 Greeks had been deported to the interior and another 164,000 to Greece during the war.[68] The Greek government maintained that

280,000 Ottoman Greeks had been deported in 1914, before the war, and about 500,000 during the war.[69] Of the latter, according to the Greek Central Relief Commission, 197,399 had been expelled from Thrace.[70] In sum, it is likely that approximately half a million Ottoman Greeks were deported during the Great War. Of these, certainly tens of thousands, and perhaps hundreds of thousands, died.[71]

Postwar Greek Return

George Horton, the philo-Hellenic US consul-general in Smyrna, endorsed the Ottoman Greek refugees' postwar "right of return" to their homes on the grounds that, "from the dawn of history, . . . they are the race best fitted to develop the coast of Asia Minor. . . . The present Turkish occupants have made a hash of the pretty houses and villages and well cultivated vineyards and farms."[72] Horton explained that the muhacirs settled along the Ionian coast were mostly "mountaineers" from Macedonia "with little or no knowledge of agriculture." So they "stripped" Greeks' farms "like locusts."[73]

In November 1918, with the convening of the Paris peace conference, the victorious powers agreed that surviving Greek deportees should be allowed to return to their homes.[74] "The majority died," Webb wrote in January 1919, "as it was intended by Turks and Germans that they should." But the number remaining made for a Greek-returnee problem "almost [of the] same magnitude" as the Armenian. Webb calculated that there were "some 200,000" survivors of the January–June 1914 deportations and 150,000–200,000 survivors from the "half a million" deported during the war.[75]

The British moved swiftly. In winter 1918 Webb put Commander C. E. Heathcote-Smith in charge of Greek repatriation and sent him on a tour of villages near Constantinople. The Turks, still in shock from defeat, collaborated, or appeared to collaborate, instructing all governors to assist the return and hand over orphans, whether homeless or taken by Muslim families.[76] Governors were also ordered to restore churches, schools, and confiscated property.[77]

The orders, however, were not always taken seriously or acted upon. For example, when 200–300 Greek families returned to Büyükdere, they found 150 of their houses still occupied and the police "helping the Turkish tenants to remain." In Pyrgos village 200 Greeks were driven off while attempting to regain their homes. Heathcote-Smith arrived a fortnight later and, aided by Turkish officials, managed to resettle 120 families. But even when Greeks were able to regain their homes, there were problems: their houses were damaged, and they had outstanding bills to pay. Altogether, Webb was not sanguine. "The Turkish authorities," he wrote, "pursue a policy of active obstruction feebly disguised by official assurances of their good intentions."[78]

There were notable successes, but rarely total ones. At Ayvalık 8,000–12,000 Greeks returned, though only a "few families" made it back to adjoining Mosko Island, which Heathcote-Smith described as "now a perfect desert."[79] A March 2, 1919, visit by Lieutenant Perring to the Marmara Islands netted immediate results for the 2,900 or so Greek returnees, though they constituted only a tenth of the islands' prewar Greek population. Accompanied by Turkish officials, he secured the speedy restoration of homes, "including furniture," and even the liberation of "all Christian girls" from Muslim households.[80]

The British could not solve every repatriation problem—not even close. But returnees were still grateful. At Maltepe, on the northern shore of the Sea of Marmara, Greek returnees demonstrated their appreciation for the British by parading through the street, cheering, firing shots in the air, and waving a Greek flag. Repatriation agents warned local priests to avoid such exhibitions, as they would "excite the fanaticism of the Turks, thus making our task of repatriation harder."[81]

As a rule, Turks resisted Greek repatriation, with or without British assistance, especially in sites inundated by muhacirs. Around Smyrna, "no Greeks" had returned by late February 1919, whereas, according to Turkish figures, 91,000 muhacirs had settled in the district since 1913, 22,000 of them in empty Greek homes. The director of the Constantinople government's Turkish Refugee Department told Heathcote-Smith that "the Greeks could not return," as the Ottoman and Greek governments had reached a population-exchange agreement in 1914. But this wasn't the Greek government position—and, in fact, no agreement had been reached in 1914. Indeed, the Greeks invaded Smyrna in May 1919 in part with the aim of facilitating the return of Ionian refugees.[82]

Further afield, where Britain's writ was still weaker, the Turks were even more obstructive. By late January 1919, between 10,000 and 40,000 Greeks had returned to Samsun and Bafra, many living in makeshift "mud huts" and in the street, as usurping Turks, "gypsies," and Albanians, "with the connivance of the authorities," refused to vacate their homes. The kaymakam of Bafra reportedly told returnees "to go and live with the Albanians and become their servants." A number of Bafra Greeks were killed trying to regain homes, even as some empty Armenian homes were being torn down and "sold for wood."[83] Kapancızade Hamid Bey, the governor of Samsun, was set against any Greek revival in the city. He did not see Greeks as refugees trying to go home, but as enemies of the state: "It seemed as though the Samsun area was already in the hands of the Pontus rebels," he wrote in light of the ongoing repatriation.[84]

The situation in Kastamonu vilayet was little better. Returning Greeks were "in a very pitiful condition," though the Turkish authorities provided them with transport and "repatriation expenses." Greek children were "nearly naked, their scraps of clothing consisting of pieces of sacking, curtains, cushion covers and strips of mattress cloth."[85] In Merzifon and its environs, Greek refugees were returning "to wrecked homes and ruined villages." The returning refugees formed "bands" to defend themselves and reclaim their property, giving the Turks a "pretext" for violence.[86]

Conditions varied from place to place, depending on what had happened during the war, the character of the Turks in charge, and past and present economic and social relations. In Milas, south of Smyrna, all the wartime deportees returned, and by April 1919 the town had 5,600 Turks, 2,200 Christians, and 1,000 Jews. The Greeks' only complaint was that they were forced to close their shops at one o'clock in the afternoon. But in the nearby Greek village of Kuluk, "practically all" was in ruins. Only one Greek woman remained, a servant of the Turkish port officer. At Bodrum, which had a prewar Christian population of 4,400, only 750 "remain[ed]," or had returned, in April 1919. They lived alongside 7,000 Turks, 3,000 of whom were muhacirs from Erzurum and Van. At Scala Nouva only 150–200 Greeks, from a prewar population of 7,000–10,000, remained at the time of the armistice. About 1,300 Greeks returned thereafter. They lived "in a most direful state of poverty, families of ten or twelve . . . in small rooms without light or ventilation." Many of them were "very ill." But the Turkish quarter was "flourishing." During the war the Turks in Scala Nouva had occasionally exhumed "the bodies of Christians the third day after their burial, crucif[ied] them on the Church wall and [thrown] stones at them." A British officer recommended barring a Greek return to southern Ionia unless homes and employment were assured.[87]

Just about everywhere, return led to friction, and Turks displayed "a spirit of arrogance and hostility." Constantinople was busy arming the Turks and "threats and acts of violence are the order of the day," a relief officer wrote, describing the context in which the repatriation effort played out.[88] Unsurprisingly, returnees sometimes resorted to force of arms. For instance in mid-February a band of fifty Greek refugees took over Arquoi (Akköy), to which they were returning from the island of Samos. The refugees, most of them demobilized soldiers, drove out the Turkish officials, confiscated military stores, and killed a Turkish soldier and several gendarmes. The Turks mobilized troops, but the British intervened, prevented a clash, and forced the refugees to return to Samos.[89]

The Turks claimed that by the end of February 1919, 62,721 Greeks had returned, with Ottoman government aid, to their homes around Asia Minor. Another 15,000 had returned on their own steam.[90] The Turks complained that the Greeks had not, reciprocally, helped exiled Turks return to their homes in Thrace, so Turkey had a problem helping Greeks—some of whom had fought against Turkey—return home.[91]

According to the Greek government, most deportees' real estate, with British help, had been restored to returning owners. But other property—fishing boats, farm animals—had not. Some Ottoman Greeks used grants and loans from the Greek government's Central Relief Commission, to buy back their own farm animals.[92] By and large, though, Greece was too poor to aid returnees.

The pace of repatriation to Ionia picked up after the Greek occupation of Smyrna. But, wishing to avoid friction, the Greek High Commission in Constantinople did not encourage such return. The high commission also obliged returnees they were assisting not to oust Muslim squatters "until a new [place] can be found" for them. Some returnees tried to force out squatters, leading to trouble.[93]

Bristol, who regarded "the Greek people" as "worthless" and "good-for-nothing," generally opposed Greek repatriation.[94] He called it "a mistake" that would cause more harm than good, at least until "a suitable government"—that is, a Western mandate—"was established."[95] Consul-General Horton disagreed. In March 1920 he toured the area south of Smyrna—St. George Çiftlik, Vourla, Alatesta, Lidja—and reported that the Greeks had "begun to restore their ancient civilization." "After six years of Turkish occupation" and muhacir settlement all had been in ruins. It looked like "Pompei." The returning Greeks were now "working like bees" to repair farmhouses and fields. As for the muhacirs, Horton said, they were not being expelled; they were "leaving of their own accord. It was a case of leaving or starving to death."[96] Horton discovered "feverish activity" of reconstruction north of Smyrna, in Phocia, Dikili, and Bergama. To Phocia, of the original 8,000 Greeks, 5,500 had returned by April 1920; to Bergama, some 6,000 of the original 13,000. The Greek occupation authorities dismantled Greek brigand bands operating in the area.[97]

But by the start of 1921, Greek repatriation had been reduced to a thin trickle. Then it ceased altogether. American diplomats believed that the Nationalist government intended not merely to block Greek repatriation, but to empty the country of its Greek population altogether.[98]

Deporting the Greeks, 1919–1923

As Greeks were trying to get home, the Turks were working to deport them. More than a million Greeks were uprooted during 1919–1923. The process began before the Smyrna landing with uncoordinated bouts of intimidation at various sites. During spring 1920 sporadic depredations transformed into a deliberate campaign, spearheaded and then orchestrated by the Turkish Nationalist movement and government. The campaign unfolded in a number of waves, the first in summer 1920. Further waves followed in the spring and summer of 1921 and 1922. The decisive wave—marked by the destruction of Smyrna and of the Pontic Greek community—was unleashed in autumn and winter of 1922–1923. The first waves were partly linked to the shifting tides of the Greco-Turkish war in Anatolia; the last began alongside the Greek army's defeat in August–September 1922 and was influenced by the subsequent

Allied-Turkish peace negotiations at Lausanne. This was followed, in 1923–1924, by a final Turkish campaign to rid the country of its remaining Christian communities. The 1920–1922 period was characterized by endless, deadly treks from the population centers along the coasts to the harsh mountains of the interior. Then, in late 1922 and early 1923, Greeks in the interior and the smaller coastal settlements were deported to ports on the Black Sea, Aegean, and Mediterranean and thence, most of them, to Greece. There were also smaller deportations southward, by land, to Syria. All the waves were characterized by murderousness, resulting in hundreds of thousands of deaths.

1919–1920

Within weeks of the end of the Great War, Turks launched sporadic attacks on Greeks around Anatolia and Edirne vilayet. Most of the assailants were brigands and demobilized soldiers. In the Tsinik area near Samsun, according to a British observer, the Ottoman authorities had armed the Turkish villagers, and there was "a carefully laid down plan . . . to eliminate the Greek and Armenian elements from this district."[99] In Edirne province, life for Christians was "a continual night-mare," a British officer reported in March 1919.[100]

Initially the brigandage may have been largely criminal, but by late spring it gave way to politically motivated violence, often organized by local CUP apparatchiks. Central-government officials apparently contributed; indeed, some brigands claimed that they were in the pay of Constantinople. The brigands extorted, robbed, and beat Christians. In the case of Vasili Poulou, of Pasha Keuy (Paşaköy), they also cut off ears: "We could easily kill you," the brigands told him. "But instead we are cutting off your ears so that you can go to the British and French and complain." Brigands also turned to arson and often operated hand in hand with local gendarmes.[101] The goal appeared to be to drive the Greeks out.

Athens charged that "the persecutions became . . . more ferocious" after the start of the Kemalist rebellion in spring 1919.[102] By September the British were reporting that "public security all along the Black Sea Coast was very bad." The state was encouraging the brigands by pardoning their crimes and hiring them for official jobs: reportedly 80 percent of the gendarmes were "former brigands," who devoted "most of their energies to rounding up odd

Christians."[103] The Christians were "terrified. . . . Every district has its band of brigands now posing as patriots. . . . Behind all these elements of disorder stands Mustapha Kemal," the British concluded. Turks were busy boycotting Christians and repossessing property recently restored to them.[104]

By early 1920 the Kemalist policy of intimidating the Greeks into flight was in full swing. In March representatives of fifty-one Greek communities in Cappadocia, Konya vilayet, appealed to the great powers for protection, saying that "emissaries" of Kemal preached in schools "the immediate extermination of all the Greeks in the country. The most fanatical and sanguinary went so far as to insist upon the immediate carrying out of this massacre 'en bloc.'"[105] Nationalist army officers near Samsun toured the villages saying that "the Christians [were] the cause of the [Allied] occupation of Constantinople and advocated their extermination." At Ünye and Fatsa, Turks posted placards blaming the Christians "for all their troubles."[106] The Kemalists arrested and exiled to Ankara Polycarpos, the Greek bishop of the mixed town of Ordu.[107] The Turks walked about the town "fully armed"— except when an Allied ship was in port. "They are on their good behavior until the ships leave. . . . The Christians feared to venture out of town.[108]

In Samsun the Nationalists, stressing the "religious side of the question," inflamed the Turkish population "by preaching a Holy War. . . . The Greeks are accused of violating Turkish women, and of destroying the Holy Tombs of Sheikhs at Broussa and other captured towns."[109] The mutesarrif of Samsun, Nafiz Bey, spoke more or less openly of massacring the local Greeks should the Greek Navy try to land troops, and Nationalist members of Kemal's parliament in Ankara proposed a law calling for the deportation of all Christians from the Black Sea area.[110] No such law was passed; Kemal preferred less publicized methods. Here and there, there were fatalities. In Domuz-Dere seven Greek charcoal-sellers and two children were murdered.[111] By spring there were full-scale massacres. At Gelebek station (Haçkiri), in April, some 500 Christians were reportedly murdered by irregulars.[112]

According to British officials, Italians, in their zone of occupation south of Smyrna, were facilitating Nationalist attacks on Greeks. In the village of Tomatia, Turkish brigands killed 85 peasants and stole tobacco, wheat, farm animals, and 750 beehives. Italian troops looked on and then disarmed the Greeks when they retaliated and torched a Turkish village.[113]

Systematic ethnic cleansing of Greek villages appears to have begun in March 1920 near the Greek-Turkish front lines in Izmit sanjak. The frequency and intensity of persecution increased in June–July, according to an Allied commission that investigated two months later. The perpetrators were brigands often assisted "by the Turkish villagers." All the while the Turks complained of Greek atrocities. In March the Turkish Foreign Ministry alleged beatings, rape and torture by Greek soldiers.[114] But the commission found that atrocities "on the part of the Turks have been more considerable and ferocious than those on the part of the Greeks." The commission's report detailed more than a dozen Greek villages cleansed around Adapazarı and several south of Izmit.[115]

As Nationalist strength grew, so did "Nationalist persecutions and excesses."[116] At Ortaköy, there were repeated bouts of murder and depredation. Twenty were killed and dozens exiled on April 12.[117] The Turks reportedly took women aside and "cut off ears and fingers to obtain the jewelry they were wearing."[118] Another 270 were killed on June 9. On July 19, 150 houses were torched, and "nearly all the young girls and women were violated and many of them afterwards were killed while others were taken into the harems of Giaour Ali and his followers."[119]

In response to the Greek army's summer 1920 advance eastward, the Nationalists engaged in "serious . . . excesses against the Christians in the districts bordering on the newly occupied territory."[120] Others suffered alongside the Greeks; for instance, the Jewish population of Nazli, some 450 strong, was deported.[121] But the Greeks fared far worse. When the Greek army entered Nazli, they found close to sixty corpses, many of them of young girls who had first been raped.[122] The rule of thumb at this time appears to have been that areas where Kemal's hold was tenuous were ravaged by anti-Christian "anarchy and brigand rule," but "little or no persecution of Christians appears to occur in those districts in which the authority of Mustapha Kemal has remained undisputed."[123]

The Turks attempted to turn against their enemies the very accusations hurled at them. During summer 1920 Turkish gendarmes and village headmen in the Aegean region reported cases of abuse, murder, and rape by conquering Greek soldiers.[124] But British officials found no evidence of this. In Thrace, they reported, the Greek troops' "behaviour . . . was exemplary." In Asia

Minor there were "occasional cases of misconduct," but the Greek authorities punished the miscreants. For instance, four Greek soldiers at Balikesir were sentenced to four and half years' imprisonment for looting.[125] The worst miscreants on the Greek side may have been a handful of Armenians recruited by the Greek army, said to have "committed atrocities on Turkish villages." The Greeks quickly packed them off to Constantinople.[126] In general Greek behavior was such that "the [Turkish] inhabitants of the occupied zone have in most cases accepted the advent of Greek rule without demur and in some cases undoubtedly prefer it to the Nationalist regime which seems to have been founded on terrorism," a British intelligence report stated.[127] One British liaison officer assigned to Greek army units advancing on Uşak, south of Kütahya, observed that the troops were "warmly welcomed by the Moslem population . . . [with] a sincere outburst of gratitude at being freed from the license and oppression of the Nationalist troops."[128]

Throughout the summer the British received reports of mass killings and expulsions of Greeks in front-line areas and on the Black Sea coast. Osman Aga, the brigand leader who was now also mayor of Giresun, reportedly pillaged coastal villages. In Giresun itself, on the night of August 13, 1920, Osman imprisoned all the Christian men. Thereafter "every evening five or six Christians" were taken out and shot, until the Christian community paid a ransom of 300,000 Turkish lira. While their husbands were in jail, "the women were violated." Greek men were deported inland from both Giresun and Samsun "at the order of Mustapha Kemal."[129]

That summer British and Nationalist troops clashed for the first time. The precipitating event came in April, when the Şeyhülislam issued a fatwa declaring Kemal and his associates rebels against the caliph.[130] The Constantinople government, supported by the British troop presence, then moved against the Nationalists in the Izmit Peninsula.[131] The Nationalists responded with a proclamation, couched in religious language, attacking the British, Greeks, French, and Italians: "They wish to convert the mosques of Fatih and Aya [Hagia] Sofia into churches, and to drive the Moslems from Constantinople . . . and to give Erzurum, Van, Bitlis, Sivas and Harput to the Armenians. . . . May God preserve the people of Mahomet."[132] The Nationalist press portrayed the British as "determined enemies of Islam . . . trying to subjugate the Islamic world."[133] On June 15 words gave way to action, as Nationalist troops attacked British outposts on the Izmit Peninsula.[134] The British responded with fire from sea and air, causing heavy Turkish losses and eventual retreat.[135] To the south, though, Nationalists took rebellious Turkish villages. In some cases, the villagers fled to neighboring Christian villages and towns for shelter. The Armenian Patriarchate reported that in one village, Pazarköy, the Nationalists had forced Turkish women and girls "to dance all naked, then they violated and murdered them."[136]

British intelligence noted "a decided change" in Nationalist policy toward the Christian population, against the backdrop of the Greek army's major summer offensive. According to an American witness, when the Greek army marched into Bursa on July 8, the troops and Bursa Greeks displayed "perfectly wonderful self-control" toward the town's Turkish inhabitants, "especially when you think what they have to remember of wrongs done them and their families."[137] Nonetheless Ankara resolved to destroy "non-Muslim villages as a reprisal for the destruction of Muslim villages in the occupied areas."[138]

One outcome of the growing Nationalist anger appears to have been a series of massacres by Turkish regulars and irregulars in the Izmit Peninsula.[139] At Fulacık, in June, the Turks "hanged 400 of the inhabitants." Soon after, some 600 were killed in Geyve and its vicinity.[140] In what is likely an exaggeration, a native of Geyve-Etchme (Eşme) related that on July 11, 7,300 Armenians and Greeks in Geyve-Ortaköy were pushed into a church and burned alive. He added that, the day before, the Turkish authorities, using deceit, had transferred to Etchme the inhabitants of neighboring villages, tied the men together, then massacred them at the Kara-Tchai (Karaçay) pass. Women were also murdered. Villagers who fled to the mountains were hunted down and killed. The villagers of Pamucak, after offering resistance, were piled into the church and massacred. Muslims carried off the women and girls.[141] Although some of the allegations may have been exaggerated, there are perfectly credible reports of atrocities. Clearly, thousands of villagers were forced to flee to Izmit.[142] And the depredations described at Geyve are in keeping with what is known from other sites, qualitatively if not quantitatively.

For instance, at Akhisar, occupied by the Nationalists on July 1, 1920, the men were tied in twos and marched to the well of Yeghise, then cut to pieces

with swords. The following day, Akhisar's women and children were taken
to a silk factory and massacred. Altogether some 350 Armenians and a handful
of Greeks were killed. Muhacirs then occupied the empty houses. Five "beautiful" Armenian girls were spared, as was an eight-year-old who screamed
she wanted to embrace Islam.[143] According to one report, though, the children
were later slaughtered in the vegetable gardens of Geyve.[144]

In İznik there were massacres on August 27 and at the end of September,
before the town came under Greek control.[145] A British officer later toured
the ruins. Outside town he saw a cave filled with "at least 100 . . . burnt and
mangled bodies," including of women and children. "All . . . apparently had
first had their hands and feet cut off, after that they were either burnt alive in
the cave or had their throats cut."[146] The Greek High Commission put the
total massacred at İznik at 600.[147]

On September 9, at Kütahya, the Turks arrested ninety-two Greek notables. The next day, "all males over 15 years of age were deported," and the
Turks pillaged the town.[148] According to Athens, the convoys were sent to
Sivri-Hisar, Bey-Bazar, Haimaki, Ankara, and Eskşehir. Only girls and boys
remained in Kütahya, where they were abused by Kemalist officers.[149] The
American vice consul in Smyrna wrote of the Kütahya Turks' "hideous, calculating cruelty."[150] Some Kütahya Armenian and Greek "women [were being]
kept by the Kemalists," others, apparently, had "perished through hunger and
diverse disease."[151] In the Meander Valley, southeast of Smyrna, Nationalists
massacred and deported several Greek communities. On September 10, they
slaughtered "most" remaining Christian males in Denizli. "Every kind of savagery was exercised on women, children," locals reported. The Kemalists deported the remaining Christians to Eyerdir, where refugees from Aydın and
Nazlı had already been concentrated.[152] In the Constantinople area, too, Greek
villages were raided, and men were killed and women raped. In two villages
at Yeniköy, 150 people were killed on June 28. Fifteen more were killed at
Arvanitohori on July 14.[153]

By the time Kemal's forces reached Konya and Cappadocia in September,
no one doubted what would come next. Greek community leaders appealed
to the British. "Our populations," they wrote, "find themselves totally at the
mercy of . . . Kemal. It is impossible to describe the terror, tortures, ordeals
and exactions perpetrated in that 'hunt for Christians' organized in our poor

country. Mass hangings are the order of the day. . . . Soon . . . nothing will be left but ashes and the silence of death."[154]

The most murderous Turks received the greatest rewards. In October Osman Aga went to Ankara for a meeting with Kemal; he left with a new job, as governor general of the coastal area from Inebolu to Hoppa. Kemal and Osman may not have had precisely the same priorities—the Nationalists were driven by political fervor and religious hatred, and Osman primarily by the desire to pillage. But Kemal knew how to get the worst out of his subordinates.[155]

By November rumor had it that the Nationalists had ordered "a general deportation of Greeks from the Pontus."[156] It is not clear whether any such order had in fact been given, but the signs were certainly there. Even as the ethnic-cleansing campaign slowed down in winter, the Turks took advantage of worsening conditions to score key blows against the weakening Greeks. Early 1921 saw continued pressure for mass conscription of able-bodied Greeks.[157] They were destined for labor battalions, which, "in reality," a missionary wrote, meant they would "starve or freeze to death." Maintaining a façade of legalism, in line with Ottoman traditions, the Turks routinely employed deceit. By law anyone younger than twenty was ineligible for conscription. So, in an effort to force more and younger Greeks into the jaws of labor service, the authorities forged birth certificates designating orphans "one to four years older than their real age."[158]

While the Greco-Turkish war served as background to the widespread, if occasionally haphazard, massacre and deportation of Greeks, a string of remainder Armenian communities was also destroyed. Sometimes the Armenians were specifically targeted, but more often they were swept up incidentally in the anti-Greek campaign. During 1919–1923 Greeks predominated in towns and villages with mixed Christian populations, if only because the Armenians had largely been disposed of during the war. Thus in August 1920, for example, Nationalist bands in Bolu massacred the Armenian population alongside eighty Greeks. The killing may have been instigated by Mufti Abdullah Chukri (Şükrü), a Muslim preacher from Devrek who had preached in Bolu's marketplace a few days earlier. "Holding a sword in his hand," he had urged listeners to destroy "the profaners of the holy Moslem religion."[159]

Throughout 1920 the Nationalists—in public and in conversation with outsiders—denied any genocidal purpose. In September, long after the excuse had lost all credibility, Kemal told an American missionary, Annie Allen, that the deportations were taking place "only on the frontiers"—that is, only for military reasons—and that the Nationalists "had no intention of a general deportation of their Christian subjects." The "three races, Turks, Armenians and Greeks, would live together in orderly" fashion, he said, and "hate would soon die."[160]

1921–Early 1922

The deportations and massacres tapered off in late autumn 1920, though there was an expulsion of Hellenic Greeks from Samsun at the end of the year.[161] Ethnic cleansing resumed with a vengeance in spring 1921 and encompassed all the territory under Nationalist control, not merely communities near the front lines. Jackson believed the campaign was being "carried out with all of the consequential results that occurred" during the Armenian deportations "in 1915–1916."[162] "The persecutions of 1921 were on a larger scale and more atrocious than those of 1920," a British government analysist concluded.[163]

The systematic operations of spring 1921 focused again on Pontic Ottoman Greeks. In February the Nationalist Interior Minister Fethi Bey had visited the region and then urged Kemal to authorize "more expeditious and larger scale [deportations] than hitherto."[164] Kemal apparently needed little persuasion. American officers visiting Samsun in early spring reported signs of "a definite [Nationalist] policy to exterminate the Greeks."

The officers quoted an American missionary to the effect that about 100 Greek villages south of Bafra had been destroyed in the course of a few days beginning May 17. The villagers were murdered and "the priests . . . crucified." The Greeks in the area felt that now that the Turks had finished off the Armenians, it was their turn. "The belief seems to exist that Osman Agha is in charge of the cleaning up the district," an American officer wrote, and "that there is to be a massacre of all Greeks in Samsun." Refugees from the countryside were flowing into Samsun, despite intermittent government efforts to halt the process. The Americans also got an inkling of discord within

Turkish ranks: the talk in the town was that the military wanted to exterminate the Greeks, while the local civil authorities were opposed.[165]

As in previous episodes, authorities sympathetic to the Christians did what they could, while being steamrolled by the government. Indeed, the character of the Nationalist policy in 1921 was much like that of the CUP in 1915. The Kemalists used the little evidence of dissidence they could muster—and a great many falsifications—to justify "wholesale deportations, continuous persecutions, and frequent massacres." The Turks first arrested the Greek notables and then proceeded to deport the masses.[166] There were, of course, differences between 1921 and 1915, but they were inconsequential from the standpoint of the victims. As an American missionary in Merzifon put it, "Unlike the Armenian deportations of 1915, there usually was a definite destination for these Greek deportees and there was no open and avowed policy of extermination, however much that may have been a sub-rosa policy of individuals, local governments or the national government."[167]

The campaign began in March. It may have been precipitated by the launch of the large Greek spring offensive, which began on the 23rd. The leader of the Turkish campaign was General Nureddin Pasha, a killer so ruthless that in January 1922 he was brought up by his own government on charges for "the mal-execution of his orders"—or so American diplomats were informed.[168] The Turks claimed that they were "eradicating rebellion," Greeks were massacring Turks, the Greek Black Sea fleet was periodically bombarding coastal towns, and Pontine Greeks had joined the Greek army.[169]

Western observers uniformly asserted that there was no Pontine "rebellion," either underway or in preparation.[170] The most anyone could say was that "it is probably true that Greeks in the Coast region were sympathetic with the Hellenic Greek Government. Possibly in the early days after the Armistice, some were even working towards union with the [Athens] government."[171]

But the Nationalists saw, or claimed they saw, things differently. The by-now pro-Turkish Arnold Toynbee, with mindless exaggeration, compared Greek atrocities to "the C.U.P.'s extermination of the Armenians." "The Greeks," he said, "are not different in kind from the Turks." The Turkish ethnic cleansing campaign was "partly a war measure, like and in essence not more barbarous than our own [i.e., Britain's] treatment of alien enemies, and partly a reprisal for the uprooting of the Moslem population in Europe as a result of the Balkan Wars."[172] The Turks maintained that the deportations were also an effort to force Greek brigands to give up their arms.[173]

Turks and their defenders have also sought cover by pointing to the arrival in the Black Sea in summer 1921 of a Greek naval squadron, which stopped Turkish ships, took passengers prisoner, and later lightly shelled Inebolu. This may indeed have hastened the deportation process, but it wasn't the cause of the campaign, which was launched weeks before.[174] As Count Schmeccia of the firm Lloyd Triestino in Samsun, and previously a representative of the Italian High Commission, said, the Inebolu bombardment, which produced no casualties, was merely a Turkish "excuse for the massacres."[175]

In any event, much other evidence points to Ankara's planning for that summer's destruction of the Greek communities. An Armenian report refers to a July 2 order from Ankara requiring deportation of all "adult male" Christians "throughout the interior of Anatolia," not merely in the Pontus.[176] Another report indicates that, two weeks later, Ankara ordered the "immediate deportation of all Ottoman Greeks," meaning women, children, and the elderly as well.[177] At the beginning of August, the mutessarif of Bafra told a visiting American naval officer that the deportation "of all remaining Greeks, including women and children, had been ordered by Angora." That order was apparently reinforced by another, from Nureddin Pasha, who instructed a local governor "to proceed with all dispatch to carry out the orders which had been given him or that he would shortly cease to be mutassarif." The American officer concluded that this was "part of an official plan which contemplates extermination of the Greeks."[178] There may not have been an "open and avowed policy of extermination," but there was evidence of a "popular policy" aiming at "Turkey for the Turks," as one missionary put it.[179]

Be that as it may, the largescale massacres and deportations began already in the spring, with the rural Greek communities. In the villages of the Black Sea's Düzce (Kurtsuyu) kaza, "many old men and women [were] burnt alive."[180] The Turks also attacked swaths of villages around Alaçam, Bafra, and Çarşamba and in the interior as far as Havza and Vizirköpru. The Turks took pains to make sure that there were no American witnesses. Missionaries were not allowed out of Samsun, the regional missionary center. But survivors reached the town and told their stories. American naval officers reported that the campaign was "under strict control of the military," "directed by high authority—probably Angora," and carried out, at least in part, by soldiers.[181] A purported eyewitness stated that villagers around Bafra were subjected to "incendiarism, shooting, slaying, hanging and outraging" and that the villages were "turned to heaps of ruins."[182] The American officers quoted an American missionary to the effect that about a hundred Greek villages south of Bafra had been destroyed. Villagers were being killed and "the priests . . . crucified."[183]

By summer, the campaign reached the towns. In Bafra, it kicked off with an ancient ploy, according to the Greek Patriarchate. Greek notables were invited to a dinner party at the house of one Efrem Aga, arrested, and murdered. The Turks then rounded up and massacred young Greek men.[184] On June 5 Bafra was surrounded by gendarmes, brigands, and Turkish troops—"a special corps . . . formed for the purpose of exterminating the Greek element"—who demanded that the men give themselves up.[185] Some hid. The Turks then searched the houses, pillaging and violating "the prettiest and best bred" women. The men were marched off in a succession of convoys. The first headed for the nearby village of Blezli. Seven Bafra priests were axed to death and the rest of the men killed thereafter. One, Nicolas Jordano-glon, gave the Turks 300 Turkish lira for the privilege of being shot rather than butchered with an axe or bayonet. Another 500 men, from a second convoy, were reportedly burnt alive in the church in Selamelik. And another 680 were murdered in a church at Kavdje-son.[186] Five convoys left Bafra that summer. At least two, according to the Greek representative to the League of Nations, were shot up by their escorts near Kavak Gorge, outside Samsun, killing at least 900. The survivors were sent naked, "like wandering spirits," to Malatya, Charnout, Mamuret, and Alpistan.[187] A western report claimed 1,300 Greeks were murdered in the gorge on August 15 or 16.[188] The government claimed those dead at Kavak had been killed justifiably in battle, after Greek bands allegedly attacked Turks.[189]

On August 8 the Turks collected the Bafran women and girls, "stripped and violated them and by torture compelled many to adopt Mohammed-anism." Those who refused conversion were led off "to different unknown places, where many died on the way . . . and the children were slaughtered."[190] The only Greeks allowed to stay were the sick people who paid bribes.[191] Some 6,000 Greek women and children were deported from Bafra around August 31 and a further 2,500 on September 19.[192]

A party of Americans encountered a column of 4,000 Bafran women and children, near Sivas. They had "little clothing, many were without shoes and apparently there was no food. Their faces were haggard. . . . There were about seventy old men in the party."[193] According to a Greek observer, "a small number of [Bafra] women offered to become Mohammedan in order to save their daughters and young sons but were refused. Some on the ground that they were beautiful and were to be reserved for public use and others because they were too ugly, poor, or old." Other women hid; "when they venture to come out into the streets they are seized. . . . If fine looking they are taken to harems, if not, are got rid of." Any Turk could enter Greek homes with the excuse of searching for men in hiding. But, in fact, they came to plunder, "even cutting off fingers and ears for jewelry."[194]

At nearby Çarşamba, the "good-looking women" were "rounded up at night with no clothes . . . and were being held for the pleasure of the troops under Osman Ağa." The other women were "marched off" into the interior.[195] According to a Greek observer, Osman gathered the women and children next to the Tersakan River and slaughtered them. "Eighteen brides and girls selected for their beauty . . . were distributed among the chiefs of the bandits who after indulging in their beastly lust for several days shut them up in a house in [the nearby town of] Kavza and burned them alive."

A Turkish notable told an American businessman that "what had happened made him ashamed to be a Turk."[196] There was apparently some local Muslim opposition to the Bafra deportations.[197] An American officer who regularly visited the Pontus ports wrote that he could understand the deportation of the adult males "as an inevitable consequence of the war." But "to treat poor women and helpless children . . . in such a cruel and inhumane manner is an . . . unpardonable sin against civilization."[198]

Elsewhere around Bafra, the deportations inland were regularly accompanied by mass murder. At Sürmeli, 300 were herded into houses "and burnt alive." By August all the men in the Ordu region had been exiled. Ten villages, including Bey Alan, "bought off" their harassers. But some of their men were later deported, and others fled to the hills.[199] An American naval report stated that, in the Bafra area, "as many as 90 percent of deported Greeks have been killed."[200] In February 1922 the Turks, directed by Fethi, swept Bafra's hinterland and captured those hiding in the mountains. The interior minister allegedly offered rewards to soldiers "who brought in heads. Five sacks full of heads were brought to him at Baffra; thousands of bodies . . . strewed the woods and plains of Pontus."[201]

Another focus of the campaign was Samsun, the heart of the Pontus. In early spring 1921 there were nightly murders in the streets, some witnessed by missionaries. Deportations began on May 28, when 200 Greek men were packed off, supposedly to Diyarbekir.[202] In early June Greek refugees in Samsun were told that they would soon be deported to the interior.[203] But there was local dissent. Seventy Turkish notables telegraphed Kemal, saying "it was against their religion to massacre" women and children. The dissenters recommended that the women and children actually be deported to Greece. Unusually, the dissenters were backed by the town mufti, who issued a fatwa against massacres of women and children. Kemal responded by pointing to atrocities committed by Greek against Turks and described exiling Samsun's Greeks as "a merciful act."[204] The dissenters then warned Nureddin Pasha that the deportations would trigger Greek naval bombardment. Nuredddin angrily accused them of treason. They complained to Ankara.[205] The authorities then threatened to charge the dissenters with "disloyalty." They backed down and promised not to "take further steps to oppose deportation of women and children."[206]

On June 16 police began to round up Samsun's Greek males aged 15–50.[207] On the 19th, American officers reported, about 2,000 were "marched into the interior."[208] Some were accompanied by their families.[209] By early summer all non-Ottoman Greeks of military age had been deported to Greece, "inciters" were under arrest, and Ottoman Greek males aged 18–32 had been mobilized in labor battalions. What remained were those who had paid to avoid military service, women, children, the elderly, and Greeks of "bad character." Young Greek women reportedly "provided themselves with poison, to commit suicide rather than be violated. . . . The price of sublimate and cyanide had gone up in all the drug stores."[210]

In mid-July 1921, the remaining Greeks in and around Samsun were informed that the women and children would also have to go, within three days. "Everywhere in the Greek quarter one hears women and children crying their lungs out. . . . They know that they were [sic] going to their death," a U.S. naval officer reported. "The police have directed that all valuables should be turned into the Greek church before leaving."[211] One missionary later recalled, "Our house was surrounded by these poor women, hammering at our doors . . . , holding out their children, begging us to take the children. . . . They threw their arms about our necks and we never felt so helpless."[212]

In December a missionary summed up his feelings about the authorities who sent the Greeks of Samsun to their deaths, "packed into a barn and burned alive, men, women and children." He claimed to know the men responsible. "The officers who carried out this diabolical massacre have been here again and again in my home drinking tea and telling me that all the stories about the Turks being cruel were lies," he explained. "And this at the time when they were plotting this new atrocity."[213]

The villages around Samsun were also cleansed of Greeks. One report described Turkish "excesses" as "savage beyond description. According to escaped refugees, am informed that villages from which men have been deported have been surrounded, fired into by troops and [set] afire, women and children caught escaping being forced back into flames. . . . Turks sneeringly tell Greek women to get help from Americans."[214] In two nearby towns, Sinop and Gerze, during September and October 1921, the Turks rounded up and deported "all the [stray] Christian children . . . between the ages of 9 and 12."[215]

The most notorious massacre in the Pontus that summer occurred in Merzifon, just south of the Black Sea coast. The town had a mixed population of Greeks, Armenians, and Turks, as well as an American missionary contingent, which returned after the suspension of their activities during WWI. The missionaries ran a hospital, and many worked at Anatolia College, which itself had a mixed population of students and faculty.[216] It is thanks in large part to the international missionary network that the slaughter at Merzifon became so well known.

The missionary presence may have contributed to the extreme violence in Merzifon, which lasted more than a week and resulted in deportations and more than a thousand deaths. The Great War had only increased Turkish animosity toward missionaries. The Turks knew that missionaries had witnessed and reported their wartime atrocities, and they may have sought payback. At the very least, the missionary J. Herbert Knapp thought so, alleging his brother George had been murdered in Harput in 1915 in retaliation for his testimony about atrocities against Christians.[217] Turkish newspapers whipped the people into a frenzy of hostility. As one put it in 1921, "These foreign institutions that have crawled like glittering snakes into the bosom of the fatherland are belching forth all sorts of poison in the name of education."[218] Another described "American colonies of crusaders . . . preparing a place for the culture of the microbes they aimed to produce under the mask of charity and humanity."[219]

Anti-missionary sentiment prevailed among the Merzifon Turks. A February 1921 incident was a case in point. That month a Muslim teacher at Anatolia College was murdered by an unknown assailant. The authorities searched the college and hospital for arms. None were found, but the Turks did come across literature they deemed "subversive," such as a letter from college President George E. White mentioning Kurdish tribes "reputed to have been converted from Christianity to Muslimism in the past."[220] On this basis the Turks arrested four teachers and two students, all involved in the college's Greek Literary Society. Two of the teachers and one of the students were later executed. The college and other missionary institutions were closed, and twenty-nine of the town's thirty-two missionaries expelled.[221] Even Bristol, despite his sympathies, felt the Turks in this case had been "over-zealous and unreasonable." White called the Turks "sedition-mad."[222]

It was against this background that the massacres began on July 23–24, when Osman Aga and his brigands rode into town. They spent four days pillaging and killing. Then came another four or five days at the hands of locals, assisted by gendarmes and troops. "The city was comparatively quiet" during the daytime, as Christians sheltered at home. But at night gangs broke into houses to steal, rape, and kill. The missionaries could hear "screaming and crying" from the houses. Hundreds of Greeks and Armenians fled to Anatolia College. Others sought safety in the city prison, a French school, and a site described in the record as a "large red house." Surprisingly, the refugees were treated well in the prison. But the red house was another story. Most of the Christians who had fled there were young girls; "all . . . were violated and many . . . were taken by the brigands when they left the city." Brigands also abducted "any desirable girls" from the French school, which was later torched. The men and boys they took out and shot. Although much of the killing was carried out by townspeople, the local Turkish officials said they were "powerless" to stop the massacre. The kaymakam reportedly took to his house and stayed indoors until the irregulars left town.

Altogether some 400 Armenian houses were burned down. Curiously, the Greek quarter was left untouched, perhaps evidence that the affair was organized and centrally directed. After the brigands left, the rape and killing continued in the army barracks, just outside town. Villagers and "Turkish neighbours" went on looting. "From our windows we saw streams of ox-carts and wagons bearing away loot of every conceivable description," Donald Hosford, a teacher at the college, recorded. Thieves ran off with "wood, cooking utensils, flour . . . doors and roof tiles." Wagon-loads of dead bodies were buried in pits. Some of those interred "were not entirely dead," according to one missionary. Turks moved into intact Christian houses.

Before the massacre, Merzifon was home to 2,000–2,500 Christians. "Almost all the men were killed," along with some women and children. Afterward, the remaining Greeks were deported. The women and children were transferred to the villages of Hadji Keuy (Hacıköy) and Gumush-Madin (Gümüş Maden), and the men marched off toward Amasya. Some 700 Armenians were left in the town, almost all women and children. The affair was enough to convince the American missionary Gertrude Anthony that "the plan of the Young Turk Committee in 1915 has not been abandoned by these Turks . . . now in power. . . . The Christians in Asiatic Turkey are doomed."[223]

The Nationalists initially denied the massacre. "It is not exact that the population of Merzifoun has been massacred and dispersed," Youssouf Kemal, the Nationalist minister of foreign affairs, announced. It was a "legend."[224] Later, after telling evidence had surfaced, the Nationalists switched tack and argued that "the troops simply got from under control." Alternatively, they also claimed that brigands were to blame—not the "army." Besides, if it had been the army, the offenders were soon sent into battle "and most . . . were killed."[225]

Soon afterward Osman and his brigands moved to the area of Tirebolu and Giresun, where, after killing many Greeks and deporting others, he took the most beautiful women for himself and his men.[226] He was subsequently welcomed with great fanfare in Ankara and placed in command of 6,000 men. According to an American missionary, his portrait appeared on a Nationalist postage stamp.[227]

The campaign spread quickly from the Black Sea coast to other areas of Anatolia under Nationalist control. In April 1921, after "incendiary speeches," a Turkish mob carried out a pogrom in Adalya, killing thirty Greeks and wounding 80 others.[228] In July 400 were deported.[229] In June it was reported that villages in the Bilecik area had been depopulated, with some villagers massacred. South of Izmit, thirty-seven villages were torched; 12,493 Greeks were reported dead and 2,551 missing.[230] In Eskişehir Greeks were hanged or shot and a portion of the population deported. Women and children "forced to disavow the Patriarchal authority were saved from deportation and massacre."[231] During March and April the Turks first deported notables from the Konya and Şile areas and then all men aged "from 10 to 80 and above" from Konya, Şile, Akşehir, Ilğin, Karaman, and Ereğli. It appears that only bank and railway employees were exempted.[232] Armenians, too, were deported from Konya and Afyon-Karahisar.[233]

Amid "scenes of confusion, panic and terror" the Christians of Izmit— 21,000 Greeks and 9,000 Armenians—escaped as the Turks advanced on the town at the end of June.[234] Thousands of farm animals, driven to Izmit by Greeks from surrounding villages, ended up dead on the shoreline: "exposed to the blazing sun and without food," they drank sea-water.[235] The townspeople feared massacre and fled, by sea, to Volo, Tekirdağ, Constantinople, and the Aegean islands.[236] In Bursa missionaries reportedly found eight hundred Greek and Armenian girls aged ten to sixteen who were raped and then "stamped by [the Turks] on the forehead with burning iron as a sign of their dishonor."[237]

While some Western observers viewed the Turkish campaign in Izmit as "retaliation" for Greek atrocities that spring in the Yalova-Izmit area, others, probably most, framed it differently: "The Turks are carrying out the extreme Moslem doctrine of the book or the sword" that is, conversion or death, "and are pursuing a definite policy of clearing their territories of all Christian populations."[238] It is possible that both views were to some degree correct, the Greek atrocities explaining the timing of the Turkish atrocities, while ideology provided a popular justification for the campaign.

As with the destruction of the Armenians during the Great War, the expulsion and murder of the Anatolian Greeks was in part driven by the enticing vision of plunder. The state, local officials, and the victims' Turkish neighbors all had much to gain. In the short term, Turks benefited from appropriated houses, lands, and household goods. In the long term, they replaced urban Greek and Armenian craftsmen, traders, and professionals. In some cases, local authorities even forged letters purporting to be from deportees asking their remaining relatives for funds.[239]

In addition to securing economic gain, the Turks had opportunities to carry out economic destruction, harming their enemies. The Greek villages of the Pontine coast traditionally produced "most of the higher grades of tobacco in Asia Minor." Their ruination did serious harm to U.S. tobacco firms. The Samsun deportations, in particular, deprived tobacco companies of their "expert sorters." The U.S. High Commission remonstrated with the authorities.[240] Bristol's aide, Lieutenant Dunn, told Youssouf Kemal that even if "the deportations were justified in principle as a military measure" the tobacco workers were not involved in any kind of revolutionary organizing. The foreign minister agreed to end deportation of the sorters, which he claimed was a mistake caused by local officials' exaggerated zeal, and to retrieve those already deported.[241] Dunn still considered Youssouf Kemal "spy and sedition mad."[242]

Youssouf Kemal also told Dunn that Ankara had not ordered deportations of women. Yet, in February 1922, when a journalist inquiring about deportations asked him, "What are the women and children guilty of?" he replied, "The military command . . . has . . . judged [it] necessary to deport them, so that they do not interfere with military operations." After all, he said, "There are many spies among the Christians, and this is the main cause of the deportations."[243] Youssouf Kemal might also have been worried about armed Greeks banding together in the mountains. A British observer put their number at 20,000–30,000.[244]

A British government analyst estimated that "well over 35,000 Greeks" were deported from the Pontus in 1921. The balance of the deportees had been "massacred . . . in circumstances of utmost barbarity."[245] Jackson thought the problem even worse: he reported in late March 1922 that American missionaries arriving in Aleppo from Harput said that "at least 75,000 Greeks" had been deported in the previous months from the Pontus, of whom only "20,000" had survived. The authorities had taken care to launch the deportations "in the face of blizzards," often "outraged" the women, and prevented food from reaching them.[246] Of the 720 majority-Greek villages in the Pontus, 420 had been "burnt or destroyed, the men killed or deported, and the women removed" and the other 300 partially destroyed, only the men deported.[247] Western and Japanese diplomats protested to no effect. In July Bristol thought that he had succeeded in getting the deportations suspended, but the facts demonstrate otherwise.[248] Rumbold recognized that protests "only provoke counter accusations" from the Turks in "an almost insolent tone."[249]

The campaign largely died down in the winter, as bad weather threatened escorting gendarmes.[250] But even then, the deportation and killing continued, as the Turks worked to clear out Pontic women and children who had escaped cleansings of 1921. A January 1922 case is illustrative. After the government had proclaimed an amnesty allowing women to return home, a group of about a thousand women who had taken refuge in the mountains made their way back to Samsun. They were "ill, in starving condition and mere living skeletons"; the "majority . . . were very badly wounded," some having lost arms or legs. Eight-to-ten died daily. Officials promised that they would be "free of molestation," but soon "the whole band was deported to the interior."[251] A British official suggested that the Turks had only allowed women and children a temporary reprieve in hopes that male brigands in the hills would "come out of hiding" to join them.[252] One woman actually spared was the mutesarrif of Samsun's alleged "Greek mistress."[253] Elsewhere, on February 15, 200–300 brigands headed by Osman rode into Ordu, a village largely emptied of men but left "with a lot of Turkish [sic: Greek?] women." According to a survivor, Osman and his raiders had come "to carry off the plunder." The brigands torched all except two houses, into which about 170 women and children, and a handful of men, were herded. The houses were then set alight. Fifteen or so young girls were taken aside and "subjected to the most horrible treatment that night, and all butchered the next day." However, it was rumored that five or six girls were in fact spared "for the harem of the Pasha." Nine neighboring villages received the same treatment.[254]

The deportations of 1921 were preceded and accompanied by what a British diplomat described as "wholesale executions" of Greek notables. Sometimes the Nationalists tried notables in kangaroo-court proceedings— so-called Independence Tribunals, against whose judgements there was no appeal. One report holds that about 250 Greeks were hanged in Amasya in

September 1921; another source puts the number at 168. Among them was the Metropolitan of Samsun, Platon. The Turks extracted his gold teeth.[255] In Ordu 190 "prominent Greeks" were reportedly hanged.[256] In Tokat, ten were executed.[257] Seventy-nine were condemned to death in Samsun, "hanged naked and in batches, all the condemned having to undergo the terrible ordeal of standing by and witnessing the executions until their own turn arrived." In one case, a father and son were reportedly given the option of deciding which of them would go first.[258] Seven priests from Alaçam, Bafra, and their environs were crucified in the marketplace of Gözköy, according to the Greek Patriarch in Constantinople.[259] Another priest was reportedly crucified in Topedjik. The Nationalists treated Christian clergy with particular brutality. Many were murdered; others were exiled or imprisoned, including a number of Greek and Armenian prelates.[260]

At times in 1921, the Kemalists exploited Muslim rebellions to persecute Christians. For example, when Kurds near Dersim attempted to resist Nationalist forces, the Turks accused Christian villagers in Kizik, Bazar-Selen, and Inönü of "connivance." The Nationalists imprisoned the Christian men and deported the women to Mamuret-ül-Aziz. Most of the men were subsequently killed.[261]

In early spring 1922 the Turks renewed the mass deportations with the aim of definitively solving the Greek problem as quickly as possible. As Rumbold put it in February, "Many people in Anatolia and at Constantinople considered that history had intended that the old Ottoman Empire composed of so many heterogeneous elements should disappear. Nationalists accepted this fact. A new Turkey had arisen which repudiated bad traditions of [the] former Ottoman Empire."[262] But the perpetrators did not want to be too blatant. They set in motion a variety of conflicting measures and issued contradictory statements about their intentions, leaving Western observers at least briefly confused about what was happening.[263] Sometimes Christians were ordered to stay put or return to towns or relocate within a given town. But mostly people were deported or massacred.

On April 10 or 11, a reported 1,324 Greeks, "mostly women and children . . . [with] a few old men," were deported from Samsun. Near East Relief took on twenty-seven orphans and attempted to provide aid to those departing, but some of the exiles "were said to be so weak they could not walk

A Greek refugee.

out to the truck for their bread. A few of the worst cases were sent out in carts."
The rest walked.[264] Another 1,462 Greek women and children, many of them
recently arrived from the mountains, were deported inland on April 15. "The
deportation was conducted in a quiet and orderly manner," according to a witness, but the wife of a Turkish officer later reported that Greeks had been

"marched into the hills near Kavak and murdered."[265] In Mamuret-ül-Aziz vilayet many Christians were forced to convert.[266]

By May Rumbold was reporting that fresh "outrages are starting in all parts of Asia Minor from northern sea ports to southeastern districts." Citing Mark Ward, the Near East Relief director in Harput, he explained that the Turks, were "accelerating their activities in this respect before [a] peace settlement" was reached with the Allies. "The Turks appear to be working on a deliberate plan to get rid of minorities." The Turks would collect Greeks from Samsun and Trabzon in Amasya and then march them "via Tokat and Sivas as far as Caesarea [Kayseri], and then back again until they are eventually sent through Harput to the east. In this manner a large number of deportees die on the road from hardships and exposure. The Turks can say that they did not actually kill these refugees, but a comparison may be instituted with the way in which the Turks formerly got rid of dogs at Constantinople by landing them on an island where they died of hunger and thirst." According to Rumbold, Turkish officials told Ward that "in 1915 Turks had not made a clean job of massacres . . . next time Turks would take care to do their work thoroughly."[267]

Trabzon and its hinterland were a focus of the new deportations. In 1921 the deportation plans had been suspended there because of protests by local notables.[268] At one point the Trabzon Turks had collected hundreds of Christian boys aged eleven to fourteen and imprisoned them "in a filthy dungeon underground" from which they were to be sent to an "internment camp" near Cevizlik. But prominent Cevizlik Turks came to Trabzon to protest against the "unparalleled inhumanity" at the camp. They were "beaten and sent away," but Trabzon's mayor was said to have done what he could to "protect little boys," and the vali also reportedly "opposed . . . massacres and persecutions." However, he ultimately was "powerless," according to Rumbold. "His predecessor tried" to halt the atrocities "and was removed."[269] By early May 1922, Rumbold wrote, "the whole Greek male population from the age of 15 upwards" was "being deported."[270] An American related that they were being deported in groups of fifty every few days. "This will continue until the entire Greek male population" is gone, he was told by a party unnamed in the available documentation.[271]

With the men gone, the women who remained were forced, at least for a time, to become breadwinners. But there were no fields to work: either they had been confiscated or were too dangerous to venture to. So they and their children begged in the streets or worked as hamals (porters) and "perform[ed] other duties" typically carried out by men.[272] There was constant sexual predation. The missionary Ethel Thompson noticed that girls "disfigured their faces with dye to hide their good looks." The Turks "boasted openly of the number of women they had taken."[273]

Dr. Herbert Adams Gibbons, who taught at Robert College and reported for the *Christian Science Monitor,* left a striking description of Trabzon in May. Almost all the Armenians were gone, he said. In 1919 the Turks began to "slowly—*yavaş yavaş*"—deal with the Greeks. After the men were deported, Trabzon was left, in spring 1922, with "half a dozen priests and ten other men and boys"; there was "not one doctor . . . [or] teacher." It was left to women to "eke out a living . . . digging ditches, acting as masons' helpers, and . . . [as] longshoremen in the port." Gibbons also found that "a few shops are run by Greek women."

At this stage the Turks were "going after the little boys":

It used to be conscription that was invoked as an excuse to take the men. When they got down to deporting the boys from 15 to 18, the Turks said that it was to give them preliminary training. Now—as I write—they . . . are seizing the boys from 11 to 14. The poor little kiddies are gathered together like cattle, and driven through the streets to the Government House, where they are put in a filthy dungeon. . . . If precedent is followed, these children will follow their elders to a barbed wire enclosure in the vicinity of Cevizlik . . . where they will regrettably die of an epidemic. . . . No food is given [there].

Gibbons added that there were a great many "good Turks." These include Trabzon Mayor Hussein Effendi, and the vali, Ebou Beker Hakim Bey, both of who opposed the persecution. "The Anatolian Turk is a fine fellow, who, unless incited to it by an appeal to his fanaticism, wouldn't hurt a fly. But the great mass of Turks are unfortunately ignorant and indolent—and they can be . . . —despite their instinctive kindliness and tolerance—worked upon to do the most terrible things" when the "mob spirit is aroused."[274]

It was just such a spirit that befell the Trabzon vilayet village of Cevizlik. On its outskirts, two women witnessed seventeen men beheaded. Thereafter, they related to Near East Relief, "The soldiers ran a bayonet through from one ear to the other, a long stick was placed through each head, and then the soldiers paraded before the officers with these heads. . . . These two women also saw four girls from fifteen to eighteen years of age taken by officers for immoral purposes" and then "put to death." In addition there were "three children, nine, ten and twelve years of age killed before the[ir] eyes."[275]

By June 1922 American missionaries were reporting from the Pontus that all the villages were empty.[276]

Convoys

As bad as the situation became in the towns and villages of the Pontus, sources indicate that most loss of life occurred on the road. As one missionary put it, the Turks sought the same outcome for the Greeks as they had the Armenians during the world war, but the Turks were "trusting to starvation and exposure to do the work of the sword."[277]

An estimated 70,000 Pontus deportees passed through Sivas, the women and children "hungry, cold, sick, almost naked, vermin-covered." According to Theda Phelps, a missionary who witnessed the convoys, about 1,000–2,000 Christians arrived each week in such a state that "they little resembled human beings." The authorities allowed Near East Relief to open temporary shelters for those suffering from "typhus, small-pox, dysentery, pneumonia and influenza"—before the survivors were launched back onto the roads. Phelps described one such shelter, an Armenian church. It was "black as any hole in Calcutta could have been. . . . Sick, dying and dead all in one mass, huddled together under a very few unspeakably filthy quilts." Phelps spoke with a woman from Bafra, who told her that she had forced her two children to walk the snow-covered mountain paths because she saw that "the children who were being carried were all freezing to death." For Phelps and some other missionaries, this degree of misery was quite a shock. A British diplomat said that missionaries who had initially "appreciated the Turkish case" wound up "horrified." "Miss Phelps, indeed, admitted that she had left Angora" in autumn 1921 "with a firm belief . . . that Mustapha Kemal's Government would bring about a regeneration of Turkey. On arriving in Sivas she was rapidly disillusioned."[278]

Another missionary, who travelled in August 1921 from Samsun to Sivas, described what she saw along the way: "We crossed Anatolia under a blazing sun, passing groups" from the "Black Sea ports . . . driven by Turkish gendarmes. The dead bodies of those who had dropped during the hard tramp were lying by the roadside. Vultures had eaten parts of the flesh so that in most cases merely skeletons remained." By early September she was in Harput, where she encountered "a city full of starving, sick, wretched human wrecks." "These people were trying to make soup of grass and considered themselves fortunate when they could secure a sheep's ear to aid it . . . the only part of the animal [traditionally] thrown away in Anatolia. . . . I shall never forget the look of a black hairy sheep's ear floating in boiling water . . . and these poor wretches trying to obtain nourishment by eating it. The Turks had given them no food on the 500 mile trip from Samsun." The survivors were those who had enough money to bribe guards for food. "Those without money died by the wayside. In many places, thirsty in the blistering sun and heat, they were not allowed water unless they could pay for it."[279] Another observer in Harput, probably the missionary Dr. Ruth Parmelee, said that arriving women and children were "practically naked, sometimes in snow up to the knees, with just some sacking as covering." They had been deported "in a blizzard"; on the roads, "a carriage has sometimes to zigzag to avoid passing over" the corpses.[280]

Bessie Bannerman Murdoch and J. Herbert Knapp, two missionaries stationed in Arapgir, witnessed the regular passage of Convoys in 1921. Each consisted of several hundred deportees, hailing from Konya and Ordu. Most of the marchers were Greeks, though often the convoys contained Armenians as well. Usually the group was exclusively military-aged men or else women, children, and old people. All were escorted by gendarmes. The missionaries recalled "one large drove" of about 1,000 deportees in late fall, 1921, "herded on a hill above [Arapgir] within 200 yards of a running ditch of water. They were not allowed to get water from this ditch and were compelled to buy their water from vendors. . . . A few days afterwards they were started on their way towards Harput . . . middle-aged and old women and men [and] . . . younger women and children, carrying on their backs large loads of bedding, food and fagots, and in their hands pots and kettles and perched upon their load a child . . . the roads were left strewn with their dead bodies the next day. . . . Many of the women were unable to carry their children along and they were obliged to leave them by the roadside, and we took in our orphanage about 20 of these." Several of them died. There was "one instance of a woman who came to us with three children, asking us to take care of one of them . . . whom she was willing to leave behind. She selected the oldest one, a boy of about eleven, but in parting with him she finally decided she couldn't be separated and took him along. . . . We were convinced . . . [that the Turks'] intention was to subject them to such exposure that they would perish."[281]

But starvation and exposure did not entirely replace the sword. As we have seen, there were the massacres in and around Kavak Gorge. Elsewhere, a deportee attached to the third convoy from Samsun wrote that "660 were killed" by gendarmes as the column was descending a mountain. He survived by feigning death. The "guards came up and stripped us of all our clothes leaving us our shirts and pants only which were soaked with . . . blood." Those who remained, "left without food or water and almost naked," were pushed on to Sivas and Kangal. He himself escaped to the mountains.[282]

Cosmos Lilidas, a nineteen-year-old relief worker, related another tale of unlikely escape. His convoy, probably the second from Samsun, left town around June 20. One day "the guards suddenly opened fire" while the convoy stopped for lunch near Djinbush. The assailants "then went about with knives and bayonets making sure that those . . . shot were dead." Lilidas rolled over in a ditch to play dead, but the Turks "stabbed [him] in the arm and back." The convoy then resumed its march southward, "292 remaining out of the thousand." Lilidas survived his wounds and eventually reached Sivas.[283]

During 1919–1923, as during 1915, the Turks often resorted to deceit. Two witnesses related that in August 1921 the authorities in Trabzon ordered all adult Greek men to present themselves for paid labor on fortifications. Five hundred or more complied; they were immediately imprisoned and their homes pillaged. The men were then deported to the interior in groups of fifty and forced to march for seven days "without as much as a morsel of bread." One night they were taken away in groups of ten and shot.[284]

Muslim civilians occasionally participated in the killings. A Greek witness described the death by stoning of a deported priest who had fallen down from exhaustion: "The soldiers dragged him to the side" of the road "and began to beat him with their rifle butts. . . . Turkish children . . . ran down to the scene. The soldiers withdrew . . . and the children began at once to stone the body which was in its death throes. For some time we could hear the dull thud of the stones as they began to accumulate atop the priest."[285]

Convoy guards made up rules and practices in an ad hoc manner. Generally, the Turks provided convoys neither food nor water, though occasionally deportees were allowed to purchase both. NER workers were often forbidden to supply food, clothing, and water, but occasionally there would be no such prohibition.[286] Sometimes Turkish officials allowed columns to rest in towns. Families were allowed to leave convoys and stay indefinitely in some places—usually for a fee. In most locations, officials quickly drove deportees back onto the roads. Here and there NER orphanages were allowed to take in deportees; elsewhere, this was forbidden. At one point NER in Harput was given an old German missionary building and allowed to take in a number of Greek children. "But in a very few days the building was empty," American Missionary Ethel Thompson reported. "The Turks had driven the children over the mountain."[287]

Ill-treatment of children was common. On February 5, 1922, Thompson ventured out on horseback to visit an outlying Christian orphanage. Five minutes outside of Mezre, she reached a watershed where some "300 small children who had been driven together in a circle" were being "cruelly" beaten by twenty gendarmes wielding heavy swords. When a mother rushed in to save a child, she was also beaten. "The children were cowering down or holding up little arms to ward off the blows," Thompson reported. "We did not linger." She pointed out that the missionaries appealed to be allowed to take in Greek children whose mothers had died, but the missionaries were almost "always refused."[288]

The most detailed and comprehensive description of the convoys during August 1921–February 1922 comes from two NER missionaries stationed in the Harput area, Major F. D. Yowell and Dr. Mark Ward. After they were expelled by the Turkish authorities in March 1922, they presented their findings to Jackson and Bristol. The British High Commission in Constantinople described the two missionaries' reports as highlighting "the deliberate attempt of the Angora Government to exterminate the Greek population of Anatolia."[289]

Yowell and Ward described, among other things, the severe restrictions the authorities imposed on NER operations.[290] Before the Kemalists took over, the Harput authorities had been "friendly" and had assisted NER. But "since the Nationalists have been in control . . . the local politicians who took part in the deportations and massacres of Armenians in 1915 and 1916 have gradually returned to power," Ward wrote.[291] He noted that many of the better-educated Muslims, including Muslim clerics, opposed the government's treatment of NER.[292]

In May 1922 Yowell and Ward published some of their findings in the *New York Times* and the *Times* of London, causing the Turks and the American High Commission much embarrassment, in addition to some awkwardness for NER itself. They first obtained NER permission to "release . . . such news material as may possibly awaken the conscience of the American people." Yowell was "speaking merely as an American citizen," Harold Jaquith, head of NER in Turkey, noted, and not on behalf of the organization.[293]

Yowell and Ward reported that, of 30,000 Greek deportees who had passed through Sivas in early summer 1921, 5,000 had died before reaching Harput and another 5,000 had escaped the convoys. Of the 20,000 who reached Harput, 2,000 died there and 3,000 were scattered around the vilayet. The remaining 15,000 trudged on to Diyarbekir. Of these, 3,000 died on the way, 1,000 died in Diyarbekir, 2,000 remained in Diyarbekir, and the remaining 9,000 were sent toward Bitlis. What had happened to them was unknown. But "the deportees all know that they were being sent there to die. The Turkish officials all know it," the missionaries reported. "The Turkish authorities were frank in their statements that it was the intention to have all the Greeks die and all of their action—their failure to supply any food or clothing—their strong opposition to relief by the N.E.R.—their choice of routs [*sic*], weather, etc.—concentrations in unhealthful places, and last of all their deliberate choice of destination, Bitlis, a place almost totally destroyed, with no industry and located far up in the mountains, seem to fully bear this statement out."[294]

The core of the report constituted extracts from Ward's diary, which detailed the convoys passing through Harput—their composition, origin, destination, and, occasionally, fate. Initially, during May–June 1921, the convoys were mostly Armenian, from the Konya area. By July, they were predominantly Greek, from the Pontus. On June 3, Ward recorded, a convoy of 125 Greeks and 187 Armenians, from Eskişehir and Kütahya, reached town. "They have been eating grass, having no money to buy bread as they were robbed on the way." On June 20 a small convoy of twenty, from Konya, reached Ward's hospital to be deloused. The group included businessmen, an engineer, and "the well-known Professor Haigazian, president of the American College in Konia," who was ill. Ward wanted to admit him, but the Turks sent him to a quarantine camp. Most of the party was sent away on the 28th, but Haigazian was permitted to remain in exchange for a fee paid in gold. "The following day we got him to our hospital," Ward wrote. But "by that time the rash of typhus had appeared. . . . He died on the 7th of July. We were permitted to bury him." On November 10, 1,700 Christians passed through; "they were 2,000 when they left Diarbekir." On December 31, 300 arrived from Konya. "They left January first for Bitlis but at the foot of the mountain it is reported they were robbed and afterwards many died on the mountain roads from exposure." In all, Ward recorded 20,526 deportees passing through Mezre-Harput between May 1921 and February 1922, about 18,000 of them Greeks and 2,000 Armenians.[295]

Ward and Yowell noted that sexual predation against women in the convoys was frequent. "All along the route . . . Moslems visit the various groups and take of the women and girls whomsoever they want for immoral purposes," they wrote.[296] A Greek observer reported that "many parents killed their sons and daughters, unable to see them violated by the Turks."[297] One NER missionary described three teenage girls she found in a cave outside Sivas: two had been clubbed to death, perhaps after being raped.[298]

The Grand National Assembly in Ankara condemned the Ward-Yowell allegations at a secret session on May 18, 1922. Interior Minister Fethi claimed, "No Christians, Greek or Armenian, had been illegally punished." If some had been deported "provisionally from the sea coast, it was solely in the interests of safeguarding [Turkish] independence." He "received an ovation from the deputies."[299] Kemal himself denounced the "lying Yowell" and his "calumnious statement" that "Turkey is unjust to Christians."[300] The Nationalists went so far as to forge and publish a letter in which Jaquith—they misspelt his name "Jacquith"—supposedly avowed that Turkey's Christians "pass their lives in perfect peace and tranquility. They maintain the best of relations with their Moslem neighbors."[301]

The Turks dismissed Ward and Yowell as "pro-Greek" and spoke instead of Greek persecution of Muslims.[302] Rumbold dismissed the Turkish charges as "designed to divert attention from Turkish atrocities."[303] The Turks were especially stung by accusations that they had abused women. Shortly after the session on Ward and Yowell's report, Ankara declared, "The accusation that Christian women and girls have been used for immoral purposes by the Turks is entirely false."[304]

Bristol joined the Turks in decrying the missionaries' report. He told Ward that he regarded the publication as a British government "intrigue" that, "if successful, would greatly strengthen the English position in the Near East, injure the prestige of American interests considerably, place the Turkish Nationalists very much on the defensive and give the English . . . an excuse . . . to stop the present negotiations for peace and even to back the Greeks in their war on Turkey. The total result would be the resumption of hostilities in Turkey with more people killed, more of Anatolia devastated, more refugees and more misery."[305] Bristol acted to discredit the Ward-Yowell reports.[306] American missionaries came to dislike Bristol intensely but were careful not to show it, given his influence. Hosford no doubt was correct in claiming to "represent the opinion of the large majority of Americans in Anatolia when I say that he is . . . grossly unfair to the minority peoples in Asia Minor." He called for Bristol's replacement.[307] On the British side, the reports triggered demands for an international commission of inquiry. But Bristol vetoed the idea, and the French pressed instead for an investigation of Greek massacres of Turks.[308]

The Turks devoted considerable energy to covering up their atrocities. Jaquith, who spent seven weeks traveling around eastern Anatolia in summer 1922, wrote that the Yowell-Ward reports gave only "a portion of the truth; they described only facts either witnessed or definitely ascertained. There had been no eyewitnesses of what had occurred in out-of-the-way places." Jaquith himself had "noticed along the sides of the roads thousands of shallow mounds round many of which lay skulls and bones uncovered by the wandering pariah dogs. This evidence the Turks had not had the patience or the time to conceal." But in other ways, "pains had been taken . . . to remove anything in the way of evidence." For example, deportees were removed from towns he was about to visit.[309] An American missionary, Jeannie Jillson, told visiting American naval officers about one attempted cover-up. The story began with a handful of Armenian men and women deported from Bursa to Mudanya. The Turks executed the men. An American identified as "Captain Coocher" photographed the bodies. The Turks then attempted to confiscate the photos. A man carrying Coocher's mailbag was then arrested in Mudanya but managed to escape and return the mailbag to Coocher.[310]

In 1922 the Turks began to evict "all orphans over the age of fifteen" from the missionary orphanages. This meant that young girls were "thrown into the streets and either face[d] starvation, or a return to their former position of slaves to Turks. . . . Many of the boys would[,] . . . to get a living[,] have to work for Turks and eventually become Moslems," a missionary wrote.[311]

The Turks also brutally mistreated the Greek soldiers they took as prisoners of war. The facts of the situation emerged mainly after PoWs were exchanged in 1923 once the Greco-Turkish hostilities concluded. An international commission—consisting of Swedish, Swiss, British, French, Italian, and Greek officers—questioned soldiers returned from captivity. Their depositions were more or less identical. Turkish troops often murdered surrendering Greeks, peasants attacked and often robbed them of clothing, and guards murdered stragglers. Sometimes the prisoners' genitals were cut off and stuffed in their mouths. Officers were often taken aside and executed, as were prisoners with Anatolian or Thracian accents, whom the Turks regarded as traitors. PoWs were routinely subjected to hard labor; "our guards whipped us with zest," one testified. All were ill-fed, and many died of disease. Bodies were not buried but instead thrown into ditches. Turkish troops often extracted gold fillings and sometimes killed prisoners in the process.[312] One Greek officer later wrote that Turkish civilians "bought" Greek PoWs for five or fifty piastres, "according to rank," and then threw them off cliffs and shot at them as they fell. The officer complained that, in the West, there was a "conspiracy of silence" about Turkish "barbarity."[313]

According to the international commission, some 54,000 Greek soldiers went missing during the war. Of these, 20,000 were massacred by Turkish mobs on the way to prison camps. Of the 32,000 that the Turks admitted taking prisoner, more than half died in captivity. Of more than 2,000 officers captured, only 750 were alive in summer 1923.[314]

The Destruction of Smyrna

Smyrna was burned to the ground by Muslim conquerors in 1084 and 1130, and in 1402 Tamerlane razed it once more. He slaughtered many of its Christian inhabitants, in line with the Prophet Mohammed's instruction, "When you encounter a nonbeliever, strike his neck."[315] It would burn again in 1922, immediately after the Nationalists retook the city from the Greek army.

In the aftermath of World War I, and for decades preceding, Smyrna was the largest city in western Anatolia and Turkey's main commercial center on the Aegean. According to the general manager's office of the Ottoman Railway, in early 1921 Smyrna had a population of 411,000, dominated by Greeks (205,000) and Turks (161,000). There were also 15,000 Armenians and 30,000 Jews, not to mention thousands of expatriate Italians, British, French, and Americans.[316] It was a city known for its cosmopolitanism and had not been a site of significant anti-Armenian violence during the war.

Yet ethnic tension was hardly unknown in Smyrna, and, following the signing of the 1918 armistice, the Greek and Turkish communities were on edge. Both were arming, and violent incidents between Muslim muhacirs and returning Greeks were becoming routine. In December 1918 Muslims responded to a Greek demonstration in nearby Sokia (Söke) by murdering twelve Greeks. In Pirgi (Chios) Turks murdered the Greek mudir.[317] The following February or early March, there was a series of clashes near Sokia after Turks humiliated a Greek-refugee couple. "They were stripped and paraded through the village [of Yerenda], the woman riding a horse and the man tied to its tail."[318]

The Turks learned of the Greek landing the day before it happened. Gough-Calthorpe informed Aydın's vali, Rahmi Bey, that the Greeks would be occupying the area on the basis of Article 7 of the armistice agreement. The aim was to secure law and order, but Lloyd George also hoped to preempt a threatened Italian occupation of the city, pursuant to the Anglo-French promise embodied in the 1917 Saint Jean de Maurienne Agreement.[319] On May 15, 1919, The Greek flotilla was escorted into Smyrna by Allied warships, which also sent ashore small contingents to guard their consulates.[320] The local Turkish commander, General Ali Hadir Pasha, ordered his troops not to resist. They complied, remaining in barracks, as three regiments of Greek troops occupied the city and its environs.

Local Christians cheered the invaders, while Turks looked on glumly. Bristol called the occupation "a great crime," but it enjoyed the overwhelming support of the vilayet's Greeks, who had been actively persecuted since 1914.[321] The Turks, for their part, feared Greek revenge. Horton feared they were unwilling to accept their "former slaves" as masters.[322] The two groups "loathe each other," he said.[323] With the occupation of Smyrna, in Churchill's later description, Greece had "gained the Empire of her dreams," but it was to end in tragedy.[324]

After the orderly Greek disembarkation, a shot or two rang out; who fired is unclear. The Greek troops, accompanied by local irregulars, occupied the konak and fired on the barracks. The Turks surrendered. Smyrna's officials, including the vali, were removed from their offices, robbed, and detained after suffering jeers and beatings from the crowds. About thirty were murdered.[325] Disarmed troops and officials were then marched to the quay and put on a steamer, where they were held, with little food or water, for two to three days before being released. The takeover was accompanied by the pillage of Turkish shops and houses. Turkish officers were de-fezzed and beaten and some Turkish shopkeepers and bystanders were killed. The vali later claimed that some women were raped.[326] One local recalled that he saw about a dozen Turks killed "or kicked into the sea and shot."[327] Toynbee conjectured that at least 200 Turks had been murdered, most or all by Greek civilians.[328]

The Greek army eventually restored calm on orders from Gough-Calthorpe.[329] "Orders were given that all stolen property . . . be returned . . . or those found in possession . . . would be shot."[330] By mid-August the Greeks had tried and convicted seventy-four people for crimes in Smyrna on May 15–16: forty-eight Greeks, thirteen Turks, twelve Armenians, and a Jew. Three, all Greeks, were condemned to death.[331] Local Greeks were unhappy with these measures. In the weeks after the crackdown, Greek villagers raided their Turkish neighbors in the Smyrna countryside, stole cattle, and, here and there, committed murder.[332]

Some Anatolian Greeks volunteered as irregulars, joining the invading Greek army.

Meanwhile, Greek forces were pushing inland. At Nazili, occupied on June 3, Greek troops exposed "certain parts of their body to the Turkish women." According to the Turkish authorities, a Turk who complained was shot. The Turks further charged that the Greeks systematically searched for arms, stole belongings, and killed householders. Near Nazili the Greeks reportedly killed forty Turkish hostages. Villages in the area suffered greatly as they changed hands between warring parties. Over the summer Nazili experienced heavy shelling. According to the Turks, 200 Muslim girls were raped and then murdered there, while other villages were torched.[333]

The Turks also accused the Greek army of levelling Aydın town and massacring civilians there. But the story was more complicated. When Turkish irregulars retook the town in July, armed locals joined in, firing from rooftops and windows at the retreating Greeks. In retaliation, they set fire to the Turkish quarter. The Turks then torched the Greek quarter and massacred the remaining inhabitants. Even Toynbee refused to sugarcoat what the Turks did to Greek noncombatants: "Women and children were hunted like rats from house to house, and civilians . . . were slaughtered in batches—shot or knifed or hurled over a cliff. . . . Many of the women . . . were violated."[334] The retreating Greek units refused to allow Greek locals to leave with them; they were subsequently deported to the interior by the Turks. The Turks took thousands of Greeks hostage in Denizli and Nazili, threatening them with massacre if more Muslims were killed.[335]

Nonetheless Constantinople complained to the Allies, submitting a detailed summary of Turkish casualties for investigation. According to the complaint, in "the City of Smyrna and the Surrounding Districts," 675 Muslims were massacred and 34 were "lost," while 13 girls were "violated." In Menemen kaza 929 Muslims were massacred. In Manisa kaza forty-three Muslims were killed and eleven girls violated. In Aydın kaza "a few thousand were massacred, a few thousand wounded and the rest lashed." More vaguely, the Turks spoke of "several thousands" more massacred on "various roads . . . or thrown [in]to the sea."[336]

The Allies established a commission of inquiry chaired by Bristol, which also included three generals, British, French and Italian. They spent August–October 1919 questioning Allied officers, Turks, and Greeks. Overall, the commission endorsed the Turkish version of events but also found fault with the Turks. "The Greek command tolerated the actions of the armed Greek civilians [in Smyrna] who, on the pretext of helping the Greek troops, freely pillaged and committed all sorts of excesses," according to the report. But the report also charged the Turks with massacring "some Greek families" in Nazili. The commissions accused the Greeks of "numerous outrages and crimes" during the evacuation of Aydın, where the Turks, led by one Yuruk Ali, were charged with torching the Greek quarter. They "pitilessly shot down a great number of Greeks." The commission affirmed the Turkish charge of a Greek massacre in Menemen but said that it wasn't organized by the Greek command and was a result of panic. A separate French investigation concluded that 200 Turks had been murdered there.[337] The commission made no mention of some 3,000 Aydın Greeks—men, women, and children—allegedly murdered, nor of 800 women and children deported inland. "Now Aidin is a vast cemetery," the Greek Patriarchate lamented.[338]

The commission concluded that responsibility for the Greek atrocities lay chiefly with the Greek army. The Turks were held partially responsible for what happened in Smyrna city because the local authorities had failed to prevent criminals escaping from prison and taking up arms before the Greek army arrived. Importantly, the Greek army had advanced beyond the sanjak of Smyrna, to Aydın, Manisa, and Kasaba, outside the remit of the Allied authorization. The Greek invasion, mounted ostensibly to maintain order, turned into a "conquest and crusade," the report said. The commission ruled that the annexation by Greece of the areas occupied would be "contrary to the principle proclaiming the respect for nationalities" and proposed that the Greek army be replaced by Allied troops.[339]

Although the report blamed mutual "religious hatred" for persecution on both sides, it was hardly impartial. Bristol had already reached his conclusion months before the investigation. In May 1919 he wrote that the Greeks' behavior was "disgraceful," that "they murdered Turks . . . [and] forced" captured Turkish troops "to sing out 'Long live Venizelos' in the Greek language. They killed some of these soldiers [and] . . . killed people and looted houses and shops in the surrounding villages."[340] The report was never published, but it certainly affected Allied officials' attitudes during the following months.

During the next three years the Greek zone of occupation was relatively tranquil. Indeed, Horton thought that Smyrna—under newly appointed Greek high commissioner Aristeidis Stergiadis, a highly efficient, principled, but temperamental administrator—was "better governed than I have ever seen it, probably better than ever in its history. . . . Stergiadis and his aides are making a great and honest effort to see justice done to Turks . . . and the conduct of Greek gendarmes . . . throughout the occupied region is worthy to [*sic*] all praise."[341]

The Greek administrators did their best to maintain law, order, and justice. They shunned a policy of expulsion, as might have been expected from a vengeful occupier. Indeed, many local Greeks pressed for expulsions, but the authorities held firm. The new administration did, however, resettle in the area about 100,000 Greek refugees ejected from Asia Minor during or before the war.[342] This entailed the eviction of many Muslims squatting in Greek homes and lands. There was a good deal of violence as well. Roving Turkish brigand bands and rebellious villagers persistently attacked Greek villagers, gendarmes, and troops behind the lines while the Turkish and Greek armies faced off to the east. This often led to Greek reprisals, sometimes culminating in small massacres and torching of Turkish villages.[343]

The three years of Greek rule ended with the Turkish reconquest of Smyrna in September 1922. The restoration of Turkish control brought massacre and mass deportation, the destruction of much of the city, and the complete exodus of the remaining Christians of Anatolia. Western residents, diplomats, naval officers, and missionaries witnessed much of what happened in Smyrna and recorded in diaries, letters, and memoranda what they had seen or been told by others.

The crisis began with the defeat of the Greek army at Afyon Karahisar in the last week of August. The army broke and fled to the coast, funneling mainly into Smyrna, Ionia's largest port. On their way westward, Greek soldiers torched Turkish villages, leaving behind scorched earth. "Inhabitants who failed to escape were slaughtered," the British vice-consul reported.[344] In some places, it was reported, the Greeks "collected Moslems in mosques to which they subsequently set fire."[345]

The retreating army pulled in its wake a "helter-skelter rush of the bulk of the Christian population" from the hinterland.[346] Some left on orders from Greek officials. But most simply feared massacre. Chrysostomos, the Greek Orthodox bishop of Smyrna, had warmly welcomed the Greek landing back in May 1919 as fulfilling "the desire of centuries." But he now believed that "the Greeks will be delivered to . . . destruction. Hundreds of thousands . . . will perish."[347] Refugees began pouring into Smyrna on September 3. Within two days its streets were "filled with carts, wagons, vehicles of all kinds that could carry anything—all loaded with goods and fleeing families . . . trying to get to steamers. The quay . . . was packed with baggage and people."[348] They also arrived on trains, the carriages so crowded "that the dead bodies were passed out at stations on their way."[349]

The senior British officer in Smyrna, Admiral Osmond de Beauvoir Brock, described the Greek troops passing through on their way to the harbor as an "undisciplined rabble." But they behaved themselves, contrary to expectations. Perhaps, Brock suggested, they were too "weary, footsore and dispirited" to act out.[350] Greek administrators "neatly" packed up their records and belongings and left. Chrysostomos wrote Venizelos, "Hellenism in Asia Minor, the Greek state and the entire Greek nation are descending now to a hell."[351] In the following days, European and American nationals, chaperoned by contingents of their marines and officials, were ferried to their gunboats offshore.

Starting on September 6, the Greek army embarked on ships from Smyrna, Çeşme, and Vurla. On the evening of September 8 the last Greek warship steamed out of Smyrna. Stergiadis preferred to leave for exile in France aboard on HMS *Iron Duke*. He never set foot in Turkey or Greece again.[352]

Smyrna's Turks feared massacre, but the evacuation passed smoothly. There was no violence despite the authorities' apparently "indiscriminate" arming of the Christian population and despite Christian threats "openly shouted in all corners of the town."[353]

Turkish Occupation and Massacre

The advance guard of the Turkish army, the 1st Cavalry Division, entered Smyrna at eleven o'clock in the morning, September 9. They were on horseback at a light trot, swords drawn and four abreast. They encountered no opposition. "They were a hard, dusty, seasoned looking bunch of men," an American officer recorded. "Their uniforms were dirty but their equipment, rifles and sabres were clean."[354] They were "greeted by large throngs of all people on the quay, and resembled more a parade, rather than a victorious entrance to a conquered city."[355] Thousands of Greeks and Armenians fled to churches, schools, and consulates for safety, and hundreds congregated on barges moored in the harbor.[356] At the dockside "the cafes and stores were open and well patronized with calm looking people taking their morning coffee and reading the papers."[357] Two officers, a Greek and a Turk, rode down the quay together and tried to reassure the inhabitants.[358]

At one point a bomb, or bombs, were thrown at the cavalcade, apparently by Armenians. Several Turks were injured. One or two shots rang out.[359] U.S. Vice-Consul E. C. Hole remarked that the Turkish column was so disciplined that it didn't even retaliate. But in the inner streets and alleys, local Turks descended into what one observer called "hooliganism."[360] As many as 150 Armenians were murdered, and Turkish soldiers, who began to deploy around town, raped many Armenian women.[361] Turks fired at a Greek church, killing several Christians.[362] An American naval captain described what he saw that day:

> On my afternoon round the . . . killing was apparent. On nearly every street were lying bodies of men of all ages . . . most of whose wounds were from . . . close ranged shots . . . in the face or in the back. There were no uniformed Turks in these shooting parties. . . . The Armenian quarter being infested with Turks in civilian clothes with rifles and shotguns, . . . [the Turks would] halt a man, rifle his pockets while two held him and then . . . they fired. I saw three killings. . . . As day progressed the shooting became more frequent[,] likewise [the] dead.[363]

That night Turks began looting the Armenian quarter and "killing the inhabitants."[364] The Turkish commanders promised Western representatives they would restrain their people and on September 10 proclaimed that "anyone who killed a Christian would be executed." Some Turkish officers tried to maintain order.[365] But with the arrival that day of the 8th Infantry Division, robbery and looting by troops and locals multiplied. One missionary wrote that as the column of infantrymen passed her house in the suburb of Paradise (Cennet Çeşme), "we saw groups of five or six drop out of line, break into all the houses on the corner, come out laden with all they could carry and drop back into the marching column." The Turkish guards assigned to the missionary International College even "robbed our little old grocer."[366]

Lieutenant Commander H. E. Knauss of the U.S. Navy drove south to Paradise that day and recorded: "En route we passed many dead on streets. . . . The smaller shops were being looted. Invariably, the owner was lying dead. . . . An old woman about seventy years old was still kneeling but dead and later another old woman was lying dead in [a] ditch. . . . In an enclosure, several small Turkish boys were throwing stones at a man shot through the head and evidently not quite dead." Knauss later toured the Armenian quarter "and found many new bodies along streets that were not there on my morning inspection." Looting was widespread, "by irregulars, regular civilians and brigands. There were no Turkish officers seen." He witnessed "four people killed in cold blood."[367]

In Smyrna's suburbs, "many Greek houses were in flames, and the corpses of men, and some women, also were frequently seen." In the harbor Turkish tugs pulled in the barges filled with fleeing Christians, and the men aged eighteen to forty-five were "taken off and marched in companies to the konak." Dr. Wilfred Post, an NER worker, wrote, "We saw a number of recently killed men strewn along the quay. We heard many shots in the direction of the konak, and were afterwards told that a considerable number of these unfortunate men had been executed."[368] According to one witness, the Turks set alight one of the barges killing hundreds.[369]

One of those murdered on September 10 was Bishop Chrysostomos. He had been summoned to the konak to meet the new military governor, 1st Army Commander Nureddin Pasha. The general reportedly spat on the bishop's outstretched hand and handed him over to a waiting mob, who cut off his beard, gouged out his eyes, and cut off his ears, nose, and hands before finishing him off.[370] His body was then dragged through the streets and hacked to pieces by "the infuriated rabble."[371] Nureddin, "a forceful, ambitious, xenophobic and cruel soldier," had during the world war been military commandant in Ionia, possibly responsible for the expulsion of Greeks from the coast.[372]

That same day, Mustafa Kemal arrived in Smyrna for a conference with Nureddin. That evening Turkish commanders discussed "the deportation of the Armenians."[373] Kemal may have attended and "authorized pillage," which that night went "from bad to worse."[374] The conclave's decisions were translated into action the following morning, September 11. Turkish soldiers cordoned off the Armenian quarter and began "a systematic hunt." Turkish troops moved from house to house, flushing out and robbing inhabitants and raping women. A large number of Christian men were shot, and women and children were then "herded together and marched away."[375] One Turkish witness recalled, "Almost every night the Greek men were being taken in groups past our doorstep, with their hands tied. . . . They were taken up to the mountains and shot."[376] In the evening the troops were ordered to use cold steel rather than live fire, apparently to avoid attention.[377]

According to one European, who left town on September 14 after Turks had murdered his mother and caused the suicide of his two sisters, hundreds of Armenians were murdered in St. Stephano Church, some of them burnt alive.[378] NER's William Peet wrote that he was told by an eyewitness that the Armenians "were hunted like rabbits."[379] Knauss described a rape-murder of a fifteen-year-old girl witnessed by one of his men: "The Turks had taken [her] from her father and mother into an alley. Her shrieks were plainly heard, then the Turks returned and one of them wiped a bloody knife on the mother's forearm, then led them down the street."[380] Armenians that day "were gathered together by groups of 100, marched to the konak . . . and put to death."[381] Other groups of Armenians and Greeks were "marched out of the city to face firing squads."[382] Horton reported that Americans had seen "nine cartloads of dead bodies" being taken away near the konak.[383] Horton was deeply affected. An Armenian witness described him as "the saddest man" in Smyrna.[384]

Post, of NER, and other leading Americans—Jaquith, vice-consul Maynard Barnes, Lieutenat A. S. Merrill, Major C. Claflin Davis of the American Red Cross, and Arthur Japy Hepburn, Bristol's naval chief of staff—met with Nureddin that afternoon. Echoing Bristol's thinking, Hepburn said "the best solution" was a return of the refugees to their homes with a guarantee of safety. Nureddin dismissed this as "out of the question."[385] Post later described the meeting as "far from satisfactory." The pasha was in a "fanatical and cynical mood" and said "that whatever the troops in Smyrna might do, was as nothing [compared] to what the Greeks had done in the interior." He "emphatically said that the Turks had no further use for the Christian population."[386] "Bring ships and take them out of the country. It is the only solution," Hepburn reported Nureddin as saying.[387] According to Davis, Nureddin had in mind not only the refugees in Smyrna but all the Christians of Anatolia. Davis cabled Bristol that evening: "Believe this is final decision [of the] Nationalist Government as solution of race problem."[388] The American officers, again reflecting Bristol's views, made clear that they cared about the safety of American nationals but were not interested in the fate of the Ottoman Christians. They pressed Western journalists to report that the Turks were behaving appropriately toward Smyrna's population.[389]

That day or the next, Kemal, at a meeting with Barnes and Lieutenant Commander Halsey Powell, the senior U.S. naval officer in situ, echoed Nureddin's position. "Each individual Turk and each individual Greek are now enemies," he said. "In the past it was the rule . . . that the Turk and the Greek lived together in peace and in friendship. But this has all been changed by the Greek occupation and by the irregularities committed during this occupation, and later during the evacuation of the Greek army. The situation now demands that the Greeks and the Armenians leave Anatolia."[390]

At his meeting with the Americans, Nureddin had assured them that he would issue a proclamation to restore order. The order was duly issued, but the looting and murder continued. Post recorded:

> Almost every street was blocked by a mass of debris from the looted houses . . . and there were numerous corpses. . . . Not one Armenian house in five had escaped. . . . On looking more closely at the houses I saw written in chalk, in Turkish characters, on a number of them . . . the words "Jewish house"—evidently a warning to the looters to respect non-Christian property, and a clear indication that the destruction had been carefully and systematically planned. Here and there young girls were being led away by the soldiers.

By the time of the meeting, the men had all been detained, and "multitudes of women and children had been driven out of the Christian quarters of the city." Some hid in cellars for fear of marauding bands. "The stench from dead bodies was everywhere . . . the filth in the schools, churches and other places where refugees were . . . huddle[d] together was indescribable."[391]

Thousands of refugees were concentrated in havens in the Armenian quarter and on the waterfront: consulates, schools, relief institutions, and the American Tobacco Company warehouse. But these quickly became overcrowded, forcing many to remain outside. Minnie Mills, an American missionary, observed men and women seeking entry into her building. Some, she said, were killed "under our windows."[392]

Already on September 10, the Turkish military had overrun the Greek Hospital, "taken the patients out, and laid them in the street, saying that they could look after themselves."[393] The looting, by civilians and soldiers, went on for days. Nureddin told complaining Westerners that "the troops were promised" a free hand.[394] One missionary later wrote, "I did not know then that a victorious army over here is allowed three days of looting."[395] Hepburn commented that "it was apparent to everybody that order could be restored within two hours if the authorities" so decided.[396]

On September 11 Turkish troops and brigands occupied Paradise. They looted houses and severely beat the Canadian president of International College, Alexander MacLachlan, who was robbed of his coat, trousers, shoes, watch, and gold ring. A Turkish officer saved him as he was about to be killed.[397] MacLachlan, incidentally, was among the many Westerners in Smyrna who in 1919 had protested in advance against the prospective Greek occupation.[398]

On September 12, 1922, the second day of the systematic massacre, the Turks behaved "more discreetly."[399] Or as Barnes put it, "bayonets and knives had largely supplanted the rifle and revolver." Again, the focus was on the Armenians. "The Greek, relatively speaking, remained unmolested," Barnes reported. Perhaps the Turks were influenced by the presence of Greek and Allied gunboats offshore, or maybe they worried that Allied intervention was still a possibility, if a remote one. The Armenians enjoyed sympathy but, unlike the Greeks, had no allies.

The killings continued for days, but on a reduced scale. Barnes witnessed a particularly cruel murder on the morning of September 14:

> I saw on the quay, circulating through the refugees in search of Armenians, five groups of Turkish civilians armed with clubs then already covered in blood. One of these groups fell upon an Armenian and clubbed him to death. The proceeding was brutal beyond belief. I do not believe there was a bone unbroken in the body when it was dragged to the edge of the quay and kicked into the sea. In this group were boys of no more than twelve or thirteen . . . each with his club, participating . . . as heartily as did the more mature individuals. One of the men . . . explained that the victim was an Armenian, and then he shrugged his shoulders.

Barnes was an evenhanded observer, in the sense that he did not perceive criminality only on the part of Turks. "During these days," he wrote, referring to September 9–13, "the Armenians continued to throw bombs and to snipe."[400] But no other eyewitnesses recalled this. E. M. Yantis, manager of the Gary Tobacco Company in Smyrna, claimed later that the behavior of

Turkish regulars was generally impeccable, responsibility for the killings lying with civilians and brigands.[401] The weight of eyewitness testimony is decidedly against him.

Among the "outstanding features of the Smyrna horror," Horton wrote, was "wholesale violation of women and girls." The charge is based on the findings of M. C. Elliott, an American physician who examined "hundreds" of girls during and after the massacre.[402] Charles Dobson, a New Zealand pastor, described gang rape by troops as "typical." On September 13 or 14, aboard the *Bavarian* in Smyrna Harbor, he met "a woman and her daughter, each of whom had been ravished by fifteen Turkish soldiers." On September 12 he had seen carts loaded with "bodies of women and babies and also of young girls who had patently been violated before being killed."[403]

Some analysts, such as Rendel, thought "the massacres . . . may be regarded to a large extent as retaliation for the widespread destruction caused by the Greek army in its disorderly retreat."[404] Mark Prentiss, an NER man and *New York Times* correspondent, implied the same when he telegrammed that after the fall of Smyrna he travelled through territory evacuated by the Greeks and found villages "sacked burned. Have interviewed many old men and boys beaten shot stabbed and girls outraged by Greek soldiers."[405] But while there is no doubt that Greeks committed crimes against Turks in the course of their occupation and withdrawal, the Turkish behavior in Smyrna cannot be considered merely retaliatory. Turks, after all, had been massacring, raping, and plundering Christians for decades.

The Fire

When a large fire broke out in Smyrna on September 13, few were surprised. In Turkey—as in many other places—scorched-earth tactics were a familiar component of armed conflict. During World War I, Turks often accused Armenians of "setting huge fires" in towns they were evacuating.[406] In August 1914, as the Turks were preparing to enter the war, they contemplated burning down Smyrna so that the British would be unable to take it. Vali Rahmi Bey told the London *Times*'s Erle Whittall that he "would destroy the town rather than let it fall into enemy hands." Burning Smyrna, Rahmi said, was "a most natural measure," and he "had all his plans ready." Such plans included removing the inhabitants to the interior. Moukhtar Bey, former Turkish minister in Athens, made a similar statement. At about the same time, Morgenthau learned of developing Turkish plans to destroy Beirut and Mersin. Talk of this sort caused panic, which was exactly the point. In October 1914, days before the Ottomans joined the fray, Talât informed Morgenthau that the threat to destroy Smyrna was intended above all to alarm the Greeks. Talât told the ambassador he wanted the Greeks to "leave the city . . . and [to] make it a Moslem instead of a Christian city." Some well-to-do Christians did indeed leave Smyrna in response to Rahmi's comments.[407]

The Greeks and Armenians also reportedly threatened to torch Smyrna if the Turks retook it.[408] An American missionary said "there had been a determined effort . . . by the Greeks to organize a band for the burning of Smyrna, should the Greek troops . . . leave." He also "heard several of the Greek officers make the statement that the Armenians would burn the city if the local Greeks [lacked] the courage."[409] After the Greek military collapse, Horton cabled, "When demoralized Greek army reaches Smyrna serious trouble more than possible and threats to burn the town are freely heard."[410] On September 8 Bristol told Max Aitken, the British press baron, that "there was a danger the city might be burned."[411] The retreating Greek army reportedly had already burned Aydın and Nazili.[412]

The first fires were set on the morning of the 13th. The Turks had entered the city four days earlier and were just then beginning to clear the streets of the dead. They piled up the bodies and burned them.[413] Around noon fires were spotted at "several points" in the Armenian Quarter.[414] The fires generated a mass "stampede" toward the dock, with thousands of Christians evacuating the cellars, churches, and Western institutional buildings they had holed up in. As of four o'clock in the afternoon "it was evident the city was doomed," Post wrote. The fires had coalesced and "a terrific wind" was carrying it toward the quay.[415]

By evening "the quay was . . . congested" with evacuees, and by midnight "the broad waterfront street appeared to be one solidly packed mass of humanity, domestic animals, vehicles and luggage." At this stage, "the appalling nature of the catastrophe began to make itself felt." Hepburn wrote that, "separated from the crowd by a few short unburned blocks, the city was a mass of flames driving directly down upon the waterfront before a stiff breeze.

Mingled with the noise of the wind and flames and the crash of falling buildings were the sounds of . . . rifle fire or the explosion of small-arms ammunition and bombs in the burning area. High above all other sounds was the continuous wail of terror from the multitude."[416] Arthur Maxwell, a British officer watching from the *Iron Duke,* later testified that he saw Turkish troops dousing refugees on the quay with "buckets of liquid" and then igniting them. Other Turks threw kerosene on a raft crowded with refugees.[417]

In some places Turkish troops prevented Christians from escaping the flames and reaching the waterfront.[418] But tens of thousands made it to the quay. There they were trapped. The routes north and south were blocked by Turkish positions and machine guns; those east by the conflagration and west by the sea. Some threw themselves into the water. Post watched the scene from an American destroyer, binoculars in hand:

> The volume of shrieks and wails [that] rose from a quarter of a million throats was heart-rending, and could be heard above the roar of the fire and the constant rattle of what sounded like machine guns. . . . It seemed as though the mass of people on the quay would certainly perish between the fire and the sea. But as though by a kindly act of providence, as the flames approached the water's edge a counter current of air seemed to carry them vertically upwards, so that comparatively few people were burned. . . . Suddenly we were horrified, as we looked through our glasses, to see groups of soldiers gathering embers together along the sea front . . . and pouring some kind of liquid on them, apparently kerosene, deliberately set fire to the unconsumed houses along the water front. I saw at least twenty such fires started all along the quay. It looked like a deliberate effort to burn the Christians, but as the soldiers could more easily have fired into the crowd, or forced them into the water, their action may perhaps have been instigated merely by the desire to leave nothing of the Christian and foreign quarters.[419]

The crowd dockside was "demented by fright. Some ran aimlessly about clutching their bundles despite the fact that these were alight; some fell or jumped into the water; the majority made no effort to escape, being literally petrified by terror. A few had escaped in small boats." Some reached the *Iron*

Duke, where "every effort [was] made to quiet the women, who were very hysterical; most of them had lost their husbands and children." Eventually, Brock and other American, Italian, and French naval commanders ordered small boats to shore to rescue the Christians.[420] As Davis tells it, an aide came up and said, "My God, Admiral, they are throwing kerosene over the women and children; we have got to send in the boats."[421]

By morning on September 14 the quayside stank like "a reeking sewer. It was the smell of burning buildings and burning flesh, feces and urine. The smell grew worse over the following days as the crowd, waiting for their salvation, relieved themselves on the quay or into the sea. The stench was accompanied by a continuous wailing and moaning. Sailors on the gunboats turned up the volume on their gramophones to drown out the noise. The gunboats raked the quayside with their searchlights, perhaps hoping to deter the Turkish troops from attacking the refugees.[422]

"Many thousands" were saved that day. *HMS Serapis* took aboard a large number of women and children, but there were almost none between the ages of fifteen and thirty-five.[423] Turks had been plucking out girls and young women from the mass on the quay. Many were never seen again.[424] That night, according to an American officer, "separate fires were observed to start in locations distant from the general conflagration, plainly indicating incendiarism." Hepburn was told that "every able-bodied Armenian man was being hunted down and killed wherever found; even small boys . . . armed with clubs were taking part." He also "witnessed from the ship . . . a man in civilian clothes being . . . bound and thrown over the seawall and shot" by soldiers.[425]

In short, between September 9 and 12, the incoming Turkish troops shot and killed thousands of Christians, raped hundreds if not thousands of girls and woman, and pillaged the Christian suburbs and quarters of town. Thousands of Christians were led away under guard to the interior. Then, on September 13, as tens of thousands of Greeks and Christians rushed to the quayside in hope of maritime salvation, fires were set in various parts of the Christian quarters and among the buildings along the quayside, while bands of Turkish thugs murdered stray Armenians. Joined by soldiers, they raped Christian women and girls plucked from the mass of humanity on the crowded, noisy, stinking quay.

Remarkably the Turkish government filed insurance claims in an effort to receive compensation for Christian-owned properties destroyed in the Smyrna fire. The Turks argued that the occupants had fled their homes before the fire had started, and because the properties were "abandoned," title automatically passed to the government.[426] NER pressed its own claim, asking the U.S. State Department to take steps to assure that Armenians' property titles be secured for surviving orphans and NER itself, which was expending huge sums on their upkeep.[427] Nothing came of either legal maneuver.

Almost immediately, a controversy sprang up about the origin of the fire, which completely obliterated the Christian quarters of the city, though left its poorer Turkish neighborhoods intact. Who was responsible? Turks, Greeks, and Armenians all seemed to have reasons for setting the town alight, and all had, in one place or another during the previous years, committed large-scale arson.

Paul Grescovich, an Austrian-born engineer and head of the Smyrna Fire Department, apparently told an NER worker that on September 13, the day the fire started, the Turks had reported killing a number of young Armenian men "setting fires." According to this account, some were disguised as women or as Turkish soldiers or irregulars. Grescovich claimed he had found petroleum-covered rags and bedding in buildings evacuated by Armenian refugees. Smyrna's new military governor, Kâzım Pasha, said he ordered his soldiers to prevent incendiarism, and Turkish officers uniformly denied having torched the town. They said that burning Smyrna was contrary to their interests. Grescovich criticized the Turkish military for failing to prevent the fire and for responding to it negligently and ineffectively. But he found no evidence that Turks—soldiers or civilians—had started it.[428] On September 15 Kâzım told Lieutenant Merrill and a journalist that he had arrested twenty-two Armenians who had confessed to "belonging to a [secret] society of 600 Armenians who had planned and executed the burning of Smyrna." He promised to present the arsonists, but he never did.[429]

Bristol, too, saddled Armenians with responsibility, explaining that they had "set fire to their churches and some of their houses with the idea of preventing these buildings and houses getting into the hands of the Turks." This led to the big fire, but Bristol did "not think that the Armenians intended to burn the whole of Smyrna."[430] He added, "All the different races took a hand in this work. The Greeks and Armenians when they found they had to leave their homes set fire to them. . . . The Turks in many cases burned buildings to cover up murders and crimes, or just for the sake of wanton destruction."[431] Hepburn, possibly influenced by his superior, wrote that individual Turkish soldiers may have set some of the fires, but this did not indicate "an organized plan to burn the city." He dismissed as "far-fetched" the argument that burning Smyrna was part of a Turkish policy to "rid the country of all non-Moslems."[432]

British Army headquarters in Constantinople largely agreed with Bristol and Hepburn. Basing its conclusions on a report from an unnamed agent, the British determined that both Turks and Armenians had started fires, neither with the intention of torching the city. The fires got out of control and "the whole town was soon embraced by the conflagration, in spite of all the efforts of the Turkish troops."[433]

But an overwhelming number of eyewitnesses told a completely different story: of deliberate Turkish authorship and responsibility. The Armenian memoirist Abraham Hartunian said he saw Turks "driving wagonloads of bombs, gunpowder, kerosene, and all else necessary to start fires" through the streets on September 11.[434] Anita Chakerian, who taught at the women's college in Smyrna, saw Turkish soldiers drag sacks into buildings in various corners, suggesting some sort of plot afoot.[435] Missionary Minnie Mills, inside the Armenian quarter, saw on September 13 "a Turkish officer enter a house with small tins of petroleum or benzene . . . and in a few minutes the house was in flames. Our teachers and girls saw Turks in regular soldiers' uniform and in several cases in officers' uniforms with long sticks with rags at the end which were dipped in a can of liquid and carried into houses which were soon burning."[436] Missionaries said the fire began in four different locations more or less simultaneously, indicating deliberation and organization. Post reported that firefighters in the Armenian quarter "seemed" to be "playing with the fire, rather than actually trying to put it out."[437] One witness related that after the fire was well under way, "Turkish soldiers came . . . [to] the waterfront and poured kerosene . . . all along the street." This witness also claimed "fires were helped along by the troops in the Armenian quarter . . . and Turkish officers said that it was a good idea to clean it all out."[438]

Hole thought "the conflagration was encouraged to spread to the European quarter by the liberal use of oil. The street that runs parallel to the consulate building was saturated." He noted that the bundles refugees carried to the seafront "must also have been sprinkled with petrol." Hole, too, witnessed clear signs of arson. "In the quarter at the back of the harbor, I saw a number of buildings take fire in the same manner, there being no fire which could possibly have been communicated to them in the ordinary way." It was obvious to him that Turks were responsible. They "wished to drive out any stray [Christian] fugitives who had succeeded in evading them or merely to cover up their tracks."[439] Rumbold, perhaps basing himself on Hole's reports, concluded, "There seems no doubt that Turks . . . burnt the Armenian and European quarters of the town."[440]

Post, who believed that the Turks had started the fire to cover up traces of their misdeeds, was probably wrong to condemn the whole of the Smyrna fire brigade.[441] Some—Greeks and Turks—vigorously tried to douse the flames. But other Turks who should have been battling the flames, or at least working to rescue civilians, were witnessed doing the opposite. According to Sergeant Tchorbadjis (Çorbacı), a Turkish member of the fire brigade who testified at an insurance trial in London two years after the destruction of Smyrna, said he saw Turkish soldiers igniting fires as he and his fellows put them out elsewhere. He said he "found bedding on fire" on the roof of an Armenian church. "Then I went down into one of the rooms and saw a Turkish soldier . . . setting fire to the interior of a drawer."[442] Another firefighter, Emmanuel Katsaros, was hosing down the Armenian Club when two soldiers entered carrying tins of petroleum. He saw them dousing a piano with the liquid. "We are trying to stop the fires, and . . . you are setting them," he told the solider, who replied, "You have your orders and we have ours."[443]

Probably the strongest indication of Turkish culpability is that Turkish quarters of the city were completely untouched by the fire.[444] It is no wonder the missionary Peet saw the fire and massacres in Smyrna as proof of Turkey's "deliberate purpose . . . to exterminate the Christians within their borders."[445]

Expelling Greek Men, Women, and Children

In the days after the Turks retook Smyrna, they deported inland many thousands of Ionian Greeks. Along the coast and in the inland villages, they detained all men aged eighteen to forty-five, and sometimes older. Many were executed immediately. Some were sent inland and then executed. And some were marched into the interior as prisoners of war destined for labor battalions.[446] The Greek government estimated that more than 100,000 men from Smyrna were driven inland, perhaps an exaggeration.[447] But without doubt "practically all males between 18 and 45" who were not immediately executed "were removed to concentration camps" and formed into labor battalions.[448]

After the signing of the Greco-Turkish armistice on October 11, League of Nations High Commissioner for Refugees Fridtjof Nansen—a famed Norwegian explorer and scientist—demanded the release of the prisoners in the labor battalions. He argued that the women and children who had reached Greece needed their men: they could not be productively resettled without breadwinners.[449] Meanwhile, the deported men were, according to Bristol "treated like animals."[450]

Thousands, perhaps tens of thousands, of women and children were also deported inland. It began within a few days of the Turkish takeover of Smyrna. The Turks gathered women and children from the quay, fields, and streets, and "drove them off."[451] Immediately after the fire, one Christian eyewitness reported that "the road to Paradise was literally filled with women and children, together with older men, being led off under guard towards the interior."[452] On September 18 Lieutenant Commander Knauss saw "the road to Dadagatch [Dadaağaç] . . . filled with women and children being driven towards the interior."[453] Even Bristol understood that deportation to the interior "means certain death, either from starvation or at the hands of enraged Turks."[454]

One of the columns departing Smyrna numbered 4,000 at the outset. The survivors reaching Kayseri two months later, on November 19, numbered just 700. Initially there had also been men in the convoy, but they had been separated and taken away. The deportees were given no food. Of the women, "over half . . . died on the road," missionaries in Kayseri reported. Those who were hospitalized "all cried for bread and suffered most terrible pain, their mouths were bleeding. Teeth loose, bodies covered with sores, filth and lice." At Kayseri, ten died each day; many more "are going to die," the hospital director predicted.[455]

It was not just Smyrna that experienced deportations. The Turks were determined to leave no Greeks on the seacoast.[456] The *New York Times* reported on October 15 that the Turks had ordered all Christians out of the entirety of southwestern Anatolia—including towns such as Antalya and Makri—within seven days. Army-aged men, of course, were also deported inland.[457] At the end of October, some 7,000 women and children from the Moschonissia Islands, off Ayvalık, and the village of Yenitsarohori (Küçükköy) were reportedly deported inland.[458]

In sum the Nationalist army, assisted by locals, destroyed a great number of Armenians and Greeks during September–October 1922. The systematic "hunt" in the residential districts of Smyrna, the round-up and massacre of Greek army-age men, the fires in the Christian quarters, the murder of Christians fleeing their sanctuaries toward the dock, the shooting and burning on the quayside and in the waters offshore, and the travails of the deportees—all contributed to a massive death toll.

Bristol, in his wonted manner, downplayed Turkish atrocities, arguing that reports "greatly exaggerated" the losses. He asserted an overall death toll of 2,000–3,000 and claimed "there was no general massacre, and only killing of individuals."[459] But a host of on-the-spot witnesses described a different reality. A British relief officer, Lieutenant Hadkinson, estimated that 25,000 died on the night of September 13 alone when, he said, Turkish soldiers and locals prevented Armenians and Greeks from reaching the dock from quarters engulfed by fire.[460] One Smyrna notable pointed out that 10,000–12,000 Greeks and Armenians were taken away as prisoners and had since "disappeared."[461] Horton seemingly endorsed a high, and probably exaggerated estimate of the Smyrna death toll—a hundred-thousand.[462] There is no knowing the true number. But Churchill at the time described Turkish actions in Smyrna as "a deliberately planned and methodically executed atrocity." He put no figures to his assessment, though he was convinced that elimination of Christian life in Smyrna had "few parallels in the history of human crime."[463]

The Exodus

Aside from the Ionian Greeks deported to the Anatolian interior, the great majority of the inhabitants of Smyrna and its hinterlands were transported westward, to the Greek Aegean islands and the Greek mainland. In September 1921 Hamid Bey, the Nationalist representative in Constantinople, told Bristol that "in the bottom of their hearts the Turks wished that these people would leave the country."[464] The wish was fulfilled the following year.

In late spring 1922, as Greek arms began to falter, the Allies began to consider the possibility of a wholesale Christian exodus from western Anatolia. The British put the numbers involved at 650,000: 350,000 from Smyrna, 136,000 from Bursa; 120,000 from Balikesir; and 44,000 from the regions of Kütahya, Afyon-Karahisar, and Eskişehir. The Allies generally opposed such an exodus, which would be enormously difficult given the costs of transport and transitional and long-term refugee maintenance and the challenge of securing ultimate destinations.[465] But circumstances conspired to thwart their wishes. In the end it was the Allies themselves who carried out the massive transfer of the western Anatolian Christians to Greece. Most were Greeks, but there were also tens of thousands of Armenians.

Christians were already pouring out of Smyrna before the Nationalist forces arrived in early September. Among these emigrants was a small number of wealthier Smyrniot Christians and a large number of Greeks from the interior who had descended on the city. Barnes put the number leaving before the Turkish reconquest at 75,000. But that left about 150,000 locals and 100,000 refugees in the town and its suburbs.[466] As the Turks approached, many fled the suburbs for the city center and the port. On September 9 Christians began boarding boats.[467] Among the first post-conquest departees were hundreds of European and American nationals. The Americans, with gunboats in the harbor, established their forward headquarters next to the quay in the Smyrna Theatre. At the entrance hung an electric sign in block letters two feet high, reading "Le Tango de la Mort."[468]

The following days were marked by a chaotic maritime exodus against the backdrop of urban massacre and catastrophic conflagration. On September 16 the Turks proclaimed:

Greeks and Armenians living in the part of the country rescued and cleansed by our army, and those Greeks and Armenians brought to Smyrna and to our coast towns by the enemy army . . . are persons who . . . openly joined the Greek army and have thus taken up arms against us, burned our cities and tortured and persecuted the innocent inhabitants. . . . In order not to allow these persons to join the Greek army again . . . those males who are between the ages of eighteen and forty-five will be placed in garrisons as prisoners of war. . . . Permission to leave Turkey is hereby granted to all [other] Greeks and Armenians be they from Smyrna or from the interior. This permission is valid until September 30, 1922. It is hereby declared that those, who after [that] date . . . are in a position of impairing the public peace and tranquility and the security of our military operations, will be deported [to the interior].

The order also applied to "Jews of Hellenic nationality."[469]

The proclamation, Barnes wrote, "made immediate evacuation imperative."[470] Hepburn wrote ominously, "Unless action were taken immediately, there would be no refugee problem in sight within a week."[471] Western representatives attempted to negotiate with the Turks, but they insisted on the departure of all Christians, regardless of the consequences. Bristol reported Hamid Bey telling him, the Turks "preferred less prosperity to greater prosperity coupled with these undesirable elements" remaining.[472]

The deadline of September 30 stuck, and masses of refugees were soon rushing out of Smyrna. By September 19, about 30,000 had been taken off by British, American, French and Italian destroyers. On September 24, Greek steamers escorted by Allied naval craft began shuttling between Smyrna, Piraeus, and Salonica.[473] Many refugees were first transported to Mitylene, from which they were later dispersed westward.

American officers who witnessed the scene at the embarkation gate remarked on the "at times very severe" behavior of Turkish troops engaged in crowd control. According to one officer, "The force used was a leather strap, a cane, the butt of a rifle, or even sometimes a bayonet, and in one or two instances by shooting." But the Turks were doing more than managing crowds. "Robbing at the gates and in the yard was rather the rule than the exception," Lieutenant Commander Powell wrote. Occasionally, Turkish officers intervened, but often they looked away, and sometimes they participated.[474]

Under Powell's command the USS *Edsall* put twenty men ashore to "assist in patrolling and in preventing undue violence." He wrote:

> As soon as the harbor gates were opened, the crowd became a mob; women were knocked down, were walked over, children were torn from their arms . . . and they were pushed through screaming and crying. Many lost their bundles which added to the confusion, by causing others to stumble over them. . . . The Turkish troops weeded out the males. . . . Families were broken up without regard. There were a few cases of shooting where men . . . were selected out and tried to escape.[475]

Left behind on the quay was

> a crowd of panic-stricken women and old men, with hordes of children . . . carrying all their worldly possessions. . . . The majority . . . had been under guard since the fire . . . exposed to robbery, outrage and violence. . . . Robbery was continuous. . . . Turkish officers . . . were as bad as—or worse than—their men. . . . The conduct of the police officer at the police barrier was very restrained, and he was on the whole most generous. . . . On the other hand, his subordinates and the soldiers were brutal. . . . The contradictory nature of the Turk's character is exemplified by the numerous cases . . . of Turkish police and soldiers throwing themselves on the ground outside the gates to save a child that had fallen and was being trodden underfoot; five minutes later the same man would quite likely kick a cripple in the stomach. I myself saw an exceptionally brutal policeman carry a lost child up and down the jetty until he found the parents.[476]

An American missionary recalled "Turkish soldiers carrying the bundles of the refugees and assisting the sick and old people."[477] Some of the Allied shore parties interacted socially with Turkish soldiers and officials. HMS *Curacoa* dispatched a soccer team, which was beaten two-to-one by the Turks.[478]

By September 30 more than 190,000 Ottoman Christians, almost all Greeks, had been evacuated. Another 21,000 British, French, and Italian citizens and "protégés" had also left.[479] But refugees from towns and villages in the interior continued streaming to the coast. Pressed by the Allies, the Turks extended the deadline to October 10.[480] By October 9 Allied warships and steamers had taken some 240,000 Christians from Smyrna, Ayvalık, Çeşme, Vurla, Makri, and Antalya.[481] The Greeks of Ayvalık apparently decided in early September to stay put, but the Turks ordered them out.[482] "Infidel Smyrna" had become Turkish Izmir, as CUP leaders had advocated at the secret War Ministry meetings chaired by Enver Pasha in May, June, and August 1914, when the "elimination of the non-Turkish masses" had been discussed.[483]

The exodus from most of the coast was more orderly than from Smyrna. American officers aboard USS *Lawrence* remarked on the "splendid conduct of the Turkish military" during the evacuation of the 15,000 Greeks from Ayvalık on October 8–9. Civil officials, however, relieved evacuees of "money and jewels."[484] As in Smyrna, the Turks marched off all army-age men to the interior. Of the 3,000 taken, only 23 reportedly survived. The town's Greek orthodox clergy were all massacred.[485]

Eastern Thrace also emptied of Greeks. The Mudanya armistice mandated the evacuation of the Greek army from eastern Thrace and placed the territory under Turkish rule.[486] In addition, after the Greek rout, the Kemalists advanced northward, toward the Allied-held zone along the Dardanelles and Sea of Marmara, threatening Eastern Thrace. Greek civilians decided to leave with the soldiers rather than face a possible Kemalist assault and further Turkish depredations. By October 28, 250,000 Greeks had departed for Western Thrace, in orderly fashion and overseen by Allied forces.[487] Another 70,000 left for Greece via Tekirdağ from the Bursa area.[488] In Thrace the young Ernest Hemingway was on hand to witness "twenty miles of carts drawn by cows, bullocks and muddy-flanked water buffalo, with exhausted, staggering men, women and children, blankets over their heads, walking blindingly [*sic*] along in the rain beside their worldly goods. . . . It is a silent procession. Nobody even grunts. It is all they can do to keep moving."[489]

The resettlement of the Thracian evacuees, assisted by Greek troops and brigands, resulted in the displacement of many Bulgarian villagers. It was a rough process. Some were murdered, and girls were raped. According to an

American official, there was "a systematic policy of denationalization and extermination of the Bulgarians . . . applied without scruple and without any
pity."[490] Animosity between the two peoples had been simmering for the previous decade, as the Bulgarians had turned against their former allies in the
Second Balkan War, attacking Greece in June 1913.

Back in Smyrna the new Turkish administration devoted considerable energy to cleaning up after the fire, but also to ridding the city of the vestiges of
Christianity. Rumbold described the situation as "a reign of terror." Remaining
Christians and their tenants were summarily evicted.[491] Churches were "systematically razed to the ground." Jews were allowed to stay, but the Turks
desecrated the town's Jewish and Christian cemeteries. At one Greek cemetery, "all graves and tombs had been violated, the lids to coffins having been
torn off and bodies thrown about."[492] Reportedly 20 percent of the graves at
one Armenian cemetery were opened.[493] The British and Jewish cemeteries
in the Bournabat (Bornova) quarter were desecrated. "Almost without exception, the tombstones" in Bournabat "had been smashed and overthrown . . .
and many defiled with the filth of human beings and animals."[494] A senior
British naval officer concluded, "It is impossible to believe that all this willful
damage to Christian and Jewish cemeteries could have taken place without
the knowledge of the Turkish authorities, and I consider it part of a considered
policy."[495]

The Nationalist victory and takeover of Smyrna triggered massive demonstrations among the Turks of Constantinople. "A great many windows were
smashed" at Christian-owned homes and shops. But the Allied occupation
troops curbed the rioting.[496] Greeks nonetheless fled the capital in a panic,
fearing that the Kemalists were about to descend on the city. "The Turk must
massacre and burn; Smyrna was burned; therefore the same fate awaits Constantinople" Bristol wrote, accurately capturing the reasoning underlying the
Constantinople exodus.[497] He estimated that, by early December, 75,000
Christians had left the city.[498]

With the Nationalists on the doorstep of Constantinople and the straits,
the deterioration of the Allied position in western Turkey was plain to see.
So was the divide between the two major European powers. It had only
widened since the signing of the Franco-Turkish deal over Cilicia, behind
Britain's back. Now the Allies were emphatically at loggerheads. Curzon

described a heated meeting in Paris on September 22 with French Prime Minister Raymond Poincaré. He "lost all command of his temper, and for a quarter of an hour shouted and raved at the top of his voice ... and behave[ed] like a demented schoolmaster screaming at a guilty school boy," Curzon wrote. After Curzon left the room, Poincaré came out to apologize, "explaining that he had been exasperated at the charge that France had abandoned her Ally." But then "Poincaré once more insisted on ... submission to Kemal."[499]

Suddenly the lone foreign power facing off against the Nationalists, Britain and her leaders were forced to confront the bankruptcy of their own thinking. As the cabinet put it on September 23, "It must be recognized that the policy originally adopted by the Allied and Associated Powers at the Paris Peace Conference, according to which the Turks could not be trusted in future to rule races alien to them in nationality and religion ... had failed." The British made ready to acquiesce in unimpeded Turkish sovereignty over the whole of Turkey and unsupervised rule over its non-Muslim minorities.[500] Within days the British, in the Mudanya agreement, would also concede the principle of Turkish sovereignty over Constantinople and Eastern Thrace.

The immediate precipitant to the agreement was a limited Kemalist push into the Neutral Zone at Çanak. Swinging northwards from Smyrna, Kemal threatened to cross into Thrace and drive on Constantinople. His troops pushed into the Neutral Zone, and the British fired warning salvos. But the Kemalists did not retire.[501] In London, the cabinet was reluctant to go to war: Harington had few troops, the Treasury was broke, and the public had tired of war—"Stop This New War," ran a headline in the *Daily Mail* on September 18.[502] Nonetheless, the government authorized General Charles Harington to issue an ultimatum demanding Turkish withdrawal.[503] But Harington held off, saving the day. The Nationalists stayed put, and the two sides agreed to talk.[504] The upshot was the Mudanya armistice.

After Smyrna

Smyrna convinced Western observers that Turkey's rulers were set on "the elimination of all Christians from its borders," Barton, the head of the American Board of Commissioners for Foreign Missions, wrote. "This has been largely accomplished already. The remnant will be absorbed into the Turkish race, deported from the country, or killed." He added, "The government has [also] determined that the American missionary work shall cease."[505] Rendel agreed that "the Kemalists mean to expel or deport all Christians remaining in territory over which they obtain control."[506]

In the fall of 1922, Ankara decided that the final disappearance of Asia Minor's Christians—at this point, overwhelmingly Greeks—would be accomplished not by massacre and death march but by straightforward expulsion to Greece. Smyrna had pointed the way. Kemal's timing also was linked to the forthcoming Lausanne peace conference. The Turks sought to present the Allies with a fait accompli: if there were no minorities left in Turkey, there would be no need in the treaty for a troublesome minority-protection clause. Gates, the missionary, summed up the Turkish attitude heading into the talks as, "We will show the world what the Turk[s] can do when left to themselves."[507] (As it turns out, the Treaty of Lausanne would include minority-protection provisions, but without teeth.)

Immediately after retaking Smyrna, Ankara instructed the Turkish authorities in central and eastern Anatolia to expel the remaining Christians. Unlike the Greeks deported in 1921–early 1922, these were to be directed toward the ports rather than to the interior. Slyly, the order was framed as a grant of "permission" to leave the country.[508] The announcement went out to the authorities in the provinces in early October 1922. This was "really an order for them all to get out," a missionary in Samsun wrote. The town's mutesarrif said so explicitly to officers of the USS *Overton*.[509]

The Turks were less forthcoming with the Allied plenipotentiaries in Constantinople, preferring a combination of disinformation and brazen mendacity. Refet Pasha, Ankara's representative, told Bristol that there was "no order for expulsion" and that such an order was, in any case, unnecessary as "all of the Christians . . . had been anxious to leave for some time." Ankara was merely acceding to their wishes.[510] Refet also claimed, in somewhat contradictory terms, that "his government was making efforts to induce these Christians who had already left the interior cities for the coast to return to their homes" and stay.[511] The interior minister sent a circular to governors, generals, and the press stating that expelling Christians was "contrary to [the government's] decision" and that "compulsion should not be" exercised.[512]

But neither diplomats nor Christian inhabitants were taken in.[513] They recalled Constantinople's fake 1915 orders instructing officials to treat deportees humanely. Even Bristol admitted that the current instructions were "really . . . an order of expulsion."[514] He was "certain that [the] Nationalist Government wishes [to] get rid of entire Greek and Armenian population."[515] The French high commissioner, General Maurice Pellé, said he had heard that "in all parts of Anatolia from Mersina to Trebizond" Christian men aged eighteen to forty-five were to be "made prisoners," and the rest were to be "expelled from the country."[516] Bristol complained that this would "create over a million refugees" and constitute an obstacle to "a settlement."[517] But the Allies had no leverage with which to negotiate a better outcome.

Along the Black Sea coast, the Christians were bluntly told that they had thirty days to leave, otherwise they would be marched to the interior. All knew what that meant. The order encompassed the Christians working in missionary institutions and the many thousands of orphans in their care. Rumbold, probably exaggerating the number of Christians left to expel, thought the order would affect "over one million Christians in Eastern Anatolia."[518]

Throughout Anatolia, the orders received the approval and reinforcement of the Muslim public. Newspapers lambasted the Christians, and neighbors threatened them with massacre. In November 1922 Jackson cataloged a litany of persecutions, big and small. Christians, he said, were excessively taxed, "beaten, robbed and [left] with no redress. A persistent boycott exists against them, preventing them from selling anything . . . at any price; also, whatever they are obliged to purchase from a Moslem they are forced to pay from ten to twenty times the value thereof." In short, "there is a clear understanding among the Turkish authorities and the Mohammedan population that everything possible is to be done to oblige the Christians to leave."[519] Turks wishing to purchase the departees' houses were threatened with reprisals.[520]

The exile was to be a repeat of the Cilician Armenians' November–December 1921 rush to Mersin, Alexandretta, and subsequent seaborne flight, but on a vaster scale and spread out over a longer timeline. As Christians—mostly Greeks, but also some Armenians and Assyrians—headed from the interior to the Black Sea and Mediterranean, a missionary reported the "wildest scenes": "all roads leading to Samsun are crowded with long lines of refugees laden with bundles, many with oxcarts piled high." The exceptions, of course, were army-aged men. "Men are not even allowed to come with the refugee columns," the missionary wrote. "Only women, children and the infirm are reaching Samsun."[521] Greek villagers near Trabzon reportedly were loath to leave their homes, but "their Turkish neighbors . . . urge them to leave in order to get their property."[522] Most headed for the ports, but a few journeyed by land southward, toward Aleppo.[523] Jackson reported that the latter were sometimes given the option of staying put—if they converted.[524]

Tens of thousands of Greek refugees packed Samsun, waiting for boats out. Occasionally, they were harassed or attacked by Turks. One witness saw "a lot of young Turks stoning the refugees in the square near the customs house. Later . . . an Armenian doctor . . . reported that a lot of young Turkish boys . . . had been assaulting refugees around the Armenian Church . . . until the police . . . put a stop to it."[525] The streets were crowded with women selling household goods. An American naval officer commented, "The present . . . stir reminds one of biblical times, [the] harassing of the Christians. It seems strange to me that we Christian nations should . . . countenance the denial of [this] part of the world to Christians. . . . The Christians are calm but downcast." A missionary told the officer that the Turks were "already beginning to squabble amongst themselves over the spoils."[526]

Nasty incidents were reported from Mersin. An American officer wrote, "The Turkish military entered the churches and refugee dumps and take young girls. Five were taken from [the Georgian Greek] Church last night. Three returned this morning and complained to the Spanish consul. . . . The other two have not yet returned." The officer later met one of the girls: "She appeared about twenty years of age and was a cumberly [sic, comely?], bucksome lass. She stated . . . she was taken [by four gendarmes] to a Turkish house where there were two more gendarmes and a civilian. She . . . said they used her repeatedly, until this morning when she was released." Another of the girls, a twenty-year-old Greek from Denizli, told the same story. Two of her rapists were soldiers, "Suleiman Onbachi and Imzebeit Tehaouchou." The American officer was also told that "bands of civilians" waylaid Christian women who went to use lavatories outside the refugee compounds. The assailants "would throw a shawl over the woman's head and drag her to their harems. . . . At the rate of the stories I have heard the harems should now be overflowing." On November 28 the officer recorded the text of a Turkish poster hung on Christian houses:

To the Greeks and Armenians. Ingrate Criminals of Mersina. The Nationalists [*sic*] Government has pardoned you for the innumerable atrocities against Mussulmen during the [French] occupation. . . . This noble pardon has not been appreciated, you have remained tranquil but continued with traitors' acts against this government and nation. . . . You have burned towns and villages and . . . soiled the honor of our daughters and wives. . . . All the blood in our veins cries unmercifully for revenge. . . . Mussulmen do not want to see you in their country. . . . Go or you will know the . . . Bloody sword.

The American officer, who described himself as formerly "pro-Turk," now considered them "savages and barbarians."[527]

The harassment and incitement were intended to induce emigration, but they also pushed Turks to the edge of massacre. The government hoped to avoid any such incidents during the sensitive peace talks. The Nationalists had to walk a fine line, which in practice meant enraging the populace and then reining it in. Thus the following summary, from Jackson, of Adana and Antep newspapers pushing anti-Christian propaganda in late 1922: "Moslem hearts filled with hatred [of] Armenians and Greeks who are accused [of] destroying Turkish homes, violating women, girls, imprisoning, maiming. Murdering . . . intriguing with the British and Greeks . . . burning Smyrna. . . . Calling Christians villains, assassins, serpents, insisting they leave the country."[528] Such rhetoric helped to inspire a Muslim mob that invaded the Christian neighborhoods of Adana in mid-November, but Turkish police drove the rioters out.[529]

Toward the end of 1922 NER workers made haste to ship out orphans quickly.[530] The missionaries knew that, if left behind, the orphans would fall into Turkish clutches. The Turks were rounding up orphans, especially those under fourteen years old, and placing them in Muslim orphanages or homes. Occasionally the Turks "poached" orphans directly from NER institutions. A *New York Times* correspondent likened the Turkish harvest of Christian orphans to a revival of "the janissary system." Dr. Cevdet Bey, Ankara's Commissioner for Deportees, forcibly took girls from NER institutions to serve supper in his home and "kept" them there "till morning."[531]

Ankara was eager to rid Anatolia of its Christians before the Lausanne Conference ended.[532] By December 1922, a month into the conference, the

Turkish officials in Crete with a child described in the source caption as the "sole survivor" of an alleged Christian massacre of Turks.

evacuation was in full swing. Jaquith described what he saw: "Death is over-taking thousands of the children and the aged infirm on the frozen roads of Anatolia. . . . Moving over the worst mud roads in the world, I saw a crowd of broken civilians more depressing than an army in hard-pressed retreat. Women about to become mothers tramped in snow up to their knees. Tired children dropped weary by the wayside, and girls of tender years bore men's burdens."[533]

At the ports the waiting refugees suffered intimidation, robbery, and violence.[534] In March 1923 a group of Turkish children attacked a party of

Armenian orphans out for a walk in Samsun. Turkish mothers joined in.[535] An American officer recorded a vicious assault on a group of Greeks defending themselves against an "intoxicated Turkish soldier" who had shot one of them. A "gang of hamals, boot blacks, police, Turkish soldiers and even" women attacked the Greeks and beat them. Some 200 Greeks were arrested, and 1,500 were driven out of a shelter onto a beach "without cover." There the attack continued. Eight women and girls were taken "away."[536]

Other incidents were reported at Mersin's refugee encampments.[537] "Practically all" the refugees heading southward for Mersin, Alexandretta and Aleppo were robbed en route by "gendarmes or civil bandits." A few were murdered, and "women and girls violated."[538] Greek refugees often wore cheap clothes—finery invited depredation.[539]

In the ports Western eyes kept the authorities and everyday Turks in check. But in the interior brutality was common. Troops, gendarmes, and brigands harassed and murdered, whether because they wished to speed up Greek departure or because such behavior was simply endemic. In April 1923 near Havza, nineteen young villagers were murdered.[540] In May, at Gurumza, villagers and brigands killed between sixty and ninety Greeks.[541]

The degree of refugees' suffering was determined to an extent by class. The poor reached exit ports—Giresun, Ordu, Ünye, and others—on foot. Those who could afford to came on freight trains or in carriages. From the trains they might be herded by stick-wielding soldiers to makeshift camps or directly to the harbor.[542] On the steamers the moneyed minority enjoyed cabins, but most refugees languished on crowded decks. The conditions were often appalling. One boat carrying 2,000 passengers from the Black Sea to Piraeus arrived with 1,600 cases of typhus, smallpox, and cholera. A U.S. Navy officer called it a "death ship."[543]

Most Anatolian refugees subsisted for weeks or months in camps on the edges of ports, enduring hunger and disease as they waited for a chance to ship out. At Mersin a large number lived in an empty factory on the outskirts of the city. They lived on dark bread and soup dispensed by American missionaries and a Greek aid group and on cabbage and mustard they collected from the fields. "It is a common sight to see a little weak, anemic, dirty and emaciated girl hovering around a charcoal fire trying to cook a few leaves of mustard or cabbage in a tin cup," an American naval officer wrote.[544]

The locals and the mayor complained about the scourge of beggars.[545] The French at one point offered to transport the Mersin refugees to Morocco, Algiers, West Africa, but the refugees preferred "starvation . . . to a journey to Morocco," where they expected they would again be persecuted by Muslims.[546] The situation in Alexandretta was arguably even worse than in Mersin: refugees lived in "hovels built of gunny sacks, tin cans and rubbish all around the town and on the edge of the swamps." Many were sick.[547]

A missionary described the authorities' attitude toward the refugees as "indifferent," but this wasn't quite right. Officials were interested in the refugees, to the extent that they could derive some benefit. Mersin authorities exacted exorbitant fees for passports and allowed the boatmen to charge outrageous sums for ferrying refugees to steamers.[548] In Samsun Armenian adults who had avoided military service were prevented from leaving until they paid a fee. Boatmen rifled the refugees' belongings.[549] The Turks often exacted lighthouse and sanitation taxes before allowing departure. At Mersin in late November 1922, the Turks were charging sixty piastres per orphan for ferrying them to the steamships.[550]

Refugees often lacked funds to pay passage on the outbound steamers. This, in addition to constant arrivals from the interior, resulted in crowding on the docks. During October 1922–March 1923, there were always more refugees in the ports than there were berths available. As they waited, they squatted in alleyways, empty lots, vacant buildings, and churches and other public spaces. An American officer came away from a Samsun church with a low opinion of everyone involved: "Filth is everywhere. The refugees will do nothing to help themselves. Women and children are sick and lie on their packs. . . . All of it is as repulsive [a] sight as I've ever seen. . . . The Turks are doing nothing."[551]

NER provided a measure of relief. In March 1923 NER managed to feed 9,000 refugees in the port of Samsun one hot meal a day. But another 4,000 received no aid. Under NER supervision, most of the Samsun refugees were vaccinated and deloused at least once. NER paid orphans' passage and sometimes covered costs for other refugees. In an effort to speed the removal, the mutesarrifs constantly pressed NER to appeal to Western governments and prelates for ships.[552]

American officers on gunboats in the Black Sea often helped facilitate embarkations, cajoling officials or arranging refugees' passage aboard Greek, British, Russian, and Turkish steamships. American naval captains might have shuttled refugees themselves, but Bristol forbade this.

As the months dragged on, the Turks turned to a combination of carrots and sticks in an effort to complete the exodus. Eventually poor refugees were allowed to board steamers without charge. So eager were the Turks to see the Greeks' backs that they sometimes allowed men of military age to leave if they paid the exemption tax of 300 Turkish lira, though more often they were detained.[553] The Turks also used brute force to maintain the momentum. In Trabzon and its suburbs in February 1923, 700 families were "turned out of their houses."[554] In April a recalcitrant captain of a French-flagged steamer was forced "by the point of the revolver" to take on several hundred refugees. Something similar occurred in Samsun.[555] Turks brandished liberally the threat of deportation inland, both to get the Greeks moving and to persuade the Allies to expedite the process.[556]

By the close of 1922, tens of thousands had fled the country, but there were still many thousands to go. In January 1923 American diplomats estimated that 3,000–5,000 refugees from the interior were still arriving at the ports each week.[557] In March some 8,000 refugees were awaiting boats out in Alexandretta, and 3,500 in Mersin.[558] Ten-thousand awaited passage in Samsun, 3,000 in Trabzon, 1,500 in Ordu, 500 in Ünye, and 300 in Fatsa.[559] And there were still 60,000 refugees in Aleppo, 50,000 of them Armenians, and 23,000 in Constantinople.[560] In April embarkations were impeded by the problem of passage fees and Greece's momentary unwillingness to take in more refugees. The country was already hosting more than a million and announced that it would take in no more until an official population exchange was implemented, with Muslim departures from Greece, Macedonia, and Thrace creating space in which to absorb Greek refugees.[561] In early April Ankara instructed local governors not to ship refugees to Constantinople on their way out of the country.[562] The city was becoming overcrowded, and refugees were dying at a rate of nearly 600 a week from smallpox and typhus.[563] Local Turkish authorities regarded Constantinople as a way station and were not interested in holding refugees who could no longer be sent on.

Officials reacted to the temporary closures of Greece and Constantinople by threatening to deport to the interior the Greeks waiting at the ports. "Since the city [of Constantinople] is not desirous of more people, and because a contagious disease has broken out lately among these people, therefore all those who intend to leave the country ought to do so in a few days' time," read an official proclamation plastered on the walls of Samsun in mid-March 1923 "Otherwise they will be compelled to return to their homes."[564] Such internal deportations would result in a death rate of "fifty per cent or more," the Americans feared.[565] They lodged protests, and the Turkish officials agreed to wait.[566]

The Christians, of course, overwhelmingly were eager to leave. "They live in constant fear," as one missionary put it. "They know that at any time they may be dragged from their homes and suffer" massacre or deportation inland.[567] There were occasional exceptions, though. Some wealthy Greeks in Sivas, it was reported, preferred to stay.[568] After all, the journey was impoverishing; émigrés forfeited their real estate and had no choice but to sell off personal effects at great loss. What faced them in exile was at best unclear.[569]

In some respects the condition of the waiting emigrants in the Pontus ports gradually improved. At the end of 1922 the Turkish authorities launched a vaccination campaign. In Samsun, in spring 1923, missionaries cut the refugees' hair: "close cuts on males and bobbed on females." Missionaries also "delouse[ed] all clothes and effects," washed scalps in kerosene for the same purpose, and gave refugees "hot baths."[570] In May American officers reported that refugee buildings in Samsun were "scrubbed clean." Although the refugees were "in rags," they were "clean" and healthy, especially the Armenians. "Many of these people are better off than they have ever been," the officers judged.[571] Local authorities sometimes provided shelter in disused mills, khans, school buildings, and other spaces but rarely supplied food or water. Occasionally, they provided medical services, but almost never in Turkish hospitals.[572] By summer refugees in Ünye, Fatsa, and Giresun were reported to be well-fed and almost disease-free. Many even found work.[573]

But on the Mediterranean coast, severe problems persisted. In Turkish-ruled Mersin in April 1923, about 20 percent of the 3,500 refugees were sick and others "weak and anemic." A few died each day.[574] In French-ruled Alexandretta, where most of the 14,000 Armenian refugees lived in two camps on the edge of a swamp, malaria and typhus were rife. Children were "distressingly undernourished and many have dropsy." The refugees lived in huts "built of straw, old boards, old sheet iron." They slept on boards "resting on stakes" to keep off the water-logged ground.[575] Armenian refugees were gradually moving out to villages.[576]

Sanitary conditions were also poor in Constantinople. While the town's 5,000 or so Armenian refugees were properly cared for, the 25,000 Greeks, it was reported in March 1923, were uniformly filthy. Many arrived diseased and were crammed into "draughty, barn-like buildings," with barely enough food. Babies and the elderly died off rapidly. Some 6,000 Greeks living next to the Selimiye barracks were dying at rates of up to seventy a day. Arthur Ringland, who would go on to found the international relief agency CARE, described conditions as "shocking, scandalous and a reproach." Corpses lay unburied for days, perhaps because the Turks charged fifty piastres to bury a child and a lira per adult.[577] Thousands lived in ships in the harbor, which were little better. "The filth and offal thrown from disease-laden ships is devoured by fish which in turn are eaten by the people of the city," Post wrote.[578]

By early summer 1923 there remained about 81,000 Christian refugees in Asia Minor, of whom 60,000 were Greek. There were large concentrations in the ports and in some inland locations such as Gümüşhane and Kayseri and its surroundings. There was also the 50,000 Armenian refugees in Aleppo, along with 12,000 Greeks.[579] By August most of the Greeks had been shipped off to Greece, though "the poorest and weakest in health, mostly women and children," remained, begging.[580]

In December 1922 the Greek Government reported that it had taken in 868,186 refugees.[581] By March 1923 the total had reached 1,150,000.[582] The deportees from Ionia and the Pontus included few young women and almost no able-bodied men between the ages of fifteen and fifty. An American who toured the Aegean islands that November reported, "There are scarcely five per cent of males over 14 years of age. The men are such pathetic wrecks, blind, more helpless than the women. . . . Of girls there are [very few] between the ages of 14 and 18."[583] The refugees from Eastern Thrace, however, included a normal proportion of able-bodied men and young women.[584]

The deportations resulted in a refugee-maintenance problem well "beyond [the] power" of a small, poor country such as Greece.[585] At the end of 1922, the Greek and Armenian refugees lived in public buildings, tent camps, and under trees in the Aegean islands and on the Greek mainland. In Athens the ruins of the Parthenon accommodated some, as did the velvet-lined boxes and the orchestra in the National Opera House.[586] The government even forced some homeowners to take in and feed refugees, gratis.[587]

In Salonica, where some 30,000 refugees were accommodated in October 1922 in huts on the grounds of the old British Army hospital, "practically all . . . are crawling with vermin, having no clothes to change into. There is no water for washing and hardly enough for drinking. There is no soap. There are no disinfectants. . . . The very rudiments of sanitation . . . do not exist." The huts had no floors; doors and windows were absent as well, carried off by previous inhabitants. Others in Salonica lodged in mosques, schools, and synagogues.[588] Conditions were such that some refugees were "very anxious to get back to Asia Minor," even "willing to swim." By February 1923 the city had 120,000 refugees.[589]

Western aid agencies took on part of the burden, and were nearly overwhelmed themselves. The American Red Cross was feeding about half a million.[590] During the initial weeks of the exodus, the camps were "appalling."[591] The director of the American Red Cross in Constantinople described a camp outside Salonica, inhabited mostly by Greeks from the Caucasus, as "one great hospital." Many of the residents "we found lying in the barracks absolutely nude with nothing but a quilt thrown over them. Many were suffering from typhus, influenza and pneumonia, the death rate averaging 40 persons per day. . . . This is a death rate of over one hundred per cent a year."[592] The Greek government supplied a little bread and sometimes cooked meals. Little work was available. Armenian clerics provided refugees with "olives [and] medicine."[593]

In summer 1923 there was a mini-crisis when the Greek government refused to take in additional refugees. In response the Turks stopped transfers from the interior, and NER threatened to pull out of the Pontus and stop relief.[594] The Greeks immediately relented.[595] The Turks then renewed the movement of Christians from the interior to the coastal towns.[596] A party of 179 that reached Trabzon told "horrible tales of the atrocious treatment they received. They claim that many young girls and boys still remain[ed] in the Kurdish villages, held as slaves."[597]

By late 1923 the refugee situation in Greece had improved. Refugees were siphoned off to empty Bulgarian and Muslim farms in Western Thrace and Macedonia, where they were permanently resettled. A year after Smyrna, an American relief committee thought it "obvious that the refugees from Turkish territory . . . have demonstrated almost unbelievable ability to assimilate themselves with the help of the Greek Government." The relief agencies had provided sustenance and health care, and the government shelter and stability.[598]

Altogether between 1919 and summer 1923, about 1.5 million Greeks were cleansed from Asia Minor and Eastern Thrace. Almost all were resettled in Greece. But several hundred thousand Ottoman Greeks had died. Either they were murdered outright or were the intentional victims of hunger, disease, and exposure. Without doubt, the exodus badly disrupted the Turkish economy, at least at first.[599] On the other hand, the state and its Muslim inhabitants gained vast amounts of property. Across the sea the refugee influx strained Greece's resources to the limit and no doubt caused much economic grief. But, in the long run, the vast increase in manpower was a boon to the Greek state and economy.

Exchange

The last stage of the Greek evacuation of Anatolia began in October–November 1923 with the implementation of a population-exchange agreement *(mübadele)* between Greece and Turkey. Rendel considered the notion of an agreed "exchange" to be "ironic," given that, by the time it was signed, most of "the Greeks were already expelled."[600]

Nonetheless, despite the killings and coerced removals, a few had remained in Turkey. The Turks were intent on clearing out these stragglers. Their position was bluntly set out in an article, "The Conversion of Senator Borah," published in *The International Interpreter*, during the Lausanne negotiations:

Of all the germs of disturbance, the Greek is by far the most dangerous. He is foreign in blood and religion; in buying and in selling he is incessantly active, and together with the Armenian he gathers in the piasters of the 'Faithful.' In one way and another this leads to trouble, to

accusation—false of course—of massacres, and to interference from
without. And, even worse than this, the Greek is a near neighbor who
actually claims the soil. Who declares that he had an empire in Anatolia
centuries before the Turks were heard of, when they were just wandering
bands of horsemen in Khorassan, in Armenia, or along the upper streams
of the Euphrates. He goes so far as to pretend that the city of Istanbul,
which he names Constantinople, is by rights his, and the great mosque
on the Bosporus, St. Sophia he calls it, the metropolitan cathedral of his
faith. Therefore he must go, and go at once, and as quickly from Constantinople as from Smyrna.[601]

The population exchange was settled within the context of the Lausanne
negotiations, on January 30, 1923, with implementation to begin May 1. The
agreement provided for the compulsory removal of the minority populations from Turkey and Greece, except Greeks from Constantinople and
Muslims from Western Thrace. All "able-bodied" Greek detainees in Turkey
were also to be released. "The exchange of populations was a horrible thing,"
Bristol wrote, but there was "a silver lining, being the means for finally
solving the race problem in this part of the world."[602]

The population exchange was a long time in coming. Venizelos, who signed
the agreement on behalf of Greece, had been pursuing such a deal since at
least 1914.[603] Talk of the idea was fitfully renewed in late 1919 against the
backdrop of the investigation into Greek atrocities during the occupation of
Smyrna.[604] Article 143 of the 1920 Treaty of Sèvres provided for "a special
arrangement relating to the reciprocal and voluntary emigration of the populations of Turkish and Greek race in the territories transferred to Greece and
remaining Turkey respectively."[605]

But while Sèvres was a dead letter, the idea of exchange was not. Many
observers, from a variety of political persuasions, felt it was a worthwhile
endeavor. Arnold Toynbee, who sympathized with the Turkish Nationalists, grudgingly approved.[606] The missionary William Peet, who tended to
sympathize with the Christians, thought that, to assure a lasting peace, it
was necessary that the minorities emigrate each to "the area controlled by
people of their own race."[607] The great powers agreed. Nansen, the League
of Nations High commissioner for refugees, thought that to "unmix the

populations . . . will tend to secure the true pacification of the Near East."[608] For his part, Rendel dispensed with politic language. He knew the problem was principally Turkey's behavior toward its Greeks. "We are no longer able to obtain any effective protection for the Greek minorities in Turkey, and the Kemalists are adopting a policy of violent xenophobia which makes them eager to expel or otherwise eliminate all non-Turkish elements," he wrote in November 1922. "It is therefore an urgent matter to provide for the departure of the remaining Greek minorities from Anatolia." Rendel hoped this would include detained army-age men, prisoners of war, and "Islamized" Christian women and children in Turkish homes.[609]

The British ambassador in Athens, Francis Lindley, had proposed the exchange idea afresh in February 1922.[610] But Venizelos was troubled by the prospective demographic asymmetry. There were only 200,000 Turks in Greece, he said in mid-October, but there were 800,000–900,000 Greeks in Eastern Thrace and Constantinople. A one-for-one exchange would leave hundreds of thousands of Greeks in Turkey. That would be no solution to the minorities problem.[611] Others believed the population figures were less divergent, though, and the numbers were changing radically in the last months of 1922, as hundreds of thousands of Greeks fled Turkey or were expelled. In November 1922 the British Legation in Athens estimated that about 500,000 Muslims lived in Greece.[612] That same month Rendel estimated that 500,000–600,000 Greeks remained in Asia Minor, most of them detained army-aged men and young women and children.[613]

Formal consideration of an exchange began in late 1922, during the Lausanne negotiations and hard on the heels of the exodus from Smyrna. The Allied high commissioners discussed the idea with Nansen. Both the Greek and Turkish governments "seemed to agree . . . in principle," Rumbold said. From the beginning the Turks wanted "all Greeks" to leave, from Constantinople as well as Anatolia. French High Commissioner Maurice Pellé objected that Greece couldn't accommodate so many arrivals.[614] The high commissioners and Nansen agreed to call on the two governments to set up a joint commission, with League of Nations representatives, to iron out the details.[615]

When Nansen met the Nationalists' Hamid Bey in Constantinople on October 31, 1922, that city's Greeks remained the major sticking point. The Turks still sought a "compulsory exchange of whole of Mussulman inhabitants now living in Greece, Macedonia and islands etc. for total Greek population in Turkish dominions including Constantinople."[616] Greece still wanted Constantinople's Greeks exempted.[617] Nansen submitted a seventeen-article draft treaty, which omitted Constantinople's Greeks from the terms of exchange.[618] The Turks turned it down and the negotiation collapsed. If there was to be an exchange agreement, it would have to be within the wider framework of Lausanne, which would enable the kind of horse-trading necessary to reach a deal.[619]

There were areas of complication aside from the fate of Constantinople Greeks. One concerned the potential transferees themselves: not all wanted to move, in spite of the persecution they had experienced. There were many Muslims in Greece, some of them Greek-speaking, who wanted to stay. The largest concentration was in Macedonia. Toward the end of 1922, as Turkish pressure on Anatolia's Greeks mounted and the idea of compulsory exchange took hold, the Greeks began to pressure Macedonia's Muslims to leave. The government billeted refugees in Muslim villages, requisitioned houses, extracted money and goods from Muslims for refugee upkeep, and used troops to aggressively disarm Muslims. Occasionally there were beatings and rapes. "The great majority of the Turkish-speaking Moslems now wish to go," an American observer reported.[620] But beyond Macedonia were many Turks who refused to decamp.[621] In Crete, Muslim landowners wished to stay (while working class Turks were eager to leave).[622] At the same time, many Greek refugees, after months of exile and harsh conditions, wanted to return to Asia Minor come what may. In January 1923 refugees demonstrated in Athens against the prospective agreement, which would see them permanently resettled in Greece.[623] One Westerner reported from a refugee camp in Greece, "All are longing to return to Asia Minor, which they regard as their country. . . . The terrors of the Smyrna flames would appear to be short lived."[624]

Whereas Turkey opposed the repatriation of Greek refugees and demanded that the exchange be compulsory, the Allies and Greece hoped for a voluntary exchange. Ultimately, the two sides met in the middle: exchange would be compulsory, with some exceptions. Greeks could stay in Constantinople if they wished, and Muslims in Western Thrace.[625] On the matter of compulsion, Curzon said, "All those who had studied the matter most closely seemed to agree that the suffering entailed, great as it must be, would be repaid by the advantages which would ultimately accrue to both countries from a greater homogeneity of population and from the removal of old and deep-rooted causes of quarrel."[626] (Reality took a path quite different from the one envisioned in the population exchange. Today about 100,000 Muslims live in Western Thrace, while steady Turkish pressure has reduced the Greek population of Constantinople to insignificance. In 1955 tens of thousands fled after a large-scale pogrom, and in 1964 the Turks expelled thousands of residents who held Greek passports. Today, Constantinople's Greek population numbers some 2,000.[627])

The final agreement, an annex to the Lausanne Treaty known as the Convention Concerning the Exchange of Greek and Turkish Populations, also provided for the release and repatriation of able-bodied Greek detainees—"hostages" and prisoners of war. And property lost on both sides would be assessed and compensated to a degree. But the convention made no mention of Greek women and children in Muslim homes.[628] The accord was extremely unpopular in Greece, partly because the country was already chockful of refugees.[629]

Within days of signing, the Turks violated the language and spirit of the agreement with "fresh deportations" from the Pontus in advance of the exchange's implementation date. The Turks maintained that the Pontine Greeks were leaving of their own accord.[630] The Greeks countered by holding back repatriation of civilian hostages and Turkish prisoners of war.[631] The Turks responded in kind.[632] The Greeks then threatened to expel Muslims to make room for the Greeks being expelled.[633] Bizarrely, even at this late date Bristol appeared to believe that the Turks would allow exiled Christians to return and that they would want to. "By taking an oath of allegiance to the new Turkish Government," they might "reestablish themselves in the properties that they had abandoned," he wrote.[634]

The exchange convention was activated slowly. People were moving on their own, but lack of funds, housing, and transport slowed the formal process. Although implementation was officially set to begin on May 1, 1923, no transfers took place until after the League of Nations Commission for the Exchange of Greek and Turkish Populations convened on October 8. Its members anticipated that "some years" would pass before the convention's full execution.[635]

The first installment of the exchange, supervised by NER, took place in October–November 1923. From Mitylene, 7,024 Muslims and their livestock were ferried to Ayvalık. From the Pontus, 7,491 Greeks were shipped to Greece. The embarkation at Samsun was rough-edged. There were police searches and robberies on the quays, though the malefactors were eventually arrested. In both Samsun and Trabzon, NER had to pay tolls for the quays and quarantine—payments the Greeks did not exact from departing Turks.[636] The ships to Greece were overcrowded.[637] Morgenthau, now heading the international Refugee Settlement Commission orchestrating aid for Greek transferees, described the arrival in Salonica of one boatload: "A more tragic sight could scarcely be imagined. I saw 7,000 crowded in a ship that would have been taxed to normal capacity with 2,000. They were packed like sardines . . . , a squirming writhing mass of human misery. They had been at sea for four days. . . . There had been no food . . . ; there was no access to any toilet. . . . They came ashore in rags, hungry, sick, covered with vermin, hollow-eyed, exhaling the horrible odor of human filth—bowed with despair."[638] For their part, Turks coming from Mitylene complained of Greek "terrorism."[639] Rendel dismissed this as "propaganda."[640]

The Turks often mismanaged the absorption of their refugees. In Smyrna "the immigrants are greeted on arrival with tea and cakes, speeches and flags, and then sent up country very often to starve," the British consul-general said. Some Cretan Muslims, after reaching Smyrna, crossed over to Mitylene and "implored to be admitted back into Greece even at the price of conversion to Christianity."[641] In some places, Turks were unhappy with the resettlement in their midst of Muslims from Macedonia or Crete. In place of "Turkey for the Turks," they raised the cry of "Anatolia for the Anatolians."[642] In Greece, too, where matters were better organized, the immediate lot of the new transferees was not always happy. They arrived destitute, and Greece had few resources with which to assist them.[643]

The Last Wave

By the end of 1923, Christians had been almost completely cleansed from Anatolia. From a population of several million before the decade of systematic deportation and massacre, just a few tens of thousands remained, most of them in its southeastern corner. A larger Christian concentration, in the hundreds of thousands, remained in Constantinople. All were subjected to intimidation.

In Constantinople, where Turkey had reluctantly agreed that Greeks would enjoy residence and security, well-to-do Greeks were "subjected to a persistent form of blackmail. The majority of Greeks pay up. The blackmail usually takes the form of subscriptions to schools, etc. which do not exist. . . . No one dares to complain. . . . The poorer class of Greek, the small shopkeeper, is usually turned out of his shop and a Turk installed in his place." Off the coast, "the majority of shopkeepers on the islands . . . have been arrested and taken to Ismid. Fourteen Armenians, including a doctor, were taken from Maltepe to Ismid and hanged for treason. All the Greeks who cannot pay the military service exemption tax are escaping as fast as possible. It seems quite plain here that everything is being done to drive the Greeks away."[644]

On occasion intimidation took a spontaneous form. On October 6, 1923, the day Turkish troops took over Constantinople from the Allied occupation, a Turkish mob rushed Taksim Square, tearing down awnings in blue and white, the colors of the Greek flag. "All Greek signs" were removed. The Turkish public was taking a vigilante approach to the enforcement of new regulations requiring that "all notices and signs in a foreign language" be removed from Constantinople. In addition, "quite frequently some Turk would knock a hat from a civilian's head and tramp on it. Many women were insulted." But by and large, the police curtailed violence.[645]

In Anatolia the remaining Christian pockets faced more direct intimidation, ending in expulsion. In early 1924 the authorities launched a general round-up aimed at clearing the Urfa, Mardin, and Diyarbekir districts. This was to be "the last clean sweep of Christians from the Ottoman dominions," according to the British consul in Aleppo. "So much for the minority provisions of the Treaty of Lausanne," Rendel wrote.[646]

The process was, by now, entirely familiar. In March the Turks imposed severe restrictions on Christians, mostly Assyrians, in the Diyarbekir-Mardin area.[647] Perhaps hoping to intimidate Christians into flight, the Turks also floated the idea that Armenians would no longer be allowed to live east of a line between Samsun and Lefke and that Greeks would be barred from resettling outside Constantinople in the future, which the exchange agreement did not stipulate.[648] British diplomats wrote that Turks were engaged in "secret terrorism and victimization" and were seizing all Christian buildings and endowments in eastern Turkey.[649]

Other tried-and-true methods included boycotts and murder. In February or March 1924, five Armenians were killed in Urfa. During the subsequent deportations, Armenians were allowed to take only "the clothes they stand in."[650] In September it was reported that "no native Christians remain in Samsoun." The lone church service on Sundays was performed by a Catholic priest, with only foreigners attending.[651] A British official travelling in southern Turkey that month reported seeing 2,000 Greek and Armenian refugees living in cattle trucks at Yenice in "the most filthy conditions." They had almost no food and were left to eat melon rinds. At Mersin the official saw a camp with some ten-thousand Christian refugees, plagued by disease, consuming water "unfit to drink." They were probably awaiting shipment to Greece within the framework of the exchange agreement.[652]

During September–October 1924 the exchange process experienced a snag. The trouble was compulsory transfer to Greece of those the Turks deemed nonresident Greeks in Constantinople. The Turks did not consider them "established residents" (établis), because they were not included in the Constantinople Civil Registers before October 30, 1918. Perhaps a hundred-thousand of the city's Greeks were so registered, leaving thousands open to deportation according to the Turkish definitions.[653] Acting unilaterally, the Turks on October 18 rounded up 4,500 "exchangeables" and interned them at Balıklı. "One procession," the London Times reported, "was headed by a baker's boy, still white with flour and holding a loaf. In another convoy was a child suffering from smallpox who was dragged in a bed."[654] Before the League of Nations ruled on the matter, the Turks shipped out more than 3,000 Constantinople Greeks.[655]

Otherwise the exchange proceeded smoothly. In December Greece reported that about 150,000 Greeks had moved to Greece between October 7 and the end of November under the terms of the agreement. Another 28,000 "non-exchangeables," as defined by Greece, left for Greece between October 7, 1923, and November 30, 1924. These joined the more than 1.2 million who had left for Greece since August 26, 1922. By mid-1926 about 189,000 Greeks had moved from Turkey to Greece and 355,000 Muslims, mostly Turks, from Greece to Turkey under the agreement.[656]

Greeks Kill Turks

All Western observers agreed that Turkish atrocities against Greeks during 1919–1923 were "on a very much greater scale than those committed by the Greeks."[657] But there were, to be sure, several series of Greek atrocities. Starting with the May 1919 invasion of Smyrna, Greek irregulars and the Greek army deported Turkish villagers and townspeople, looted and torched villages, and occasionally murdered and raped. The atrocities occurred in waves, usually linked to Greek military advances or retreats, and to Turkish guerrilla operations and atrocities.

With the expansion of the Greek zone in June–July 1919 came a number of massacres. But as the occupation consolidated and extended eastward over the next few months, the Greek army by and large maintained discipline among troops and irregulars. The Turks complained of heavy-handed arms searches, beatings, robbery, and crop damage, but not of massacres or mass executions.[658] Much of the pillaging appears to have been done by Greek brigands. The Stergiadis administration was so thorough in identifying Greek offenders, and so harsh in punishing them, that local Greeks complained that "the authorities are now more severe towards them than towards the Turks."[659] In April 1920, for example, three Greek brigand leaders were publicly executed.[660] But Toynbee maintained that many brigand bands in the Greek zone—some comprising only Greeks, others mixed Turks and Circassians—were organized by the Greek military.[661]

Over the next two years, Turks abandoned dozens of villages as the Greeks advanced westward past them, toward Ankara. Usually the Turks were ordered out by Nationalists, but sometimes the Greek army expelled them or otherwise pressed them to leave. West of the front line, Turks occasionally attacked Greek columns or trains, triggering reprisals, including mass arrests and the destruction of villages. Occasionally Turkish women were raped.[662] In Gemlik and Orhan Ghazi kazas, in Bursa vilayet, Greek and Armenian bands killed and robbed Turkish travelers and raided villages. The Turks complained that the Greek army had disarmed the Muslim population but not the Christians. On September 7 brigands torched the villages of Tutluca, Bayir-Keuy, and Paşayaylası; massacred dozens of their inhabitants; and carried off Muslim girls. The Greek authorities arrested thirty Armenian and Greek brigands suspected of attacking Tutluca.[663] In November, in Bandırma and its surroundings, locals and soldiers assaulted and murdered Turks before the Greek army restored order.[664] In other areas such as Aydın and Nazilli, Greek administration was sufficiently benign and effective that Turkish refugees were attracted back to their homes.[665]

Greek depredations were most frequent during the army's retreats. Greeks would raid Turks in response to acts of sabotage. Especially during the final retreat to the coast, the Greeks, as a matter of official policy, scorched the earth behind them in order to deny the advancing Turks food and shelter.[666] Already in early January 1921 Rumbold wrote that the Greeks were gradually turning their "zone of operations . . . to . . . a wilderness."[667]

As the war dragged on, with the Greek army suffering heavy casualties and the Turks massacring Greeks along the front lines and in the Pontus, Greek brutality increased. As one British Smyrniot wrote in April, "Flogging has become shooting and there is now a reign of terror throughout all the [Greek-occupied] country."[668] One factor here may have been the large number of Anatolian Greeks newly enlisted—usually under compulsion—in the Greek army.[669] The Anatolian Greeks no doubt had vengeance in their hearts.

In the Edirne-Thracian borderlands, crime appears to have been common. The Turks accused the Greeks of mass arrests, beatings, robbery, and occasional rape.[670] In Söğüt, near Bilecik, the Greeks blew up the tomb of Ertoğrul, father of Osman, founder of the Ottoman dynasty.[671]

In spring 1921 Turkish leaders accused Greek irregulars of several heinous acts. Allegedly they threw inhabitants of the village of Tcherkess-Muslim into a fire and cut off women's breasts there. They set fire to notables in Tcigilli. Near Gumuldjina they forced a shoemaker to walk barefoot on live coals.[672] In Beicos (Beykoz) Greeks cut crosses on the faces of murder victims.[673] And in Kodjai Dir, near Yalova, 1,500 Turkish men, women, and children were assembled in a building and burned alive.[674]

The veracity of these assorted accusations is questionable. Routinely, the Turks threw out general charges, such as a Greek "preconceived plan" to exterminate "the Turkish element."[675] But when the Turks gave specifics—as in March 1922, when the mutesarrif of Samsun told an American officer that Greek brigands had "killed 10,000 Turks" in the Bafra area—they were almost never confirmed by Western diplomats, missionaries, or journalists.[676]

Western diplomats came to believe that most Turkish charges were fraudulent, invented to offset Western accusations of Turkish atrocities.

But there were occasional Western confirmations of Greek atrocities. A number of factors contributed to the Greek violence. The Greek soldiers responsible included a large number of raw recruits and some recent Anatolian Greek recruits. Morale occasionally was low following the failure of Greek offensives. The area of occupation was manned with insufficient forces, making population control more difficult. And the cumulative effects of protracted battle and occupation took their toll.[677] The Greeks also felt justified by their historic claims and their own suffering. As Constantine, the Greek king, put it in a private letter:

> It is extraordinary how little civilized the Turks are. . . . It is high time they disappeared once more and went back into the interior of Asia whence they came. . . . There are still some villages where dangerous fanaticism still reigns, and the Turks go out by night and massacre, in the most atrocious manner, our men or the lorry drivers who happen to be isolated; they mutilate them or even skin them, which enrages our soldiers to such an extent as to give rise to disagreeable reprisals. . . . That is the reason we have so few prisoners—they are all massacred on the spot.[678]

One Greek atrocity occurred along the southern shore of the Sea of Marmara during March–May 1921. In the Yalova-Izmit area, Greek brigands, often commanded by regular officers, destroyed dozens of villages in a process of systematic ethnic cleansing. The Greeks took a leaf out of the Turkish playbook and deported Turkish civil and religious notables.[679] The Allies sent commissions of inquiry to investigate "alleged excesses" by both Muslims and Christians.[680] In Yalova-Gemlik the commission visited torched villages and interviewed Muslims, Armenians, and Greek refugees, as well as Greek officers. One Greek officer "acknowledged" having had four Turks shot. Near Kumlar, the commissioners found "28 bodies of old men and women who had been recently shot or knocked on the head." Some had apparently been killed while the commission was in the area. Dozens of Muslim villages had been looted and burned "by Christian bands" and their populations scattered. The

Greek commandant of the Bazar Keui (Pazarköy) area said that his orders were to "evacuate the Turkish population . . . within his sector" after Turks had attacked Christian villagers and the army's lines of communications.[681]

The commission concluded that, in the Gemlik-Yalova area, the Greek authorities were implementing a policy of "destruction of [the] Moslem element, Greek troops and brigands appearing to act . . . in complete accord."[682] One Greek general told the commissioners that they were carrying out "reprisals."[683]

The Allied commission of inquiry in Izmit stated in its interim report that "both Greek regular officers and men" had committed rape, robbery, and other acts of violence. Several women testified that they had been "raped five times." At Darlık village, a woman and a young girl "were killed after having been raped." Greek troops or irregulars murdered a number of men. In many villages the Greeks stole property, sometimes using torture or murder to extract information about valuables. At Tchboukli (Çobuklu?), near Beykoz, there had been "widespread murder." Eighteen Turks were imprisoned for ten days in an underground cistern; most of them were eventually killed.[684] The commission found that Greek troops had committed murders and rapes in Beykoz in July–August 1920 and again in March–April 1921. The Greek army had used bands of Circassian Muslims to raid Turkish villages.

As bad as it all was, the commission, in its final report, concluded that Turkish behavior in the region had been worse. While there was "credible evidence" that both Greeks and Turks had committed crimes during the previous twelve months, "it appears that those on the part of the Turks have been more considerable and ferocious than those on the part of the Greeks." The Greeks claimed that 12,000 of their villagers were massacred and 2,500 were missing.[685]

An International Red Cross official, Maurice Gehri, accompanied the Yalova-Gemlik commission and produced a detailed report of his own. He saw burning villages, Turkish corpses, and frightened civilians. The villagers spoke of Greek killings, robbery, and rape.

Gehri noted that the area had been occupied by the Greek 10th Division, which comprised mainly Anatolian Greeks, who seemed especially violent. It seemed to Gehri that they shared an ethos communicated to him by

Monsignor Vassilios, the archbishop of Nicaea: "The Greek army has been much too mild in the repression. I, who am not a soldier but an ecclesiastic, I should like to have all the Turks exterminated, without sparing one." On a second visit to Yalova, Gehri was accompanied by the Toynbees, Arnold and his wife Rosalind. At Ak-Keui (Akköy), the group, despite a Greek escort, was led by "two courageous [Turkish] boys" to the graves of sixty murdered Turks.[686] In his report Gehri concluded, "Elements of the Greek army of occupation had, for two months, been pursuing the extermination of the Moslem population of the peninsula." Gehri didn't know whether the policy originated with the 10th Division or the Greek high command.[687]

According to Rosalind, clearly shocked by her first encounter with this brutality, the Greeks "must have killed about 5,500" Yalova-area Turks during the previous six weeks and perhaps as many in the Gemlik area. She implied that these were "Gehri's figures," though they do not appear in his report. She described what had happened as "the methodical and diabolical system of extermination of the whole Moslem population." Arnold's articles, published at the time in the *Manchester Guardian,* were similar in tone, offsetting the general philo-Hellenism of the Western press during those months.

Rosalind's notes appear mainly in a letter she sent her father, the classicist Gilbert Murray. The letter is full of emotional description. She calls Yalova's Christian civilians "semi-human": "They had ghastly bestial faces as though they had been drinking blood; the whole crowd often seemed demoniac . . . as though . . . changing back into wild beasts . . . that were obscene and unnatural, and beyond belief." The contrast to the way she described Turkish refugees was stark:

> The Turkish Women of that district dress still like the Virgin Mary . . . exactly like the typical Italian Madonna, and there they sat . . . several hundred of them, patiently for hours and hours, most of them with children in their arms; they were white with terror, extraordinarily still and quiet . . . and all around them surged this crowd of diabolical "Christians" threatening and jeering. . . . Men stood beside them, bearded, bronzed, with again those patient suffering faces—like Holy families or flights into Egypt—and above the beach . . . were a crowd of "Christian"

women, gay looking, gaudily dressed, laughing and jeering. . . . Arnold
says he has heard descriptions of that queer bestial look on the Turks'
faces during the Armenian Massacres [of 1915–16]—it is evidently a
phenomenon that goes with massacres.[688]

At Armutlu, near Gemlik, Rosalind discovered Greek and Turkish villagers
who were friendly with each other. During the world war, she heard, the local
Turks had pleaded with the authorities and saved their Greek neighbors from
deportation. But during the Greek occupation, Armenian brigands had gathered the Muslim inhabitants of one village in a house and thrown bombs inside. In Armutluoudlou women "were requisitioned" by Greek soldiers.[689]

The Allied investigations appear to have had little impact on the behavior
of Greek troops and irregulars along the Marmara. A subsequent Allied commission of inquiry found that on June 10 Greek "brigands" raided Arablar
and murdered fourteen or fifteen villagers and abducted several women.[690]
According to Ankara, on June 27–28, just before the Greek army evacuated,
Christians slaughtered some 300 Turks in Izmit.[691] The Toynbees reached
Izmit on June 29. Arnold wrote that he had "never seen anything so horrible."[692] Rosalind described the carcasses of oxen and cows "apparently . . .
burned alive"; a burnt kitten (the "most painful and unforgettable thing we
saw," she recorded); the courtyard of the main mosque "strewn with slaughtered pigs" and Korans "torn to bits"; the cemetery littered with sixty-five
bodies, some without hands and feet, one with a beard "like Christ's in many
entombment pictures."[693]

The Toynbees later wrote up memos on dire events in other areas and sent
them to Bristol. Arnold claimed "groups of a dozen to thirty villages at a time
are being raided, plundered, the population massacred wholly or in part,
women violated, people of both sexes occasionally tortured. The survivors
are marched down to Smyrna as 'prisoners of war,' many disappearing on the
way. The rest are shipped—no one knows where."[694] Rosalind wrote of deportations, mainly of notables, from in Kasaba, Manisa, Nif, Alaşehir, Salihli,
Uşak, Kula, Mamara, Akhisar, Tira, Odemiş, Barindir, Torbalı, and Aydın. But
the Toynbees, by their own admission, never visited these places. Instead they
were fed information by leading Smyrna Turks such as Dr. Husni Bey, a large
landowner who had been "completely ruined" and occasionally jailed by the

Greeks, and Ramzy Bey, a barrister. The Toynbees conceded that they had not independently verified any of this information.[695]

Arnold recommended Greek evacuation of Anatolia and stationing Allied troops in the area because "the native Greek population would not [otherwise] be safe." Such insecurity, however, was "hardly a reflection on the Turk—it is only to say that he is human and would be tempted to take revenge for the intolerable treatment he has been undergoing."[696] Arnold believed—or said he believed—that the Greek atrocities were "organized" from above and that the Greeks had systematically unleashed a "war of extermination" against the Turks throughout the areas that they had evacuated in northwestern Anatolia.[697]

British officials rejected the Toynbees' claims. Rendel described Arnold as "notorious for virulent hatred of Greece, for passionate championship of the Turks and for total lack of balance and judgment on any questions connected with the Greco-Turkish conflict."[698] It seemed the London University historian was making amends for earlier writings that had embarrassed the Turks.[699] As a Foreign Office official in charge of political intelligence on the Ottoman Empire during the Great War, Toynbee had been a strident critic of Turkey and had aided Lord Bryce in compiling *The Treatment of Armenians in the Ottoman Empire 1915–16,* a British Government publication documenting atrocities against the Armenians.

Bristol, however, found the Toynbees' claims more amenable and forwarded them to Washington.[700] In June 1921 he wrote, "The Greeks and Turks practice the same methods of murdering the civil population and destroying cities and towns."[701] The fact that Muslims had killed "thousands" whereas Christians had killed only "hundreds" was of no consequence; "it was as bad to steal five cents as five dollars." Bristol concluded that "the Christian races" in Asia Minor "are just as bad as the Moslem races."[702] He invited American journalists, such as the *New York Tribune*'s John Dos Passos, to Izmit to find out the truth. "I pointed out to him how regrettable . . . it was that the true picture of conditions out here was not before our people at home and instead they were deceived by Greek and Armenian propaganda."[703] Bristol also argued that Greek atrocities had triggered Turkish "reprisals" in the Pontus.[704] Arnold Toynbee implied the same when he wrote, "The Greek organized atrocities began about April 18, 1921, the Turkish about June 1, 1921."[705]

The Greek army carried out a systematic scorched-earth policy when it retreated from the Sakarya-Sivrihisar area in summer 1921. Some 250 villages were wholly or partly torched. In most, according to Turkish testimony, there had been killings and rapes, and mosques were destroyed, despoiled, or damaged. In one village, Gecek, soldiers "tore to pieces and burned." American missionaries visited several villages and confirmed a range of allegations but reported no massacres.[706] The British consul-general in Smyrna, Harry Lamb, described Greek policy: "They are decided to leave a desert behind them. . . . Everything which they have time and means to move will be carried off to Greece; the Turks will be plundered and burnt out of house and home."[707]

The Greek army again adopted a scorched-earth policy during its retreat to the Ionian coast in August–September 1922. "Retreating Greek army burned eighty percent of the smaller villages[,] nearly every *chiftlik* [farm] and partially burned almost all larger ones," a missionary wrote. "We did not pass a single inhabited place on the road from Broussa."[708] At Bandırma, two-thirds of the houses were torched, according to a French consul.[709] At Karacabey in October Turks told an American officer that Greeks had murdered 300 people and torched the town. To the south, the Turks said, Greeks burned the towns of Manisa, Kasaba, Salihli, and Alaşehir; murdered Turks; and raped hundreds of girls. In Manisa some of the raped girls were "compelled to drink petroleum and . . . were set on fire." At Salihli, an American lieutenant named Perry saw one or two disinterred bodies and was persuaded by Turkish eyewitnesses of the veracity of at least some of the allegations.[710] Rendel noted that "the Greek [government] admit the destruction caused by the Greek army in its retreat."[711]

An indication of the difference in levels of atrocity committed by the two sides is provided, by default, in a letter sent by Thracian Turkish notables to Bristol in July 1922. The letter speaks generally of "misdeeds, the likes of which do not exist in the annals of history" and then gives details: "A Greek officer, two sergeants, two interpreters and a secretary have occupied the building of the Mussulman Community of Eskidje." Or "a society has been formed with the pretext of finding clothing for poor children. This society obliges the Moslems to give a minimum sum of 10 drachmas per person. [An] officer's wife, accompanied by two soldiers, penetrates into houses and herself gathers this tax." Most of the alleged offences listed were similarly trivial. The complaint also alleged beatings of Turkish peasants, sometimes resulting in individual deaths, and occasional rapes. There is no mention of organized massacres or mass rape or mass torture.[712]

There were other differences. For one, the Greeks punished, or tried to punish, perpetrators. For instance, after the Yalova-Gemlik incidents, the 10th Division commander, General Georgios Leonardopoulos, was removed from his post, "severely censured," and sent back to Athens. Two alleged massacre perpetrators were arrested and faced court-martial.[713] The Turks, as far as is known, never punished perpetrators of anti-Christian atrocities.

For another, while Westerners were able to verify some relatively small-scale instances of persecution, efforts to confirm the worst Turkish charges failed repeatedly. General Harington, the British commander in Constantinople, wrote that Turkish allegations of Greeks burning villages in Eastern Thrace have "so far" not been "confirmed" by Allied air reconnaissance or the Allied commissions. The British diplomat Eyre Crowe summarized all this understatedly: Turkish anti-Greek "allegations [regarding Thrace] . . . are seldom confirmed." Indeed, local Turks were generally so well treated that they displayed "unwillingness" to leave Greek territory, "where they enjoy considerable prosperity and privileges, and full political rights."[714] Hole reported from Salonica that there is "but very slight foundation for the allegations" of massacre, though there was "brigandage," and Greek refugees occasionally forcibly entered Turkish homes.[715]

An illustrative case is the Turks' dramatically inflated story of the travails of Cretan Muslims under Greek rule. According to the British consul general in Crete, the Turks claimed that the Greeks were engaged in a "reign of terror" with "armed bands proceed[ing] up and down about the country, killing and wounding Mussulmans." The diplomat called this "a great exaggeration."[716] He reported in March 1923 that, since September 1, there had been only four murders in the Canea (Chania) district, one of which was "a vulgar '*crime passionnel*.'" He wrote, "In view of the amount of bloodshed which goes on normally in Crete between Christians, these figures really cannot be considered in any way out of the ordinary."[717]

The British chargé d'affaires in Athens, Charles Bentinck, was astounded by the chutzpah underlying Turkish allegations of Greek abuses. He had seen the difference in Turkish and Greek behavior with his own eyes, embodied by the prisoners of war at Piraeus. The Greek arrivals looked like "human wrecks." The departing Turks, on their way to Constantinople, resembled "nothing so much as fatted cattle."[718]

Conclusion

Between 1894 and 1924 the Christian communities of Turkey and the adjacent territories of eastern Thrace, Urmia, and parts of the Caucasus—Armenians, Greeks, and Assyrians—were destroyed, in staggered fashion, by successive Ottoman and Turkish governments and their Muslim agents. The process of ethnic-religious cleansing was characterized by rounds of large-scale massacre, alongside systematic expulsions, forced conversions, and cultural annihilation that amounted to genocide. At the end of the nineteenth century, Christians had constituted 20 percent of the population of Asia Minor. By 1924 their proportion had fallen to 2 percent.[1]

The destruction of the Christian communities was the result of deliberate government policy and the will of the country's Muslim inhabitants. The murders, expulsions, and conversions were ordered by officials and carried out by other officials, soldiers, gendarmes, policemen and, often, tribesmen and the civilian inhabitants of towns and villages. All of this occurred with the active participation of Muslim clerics and the encouragement of the Turkish press.

This is the inescapable conclusion that emerges from the massive documentation—American, British, French, German and Austro-Hungarian—that we have studied over the past decade. The hundreds of thousands of reports, letters, and diary entries produced by Western diplomats, officers, missionaries, businessmen, and travelers who lived in Turkey or passed through it—especially Anatolia—during 1894–1924 are clear and unchallengeable. Moreover, the Ottoman-Turkish archives, which over the past century have been purged of directly incriminating evidence, corroborate this conclusion through a mass of indirectly supportive documentation.

The number of Christians slaughtered between 1894 and 1924 by the Turks and their helpers—chiefly Kurds but also Circassians, Chechens and, on occasion, Arabs—cannot be accurately tallied and remains a matter of dispute. For decades, Armenian spokesmen and historians have zoomed in on World War I and have referred to 1-1.5 million Armenians murdered during 1915–1916, the core genocidal event during the 30-year period. Recent works, including by Armenian historians, have revised that figure substantially downwards. A major initial problem is that there are no agreed figures for the number of Armenians in the Ottoman Empire in 1914. Secondly, no proper count was made of the number of Armenians who survived and reached foreign lands. Most historians estimate that on the eve of WWI, there were 1.5–2 million Armenians in the empire, mostly in Anatolia, and that between 800,000 and 1.2 million of them were deported. Raymond Kevorkian has written that 850,000 were deported and that "the number of those who had perished exceeded 600,000" by late 1916.[2] Presumably he believes that more died during the following years. Fuat Dündar maintains that about 800,000 were deported and that altogether 664,000—consisting of those who were slaughtered in place, died during the deportation marches, or died in their places of resettlement—were dead by war's end.[3] Taner Akçam has estimated, mainly on the basis of Talât's calculations in late 1917, that some 1.2 million Armenians were deported. Of these only 200,000 or so were alive by late 1916, implying that one million were murdered in 1915–1916.[4] None of these estimates include the number of Armenians killed before and after World War I.

There is general agreement that about a quarter of a million Armenians fled the empire during the war, most of them to Russia, and that a similar number survived the deportations. Moreover about 300,000 Armenians remained in Turkey through the war, never deported. A hundred thousand of them were in Constantinople and smaller numbers lived elsewhere, mainly in Smyrna, Edirne, and Konya.[5] Looking at the whole 1894–1924 period, to those murdered during the Great War should be added at least 200,000 Armenians who died during and as a result of the massacres of 1894–1896 and their aftermath. Another 20,000–30,000 were slaughtered in 1909 during the Adana pogroms. Many thousands more were slaughtered by the Turks during 1919–1924. It is therefore probable that the number of Armenians killed over the thirty-year period, 1894–1924, exceeded one million, perhaps substantially. In this number we include not only those murdered outright but also those deliberately placed in circumstances of privation and disease that resulted in death.

The number of Greeks murdered during 1894–1924 is also uncertain, for many of the same reasons. The number of Greeks living in the Ottoman Empire in 1913 is in dispute, though most historians speak of 1.5 to 2 million. Few Greeks were killed in 1894–1896. But hundreds, and perhaps thousands, died during the first half of 1914 as the Turks tried to ethnically cleanse the Aegean coast and western Asia Minor. Many tens of thousands, and perhaps hundreds of thousands, were murdered by the Turks during the Great War, in the course of the brutal deportations inland of Greek coastal communities and in the army's labor battalions. Most significantly hundreds of thousands were murdered during 1919–1924, when the Turks systematically massacred army-aged men and deported hundreds of thousands of men, women, and children to the interior and then, in a second stage, to the coasts, from which the survivors were shipped off to Greece. Prominent among the victims in 1920–1922 were those deported from the Pontic coast and Smyrna.

Tessa Hofmann, a historian of the ethnic cleansing of the Ottoman Greeks, has argued that there were 2.7 million Greeks in the Ottoman Empire before 1914, and 1.2 million reached Greece in 1922–1925; hence, 1.5 million were murdered.[6] But the figure 2.7 million is likely an exaggeration. Moreover, several hundred thousand Ottoman Greeks fled to Russia and other countries during 1914–1924, and several hundred thousand escaped deportation altogether.

Most Greek historians accept the League of Nations' estimate from 1926 that about half of Asia Minor's estimated 2,000,000 Greeks died during 1914–1924.[7] At the opposite extreme, Justin McCarthy, a pro-Turkish demographer and historian, has written that "between 1912 and 1922, approximately 300,000 Anatolian Greeks were lost . . . from starvation, disease and murder."[8] This phrasing omits from the count Greeks murdered before 1912—admittedly, a very small number—and those killed after 1922, a larger number. McCarthy also omits altogether what befell Greeks in Thrace, Constantinople, and the Caucasus.

The number of Assyrian Christians murdered during 1894–1924 is also uncertain. Donald Bloxham has estimated that "perhaps 250,000" Anatolian and borderlands Persian Assyrians, of a total population of 619,000, were massacred by the Turks and their helpers during World War I.[9] But his estimate does not appear to take account of Assyrians massacred before the war or during 1919–1924.

The preceding assessments suggest that the Turks and their helpers murdered, straightforwardly or indirectly, through privation and disease, between 1.5 and 2.5 million Christians between 1894 and 1924.[10]

In recent decades historians have written well and persuasively about the Armenian Genocide of 1915–1916. But what happened in Turkey over 1894–1924 was the mass murder and expulsion of the country's *Christians*— Armenians, Greeks, and Assyrians. All suffered massive loss of life, all were equally shorn of their worldly goods, and nearly all who survived—save the Christians of Constantinople—were expelled from the country. In the wake of their demise, the ethnic-religious infrastructure and culture of all three groups were erased, their homes, neighborhoods, towns and villages, churches, schools and cemeteries demolished or appropriated and converted to Muslim use. In the end, no denomination was shown "favoritism"; all suffered the same fate.

It is true that the ruling Turkish elite was consistently most hostile to the Armenians, who suffered the largest number of fatalities during the thirty-year period. And the purge of the Christians kicked off in 1894–1896 with the mass murder of Armenians, though some Assyrians also were killed. During the following decades the Turks and their helpers intermittently killed and expelled Armenians en masse, all the while designating them a disease that deserved and necessitated extirpation. (The Turks' language—"cancer," "microbes"— would be echoed years later in the Nazis' description of the Jews.) Even in 1922, when few Armenians remained in the country and the Greek Army had just massacred Muslims in its helter-skelter retreat to the Ionian coast, the Turks initially and deliberately murdered thousands of Armenians and only subsequently turned their guns and knives on Smyrna's Greeks. Overall, during 1894–1924, the Turks seem to have murdered most of the empire's

Armenians while expelling rather than murdering most of its Greeks. Another indication of the overriding animosity toward the Armenians is that, through much of this period, they were barred from leaving the country—and marched to destruction—whereas Greeks were generally encouraged to expatriate.

There are several reasons for this differential treatment. Some are rooted in specific circumstances of time and place; others are more general. Most importantly the Armenians posed the first nationalist challenge to the Ottoman Empire and did so in its Asiatic core. Their intellectual elite took to nationalism a decade or two earlier than the Ottoman Greek elite (and, for that matter, the intellectual fathers of Arab nationalism). Moreover, the Armenian nationalist claim was for autonomy or even independence in the Turks' Anatolian heartland, not in its coastal peripheries. And the Armenians resorted to terrorism. This terrorism was no doubt a consequence of the Armenians' desperation, a desperation partly resulting from the blighting vassaldom of their rural masses. Unlike the Ottoman Greeks—who, since 1830, had the Kingdom of Greece to look to—the Armenians had no homeland to offer succor or haven. Eastern Anatolia, and perhaps Cilicia, was their homeland, as the Turks understood. And these were, of course, parts of the Turks' own homeland. So, from the start, the Turks viewed the Armenian nationalists as a dire threat to the empire's territorial integrity, indeed existence. The Turks' worries may have been exaggerated, even paranoid. But many felt them sincerely, much as many Nazis later took seriously the absurd notion of a Jewish "threat" to Germany.

To these reasons must be added the Turks' feeling, from 1914 on, that the Armenians had betrayed them. Armenian politicians, who had also sought Abdülhamid's removal, had been allies of the rebellious Young Turk leadership in the years before the CUP seized power, and even in the first years following their successful power-grab. But, at the same time, in the 1890s and early 1900s, the Armenians had often pleaded for Russian or Western diplomatic, political, and military intervention on their behalf—which the Turks regarded as treasonous. And in 1914–1916, the CUP trumpeted the Armenians' alleged aid to the Russian armies fighting Turkey in the east, beginning with the Battle of Sarıkamış.

Though the Balkan Wars, in which Greece participated, gave the Ottomans a serious scare, the Ottoman Greeks posed no serious threat to the empire, having produced in Anatolia no operative national movement or terrorism before 1919. To be sure, some Ottoman Greeks during these wars had openly displayed pro-Greece sentiments. But that was it: no rebellion, no terrorism. Moreover, the Ottoman Greeks were to a degree a protected species. Before World War I, the Turks worried that wholesale massacres of Ottoman Greeks might lead to war with Greece and to retaliatory Greek persecution of Muslims. And during August 1914–May 1917, the Turks' desire to maintain Greek nonbelligerence was even stronger, as Greece's entry into the world war on the Allied side might tilt the odds against them.[11] In any event, during World War I there was no Ottoman Greek insurgency in Anatolia.

Nonetheless, in the first half of 1914 and during the Great War itself, the Turks made centrally orchestrated efforts to rid Anatolia of at least some of its Greeks, and hundreds of thousands were indeed hounded into the interior or out of the country, or killed.

Then in 1919, against the backdrop of the war against the invading Greek army, the gloves came off. The Greek seizure of Smyrna and the repeated pushes inland—almost to the outskirts of Ankara, the Nationalist capital—coupled with the largely imagined threat of a Pontine breakaway, triggered a widespread, systematic four-year campaign of ethnic cleansing in which hundreds of thousands of Ottoman Greeks were massacred and more than a million deported to Greece. Whereas during the war the Ottomans could march the Armenians to empty marchland deserts, afterward, there were no such places left. The Greek "problem" had to be solved within the boundaries of a newborn Turkey, by murder or forced assimilation (conversion), or else by expatriation to Greece. Initially the Greeks of the littoral, especially in the Pontus, were deported inland, with genocidal intent. Adult men were usually first taken aside and murdered, while the convoys consisting of women, children and the elderly were brutally marched hither and thither across the sunbaked plateaus and snow-covered mountains or dispersed in Muslim villages. Then in late 1922–1923, Nationalist policy changed. While the Turks continued killing many thousands of men from Ionia and the Pontus, women, children, and the elderly were driven from the interior and the coastal towns and deported to Greece. This last stage meant ethnic cleansing through exile rather than genocide. But throughout 1914–1924, the overarching aim was to achieve a Turkey free of Greeks.

The dispatch of the Armenians began earlier and was more thorough, partly because they enjoyed no concrete foreign protection. Throughout 1894–1924, the Western Powers and Russia, while often intervening diplomatically, failed to send troops or gunboats to save them. The Turks were free to murder or deport Armenians at will. The repeated Russian invasions of the Van-Urmia-Erzurum areas during World War I probably saved some Christian lives, but this was incidental to their war-making. The primary objective was strategic rather than humanitarian. The Armenians were abandoned to their fate, as the Turks, since 1894–1896, understood they would be.

As we have said, historians have tended to focus on what befell the Armenians, specifically in the years 1915–1916. But the mass murder of the Armenians in the Great War was not an aberration—as, say, the Holocaust of 1940–1945 was in the course of modern German history. The Turks systematically murdered Armenians en masse before, during, and after 1915–1916. We believe the story must be viewed as a whole, beginning in 1894 and ending in 1924, and that one needs to look at the whole thirty-year period in order to properly understand the events of 1915–1916. Looking at the Armenian segment of what unfolded, historian Richard Hovannisian has written, accurately in our view, that there was a "continuum" of genocidal intent and a "continuum of ethnic cleansing," aiming at the "de-Armenization of the Ottoman Empire and the Republic of Turkey," stretching from 1894 to the 1920s, even if "it is unlikely that the sultan [Abdülhamid II in the 1890s] thought" in terms of complete extermination.[12] We would add, however, that it was not so much "de-Armenization" as de-Christianization that the Ottoman and Nationalist Turks were after.[13]

Viewed in retrospect, the 1894–1896 massacres pointed the way to 1915–1916, and 1915–1916 pointed the way to 1919–1924. On various levels 1894–1896 was a trial run. Abdülhamid was quoted as saying, "The only way to get rid of the Armenian question is to get rid of the Armenians."[14] The 1890s persuaded the next generation of Muslims and Christians that genocide was possible—the populace and troops would do the job, the great powers would not interfere, the Armenians would not resist—and conditioned the Muslims for the next stage by dehumanizing and marginalizing the Armenians. In 1915–1916 the Turks were killing what some of them referred to as "infidel dogs." The killing and massive confiscation of Christian property during WWI, by individuals and the state, were merely a repetition, albeit expanded, of what had happened in the 1890s, as was the rape and acquisition of Armenian women for immediate or long-term use.

During the Great War the Young Turk leadership understood and acknowledged the connection between 1915–1916 and 1894–1896, and, indeed, saw themselves as improving on what Abdülhamid had begun. "I have accomplished," Talât reportedly told friends, "more toward solving the Armenian problem in three months than Abdul Hamid accomplished in thirty years."[15] On May 12, 1915, as the mass deportations were getting under way, Vartkes Serengulian, the Armenian parliamentarian, anticipating massacres, asked Talât, "Will you continue the work of Abdul Hamid?" Talât replied, "Yes."[16]

Likewise the Armenian massacres of 1915–1916 paved the way for the anti-Greek (and anti-Armenian) atrocities of 1919–1924, in which many of the earlier measures were replicated: mass arrest of local leaders, initial killing of adult men, the use of lethal convoys, and so on.

What drove the successive Turkish governments and the Turkish people in 1894–1896, 1914–1918, and 1919–1924 to "de-Christianize" the Ottoman Empire and Turkish Republic? To be sure, there was a common political impulse and motive during the reigns of Abdülhamid, the CUP, and Mustafa Kemal. Most Turks, including the country's leaders, genuinely feared that the Christian minorities, especially the Armenians, were destabilizing the empire and later Turkey. The Turks believed the Christians' actions threatened their country with dismemberment, through a combination of internal subversion and precipitation of Western and Russian intervention.

Another key factor was the ideology of Muslim supremacy. All three regimes, and the Muslim populace, regarded Christian subservience as a state of nature. That had been the empire's experience for centuries. Christian victories and depredations against Muslims—as had occurred in the nineteenth and early twentieth centuries in North Africa, the Balkans, Crete, and the eastern marchlands—were unintelligible subversions of the worldview Muslims had been brought up with. And Christian iterations of equality with Muslims, as prompted and backed by the Christian great powers and enacted as law in nineteenth-century imperial reforms, were an affront to Allah's will and the natural order, based on the time-honored traditions of Christian dhimm-itude. As aggrieved Turkish notables from Kastamonu put it in 1920—against the backdrop of the Franco-Turkish war in which Armenians, too, periodically fought the Turks—"The Armenians, whom we have always protected, now rise against their former masters, they massacre and plunder the [Muslim] inhabitants. . . . We just wonder if an instance of this kind has ever been witnessed in the history of Islam."[17]

After the ethnic cleansing of the Christians, Kemal came to be identified with secularism and modernity. But Kemal, like the CUP leaders, had been brought up Muslim and shared an Islamic world view, as well as a history of familial dispossession and refugeedom at Christian hands in the Balkans. During the Great War, and in the years immediately before and after, these leaders shared with the Muslim population at large a deeply ingrained feeling that the natural order had somehow been overthrown and that matters had to be put right. Such sentiments also underpinned the repeated abuses of the minute Christian communities living in Turkey during the later republican years, from the "wealth tax" of the 1940s to the pogroms of the 1950s and 1960s.

Those who orchestrated the mass murder and expulsions, from Abdülh-amid through the CUP triumvirs to Kemal, were motivated by the desire to maintain the territorial integrity of the empire and then of the Turkish state. Imperial, religious, and nationalist considerations motivated them to roll back foreign control, interference, and influence. Their memories comprehended the gradual diminution of Ottoman-Turkish domains as a result of internal Christian rebellion (Greece, Serbia, Crete), external Christian invasion (Russia in the western and eastern marchlands, Britain in Egypt-Palestine-Syria-Iraq), and the occasional partnership between the two (British and Russian support for internal Christian subversion or rebelliousness).

This political-religious motive shifted from "imperial" to "nationalist" during the years immediately preceding the outbreak of World War I, when the Turks, under the CUP, adopted nationalism as a unifying principle, gradually replacing Ottoman imperialism. The subsequent anti-Greek and anti-Armenian campaigns, leading to expulsion and mass murder, were in large measure driven by this nationalism and its exclusionist ("Turkifying") mentality. But the nationalism that drove the murderous campaigns of 1909 and

1914–1924 also had a religious undertone, as nationalism in most Muslim Middle Eastern countries in the twentieth century always had. To put it another way, given the non-separation of church and state in the Muslim Middle East, the nationalist politics of the region have often been underwritten by, and are inseparable from, Islamic beliefs. Hence in the anti-Christian urban pogroms of 1894–1896 and 1919–1922, Turkish Muslim clerics and seminarians were prominent among the killers and jihadist rhetoric was prevalent, if not dominant, in sermons, billboards, and the Turkish press. Hence, too, religious conversion was often the desired result of depredations. (It is perhaps worth noting that we have encountered no evidence, not one case, of Greeks or Armenians forcing Muslims to convert to Christianity anywhere in the Ottoman Empire during 1894–1924. We find no such instances even in the areas of western Anatolia and Cilicia where Christians—Greeks and Frenchmen—dominated during 1919–1922. Nor, it should be added, have we found cases of Christian priests leading the infrequent massacres of Muslims that occurred between 1894 and 1924.)

To judge from the available documentation, among most of the actual perpetrators of the mass murder and mass expulsion of Christians throughout the thirty-year period, the overriding motivation was religious. The perpetrators viewed the Christians, of all denominations, as infidels who, insurgent or resurgent, should be destroyed. The perpetrators believed they were acting in defense of Islam and in defense of the sacred Islamic domain. For most, the slaughter of Christians, innocents as well as combatants, was imperative in a state of declared jihad. And, of course, the fact that conversion to Islam, in many cases, was sufficient to redeem potential victims and take them into the fold is also proof of the religious impulse underlying Turkish Muslims' actions. Indeed, some Western observers at the time situated the ethnic cleansing of Turkey's Christians within the wider context of a reborn clash of civilizations between the Muslim East and the Christian West.[18]

The Thirty-Year Genocide can be seen as the most dramatic and significant chapter in the de-Christianization of the Middle East during the past two centuries. It was not the last, though. The destruction of Syria's and Iraq's significant Christian communities—which started with the Syrio-Lebanese pogroms in the mid-nineteenth century—is today nearing completion, as is the de-Christianization, demographically speaking, of Syria, Iraq, and

Palestine. For example, Bethlehem, once an overwhelmingly Christian town, is now majority Muslim. These may be the final stages of the Arab and Turkish "awakenings."

It is not by accident that the Ottoman Empire declared jihad against the Allied powers in November 1914, days after entering World War I. Some of the CUP leaders may have been atheists, but even they could not imagine a state that was not based, to some extent, on Islamic solidarity, and they were keenly aware of what it would take to mobilize mass enthusiasm, hatred, and sacrifice. As Enver put it in early August 1914, "War with England is now within the realm of possibilities. . . . Since such a war would be a holy war . . . it will definitely be pertinent to rally the Muslim population . . . [and] invite everyone to come to the state's defense in this war."[19] The Şeyhülislam's fatwa calling for jihad against the Allied powers followed. That fatwa did not specifically refer to the empire's Christian minorities. But it didn't have to. By 1914 the Turkish masses had been conditioned to regard their Christian neighbors as potentially or actually subversive and rebellious, helpmates of the enemy without. It was only natural that removing or destroying them would be a necessary part of the holy war, which the Turkish leadership and masses viewed as a defensive, existential struggle.

Proofs that the Ottoman and Turkish leaders, from Abdülhamid to Mustafa Kemal, saw the problem as one of *the Christians* rather than of the Armenians or Greeks or Assyrians, are abundant, not only in their actions but also in their words. Abdülhamid II, according to his private secretary, believed that "within the limits of our State, we can tolerate but members of our own [Turkish] nation and believers in our own [Muslim] faith."[20] As to the CUP triumvirs, the German ambassador in Istanbul reported that in June 1915 Talât had told one of his embassy staff, "The Turkish Government intended to make use of the World War to deal thoroughly with its internal enemies, the Christians of Turkey."[21] Ambassador Morgenthau lumped the three CUP leaders—Enver, Talât, and Cemal—together when he explained and defined their goal, in his wartime memoir:

> Their passion for Turkifying the nation seemed to demand logically the extermination of all Christians—Greeks, Syrians, and Armenians. Much as they admired the Mohammedan conquerors of the fifteenth and

sixteenth centuries, they stupidly believed that these great warriors had made one fatal mistake, for they had had it in their power completely to obliterate the Christian populations and had neglected to do so. This policy in their opinion was a fatal error of statesmanship and explained all the woes from which Turkey has suffered in modern times.[22]

And Kemal, routinely careful in his public pronouncements, in September 1922 told Westerners that the country's *Christians* "had to go." By then, of course, most had already "gone" under duress, either overseas or deep into Turkey's soil.

The mass slaughter and expulsion during 1914–1924 of the Assyrians is the definitive "tell," indicating that what the Turks sought was the elimination of Turkey's Christians in toto, not this or that ethnic group that happened to adhere to Christianity. The Assyrians had no "national" political agenda and were not thought by the Turks to have one. They did not engage in terrorism. And they were so dispersed and demographically insignificant as to threaten no one. Nonetheless they were murdered and expelled en masse.

Many in the West added a racial veneer to the explanation of Turkish behavior: the murderousness was an expression of the Turks' "character"; here was "the terrible Turk" unchained. Most memorable in this respect was the anti-Turk charge sheet drawn up in the 1870s by Gladstone in his pamphlet, "Bulgarian Horrors," which alleged the massacre of tens of thousands of Christian innocents. Harold Nicolson, a cultivated British diplomat, later put it very clearly: "Long residence in Constantinople had convinced me that behind his mask of indolence, the Turk conceals impulses of the most brutal savagery. . . . The Turks have contributed nothing whatsoever to the progress of humanity; they are a race of Anatolian marauders."[23]

But whether or not one believes that a nation can have an inherent character and exhibit constant and predictable behavioral patterns, the destruction of Turkey's Armenian, Greek, and Assyrian communities during 1894–1924, like most great historical events and processes, was multilayered in its motivation. And somewhat different motives or emphases powered the different sectors of the Ottoman Muslim population. To be sure, religion and politics were prevalent throughout both the organizers and the perpetrators. But there were additional factors.

Kevorkian and other historians have pointed to "the construction of a Turkish nation-state—the supreme objective of the Young Turks," as an additional motive of the CUP leadership in the post-Hamidian massacres. Indeed, Kevorkian designates the 1915–1916 genocide "the act that gave birth to the Turkish nation," the bloody handmaiden of the republic. And he rightly points to another major motive: expropriation of Christian property. This was one of "the major objectives of the Young Turk policy of ethnically homogenizing Asia Minor."[24]

Economics drove Turks on two levels, national and personal. Nationally, the rulers, from Abdülhamid and the CUP through Kemal, all sought to lay their hands on the vast wealth Christians possessed—land, houses, money, businesses. In part, they hoped that the transfer of assets from Christian to Turkish hands would help empower Turks and foster a "national" and "modernized" *Turkish* economy.[25] By the fin de siècle, the minority communities appeared to have too much economic power and too many financial assets: in 1900 twenty of twenty-one metalworking factories in the empire were owned by Christians; in Bursa, thirty-three raw-silk manufactories were owned by Christians and only six by Muslims. (Two were owned by the government.)[26] But the Turkish leaders—especially Kemal—were also driven by other economic considerations. They needed money to finance their successive, impoverishing wars, and they had to house and put on their feet the destitute Muslim muhacirs who had been cast out of the Balkans and Caucasus.

Alongside national considerations, there was the personal motivation of greed. Among the perpetrators—local officials, soldiers and gendarmes, mob members, and Kurdish tribesmen—there was envy of the better-off, or allegedly better-off, Christians and the desire to despoil them of their lands and houses, household possessions, money, and farm animals. Almost every attack on Christians during 1894–1896 and 1919–1923 was accompanied or followed by massive looting, and in some cases the assaults were actually preceded by a call to loot. During 1914–1916, too, a great deal of "neighborly" plunder accompanied the exit of the Greek and Armenian deportees.

Similarly a desire for revenge was operative on the national and personal levels. Destroying the Ottoman Christians was payback for the territorial losses and humiliations meted out to the empire and the Turks since the 1820s by the Christian powers and rebellious Christian minorities, from the Balkans to the Caucasus. And millions of Turks—including muhacirs and CUP leaders—had personal accounts to settle with Christians whose "cousins" had dispossessed them and their families and driven them to Anatolia.

Punishment and deterrence were also important motivators for those un-leashing the anti-Armenian pogroms, especially in 1894–1896. Massacres would dampen Armenian enthusiasm to push for "reforms," let alone inde-pendence, and for individual civil rights. Moreover, once embarked on genocide, the CUP leaders understood that they could not look back, and the mission had to be completed; Armenians left alive would doubtless seek revenge.

The perpetrators included Ottoman and Turkish regular troops; Turkish irregulars, including Kurdish Hamidiye regiments; Kurdish tribesmen; Turkish, Laz, Arab, Chechen, and Circassian villagers; many Muslim towns-people, and muhacirs. In 1894–1896 the massacres were carried out initially by soldiers and Hamidiye cavalry, and then by a mix—different in different sites—of soldiers, gendarmes, and civilians. In 1909 the main perpetrators were Turkish and Kurdish civilians and army units sent "to restore order." In 1915–1916 the murderers were a mix of Turkish soldiers and gendarmes; Kurdish, Turkmen, and, occasionally Arab tribesmen; Special Organization members; and Chechen and other irregulars. In 1919–1923 the killers were soldiers and Nationalist irregulars, gendarmes, Kurdish tribesmen, and villa-gers and townspeople.

Among perpetrators and local officials alike, sexual gratification seems to have played a major role in the assault on the Christians, to judge by the sheer volume of rapes and abductions during the successive bouts of violence. It is probable that rape and the abduction of women and children also served as an assertion of social and religious mastery, especially in societies governed by traditional repressive sexual norms. Perhaps it was understood in some levels of Turkish officialdom that the production of babies thus engendered would enhance Muslim numbers and help in the destruction of the Christian communities. The bouts of violence were characterized by an atmosphere of absolute sexual permissiveness vis-à-vis Christians. We have encountered no evidence that any Muslim in the Ottoman Empire or Turkey was punished for raping, abducting, or enslaving a Christian during 1894–1924. Indeed, rape and abduction throughout the period seem to have been tacitly approved, if not promoted, by the Ottoman and Turkish authorities. Such acts were never publicized or condemned by Ottoman or Turkish spokesmen. Rather, as with the mass murders, the official line was consistently one of blanket denial while charging Christians with the very offences Muslims committed against them.

Following World War II, commentators compared the Armenian genocide to the Nazi destruction of European Jewry. Even the term "Holocaust"—Greek for conflagration—was occasionally used in descriptions of the 1894–1923 massacres of Christians; the massacres often saw Christians burnt to death in churches. Indeed, Hitler at one point reportedly referred to the "annihilation of the Armenians" when envisioning the coming destruction of Europe's "lesser" peoples. And throughout the 1920s and 1930s, the German ultra-nationalists, especially the Nazis, revered Kemal. They held up the Turkish "purification" of Anatolia, of its Armenians and Greeks, as a model in achieving the desired *völkisch* state.[27] Without doubt the twentieth-century wars in which the Germans and Turks participated brutalized both peoples, a pre-condition for implementing genocide.

But the Holocaust and the Thirty-Year Genocide were different in important ways. For one thing, Hitler's racist views led to the biological definition of the Jews and to their destruction. Jews who had converted, or whose parents had converted, to Christianity were not usually spared, and conversion offered no path to safety. In Turkey, by contrast, conversion sometimes assured salvation, and Turks and other Muslims willingly, indeed eagerly, took in Christian women and children and turned them into Muslim Turks, Kurds, or Arabs. Such integration or absorption of Jews into the German national body under the Nazis was unthinkable; the Nazis, indeed, treated sex between Aryans and Jews as a crime. (However, it is also worth noting that the Nazi Germans kidnapped as many as 200,000 Slavic children for "adoption" and "Germanization" during 1940–1945, in a practice resembling the Turks' with respect to Christians during and after WWI.[28]) The Turks, if anything, promoted cross-religious and cross-racial sex between

Muslim men and Christian women, with the offspring automatically bolstering Muslim numbers.

The two genocides differed also in their degree of efficiency. The Armenian and Greek deportation-and-murder processes, while centrally organized, first from Constantinople, then from Ankara, were somewhat chaotic, reflecting the relatively slipshod nature of Ottoman and Turkish administrations, the difficult geography of Anatolia, and the comparative backwardness of its communications networks. At times, too, there seems to have been a measure of dissonance at the top. In 1915–1916, while Talât and Enver were as one regarding the anti-Armenian policy and its execution, the third CUP triumvir, Cemal appears at times to have preferred utilizing Armenians as laborers rather than killing them. Occasionally, from his perch in Greater Syria, he disobeyed or circumvented Talât's murderous directives. But chaos also affected areas beyond Cemal's domain. Contradictory orders sometimes emanated from Constantinople, usually after complaints by ambassadors. One day the localities were ordered to murder all Armenians; the next, orders arrived exempting Protestants and Catholics. Here, conversion assured salvation; there, executions followed hard upon conversions. Corruption, too, took its toll, with wealthy Christians managing to abort or at least delay death by paying bribes. And the weather occasionally interfered. Gendarmes were sometimes averse to deportation marches through snowcapped mountains, which led to delays, though rarely to long-term salvation.

The destruction of Europe's Jews and other "racial inferiors" was carried out far more methodically and systematically, with a uniformity of purpose and method at each stage, and in concentrated fashion over a five or six year period. The Nazis managed to kill 6 million Jews and millions of others, whereas the Turks killed "only" a third or quarter of that number in staggered fashion over a thirty-year period. To be sure, some of the means the Nazis employed changed as the process unfolded. At the start, in 1940–1941, Jews were killed by gunfire and, in the ghettos and concentration camps into which they had been herded, hunger and disease. The shootings and ghettoization were then replaced by gassing in extermination camps, though concentration camps and forced labor continued to exist and exact a major toll in blood well into 1945.

Throughout, the process was marked by clear, stringent organization from the top and executed with consistency by the units in the field, primarily the SS but also the Wehrmacht and the order police and their non-German auxiliaries. The Jews, in the hundreds of thousands, and then millions, were methodically murdered, a virtual production line of death. Almost no one managed to escape from the death camps, and very few survived mass shootings. There were no deviations from the system or purpose; almost no one was spared. Bribes were of no use, and humanity rarely came into play. The perpetrators simply, meticulously did their job. There was almost no dissent and even less disobedience. All acted like cogs in an efficient machine. During the Turkish genocide, sympathetic Muslims managed to save some Christians, and humane officials resisted or delayed orders to deport and kill.

The anti-Jewish campaign was not based on personal sadism, of the sort exhibited by SS officer Amon Goeth in *Schindler's List* (1993). (In this sense the movie was misleading.) Cruelty was pervasive, of course, and massive suffering was inflicted. But suffering was not the perpetrators' purpose. In most cases the process was impersonal and cold, and geared only to extermination. The Turks' mass murder and deportation of the Christians during 1894–1924, on the other hand, was highly upfront and personal and involved countless acts of individual sadism. Where the Nazis used guns and gas, many of the murdered Christians were killed with knives, bayonets, axes, and stones; thousands were burned alive (the Nazis burned corpses); tens of thousands of women and girls were gang-raped and murdered; clerics were crucified; and thousands of Christian dignitaries were tortured—eyes gouged out, noses and ears cut off, feet turned to mush—before being executed. In terms of the behavior of the perpetrators, on the level of individual actions, the Turkish massacre of the Christians was far more sadistic than the Nazi murder of the Jews.

Another major difference is that many Armenians and Greeks—especially in 1894–1896, 1909, and 1919–1923—were murdered by civilians, not soldiers or gendarmes, and here and there women and children participated in the killings. Only in 1915–1916 was the murder, of Armenians, handled primarily by the military, paramilitary units, and gendarmes, though Turkish villagers and Kurdish tribesmen also took part. Throughout, the bulk of Turkey's civilians saw what was happening to their neighbors, or otherwise knew, and largely approved of it.

During the Holocaust German civilians were almost never involved in the killing, which occurred mainly in Poland and the Soviet Union. (Of course, this later enabled many Germans to claim they had not known what was going on.) At worst they saw their Jewish neighbors being rounded up and sent off; they rarely witnessed an actual killing. In Turkey the whole death-dealing process was routinely accompanied by robbery and looting for personal gain by townspeople, villagers, and tribesmen. The number of Muslim civilians personally involved, directly and indirectly, in the deportation and mass murder of Christians during 1894–1924 must have been enormous.

Lastly, the two genocidal processes—against the Jews and against the Christians—occurred on very different time-scales. The murderous persecution of the Jews lasted five years or, if one begins the count from Kristallnacht in November 1938, seven years. The Christians of Turkey suffered three decades of persecution even though there were years of relative "quiet" between each murderous bout. This meant that the Armenians—less so the Greeks and Assyrians—underwent an almost unrelenting torment: an Armenian woman from eastern Anatolia, born in the 1880s, would likely have seen her parents killed in 1895 and her husband and son massacred in 1915. If she survived, she probably would have been raped and murdered in 1919–1924. Certainly she would have been deported in that last genocidal phase. For most Greeks and Assyrians, the period of acute persecution would have been restricted to a "mere" ten years, from 1914 to 1924.

All this said, there were many points of similarity between the two genocides. Much as the Nazis saw the Jew as both an external enemy, controlling both Anglo-American capitalism and Soviet Bolshevism, and an internal enemy, polluting German blood and culture, so the Turks saw the Christians as both the external threat and the subversive internal enemy. During both genocides the great powers were aware of what was happening—in Turkey, in real time; during the Holocaust, certainly from 1942—but did next to nothing to save the victims. The exception was the French sealift of Armenians off Musadağ in 1915.

Both the Nazis and the Turks benefitted from the docility of their victims. After the Holocaust, many Zionists in Palestine and later Israel blamed the

Jews of Europe for going "like lambs to the slaughter," almost like unresisting collaborators in their own deaths. The anti-German uprisings in Warsaw, Bialystok, and several other sites, and the activities of a few Jewish partisan groups, were the rare exceptions rather than the rule. Likewise the vast majority of Armenians, Greeks, and Assyrians went to their deaths unresisting; the preemptive rebellions in Zeytun and Van in 1915, and the resisters on Musadağ, were also almost unique. In both cases the power of the state and the situation of the victim populations were such that effective resistance was impossible. Neither the Jews in Europe nor the Christians in Turkey were "nationally" organized or armed.

But there was a difference relating to the two victim populations. During the Holocaust, the Germans found, and made devilish use of, Jews to assist them in the work of destruction. Prominent, usually older, Jews served in the ghettoes' Jewish councils *(Judenrats),* where they "managed" the internal life of the ghettoes and often, on demand, supplied the Germans with lists of Jews destined for "resettlement." The Judenrats ran ghetto police forces composed of young Jews with truncheons, who helped maintain order and also occasionally helped the Germans round up their coreligionists for deportation to the death camps. And, in the extermination camps, *kapos,* many of them Jews, helped with the disposal of the victims' belongings and corpses and in the maintenance of the death facilities—the gas chambers, crematoria, and so on. The council members, ghetto policemen, and Kapos were driven by an instinct to save themselves for as long as possible but often also, in the case of the Judenrats and police, by a desire to assist their communities or relatives and friends.

During the Thirty-Year Genocide, Armenians, Greeks, and Assyrians were not recruited, and did not "assist," their murderers in such institutionalized ways, according to the evidence we have seen. But, to be sure, there were individual Christians who informed on other Christians and handed them over for destruction.

In the course of the massacres, both the Germans and the Turks employed deceit to smooth the path of murder, to stanch potential trouble and rebelliousness on the part of the victims. The Germans told the Jews they were being "resettled in the East" and that "work leads to freedom"; the Turks told the Armenians they were being resettled in the southeast or in Konya, and

Greeks were often led to believe that they were merely being deported just before they were actually executed. In many cases Armenians were told that bribes or conversion would lead to salvation, but they were often murdered after paying bribes or converting.

Both the Germans and the Turks tried, during the years of massacre, to hide what they were doing from the prying eyes of outsiders. The Turks made sure that much of the killing was done well outside cities where consuls and missionaries roamed; the Germans sequestered their murderous enterprise in closed-off ghettoes and camps, mostly in Poland and the conquered parts of the Soviet Union. Both peoples subsequently tried to cover up and expunge the physical traces of the mass killings, by burial and with lime and fire. Both, in describing what happened and in the language used in operational orders and reports, deployed euphemisms. It must be pointed out, though, that much of the original Turkish documentation is inaccessible; perhaps the Turks also used more explicit terms.

While the Germans did not employ forced marches as a means of killing—as did the Turks with the Armenians and Greeks—many Jews died in the marches westward in 1945 as death and concentration camps were dismantled in the east. Both genocides witnessed the assembly of victims in concentration camps or special areas as a preliminary to the coup de grace. In the case of the Turks, these concentration camps were usually open fields, sometimes marked off by barbed wire, in which deportation convoys were halted for a night or a week or months. Often the camps were near railway terminals, in which the inmates died of disease, exposure, and starvation, much as many Jews died of the same causes in the ghettos and concentration camps of Central and Eastern Europe.

In the course of both genocides, the perpetrators looted the victims' property on a large scale; mass murder produced economic gain. In both, gold teeth, and occasionally swallowed jewelry, were extracted from the dead. But it would appear that German soldiers and civilians enjoyed far less personal economic gain than did their Turkish counterparts. Looted Jewish property almost always went to the state or to the leadership, whereas during the Thirty-Year Genocide, plundered property was "shared" between the state and countless Muslim civilians, officials, gendarmes, and soldiers.[29]

There were similarities also in the composition of killing squads. Both Turks and Germans deployed special-operations units, not just regular troops. During the Holocaust, initially, much of the killing was carried out in the East by specially formed Einsatzgruppen; in the Ottoman case, the shadowy Special Organization served a similar purpose, though its operatives largely used local troops, gendarmes, and Kurdish hirelings to do the killing. During both genocides, the chief perpetrators—Germans and Turks—used other ethnic groups as auxiliaries—Poles, Ukrainians, Lithuanians, and Frenchmen; Kurds, Circassians, and Chechens—to round up the victims and murder them.

And, lastly, both peoples, after defeat by the Allies and appropriate regime changes, tried some of the perpetrators, though the postwar Turkish governments quickly abandoned the effort and punished almost nobody whereas the Germans, after initial hesitation, persisted. They tried and punished Nazis for decades. Nonetheless, many Nazis, including actual perpetrators, were reemployed in the bureaucracies of East and West Germany and Austria in the decades after World War II. In the Turkish case, the most prominent World War I–era perpetrators were assassinated by Armenian avengers, but others often resurfaced in the state apparatus under Mustafa Kemal during the 1920s. And whereas the German people acknowledged collective guilt, expressed remorse, made financial reparation, tried to educate itself and future generations about what had happened, and has worked to abjure racism, successive Turkish governments and the Turkish people have never owned up to what happened or to their guilt. They continue to play the game of denial and to blame the victims.

We set out to discover what happened to the Armenians in Anatolia during World War I. Our investigation convinced us that the story cannot be confined to 1915–1916 or to the Armenians and that the Turks' genocidal ethnic-religious cleansings were designed to deal with all the country's Christians and were implemented by successive governments over a thirty-year period. Since the bouts of atrocity were committed under three very different ideological umbrellas, we must resist the temptation to attribute what happened to an aberrant ideology or to an evil faction or person. Clearly Islam was the banner under which, for a great majority of the executioners, the atrocities were perpetrated. But "Islam" in itself is not a sufficient explanation. After all, for centuries the Muslim Ottomans ran an empire that respected religious minorities and protected and allowed them a measure of autonomy, as long as they accepted subordination and obedience. As we have tried to show, it was the specific convergence in the late nineteenth and early twentieth centuries of a declining, threatened Islamic polity and people and the rise of modern nationalisms and greed that brought forth this protracted evil.

We approached this study with no political agenda. Our sole purpose was to clarify a fateful period of history. But in the years since we embarked on this journey, the true dimensions of the tragedy gradually unfolded before our eyes, document after document. We hope that this study illuminates what happened in Asia Minor in 1894–1924, that it will generate debate and, in Turkey, reconsideration of the past.

Abbreviations

BOA	Başbakanlık Osmanlı Arşivi (Prime Ministry's Ottoman Archives)
A. MKT. MHM	Grand Vizier's Chamber, Important Affairs Office Documents
DH. EUM	Interior Ministry, Public Security Directorate
DH. EUM. 2Şb	Interior Ministry, Public Security Directorate, 2nd Bureau
DH. EUM. AYŞ	Interior Ministry, Public Security Directorate, Public Order Bureau
DH. EUM. MEM	Interior Ministry, Public Security Directorate, Officer Chamber Documents
DH. EUM. SSM	Interior Ministry, Public Security Directorate, Traffic and Passages Chamber
DH. I. UM	Interior Ministry, General Directory Papers
DH. KMS	Interior Ministry, Directorate of Special Section
DH. ŞFR	Interior Ministry, Cypher Section
HR. SYS	Foreign Ministry, General Intelligence Section, Political Documents
IAMM	Directorate for the Settlement of Tribes and Immigrants
I. HUS	Privy Directives
Y. A. HUS	Yıldız Palace, Grand Vizier's Office, Requests / Petitions
Y. A. RES	Yıldız Palace, Grand Vizier's Office, Official Submissions
Y. EE	Yıldız Essential Papers
Y. MTV	Yıldız Diverse Submissions
Y. PRK. ASK	Yıldız Occasional Documents, Military Submissions
Y. PRK. BŞK	Yıldız Occasional Documents, Chief Scribal Department Submissions
Y. PRK. UM	Yıldız Palace, Retail notes of all vilayets
Y. PRK. ZB	Yıldız Occasional Documents, Police Ministry Submissions
Bodl. MS	Bodleian Library MS Collections
Lord Bryce Papers	
Rumbold Papers	
Toynbee Papers	

British Documents on Ottoman Armenians	Şimşir, *British Documents on Ottoman Armenians,* Vol. 1: *1856–1880*
DE / PA-AA-BoKon /	Deutschland, Politisches Archiv des Auswärtiges, Botschaft-Konsulat (Political Archive of the German Foreign Office, Embassy-Consulate)
Ermeni Isyanları	*Osmanlı Belgelerinde Ermeni Isyanları* (Armenian Uprising in Ottoman Documents)
Ermeni-Rus Ilişkileri	*Osmanlı Belgelerinde Ermeni-Rus Ilişkileri* (Armenian-Russian Relations in Ottoman Documents)
FDRL	Franklin Delano Roosevelt Library
HM Sr. Papers	Henry Morgenthau Sr. Papers
FRUS	*Foreign Relations of the United States*
German Foreign Office	Gust, *The Armenian Genocide: Evidence from the German Foreign Office Archives, 1915–1916*
HHStA	Österreich, Haus- Hof- und Staats Archiv, Politisches Archiv, Türkei (Austrian Habsburg Archives, Political Archive, Turkey), 1848–1918
Houghton ABC	Houghton Library, American Board of Commissioners for Foreign Missions
LC	Library of Congress
HM Sr. Papers	Henry Morgenthau Sr. Papers
Bristol Papers	Mark Bristol Papers
MAE	Ministère des Affaires Etrangères (Ministry of Foreign Affairs), France
Turquie	Nouvelle Serie (NS)—Turquie
Affaires jusqu'à 1896	Affaires Politiques jusqu'en 1896—Turquie
OeUA	Ohandjianian, *Österreich-Ungarn und Armenien 1912–1918*
SAMECA	St Antony's College Middle East Centre Archive
Sevk ve Iskan	*Osmani Belgelerinde Ermenilerin Sevk ve Iskanı* (Referral and Relocation of Armenians in Ottoman Documents)
SHD	Service Historique de la Défense (Ministry of Defense), France
UKNA	United Kingdom National Archives
FO 371	Foreign Office
WO 95	War Office
USNA	United States National Archives
RG 59	Record Group 59
RG 84	Record Group 84
RG 256	Record Group 256
U.S. Official Records	Sarafian, *United States Official Records on the Armenian Genocide*

Notes

Introduction

1. Davis to Morgenthau, 30 December 1915, quoted in Suny, *They Can Live in the Desert,* 320.

2. "Report of Leslie A. Davis, American Consul, Formerly at Harput, Turkey, on the Work of the American Consulate at Harput Since the Beginning of the Present War. This Report is Prepared at the Request of Mr. Wilbur J. Carr, Director of the Consular Service," 9 February 1918, USNA RG 59, 867.4016, Roll 46. Back in December 1915, Davis briefly mentioned these lakeside trips, "where I saw the dead bodies of fully 10 thousand persons" (Davis to Morgenthau, 30 December 1915, *U.S. Official Documents,* 474).

3. Kevorkian, *Armenian Genocide,* 400.

4. This was already noted in Ambassador Henry Morgenthau's 1918 account: "The Armenians are not the only subject people . . . which have suffered from this policy of making Turkey exclusively the country of the Turks. The story which I have told about the Armenians I could also tell . . . about the Greeks and the Syrians" (*Morgenthau's Story,* 323). The Danish minister in Constantinople also noted that the government "has made xenophobia and hatred toward the Christians a leading principle in its policies" (Carl Ellis Wandel to Erik Scavenius, 14 August 1915, http://www.armenocide.de/armenocide/armgende .nsf/$$AllDocs-en/1915-08-14-DK-001).

5. Kevorkian, *Armenian Genocide;* Bloxham, *Great Game of Genocide;* Akçam, *Shameful Act;* and Suny, *They Can Live in the Desert.*

6. Akçam, "Ottoman Documents and the Genocidal Policies," 127–148. See also Üngör, *Making of Modern Turkey,* xiv.

7. Akçam, "Ottoman Documents and the Genocidal Policies," 127–148. See also Üngör, *Making of Modern Turkey,* xiv.

8. Akçam, *Shameful Act,* 270.

9. Arnett (Ankara and Istanbul) to Department of State, 12 July 2004, published by Wikileaks, https://wikileaks.org/plusd/cables/04ISTANBUL1074_a.html.

1. Nationalist Awakenings in the Nineteenth-Century Ottoman Empire

1. The description of events here and in the following pages is based largely on Hanioğlu, *Brief History of the Late Ottoman Empire,* 109–135; Quataert, *Ottoman Empire,* 54–73; Shaw, *History of the Ottoman Empire and Modern Turkey,* 146–193; and Reynolds, *Shattering Empires,* 8–18.

2. On Krikor Odian, see Suny, *They Can Live in the Desert,* 61–62.

3. Gladstone, *Bulgarian Horrors,* 10. The number of casualties caused by the rebellion and its suppression is unclear. Misinformation was apparently peddled by all sides (see Millman, "The Bulgarian Massacres Reconsidered").

4. Akçam, *Shameful Act*, 37; and Lewy, *Armenian Massacres*, 7–8.

5. For the text of the treaty see Holland, *European Concert*, 335–348.

6. Berlin Treaty, 1878, article LXI. See also Akçam, *Shameful Act*, 39.

7. Lewy, *Armenian Massacres*, 8.

8. It should be noted here that not all Armenian researchers fully subscribe to the "Armenian" version, and certainly not all Turkish scholars accept the "Turkish" narrative.

9. Augustinos, *Greeks of Asia Minor*, 77, 80–82, and 91–107.

10. Levy-Daphny, "What Will You Leave?"

11. "Dragoman" is a Latinized corruption of the Ottoman *tercüman*, meaning interpreter—often used to describe those representing the Ottoman government and Western ambassadors in negotiations.

12. Artinian, *Armenian Constitutional System*, 8–9.

13. See Wharton, *Architects of Ottoman Constantinople*.

14. Artinian, *Armenian Constitutional System*, 21–24; Çaksu, "Janissary Coffeehouses," 120.

15. Lewis, *From Babel to Dragomans*, 25; and Quataert, *Ottoman Empire*, 47–48.

16. Originally the word is the plural of the Arabic *sinf*, meaning, type, grouping, etc. In Ottoman Turkish the word meant a guild or guilds; in modern Turkish it means artisans and day-workers.

17. Artinian, *Armenian Constitutional System*, 25. Wharton points out that there were two distinct groups of amiras—one, of bankers, merchants, and commercial agents; the other, of state employees, such as architects and technocrats. The latter group often served as mediators between amiras and esnafs (Wharton, *Architects of Ottoman Constantinople*, 145).

18. Stamatopoulos, "From Millets to Minorities"; Braude, "Foundation Myths." During the second half of the nineteenth century, "millet" came to be used interchangeably with "nation."

19. Haddad, "Nationalism in the Ottoman Empire," 15.

20. Dündar, *Crime of Numbers*, 177–183. The six so-called "Armenian vilayets" were Van, Erzurum, Sivas, Bitlis, Mamüret-ul-Aziz, and Diyarbekir.

21. Davison, "Nationalism as an Ottoman Problem," 28–30.

22. Mutlu, "Late Ottoman Population," 11. Augustinos says that the Greek Orthodox constituted 8.3% of Asia Minor's population at the start of the twentieth century (Augustinos, *Greeks of Asia Minor*, 21).

23. Gaunt, *Massacres*, 28.

24. Hanioğlu, *Brief History of the Late Ottoman Empire*, 69–70, 88; Quataert, *Ottoman Empire*, 63, 107.

25. Göçek, "Ethnic Segmentation," 509–511.

26. Kitromilides, "Greek Irredentism," 5. See also Davison, "Nationalism as an Ottoman Problem": "there are many Armenian villages where only Turkish is spoken and many Greek villages where the inhabitants have forgotten the speech of their race" (32).

27. Augustinos, *Greeks of Asia Minor*, 152–156. Kitromilides, "Greek Irredentism," 7.

28. It is not clear how "official" and programmatic was this "policy" between 1830 and World War I. Kitromilides, for example, writes that "the process was the result not of a consciously planned and executed state policy, but of individual initiatives and voluntary organization" (Kitromilides, "Imagined Communities," 50).

29. Dontas, "Greece."

30. Koliopoulos, "Brigandage and Irredentism," 86.

31. Smith, *Ionian Vision*, 2–3.

32. Koliopoulos, "Brigandage and Irredentism," 78.

33. Kofos, "Patriarch Joachim III," 110.

34. See Gondicas and Issawi, *Ottoman Greeks*, 163.

35. Toynbee, *Western Question*, 128.

36. Kitromilides, "Greek Irredentism," 9, makes this point.

37. Koliopoulos, "Brigandage and Irredentism," 82.

38. Kofos, "Patriarch Joachim III," 111; and Kitromilides, "Greek Irredentism," 11.

39. As late as 1902, the Greek consul-general in Smyrna was struck by "the sparse knowledge of Greek, even among community leaders, priests and members, and by the political unawareness of members of school committees" and "dismayed by the [locals'] absence of feeling of attachment to Greece" (Kitromilides, "Imagined Communities," 48–49).

40. Toynbee, *Western Question,* 131–132.

41. Augustinos, *Greeks of Asia Minor,* 242n30.

42. Augustinos, *Greeks of Asia Minor,* 198–199.

43. Artinian, *Armenian Constitutional System,* 23–24.

44. Georgelin, "Armenian Inter-Community Relations," 181–183.

45. Artinian, *Armenian Constitutional System,* 28–30.

46. The name Apostolic refers to the purported establishment of Armenian Christianity by two of Christ's apostles, Bartholomew and Thaddeus, in the first century. Gregorian harks back to the beginning of the fourth century, when St. Gregory the Illuminator is said to have converted the king and court of Armenia to Christianity and later to have been appointed the first head of the Armenian church.

47. Whooley, "Armenian Catholic Church"; and Deringil, *Well-Protected Domains,* 119–123. After World War I, in which Anatolia's Catholic Armenian population was decimated, the patriarchate was moved back to Lebanon. See also Gürün, *Armenian File,* 74–75; and Şahin, *Katolik Ermeniler.*

48. Arpee, "Century of Armenian Protestantism," 150–167; Artinian, *Armenian Constitutional System,* 31–44; Makdisi, "Reclaiming the Land of the Bible," 682, 683; and Deringil, "Invention of Tradition," 3–29. Gürün, *Armenian File,* 41. For a description of this British and American missionary activity, see Deringil, *Well-Protected Domains,* 123–134. See also Ternon, *Bir Soykırım Tarihi,* 76–78.

49. Arpee, "Century of Armenian Protestantism," 153–155; Gürün, *Armenian File,* 42–43; and Lewy, *Armenian Massacres,* 6–7.

50. Artinian, *Armenian Constitutional System;* Göçek, "Ethnic Segmentation," 514. See also Payaslian, *History of Armenia,* 114.

51. Quataert, *Ottoman Empire,* 80–81.

52. Nationalized by the Turks in 1971, Robert College is now Bosphorus (Boğaziçi) University, but part of it still functions as a high school retaining the name "Robert College."

53. Artinian, *Armenian Constitutional System,* 72–73.

54. Hacikyan, *Heritage of Armenian Literature,* 3:226–228. See also Artinian, *Armenian Constitutional System,* 64.

55. Hacikyan, *Heritage of Armenian Literature,* 3:227–228.

56. Hacikyan, *Heritage of Armenian Literature,* 3:227–228. Also Gürün, *Armenian File,* 78.

57. Artanian, *Armenian Constitutional System,* 78–82.

58. Artanian, *Armenian Constitutional System,* 83; Gürün, *Armenian File,* 78; and Payaslian, *History of Armenia,* 114–115.

59. Artinian, *Armenian Constitutional System,* 93–103.

60. Artinian, *Armenian Constitutional System,* 104–105; and Kamouzis, "Elites and the Formation of National Identity," 19–20.

61. Gürün, *Armenian File,* 77.

62. Astourian, "Silence of the Land," 58. See also Cuthell, *Muhacirin Komisyonu;* McCarthy, *Death and Exile;* and Ternon, *Bir Soykırım Tarihi,* 105–106.

63. See Verheij, "Frères de terre et d'eau," 230. See also Suny, *They Can Live in the Desert,* 20–22; and Lewy, *Armenian Massacres,* 4.

64. Astourian, "Silence of the Land," 60 and 63.

65. Taylor to Clarendon, n.d., in *British Documents on Ottoman Armenians*, 55.

66. Ternon, *Bir Soykırım Tarihi*, 83–85.

67. Astourian, "Silence of the Land," 58–59; and Lewy, *Armenian Massacres*, 6.

68. Astourian, "Silence of the Land," 59–61. See also Ternon, *Bir Soykırım Tarihi*, 82–83. On the problems of applying the new legal system in the provinces, see Rubin, *Ottoman Nizamiye Courts*, 27–31.

69. Rassam to Layard, 15 October 1877, in *British Documents on Ottoman Armenians*, 97.

70. For Ottoman intelligence on Russian-Armenian relations, see the documents published by the Turkish State Archives in *Osmanlı Belgelerinde Ermeni-Rus İlişkeleri* [Armenian-Russian Relations in Ottoman Documents]. The authorities believed the Armenians in the east were plotting with the Russians.

71. Lewy, *Armenian Massacres*, 4–6; and Astourian, "Silence of the Land," 60.

72. Astourian, "Silence of the Land," 62–63.

73. See, for instance, Alkan, "Fighting for the Nuṣayrī Soul," 23–50; Deringil, "There Is No Compulsion in Religion," 547–575; and Deringil, *Well-Protected Domains*, 63–66.

74. Astourian, "Silence of the Land," 60–65; and Deringil, *Well-Protected Domains*, 69–92.

75. Akçam, *Shameful Act*, 39.

76. H. M. Allen, "Facts and Figures from the Province of Van," undated but from spring 1895, Bodl. MS Lord Bryce Papers 296. A detailed list of exactions by local Kurds from the Armenian village of Hassana, near Diyarbekir, is provided in "Letter to Acting Vice-Consul Boyajian," 17 November 1893, *Turkey No. 6 (1896)*, 29–31.

77. Ihrig, *Justifying Genocide*, 27.

78. Verheij, "Frères de terre et d'eau," 235–236. See also Ternon, *Bir Soykırım Tarihi*, 121–123; and Bulut ve Birol, "XIX Yüzyılın sonlarında Sivas vilayetinde Ermenilerin Faaliyetleri," 4.

79. Bulut ve Birol, "XIX Yüzyilin sonlarında Sivas vilayetinde Ermenilerin Faaliyetleri," 4; Hepworth, *Through Armenia on Horseback*, 295–298; Verheij, "Frères de terre et d'eau," 233: "L'émergence d'un militantisme politique et du nationalisme parmi les élèves des missionaires, surtout les protestants, n'était pas due au hasard."

80. Verheij, "Frères de terre et d'eau," 235–237; Ternon, *Bir Soykırım Tarihi*, 123–132; Hovannisian, "Simon Varatzian," 195–197; Bloxham, *Great Game of Genocide*, 49–51; and Lewy, *Armenian Massacres*, 11–15.

81. Payaslian, *History of Armenia*, 119–120; and Lewy, *Armenian Massacres*, 11–12.

82. Lewy, *Armenian Massacres*, 11–15; Gürün, *Armenian File*, 155–166; and Bloxham, *Great Game of Genocide*, 49–51. Bloxham claims that there is no evidence that this was their intention, but they were willing to accept such consequences of their behavior.

83. See Yildiz Saray, Justice Ministry and Grand Vizier's correspondence with the vilayets and Syriac patriarchate, October 1896, BOA, Y. PRK. UM, 32/96, 28.8.1895; BOA, Y. A. HUS, 344/4 from October 1896. These reports and letters claimed that Armenians in Muslim dress had attacked Christian churches. These impostors, it was charged, also attacked Kurds to create chaos in Mamuret-ül-Aziz vilayet. See also Testimony of Rev. Cyrus Hamlin in *New York Times*, 23 August 1895; MAE, Affaires Politiques Jusqu'en 1896, 514, 13/1/1894; and Bulut ve Birol, "XIX Yüzyilin sonlarında Sivas vilayetinde Ermenilerin Faaliyetleri," 4–5. About the intended provocation of Ottoman authorities, see Hepworth, *Through Armenia on Horseback*, 296, 339–340; and Verheij, "Frères de terre et d'eau," 234.

84. Longworth to Currie, 8 February 1895, UKNA FO 195/1936. Very few Armenians heeded the call of the revolutionaries.

85. Verheij, "Frères de terre et d'eau," 234; and Klein, *Margins of Empire*, 20–24.

86. Yildiz Saray, Justice Ministry and Grand Vizier's correspondence with the vilayets and Syriac patriarchate, October 1896, BOA, Y. PRK. UM, 32/96, 28.8.1895; BOA, Y. A. HUS, 344/4 from October 1896. See also Lewy, *Armenian Massacres*, 9.

87. Klein, *Margins of Empire,* 20–24.

88. The name "Hamidiye" is derived from Abdülhamid.

89. Klein, *Margins of Empire,* 11. See also Deringil, "Armenian Mass Conversions," 349.

90. Klein, *Margins of Empire,* 24.

91. Onal, *Sadettin Paşa'nın Anıları,* 20–23. The French vice-consul in Diyarbekir in 1901 described the regiments as "a band of official highway robbers spreading terror," killing and pillaging Christians with impunity (Travis, "Native Christians Massacred," 330).

92. Verheij, "Frères de terre et d'eau," 238. Simşir, *Kürtçülük 1787–1923,* 207–217.

93. Artinian, *Armenian Constitutional System,* 104–105; and Pamuk, "The Ottoman Empire in the Great Depression," 107–118.

2. The Massacres of 1894–1896

1. Salt, *Imperialism, Evangelism,* 31.

2. Graves to Nicolson, 26 December 1893, *Turkey No. 6 (1896),* 18.

3. For example, see Hallward to Graves, 10 November 1894, *Turkey No. 6 (1896),* 166–169, concerning Bitlis Vali Hassan Tahsin Pasha.

4. H. M. Allen, "Facts and Figures from the Province of Van," undated but from spring 1895, Bodl. MS Lord Bryce Papers 196.

5. Allen, "Facts and Figures from the Province of Van," undated but probably from spring 1895, Bodl. MS Lord Bryce Papers 196.

6. Hallward to Graves, 10 June 1895, *Turkey No. 6 (1896),* 348. See Verheij, "Les Frères de terre et d'eau," 260–262.

7. "Report of G. H. Fitzmaurice to Sir Philip Currie, Constantinople—Ourfa, March 16, 1896," Houghton ABC 16.10.1, Vol. 12.

8. C. S. Sanders, Aleppo, to H. D. Barnham, British consul, Aleppo, 11 January 1895, UKNA FO 195/1883. See also MAE, summary of report sent from Maraş to the French embassy on 4 July 1895, UKNA FO 195/1906.

9. "Report of G.H. Fitzmaurice to Sir Philip Currie, Constantinople—Ourfa, March 16, 1896," Houghton ABC 16.10.1, Vol. 12.

10. Hallward to Graves, 2 February 1895, *Turkey No. 6 (1896),* 238.

11. "Report of G. H. Fitzmaurice to Sir Philip Currie, Constantinople—Ourfa, March 16, 1896," Houghton ABC 16.10.1, Vol. 12.

12. The Committee of the Patriots of Islam, "Placard," undated but enclosed in Francis Clare Ford to Earl of Rosebery, 13 April 1893, *Turkey No. 3 (1896),* 82.

13. Unsigned but by British Embassy in Constantinople, "Precis of Events at Marsovan," April 1893, *Turkey No. 3 (1896),* 80–82; Longworth to Ford, 28 March 1893, *Turkey No. 3 (1896),* 83–85; and Longworth to Ford, 20 April 1893, *Turkey No. 3 (1896),* 95.

14. Graves to Ford, 6 May 1893, *Turkey No. 3 (1896),* 105–106.

15. Graves, "Memorandum on Armenian Troubles in Sivas and Angora Vilayets of January 1893," 1 July 1893, *Turkey No. 3 (1896),* 160–162.

16. "Inclosure 3 in No. 12," signed "The Armenian Revolutionists," attached to Longworth to Arthur Nicolson, 31 December 1893, *Turkey No. 6 (1896),* 13–14.

17. Nicolson to Earl of Rosebery, 16 December 1893, *Turkey No. 3 (1896),* 228. For a French description, see French Ambassador Laboulinière to Foreign Ministry, 19 December 1893, MAE, Affaires jusqu'a 1896, no. 513. For the Ottoman description, see BOA, A. MKT. MHM, 645/1; also quoted in *Ermeni Isyanları,* Vol. 1, 61–78. Initially the Ottomans spoke of sedition encouraged by the Armenian

Patriarchate. But later investigation put the onus on Armenian revolutionary committees and explained the commotion as a result of mutual misunderstandings.

18. Cumberbatch to Nicolson, 2 February 1894, and "Inclosure 2 in No. 33," "Petition concerning Events at Indjirli" (Yozgat), 12 December 1893, in *Turkey No. 6 (1896)*, 33–35.

19. Currie to Foreign Secretary Kimberley, draft letter conveying statement to one of his assistants, "Mr. Eliot," by Protestant Armenian "preacher" at Yozgat, Karekine (or Karekin), 17 May 1894, UKNA FO 195/1823.

20. Cumberbatch to Nicolson, 29 December 1893, *Turkey No. 6 (1896)*, 3–7.

21. Currie to Kimberley (draft dispatch), 17 May 1894, UKNA FO 195/1823.

22. Currie to Kimberley (draft dispatch), 17 May 1894, UKNA FO 195/1823.

23. Currie to Kimberley (draft dispatch), 17 May 1894, UKNA FO 195/1823; Cumberbatch to Currie, 26 February 1894, *Turkey No. 6 (1896)*, 50–52; *Ermeni Isyanları*, Vol. 1, 73.

24. Currie to Kimberley (draft dispatch), 17 May 1894, UKNA FO 195/1823. An alternative explanation of the cause of the fight at Yozgat church appears in Cumberbatch to A. Nicolson, 16 December 1896, *Turkey No. 6 (1896)*, 3–4: the Muslim assembly outside the church was triggered by an ambush of the kadi of Sungurlu, who was robbed and his "harem grossly insulted" by a band of brigands, identified as Armenians. See also Cumberbatch to Nicolson, 29 December 1893, *Turkey No. 6 (1896)*, 6–7; and "Petition of Armenians of Yuzgat to the Sultan and others, 13 December 1893," *Turkey No. 6 (1896)*, 9–10. See Cumberbatch to Currie, 26 February 1894, *Turkey No. 6 (1896)*, 50–52, for a description of the events of 1–2 February in Yozgat.

25. Cumberbatch to Nicolson, 22 January 1894, *Turkey No. 6 (1896)*, 25; and Cumberbatch to Currie, 27 February 1894, *Turkey No. 6 (1896)*, 49–50.

26. Letter from Yozgat to Cumberbatch, 24 April 1894, *Turkey No. 6 (1896)*, 77–79.

27. Cumberbatch to Currie, 13 April 1894, *Turkey No. 6 (1896)*, 69–70.

28. Terrell to (?), 20 February 1894, USNA RG 84, Turkey (Constantinople), Vol. 19.

29. Jewett to Longworth, 3 and 10 February 1894, both enclosed in Longworth to Nicolson, 18 February 1894, UKNA FO 195/1854.

30. Currie to Lord Kimberley, 14–15 October 1894, UKNA 195/1825.

31. Unsigned report from a Bitlis missionary, 18 January 1895, Houghton ABC 16.10.1, Vol. 6.

32. Hammond Smith Shipley to Graves, 15 March 1895, UKNA FO 195/1891, Tavo's testimony.

33. Kurd petition, "Through Her Majesty, the Queen of England, to the Great Powers of Europe," 27 June 1895, attached to Graves to Currie, 25 July 1895, UKNA FO 195/1892.

34. Statement by Hamms and his wife Altoon, of Geligüzan, and Ovig, of Talori, undated but probably from early 1895, Bodl. MS Lord Bryce Papers 208.

35. Unsigned report from Bitlis missionary, 18 January 1895, Houghton ABC 16.10.1, Vol. 6. For the detailed confession/testimony of Daghmatian (Damdaian) after his capture, see BOA, Y. PRK. BŞK, 35/29, 23 February 1894; *Sevk ve Iskan*, 18–48, doc. 7.

36. Statement by Hamms and his wife Altoon, of Geligüzan, and Ovig, of Talori, undated but probably from early 1895, Bodl. MS Lord Bryce Papers 208.

37. Shipley to Currie, 1 March 1895, UKNA FO 195/1887.

38. Vice-Consul Thomas Boyajian (Diyarbekir) to Graves, 16 March 1894, *Turkey No. 6 (1896)*, 73–74.

39. Statement by Hamms and his wife Altoon, of Geligüzan, and Ovig, of Talori, undated but probably from early 1895, Bodl. MS Lord Bryce Papers 208.

40. For a summary of French correspondence about these events, see Cambon to Develle, November 1894, MAE, "Documents Diplomatiques, Affaires Armeniennes, Projets de réformes dans

l'Empire Ottoman 1893–1897" (henceforward referred to as "Projets de réformes"), Bodl. MS Lord Bryce Papers 211–212, pp. 21 and 35–135. For Ottoman sources, see Rustem Paşa to Said Paşa, 5 February 1895, BOA, HR. SYS, 2814-1/12, 2814-1/13, 11; and Rustem Paşa to Said Paşa, 6–7 February 1895, BOA, HR. SYS, 2814-1/5-7. Unsigned report from a Bitlis missionary, 18 January 1895, Houghton ABC 16.10.1, Vol. 6.

41. Unsigned report from Bitlis missionary, 18 January 1895, Houghton ABC 16.10.1, Vol. 6. For the detailed confession/testimony of Daghmatian (Damdaian) after his capture, see BOA, Y. PRK. BŞK, 35/29, 23 February 1894, *Sevk ve Iskan,* 18–48, doc. 7.

42. Unsigned report from a Bitlis missionary, 18 January 1895, Houghton ABC 16.10.1, Vol. 6.

43. Unsigned report from a Bitlis missionary, 18 January 1895, Houghton ABC 16.10.1, Vol. 6. The missionary wrote that the Kurds had "written orders" from the "government" to attack the villages. The Kurds were promised spoils and relieved of liability.

44. Süreyya to Serasker, 26 August 1894, Osmanlı Arşivi, Yildiz Tasnifi, *Ermeni Meselesi,* 153–157, quoted in Verheij, "Les Frères de terre et d'eau," 243–244.

45. Zeki Paşa, commander of 4th army to the Serasker, 16 September 1894, in Verheij, "Les Frères de terre et d'eau," 243.

46. Graves (Erzurum) to Currie (telegram), and Graves to Currie (letter), both 13 December 1894, UKNA FO 195/1846.

47. Shipley to Graves, 15 March 1895, UKNA FO 195/1891. Shipley commented, "The above story . . . may or may not be true, but the fact that a similar statement has been made by other witnesses since examined shows that a belief that some such an order had been issued was certainly prevalent among the villagers."

48. Kurd petition, "Through Her Majesty the Queen of England to the Great Powers of Europe," 27 June 1895, enclosed in Graves to Currie, 25 July 1895, UKNA FO 195/1892.

49. Hallward (Muş) to Currie, 9 October 1894, UKNA FO 195/1838.

50. Unsigned report from Bitlis missionary, 18 January 1894, Houghton ABC 16.10.1, Vol. 6.

51. Statements by Hamms and his wife, Altoon, of Geligüzan, and Ovig, of Talori, undated but probably from early 1895, Bodl. MS Lord Bryce Papers 208.

52. Graves to Currie, 2 March 1895, UKNA FO 195/1891, containing the statement to Graves by Khazar of Simal. Khazar said that the local Kurds, of Simal and Shenik, had moved out of the area a week before the massacre began.

53. Hallward (Muş) to Currie, 9 October 1894, UKNA FO 195/1838; and M. Meyrier, French vice-consul in Diyarbekir, to Hanotaux, 5 October 1894, in "Projets de réformes," 15–16, Bodl. MS Lord Bryce Papers 211–212. For Ottoman reports, see Constantinople to Ottoman Embassy, London, 23 May 1894, BOA, A. MKT. MHM, 750/11. The Ottomans described the incident as a quarrel between the Kurds and Armenians, in which the army had had to intervene to restore order. Graves to Currie, 2 March 1895, UKNA FO 195/1891, statement by the Turk Mevlod Aga, on the fighting at Shenik and Geligüzan. Mevlood said that the Kurds were routinely sent in to attack the villages while the troops provided covering fire from a distance. A similar observation is provided by Ali Gulaninen Oghlou, a Turkish muleteer accompanying the Ottoman 4th Battalion, 32nd Regiment, to Talori (Oghlou's statement attached to Graves to Currie, 26 April 1895, UKNA FO 195/1891). He described soldiers setting fire to the Talori church while "preventing the inmates from escaping."

54. Graves to Currie, 2 March 1895, UKNA FO 195/1891, statement to Graves by Khazar of Simal, who survived the massacre; and Graves to Currie, 8 March 1895, UKNA FO 195/1891, statement by Hebo of Shenik.

55. Graves to Currie, 2 March 1895, UKNA FO 195/1891, statement by Mevlood Agha, a noncommissioned officer serving with the 25th Regiment, from Muş, in the Shadak area during the massacre.

56. Statement by Hamms and his wife, Altoon, of Geligüzan, and Ovig, of Talori, undated but probably from early 1895, Bodl. MS Lord Bryce Papers 208.

57. Ibid. See also order from the Imperial palace to the army commander in chief about the pursuit and destruction of "Armenian rebels" on Mt. Anduk and in valleys around Geligüzan, BOA, Y. EE, 96/1, in *Ermeni Isyanları*, Vol. 1, 95.

58. Graves to Currie, 2 March 1895, UKNA FO 195/1891, statement by Khazar of Simal.

59. Graves to Currie, 24 April 1895, UKNA FO 195/1891.

60. Statement by Hamms and his wife, Altoon, from Geligüzan, and Ovig, from Talori, undated but probably from early 1895, Bodl. MS Lord Bryce Papers 208.

61. Graves to Currie, 2 March 1895, UKNA FO 195/1891, statement by Mevlood Agha; and Shipley to Currie, 20 February 1895, UKNA FO 195/1887. The survivor, who later testified before the Ottoman commission of inquiry, was a sixteen-year-old named Ovak. He was bayoneted but managed to crawl out from under twenty bodies. The commission's government-paid doctors said Ovak's wounds were not caused by bayonets (see "Inclosure 10 in No. 1," "Medical Report," 19 February 1895, by Drs. Bessim, Vassif, and Dimitri Saridi, in UKNA FO 195/1865).

62. Shipley to Currie, 16 February 1895, UKNA FO 195/1887; and Graves to Currie, 2 March 1895, UKNA FO 195/1891, statement by Mevlood Agha.

63. Shipley to Graves, 30 March 1895, UKNA FO 195/1891; and "Inclosure 14 in No. 1," "Proces-verbal No. 26 of the Bitlis Commission of Inquiry—Sitting of February 23, 1895," UKNA FO 195/1865.

64. Graves to Currie, 2 March 1895, statement by Mevlood Agha, UKNA FO 195/1891.

65. Graves to Currie, 8 March 1895, UKNA FO 195/1891, statement by Anna of Shenik.

66. For example, a woman from Talori named Shaman related how her three-year-old son was abducted by soldiers (Graves to Currie, 24 April 1895, UKNA FO 195/1891).

67. Graves to Currie, 24 April 1895, UKNA FO 195/1891.

68. Graves to Currie, 24 April 1895, UKNA FO 195/1891, "Extract from Private Letter [from American missionary], Mush, February 15 to 27th, 1895"; and Graves to Currie, 26 April 1895, UKNA FO 195/1891, "Statement of Ali Gulaninen Oghlou."

69. Unsigned report by Bitlis missionary, 18 January 1895, Houghton ABC 16.10.1, Vol. 6.

70. Graves to Currie, 24 April 1895, UKNA FO 195/1891.

71. A long, typewritten untitled, unsigned report by an American missionary from Bitlis, 18 January 1895, Houghton ABC 16.10.1, Vol. 6, describes in gory detail the murder of a number of Sason-area priests, including Der Hohanes Mardovan.

72. For example, see Graves to Currie, 24 April 1895, UKNA FO 195/1891.

73. Unsigned report by Bitlis missionary, 18 January 1895, Houghton ABC 16.10.1, Vol. 6.

74. Ibid. See also report by French Embassy, Constantinople, to Ministry, 26 December 1894, MAE, Affaires jusqu'à 1896, no. 519.

75. Unsigned report by Bitlis missionary, 18 January 1894, Houghton ABC 16.10.1, Vol. 6. The missionary put "a safe estimate" of women and children taken by the Kurds and soldiers at "1,000." On the other hand, a number of Kurdish tribal leaders and tribes apparently protected Armenians during 1894–1896: in the Dersim, near Mount Arnos north of the Jazira; and in the Jazira itself, in Adiljevaz and Norduz, Bohtan; and in Khizan (Baibourtian, *The Kurds,* 154).

76. Hallward to Currie, 9 October 1894, UKNA FO 195/1838.

77. H. M. Allen, "Facts and Figures from the Province of Van," undated but from spring 1895, Bodl. MS Lord Bryce Papers 196; and Hallward to Graves, 19 March 1895, UKNA FO 195/1891.

78. Unsigned report by Bitlis missionary, 18 January 1895, Houghton ABC 16.10.1, Vol. 6; Graves to Currie, 27 December 1894, UKNA FO 195/1846; and Graves to Currie, 2 March 1895, UKNA FO 195/1891, statement by Mevlood Agha.

79. Unsigned, from Bitlis, 29 (?) September 1894, Houghton ABC 16.9.8, Vol. 6.

80. Graves to Currie, 27 December 1894, UKNA FO 195/1846. Graves provides a village by village count of the Armenian dead and houses destroyed. See also unsigned Bitlis missionary report, 18 January 1895, Houghton ABC 16.10.1, Vol. 6. If one adds to the number massacred in August–September those who later died of wounds, starvation, and exposure, one may easily reach the higher figure. Bergeron, the French consul at Erzurum, sums it up succinctly: "A l'heure actuelle le Sassoun ne serait plus qu'un monceau de ruines" ["At this point Sason is nothing more than a heap of ruins"] (Bergeron to Hanotaux, 24 November 1894, "Projets de réformes," 18–19, Bodl. MS Lord Bryce Papers 211–212).

81. Unsigned report by Bitlis missionary, Houghton ABC 16.10.1, Vol. 6. In Muş 1,200 of the inhabitants were reported dead from the disease.

82. Currie to Kimberley, 14–15 October 1894, UKNA FO 195/1825.

83. Terrell to Secretary of State Richard Olney, 24 October 1895, *FRUS* 1895, Part 2, 1325–1327.

84. Terrell to Secretary of State, 22 November 1894, USNA RG 84, Turkey (Constantinople), Vol. 19.

85. Terrell to Secretary of State, 29 (?) November 1894, USNA RG 84, Turkey (Constantinople), Vol. 19. See also the series of articles by Reverand Cyrus Hamlin in the *New York Times* a year later. For example, "The Sassoun Massacres: Proof of the Assertion That Armenian Revolutionaries Caused It," 23 August 1895.

86. Unsigned from Bitlis, 3 October 1894, Houghton ABC 16.9.8, Vol. 6; and Cambon to Develle, November 1894, "Projets de réformes," 21, Bodl. MS Lord Bryce Papers 211–212.

87. Unsigned report by Bitlis missionary, 18 January 1895, Houghton ABC 16.10.1, Vol. 6.

88. Hallward (Muş) to Currie, 9 October 1894, UKNA FO 195/1838. Unsigned, from a missionary in Constantinople, 31 October 1894, Houghton ABC 16.9.8, Vol. 6.

89. Unsigned from Bitlis, 3 October 1894, Houghton ABC 16.9.8, Vol. 6. The Sultan, Abdülhamid, sent a special letter of thanks to Armenians who refused to join the "rebels," 30 September 1894, BOA, A. MKT. MHM, 750/15.

90. Unsigned report by Bitlis missionary, 18 January 1895, Houghton ABC 16.10.1, Vol. 6.

91. Hampson (?) to Currie, October (?) 1895, UKNA FO 195/1887. See also Hallward to Graves, 31 January 1895, UKNA FO 195/1891.

92. Revoil to Minister of Foreign Affairs, 8 December 1894, MAE, Turquie 519; and unsigned translation of instructions for the inquiry committee, 26 December 1894, MAE, Turquie 519.

93. Hallward to Graves, 31 January 1895, UKNA FO 195/1891.

94. Occasionally, the "president" of the commission is referred to as "Shefik Bey" (Shipley to Graves, 27 April 1895, UKNA FO 195/1951). It is possible that the original president was replaced at some point.

95. Graves to Currie, 1 February 1895, UKNA FO 195/1891.

96. Shipley to Graves, 8 February 1895, UKNA FO 195/1887. See also Graves to Currie, 7 March 1895, UKNA FO 195/1891.

97. Shipley to Currie, 2 March 1895, UKNA FO 195/1887.

98. For example, statement by muleteer Ali Gulaninen Oghlou attached to Graves to Currie, 26 April 1895, UKNA FO 195/1891.

99. Shipley to Graves, 12 May 1895, UKNA FO 195/1887.

100. Shipley to Graves, 17 April 1895, UKNA FO 195/1887; and Graves to Currie, 31 May 1895, UKNA FO 195/1892. The Ottoman letter referred to is in UKNA FO 195/1892.

101. Graves to Currie, 2 March 1895, UKNA FO 195/1891, statement to Graves by Khazar of Simal; and "The Truth about Armenia," *Daily Telegraph,* 16 March 1895.

102. Graves to Currie, 30 April 1895, UKNA FO 195/1892.

103. "Through Her Majesty, the Queen of England, to the Great Powers of Europe," 27 June 1895, enclosed in Graves to Currie, 25 July 1895, UKNA FO 195/1892.

104. "The Truth about Armenia," *Daily Telegraph,* 27 February 1895.

105. "The Truth about Armenia," *Daily Telegraph,* 11 March 1895. See also statement by Anna of Shenik in Graves to Currie, 8 March 1895, UKNA FO 195/1891; and Graves to Currie, 24 April 1895, UKNA FO 195/1891.

106. Shipley to Graves, 18 June 1895, UKNA FO 195/1867. For the Turkish report of 23 July 1895, see BOA, Y. EE, 66/12; and *Ermeni Isyanları,* Vol. 1, 97–128.

107. Graves to Currie, 12 August 1895, UKNA FO 195/1892.

108. Boyajian to Graves, 29 October 1895, UKNA FO 195/1846.

109. Hallward to Currie, 10 December 1894, UKNA FO 195/1846.

110. Currie to Kimberley, 14–15 October 1894, UKNA FO 195/1825; and Graves to Currie, 27 December 1894, UKNA FO 195/1846.

111. Hallward to Graves, 19 March 1895, UKNA FO 195/1891.

112. Graves to Currie, 8 August 1895, UKNA FO 195/1892. See also Summary of two (unsigned) French reports dated 10 and 14 June 1895 on continued troubles in Sason, UKNA FO 195/1906.

113. Graves to Currie, 1 July 1895 and 20 July 1895, UKNA FO 195/1892; and BOA, Y. A. HUS, 331/61, 1 July 1895. See also Graves to Currie, 21 July 1895, UKNA FO 195/1892; Hampson (Muş) to Currie, 28 July 1895, UKNA FO 1887; and Hampson (Muş) to Currie, 16 October 1895, UKNA FO 195/1887.

114. "Extract from a private letter dated June 24th 1895," UKNA FO 195/1892.

115. "The Truth about Armenia," *Daily Telegraph,* 16 March 1895.

116. Graves to Currie, 1 April 1895, *Turkey No. 1 (1896),* 20–21 and 24–26.

117. "Resume of a Report received from Keghi," 4 February 1895, *Turkey No. 1 (1896),* 24.

118. Hampson to Graves, 25 August 1895, *Turkey No. 2 (1896),* 17–18; and Hampson to Cumberbatch, 9 October 1895, *Turkey No. 2 (1896),* 98–99.

119. Hampson to Currie, 28 July 1895, UKNA FO 195/1887; Cambon to Foreign Office, 3 September 1895, MAE, Turquie 523, 240; and Bergeron, Consul in Erzurum, to Cambon, 8 August 1895, MAE Turquie 523, 245.

120. Hallward to Graves, 2 February 1895, *Turkey No. 6 (1896),* 237–239.

121. Henry D. Barnham (Aleppo) to Currie, 1 June 1895, *Turkey No. 6 (1896),* 320.

122. Terrell to Olney, 1 October 1895, USNA RG 84, Turkey (Constantinople), Vol. 20; Cambon to Foreign Office, 30 September 1895, MAE, Turquie 523, 403–404; Terrell to Olney, 24 October 1895, *FRUS* 1895, Part 2, 1325–1327; and Dwight, "Bad Days at Constantinople," undated, Houghton ABC 16.10.1, Vol. 5. See also Ottoman police reports about preparations before the demonstration, 26 September 1895, BOA, Y. PRK. ASK, 106/67.

123. Currie to Salisbury, 3 October 1895, *Turkey No. 2 (1896),* 30–35.

124. Currie to Salisbury, 1 October 1895, *Turkey No. 2 (1896),* 22. "Inclosure 2 in No. 50. Petition," 30 September 1895, *Turkey No. 2 (1896),* 32–35.

125. Currie to Salisbury, 3 October 1895, *Turkey No. 2 (1896),* 30–35.

126. Cambon to Foreign Minister, 30 September 1895, MAE, Turquie 524, 11–13. See also later detailed reports: Cambon to Foreign Minister, 2 October 1895, MAE, Turquie 524, 27–31; and Currie to Salisbury, 1 October 1895, *Turkey No. 2 (1896),* No. 30, 22.

127. Cambon to Foreign Minister, 30 September 1895, MAE, Turquie 524, 11–13.

128. Currie to Salisbury, 1 October 1895, *Turkey No. 2 (1896),* No. 30, 22.

129. Cambon to Foreign Minister, [?Paris?] 30 September 1895, MAE, Turquie 523, 11–13.

130. Cambon to Foreign Minister, 30 September 1895, MAE, Turquie 523, 11–13.

131. Cambon to Foreign Minister, 2 October 1895, MAE, Turquie 524, 11.

132. Cambon to Foreign Minister, 2 October 1895, MAE, Turquie 524, 11.

133. Henry Dwight, "Bad Days at Constantinople," undated, Houghton ABC 16.10.1, Vol. 5.

134. Cambon to Foreign Minister, 2 October 1895, MAE, Turquie 524, 11–13 and 58.

135. Currie to Salisbury, 2 October 1895, *Turkey No. 2 (1896)*, 22–23.

136. Terrell to Olney, 8 October 1895, USNA RG 84, Turkey (Constantinople), Vol. 20.

137. Cambon to Foreign Minister, 2 October 1895, MAE, Turquie 524, 11–13.

138. Cambon to Foreign Minister, 2 October 1895, MAE, Turquie 524, 11–13; and Ottoman reports, 5 October 1895, BOA, Y. PRK. ZB, 16/49. See also instructions against letting those besieged in the churches leave with their weapons, 6 October 1895, BOA, Y. A. RES, 76/54.

139. Terrell to Olney, 1 October 1895; Terrell to Olney, 3 October 1895; and undated "Copy of Telegram," Terrell to Olney, Washington, all three in USNA RG 84, Turkey (Constantinople), Vol. 20; and Dwight, "Bad Days at Constantinople," undated, Houghton ABC 16.10.1, Vol. 5.

140. Terrell to Richard Olney, 8 October 1895, enclosure, "Translation from the *Sabah* of October 5," USNA RG 84, Turkey (Constantinople), Vol. 20; and Dwight to Currie, 12 October 1895, UKNA FO 195/1907.

141. Dwight to Currie, 12 October 1895, UKNA FO 195/1907. For the Ottoman description of events see Police Minister *(Nazir-i zabtiye)* Nazim's report, 5 October 1895, BOA, Y. PRK. ZB, 16/51. Its gist is that, amid shouts of "long live Armenia," Armenians attacked Muslims who then defended themselves.

142. Cambon to Foreign Minister, 3 October 1895, MAE, Turquie 524, 39–49.

143. Terrell to Olney, 8 October 1895, USNA RG 84, Turkey (Constantinople), Vol. 20.

144. Dwight, "Bad Days at Constantinople," undated, Houghton ABC 16.10.1, Vol. 5.

145. Terrell to Olney, 8 October 1895, USNA RG 84, Turkey (Constantinople), Vol. 20; and J. W. Whittall to Currie, 14 October 1895, UKNA FO 195/1907.

146. Currie to Salisbury, 22 October 1895, Inclosure 2 in No. 204, "Vizirial Order addressed to the Valis of Erzerum, Van, Bitlis, Diyarbekir, Mamuret-ul-Aziz, and Sivas, and to the Inspector, Shakir Pasha," and Inclosure No. 3 to No. 204, "Scheme of Reforms," *Turkey No. 1 (1896)*, 160–176.

147. Dadrian, *History of the Armenian Genocide,* 163.

148. Terrell to Olney, 24 October 1895, *FRUS* 1895, Part 2, 1325–1328. See also Fuller (Aintab) to Smith, 31 October 1895, Houghton ABC 16.9.5.

149. Unsigned, undated memorandum headed "Trebizond, October 9, 1895," UKNA FO 195/1907. It was probably written by a missionary. See also Cambon to Foreign Minister, 15 December 1895, MAE, Turquie 525, 287–288. The French consul, Villière, said, "The taste for pillage has developed among the Turkish population to an alarming degree." He noted that the Turks had targeted other Christian populations, including the region's Greeks, many of whom fled to Russia.

150. Longworth to Currie, 17 December 1894, UKNA FO 195/1854.

151. Terrell to Olney, 16 December 1895, USNA RG 84, Turkey (Constantinople), Vol. 20.

152. Cambon to Foreign Minister, 12 December 1895, MAE, Turquie 525, 284–300.

153. Barnham to Currie, 24 November 1895, *Turkey No. 2 (1896)*, 227.

154. Longworth to Herbert, 6 November 1895, UKNA FO 195/1902.

155. Hampson to Cumberbatch, 3 December 1895, UKNA FO 195/1893.

156. Hampson to Cumberbatch, 7 January 1896, UKNA FO 195/1941.

157. Fitzmaurice (Urfa) to Currie, 6 September 1896, UKNA FO 195/1930. For a copy of an Ottoman circular, perhaps the one referred to by Fitzmaurice, see police report, 20 February 1896, BOA, Y. PRK. ASK, 106/67.

158. Fontana to Currie, 19 May 1896, with two attached signed depositions, UKNA FO 195/1944.

159. Longworth to Currie, 9 October 1895, UKNA FO 195/1902. For an Ottoman description of these events, see report sent to the grand vizier's bureau (Sadaret Mektubi, Mühimme Kalemi), 14 October 1895, BOA, A. MKT. MHM, 638/7; see also petitions submitted to the Sultan, 19 October 1895,

BOA, Y. MTV, 130/10. For the French take, see consul in Trabzon to Cambon, 15 October 1895, MAE, Turquie 524, 280–297.

160. Unsigned, undated memorandum headed "Trebizond, October 9, 1895," UKNA FO 195/1907.

161. Longworth to Currie, 5 October 1895, UKNA FO 195/1902; and "Report on the Armenian Troubles at Trebizond, Signed by the Civil and Military Officials, the *Ulema*s, and Notables of the *Vilayet* (Mussulman, Greek, Orthodox, and Catholic)," enclosed in Mavroyeni Bey, Ottoman ambassador to Washington, to Olney, 27 December 1895, *FRUS* 1895, Part 2, 1418–1420.

162. The French consul claimed the vali menaced the Trabzon Armenians until they handed over the suspects (consul to Cambon, 15 October 1895, MAE, Turquie 524, 280–297).

163. "Report on the Armenian Troubles at Trebizond, Signed by the Civil and Military Officials, the *Ulema*s, and Notables of the *Vilayet* (Mussulman, Greek, Orthodox, and Catholic)," enclosed in Mavroyeni Bey to Olney, 27 December 1895, *FRUS* 1895, Part 2, 1418–1420.

164. Longworth to Currie, 5 October 1895, UKNA FO 195/1902.

165. "Report on the Armenian Troubles at Trebizond, Signed by Civil and Military Officials, the *Ulema*s, and Notables of the Vilayet (Mussulman, Greek, Orthodox, and Catholic)," *FRUS* 1895, Part 2, 1418–1420; and petitions and report by Trabzon Vali, Mehmet Kadri, to Grand Vizier, 19 October 1895, BOA, Y. MTV, 130/10.

166. Unsigned typewritten report probably by an American missionary, Trebizond, 9 October 1895, UKNA FO 195/1907.

167. Herbert to Salisbury, 9 November 1895, UKNA FO 195/1870; and Longworth to Herbert, 2 November 1895, UKNA FO 195/1902.

168. Longworth to Herbert, 14 November 1895, UKNA FO 195/1902. See also Cambon to Foreign Minister, 18 December 1895, MAE, Turquie 525, 310; and Deringil, "Armenian Question Is Finally Closed."

169. Longworth to Currie, 12 October 1895, UKNA FO 195/1902.

170. Cambon to Foreign Minister, 16 March 1896, MAE, Turquie 527, 95–96.

171. Longworth to Currie, 7 February 1896, UKNA FO 195/1936. Some, if not all of the Turkish and Greek dead were apparently killed by Turks (Longworth to Currie, 12 October 1895, *Turkey No. 2 (1896)*, 87–88; and Kadri to Grand Vizier, 19 October 1895, BOA, Y. MTV, 130/10). See also Cambon to Foreign Minister, 31 October 1895, MAE, Turquie 524, 271–272.

172. Longworth to Herbert, 2 November 1895, UKNA FO 195/1902.

173. Longworth to Currie, 18 October 1895, UKNA FO 195/1902.

174. Longworth to Herbert, 2 November 1895, UKNA FO 195/1902.

175. Longworth to Currie, 9 October 1895, UKNA FO 195/1902.

176. "Report on the Armenian Troubles at Trebizond, Signed by the Civil and Military Officials, the *Ulema*s, and Notables of the *Vilayet* (Mussulman, Greek, Orthodox, and Catholic)," enclosed in Mavroyeni Bey to Olney, 27 December 1895, *FRUS* 1895, Part 2, 1418–1420. Also, see report by Mehmet Kadri to Grand Vizier, 19 October 1895, BOA, Y. MTV, 130/10.

177. Grand Vizier, "Account of the Trebizond Massacres," undated, *Turkey No. 2 (1896)*, 118–122; and Cambon to Foreign Ministry, 29 October 1895 and 31 October 1895, MAE, Turquie 524, 227, 271.

178. Quoted in Ihrig, *Justifying Genocide*, 38.

179. Longworth to Currie, 9 October 1895, UKNA FO 195/1902. The Greeks later denied participation in the killing and looting, but Longworth stuck to his guns, writing, "That Greeks participated in the looting is unquestionable" (Longworth to Currie, 23 April 1896, UKNA FO 195/1936).

180. Longworth to Currie, 12 October 1895, UKNA FO 195/1902.

181. Longworth to Currie, 9 October 1895, UKNA FO 195/1902.

182. Longworth to Currie, 12 October 1895, UKNA FO 195/1902; and collection of reports from Trabzon, October–November 1895, "Projets de réformes," 199–200, Bodl. MS Lord Bryce Papers 211–212.

183. Longworth to Currie, 8 February 1896, *Turkey No. 8 (1896),* 61.

184. Longworth to Herbert, 2 November 1895, UKNA FO 195/1902. For the French take, see reports from Trèbizonde, October-November 1895, "Projets de réformes," 199–200, Bodl. MS Lord Bryce Papers 211–212. Lepsius also concluded that the killing began and ended "at the signal of a trumpet." Ihrig, *Justifying Genocide,* 50.

185. Sanders to Barnham, 11 January 1895, UKNA FO 195/1883.

186. Lucius O. Lee (Maraş) to Judson Smith, 30 October 1895, Houghton ABC 16.9.5.

187. F. W. Macallum (?) to Smith, 6 November 1895, Houghton ABC 16.9.5.

188. Extract from Lee (Maraş) to ?, 13 November 1895, *FRUS* 1895, Part 2, 1359.

189. Unsigned but probably by Lee, undated, "The Massacre in Marash," Houghton ABC 16.9.5; and summary of reports from 23 October, 3 November, and 18 November 1895, in "Projets de réformes," 208, Bodl. MS Lord Bryce Papers 211–212. The Ottoman Army comprised various Muslim groups, including Arabs.

190. Unsigned letter from Maraş American missionary, 28 November 1895, *FRUS* 1895, Part 2, 1434–1437; Marsden (?) to ?, undated, Houghton ABC 16.10.1, Vol. 6; and extract from Lee to ?, 20 November 1895, *FRUS* 1895, Part 2, 1387.

191. Unsigned, undated, handwritten memorandum (probably by Lee), "The Massacre in Marash," Houghton ABC 16.9.5. See also Deringil, "Armenian Question Is Finally Closed."

192. Currie to Salisbury (quoting a cable from Barnham), 30 January 1896, UKNA FO 195/1914; and instructions from Grand Vizier's office to Maraş vilayet, 18 November 1895, BOA, A. MKT. MHM, 647/12.

193. Lee to Smith, 9 February 1896, Houghton ABC 16.9.5. French missionaries later concluded that 856 had been killed and 140 houses levelled (Barnham to Currie, 6 January 1896, UKNA FO 195/1932).

194. Lee to Whittall, 28 March 1896, UKNA FO 195/1950; and Lee to Smith, 30 March 1896, Houghton ABC 16.9.5.

195. Thomas D. Christie (Tarsus) to McWilliams, 20 November 1895, Houghton ABC 16.9.5.

196. Unsigned, undated letter or memorandum, by a Maraş American missionary, Houghton ABC 16.10.1, Vol. 5.

197. Ibid.; and Barnham to Currie, 31 December 1895, UKNA FO 195/1883.

198. Macallum to Smith, 31 July 1896, Houghton ABC 16.9.5.

199. Barnham to Currie, 6 January 1896, UKNA FO 195/1932.

200. Marsden (?) to ?, undated, Houghton ABC 16.10.1, Vol. 6.

201. Barnham (Aleppo) to Currie (quoting a "private and confidential" letter from Maraş, probably from Lee), 25 November 1895, UKNA FO 195/1883. One missionary, probably Lee, wrote that "the massacre was . . . carefully planned by the authorities" (unsigned, undated "The Massacre in Marash," Houghton ABC 16.9.5).

202. Barnham to Currie, 6 January 1896, UKNA FO 195/1932.

203. Lee to Smith, 30 March 1896, Houghton ABC 16.9.5.

204. Macallum to Smith, 26 November 1895, Houghton ABC 16.9.5.

205. "Extract from a private letter from Mr. [Thomas] Boyajian [the former British vice-consul at Diyarbekir], dated July 15th, 1895, Kharput," UKNA FO 195/1892. See also French report on Harput from 28 June 1895, UKNA FO 195/1906.

206. Barnum to Dwight, 2 October 1895, attached to Dwight to Currie, 16 October 1895, UKNA FO 195/1907.

207. Unknown author, "Extracts from Private Letters from Kharput," 19 August and 12 August 1895, *Turkey No. 2 (1896)*, 10–11. Father Adorno, a Capuchin monk, described how revolutionaries arrived in town and animated the Armenians with talk of independence and bombings (Boulinière to Hannotaux, 23 May 1896, MAE, Turquie 528, 118–119).

208. "Private letter from Kharpout, October 25th & 26th, 1895," 28 October 1895, UKNA FO 195/1893.

209. Gates to Terrell, 19 November 1895, *FRUS* 1895, Part 2, 1370–1375. The massacre at Bitlis occurred on October 25. Hundreds were murdered.

210. Cumberbatch to Currie, 1 February 1896, UKNA FO 195/1941, enclosing the translation of a letter from an unnamed Shepik Armenian, from 31 December 1895, describing what happened; and Gates to Terrell, 19 November 1895, *FRUS* 1895, Part 2, 1371–1372, regarding other villages. American missionaries in Harput later put the total number of Christians killed in the mission district during October–November at 15,834, the figure including those killed in Diyarbekir (2,000), Malatya (5,000), and Arabkir (4,000). For some reason the figure excluded Harput town ("List of Houses burnt and of Persons killed in the District of the American Mission of Kharput," enclosed in Cumberbatch to Currie, 8 January 1896, *Turkey No. 8 (1896)*, 11).

211. Gates to Terrell, 19 November 1895, *FRUS* 1895, Part 2, 1370–1375; Cambon to Foreign Minister, 14 November 1895 and 12 December 1895, MAE, Turquie 525, 75–76 and 286; and "Affidavit of Rev. H. N. Barnum," 17 September 1896, *FRUS* 1896, 888–889.

212. "Affidavit of Mrs. Mary E. Barnum," 17 September 1896, *FRUS* 1896, 890.

213. Gates to Terrell, 19 November 1895, *FRUS* 1895, Part 2, 1370–1375.

214. Fontana to Currie, 25 April 1896, and Fontana, "Summary of Evidence," UKNA FO 195/1944.

215. Unsigned but apparently by a missionary named von Fischer, "Inclosure 1," Harput, 26 November 1895, in Terrell to Olney, 15 December 1895, *FRUS* 1895, Part 2, 1395–1397.

216. Wheeler to Dr. and Mrs. Barton, 30 December 1895, Houghton ABC 16.9.8, Vol. 8.

217. Gates to Terrell, 19 November 1895, *FRUS* 1895, Part 2, 1370–1375; and Emily Wheeler to ?, 4 December 1895, Houghton ABC 16.9.8, Vol. 7.

218. Fontana to Currie, 25 April 1896, and Fontana, "Summary of Evidence," UKNA FO 195/1944; and summary of reports on Harput, 10–11 November 1895, in "Projets de réformes," 203, Bodl. MS Lord Bryce Papers 211–212.

219. Barnum to Terrell, 21 November 1895, *FRUS* 1895, Part 2, 1380–1381. See also Cambon to Foreign minister, 12 December 1895, MAE, Turquie 525, 286–287.

220. ? (Harput) to Terrell, 9 December 1895, enclosed in Terrell to Olney, 29 December 1895, *FRUS* 1895, Part 2, 1423–1427.

221. Fontana to Currie, 25 April 1896, UKNA FO 195/1944.

222. Gates to Terrell, 25 November 1895, *FRUS* 1895, Part 2, 1392–1395.

223. Gates to Smith, 30 November 1895, Houghton ABC 16.9.8, Vol. 5. Cambon reported that the authorities had assured the Kurds that they would not be punished if they attacked the Christians (12 December 1895, MAE, Turquie 525, 284–293).

224. Fontana to Currie, 25 April 1896, and Fontana, "Summary of Evidence," UKNA FO 195/1944.

225. "Extract from another letter evidently written by Hafiz Mehmet . . . ," 23 November 1895, UKNA FO 195/1944.

226. Unknown author, "Letter received from Kharput," 13 November 1895, *Turkey No. 2 (1896)*, 206–207.

227. ? to Terrell, 9 December 1895, enclosed in Terrell to Olney, 29 December 1895, *FRUS* 1895, Part 2, 1423–1427.

228. Gates to Terrell, 25 November 1895, *FRUS* 1895, Part 2, 1392–1395.

229. Fontana to Currie, 25 April 1896, and Fontana, "Summary of Evidence," UKNA FO 195/1944.

230. Gates to Terrell, 19 November 1895, *FRUS* 1895, Part 2, 1374. A French investigation later put the number of conversions in the Harput region at 12,500 (June 1896, MAE, Turquie 528, 320).

231. "Inclosure 1," Harput, 26 November 1895, in Terrell to Olney, 15 December 1895, *FRUS* 1895, Part 2, 1395–1397; and Fontana to Currie, 25 April 1895, and Fontana, "Summary of Evidence," UKNA FO 195/1944.

232. ? (Harput) to Terrell, 9 December 1895, enclosed in Terrell to Olney, 29 December 1895, *FRUS* 1895, Part 2, 1423–1427; and Deringil, "Armenian Question Is Finally Closed," 354.

233. Cumberbatch to Currie, 10 March 1896, UKNA FO 195/1941.

234. ? (Harput) to Terrell, 9 December 1895, enclosed in Terrell to Olney, 29 December 1895, *FRUS* 1895, Part 2, 1423–1427.

235. ? (Harput) to Terrell, 9 December 1895, enclosed in Terrell to Olney, 29 December 1895, *FRUS* 1895, Part 2, 1423–1427; and ? (Harput) to Terrell, 18 December 1895, enclosed in Terrell to Olney, 10 January 1895, *FRUS* 1895, Part 2, 1452–1453.

236. "Inclosure 2 in No. 11," attached to Cumberbatch to Currie, 11 March 1896, *Turkey No. 8 (1896),* 105.

237. Unsigned, undated memorandum, probably by a missionary, from late January 1896, Houghton ABC 16.10.1, Vol. 6; and a breakdown of these statistics is in Terrell to Currie, undated but from February 1896, UKNA FO 195/1949.

238. Carrie Bush, "Work for Orphans in the Harpoot Field," 28 July 1896, Houghton ABC 16.9.7.

239. Ibid.

240. ? (Harput) to Armenian relief Commission, 1 February 1896, UKNA FO 195/1949.

241. "Report of G. B. Fitzmaurice to Sir Philip Currie, Constantinople—Ourfa, March 16, 1896," Houghton ABC 16.10.1, Vol. 12. Fitzmaurice wrote, "I have obtained" most of the information "from Mussulman sources, or have had [it] confirmed by Mussulman authority." His description tallies with that of the French consul in Baghdad, who also relied on diverse sources (consul to Cambon, 23 February 1896, MAE, Turquie 527, 160).

242. "Report of G. H. Fitzmaurice to Sir Philip Currie, Constantinople—Ourfa, March 16, 1896," Houghton ABC 16.10.1, Vol. 12.

243. Shattuck to Friends, 4 November 1895, Houghton ABC 16.9.5.

244. "Report of G. H. Fitzmaurice to Sir Philip Currie, Constantinople—Ourfa, March 16, 1896," Houghton ABC 16.10.1, Vol. 12.

245. "Copy of Journal of Miss Corinna Shattuck of the American Mission at Aintab, Five Terrible Weeks at Ourfa," UKNA FO 195/1907.

246. Ibid. See also Pognon, the consul in Baghdad, to de la Moulinière, 23 February 1896, MAE, Turquie 527, 158–160.

247. "Report of G. H. Fitzmaurice to Sir Philip Currie, Constantinople—Ourfa, March 16, 1896," Houghton ABC 16.10.1, Vol. 12; and "Copy of Journal of Miss Corinna Shattuck of the American Mission at Aintab, Five Terrible Weeks at Ourfa," UKNA FO 195/1907. The first massacre was succinctly reported in an Ottoman telegram on 29 October 1895, blaming the Armenians (see Nazim, *Ermeni Olayları Tarihi,* vol. 1, 99).

248. "Report of G. H. Fitzmaurice to Sir Philip Currie, Constantinople—Ourfa, March 16, 1896," Houghton ABC 16.10.1, Vol. 12.

249. Shattuck to "Friends," 4 November 1895, Houghton ABC 16.9.5; and French consul, Baghdad, to ?, undated, MAE, Turquie 527, 158–159, conveying the gist of the Capuchin novice's report.

250. "Report of G. H. Fitzmaurice to Sir Philip Currie, Constantinople—Ourfa, March 16, 1896," Houghton ABC 16.10.1, Vol. 12.

251. Shattuck to "Friends," 7 January 1896, Houghton ABC 16.9.5. See also Cambon to Foreign Minister, 8 January 1895, MAE, Turquie 526, 37–38. The French consul in Baghdad wrote that the protection afforded the missionaries was a proof of the authorities' complicity in the massacre (MAE, Turquie 527, 159).

252. "Report of G. H. Fitzmaurice to Sir Philip Currie, Constantinople—Ourfa, March 16, 1896," Houghton ABC 16.10.1, Vol. 12.

253. Shattuck to "Friends," 7 January 1896, Houghton ABC 16.9.5.

254. "Report of G. H. Fitzmaurice to Sir Philip Currie, Constantinople—Ourfa, March 16, 1896," Houghton ABC 16.10.1, Vol. 12.

255. "Report of G. H. Fitzmaurice to Sir Philip Currie, Constantinople—Ourfa, March 16, 1896," Houghton ABC 16.10.1, Vol. 12; and Barnham to Currie, 6 January 1896, UKNA FO 195/1932.

256. Barnham to Currie, 10 January 1896, UKNA FO 195/1932.

257. ? to ?, 3 February 1896, UKNA FO 195/1949.

258. Shattuck to ?, 22 March 1896, Houghton ABC 16.9.5.

259. Fitzmaurice to Herbert, 27 June 1896, *Turkey No. 8 (1896),* 270.

260. "Report of G. H. Fitzmaurice to Sir Philip Currie, Constantinople—Ourfa, March 16, 1896," Houghton ABC 16.10.1, Vol. 12.

261. Fitzmaurice (Urfa) to Currie, 10 September 1896, UKNA FO 195/1930.

262. Shattuck to Judsen Smith, 1 February 1896, Houghton ABC 16.9.5.

263. Currie to Salisbury, c. 9 January 1896 (draft telegram), UKNA FO 195/1914.

264. Boyajian to Currie, 26 March 1895, UKNA FO 195/1887; Armenian Patriarchate, "Occurrences in 1895 in Asia Minor," undated but from 1896, 327; and summaries of reports on events in Diyarbekir, November-December 1895, "Projets de réformes," 204–205, Bodl. MS Lord Bryce Papers 211–212.

265. "The Martyrdom of Protestant Preachers in the Region of Diyarbekir," unsigned and undated, Houghton ABC 16.10.1, Vol. 6; and Armenian Patriarchate, "Occurrences in 1895 in Asia Minor," undated, *Turkey No. 2 (1896),* 327. See also de Courtois, *Forgotten Genocide,* 110.

266. A series of Ottoman reports to the grand vizier's office on "clashes" between Muslims and Christians, early November 1895, BOA, A. MKT. MHM, 636/11, 14, 16, 17, 44. One of the reports is by an Iranian consul concerning "Armenian provocations." Another describes steps taken to stop Kurdish attacks on Armenian villages. See also Hallward to Cumberbatch, 17 March 1896, *Turkey No. 8 (1896),* 126–127; and summaries of reports from November–December 1895, in "Projets de réformes," 204–205, Bodl. MS Lord Bryce Papers 211–212.

267. Kieser, *Talaat Pasha,* 103–104.

268. An unsigned letter from Mardin, 25 November 1895, *FRUS* 1895, Part 2, 1408–1410; and "The Martyrdom of Protestant Preachers in the Region of Diyarbekir," unsigned and undated, Houghton ABC 16.10.1, Vol. 6. See also reports to Grand Vizier's office about attacks against Assyrians, 26 November 1895, BOA, A. MKT. MHM, 619/23; attacks on villages in the area of Lice, 14 December 1895, BOA, A. MKT. MHM, 613/23, 636/17; and orders to prevent future attacks, 21 November 1895, BOA, A. MKT. MHM, 636/33.

269. De Courtois, *Forgotten Genocide,* 114–118; and Gaunt, *Massacres,* 43.

270. In his report to the grand vizier, the vali of Diyarbekir estimated that 70 Muslims and "over 300" Armenians had been killed in the province, 5 November 1895, BOA, A. MKT. MHM, 636/16.

271. Hampson to Cumberbatch, 11 December 1895, UKNA FO 195/1893. On Lice, see also 26 November 1895, BOA, A. MKT. MHM, 619/23.

272. Hallward to Cumberbatch, 17 March 1896, *Turkey No. 8 (1896),* 126–129.

273. Hampson to Cumberbatch, 11 December 1895, UKNA FO 195/1893. On Lice, see also BOA, A. MKT. MHM, 619/23, 26 November 1895.

274. F. D. Shepard to James Barton, 9 October 1895, Houghton ABC 16.9.5.

275. Barnham to Currie, ? November 1895, UKNA FO 195/1883.

276. Extract from letter from Fuller, Aintab, to Chas E. Swett, 9 May 1895, Houghton ABC 16.9.5.

277. Barnham to Currie, ? November 1895, UKNA FO 195/1883; and Poche to Terrell, 2 November 1895, *FRUS* 1895, Part 2, 1346–1347.

278. Fuller to Smith, 5 November 1895, Houghton ABC 16.9.5.

279. Fuller to Clark, 23 November 1895, Houghton ABC 16.9.5; and Fuller to Lord Bryce, 5 March 1896, Houghton ABC 16.9.5.

280. Fuller to Clark, 23 November 1895, Houghton ABC 16.9.5.

281. Fuller to Clark, 23 November 1895, Houghton ABC 16.9.5; and Shepard to Alice Shepard, 18 November 1895, Houghton ABC 16.9.5.

282. Saunders to Terrell, 27 November 1895, *FRUS* 1895, Part 2, 1388–1390.

283. Fuller to Clark, 23 November 1895, Houghton ABC 16.9.5; Shepard to Alice Shepard, 18 November 1895, Houghton ABC 16.9.5; and summary of report on Aleppo, September (?) 1895, "Projets de réformes," 207, Bodl. MS Lord Bryce Papers 211–212.

284. Barnham to Currie, 21 January 1896, UKNA FO 195/1932.

285. Barnham to Currie, 21 January 1896, UKNA FO 195/1932.

286. Fuller to Clark, 23 November 1895, Houghton ABC 16.9.5.

287. Barnham to Currie, ? November 1895, UKNA FO 195/1883.

288. F. D. Shepard to Alice Shepard, 18 November 1895, Houghton ABC 16.9.5.

289. Fuller to Smith, 25 December 1895, Houghton ABC 16.9.5.

290. Barnham to Currie, ? November 1895, UKNA FO 195/1883.

291. Barnham to Currie, 21 January 1896, UKNA FO 195/1932. An order from the grand vizier's office to the governors of Aleppo and Diyarbekir cited intelligence reports claiming that the outlaws *(erbab-ı fesad)* in Antep were waiting for an opportunity to renew their rebellion (26 December 1895, BOA, A. MKT. MHM, 648/6). See also Fuller to Smith, 6 February 1896, and Rebecca Kreikorian to "my Sister," 5 February 1896, both in Houghton ABC 16.9.5.

292. Fuller to ?, 17 December 1895, Houghton ABC 16.9.5.

293. Barnham to Currie, 21 January 1896, UKNA FO 195/1932.

294. "Notes on the Situation at Aintab (Province of Aleppo)," 6 February 1896, unsigned, attached to Dwight to Currie, 19 February 1896, UKNA FO 195/1949.

295. Fuller, "News Notes No. 1," 12 March 1896, Houghton ABC 16.9.5.

296. Fuller, "News Notes No. 2," 19 March 1896, Houghton ABC 16.9.5.

297. Fuller to Smith, 25 December 1895, Houghton ABC 16.9.5.

298. Catoni to Herbert, 1 July 1896, UKNA FO 195/1932.

299. Fuller to Smith, 25 December 1895, Houghton ABC 16.9.5.

300. Sanders to Barnham, 11 December 1895, UKNA FO 195/1883.

301. Barnham to Currie, 21 January 1896, UKNA FO 195/1932.

302. Barnham to Currie, ? November 1895, UKNA FO 195/1883.

303. Jewett to Longworth, 26 March 1895, UKNA FO 195/1902.

304. "The Massacre at Marsovan," undated, unsigned but by a local missionary, attached to Dodd to Terrell, 19 November 1895, *FRUS* 1895, Part 2, 1361–1363; Longworth to Currie, 17 December 1895, UKNA FO 195/1902. This figure also appears in Cambon to Foreign Minister, received on 18 November 1895, MAE Turquie 525, 96. See also summary of events in Marsovan, 5 November 1895, in "Projets de réformes," 207, Bodl. MS Lord Bryce Papers 211–212.

305. "Massacre at Gurun," unsigned and undated, attached to Fontana to Currie, 11 December 1895, UKNA FO 195/1884.

306. Bulman to Currie, 4 February 1896, *Turkey No. 8 (1896)*, 38.

307. Cambon to Foreign Minister, 26 December 1895, MAE, Turquie 525, 365.

308. Fontana to Currie, 24 December 1895, *Turkey No. 2 (1896)*, 286.

309. "Letter Received from Caesarea," 12 December 1895, *Turkey No. 2 (1896)*, 260–262; Cambon to Foreign Minister, 26 December 1895, MAE, Turquie 525, 366; and Cambon to Foreign Minister, 13 January 1896, MAE, Turquie 526, 98–99.

310. Fontana to Currie, 24 December 1895, *Turkey No. 2 (1896)*, 286.

311. Barnham to Currie, 21 January 1896, UKNA FO 195/1932; Fitzmaurice to Currie, 5 March 1896, UKNA FO 195/1930; and unsigned, "The Massacre at Biredjik," 1 February 1896, UKNA FO 195/1949.

312. Fitzmaurice to Currie, 5 March 1896, UKNA FO 195/1930; and Barnham to Currie, (probably) 21 January 1896, *Turkey No. 8 (1896)*, 48.

313. Fitzmaurice to Herbert, 22 July 1896, UKNA FO 195/1930.

314. Fitzmaurice to Currie, 8 March 1896, UKNA FO 195/1953.

315. R. Chambers (Bahçecik, Izmit) to Currie, 16 October 1895, UKNA FO 195/1907; and Currie to Salisbury, 17 October 1895, and Currie to Salisbury, 22 October 1895, both in *Turkey No. 2 (1896)*, 54–55, and 56–57.

316. Armenian Patriarchate, "Occurrences in 1895 in Asia Minor," 1896, *Turkey No. 2 (1896)*, 323. Hampson (Muş) to Cumberbatch, 29 October 1895, and 6 November 1895, both in UKNA FO 195/1893; and George Knapp (Bitlis) to Cumberbatch, 6 November 1895, UKNA FO 195/1893.

317. Longworth to Herbert, 15 November 1895, UKNA FO 195/1902.

318. Cumberbatch to Herbert, 12 November 1895, UKNA FO 195/1893; Armenian Patriarchate, "Occurrences in 1895 in Asia Minor," undated but from 1896, *Turkey No. 2 (1896)*, 322; and unsigned notes on the October-December massacres, probably by a U.S. missionary, undated, Houghton ABC 16.10.1, Vol. 5.

319. Cumberbatch to Herbert, 12 November 1895, UKNA FO 195/1893; Cumberbatch to Herbert, 4 November 1895, and V. Maximov (consul-general of Russia), A. Monaco (consul of Italy), Cumberbatch, and Roqueferrier (vice-consul of France), "Memorandum," 7 November 1895, both in UKNA FO 195/1893; "Information Furnished by the Governor-General of the Vilayet of Erzerum on the Facts Mentioned in the Memorandum Drawn Up by the Russian Consul-General, the Italian and British Consuls, and the French Vice-Consul on the Subject of the Disorders which Took Place in the Capital of the Vilayet," undated, *Turkey No. 8 (1896)*, 44–45; and "Observations by Consul Cumberbatch on the Report of the Governor-General of Erzurum, Commenting on the Consular Memorandum on the Disorders at Erzurum," attached to Cumberbatch to Currie, 6 March 1896, *Turkey No. 8 (1896)*, 94–98.

320. Fitzmaurice to Currie, 25 March 1896, UKNA FO 195/1930.

321. Gates, "Three Cities," 26 November 1896, UKNA FO 195/1953.

322. Armenian Patriarchate, "Occurrences in 1895 in Asia Minor," undated but 1896, *Turkey No. 2 (1896)*, 325.

323. Armenian Patriarchate, "Occurrences in 1895 in Asia Minor," undated but 1896, *Turkey No. 2 (1896)*, 326. Unsigned memorandum, untitled, Harput, 20 August 1896, Houghton ABC 16.10.1, Vol. 12. Unsigned, "Remarks," UKNA FO 195/1907, speaks of "5,029" killed at Malatya.

324. Fitzmaurice to Currie, 25 March 1896, UKNA FO 195/1930.

325. Jewett to Longworth, 13 November 1895, UKNA FO 195/1902; Longworth to Currie, 28 November 1895, UKNA FO 195/1902; Terrell to Olney, 12 December 1895, and enclosure, "Massacre at Sivas," *FRUS* 1895, Part 2, 1390–1391; and Armenian Patriarchate, "Occurrences in 1895 in Asia Minor," undated but 1896, *Turkey No. 2 (1896)*, 328.

326. Bulman to Currie, 31 December 1895, UKNA FO 195/1887.

327. Untitled memorandum, signature unclear (but by a U.S. missionary), 17 February 1896, Houghton ABC 16.10.1, Vol. 5.

328. ? (Tokat) to Herbert, 25 June 1896, UKNA FO 195/1951; and Longworth to Herbert, 13 July 1896, *Turkey No. 8 (1896)*, 276.

329. Barnham to Currie, 28 January 1896, UKNA FO 195/1932.

330. "Memorandum by Consul Barnham respecting the Zeitoun Insurrection, 1895–96," 18 June 1896, attached to Barnham to Salisbury, 21 June 1896, *Turkey No. 8 (1896)*, 212–213.

331. Quoted in Salt, *Imperialism, Evangelism,* 60.

332. "Memorandum by Consul Barnham . . . ," *Turkey No. 8 (1896)*, 213.

333. "Memorandum by Consul Barnham . . . ," *Turkey No. 8 (1896)*, 213–214; and Ottoman Army intelligence report about rebels and weapons in Zeytun, 6 November 1895, BOA, Y. PRK. ASK, 108/18. See also Verheij, "Les Frères de terre et d'eau," 250–251.

334. Halil Pasha (vali of Sivas) to the Imperial Palace, 30 October 1895, BOA, Y. PRK. UM, 33/21.

335. Thomas D. Christie (Tarsus) to Alex Christie, 2 December 1895, Houghton ABC 16.9.5. On the death of Father Salvatore, see also Cambon to Foreign Minister, 13 January 1896, MAE, Turquie 526, 98–99.

336. Herbert to FO, 5 November 1895, UKNA FO 195/1869; Cambon to Foreign Minister, 14 November 1895, MAE, Turquie 525, 78–79; and BOA, Y. PRK. UM, 33/22.

337. L. O. Lee (Maraş) to ?, 13 November 1895, *FRUS* 1895, Part 2, 1359.

338. J. C. Martin (Hadjin) memorandum, untitled, 23 November 1895, UKNA FO 195/1907.

339. An Ottoman report on Armenian massacres in Gercanis kaza was sent by Halil Pasha to the Palace on 25 October 1895, BOA, Y. MTV, 130/75.

340. Barnham to Currie, 26 January 1896, UKNA FO 195/1933.

341. Herbert to FO, 19 November 1895, UKNA FO 195/1870. For Ottoman instructions and accounts, 14–28 December 1895, see BOA, I. HUS, 44.

342. Barnham (Aleppo) to Currie, 6 January 1895 [should be 1896], UKNA FO 195/1932.

343. Barnham to Currie, 29 January 1896, UKNA FO 195/1932.

344. Barnham (Zeytun) to Currie, 30 January 1896, UKNA FO 195/1932. See also Cambon to Foreign Minister, 10 January 1896, MAE, Turquie 526, 52–53.

345. Barnham to Currie, 31 January 1896, UKNA FO 195/1933.

346. This description of the "revolt" is based largely on Barnham to Currie, 12 February 1896, UKNA FO 195/1932; and "Memorandum by Consul Barnham . . . ," 18 June 1896, *Turkey No. 8 (1896)*, 212–222. See also Hess, "Zeytun—its Capture and Capitulation, a Story of Heroism," 19 February 1896, Bodl. MS Lord Bryce Papers 197; and Cambon to Foreign Minister, 5 March 1896, MAE, Turquie 527, 56.

347. Lee (Maraş) to Currie, 15 February 1896, UKNA FO 195/1950; Hess, "Zeitoun—its Capture and Capitulation, A Story of Heroism," 19 February 1896, Bodl. MS Lord Bryce Papers 197; and F. W. Macallum to Currie, 19 February 1896, UKNA FO 195/1950.

348. Macallum to ?, 7 July 1896, UKNA FO 195/1951.

349. Macallum to ?, 7 July 1896, UKNA FO 195/1951.

350. F. W. Macallum (Zeytun) to Peet, 27 March 1896, UKNA FO 195/1950.

351. Barnham to Currie, 14 March 1896, UKNA FO 195/1932.

352. Barnham (Zeytun) to Currie, 1 March 1896, UKNA FO 195/1932.

353. Hallward to Graves (?), 1 December 1894, UKNA FO 195/1846; Hallward to Graves, 2 February 1895, UKNA FO 195/1891; and Hallward to Graves, 29 July 1895, UKNA FO 195/1892.

354. Hallward to Graves, 28 June 1895, UKNA FO 195/1892; and Hallward to Graves, 29 July 1895, UKNA FO 195/1892.

355. Hallward to Cumberbatch, 6 November 1895, UKNA FO 195/1893; and Hallward to Cumberbatch, 26 November 1895, UKNA FO 195/1893.

356. Hallward to Cumberbatch, 16 November 1895, UKNA FO 195/1887; Hallward to Cumberbatch, 20 November 1895, UKNA FO 195/1893; and Hallward to Cumberbatch, 26 November 1895, UKNA FO 195/1893. By mid-December 1895, "upwards of 200" villagers had been killed and no Kurds arrested (Hallward to Cumberbatch, 18 December 1895, UKNA FO 195/1893).

357. Hallward to Cumberbatch, 26 November 1895, UKNA FO 195/1893.

358. Deringil, "Armenian Question Is Finally Closed," 357–358.

359. Hallward to Graves, 29 July 1895, UKNA FO 195/1892.

360. Graves to Currie, 3 July 1895, UKNA FO 195/1892.

361. For example, Hallward to Cumberbatch, 20 November 1895, UKNA FO 195/1893.

362. Hallward to Cumberbatch, 26 November 1895, UKNA FO 195/1893.

363. Hallward to Cumberbatch, 13 November 1895, UKNA FO 195/1893. See also report by Agop M. B. of Tabriz, on the smuggling of guns from Iran, in Nazim, *Ermeni Olayları Tarihi*, vol. 1, 137.

364. Hallward to Cumberbatch, 23 November 1895, UKNA FO 195/1887. See also reports sent by the Catholicos of Akdamar to the French embassy, dated 12 May and 7 August 1895, UKNA FO 195/1906.

365. George C. Raynolds to Smith, 21 January 1896, Houghton ABC 16.9.8, Vol. 7.

366. Williams to Herbert, 28 June 1896, *Turkey No. 8 (1896)*, 271.

367. Williams to Currie, 27 May 1896, *Turkey No. 8 (1896)*, 224.

368. Dr. Grace M. Kimball, "Women's Armenian Relief Fund. Extracts from Miss Kimball's Letter. Van, 1st April 1896," UKNA FO 195/1928.

369. John W. Whittall to Max Muller, 25 April 1896, UKNA FO 195/1950.

370. John W. Whittall to Max Muller, 25 April 1896, UKNA FO 195/1950.

371. Unsigned, "From the Hantchak of Sep. 1, The Fighting Nationalists at Van," Bodl. MS Lord Bryce Papers 198.

372. Williams to Herbert, 28 June 1896, *Turkey No. 8 (1896)*, 271–273.

373. Williams to Herbert, 28 June 1896, *Turkey No. 8 (1896)*, 271–273; Report by Cambon to Foreign Minister, 17 June 1896, MAE, Turquie 528, 398; and unsigned, "From the Hentchak of Sep. 1, The Fighting Nationalists at Van," Bodl. MS Lord Bryce Papers 198.

374. Cambon to Foreign Minister, 23 June 1896, MAE, Turquie 528, 411.

375. Unsigned, "From the Hentchak of Sep. 1, The Fighting Nationalists at Van," Bodl. MS Lord Bryce Papers 198.

376. Herbert to Lord Salisbury, 23 June 1896, UKNA FO 195/1917; unsigned (but probably by Raynolds), "Report of Relief Work at Van, for the Month of August 1896," undated, Houghton ABC 16.10.1, Vol. 12; and Raynolds, "Van Station Report for the Year 1896," 24 May 1897, Houghton ABC 16.9.7. See also untitled report by Père Defrance, attached to Cambon to Foreign Minister, 9 July 1896, MAE, Turquie 529, 79–84.

377. Untitled, unsigned report (perhaps by Raynolds), 23 June 1896, Houghton ABC 16.10.1, Vol. 12; unsigned (but probably by Raynolds), "Report of Relief Work at Van, for the Month of August 1896," undated, Houghton ABC 16.10.1, Vol. 12; and Raynolds, "Van Station Report for the Year 1896," 24 May 1897, Houghton ABC 16.9.7. Raynolds pointed out that the conversions eased the relief burden as the converts did not receive aid.

378. Terrell to State Department, 1 September 1896, USNA RG 84, Turkey (Constantinople), Vol. 20.

379. Terrell to State Department, 27 August 1896, USNA RG 84, Turkey (Constantinople), Vol. 20.

380. Fitzmaurice (?), untitled memorandum, undated but c. 30 August 1896, based on a conversation with the 17 bank raiders subsequently transferred to the French vessel "SS *Gironde*," UKNA FO 195/1918.

381. Herbert to Salisbury, 31 August 1896, UKNA FO 195/1918.

382. Herbert to Salisbury, 28 August 1896 (conveying text of ambassadors' telegram to the sultan), UKNA FO 195/1918; and eyewitness account by F. S. Cobb, British postmaster, Galata, to Currie, 9 September 1896, UKNA FO 195/1952. Cobb harbored five Armenians during the rioting.

383. Currie to Salisbury, 28 August 1896, UKNA FO 195/1918.

384. Herbert to Salisbury, 3 September 1896, UKNA FO 195/1918.

385. Herbert to Salisbury, 29 August 1896, UKNA FO 195/1918.

386. ? to Ministry of Foreign Affairs, 30 August 1896, MAE, Turquie 529, 577. Ottoman documents on the affair are scarce. A selection was published in Nazim, *Ermeni Olayları Tarihi*, vol. 2, 370–406, 457–497. None of the reports mentions a massacre. See also *Ermeni Isyanları*, Vol. 2, 162–164, 185–192. These documents, signed by the mayor *(şehremini)* of Constantinople, detail Armenian crimes.

387. See Nazim, *Ermeni Olayları Tarihi*, vol. 2, 380–385.

388. Terrell to Commander Jewett, 24 September 1896, *FRUS* 1896, 864. The British estimate was 5,000–6,000 dead (Herbert to Salisbury, 3 September 1896, UKNA FO 195/1918).

389. Herbert to Salisbury, 28 August 1896, UKNA FO 195/1918.

390. Terrell to State Department, 1 September 1896, USNA RG 84, Turkey (Constantinople), Vol. 20.

391. Herbert to Foreign Office, 2 September 1896, UKNA FO 195/1918.

392. Herbert to Salisbury, 2 September 1896, UKNA FO 195/1918. See also Dadrian, *History of the Armenian Genocide*, 138–146.

393. See, for example, a letter, probably from 31 August 1896, from Armenians hiding in a church in Hassekeuy to Currie, UKNA FO 195/1951: "It is better for us to remain hungry in the church than to go out and die under the sticks of cruel men. . . . Can we be sure, in our ruined houses, of safety and protection [?]"

394. Terrell to State Department, 15 September 1896, USNA RG 84, Turkey (Constantinople), Vol. 20; and Shipley to Currie, 19 September 1896, UKNA FO 195/1936.

395. Graves to Currie, 23 September 1896, UKNA FO 195/1941.

396. Shipley to Currie, 11 September 1896 and 28 September 1896, both in UKNA FO 195/1936.

397. Terrell to State Department, 15 September 1896, USNA RG 84, Turkey (Constantinople), Vol. 20.

398. Ibid.

399. Richards (Angora) to Currie, 9 September 1896, UKNA FO 195/1934; Bulman (Sivas) to Currie, 20 September 1896, UKNA FO 195/1930; and Fuller, "News Notes No. 27," Aintab, 14 October 1896, Houghton ABC 16.9.5, Reel 653.

400. Fontana to Currie, 19 May 1897, UKNA FO 195/1981; and unsigned (but by a Harput missionary), "The Massacre in Egin," undated, Houghton ABC 16.10.1, Vol. 12.

401. Ibid.; and Fontana to Currie, 18 November 1896, "Inclosure . . . Report on the Eghin Massacre," UKNA FO 195/1944.

402. Fontana to Currie, 30 September 1896, UKNA FO 195/1944. An Ottoman report estimated that 11 Muslims had died alongside 581 Armenians (Nazim, *Ermeni Olayları Tarihi*, vol. 2, 428).

403. Dadrian, *History of the Armenian Genocide*, 146.

404. Fontana (Harput) to Currie, 14 October 1896, UKNA FO 195/1944.

405. Fontana to Currie, 18 November 1896, "Inclosure 2 in No. 1, Report on the Eghin Massacre," UKNA FO 195/1944.

406. Fontana to Currie, 30 September 1896, UKNA FO 195/1944. Unsigned (but by a Harput missionary), "The Massacre in Egin," undated, Houghton ABC 16.10.1, Vol. 12. See also Mamüret-ül-Aziz to Ministry of the Interior, 11 October 1896, Nazim, *Ermeni Olayları Tarihi*, vol. 2, 427–428, 518–520. The Turks claimed that the outbreak began when Armenian revolutionaries attacked troops. Kurdish tribesmen then joined the fray.

407. Unsigned (but by a Harput missionary), undated, Houghton ABC 16.10.1, Vol. 12.

408. Unsigned (but probably by Gates) to Peet (?), 19 October 1896, Houghton 16.10.1, Vol. 12.

409. Bulman to ?, 23 September 1896, UKNA FO 195/1993.

410. Bulman to ?, 17 August 1897, with the original letter in Turkish and an English translation of excerpts, UKNA FO 195/1993.

411. Fontana to Currie, 18 November 1896, "Inclosure 2 in No. 1, Report on the Eghin Massacre," UKNA FO 195/1944; and Fontana to Currie, 7 June 1897, UKNA FO 195/1981.

412. Unsigned (but by a Harput missionary), "The Massacre in Egin," undated, and unsigned, untitled memorandum, 29 September 1896, both in Houghton ABC 16.10.1, Vol. 12.

413. Unsigned (but probably by Gates), Egin, to Peet (?), 19 October 1896, Houghton ABC 16.10.1, Vol. 12.

414. Fontana to Currie, 18 November 1896, "Inclusure 2 in No. 1, Report on the Eghin Massacre," UKNA FO 195/1944; and Fontana to Currie, 19 May 1897, UKNA FO 195/1981.

415. Fontana to Currie, 18 November 1896, and "Inclosure 1 in No. 1," in Currie to Salisbury (received 14 December 1896), both in UKNA FO 195/1944.

416. Fontana to Currie, 19 May 1897, UKNA FO 195/1981.

417. Unsigned, untitled memorandum, 29 September 1896, Houghton ABC 16.10.1, Vol. 12.

418. Unsigned letter (from Harput missionary), 22 September 1896, Houghton ABC 16.10.1, Vol. 12.

419. Memorandum, "Drogmanat via Chancery," No. 599, 3 September 1896, UKNA FO 195/1941; Memorandum, "Drogmanat via Chancery," No. 606, 4 September 1896, UKNA FO 195/1941; and Currie to FO, 7 September 1896, UKNA FO 195/1918.

420. Graves to Currie, 11 September 1896, UKNA FO 195/1941. Graves reported that the Armenians were still panicked, thanks to newly hung posters denouncing the vali as "a partisan of the Armenians" and calling on Muslims "to renew the massacres."

421. Barnham to Currie, ? November 1895, UKNA FO 195/1883; and Barnham to Currie, 24 November 1895, *Turkey No. 2 (1896)*, 231.

422. Fontana to Currie, 26 October 1895, UKNA FO 195/1884. For two other, similar cases, see Fontana to Currie, 3 December 1895, UKNA FO 195/1884; and Fontana to Currie, 30 January 1896, *Turkey No. 8 (1896)*, 25.

423. Hampson to Cumberbatch, 13 November 1895, UKNA FO 195/1893; Hamson to Cumberbatch, 15 November 1895, UKNA FO 195/1887; and Cumberbatch to Currie, 25 November 1896, UKNA FO 195/1893.

424. Hampson to Cumberbatch, 15 November 1895, UKNA FO 195/1887; and Hampson to Cumberbatch, 16 November 1895, attached to Cumberbatch to Currie, 25 November 1895, UKNA FO 195/1893.

425. Richards to Currie, 9 September 1896, UKNA FO 195/1934. Richards to Currie, 21 September 1896, and Richards to Currie, 20 September 1896, both in UKNA FO 195/1934. Richards reported that the Jews, "as usual, were the first to arrive on the scene, their object being to profit by the obscurity and confusion to appropriate any articles of minor value which might be rescued from the flames."

426. For example, after a Muslim attack on Christians in Tokat on March 19, 1895, the Turks and Armenians both reported one Armenian death, but the injury count differed greatly. Armenian clergymen reported fifty "seriously injured" by bayonets and many more lightly wounded, but the vali told diplomats that only eleven Armenians had been lightly injured. The clergy's account names each of the seriously injured and details their injuries. See "Translation of the Vali's Report on the Tokat Disturbance of March 19, 1895" and "Translation of Report by the Tokat Armenian Clergy to their Bishop at Sivas," both undated, but enclosed in Currie to Kimberley, 27 April 1895, *Turkey No. 6 (1896)*, 284–288.

427. Lepsius defined it as *vernichtungsmasregel* which Ihrig translates as "annihilatory administrative measure" (Ihrig, *Justifying Genocide*, 51).

428. It is worth noting that in November 1895 Cumberbatch entered a dissenting opinion, arguing, "As far as I know, there is no proof of direct government instigation as is generally, and perhaps naturally, insisted upon by Armenians and their friends, both as regards the Kurdish raids and the massacres in the towns" (Cumberbatch to Currie, 26 November 1895, UKNA FO 195/1893).

429. Hallward to Cumberbatch, 11 December 1895, *Turkey No. 2 (1896)*, 288–289.

430. Terrell to Dwight, 30 July 1894, USNA RG 84, Turkey (Constantinople), Vol. 269.

431. Onal, *Sadettin Paşa'nın Anıları*, 21–22.

432. Cumberbatch to Currie, 10 January 1895, *Turkey No. 6 (1896)*, 199.

433. Onal, *Sadettin Paşa'nın Anıları*, 30–32, 48–50, 74.

434. Longworth to Currie, 17 December 1894, UKNA FO 195/1854.

435. Longworth to Currie, 8 February 1895, UKNA FO 195/1936.

436. Horton to Bristol, 4 August 1922, USNA RG 84, Turkey (Constantinople), Vol. 459.

437. Henry Dwight, "The Situation in Turkey in November," 27 November 1895, UKNA FO 195/1907. Western diplomats occasionally conjectured that the massacres were part of an Ottoman policy to "stamp out the Christian element as far as possible on their Eastern frontier" (Hallward to J. S. Shipley, 11 December 1894, UKNA FO 195/1846), perhaps out of fear that the existence of large concentrations of Armenians in the east would facilitate eventual Russian conquest of the area.

438. Unsigned, "Inclosure 2 in No. 300. Letter from Sivas, 12 February 1895," attached to Longworth to Currie, 18 February 1895, *Turkey No. 6 (1906)*, 236–237.

439. Currie to Salisbury, c. 9 January 1896 (draft telegram), UKNA FO 195/1914.

440. Fitzmaurice (Aleppo) to Currie, 30 September 1896, UKNA FO 195/1930.

441. McGregor to Consul General Drummond Hay, 16 April 1895, *Turkey No. 6 (1896)*, 292–293.

442. Fitzmaurice to Currie, 2 February 1896, UKNA FO 195/1946.

443. Fontana to Currie, 26 October 1895, UKNA FO 195/1884.

444. Cumberbatch to Currie, 4 February 1895, and Cumberbatch to Currie, 7 February 1895, in *Turkey No. 6 (1896)*, 224 and 224–225.

445. Cumberbatch to Currie, 6 January 1896, and attached memorandum by Cumberbatch, "Forced Conversions . . . ," 6 January 1896, UKNA FO 195/1941.

446. Hartunian, *Neither to Laugh nor to Weep*, 13–14. The literal meaning of "Muhammede salavat" is "prayer be upon Muhammad."

447. Terrell to Olney, 16 December 1895, and attached "Attacks on Christianity in Turkey," 14 December 1895, *FRUS* 1895, Part 2, 1398–1400; and summary of report on Missis, mid-November 1895, "Projets de réformes," 209, Bodl. MS Lord Bryce Papers 211–212.

448. Barnham to Currie, 11 August 1895, UKNA FO 195/1883.

449. In June 1896 the French estimated the total number of forced conversions during the previous months at 40,950: 5,200 in Erzurum; 1,600 in Sivas; 12,500 in Harput; 7,500 in Diyarbekir; 6,500 in Bitlis; 3,000 in Van; 1,500 in Aleppo; 3,000 in Adana; 150 in Ankara (table attached to Barthélemy to Cambon, 6 June 1896, MAE, Turquie 528, 319). See also Deringil, "Armenian Question Is Finally Closed," 347–349. Üngör, *Making of Modern Turkey*, 19, estimates that 25,000 Christians were converted in Diyarbekir vilayet alone during the Hamidian massacres.

450. Currie to Salisbury, 6 March 1896, *Turkey No. 8 (1896)*, 67.

451. Cumberbatch to Currie, 26 February 1896, *Turkey No. 8 (1896)*, 78. For a list of conversions in the Van area, see reports sent by the Catholicos of Akdamar to the French embassy, 12 May and 7 August 1895, UKNA FO 195/1906.

452. Currie to FO, 13 December 1895, UKNA FO 195/1871.

453. Unsigned, "Letter dated Aintab, February 6, 1896," *Turkey 8 (1896),* 84.

454. Graves to Currie, 17 January 1895, UKNA FO 195/1891; and Graves to Currie, 28 February 1895, UKNA FO 195/1891.

455. Cumberbatch to Currie, 2 December 1895, UKNA FO 195/1893.

456. Bulman to Currie, 4 February 1896, UKNA FO 195/1930.

457. Dwight to Currie, 27 November 1895, UKNA FO 195/1907.

458. Cumberbatch to Currie, 6 January 1896, and attached memorandum by Cumberbatch, "Forced Conversions to Islamism in Kharput District. Additional Details," 6 January 1896, UKNA FO 195/1941.

459. Cumberbatch to Currie, 2 December 1895, UKNA FO 195/1893.

460. Cumberbatch to Currie, 12 December 1895, UKNA FO 195/1893.

461. Fontana to Currie, 15 June 1896, UKNA FO 195/1944.

462. Currie to Salisbury, draft telegram, c. 9 January 1896, UKNA FO 195/1914.

463. Deringil, "Armenian Question Is Finally Closed," 369–371.

464. A. J. Arnold, general secretary, Evangelical Alliance, "Extracts from Letters of Correspondents in Turkey," March 1896, UKNA FO 195/1928.

465. Currie to Salisbury, 29 January 1896, *Turkey No. 5 (1896),* 1.

466. Currie to Salisbury, 3 February 1896, *Turkey No. 5 (1896),* 1.

467. Fitzmaurice (Aleppo) to Currie, 9 April 1896, *Turkey No. 5 (1896),* 16–17.

468. Currie to Salisbury, 31 March 1896, *Turkey No. 8 (1896),* 113.

469. Vice consul J. H. Monahan to ?, 28 February 1897, and Monahan, "Memorandum: Forced Conversions in Bitlis Villages," May 1897, both in UKNA FO 195/1993.

470. Hampson to Cumberbatch, 2 March 1896, *Turkey No. 8 (1896),* 106.

471. Hallward to Currie, 21 April 1896, UKNA FO 195/1930.

472. Fontana to Currie, 2 May 1896, *Turkey No. 8 (1896),* 179.

473. Unsigned but by the ABC HQ, Constantinople, "The Orphans of Asiatic Turkey," 6 August 1896, UKNA FO 195/1953. The report states that very young girls were abducted and enslaved, serving initially as apprentice servants in households. After maturing they were handed over to the harem of some "wealthy debauchee" or sold off as wives "for the gold her flesh would bring in the [marriage] market."

474. Unsigned, "In Asiatic Turkey and the Transcaucasus in 1889–1890," undated, USNA RG 59, 867.4016, Roll 46.

475. See, for example, the "Armenian population of Karahissar" to Longworth, 2 July 1894, UKNA 195/1894, relating to the May 1894 rapes of two Armenian women washing laundry by a group of "government officials" led by "the son of Agadjouk," presumably a Kurdish leader near Karahissar. A few days later, soldiers "outraged" two Armenian women near the village of Anerzi.

476. Hallward to Graves, 19 March 1895, *Turkey No. 6 (1896),* 267–268. See also Armenian Patriarch to Cambon, 8 January 1896, MAE, Turquie 526, 54.

477. Hallward to Graves, 10 June 1895, *Turkey No. 6 (1896),* 349.

478. Christie to Major Massy, 15 July 1896, UKNA FO 195/1930.

479. Gates to Currie, 16 January 1896, UKNA FO 195/1949.

480. Fontana to Currie, 11 April 1897, UKNA FO 195/1981.

481. Unsigned, "Something about Silvan [Silouan] District," Mardin, August 1896, Houghton ABC 16.10.1, Vol. 12.

482. "Report on the state of affairs in the Vilayet of Mamuret-ul-Aziz," c. April 1896, *Turkey No. 8 (1896),* 180. See also "Inclosure No. 2 in No. 213, Vilayet of Diyarbekir," c. April 1896, *Turkey No. 8 (1896),* 180, for a case in Nor-Kegh, Palu district.

483. Bulman to Currie, 4 February 1896, *Turkey No. 8 (1896),* 38.

484. "Communication Received from the Sublime Porte," 1 August 1896, *Turkey No. 8 (1896)*, 293.

485. Hallward to Herbert, 25 August 1896, UKNA FO 195/1930; and Hallward to Currie, 3 April 1896, UKNA FO 195/1930.

486. Herbert to Salisbury, 4 August 1896, *Turkey No. 8 (1896)*, 291.

487. "Translation of Circular," undated, but attached to Fontana to Currie, 11 October 1897, UKNA FO 195/1981.

488. Fontana to Currie, 21 December 1897, UKNA FO 195/1981.

489. For example, see Hallward to Currie, 20 March 1896, UKNA FO 195/1930.

490. Waugh to Currie, 6 September 1897, UKNA FO 195/1993.

491. Cumberbatch to Nicolson, 8 January 1894, *Turkey No. 6 (1896)*, 15–16.

492. "Armenians of Shebin-Karahissar to Consul Longworth," 2 July 1894, and "Letter to Consul Longworth," 21 July 1894, both in *Turkey No. 6 (1896)*, 122–123, 123–124.

493. Currie to Salisbury, 4 July 1895, and appended "List of the Armenians exiled to Acre (fortress)," *Turkey No. 6 (1896)*, 351–354. Acre was a favorite destination for banishment. For instance, in 1868 the Ottomans exiled there the founder of the Baha'i faith, Baha'ullah.

494. Graves to Currie, 9 March 1894, *Turkey No. 6 (1896)*, 55.

495. "Memorandum respecting the state of things at Yuzgat, May 1894," *Turkey No. 6 (1896)*, 90.

496. A. Tulle, "News Notes No. 2," 19 March 1896, UKNA FO 195/1950.

497. Catoni (Alexandretta) to Currie, 14 January 1897, UKNA FO 195/1975.

498. Bulman to ?, 19 August 1896, UKNA FO 195/1930.

499. Richards to Currie, 20 May 1896, UKNA FO 195/1934.

500. Consul to Currie, 7 February 1896, UKNA FO 195/1936.

501. Graves to Currie, 12 September 1896, UKNA FO 195/1941.

502. Roqueferrier to Cambon, 10 February 1896, MAE, Turquie 527, 34–42.

503. Fitzmaurice to Currie, 10 September 1896, UKNA FO 195/1930.

504. See, for example, Graves (Erzurum) to Currie, 12 September 1896, UKNA FO 195/1941.

505. Bulman to ?, 19 August 1896, UKNA FO 195/1930. See also MAE, Turquie 527, 40.

506. Cumberbatch to Currie, 22 February 1896, UKNA FO 195/1941.

507. Henry Barnham (Aleppo) to Currie, 16 January 1897, UKNA FO 195/1976.

508. Memorandum, Drogmanat via Chancery, 9 October 1896, UKNA FO 195/1941.

509. Memorandum, Drogmanat via Chancery, 9 October 1896, and Graves to Currie, 16 October 1896, both in UKNA FO 195/1941.

510. Graves to Currie, 16 October 1896, UKNA FO 195/1941.

511. Longworth to Currie, 18 November 1896, UKNA FO 195/1936.

512. Fuller to Terrell, 26 November 1896, UKNA FO 195/1953; and Fuller to Smith, 28 October 1896, Houghton ABC 16.9.5. The vali of Aleppo told missionaries that he had received "stringent orders from Constantinople" to prevent the group's emigration (Longworth to Currie, 19 November 1896, UKNA FO 195/1953).

513. Unsigned but by ABC HQ, Constantinople, "The Orphans of Asiatic Turkey," 6 August 1896, UKNA FO 195/1953.

514. Chambers (Bahçecik, Izmit) to Currie, 28 January 1896, UKNA FO 195/1949; and Cumberbatch to Currie, 22 February 1896, UKNA FO 195/1941.

515. For example, Americus Fuller to ?, undated (probably from July 1896), Houghton ABC 16.9.5; and Cumberbatch to Currie, 22 February 1896, UKNA FO 195/1941.

516. Correspondence between British Colonial Secretary Joseph Chamberlain and British High Commissioner Walter Sendall, starting with Chamberlain to Sendall, 18 March 1896, in UKNA FO 195/1952. Sendall argued that there was a lack of arable land and the local population might not be

hospitable: "The Armenian is not liked either by the Christian or the Moslem Cypriot." He pointed out that the establishment in 1883 of a settlement of Jewish immigrants from Russia had failed.

517. See Earl of Aberdeen to Joseph Chamberlain, 21 August 1896, and John McGee, Clerk of the Privy Council, "Inclosure No. 2 in No. 1, Extract from a Report of the Committee of the Honourable the Privy Council, approved by the Governor-General on the 14th August 1896," both in UKNA FO 195/1928.

518. Akçam, *Shameful Act,* 30. Ihrig, *Justifying Genocide,* 34, puts the death toll at between 80,000 and "over 200,000." McCarthy, *Death and Exile,* 119–120, writes that during the 1890s, Armenian rebellions were "common all over the east" of Turkey, which is nonsense. He also writes, "In general, the Armenian population seems to have suffered the worse mortality," which, implying some sort of equivalence between the activities of Armenian rebels and Turkish authorities, is worse than nonsense.

519. Cumberbatch to Currie, 7 January 1896, and "Inclosure 2 in No. 7," both in *Turkey No. 8 (1896),* 7–10. See also Ihrig, *Justifying Genocide,* 42.

520. "Inclosure 2 in No. 8, List of Houses burnt and of Persons killed in the District of the American Mission at Kharput," *Turkey No. 8 (1896),* 11.

521. Longworth (Trabzon) to Currie, 8 February 1896, and attached "Depredations committed on Armenians in Karahissar-Sharki District of the Sivas Vilayet," *Turkey No. 8 (1896),* 59–60.

522. Longworth to Currie, 7 February 1896, and "Inclosure 2 in No. 49," both in *Turkey No. 8 (1896),* 41–42.

523. Unsigned, "Statistics of Disorders in the Sivas *Vilayet,* 1895–1896," undated, UKNA FO 195/1930.

524. Terrell to Currie, undated but from February 1896, UKNA FO 195/1949.

525. Quoted in Ihrig, *Justifying Genocide,* 49.

526. Waugh to Currie, 6 September 1897, UKNA FO 195/1993.

527. Crow to Currie, 3 October 1897, UKNA FO 195/1993.

528. Longworth to Currie, 23 October 1897, UKNA FO 195/1993.

529. Fontana to Currie, 23 January 1897, UKNA FO 195/1981.

530. Unsigned, "Precis of Proceedings of the Tokat Commission, which sat from April 21st to May 27th, 1897," UKNA FO 195/1993.

531. Bulman to Currie, 8 April 1897, UKNA FO 195/1993.

532. Bulman to Currie, 26 April 1897, UKNA FO 195/1993. Western newspapers reported a death toll of 700–900.

533. Unsigned, "Precis of Proceedings of the Tokat Commission . . . ," UKNA FO 195/1993.

534. Unsigned, "Precis of Proceedings of the Tokat Commission . . . , which sat from April 21st to May 27th, 1897," UKNA FO 195/1993.

535. Bulman to Currie, 14 April 1897, UKNA FO 195/1993.

536. Bulman to Currie, 14 April 1897, UKNA FO 195/1993.

537. In August 1896 the American Board of Commissioners for Foreign Missions estimated that the "massacres of 1895" had orphaned "at least 50,000 Christian children under twelve years of age" (unsigned but by the mission HQ in Constantinople, "The Orphans of Asiatic Turkey," 6 August 1896, UKNA FO 195/1953).

3. A More Turkish Empire

1. Ahmad, *Making of Modern Turkey,* 39.

2. Suny, *They Can Live in the Desert,* 206–207.

3. Rogan, *Fall of the Ottomans,* 24.

4. Quoted in Pentzopoulos, *Balkan Exchange,* 53.

5. Zürcher, *Young Turk Legacy and Nation Building*, 120.

6. Suny, *They Can Live in the Desert*, 190.

7. Suny, *They Can Live in the Desert*, 183–185.

8. McCarthy, *Death and Exile*, 109–134.

9. Ginio, "Paving the Way for Ethnic Cleansing."

10. Suny, *They Can Live in the Desert*, 175.

11. Wangenheim to Theobald von Bethmann-Hollweg, 15 November 1913, Enc. 2, *German Foreign Office*, 144. While Protestant and Catholic Armenian parishes thrived after the 1890s, a much smaller group joined the Greek Orthodox Church.

12. Suny, *They Can Live in the Desert*, 176; and Kevorkian, *Armenian Genocide*, 146–152.

13. The events described here and in the following paragraphs are based on Der Matossian, "From Bloodless Revolution," 152–173; and Tetsuya Sahara, "The 1909 Adana Incident (Part 2)."

14. Akçam, *Shameful Act*, 69.

15. Der Matossian, "From Bloodless Revolution," 163.

16. Gaunt, *Massacres*, 45.

17. Der Matossian, "From Bloodless Revolution," 164; Akçam, *Shameful Act*, 69–70.

18. Suny, *They Can Live in the Desert*, 182.

19. Suny, *They Can Live in the Desert*, 194.

20. Suny, *They Can Live in the Desert*, 202; and Kevorkian, *Armenian Genocide*, 153–165.

21. Ihirig, *Justifying Genocide*, 89.

22. Suny, *They Can Live in the Desert*, 203, 216–217.

23. Report of Rev. Ralph Harlow, attached to Horton to Morgenthau, 23 January 1915, Foreign Service, vol. 390, 374, emphasis in the original. See also Suny, *They Can Live in the Desert*, 185, 239.

24. Zürcher, "How Europeans Adopted Anatolia," 383; and Zürcher, "Renewal and Silence."

25. Suny, *They Can Live in the Desert*, 187. For the vengeful effect of the Balkan wars on the Young Turks, see also Üngör, *Making of Modern Turkey*, 42–50.

26. Kieser, *Talaat*, 56–57.

27. Kieser, *Talaat*, 56–57, 188.

28. Testimony of Wilfred M. Post, 11 April 1918, USNA RG 256, "Inquiry Documents," 1917–1919, no. 823, Roll 39. The (Sunni) Şeyhülislam's *fatwa* was quickly followed by jihadi *fatwas* by the leading Shi'ite clerics in Najaf and Karbala (Gaunt, *Massacres*, 62).

29. Kevorkian, *Armenian Genocide*, 141.

30. Mallet to Grey, 13 April 1920, and Dussi to consul-general, 14 April 1914, both in UKNA FO 371/2132. Q. in Mazower, *Salonica*, 316–318. Mazower points out that the deportation of the Macedonian-Thracian Turks was not initiated or supported by the Greek government. On the *muhacirs'* influence on Ottoman plans of ethnic cleansing, see Ginio, "Paving the Way for Ethnic Cleansing," 283–297.

31. Rodd to Grey, 19 August 1909, UKNA FO 371/778.

32. British consul, Adrianople, to Mallet, 31 March 1914, UKNA FO 371/2133.

33. Bjornlund, "Danish Sources on the Destruction of Ottoman Greeks," 150.

34. Kevorkian, *Armenian Genocide*, 170; and Akçam, *From Empire to Republic*, 143–146; Morris to Morgenthau, 18 July 1914, USNA RG 59 867.00, Roll 5; and Bjornlund, "Danish Sources on the Destruction of Ottoman Greeks," 147–149. The Turks denied that such a "plan" existed (see Kevorkian, *Armenian Genocide*, 243).

35. Kieser, "Dr. Mehmet Reshid," 196.

36. Kieser, *Talaat Pasha*, 174–175.

37. Bjornlund, "Danish Sources on the Destruction of Ottoman Greeks," 152.

38. Bjornlund, "Danish Sources on the Destruction of Ottoman Greeks," 143.

39. Bjornlund, "Danish Sources on the Destruction of Ottoman Greeks," 143.

40. Hofmann, "Cumulative Genocide," 51; and Kieser, *Talaat Pasha,* 176. The Greeks at the time published this cable, which Ottoman sources dismissed as a fabrication (Kieser, *Talaat Pasha,* 454n162).

41. Hofmann, "Cumulative Genocide," 51.

42. Kieser, *Talaat Pasha,* 177, 179–180.

43. Horton to SecState, c. 1 September 1918, USNA RG 59, 867.4016, Roll 46.

44. Memoranda attached to Mallet to Grey, 18 March 1914, UKNA FO 371/2126.

45. Greek Patriarchate, "Persecution of the Greeks in Turkey, 1914–1918," undated but probably from 1919, Bodl. MS Toynbee Papers 57 (hereafter Greek Patriarchate, "Persecution of the Greeks . . . ,"), 112.

46. Quoted in Ginio, *Ottoman Culture of Defeat,* 190.

47. Mallet to Grey, 27 January 1914, UKNA FO 371/2126.

48. Henry D. Barnham to Mallet, 13 February 1914, UKNA FO 371/2126.

49. G. Henry Wright, Birmingham Chamber of Commerce, to Assistant Secretary, Commercial Department, Board of Trade, Whitehall, 22 May 1914, UKNA FO 371/2126.

50. Greek Patriarchate, "Persecution of the Greeks . . . ," 55.

51. Henry D. Barnham to Mallet, 13 February 1914, UKNA FO 371/2126.

52. Horton to SecState, 21 February 1914, USNA RG 59, 867.00, Roll 5. Horton enclosed the translation of an official poster: "In the name of my religion and faith, I want to give you . . . a few words of advice. If your religion is Islam, if your faith is true, your marriage good, and your hearts filled with the light of faith in the Prophet, communicate this advice to [relatives and friends]. . . . In your heart secretly increase the hatred that necessitates this advice, in order that this religion, this Book, the Country, the Nation, may be saved. . . . The Christians have fixed a covetous eye on our country [and] are working to put out of existence our religion and Book. . . . Let us not use the cigarette paper, soap and matches sold [by Greeks]."

53. G. Henry Wright, Birmingham Chamber of Commerce, to Assistant Secretary, Commercial Department, Board of Trade, Whitehall, 22 May 1914, UKNA FO 371/2126.

54. Mallet to Grey, 26 February 1914, UKNA FO 371/2126.

55. Greek Patriarchate, "Persecution of the Greeks . . . ," 90, a letter by the metropolitans of Smyrna, Ephesus, etc. to the embassies in Constantinople, 25 June 1914.

56. Greek Patriarchate, "Persecution of the Greeks . . . ," 57.

57. Kieser, *Talaat Pasha,* 176.

58. Quoted in Hofmann, "Cumulative Genocide," 53.

59. Greek Patriarchate, "Persecution of the Greeks . . . ," 64.

60. Horton to Morgenthau, 9 June 1914, USNA RG 59, 867.00, Roll 5.

61. Horton to Morgenthau, 9 June 1914, USNA RG 59, 867.00, Roll 5.

62. Bjornlund, "Danish Sources on the Destruction of Ottoman Greeks," 152.

63. Horton to SecState, 18 June 1914, and Morris to Horton, 17 June 1914, USNA RG 59, 867.00, Roll 5. A second massacre occurred earlier, on 31 May, in Sere-Keuy (Saraköy), near Menemen (see Greek Patriarchate, "Persecution of the Greeks . . . ," 79–81; and Bjornlund, "Danish Sources on the Destruction of Ottoman Greeks," 155).

64. Mourelos, "The 1914 Persecutions of Greeks," 121–122.

65. Bjornlund, "Danish Sources on the Destruction of Ottoman Greeks," 157.

66. Greek Patriarchate, "Persecution of the Greeks . . . ," 55.

67. "Memo Compiled in Eastern Dept.," possibly from 26 February 1920, UKNA FO 371/5191.

68. Morgenthau to Lansing, 18 November 1915, FDRL, HM Sr. Papers, Letters 474. According to Erol, in line with Talaat Pasha's estimate, "some 163,975" Ottoman Greeks "escaped or migrated" to

Greece by June 1914 (Erol, *Ottoman Crisis,* 182, 286n51). According to the Greek Foreign Ministry, "60,926" Greeks were forced to flee Eastern Thrace during January–July 1914 (Mourelos, "The 1914 Persecutions of Greeks, 116). Bjornlund estimates that altogether "150–200,000" Greeks were displaced from their homes before the start of WWI (Bjornlund, "Danish Sources on the Destruction of Ottoman Greeks," 141n12, 155).

69. Einstein, *Inside Constantinople,* entry for 1 May 1915, 11.

70. McCarthy writes that the world war "in the east began on 2 November 1914, when Russian forces moved south to occupy the border regions of Bayazit, Diyadin, and Karakilise" (McCarthy, *Death and Exile,* 179). This is untrue. The war began with the shelling of Russian Black Sea ports and the sinking of Russian vessels by the newly-acquired Ottoman German battlecruiser, the *Goeben* (renamed the *Yavuz Sultan Selim*), on 29 October, the response to which were the Russian declaration of war and cross-border attacks.

71. Rogan, *Fall of the Ottomans,* 106; and Kevorkian, *Armenian Genocide,* 220.

72. Rogan, *Fall of the Ottomans,* 102.

73. Kevorkian, *Armenian Genocide,* 220.

74. Ford, *Eden to Armageddon,* 121–137.

75. Rogan, *Fall of the Ottomans,* 107.

76. Ford, *Eden to Armageddon,* 127.

77. Akçam, *Genocide of the Armenians,* 48. See also Rogan, *Fall of the Ottomans,* 114.

78. Kevorkian, *Armenian Genocide,* 221.

79. Suny, *They Can Live in the Desert,* 243.

80. Kevorkian, *Armenian Genocide,* 221.

81. Kevorkian, *Armenian Genocide,* 221–222.

82. During the Tanzimat reforms in the nineteenth century, conscription was made mandatory for members of all religions, but Christians and Jews were allowed to pay an indemnity, called "bedel," to receive exemption.

83. Adanır, "Non-Muslims in the Ottoman Army," 123–124.

84. *German Foreign Office,* 12.

85. Zürcher, "Ottoman Labour Battalions," 4.

86. Akçam, *Shameful Act,* 142.

87. Zürcher, "Ottoman Labour Battalions," 1.

88. Akçam, *Shameful Act,* 144.

89. Torosyan, *Çanakkale'den Filistin Cephesi'ne,* 147; see also 152.

90. Zürcher, "Ottoman Labour Battalions," 5.

91. Zürcher, "Ottoman Labour Battalions," 4.

92. Zürcher, "Ottoman Labour Battalions," 4. See also testimony of Klara Pfeiffer, *German Foreign Office,* 13, 584.

93. This is corroborated by vali of Mamuretulaziz to Interior Ministry, 19 June 1915, BOA, DH. ŞFR, 476/43, saying that most of the 1,500 men of the labor battalions (and Armenian revolutionaries) were deported.

94. Patriarchate report dated 30 November 1920, in Malta file of Suleiman Faik Pasha, UKNA FO 371/6501.

95. Ibid. See also Testimony of Tacy W. Atkinson, 11 April 1918, USNA RG 256, "Inquiry Documents," 1917–1919, no. 210, Roll 39. Perhaps it was their remains that Rafael de Nogales saw in late June: He was drawn to "black bundles" that "proved to be nothing less than the swollen and worm-eaten corpses of dozens and perhaps hundreds of Armenian soldiers, whom the escort had evidently led from the road and knifed without mercy" (De Nogales, *Four Years,* 149).

96. Patriarchate report dated 30 November 1920, in Malta file of Suleiman Faik Pasha, UKNA FO 371/6501. Story corroborated by Alma Johansson's report, 17 November 1915, attached to Morgenthau to SecState, 9 November 1915, *U.S. Official Records,* 333–337. See also translation of ARF report dated 5 September 1915, attached to Morgenthau to SecState, 17 September 1915, USNA RG 59, 867.4016, Roll 44; and report by Mary Riggs, "War-Time Events in Harpoot, Turkey," 19 August 1916, Houghton ABC 16.9.7, A467, Reel 716.

97. See Kevorkian, *Armenian Genocide,* 398.

98. Dadrian, *History of the Armenian Genocide,* 325–326; Dadrian, "Secret Young-Turk Ittihadist Conference," 185–186; and Dadrian and Akçam, *Judgment at Istanbul,* 184.

99. Dadrian, "Secret Young-Turk Ittihadist Conference," 185–186. See also Dadrian and Akçam, *Judgment at Istanbul,* 184. Later that year Vehib Pasha was arrested and indicted for "abuse of office." He escaped to Italy and remained in exile until the late 1930s.

100. Kunzler, *In the Land of Blood and Tears,* 16–20.

101. Morgenthau, *Ambassador Morgenthau's Story,* 302–304. See also Zürcher, "Ottoman Labour Battalions," 1.

102. De Nogales, *Four Years,* 124–126.

103. Raynolds to Friends, 26 November 1912, Houghton ABC 16.9.7, A467, Reel 715; Interior Ministry to Van vilayet, 6 March 1915, BOA, DH. EUM. MEM, 61/68; Yarrow to Friends, 4 December 1914, Houghton ABC 16.9.7, A467, Reel 717; and Elizabeth Ussher to Family (diary of the insurrection), 8 May 1915, Houghton ABC 16.9.7, A467, Reel 717.

104. Yarrow to Friends, 7 November 1914, Houghton ABC 16.9.7, A467, Reel 717.

105. Raynolds to Barton, 13 November 1914, Houghton ABC 16.9.7, A467, Reel 715.

106. Gaunt, "Ottoman Treatment of the Assyrians," 247.

107. Yarrow to Friends, 7 November 1914, Houghton ABC 16.9.7, A467, Reel 717.

108. Kevorkian, *Armenian Genocide,* 231–233; Suny, *They Can Live in the Desert,* 255–257; and De Nogales, *Four Years,* 66.

109. Anderson, "Who Still Talked," 204.

110. Undated ARF Report (but from March and April 1915), USNA RG 59, 867.4016, Roll 43; Van vilayet to Interior Ministry, 23 April 1915, BOA, DH. ŞFR, 468/76; Diyarbekir to Interior Ministry, 21 April 1915, BOA, DH ŞFR, 469/97; Mattie Raynolds to George Raynolds, 29 May 1915, Houghton ABC 16.9.7, A467, Reel 715; correspondence between Interior Ministry and Van, Erzurum, and Bitlis vilayets, 8 March 1915, BOA, DH. EUM. MEM, 61/3; Interior Ministry to Baghdad vilayet, 22 April 1915, BOA, DH. ŞFR, 468/70.

111. Van vilayet to Interior Ministry, 20 April 1915, BOA, DH. ŞFR, 468/36; 21 April 1915, BOA, DH. ŞFR. 468/55; and 22 April 1915, BOA. DH. ŞFR. 468/67.

112. Scheubner-Richter to Wangenheim, 15 May 1915, *German Foreign Office,* 178. For the development of Wangenheim's understanding of the issues, see Anderson, "Who Still Talked," 204–205.

113. Anderson, "Who Still Talked."

114. Van vilayet to Interior Ministry, 26 April 1915, BOA, DH. ŞFR, 468/126. See also Morgenthau to family, 27 April 1915, FDRL, HM Sr. Papers, Letters 474; and UK Foreign Office memo, 11 May 1915, UKNA FO 371/2488.

115. Elizabeth Ussher to family, 8 May 1915 and 30 May 1915, Houghton ABC 16.9.7, A467, Reel 717. See also Mattie Raynolds to George Raynolds, 29 May 1915, Houghton ABC 16.9.7, A467, Reel 715.

116. An Englishman claimed that "the general testimony in Van is that the Turks were entirely opposed to the whole anti-Armenian arrangement and were forced into it by the Committee of Union and

Progress" (Macallum to Bryce, 10 June 1916, Bodl. MS Lord Bryce Papers 202). Ussher also attested to the low enthusiasm of Turkish soldiers.

117. SecState, 30 April 1915, USNA RG 59, Roll 43; and Morgenthau to family, 4 May 1915, FDRL, HM Sr. Papers, Letters 474. See also Morgenthau to Sec. State, 25 May 1915, FDRL, HM Sr. Papers, Letters 473. After the war, Cevdet was accused of being part of the group that met in Erzurum to decide on the massacre of the Armenians (see Malta file of Tahsin Bey, UKNA FO 371/6501, Orders). De Nogales describes Halil Pasha as incompetent (*Four Years,* 106–107).

118. De Nogales, *Four Years,* 66, 70, 93.

119. Elizabeth Ussher to family, 8 May 1915, Houghton ABC 16.9.7, A467, Reel 717.

120. Van vilayet to Interior Ministry, 17 May 1915, BOA, DH. ŞFR, 471/77.

121. Mattie Raynolds to George Raynolds, 29 May 1915, Houghton ABC 16.9.7, A467, Reel 715; Elizabeth Ussher to family, 30 May 1915, Houghton ABC 16.9.7, A467, Reel 717; and Macallum to Lord Bryce, 10 June 1916, Bodl. MS Lord Bryce Papers 202. See also Interior Ministry's Security Directorate to Van vilayet, 3 May 1915, BOA, DH. ŞFR, 52/200.

122. De Nogales, *Four Years,* 124–126.

123. George Raynolds to Friends, 15 October 1915, Houghton ABC 16.9.7, A467, Reel 715; and Suny, *They Can Live in the Desert,* 261–263.

124. Yarrow to Barton, 26 December 1916, Houghton ABC 16.9.7, A467, Reel 717.

125. Gaunt, "Ottoman Treatment of the Assyrians," 247.

126. Report by Philip Price, 2 January 1914, SAMECA Philip Price Papers.

127. Kevorkian, *Armenian Genocide,* 586.

128. Wangenheim to Bethmann-Hollweg, 26 March 1915, *German Foreign Office,* 158; and Rossler to Bethmann-Hollweg, 12 April 1915, *German Foreign Office,* 161. See also Kevorkian, *Armenian Genocide,* 586; and Wangenheim's reported remarks cited in Morgenthau to family, 30 March 1915, FDRL, HM Sr. Papers, Letters 474.

129. Rossler to Bethmann Hollweg, 12 April 1895, *German Foreign Office,* 162; Suny, *They Can Live in the Desert,* 252–253; and Kevorkian, *Armenian Genocide,* 587.

130. Kevorkian, *Armenian Genocide,* 587.

131. Consul Jackson (Aleppo) to German Embassy in Constantinople, 30 March 1915, DE/PA-AA/BoKon/168, Fr. Alep 376 37/38 29; and Woodly to Barton, 23 September 1915, Houghton ABC 16.9.5, A467, Reel 672. See also Padel to Embassy and Wangenheim to Aleppo consulate, both 30 March 1915, *German Foreign Office,* 160.

132. Paraphrase of report received from "The Field Staff of the Caucasian Army," March 1915, UKNA FO 371/2484.

133. McCarthy, *Death and Exile,* 185, 180, 193; and Wangenheim to Bethmann-Hollweg, 26 March 1915, DE/PA-AA/R14085, 1915-A-11682.

134. Wangenheim to Bethmann-Hollweg, 26 March 1915, DE/PA-AA/R14085, 1915-A-11682.

135. Dündar, *Crime of Numbers,* 72–73.

136. Report by Dr. John Merrill enclosed in the letter sent by Jackson to Morgenthau, 21 April 1915, USNA RG 59, 867.00, Roll 6. See also Blank to Suchard, 15 April 1915, DE/PA-AA/R14086, 1915-A-17735, enclosure 3.

137. Report by M. Briquet, teacher at Tarsus College, attached to Morgenthau to SecState, 20 July 1915, *U.S. Official Records,* 110–111.

138. Dodd to Morgenthau, 6 May 1915, FDRL, HM Sr. Papers, Letters 473.

139. Lepsius to Foreign Office, 22 June 1915, *German Foreign Office,* 213.

140. Dündar, *Crime of Numbers,* 73.

141. Blank to Suchard, 15 April 1915, DE/PA-AA/R14086, 1915-A-17735, enclosure 3.

142. Merrill report enclosed in letter sent by Jackson to Morgenthau, 21 April 1915, USNA RG 59, 867.00, Roll 6. See also Blank to Suchard, enclosure 3, 15 April 1915, DE/PA-AA/R14086, 1915-A-17735.

143. Celal Bey, Memoirs, "The Armenian Affair, Its Reasons and Effects," part 2, *Vakit,* 12 December 1918. Celal published his memoirs in installments in the newspaper *Vakit.*

144. Missionary Blank in Marash to Rössler in Aleppo, DE/PA-AA/R14086, 1915-A-17735, enclosure 2 (15 April 1915). See also Jackson to Morgenthau, quoting Rev. Leslie of Urfa, 28 June 1915, USNA RG 59, 867.4016, Roll 43; and Morgenthau to SecState, enclosure 5, 20 July 1915, USNA RG 59, 867.4016, Roll 43.

145. Report by Leslie dated 28 June 1915, included in Morgenthau to Sec. State, 23 August 1915, USNA RG 59, 867.4016, Roll 43.

146. Suny, *They Can Live in the Desert,* 253; and Dündar, *Crime of Numbers,* 85.

147. Marash to Interior Ministry, 12 May 1915, BOA, DH. ŞFR, 470/134, and 17 May 1915, BOA, DH. ŞFR, 471/103. See also report submitted by ARF to Morgenthau, 20 July 1915, USNA RG 59, 867.4016, Roll 43. Later, Zeytun was renamed Suleymanli.

148. Morgenthau to SecState, 25 May 1915, USNA RG 59, Roll 43.

149. Kevorkian, *Armenian Genocide,* 587–588.

150. Appointment of Interior Ministry committee, 15 May 1915, BOA, DH. I. UM, 5–1/3.

151. Muhacir Directorate (IAMM, *Iskan-I Aşayir ve Muhacirin Müdüriyeti*) to Aleppo vilayet, 20 April 1915, BOA, DH. ŞFR, 52/48. See also Report from Aleppo vilayet to Interior Ministry, 21 April 1915, BOA, DH. ŞFR, 468/54.

152. Jackson to Morgenthau, 19 May 1915, USNA RG 59, Roll 43. See also Jackson to Morgenthau, 28 June 1915, USNA RG 59, 867.4016, Roll 43.

153. ARF Report from Antep, 19 April 1915, attached to Morgenthau to SecState, 20 July 1915, *U.S. Official Records,* 95.

4. The Eastern River

1. Celal Bey, Memoirs, "The Armenian Affair, Its Reasons and Effects," *Vakit,* 12 December 1918. Celal published his memoirs in installments in the newspaper *Vakit.*

2. Enclosure by Merrill in Jackson to Morgenthau, 21 April 1915, USNA RG 59, 867.00, Roll 6.

3. Talât to Resid, 12 July 1915, BOA, DH. SFR, 54/406; and Üngör, "Center and Periphery in the Armenian Genocide," 71–72.

4. Dündar, *Crime of Numbers,* 87–89.

5. Dündar, *Crime of Numbers,* 83.

6. "Council of Ministers" *(Meclis-i vükela)* decision, 30 May 1915, MV 198/24, *Sevk ve Iskan,* 155–157, doc. 81.

7. Dündar, *Crime of Numbers,* 103–104.

8. "Report by Eyewitness Lieutenant Sayied Ahmed Moukhtar Baas," 26 December 1916, UKNA FO 371/2768. Dündar, *Crime of Numbers,* 91, and full text, in Turkish and translation, on 217–218.

9. Akçam, *Young Turks' Crime,* 193–194.

10. Celal Bey, Memoirs, *Vakit,* 12 December 1918.

11. Lewy, *Armenian Massacres,* 162.

12. Jagow, Berlin, to Constantinople embassy, 15 January 1914, DE/PA-AA/R14083.

13. Wangenheim to Bethmann-Hollweg, 30 December 1914, DE/PA-AA/R14085.

14. Interior Ministry's Security Directorate to Van, Bitlis, and Erzurum vilayets, 17 February 1915, BOA, DH. EUM. MEM, 61/3.

15. Security Directorate to Van, Bitlis, and Erzurum vilayets, 12 April 1915, BOA, DH. ŞFR, 52/321; Army General Staff to Trabzon vilayet, 15 April 1915, BOA, DH. ŞFR, 52/15; Interior Ministry to Erzurum vilayet, 21 April 1915, BOA, DH. ŞFR, 468/46 (confirmed on 22 April 1915, BOA, DH. ŞFR, 468/66); and Interior Ministry to vali of Erzurum, 11 May 1915, BOA, DH. ŞFR, 470/122.

16. Interior Ministry's Special Bureau *(Kalem-i mahsus)* to Erzurum vilayet, 5 April 1915, BOA, DH. ŞFR, 51/215.

17. Malta file of Mahmud Kiamil Pasha opened on 29 May 1919, UKNA FO 371/6500. On the meeting (no exact date given) and on Third Army commander Kamil see, among others, Akçam, *Shameful Act,* 172.

18. Vilayet of Mamuretulaziz to Interior Ministry, 4 March 1915, BOA, DH. ŞFR, 463/117; and Finance Ministry to Sivas and other vilayets, 7 May 1915, DH. ŞFR, 52/249. See also Army General Staff to Interior Ministry, 22 July 1914, *Sevk ve Iskan,* 88–89, doc. 26.

19. Wangenheim to consul in Erzurum, 28 April 1915, DE/PA-AA/BoKon/168. These instructions were repeated a few days later (Wangenheim to consul in Erzurum, 19 May 1915, DE/PA-AA/BoKon/168). Scheubner-Richter, who opposed the massacre of Armenians on moral grounds, later became a prominent early Nazi. He was killed at Hitler's side by police during the Munich Putsch in 1923.

20. Scheubner-Richter to Wangenheim, 20 May 1915, DE/PA-AA/BoKon/169. See also a group of deported Armenians to Bishop Sambat of Erzurum, 22 May 1915, DE/PA-AA/BoKon/169, Enc. 1.

21. ARF Report dated 29 June 1915, attached to Morgenthau to Sec State, 20 July 1915, *U.S. Official Records,* 102–104. See also Scheubner-Richter to Wangenheim, 9 July 1915, *German Foreign Office,* 244–245.

22. Scheubner-Richter to Wangenheim, 22 May 1915, DE/PA-AA/BoKon/169.

23. See for example Interior Ministry to Sivas vilayet, 19 May 1915, BOA, DH. ŞFR 471/144; and Interior Ministry to Erzurum vilayet, BOA, 18 May 1915, DH. ŞFR, 53/48.

24. File on Tahsin Bey, UKNA FO 371/6501. See also Kevorkian, *Armenian Genocide,* 294–295.

25. Testimony of Victoria Khatchadour Barutjibashian, no date, but sent by Morgenthau to SecState, 10 August 1915, USNA RG 59, 867.4016, Roll 43. Scheubner-Richter wrote, "According to a statement made by the government, 14 of these people were murdered. . . . I have received private information that almost all the men were murdered" (Scheubner-Richter to Hohenlohe-Langenburg, 5 August 1915, *German Foreign Office,* 279). See also Lewy, *Armenian Massacres,* 163.

26. Victoria Khatchadour Barutjibashian, undated, sent by Morgenthau to SecState, 10 August 1915, USNA RG 59, 867.4016, Roll 43.

27. Report by eyewitness Lieutenant Sayied Ahmed Moukhtar Baas, 26 December 1916, UKNA FO 371/2768. For Scheubner-Richter's report, see Akçam, *Shameful Act,* 158; and Suny, *They Can Live in the Desert,* 279.

28. Testimony of Missak Vartanian, recorded at Pera on 10 August 1920, Malta file of Hadji Ahmet Adil, UKNA FO 371/6501.

29. Scheubner-Richter to Hohenlohe-Langenburg, 5 August 1915, Enclosure 1, *German Foreign Office,* 284–285. See also testimony of Rev. Robert Stapleton, (undated), Malta file of Tahsin Bey, UKNA FO 371/6501.

30. Testimony of Kourkin Kellerian, recorded 2 September 1920, Malta file of Madjid Bey, UKNA FO 371/6800; and Malta file of Memduh Bey, UKNA FO 371/6500. See also Lewy, *Armenian Massacres,* 164–165.

31. Evidence of Binganoush Bogosian, recorded 19 May 1919, Malta file of Ejzaji Mehmet Effendi, UKNA FO 37/6501.

32. Testimony of Mr. Saprastian, recorded at Tiflis on 15 March 1916, file of Tahsin Bey, UKNA FO 371/6501. Akçam believes that Tahsin Bey did his best to resist the deportations and killings (*Shameful Acts,* 167). Scheubner-Richter also believed that the vali was blameless, but testimony from Saprastian and others suggests otherwise (*German Foreign Office,* 280).

33. Kevorkian, *Armenian Genocide,* 313–314.

34. Colonel Stange to Military Mission in Istanbul, 23 August 1915, *German Foreign Office,* 330.

35. Colonel Stange's report, 23 August 1915, *German Foreign Office,* 328.

36. Kevorkian, *Armenian Genocide,* 314. For additional testimony about the Kemah Gorge massacres, see doctor's report from the German Red Cross Hospital in Erzincan, *German Foreign Office,* 223. See also Scheubner's remarks quoted in Ihrig, *Justifying Genocide,* 120.

37. Davis to Morgenthau, 11 June [should be 11 July] 1915, USNA RG 59, 867.4016, Roll 43; and Davis to Morgenthau, 24 July 1915, USNA RG 59, 867.4016, Roll 44.

38. Oscar Heizer to Morgenthau, 12 July 1915, USNA RG 59, 867.4016, Roll 43. Heizer wrote: "The real authority here seems to be in the hands of a committee of which Nail Bey is the head and he apparently receives his orders from Constantinople and not from the vali." See also Akçam, *Shameful Act,* 179.

39. Heizer to Morgenthau, 28 June 1915, USNA RG 59, 867.4016, Roll 43, attachment translated by the American Embassy.

40. Ibid. Another eyewitness, Mrs. Tahbazian (?), remembered the government's threat that anyone who helped Armenians "would be hanged outside his front door and his house burnt" (testimony recorded 22 January 1920, in Malta file of Hadji Bekir Mehmed Ali Bey, UKNA FO 371/6501). See also Der Matossian, "Taboo within the Taboo," 8–9.

41. Report by eyewitness Lieutenant Sayed Ahmed Moukhtar Baas, 26 December 1916, UKNA FO 371/2768; and Colonel Stange to German Military Mission in Constantinople, 23 August 1915, DE/PA-AA/BoKon/170. See also Kevorkian, *Armenian Genocide,* 469.

42. Pallavicini to Herrn Stephan Baron Burián, Vienna, 27 June 1915, HHStA, PA XII 209, No. 50/P.C., 2nd attachment (telegram dated 26 June 1915).

43. Heizer to Morgenthau, 28 July 1915, USNA RG 59, 867.4016, Roll 44. Another version of the story was told by Mrs. Tahbazian (?), testimony recorded 22 January 1920, in Malta file of Hadji Bekir Mehmed Ali Bey, UKNA FO 371/6501. See also report of the mekhitarists of Constantinople to the German Embassy, 7 August 1915, *German Foreign Office,* 292.

44. Cemal Azmi, vali of Trabzon, to Talât, 24 June 1915, BOA, DH. EUM. 2Şb, 68/39. On Cemal Azmi Bey, known as Sopalı *Mutasarrıf,* see Akçam, *Shameful Act,* 132.

45. Kevorkian, *Armenian Genocide,* 469.

46. Heizer to Morgenthau, 28 June 1915, USNA RG 59, 867.4016, Roll 43.

47. Pallavicini to Baron Burián, Vienna, 27 June 1915, HHStA, PA XII 209, No. 50/P.C. Re: Report No. 49/P.F of 24 June 1915.

48. Pallavicini to Baron Burián, Vienna, 27 June 1915, HHStA, PA XII 209, No. 50/P.C. Heizer to Morgenthau, 28 June 1915, USNA RG 59, 867.4016, Roll 43. See also Peet to Morgenthau, 15 July 1915, FDRL, HM Sr. Papers, Letters 473.

49. Heizer to Morgenthau, 3 July 1915, USNA RG 59, 867.4016, Roll 43. See also Ottoman Education Ministry to all vilayets asking for details about suitable lodgings for orphans under ten years of age, 26 June 1915, BOA, DH. ŞFR, 54/150.

50. Report by eyewitness Lieutenant Sayied Ahmed Moukhtar Baas, 26 December 1916, UKNA FO 371/2768. See also Malta file of Hadji Bekir Mehmed Ali Bey, the director of the Trabzon Customs House, UKNA FO 371/6501. He allegedly participated in "throwing into the Black Sea little children stuffed in sacks."

51. Heizer to Morgenthau, 28 July 1915, USNA RG 59, 867.4016, Roll 44.

52. Bergfeld to Bethmann-Hollweg, 25 July 1915, *German Foreign Office,* 263.

53. "Report by Eyewitness Lieutenant Sayied Ahmed Moukhtar Baas," 26 December 1916, UKNA FO 371/2768.

54. Heizer to Morgenthau, 28 July 1915, USNA RG 59, 867.4016, Roll 44; and Lewy, *Armenian Massacres,* 179–180.

55. Bergfeld to Bethmann-Hollweg, 25 July 1915, *German Foreign Office,* 263.

56. Heizer to Morgenthau, 28 July 1915, USNA RG 59, 867.4016, Roll 44.

57. Kwiatkowski to Minister in Vienna, 31 July 1915, HHStA, PA XII 209, No. 46/P.

58. Heizer to Morgenthau, 10 July 1915, USNA RG 59, 867.4016, Roll 43. Mrs. Tahbazian (?), testimony recorded 22 January 1920, in Malta file of Hadji Bekir Mehmed Ali Bey, UKNA FO 371/6501.

59. "Report by Eyewitness Lieutenant Sayied Ahmed Moukhtar Baas," 26 December 1916, UKNA FO 371/2768.

60. Ibid. See also Austrian Consul Kwiatkowski's report, quoted in Akçam, *Shameful Act,* 144.

61. Heizer to Morgenthau, 28 July 1915, USNA RG 59, 867.4016, Roll 44.

62. Barton to Bryce, 6 June 1916, Bodl. MS Lord Bryce Papers 202.

63. Unsigned, "Weekly Report on Turkey and other Moslem Countries," 20 March 1918, UKNA FO 371/3400.

64. Malta file of Fazıl Berki Bey, interned 2.6.1919, UKNA FO 371/6500. See also Dadrian, "Role of Turkish Physicians," 174.

65. Sivas vilayet to Interior Ministry, 19 May 1915, BOA, DH. ŞFR, 471, 144.

66. Dadrian, "Secret Young-Turk Ittihadist Conference," 191.

67. Testimony of George E. White, 10 April 1918, USNA RG 256, "Inquiry Documents," 1917–1919, no. 818, Roll 39.

68. Report from 31 May 1915 of Dr. C. E. Clark, attached to Morgenthau to SecState, 12 June 1916, *U.S. Official Records,* 509–513. See also testimony of George E. White, 10 April 1918, USNA RG 256, "Inquiry Documents," 1917–1919, no. 818, Roll 39.

69. Armenian Patriarchate to Morgenthau, 15 June 1915, *U.S. Official Records,* 98.

70. Report of Dr. C. E. Clark, 31 May 1916, *U.S. Official Records,* 509–513; and Partridge to Peet, 3 July 1915, *U.S. Official Records,* 72–74.

71. ARF report dated 15 June 1915, attached to Morgenthau to SecState, 20 July 1915, *U.S. Official Records,* 98–99.

72. Testimony of White, 10 April 1918, USNA RG 256, "Inquiry Documents," 1917–1919, no. 818, Roll 39.

73. Ibid.

74. Mary L. Graffam to Peet, 7 August 1915, *U.S. Official Records,* 242.

75. Jackson to Morgenthau, 29 September 1915, and enclosure 4, *U.S. Official Records,* 314.

76. Report sent by teacher in Merzifon to Morgenthau, attached to Morgenthau to SecState, 26 July 1915, *U.S. Official Records,* 140–142. See also unsigned, undated report, "Conditions in Marsovan," attached to Morgenthau to SecState, 26 July 1915, *U.S. Official Records,* 140–143.

77. Statement by Dr. J. K. Marden, *U.S. Official Records,* 524.

78. Testimony of George E. White, 10 April 1918, USNA RG 256, "Inquiry Documents," 1917–1919, no. 818, Roll 39.

79. Dadrian, "Role of Turkish Physicians," 179–180.

80. Justice Ministry to Sivas vilayet, 6 July 1915, BOA, DH. ŞFR, 54/318.

81. Statement from Dr. J. K. Marden, missionary at Merzifon, attached to Maurice Francis Egan (minister in Copenhagen) to SecState, 3 July 1915, *U.S. Official Records,* 525; and Dündar, *Crime of Numbers,* 98–101.

82. American consular agent in Samsun to Morgenthau, 26 August 1915, *U.S. Official Records*, 323, 410.

83. Mary L. Graffam to Peet, 7 August 1915, *U.S. Official Records*, 240–244. See also Suny, *They Can Live in the Desert*, 310.

84. Murat Bardakçı, *Talât Paşanın Evrak-ı Metrukesi*, 77.

85. Testimony of George E. White, 10 April 1918, USNA RG 256, "Inquiry Documents," 1917–1919, no. 818, Roll 39.

86. Riggs to Barton, 3 February 1913, Houghton ABC 16.9.7, A467, Reel 715.

87. Kevorkian, *Armenian Genocide*, 382.

88. Vali of Mamuretulaziz to Interior Ministry, 6 March 1914, BOA, DH. ŞFR, 463/117.

89. Interior Ministry to Mamuretulaziz vilayet, 6 May 1915, BOA, DH. ŞFR, 470/2.

90. Statement of Mehmed Namık Bey, former director of police in Harput, (date unclear), and other testimonies in Malta file of Saghir Zade Sabit Bey, interned on 2.6.1919, UKNA FO 371/6500. On Sabit, see Report of Leslie Davis, American Consul, Formerly of Harput, 9 February 1918, USNA RG 59, 867.4016, Roll 46, 7. Akçam, *Shameful Acts*, 150.

91. Sabit to Talât, 28 July 1915, in Malta file of Saghir Zade Sabit Bey, UKNA FO 371/6500.

92. The government claimed, in a "Red Book" published in 1916, to have found dynamite and more than 5,000 firearms in the vilayet, but, as Ehmann notes, in reality little compromising material was discovered (Lewy, *Armenian Massacres*, 168–169).

93. Statement of Police Director Mehmet Namik Bey, Malta file of Sashin Zade Sabit Bey, UKNA FO 371/6500.

94. Ehmann to Wangenheim, 18 May 1915, DE/PA-AA/BoKon/168, embassy register A53a/1915/3343. See also Jacobsen, *Diaries of a Danish Missionary*, 62–63.

95. Davis to Morgenthau, 30 June 1915, *U.S. Official Records*, 455.

96. Jacobsen, *Diaries of a Danish Missionary*, 65.

97. Ernest Riggs to Peet, 19 July 1915, Houghton ABC, 16.9.7, A467, Reel 715. See also Jacobsen, *Diaries of a Danish Missionary*, 71; and Testimony of Tacy W. Atkinson, 11 April 1918, USNA RG 256, "Inquiry Documents," 1917–1919, no. 210, Roll 39.

98. Riggs to Peet, 19 July 1915, Houghton ABC, 16.9.7, A467, Reel 715.

99. Testimony of Tacy W. Atkinson, missionary in Harput, 11 April 1918, USNA RG 256, "Inquiry Documents," 1917–1919, no. 210, Roll 39.

100. *Muhacirs* Directorate to Sivas, Trabzon, and Mamuretulaziz vilayets and to Canik *mutasarrıflık*, 27 June 1915, BOA, DH. ŞFR, 54/202.

101. Report of Leslie A. Davis, 9 February 1918, USNA RG 59, 867.4016, Roll 46, 27–29.

102. Entry for 3 June 1915, Jacobsen, *Diaries of a Danish Missionary*, 72.

103. Ibid. See also Report of Leslie A. Davis, 9 February 1918, USNA RG 59, 867.4016, Roll 46, 23; and Jacobsen, *Diaries of a Danish Missionary*, 72.

104. Davis to Morgenthau, 24 July 1915, USNA RG 59, 867.4016, Roll 44. See also Akçam, *Shameful Act*, 202.

105. Jacobsen, *Diaries of a Danish Missionary*, 73–75. See also testimony of Tacy W. Atkinson, 11 April 1918, USNA RG 256, "Inquiry Documents," 1917–1919, Doc. 210, Roll 39; and Davis to Morgenthau, 24 July 1915, USNA RG 59, 867.4016, Roll 44.

106. Testimony of Mary W. Riggs, 15 April 1918, USNA RG 256, "Inquiry Documents," 1917–1919, Roll 39.

107. Jacobsen, *Diaries of a Danish Missionary*, 75.

108. Talât to Mamuretulaziz vilayet, 18 August 1915, *Sevk ve Iskan*, 221, doc. 170.

109. Report of Leslie A. Davis, 9 February 1918, USNA RG 59, 867.4016, Roll 46, 36–37. See also Talât to Diyarbekir and Mamuretulaziz vilayets, 31 July 1915, *Sevk ve Iskan*, 202, doc. 142.

110. Testimony of Tacy W. Atkinson, missionary in Harpoot, 11 April 1918, USNA RG 256, "Inquiry Documents," 1917–1919, no. 210, Roll 39.

111. Davis to Morgenthau, 11 July 1915, USNA RG 59, 867.4016, Roll 43. See also Jacobsen, *Diaries of a Danish Missionary*, 73–75.

112. Jackson to SecState, 16 October 1915, USNA RG 59, 867.4016, Roll 44.

113. "Report by Eyewitness Lieutenant Sayied Ahmed Moukhtar Baas," 26 December 1916, UKNA FO 371/2768.

114. Malta file of Saghir Zade Sabit Bey, UKNA FO 371/6500.

115. Miss Alma Johanson's Report, 17 November 1915, USNA RG 59, 867.4061, Roll 44. See also another report by Alma Johanson, *U.S. Official Records*, 334.

116. Davis to Morgenthau, 24 July 1915, USNA RG 59, 867.4016, Roll 44.

117. Report of Leslie A. Davis, 9 February 1918, USNA RG 59, 867.4016, Roll 46, 657. See also Dadrian, *History of the Armenian Genocide*, 241–242.

118. Report of Leslie A. Davis, 9 February 1918, USNA RG 59, 867.4016, Roll 46, 76.

119. Sabit to subordinates (?), 4 October 1915, Malta file of Saghir Zade Sabit Bey, UKNA FO 371/6500.

120. Talât to valis, 2 January 1916, Malta file of Saghir Zade Sabit Bey, UKNA FO 371/6500.

121. Sabit to *mutasarrıf* of Malatya, 7 January 1916, Malta file of Saghir Zade Sabit Bey, UKNA FO 371/6500.

122. The term was first used in the Joint Allied Declaration on 24 May 1915: "For about a month the Kurd and Turkish populations of Armenia have been massacring Armenians with the connivance and often assistance of Ottoman authorities. . . . In view of those new crimes of Turkey against humanity and civilization, the Allied governments announce publicly to the Sublime-Porte that they will hold personally responsible . . . all members of the Ottoman government and . . . their agents" (from the French, notice to the American State Department, USNA RG 59, 867.4016, Roll 67).

123. Davis to Morgenthau, 24 July 1915, USNA RG 59, 867.4016, Roll 44. About the killing of the gendarmes see also Davis to Morgenthau, 23 August 1915, USNA RG 59, 867.4016, Roll 44; and Report of Leslie A. Davis, 9 February 1918, USNA RG 59, 867.4016, Roll 46, 54–56.

124. Sarafian, ed., *Talât Pasha's Report*, 52.

125. Kevorkian, *Armenian Genocide*, 363.

126. Jackson to Morgenthau, 3 August 1915, USNA RG 59, 867.4016, Roll 44, 1766; and Gaunt, *Massacres*, 164–165.

127. Üngör, "Center and Periphery in the Armenian Genocide," 71–72; and Güngör, "Bir Canlı Tarih Konuşuyor," 2444–2445; and Suny, *They Can Live in the Desert*, 291.

128. Acting Vice-Consul Hurst to Sir L. Mallet, 16 May 1914, UKNA FO 371/2135.

129. Mugerditchian, *Diyarbekir Massacres*, 13.

130. Mugerditchian, *Diyarbekir Massacres*, 10–11. Kevorkian points out that Feyzi Bey was Ziya Gökalp's uncle (Kevorkian, *Armenian Genocide*, 357).

131. According to Gaunt, Hamid Bey may have resigned following the mid-February hanging of 12 Assyrian youths for evading conscription (Gaunt, *Massacres*, 154–155).

132. See Kevorkian, *Armenian Genocide*, 358.

133. Kaiser, *Extermination of Armenians*, 141–152.

134. Extract from a statement by former kaymakam Shefik Bey, (undated), and statement by Mihran Boyadjian, former inspector of the vilayets of Bitlis, and Mosul, (undated), both in Fezi Bey's Malta file, UKNA FO 371/6500.

135. Mihran Boyadjian's statement, in Fezi Bey's Malta file, UKNA FO 371/6500; and Mugerditchian, *Diyarbekir Massacres*, 27.

136. Veli Nejdet's Malta file, UKNA FO 371/6500.

137. Mugerditchian, *Diyarbekir Massacres,* 27. "Battalions" is clearly an exaggeration.

138. Kaiser, *Extermination of Armenians,* 163–165.

139. Suny, *They Can Live in the Desert,* 293. On weapons searches, see Reşid to Interior Ministry, 29 April 1915, *Sevk ve Iskan,* 143, doc. 74. De Nogales noted that the weapons found were mostly fowling guns, which were permissible. Kaiser, *Extermination of Armenians,* 175.

140. Mugerditchian, *Diyarbekir Massacres,* 27. See also Morgenthau to family, 9 August 1915, FDRL, HM Sr. Papers, Letters 475. For descriptions of searches, see Diyarbekir vilayet to Interior Ministry, 29 April 1915, BOA, DH. ŞFR, 468/179; and Diyarbekir vilayet to Interior Ministry, 5 May 1915, BOA, DH. ŞFR, 469/121.

141. Testimony of Dr. Floyd O. Smith, missionary in Diyarbekir, 21 September 1915, USNA RG 256, "Inquiry Documents," 1917–1919, no. 822, Roll 39.

142. Mugerditchian, *Diyarbekir Massacres,* 36. On the torture of the bishop, see also report by Mr. Alberto, former Beirut head of Tombac Regie, the state tobacco company, forwarded by Elliot, British consul at Mitylene, 4 May 1916, UKNA FO 371/2770.

143. Mugerditchian, *Diyarbekir Massacres,* 37–38. See also Smith to Barton, 18 September 1915, Houghton ABC, 16.9.7, A467, Reel 716. On claims that the detainees belonged to Armenian armed gangs, see Diyarbekir to Interior Ministry, 25 May 1915, BOA, DH. ŞFR, 472/67. On the deportation of the missionaries, see also de Nogales, *Four Years,* 146.

144. Gaunt, *Massacres,* 163–164.

145. Mugerditchian, *Diyarbekir Massacres,* 35–45; Kaiser, *Extermination of Armenians,* 184–185; and Diyarbekir vilayet to Talât, 4 August 1915, BOA, DH. ŞFR, 482/83. See also Gaunt, *Massacres,* 151–152 and 163, for a variant of this story.

146. Gaunt, *Massacres,* 167–168.

147. Gaunt, *Massacres,* 172–173; and de Courtois, *Forgotten Genocide,* 166–168.

148. Malta file of Bedri Bey, UKNA FO 371/6500; Kaiser, *Extermination of Armenians,* 309–317; and Gaunt, *Massacres,* 173.

149. Gaunt, *Massacres,* 173–175; and de Courtois, *Forgotten Genocide,* 168–172.

150. Gaunt, *Massacres,* 182, 188–189.

151. Gaunt, *Massacres,* 243–244.

152. Gaunt, *Massacres,* 227.

153. This description is based largely on Gaunt, *Massacres,* 273–294. See also de Courtois, *Forgotten Genocide,* 184–191; and German correspondence from November 1915, *German Foreign Office,* 435–438.

154. Morgenthau to family, 22 June 1915, FDRL, HM Sr. Papers, Letters 475, 729.

155. De Nogales, *Four Years,* 139.

156. De Nogales, *Four Years,* 145–147.

157. Calthorpe to Curzon, 2 July 1919, UKNA FO 371/4192.

158. Dündar, *Crime of Numbers,* 188.

159. Üngör, *Making of Modern Turkey,* 85.

160. Gaunt, *Massacres,* 178–179.

161. Quoted in Kevorkian, *Armenian Genocide,* 379.

162. Leslie to Bell, 9 June 1915, Houghton ABC, 16.9.5, A467, Reel 671.

163. Leslie to Barton, 6 October 1914, Houghton ABC, 16.9.5, A467, Reel 671.

164. Security Directorate to the vilayets of Marash, Adana, and Aleppo, 26 April 1915, BOA, DH. ŞFR, 52/112.

165. Leslie to Jackson, 6 August 1915, LC, HM Sr. Papers, Reel 32. See also Ministry of Interior to Erzurum, Van, and Bitlis vilayets, 23 May 1915, orders to deport their Armenian populations to Urfa, Deir Zor, and Mosul, General Directorate of the State Archives, in Bryce, *Treatment of Armenians,* 36.

166. Leslie to Morgenthau, as attachment to letter from Morgenthau to SecState, 28 June 1915, USNA RG 59, 867.4016, Roll 43. See also Vice Consul Samuel Edelman, Aleppo, to Morgenthau (?), 26 August 1915, *U.S. Official Records,* 278–279; and Jackson to Secstate, 4 March 1918, "Armenian Atrocities," *U.S. Official Records,* 587.

167. Testimony of Elvesta T. Leslie, 11 April 1918, USNA RG 256, "Inquiry Documents," 1917–1919, no. 814, Roll 39.

168. Haydar to Talât, 18 September 1915, *Sevk ve Iskan,* 264, doc. 208.

169. Jackson to Morgenthau, 10 August 1915, USNA RG 59, 867.4016, Roll 44. Jackson gives their numbers as 140 British, 157 French, 112 Russians, and 18 Montenegrins. See also Leslie to Jackson, 6 August 1915, LC, HM Sr. Papers, Reel 32; Morgenthau to family, 17 August 1915, FDRL, HM Sr. Papers, Letters 475; and Morgenthau to SecState, 20 August 1915, USNA RG 59, 867.4016, Roll 43.

170. Leslie to Jackson, 6 August 1915, LC, HM Sr. Papers, Reel 32. See also hearsay report of "F.," a hospital worker from Antep, who heard the same description in Urfa a year later (Personal Observations, (undated), Houghton ABC 16.9.5, A467, Reel 671). See also Jeppe to Rössler, 18 June 1915, *German Foreign Office,* 221.

171. Enclosure 1 to letter from Rössler to Bethmann-Hollweg, 11 August 1915, *German Foreign Office,* 299–300.

172. Kunzler to consul, 23 August 1915, enclosed in Rössler to Bethmann-Hollweg, 3 September 1915, *German Foreign Office,* 346; letter from Vice Consul Edelman, 26 August 1915, USNA RG 59, 867.4016, Roll 44; and Leslie to Morgenthau, 24 August 1915, included in Morgenthau's report to SecState, 20 October 1915, USNA RG 59, 867.4016, Reel 44. See also undated hearsay report of "F.," a hospital worker from Antep, who heard the same things in Urfa a year later ("Personal Observations," Houghton ABC, 16.9.5, A467, Reel 671).

173. Interior Ministry to mutasarriflik of Urfa, 21 August 1915, BOA, DH. ŞFR, 55 / 47.

174. Enver to Foreign Office, 21 October 1915, *Sevk ve Iskan,* 292–293, doc. 236 (Kuvve-i inzibatiyenin her tarafdan ateşle karşılanması); "Note Verbale" from the Ottoman Foreign Ministry to the embassies, 11 October 1915, USNA RG 59, 867.4016, Roll 44; and "Memorandum on the Armenian Question," 8 November 1915, *U.S. Official Records,* 384–385. See also Demirel ve Takkaç, "Ermeni Tehciri Anıları Uzerine"; Dadrian, "Armenian Question," 67; and de Nogales, *Four Years,* 153.

175. Jackson to SecState, 4 March 1918, "Armenian Atrocities," *U.S. Official Records,* 587. The report on Kurdish losses seems exaggerated.

176. American Consul in Beirut to Morgenthau, 5 October 1915, USNA RG 59, 867.4016, Roll 44. See also Smyrna consulate to State Department, 15 January 1916, USNA RG 59, 867.4016, Roll 44; and Fakhri Pasha's Malta file, UKNA FO 371 / 6500.

177. Jackson to SecState, 4 March 1918, "Armenian Atrocities," *U.S. Official Records,* 587.

178. Enver to Foreign Office, *Sevk ve Iskan,* 292–293, doc. 236. For a description of the fighting, see Consul Dandini, Aleppo, to Stephan Baron Burián, Vienna, 25 October 1915, *OeUA,* Z. 15 / P; Morgenthau to his children, 27 October 1915, FDRL, HM Sr. Papers, Letters 475; and Report by Mr. Alberto, former Beirut head of Tombac Regie, the state tobacco company, who said he had been in Urfa at the time, sent by Elliot, British consul at Mitylene, 4 May 1916, UKNA FO 371 / 2770. See also Dadrian, "Armenian Question," 76; and Erickson, "Armenians and Ottoman Military Policy," 165; and Report by W. G. Holloway, one of the Urfa hostages, 10 February 1919, USNA RG 84, Vol. 400 (Turkey).

179. Jackson to SecState, "Armenian Atrocities," 4 March 1918, *U.S. Official Records,* 587; Enver to Foreign Ministry, 21 October 1915, *Sevk ve Iskan,* 292–293, doc. 236; report by an eyewitness, Smyrna consulate to State Department, 15 January 1916, USNA RG 59, 867.4016, Roll 44; and testimony of Alen Bayatian, undated, Malta file of Fakhri Pasha, UKNA FO 371 / 6500. Bayatian implicated Fakhri in the massacre of 200 boys and men on Tell Fudar, near Urfa.

180. Testimony of Elvesta T. Leslie, 11 April 1918, USNA RG 256, "Inquiry Documents," 1917–1919, no. 814, Roll 39.

181. Ibid.

182. "A Missionary Poisoned," *New York Times,* 13 November 1915; Jackson to Secstate, "Armenian Atrocities," 4 March 1918, *U.S. Official Records,* 587; and Smyrna consulate to State Department, 15 January 1916, USNA RG 59, 867.4016, Roll 44.

183. Talât to Urfa *mutasarrıflık,* 6 November 1915, *Sevk ve Iskan,* 316–317, doc. 257.

184. Sarafian, ed., *Talât Pasha's Report,* 56.

185. Der Matossian, "Taboo within the Taboo," 9–10. See also Interior Ministry to governor of Urfa, 27 October 1915, BOA, DH. ŞFR, 57/135.

186. Jackson to Secstate, "Armenian Atrocities," 4 March 1918, *U.S. Official Records,* 596.

187. Werfel, *Forty Days of Musa Dagh.*

188. Kevorkian, *Armenian Genocide,* 611.

189. Official government deportation decision, MV 198/24, 30 May 1915, *Sevk ve Iskan,* 155–157, doc. 81. Kevorkian, *Armenian Genocide,* 611.

190. Kevorkian, *Armenian Genocide.* See also Jackson to Morgenthau, 19 August 1915, USNA RG 59, 867.4016, Roll 46.

191. Jackson to Morgenthau, 19 August 1915, USNA RG 59, 867.4016, Roll 46.

192. Jackson to SecState, addendum to dispatch on "Armenian Atrocities," 27 May 1918, *U.S. Official Records,* 600–601.

193. Ibid.

194. G.O.C. Egypt (?) to Henry McMahon, 10 September 1915, UKNA FO 371/2490.

195. Exchange of cables between General Maxwell, Earl Kitchener, McMahon, Lord Bertie, Commander-in-Chief East Indies, Admiralty, Foreign Office, and War Office, 10–14 September 1915, UKNA FO 371/2490.

5. The Western River, and Downstream

1. Security Directorate to valis and mutesarrifs, 24 April 1915, BOA, DH. ŞFR, 52/96, 97, 98. This is why Armenians around the world annually commemorate the genocide on 24 April.

2. See Balakian, *Armenian Golgotha,* 61–65.

3. Security Directorate to Ankara vilayet, 25 April 1915, BOA, DH. ŞFR, 52/102.

4. Unsigned, "Addendum to 'Report of an inhabitant of Athlit, Mount Carmel, Syria,'" undated but stamped "M.I.2.b, 27 November 1916," UKNA FO 371/2783.

5. Talât to several valis and mutesarrifs, 6 November 1915, *Sevk ve Iskan,* 315, doc. 255.

6. ARF (Dashnak) report, 15 October 1915, USNA RG 59, 867.4016, Roll 44.

7. Akçam, *Shameful Acts,* 107.

8. Adil, vali of Edirne, to Interior Ministry, 2 May 1915, *Sevk ve Iskan,* 147, doc. 74; and Ali Fethi, ambassador to Sofia, to Interior Ministry, 21 December 1914, *Sevk ve Iskan,* 97, doc. 33.

9. Aktar, "Debating the Armenian Massacres," 259.

10. US consul Charles Allen, Adrianople, to Ravndal, American Consul General, Constantinople, 23 October 1915, USNA RG 59, 867.4016, Roll 44; and Pallavicini to Burián, 7 November 1915, *OeUA,* 257–262 (HHStA PA XII 93/P.B).

11. Allen to Ravndal, 5 March 1915, *U.S. Official Records,* 493. See also Akçam, *Shameful Acts,* 107.

12. Dündar, "Pouring People into the Desert," 283–284; and Sarafian, ed., *Talât Pasha's Report,* 10, 12, and 20.

13. ARF, Sofia, report dated 5 June 1915, attached to Morgenthau to SecState, 20 July 1915, *U.S. Official Records,* 91–94.

14. Malta file of Zekeria Zihni Bey, Report no. 00599, UKNA FO 371/6500.

15. Allen to Ravndal, 29 October 1915, USNA RG 59, 867.4016, Adrianople, Vol. 1; George Barclay, Bucharest, to FO, 18 December 1915, UKNA FO 371/2488; and Nadamlenzki to Pallavicini, 29 October 1915, *OeUA,* 257–262 (HHStA PA XII Z95/P, depeche No. 22 u 23). Nadamlenzki was unimpressed by the show of civility. He described the sick and elderly being pulled out of their beds.

16. Barclay to FO, 18 December 1915, UKNA FO 37/2488.

17. Dadrian, "Documentation of the World War I Armenian Massacres," 573 (based on protocols cited in *Takvim-i Vekayı,* no. 3772, 3–6). See also Dadrian and Akçam, *Judgment at Istanbul,* 118, 146.

18. Nadamlenzki to Pallavicini, 29 October 1915, *OeUA,* 257–262.

19. Allen to Ravndal, 29 October 1915, USNA RG 59, 867.4016, Adrianople, Vol. 1; and Pallavicini to Foreign Ministry, 13 November 1915, *OeUA,* 277.

20. Morgenthau to family, 15 November 1915, FDRL, HM Sr. Papers, Letters 475.

21. Nadamlenzki to Pallavicini, 3 March 1916, *OeUA,* 335–336; Nadamlenzki to Pallavicini, 8 March 1916, *OeUA,* 337–338; Pallavicini to Burián, 10 March 1916, *OeUA,* 337–338; and Allen to Ravndal, 5 March 1916, USNA, RG 84, Vol. 391.

22. Nadamlenzki to Pallavicini, 3 March 1916, *OeUA,* 335–336.

23. Notes by Mordtmann, 4 August 1915, *German Foreign Office,* 277.

24. Mutesarrif of Izmit to Interior Ministry, 20 May 1915, BOA, DH. EUM. 3 Şb.5/56; and Morgenthau to family, 22 July 1915, FDRL, HM Sr. Papers, Letters 475, 789.

25. Morgenthau to SecState, 11 August 1915, *U.S. Official Records,* 77; Morgenthau to family, 9 August 1915, FDRL, HM Sr. Papers, Letters 475.

26. Talât to Izmit mutesarriflik, 9 August 1915, *Sevk ve Iskan,* 207, doc. 149.

27. Morgenthau to family, 9 August 1915, FDRL, HM Sr. Papers, Letters 475.

28. Ibid.; and ARF report dated 2 August 1915, attached to Morgenthau to SecState, 10 August 1915, *U.S. Official Records,* 162. See also Dadrian and Akçam, *Judgment at Istanbul,* 216–217, 219–220; Malta File of Hodja Rifaat Effendi, UKNA FO 371/6500; and report of Lieutenant C. E. S. Palmer, 18 December 1918, UKNA FO 371/4157. See also notes by Mordtmann, 4 August 1915, *German Foreign Office,* 213.

29. Dodd to Morgenthau, 15 August 1915, *U.S. Official Records,* 192.

30. Morgenthau to SecState, 9 November 1915, enclosure no. 3, *U.S. Official Records,* 341, 343.

31. Dodd to Morgenthau, 15 August 1915, *U.S. Official Records,* 192–193. See also Post to Morgenthau, 3 September 1915, *U.S. Official Records,* 248.

32. Izmit vilayet to Interior Ministry, 29 August 1915, BOA, DH. ŞFR, 666/86; Morgenthau to family, 13 September 1915, FDRL, HM Sr. Papers, Letters 475; and Report of Lieutenant C. E. S. Palmer, 18 December 1918, UKNA FO 371/4157.

33. Morgenthau to family, 13 September 1915, FDRL, HM Sr. Papers, Letters 475.

34. Heinrich Albertall to Foreign Ministry, 25 September 1915, *OeUA,* 234–236.

35. Ali Suad, mutesarrif of Zor, to Interior Ministry, 7 February 1916 and 12 February 1916, in *Sevk ve Iskan,* 350–351, docs. 278, 281.

36. Report of Lieutenant C. E. S. Palmer, 18 December 1918, UKNA FO 371/4157.

37. Sarafian, ed., *Talât Pasha's Report,* 26.

38. Dadrian and Akçam, *Judgment at Istanbul,* 203, 206, 208, and 318.

39. Trano, Austro-Hungarian consular agent, Bursa, 16 August 1915, *OeUA,* 201–202; and Dadrian, "Documentation of the World War Armenian Massacres," 572.

40. Two enclosures by the consular agent in Bursa, attached to Pallavicini to Burián, 24 August 1915, *OeUA,* 216–217.

41. Post to Morgenthau, 3 September 1915, *U.S. Official Records,* 246–249.

42. Morgenthau to family, 13 September 1915, FDRL, HM Sr. Papers, Letters 475. See also Talât to valis, 8 September 1915, *Sevk ve Iskan,* 244, doc. 188; and Talât to valis and mutesarrifs, 18 / 19 September 1915, *Sevk ve Iskan,* 264, doc. 209.

43. Bursa (Hüdavendigâr) vilayet to Interior Ministry, 24 October 1915, *Sevk ve Iskan,* 298, doc. 244.

44. Morgenthau, *United States Diplomacy on the Bosphorus,* 380.

45. Akçam, *Shameful Act,* 135.

46. Bardakçi, *Talât Paşanın Evrak-ı Metrukesi,* 77; and Sarafian, ed., *Talât Pasha's Report,* 24, 27.

47. Talât to Ankara vilayet, 25 April 1915, *Sevk ve Iskan,* 127, doc. 58; and Talât to Ankara and Kastamonu vilayets, 10 May 1915, *Sevk ve Iskan,* 135, doc. 68.

48. Fifth session of military court, *Takvim-i Vekayı* no. 3554, 14 May 1919, translated in Akçam, *Shameful Act,* 164.

49. Balakian, *Armenian Golgotha,* 82–83.

50. Akçam, *Shameful Act,* 156. See also Balakian, *Armenian Golgotha,* 82–89.

51. Consul in Konya to Morgenthau, 8 September 1915, USNA RG 59, 867.4016, Roll 44; ARF (Dashnaksutyun) Report, dated 29 September 1915, attached to Morgenthau to SecState, 9 November 1915, *U.S. Official Documents,* 341–342. See also Report of Stephan Semoukhine, Steward of the Russian Embassy, who had been exiled to Ankara with 129 other Russian Armenians, attached to Morgenthau to State Department, 13 November 1915, USNA RG 59, 867.4016, Roll 44.

52. Palmer to British High Commissioner, 9 January 1919, UKNA FO 371 / 4157.

53. Talât to several vilayets and mutesarrifliks, 3 August 1915, *Sevk ve Iskan,* 205, doc. 146. Despite the initial exemption orders, almost all the vilayets deported their Armenian Catholics.

54. Morgenthau to wife, 13 September 1915, FDRL, HM Sr. Papers, Letters 475. See also ARF Report, dated 29 September 1915, attached to Morgenthau to SecState, 9 November 1915, *U.S. Official Documents,* 341–342; and "Report of Difficulties in Armenia," November-December 1915, USNA RG 59, 867.4016, Roll 44.

55. Contained in Clayton to FO, 19 May 1918, UKNA, FO 371 / 3400.

56. Atıf to Interior Ministry, 17 September 1915, *Sevk ve Iskan,* 252, doc. 195.

57. Semoukhine report, attached to Morgenthau to State Department, 13 November 1915, USNA RG 59, 867.4016, Roll 44.

58. Sarafian, ed., *Talât Pasha's Report,* 38.

59. Konya had a sizable Greek population of around 70,000, but at this stage it was left alone.

60. Dodd testimony, 21 December 1917, USNA RG 256, "Inquiry Documents," 1917–1919, no. 809, Roll 39.

61. Cited in Morgenthau to SecState, 24 September 1915, USNA RG 59, 867.4016, Roll 44.

62. Dodd to Morgenthau, 8 September 1915, USNA RG 59, 867.4016, Roll 44.

63. Dodd to Morgenthau, 8 September 1915, USNA RG 59, 867.4016, Roll 44.

64. Samih, vali of Konya, to Interior Ministry, 23 October 1915, *Sevk ve Iskan,* 295, doc. 239; Dodd to Morgenthau, 8 September 1915, USNA RG 59, 867.4016, Roll 44; and Dodd to Morgenthau, 15 August 1915, *U.S. Official Records,* 192–193.

65. Kayseri mutesarrif, Zekai, to Interior Ministry, *Sevk ve Iskan,* 260, doc. 202; Karashisar mutesarrif, Şevket, to Interior Ministry, 18 September 1915, *Sevk ve Iskan,* 260–261, doc. 203.

66. On Protestants: Talât to valis, 2 August 1915, BOA, DH. ŞFR, 55 / 19. On soldiers' families: Talât to valis and mutesarrifs, 15 August 1915, *Sevk ve Iskan,* 215, doc. 160. See also Dodd to Morgenthau, 15 August 1915, USNA RG 59, 867.4016, Roll 44.

67. Dodd testimony, 21 December 1917, USNA RG 256, "Inquiry Documents," 1917–1919, no. 809, Roll 39.

68. Dodd to Morgenthau, 8 September 1915, USNA RG 59, 867.4016, Roll 44. See also Balakian, *Armenian Golgotha,* 444.

69. Celal Bey, Memoirs, "The Armenian Affair, its Reasons and Effects" part 2, *Vakit,* 12 December 1918.

70. Dadrian and Akçam, *Judgment at Constantinople,* 280.

71. Testimony of Wilfred M. Post, USNA RG 256, "Inquiry Documents," 1917–1919, no. 823, Roll 39.

72. Konya acting vali's scribe, Naci, to Interior Ministry, 16 October 1915, *Sevk ve Iskan,* 287, doc. 227. Testimony of Wilfred M. Post, USNA RG 256, "Inquiry Documents," 1917–1919, no. 823, Roll 39.

73. Sarafian, ed., *Talât Pasha's Report,* 34.

74. Kayseri mutesarrif, Ahmet Midhat to Interior Ministry, 2 May 1915, BOA, DH. EUM. 2. Şb, 7/25. See also weapons found in the Develi (Everek) area, Develi Kaza report, 16 April 1915, BOA, DH. EUM. 2 Şb, 6/1; Security Directorate to several vilayets and mutesarriflik, 28 February 1915, DH. ŞFR, 50/127; and Frieda Wolf-Hunecke's Report on Everek, attached to Morgenthau to SecState, 20 July 1915, USNA RG 59, 867.4016. See also Morgenthau to family, 5 July 1915, FDRL, HM Sr. Papers, Letters 475; Erickson, "Armenians and Ottoman Military Policy," 152, 155; and Wangenheim to Bethmann-Hollweg, 8 May 1915, *German Foreign Office,* 176.

75. Kayseri mutesarriflik to Interior Ministry, 4 May 1915, BOA, DH. ŞFR, 469/108.

76. Testimony of Stella Loughridge, 21 June 1918, USNA RG 256, "Inquiry Documents," 1917–1919, no. 803, Roll 39.

77. Report of American missionary from Talas, in American High Commissioner Heck to William Sharp, American ambassador in Paris, 30 January 1919, USNA RG 84, Vol. 400 (Turkey). See also testimony of Loughridge, 21 June 1918, USNA RG 256, "Inquiry Documents," 1917–1919, no. 803, Roll 39; and Testimony of Clara Richmond of Talas, 11 May 1918, USNA RG 256, "Inquiry Documents," 1917–1919, no. 807, Roll 39.

78. ARF report, "The Horrors of Cesarea," attached to Morgenthau to SecState, 17 September 1915, *U.S. Official Records,* 259.

79. Richmond gives the date as August 8, 1915. A few days prior to this date, notices were posted in the market (Richmond testimony, 11 May 1918, USNA RG 256 "Inquiry Documents," 1917–1919, no. 807, Roll 39).

80. Testimony of Clara Richmond, 11 May 1918, USNA RG 256, "Inquiry Documents," 1917–1919, no. 807, Roll 39.

81. Report of American missionary from Talas, attached to Heck to Sharp, 30 January 1919, USNA RG 84, Vol. 400 (Turkey). See also Army General Staff to Interior Ministry, 27 February 1916, *Sevk ve Iskan,* 355, doc. 284; Army report about the destruction of a cave in which rebels fortified themselves, 27 February 1916, *Sevk ve Iskan,* 355, doc. 284; and testimony of Stella Loughridge, 21 June 1918, USNA RG 256, "Inquiry Documents," 1917–1919, no. 803, Roll 39.

82. Security Directorate to Ankara vilayet, 9 August 1915, BOA, DH. ŞFR, 54A/326. For an eyewitness deposition about these massacres, see testimonies in "Enclosure 8," attached to Büge to Bethmann-Hollweg, 1 October 1915, *German Foreign Office,* 406.

83. Zekai, mutesarrif of Kayseri, to Interior Ministry, 18 September 1915, *Sevk ve Iskan,* 260, doc. 202.

84. Wingate, American Mission in Talas, Kayseri, to Morgenthau, 16 November 1915, *U.S. Official Records,* 349.

85. Testimony of Clara Richmond, 11 May 1918, USNA RG 256, "Inquiry Documents," 1917–1919, no. 807, Roll 39.

86. Report of American missionary from Talas, attached to Heck to Sharp, 30 January 1919, USNA RG 84, Vol. 400 (Turkey). See also Akçam, *Shameful Acts,* 176–177.

87. Security Directorate to Kayseri mutesarriflik, 14 July 1915, BOA, DH. ŞFR, 54/427.

88. Wingate, American Mission in Talas, Kayseri, to Morgenthau, 16 November 1915, *U.S. Official Records,* 349.

89. Balakian, *Armenian Golgotha,* 169–170. The story of this convoy passing through Talas is also told in Report of American Missionary from Talas, attached to Heck to Sharp, 30 January 1919, USNA RG 84, Vol. 400 (Turkey).

90. Bardakçi, *Talât Paşa'nın Evrak-ı Metrukesi,* 77; Zekai to Talât, 18 September 1915, *Sevk ve Iskan,* 260, doc. 202; and Der Matossian, "Ottoman Armenian Kesaria/Kayseri," 209, Table 1.

91. The events described here and in the following paragraphs are based on Der Matossian, "From Bloodless Revolution," 152–173; and Sahara, "1909 Adana Incident (Part 2)."

92. Gaunt, *Massacres,* 45.

93. Der Matossian, "From Bloodless Revolution," 164; and Akçam, *Shameful Act,* 69–70.

94. Numbers are disputed. The American mission in Adana estimated that the towns Adana, Maraş, and Hacin contained 195,200 Armenians. Armenian leader Nubar, quoting the patriarchate, spoke of 407,000: "The Pre-War Population of Cilicia," Bodl. MS Toynbee 44, Stats.

95. Report by Simon Agabalian, 12 March 1915, attached to Eugen Büge to Wangenheim, 13 March 1915, *German Foreign Office,* 154–155. See also report from Dörtyol, 12 February 1915, BOA, DH. EUM. 6. Şb, 3/8; and Erickson, "Captain Larkin and the Turks."

96. Talât to valis and mutesarrifs, 28 February 1915, BOA, DH. ŞFR, 50/127, and 2 March 1915, DH. EUM. 2. Şb, 5/14; and Report by Simon Agabalian, 12 March 1915, attached to Büge to Wangenheim, 13 March 1915, *German Foreign Office,* 153–155. See also Lewy, *Armenian Massacres,* 183; Erickson, "Armenians and Ottoman Military Policy," 154–155; Demirel ve Takkaç, "Ermeni Tehciri Anilari Uzerine," 27; and Hoffmann, vice-consul in Alexandretta, to Wangenheim, 7 March 1915, DE/PA-AA-BoKon/168.

97. For the search orders, see Hakki, to Talât, 16 April 1915, BOA, DH. EUM. 2. Şb, 7/21; and enclosure to report of ARF, Sofia, 2–15 June 1915, USNA RG 59, 867.4016, Roll 43.

98. Talât to Cemal, commander of the 4th Army, 24 April 1915, *Sevk ve Iskan,* 143, doc. 74; and enclosures in Max von Oppenheim to Bethmann-Hollweg, 29 August 1915, *German Foreign Office,* 338–340.

99. See ARF report, 15 June 1915, attached to Morgenthau to SecState, 20 July 1915, *U.S. Official Records,* 98–101; Nathan to Morgenthau, 24 May 1915, USNA RG 59, 867.00, Roll 6; and Hoffmann to Wangenheim, 29 May 1915, DE/PA-AA-BoKon/169, Embassy register A53a/1915/3464. See also Lewy, *Armenian Massacres,* 184; and Testimony of Harriet J. Fischer, 13 April 1917, USNA RG 256, "Inquiry Documents," 1917–1919, no. 813, Roll 39.

100. Nathan to Morgenthau, 24 May 1915, USNA RG 59, 867.00, Roll 6.

101. Government decision to deport Armenians, 30 May 1915, *Sevk ve Iskan,* 155, doc. 81. In the original document, the actual phrase is "*nefs-i Adana, nefs-i Sis ve nefs-i Mersin müstesna olmak üzere Adana, Mersin, Kozan, Cebel-i Bereket livaları*" ("the districts of Adana, Mersin, Kozan, and Cebel-i Bereket, except the towns of Adana, Sis, and Mersin specifically").

102. Testimony of "Miss Y.," in Bryce and Toynbee, eds., *Treatment of Armenians,* 506; and Nathan to Morgenthau, 7 August 1916, USNA RG 59, 867.4016, Roll 43.

103. Testimony of Elizabeth Webb, 1 June 1918, USNA RG 256, "Inquiry Documents," 1917–1919, no. 819, Roll 39.

104. Talât to Ismail Hakki Bey, 4 August 1915, BOA, DH. ŞFR, 54-A/271; Interior Ministry to the valis and mutesarrifs, 15 August 1915, BOA, DH. ŞFR, 55/20; and Ismail Hakki Bey to Talât, 18 September 1915, BOA, DH. EUM. 2. Şb, 68/77.

105. Talât to valis and mutesarrifs, 3 August 1915, BOA, DH. ŞFR, 54-A/252; Lewy, *Armenian Massacres,* 184–185; Büge to Hohenlohe-Langenburg (Istanbul), 12 August 1915, *German Foreign Office,* 303–304; and Chambers to Barton, 31 October 1915, Houghton ABC 16.9.5, A467, Reel 669.

106. Büge to Constantinople Embassy, 10 September 1915, *German Foreign Office*, 377. See also Testimony of Harriet J. Fischer, 13 April 1917, USNA RG 256, "Inquiry Documents," 1917–1919, no. 813, Roll 39.

107. Chambers to Barton, 18 October 1915, Houghton ABC 16.9.5, A467, Reel 669.

108. Talât to Cemal, 28 November 1915, *Sevk ve Iskan*, 322–323, doc. 265. See also Testimony of Elizabeth Webb, 1 June 1918, USNA RG 256, "Inquiry Documents," 1917–1919, no. 819, Roll 39.

109. Kevorkian, *Armenian Genocide*, 641–646, 673, 678–681; and Akçam, *Shameful Act*, 185–186.

110. Unsigned, "Addendum to 'Report of an Inhabitant of Athlit, Mount Carmel, Syria,'" undated but stamped "M.I.2.b, 27 November 1916," UKNA FO 371/2783.

111. Telegram from Adana, received in Washington D.C., 16 February 1916, Houghton ABC 16.9.5, A467, Reel 672.

112. Talât to valis and mutesarrifs along the railway in Anatolia, 16 January 1916, BOA, DH. ŞFR, 60/45; and Morgenthau to SecState, 21 July 1916, USNA RG 59, 867.4016, Roll 45.

113. Sarafian, ed., *Talât Pasha's Report*, 55.

114. Celal Bey, Memoirs, *Vakit*, 12 December 1918; and Malta file of Mufti Zade Shukri Bey, UKNA FO 371/6500.

115. Bekir Sami to Talât, 18 September 1915, *Sevk ve Iskan*, 254–255, doc. 199.

116. Rössler to Bethmann-Hollweg, 27 July 1915, *German Foreign Office*, 265. See also Rössler to Embassy, 30 July 1915, *German Foreign Office*, 274–275; and Malta file of Mufti Zade Shukri Bey, UKNA FO 371/6500. See also Kurt, "Curious Case of Ali Cenani Bey," 62–63, 68–69.

117. Jackson, "Armenian Atrocities," 4 March 1918, *U.S. Official Records*, 586.

118. Malta file of Ahmet Bey, UKNA FO 371/6500.

119. Malta file of Ahmet Bey, UKNA FO 371/6500. The documents cited in this file were clearly taken from the Naim-Andonian collection, which some researchers, most prominently Orel and Yuca, claim are forgeries *(Talât Pasha "Telegrams")*. These claims were effectively countered by Dadrian in "Naim-Andonian Documents."

120. Malta file of Ahmet Bey, UKNA FO 371/6500.

121. See, for example, memorandum of Walter M. Geddes, an American businessman, attached to Horton to SecState, 8 November 1915, *U.S. Official Records*, 381. See similar descriptions in Rössler to Bethmann-Hollweg, 9 February 1916, *German Foreign Office*, 542–543; and de Nogales, *Four Years*, 170–171: "It was terrible to see some of the stragglers. . . . After crawling for a long time like wounded animals, shrieking to their families, they finally fell at the roadside, to die and become carrion."

122. Rössler to Hohenlohe-Langenburg, 27 September 1915, *German Foreign Office*, 382.

123. Geddes memorandum, attached to Horton to SecState, 8 November 1915, *U.S. Official Records*, 381.

124. Jackson, "Armenian Atrocities," 4 March 1918, *U.S. Official Records*, 588.

125. De Nogales, *Four Years*, 175, 179–180.

126. Jackson, "Armenian Atrocities," 4 March 1918, *U.S. Official Records*, 588; and Kevorkian, *Armenian Genocide*, 645.

127. Jackson, "Armenian Atrocities," 4 March 1918, *U.S. Official Records*, 591. See also Rohner to Peet, 17 January 1916, attached to Peet to Consul-General Mordtmann, 10 February 1916, *German Foreign Office*, 556–557. See also Kieser, "Beatrice Rohner," 224–225.

128. Jackson, "Armenian Atrocities," 4 March 1918, *U.S. Official Records*, 591.

129. Jackson, "Armenian Atrocities," 4 March 1918, *U.S. Official Records*, 591. See also Kevorkian, *Armenian Genocide*, 643.

130. Rössler to Bethmann-Hollweg, 30 November 1915, *German Foreign Office*, 488.

131. Kieser, "Beatrice Rohner," 224–225.

132. Kieser, "Beatrice Rohner," 225–227. Rössler to Hollweg, 20 September 1916, *German Foreign Office,* 650–651.

133. Diamadis, "Children and Genocide," 328–329.

134. Jackson's Report, 4 March 1918, *U.S. Official Records,* 594. See also Philip Hoffman to SecState, 1 September 1916, *U.S. Official Records,* 534; and Kieser, "Beatrice Rohner."

135. Kieser, "Beatrice Rohner," 228–229.

136. Sarafian, ed., *Talât Pasha's Report,* 55. The report gave the following figures for Armenians in Aleppo vilayet in 1917: Aleppo (native) 13,679; from Adana 4,757; Izmit 862; Kayseri 838; Diyarbekir 796; Sivas 681; Elazig 606; Konia 469; Ankara 373; Erzerum 257; Bitlis 216; Hudavendigar 192; Niğde 167; Eskishehir 129; Karesi 83; Kastamonu 82; Constantinople 73; Afyon Karahissar 52; Aydin 34; Syria 30; Janik 6. The total is 24,382.

137. Jackson to Morgenthau, 3 August 1915, USNA RG 59, 867.4016, Roll 44. See also Charles Brissel, American consul, Baghdad, to Morgenthau, 29 August 1915, *U.S. Official Records,* 263. On the sale of children, see also Rössler to Bethmann-Hollweg, 31 July 1915, *German Foreign Office,* 275. Kevorkian, *Armenian Genocide,* 664.

138. Jackson to Morgenthau, 3 August 1915, USNA RG 59, 867.4016, Roll 44.

139. Security Directorate to Mutesarriflik of Zor, 24 July 1915, BOA, DH. ŞFR, 54A/91.

140. Jackson, "Armenian Atrocities," 4 March 1918, *U.S. Official Records,* 590.

141. Kieser, "Beatrice Rohner," 226.

142. Kevorkian, *Armenian Genocide,* 651.

143. Morgenthau to wife, 16 October 1915, FDRL, HM Sr. Papers, Letters 475.

144. Report by Dr. Schacht, captain, (Ottoman) medical corps, "Migration of the Armenians to Der-el-Zor," 11 November 1915, attached to Rössler to Bethmann-Hollweg, 16 November 1915, *German Foreign Office,* 464. See also Suny, *They Can Live in the Desert,* 315–316.

145. Report by W. Spieken, 2 September 1915, enclosed in Rössler to Bethman-Hollweg, 3 September 1915, *German Foreign Office,* 355.

146. Vali of Damascus, Hulusi Bey, to Interior Ministry, 19 September 1915, BOA, DH. ŞFR, 56/77. About Cemal's attitude, see Metternich to Bethmann Hollweg, 7 December 1915, *German Foreign Office,* 491; and Kaiser, *At the Crossroads of Der Zor,* 60–61.

147. Kevorkian, *Armenian Genocide,* 640. See also Akçam, *Young Turks' Crime,* 275.

148. Cited in Dadrian, "Documentation of the World War I Armenian Massacres," 558. See also Dadrian and Akçam, *Judgment at Istanbul,* 86.

149. See for example Muhacirs Directorate to the mutesarriflik of Zor, 5 July 1915, BOA, DH. ŞFR, 54/308; and Muhacirs Directorate to vilayets and mutesarrifliks, 12 July 1915, BOA, DH. ŞFR, 54/413.

150. Kevorkian, *Armenian Genocide,* 664. And see Philip to SecState, 1 September 1916, *U.S. Official Records,* 535.

151. Kaiser, *At the Crossroads of Der Zor,* 66; and Kevorkian, *Armenian Genocide,* 663–664.

152. Jackson's report "Armenian Atrocities," 4 March 1918, *U.S. Official Records,* 596. In December 1915 Jackson proposed using a code so that he could keep Morgenthau apprised of what was happening, even if his messages were subject to Ottoman scrutiny.

153. Talât to all vilayets and mutesarriflik, 15 March 1916, *Sevk ve Iskan,* 356, doc. 286.

154. Kevorkian, *Armenian Genocide,* 664. See also Dadrian, "Naim-Andonian Documents," 315.

155. Rössler to embassy, 6 April 1916, *German Foreign Office,* 573.

156. Rössler to Bethmann-Hollweg, 27 April 1916, *German Foreign Office,* 581.

157. Kevorkian, *Armenian Genocide,* 364.

158. Kevorkian, *Armenian Genocide,* 665. Hoffman, Aleppo, to German Embassy, 29 August 1916, *German Foreign Office,* 617.

159. Kevorkian, *Armenian Genocide,* 664–665.

160. Dündar, *Crime of Numbers,* 118.

161. Möhrig's report, *German Foreign Office,* 314. See also Kieser, "Beatrice Rohner," 226.

162. Kieser, "Beatrice Rohner," 226.

163. Hoffman to German Embassy, 29 August 1916, *German Foreign Office,* 617.

164. Kevorkian, *Armenian Genocide,* 665. See also testimony of Manuk Kyrmenikian, 29 October 1916, attached to Rössler to Behmann Hollweg, 5 November 1916, *German Foreign Office,* 675.

165. Preacher Vartan Geranian to Rohner, attached to Rössler to Behmann Hollweg, 29 July 1916, *German Foreign Office,* 612.

166. Kevorkian, *Armenian Genocide,* 665. See also testimony of Hosep Sarkissian, attached to Rössler to Bethmann Hollweg, 5 November 1915, *German Foreign Office,* 674.

167. Bernau, "Trip from Meskene to Der-i-Zor made from 24 August to 4 September 1916," undated, attached to Rössler to Bethmann Hollweg, 20 September 1916, *German Foreign Office,* 651–656.

168. Jackson, "Armenian Atrocities," 4 March 1918, *U.S. Official Records,* 588; and Kevorkian, *Armenian Genocide,* 645.

169. Testimony of Hosep Sarkissian, attached to Rössler to Bethmann Hollweg, 5 November 1915, *German Foreign Office,* 674.

170. Kevorkian, *Armenian Genocide,* 666.

171. Jackson's report of 3 September 1915, cited in Philip to SecState, 15 September 1916, USNA RG 59, 867.4016, Roll 45.

172. Sarafian, ed., *Talât Pasha's Report,* 58.

173. Ternon, *Bir Soykırım Tarihi,* 352.

174. Kevorkian, *Armenian Genocide,* 668.

175. Akçam, *Young Turks' Crime,* 284–285.

6. A Policy of Genocide

1. See also Hilmar Kaiser's points in an interview: Kaiser, interview by Garabet Moumdjian, January 18, 2008, Asbarez Armenian news, http://asbarez.com/56524/is-a-long-overdue-controversy-finally-settled-aram-andonians-infamous-naim-beys-real-identity-is-now-considered-revealed. Another example is the "Ten Commandments" document and the other documents obtained by the British from Ahmed Esad, head of the Second Directorate *(Ikinci şube)* in the Interior Ministry (Dadrian, "Secret Young Turk Ittihadist Conference").

2. See Bauer, *Rethinking the Holocaust,* 68–118; and Kershaw, *Nazi Dictatorship.*

3. Bloxham, "Armenian Genocide of 1915–1916," 143. Given the mass murder of Armenians in 1894–1896 and in 1909, the idea of mass murder of Armenians could not have been alien to the mindset of the CUP leadership on the eve of World War I.

4. Bloxham, "Armenian Genocide of 1915–1916," 176.

5. Dundar, *Crime of Numbers,* 72.

6. Balakian, *Armenian Golgotha,* 50–51. Also quoted in Suny, *They Can Live in the Desert,* 246. Similar stories were told by missionaries. See testimony of Stella Loughridge, 21 June 1918, USNA RG 256 "Inquiry Documents," 1917–1919, no. 803, Roll 39.

7. Akçam, *Shameful Act,* 125–126; Suny, *They Can Live in the Desert,* 148; and Bloxham, "Armenian Genocide of 1915–1916," 155–156.

8. Testimony of Tacy W. Atkinson, missionary in Harput, 11 April 1918, USNA RG 256, "Inquiry Documents," 1917–1919, no. 210, Roll 39. See also testimony of Klara Pfeiffer, *German Foreign Office,* 13, 584.

9. Akçam, *Shameful Act,* 127, 132–133, 152–153; Akçam, *Young Turks' Crime,* 184; and Dadrian and Akçam, *Judgment in Istanbul,* 116–117. See also Malta file of Fazıl Berki Bey and Malta file of Gani Bey (Malta No. 2923), both in UKNA FO 371/6500.

10. Akçam, Shameful Act, 156–157.

11. Kevorkian, *Armenian Genocide,* 244.

12. Akçam, *Young Turks' Crime,* 183.

13. Akçam, *Young Turks' Crime,* 183, 411–423; and Dadrian, "Role of the Special Organization," 66.

14. Akçam, *Young Turks' Crime,* 421–422.

15. Akçam, *Young Turks' Crime,* 154–155; and Suny, *They Can Live in the Desert,* 223–224. Mass arrests of notables occurred in the first half of April in a number of towns, including Maraş and Hacin (Kevorkian, *Armenian Genocide,* 250).

16. "Conditions in Marsovan," by American teacher at the college, attached to Morgenthau to Sec-State, 26 July 1915, *U.S. Official Records,* 143.

17. Report of Victoria Khatchadour Barutjibashian of Baiburt, undated, attached to Morgenthau to SecState, 10 August 1915, *U.S. Official Records,* 158.

18. Akçam, *Young Turks' Crime,* 292–293; Lewy, *Armenian Massacres,* 177, 219, 241.

19. Akçam, *Young Turks' Crime,* 292; and Davis to Morgenthau, 30 December 1915, *U.S. Official Records,* 473.

20. Akçam, *Young Turks' Crime,* 295.

21. Talât to all valis and *mutasarrıfs,* 11 August 1915, BOA, DH. ŞFR, 54-A/382; and Malta File of Ejzaji Mehmet Efendi, UKNA FO 371/6501. See also Leslie (?) to Morgenthau, 24 July 1915, *U.S. Official Records,* 465: "Some of the women have been brought right back here. Among these there is a pretty girl of thirteen years whose father was [killed,] one of the most prominent men . . . in this region. . . . Now at her age she is to marry one of the brutal petty officers around here and they are to live in her father's house!"

22. Testimony of Sophia (?) Tahargian (?) in Malta file of Hadji Bekir Mehmed Ali Bey, UKNA FO 371/6501.

23. Watenpaugh, "Are There Any Children for Sale?" 291–292.

24. Mary L. Graffam to Peet, 7 August 1915, attached to Morgenthau to SecState, 13 September 1915, *U.S. Official Records,* 243–244.

25. Heizer, Trabzon, to John Arabian, Rhode Island, 13 November 1915; Heizer to A. G. Ballarian, 13 November 1915; and Heizer to Morgenthau, 1 December 1915 and 24 December 1915, all in USNA RG 84, Trebizond, Vol. 19.

26. Wingate, American Mission, Talas, to Morgenthau, 16 November 1915, *U.S. Official Records,* 349.

27. Assyrian plea to the American consul in Tabriz, Persia, 9 June 1914, USNA RG 59, 867.4016, Roll 43. See also Rev. Leslie's report from Urfa, 14 June 1915, cited in Jackson to Morgenthau, 28 June 1915, *U.S. Official Records,* 84–85; and testimony of Issa el-Bandec, Armenian priest at the Ourtas (Irtas) convent of Bethlehem, attached to letter from Gen. Clayton to SecState for Foreign Affairs, 20 March 1918, UKNA FO 371/3400.

28. Report by an eyewitness, Lt. Sayied Ahmed Moukhtar Baas, no date but stamped 26 December 1916, UKNA FO 371/2768. See also Malta file of Ejzaji Mehmet Efendi, CUP member from Erzincan, UKNA FO 371/6501.

29. Testimony of Shefik Bey, late kaymakam of Bulanik, in Malta file of Hodja Ilias, Deputy for Marash, UKNA FO 371/6501.

30. Testimony of Khenganie Boyadjian, 30, of Bayburt, in Malta file of Ejzaji Mehmet Efendi, UKNA FO 371/6501. See also testimony of Eftik (?) Dralian (?) of Yozgat in Malta file of Baghli Oglu Mehmet, çetebaşı in Ankara, UKNA FO 370/6501: "After having murdered her mother and three brothers, Mehmet

took the witness, bleeding and fainting . . . to his house in Yozgad and there criminally assaulted her." See also report on the "Armenian Exodus from Harput," attached to Jackson to SecState, 16 October 1915, *U.S. Official Records,* 330.

31. Patriarchate report, 21 January 1920, in Malta file of Hdji Bekir Mehmet Ali Bey, UKNA FO 371/6501.

32. Alma Johannson's report, undated, attached to Morgenthau to SecState, 9 November 1915, *U.S. Official Records,* 336.

33. Unsigned, "Addendum to 'Report of an Inhabitant of Athlit, Mount Carmel, Syria,'" undated but stamped "M.I.2.b, 27 November 1916," UKNA FO 371/2783.

34. "Arabian Report," 13 December 1915, UKNA FO 371/2781; and Intelligence Report, Sir E. Grey Bart to ?, 26 May 1916, UKNA FO 371/2777. One Mejidiye was worth 1/5 of a Turkish Lira.

35. Pamuk, *Monetary History of the Ottoman Empire,* 209.

36. Report of ARF Committee of Bucharest, no. 6, dated 5 September 1915, attached to Morgenthau to SecState, 17 September 1915, *U.S. Official Records,* 258.

37. Report of ARF no. 7, dated 28 October 1915, attached to Morgenthau to SecState, 9 November 1915, *U.S. Official Records,* 342.

38. Intelligence Report, Sir E. Grey Bart to ?, 26 May 1916, UKNA FO 371/2777.

39. Intelligence Report, Sir E. Grey Bart to ?, 26 May 1916, UKNA FO 371/2777.

40. Dodd To Morgenthau, 3 September 1915, USNA RG 59, 867.4016, Roll 44.

41. Dodd To Morgenthau, 8 September 1915, USNA RG 59, 867.4016, Roll 44. See also Morgenthau to his wife, 13 September 1915, FDRL, HM Sr. Papers, Letters 475.

42. Dündar, *Crime of Numbers,* 111.

43. Talât to valis and mutesarrifs, 22 June 1915, BOA, DH. ŞFR, 54/100. *Muhacirs* Directorate to Sivas, Trabzon and Mamuret-ül-Aziz vilayets and Canik mutesarriflik, 27 June 1915, BOA, DH. ŞFR, 54/203. See also Akçam, *Young Turks' Crime,* 291–292.

44. Talât to valis and mutesarrifs, 1 July 1915, *Sevk ve Iskan,* 184–185, doc. 122; and Akçam, *Young Turks' Crime,* 290–291.

45. Talât to mutesarrif of Kayseri, 13 August 1915, *Sevk ve Iskan,* 198, doc. 138.

46. Talât to Mustafa Abdülhalik Bey, vali of Aleppo, in Malta file of Abdülhalik Bey, UKNA FO 3711/6501.

47. Talât to the mutesarrif of Niğde, 18 August 1915, *Sevk ve Iskan,* 221, doc. 171.

48. Ministry of Education to several vilayets and mutesarriflik, 26 June 1915, BOA, DH. ŞFR, 54/150.

49. Jackson, "Armenian Atrocities," 4 March 1918, *U.S. Official Records,* 594. See also Hoffman to SecState, 1 September 1916, *U.S. Official Records,* 534; and Kieser, "Beatrice Rohner."

50. Şukru, minister of education, to valis and mutesarrifs, 26 June 1915, *Sevk ve Iskan,* 175, doc. 109; and Talât to vilayet of Mamuret-ül-Aziz, 26 June 1915, *Sevk ve Iskan,* 176–177, doc. 111. See also interior minister to mutesarriflik of Kayseri, 3 May 1916, *Sevk ve Iskan,* 366, doc. 299; and Interior minister to Bekir Sami Bey, vali of Aleppo, 9 August 1915, *Sevk ve Iskan,* 208–209, doc. 151.

51. Talât to Mutesarriflik of Kayseri, 21/23 September 1916, *Sevk ve Iskan,* 374, doc. 311.

52. Talât to Mutesarriflik of Canik, 12 November 1916, *Sevk ve Iskan,* 377–378, doc. 316.

53. Kaiser, *At the Crossroads of Der Zor,* 69–70.

54. Talât to vilayet of Sivas, 17 December 1916, *Sevk ve Iskan,* 381–382, doc. 323.

55. Çetin, *My Grandmother,* 68, 72.

56. Kevorkian, "L'extermination des déportés Arméniens," 55.

57. Talat's wife, Hayriye, later said that he routinely recited a chapter of the Koran each morning (Kieser, *Talaat Pasha*). Morgenthau wrote that Talât described himself as the most religious member of the CUP-dominated cabinet (Morgenthau, *United States Diplomacy,* 77).

58. Çetin, *My Grandmother,* ix.

59. Akçam claims that there was a systematic government policy, and that assimilation and conversion were a structural element of the genocide. But the relevant telegrams were sent only after the deportations began (Akçam, *Young Turks' Crime,* 289–291).

60. Deringil, "Study of the Armenian Crisis."

7. Historical Background, 1918–1924

1. Akçam, *Shameful Acts,* 227–228, quoting Rauf Bey.

2. Most of them soon received their comeuppance. Talât was assassinated by Armenian gunmen on 15 March 1921, and Sakir on 17 April 1922, both in Berlin. Cemal was likewise assassinated in Tiflis, Georgia, on 21 July 1922. Enver was killed in battle by the Red Army in Turkestan on 4 August 1922. Nâzım was convicted by the Turkish government of trying to kill Mustafa Kemal and hanged in Ankara in August 1926.

3. Akçam, *Shameful Acts,* 281. For a detailed description of the May and September 1915 law see also Akçam and Kurt, *Kanunların Ruhu,* 31–47.

4. "Full Text of Conditions of Armistice (which took effect from 12 Noon, 31st October 1918) as arrived at Between British Admiral and Turkish Delegates," UKNA WO 95/4515. In the negotiations the Turks successfully scotched proposals providing for Allied occupation of Sis, Zeytun, and Hacin. Rauf later said, "The armistice we have concluded is beyond our hopes" (MacMillan, *Peacemakers,* 379). Mark Sykes, the British government's Middle East troubleshooter, felt that the terms were "compatible with maintenance of Ottoman Dominion over Armenians" (Sykes to Cecil, 3 November 1919, UKNA FO 371/3403).

5. See, for example, General G. F. Milne, Commanding in Chief, Army of the Black Sea, to John de Robeck, 18 October 1919, attached to de Robeck to Curzon, 30 October 1919, UKNA FO 371/4160.

6. Lt. Col. Ian Smith, untitled memorandum, 4 March 1919, attached to Heck to SecState, 20 March 1919, USNA RG 59, 867.00, Roll 7. Of course, the Turks had suffered greatly; hundreds of thousands had died in combat and from disease.

7. Zeidner, *Tricolor over the Taurus,* 97. French rule there was in line with the 1916 Sykes-Picot Agreement that had allotted them Cilicia.

8. McMeekin, *Ottoman Endgame,* 424.

9. Smith, *Ionian Vision,* 35.

10. Smith, *Ionian Vision,* 69.

11. Fromkin, *Peace to End All Peace,* 400. An alternative take uses the phrasing: ". . . with only a child to take notes . . ."

12. Smith, *Ionian Vision,* 77–79.

13. C-in-C Mediterranean to Admiralty Intelligence, 15 June 1920, UKNA FO 371/5050.

14. Shaw, *From Empire to Republic,* vol. 1, 153, 155.

15. Barton to Bristol, 4 June 1919, USNA RG 59, 860J.01/520–860J.4016/49, Roll 4. Barton noted that "race hatred" toward the Turks was also "not lacking among the Armenians and Greeks."

16. Aktar, "Debating the Armenian Massacres," 248.

17. Aktar, "Debating the Armenian Massacres," 251–252.

18. *Meclisi Mebusan Zabıt Ceridesi* [Parliamentary Minutes], 110, as quoted in Aktar, "Debating the Armenian Massacres," 253.

19. Aktar, "Debating the Armenian Massacres," 255–259.

20. George Rendel, "Turkish Massacres and Persecutions of Minorities since the Armistice," 20 March 1922, UKNA FO 371/7876.

21. Security Directorate to governor of Konya, 2 January 1919, BOA, DH. EUM. 2 Şb, 66/24; and 20 January 1919, BOA, DH. EUM. 2 Şb. 66/31.

22. Rumbold, "Turkey, Annual Report 1920," c. March 1921, Bodl. MS Rumbold Papers 28. Rumbold served on the British Peel Commission in Palestine in 1936–1937.

23. Julian Gillespie to Bristol, 10 January 1922, USNA RG 59, 867.00, Roll 10.

24. General Staff Intelligence, Army of the Black Sea, "Weekly Report No. 69," 19 May 1920, conveying part of Kemal's speech before the Grand National Assembly, Erzurum, c. 2 May 1920, UKNA FO 371/5168.

25. Bristol, "Part Four, Report of Operations for Week Ending 18 May 1919," LC, Bristol Papers, War Diary.

26. Capt. L. LeBouvier to GS "I," GHQ, BritForce, 29 March 1919, UKNA FO 371/4157.

27. Zürcher, *Turkey, A Modern History*, 140–141.

28. Kevorkian, *Armenian Genocide*, 716–718.

29. Zeidner, *Tricolor over the Taurus*, 61–65. See also Mango, *Atatürk*, 207–209; and Kevorkian, *Armenian Genocide*, 715–720.

30. Capt. L. LeBouvier to GS "I," GHQ, BritForce, 29 March 1919, UKNA FO 371/4157.

31. Rawlinson, *Adventures in the Near East*, 180–182.

32. W. (?) Gordon Campbell, "Memorandum on the Situation in Asia Minor," 17 February 1920, UKNA FO 371/5402. Toynbee misrepresented the situation, claiming that Allied "control was working effectively until the news of the Greek landing arrived. The Turkish civil and military authorities were obeying the orders conveyed to them, troops were being disbanded, arms and ammunition called in" (Toynbee, *Western Question*, 145).

33. Rumbold, "Turkey Annual Report 1920," c. March 1921, Bodl. MS Rumbold Papers 28.

34. Webb to Curzon, 7 September 1919, UKNA FO 371/4158.

35. Lt. Patrick Slade, "Kastamouni," undated, UKNA FO 371/4158.

36. J. S. Perring, Samsun, to ?, 29 July 1919, UKNA FO 371/4158. General Staff "Intelligence," Army of the Black Sea, Constantinople, "The Nationalist Movement in Turkey," 6 January 1921, UKNA FO 371/5041.

37. Kevorkian, *Armenian Genocide*, 717.

38. Webb to Curzon, 10 October 1919, UKNA FO 371/4159.

39. Quoted in Dobkin, *Smyrna 1922*, 98.

40. Mango, *Atatürk*, 214.

41. GHQ Constantinople, to War Office, 29 January 1921, UKNA FO 371/6465.

42. De Robeck to Curzon, 18 November 1919, quoted in Smith, *Ionian Vision*, 107.

43. Akçam, *Shameful Act*, 341.

44. Kevorkian, *Armenian Genocide*, 805.

45. Akçam, *Shameful Act*, 362.

46. Akçam, *Shameful Act*, 354.

47. Lt. E. S. Dunn, "Interview with Mustapha Kemal Pasha and Submission of Formal Questions," 1 July 1921, USNA RG 84, Turkey (Constantinople), Vol. 440.

48. Lt. Col. A. Rawlinson, "Note on the Situation in Eastern Anatolia at Time of Erzerum Conference 11th August 1919," undated but with covering letter, DMI to Acting Under Secretary of State, FO, 4 September 1919, UKNA FO 371/4158.

49. Bristol, "Part Four. Report of Operations for the Week Ending 20 July, 1919," LC, Bristol Papers, War Diary.

50. Commander C. Heathcote-Smith to British High Commission, 24 July 1919, UKNA FO 371/4158.

51. Committee of the Congress, "Manifesto of the Congress of the Vilayets of Eastern Anatolia at Erzerum," 7 August 1919, UKNA FO 371/4158. See also Atatürk, *Speech Delivered by Ghazi Mustapha Kemal,* 58.

52. Mustapha Kemal, "Exhibit 'C,' Condensed Memorandum Concerning the Organization and Points of View of the League for the Defense of the Rights of Anatolia and Rumelia," undated, USNA RG 59, Unindexed Records (Central Files) Box 1, 1910–1919. Both charges were clear instances of the pot calling the kettle black.

53. "Declaration of the Congress of Sivas," USNA RG 59, Unindexed Records (Central Files) Box 1, 1910–1919.

54. Zürcher, "Renewal and Silence," 312.

55. Text of "Turkish National Pact," 28 January 1920, USNA RG 59, Unindexed Records (Central Files) Box 2, 1920–1924.

56. Rumbold, "Turkey Annual Report 1920," c. March 1921, Bodl. MS Rumbold Papers 28.

57. Rumbold to Harington, 5 June 1923, Bodl. MS Rumbold Papers 31.

58. De Robeck to Curzon, 1 March 1920, UKNA FO 371/5044.

59. Smith, *Ionian Vision,* 163–164.

60. Churchill, "Military Policy in Asia Minor," 9 October 1919, UKNA FO 371/4159. See also McMeekin, *Ottoman Endgame,* 435.

61. Stamfordham, the king's private secretary, to Rumbold, 2 April 1921, Bodl. MS Rumbold Papers 28.

62. Kemal, "High Commandment of the Ottoman Nationalist Movement and Forces," 19 March 1920, USNA RG 84, Turkey (Constantinople), Vol. 421.

63. For example, Wratislaw to FO, 1 May 1920, UKNA FO 371/5047.

64. Turkish Branch of General Wrangel's intelligence service, "International Situation," c. January 1922, USNA RG 84, Turkey (Constantinople), Vol. 459.

65. MI6 (?), "Psychologic," 16 November 1922, USNA RG 84, Turkey (Constantinople), Vol. 459, based on information/analysis by the NER's "Miss Billings, an American lady who has lived in Angora for the past year and a half."

66. Rumbold to Curzon, 20 January 1921, UKNA FO 371/6464.

67. General Staff "Intelligence," Army of the Black Sea, Constantinople, undated but reproducing essence of Col. Vitali to Italian High Commissioner, 22 April 1920, UKNA FO 371/5049.

68. De Robeck to Rumbold, 22 November 1921, Bodl. MS Rumbold Papers 29.

69. Shaw, *From Empire to Republic,* vol. 3, part 2, 1386–1387.

70. Zeidner, *Tricolor over the Taurus,* 270.

71. See, for example, "Translation from the *Yeni Gun* issued January 12th, 1920, Speech Delivered by Mustapha Kemal Pasha at Ankara," USNA RG 84, Turkey (Constantinople), Vol. 421.

72. General Staff Intelligence, Army of the Black Sea, "Weekly Report No. 69," 19 May 1920, conveying part of Kemal's speech before the National Assembly, Erzurum, c. 2 May 1920, UKNA FO 371/5168.

73. Quote in de Waal, *Great Catastrophe,* 99.

74. Bristol to Jackson, 21 June 1920, LC, Bristol Papers 32.

75. Armenian Patriarchate, untitled memorandum, undated, attached to Gates to Belin, 17 February 1921, USNA RG 84, Turkey (Constantinople), Vol. 439.

76. Bristol to SecState, 18, 28, and 29 March 1920, all in USNA RG 59, 867.00, Roll 8.

77. Kemal, untitled proclamation, 19 March 1920, UKNA FO 371/5046; and "Weekly Summary of Intelligence Issued by M.I.1.c. Constantinople Branch for the Week Ending 25th March, 1921," UKNA FO 371/5166. For descriptions of the occupation of 16 March see de Robeck to Secretary of the Admiralty, 7 April 1920, and attached letters by unit commanders, UKNA FO 371/5048; and unsigned letter

from an American missionary, Bursa, to Parsons and Peet, 20 March 1920, Houghton ABC 16.9.3, Vol. 51.

78. "Treaty of Peace with Turkey," Sèvres, 10 August 1920, *Treaty Series* No. 11 (1920).

79. Bristol to Howard Heinz, 4 May 1921, LC, Bristol Papers 34.

80. Robeck to Curzon, 9 March 1920, UKNA FO 371/5106. But others believed that the Turks were "in a minority" in "Thrace and Smyrna" (see Vansittart, untitled draft response, 13 July 1920, UKNA FO 371/5109).

81. Webb to Curzon, 8 May 1920, quoting Perring, Samsun, UKNA FO 371/5048.

82. Zürcher, *Turkey, A Modern History,* 158–160.

83. See General Garnier Duplessix (Beirut) to Paris, no. 162–164, 15 March 1921, SHD, GR N7, 4165.

84. Rumbold to FO, 5 October 1922, UKNA FO 371/7899; Rumbold, "Annual Report for Turkey for 1921," May 1922, p. 3, UKNA FO 371/7947.

85. Rendel, "French Attitude toward Minority Question," 9 August 1922, UKNA FO 371/7881.

86. Quote in Smith, *Ionian Vision,* 245.

87. Nevile Henderson, "Turkey Annual Report 1922," c. November 1923, UKNA FO 371/9176.

88. Harington to War Secretary, 20 October 1922, UKNA FO 371/9175.

89. Henderson, "Turkey Annual Report 1922," c. November 1923, UKNA FO 371/9176.

90. Lamb to Rumbold, 8 March 1922, Bodl. MS. Rumbold Papers 29.

91. Smith, *Ionian Vision,* 273.

92. Smith, *Ionian Vision,* 276.

93. Atatürk, *Speech Delivered by Ghazi Mustapha Kemal,* 566.

94. Rumbold to Ryan, 6 March 1922, Bodl. MS Rumbold Papers 29.

95. SIS, "Eastern Summary, Kemalist Plans Regarding Constantinople and Thrace," 28 September 1922, UKNA FO 371/7896.

96. Rumbold to FO, 2 October 1922, UKNA FO 371/7897.

97. "Draft Minutes of a Conference of Ministers held at 10 Downing Street . . . on Wednesday, 27th September, 1922 . . . ," UKNA FO 371/7896.

98. "Draft Conclusions of a Conference on Ministers . . . 28th September, 1922 . . . ," UKNA FO 371/7896.

99. Merrill to Bristol, 10 October 1922, USNA RG 59, 867.00, Roll 12.

100. Rumbold to FO, 6 October 1922, UKNA FO 371/7899.

101. Henderson, "Turkey Annual Report 1922," c. November 1923, UKNA FO 371/9176; and Bristol to Belin, 9 October 1922, LC, Bristol Papers 37.

102. Rumbold to FO, 15 October 1922, UKNA FO 371/7903.

103. See Kemal's description of Mudanya, Atatürk, *Speech Delivered by Ghazi Mustapha Kemal,* 569–571.

104. "Cabinet. The Near East Situation. Terms of the Mudania Convention," GHQ Constantinople to War Office, 12 October 1922, UKNA FO 371/7903; Rumbold to FO, 11 October 1922, UKNA FO 371/7902; and Henderson, "Turkey Annual Report 1922," c. November 1923, UKNA FO 371/9176.

105. Shakir Bey, vali of Edirne, to Commandant Emery, President of the Allied Mission, 13 November 1922, UKNA FO 371/7964.

106. E. K. Venizelos to Curzon, 13 October 1922, UKNA FO 371/7905; and Harington to WO, 22 October 1922, UKNA FO 371/7956.

107. G. S. Hatton, "French Troops of Occupation in the Gallipoli Peninsula," 30 November 1922, UKNA FO 371/7964.

108. Rumbold to Curzon, 17 October 1922, UKNA FO 371/7906.

109. Rumbold to Curzon, 17 October 1922, UKNA FO 371/7906.

110. Rumbold to Frank, 28 October 1922, Bodl. MS Rumbold Papers 30.

111. Henderson, "Turkey Annual Report 1922," c. November 1923, UKNA FO 371/9176.

112. "The Armenian Question before the Peace Conference," USNA RG 59, Unindexed Records (Central Files) Box 1, 1910–1919.

113. "British Statements," UKNA FO 371/6561.

114. Harbord, "American Military Mission to Armenia," 16 October 1919, USNA RG 59, Unindexed Records (Central Files) Box 1, 1910–1919.

115. "Message from the President of the United States," 24 May 1920, USNA RG 84, Turkey (Constantinople), Vol. 421; and Barton to Bristol, 2 June 1920, LC, Bristol Papers 32.

116. Quoted in de Waal, *Great Catastrophe,* 85.

117. Zeidner, *Tricolor over the Taurus,* 234.

118. "Declaration of the Armenian Patriarch," attached to Bristol to SecState, 28 April 1923, and Bristol to Secstate, 29 October 1923, both in USNA RG 84, Turkey (Constantinople), Vol. 484.

119. Charles Moser, US consul, Tiflis, to SecState, 20 December 1920, USNA RG 59, 867.00, Roll 10.

120. Entry for 6 November 1922, LC, Bristol Papers, War Diary.

121. Henderson to Rumbold, 12 December 1922, Bodl. MS Rumbold Papers 30.

122. For Kemal on Lausanne, see Atatürk, *Speech Delivered by Ghazi Mustapha Kemal,* 606–625.

123. "Minutes of the Third Meeting of the Foreign Office Ministers at the Quai d'Orsay at 3 P.M., March 23, 1922," UKNA FO 371/7858.

124. Rumbold to Curzon, 17 October 1922, UKNA FO 371/7906.

125. Rumbold to Henderson, 2 January 1923, Bodl. MS Rumbold Papers 30. After his death, Bonar Law's ashes were interred in Westminster Abbey, of which Lord Asquith said: "It is fitting that we should have buried the Unknown Prime Minister by the side of the Unknown Soldier" (Taylor, *English History,* 42).

126. "Memorandum by the General Staff on the Proposed New Treaty between the Allies and Turkey," 19 October 1922, UKNA FO 371/7952.

127. Bristol to Charles Crane, 8 January 1923, LC, Bristol Papers 38.

128. Curzon to FO, 13 January 1923, UKNA FO 371/9059.

129. Rumbold to Henderson, 30 January 1923, Bodl. MS Rumbold Papers 30.

130. Rumbold to Wingate, 27 February 1923, Bodl. MS Rumbold Papers 30–31.

131. Curzon to FO, 5 February 1923, UKNA FO 371/9064.

132. "Report by Mr. Bentinck," 7 February 1923, UKNA FO 371/9065.

133. Rumbold to Curzon, 28 April 1923, Bodl. MS Rumbold Papers 31.

134. E. G. Forbes Adam and Edmonds, "Comparison of Sevres Treaty with Last Draft of Lausanne Treaty," 16 June 1923, UKNA FO 371/9083. See similar comparison by Atatürk, *Speech Delivered by Ghazi Mustapha Kemal,* 606–625.

135. Lloyd George, "Turkey's Success at Lausanne," *Daily Telegraph,* 28 June 1923.

136. W. G. Smart, UK consul, Aleppo, to Foreign Secretary, 17 January 1923, UKNA FO 371/9129.

137. Lindsay to Ramsay MacDonald, 29 September 1924, and attached documents; and Lindsay to Austen Chamberlain, 26 November 1924, and attached enclosure, Allied Juridical Commission, "Expose des Infractions commises par la Turquie aux Clauses conernant la Protection des Minorites," 24 November 1924, both in UKNA FO 371/10228.

138. Henderson to Curzon, 18 August 1923, UKNA FO 371/9131, conveying text of Kemal's speech at the Grand National Assembly, Ankara, 13 August 1923.

139. G. B. (?) Gary, untitled report, 8 October 1923, USNA RG 59, 867.00, Roll 15.

140. Henderson to Curzon, 9 and 10 October 1923, both in UKNA FO 371/9174.

141. R. C. Lindsay, "Turkey Annual Report 1923," c. May 1924, UKNA 371/10223.

142. Zürcher, *Turkey, A Modern History,* 167–172.

8. Turks and Armenians, 1919–1924

Epigraph: William Dodd to Bristol, 9 April 1920, USNA RG 84, Turkey (Constantinople), Vol. 418. Bristol described the American missionary Dodd as "as fair-minded a man as I know" (Bristol to SecState, 26 April 1920, USNA RG 59, 860J.01/520–860J.4016/49, Roll 4).

1. Zeidner, *Tricolor over the Taurus,* 124.

2. Allenby to War Office, 28 December 1918, UKNA FO 371/3386.

3. Kevorkian, *Armenian Genocide,* 743.

4. Kevorkian, *Armenian Genocide,* 743; and "Political and Economic Intelligence Summary," 10 May 1918, Australian War Memorial 4, 1/11/3.

5. Francis Kelsey, "Incidents of the French Occupation of Tarsus," undated but attached to Kelsey to Bristol, 2 August 1920, USNA RG 84, Turkey (Constantinople), Vol. 421.

6. Hartunian, *Neither to Laugh nor to Weep,* 123.

7. Sykes to ?, 16 November 1918, UKNA FO 371/3404.

8. Sykes to ?, 25 December 1918, UKNA FO 371/3400; and Sykes (Aintab) to Clayton (Cairo), 3 January 1919, UKNA FO 371/4141.

9. Allenby to War Office, 28 December 1918, UKNA FO 371/3386.

10. Clayton to ?, 29 December 1918, UKNA FO 371/3400.

11. Commanding Officer, USS *Olympia,* to Bristol, 9 September 1919, USNA RG 59, 867.00, Roll 7.

12. Ryan, untitled memorandum, 8 August 1919, UKNA FO 371/4158.

13. Sherif to General Deedes, 8 August 1919, UKNA FO 371/4158.

14. Webb to Balfour, 22 December 1918, UKNA FO 371/4157. For Constantinople area, see Shaw, *From Empire to Republic,* vol. 1, 215–236.

15. Webb to Balfour, 11 December 1918, UKNA FO 371/3405.

16. Lt. Hadkinson, Panderma, to high commissioner, 8 August 1919, UKNA FO 371/4158.

17. GHQ Egypt to DMI, 6 March 1919, UKNA FO 371/4141.

18. Suny, *They Can Live in the Desert,* 20.

19. Zeidner, *Tricolor over the Taurus,* 40.

20. Kurt, "Curious Case of Ali Cenani Bey," 60.

21. 5th Cavalry Division, "War Diary or Intelligence Summary for Month of December 1918," entries for 16 and 17 December 1918, WO 95/4515.

22. Sykes to FO, 5 January 1919, UKNA FO 371/4141.

23. Unsigned, "Report on Situation in the District [of] Nisibin-Jerablus-Aintab-Marash-Killis," 31 December 1918, WO 95/4515. See also "Armistice Papers," 3 November 1919, BOA, HR. SYS, 2637, 3.

24. GHQ Egypt to War Office, 16 January 1919, UKNA FO 371/4141.

25. Security Directorate to Ankara vilayet, 27 February 1919, BOA, DH. ŞFR, 96, 320; and *Sevk ve Iskan,* 441–470, docs. 359–384.

26. Dodd to Bristol, 7 March 1920, USNA RG 84, Turkey (Constantinople), Vol. 415.

27. 13th Cavalry Brigade, "Intelligence Summary" for March 1919, entries for 8 and 23 March, and CO British forces Aintab, "Proclamation No. 2," 15 March 1919, both in UKNA WO 95/4518.

28. GHQ Egypt to War Office, 3 March 1919, and Lord Derby (Paris) to FO, 11 March 1919, both in UKNA FO 371/4179; Jackson (Damascus) to Secretary of State, 8 May 1919, USNA RG 59, 867.00.4016, Roll 46; GHQ, "Narrative of Action Taken by 5th Cavalry Division, 28/2/1919," undated,

WO 95 / 4515; and Major Commanding 1 / 1st Notts S. R. Yeomanry, untitled memorandum, 2 March 1919, UKNA WO 95 / 4159.

29. Wavell to high commissioner, 15 April 1919, UKNA FO 371 / 4165.

30. 5th Cavalry Division, "Intelligence Summary for Week ending 28th June 1919," 5 July 1919, UKNA WO 95 / 4515.

31. 5th Cavalry Division, "Intelligence Summary for the Week Ending 12th July 1919," 19 July 1919, UKNA WO 95 / 4515; and Eken, *Kapancızade Hamit Bey,* 41–42.

32. Two reports listing anti-Armenian incidents during December 1919–February 1920, one attached to Bristol to Secretary of State, 22 April 1920, in USNA RG 59, 860J.01 / 520–860J.4016 / 49, Roll 4.

33. Security Directorate reports, 30 February 1919, BOA, DH. EUM. SSM, 40 / 8A.

34. Bristol to Knabenshue, 23 September 1920, USNA RG 84, Turkey (Constantinople), Vol. 419.

35. Rendel, "Turkish Massacres and Persecutions of Minorities since the Armistice," 20 March 1922, UKNA FO 371 / 7876.

36. Engert to SecState, 10 March 1920, USNA RG 59, 867.00, Roll 8.

37. Rumbold to Curzon, 14 February 1921, UKNA FO 371 / 6556.

38. Circular by the patriarchate, items from Adana, dated 17 June 1919, and Yozgat, dated 19 June 1919, USNA RG 84, Turkey (Constantinople), Vol. 406.

39. De Robeck to Curzon, 1 March 1920, UKNA FO 371 / 5044.

40. Unsigned but perhaps by Paul Nilson, "Nationalist Turkish Bands Operate in Cilicia," undated but referring to events in October 1919, Houghton ABC 16.9.5, A467, Reel 669; and G.H.Q Egypt to War Office, 21 October 1919, referring to a raid by "brigands" three days earlier on an unnamed village near Adana, in which nineteen Christians, "mostly Armenians," were killed, UKNA FO 371 / 4184.

41. For return of Greeks, see Eken, *Kapancızade Hamit Bey,* 43.

42. Akçam, *Shameful Act,* 305–306.

43. Bessy Bannerman Murdoch, "Report of Work Completed at Arabkir Branch of Harput Near East Relief Unit November 1, 1919–April 1, 1922," 14 June 1922, USNA RG 84, Turkey (Constantinople), Vol. 464.

44. Numbers appended to Foreign Ministry to Heck, 27 February 1919, USNA RG 84, Turkey (Constantinople), Vol. 408. British officials questioned the figures (Deedes, "Meeting with the director of Refugee Department, Ministry of Interior, February 14th, 1919," UKNA FO 371 / 4177). See also Akçam, *Shameful Act,* 309. Richard Hovannisian (in the "Introduction" to Kerr, *Lions of Marash,* xxi) writes that "one hundred and fifty thousand" Armenians were repatriated during November 1918–November 1919.

45. Barton to Bryce, 4 May 1916, Bodl. MS Lord Bryce Papers 202. Barton wrote of "a strong movement of Armenians back to their homes."

46. Barton to Bryce, 20 June 1917, Bodl. MS Lord Bryce Papers 204.

47. "File Memo from the German Embassy in Constantinople on [Reichstag] Deputy Erzberger's Meeting[s] on 10 February 1916 Regarding Armenian and Christian Question in the Orient," *OeUA,* 308–315.

48. For the return of five Armenian families on 21 March 1916 from Izmit to Rodosto, see Prohaska, Rodosto, to ?, 28 March 1916, *OeUA,* 345–346. See also Elizabeth Webb to Barton, 27 August 1917, Houghton ABC 16.9.5, A467, Reel 672.

49. FO to Irwin Laughlin, 18 September 1918; and Reginald Wingate to British Army HQ, Baghdad, 2 September 1918, both in UKNA FO 371 / 3405.

50. Sykes (Cairo) to FO, 2 December 1918, UKNA FO 371 / 3405.

51. Sykes to FO, 13 December 1918, UKNA FO 371 / 3405.

52. DMI to Under Secretary of State, FO, 29 December 1918, UKNA FO 371 / 3405.

53. Webb to Balfour, 11 December 1918, UKNA FO 371 / 3405.

54. War Office, untitled memorandum, 10 December 1918, UKNA FO 371/3405; and Tom Hohler to George [Rendel?], 5 December 1918, UKNA FO 371/3411.

55. US consul, Salonica, to SecState, 16 December 1918, and attached report by Luther Fowle, "Memorandum Concerning Condition of Deported Armenians in Asia-Minor, and Measures for their Relief," undated, USNA RG 59, 867.4016, Roll 46; and Webb to Balfour, 22 December 1918, UKNA FO 371/4157.

56. Webb to Balfour, 22 December 1918, UKNA FO 371/4157.

57. Heck to SecState, 9 January 1919, USNA RG 84, Turkey (Constantinople), Vol. 405.

58. "GHQ Intelligence Summary, 5 February 1919," UKNA FO 371/4157.

59. Webb to Foreign Secretary, 5 April 1919, UKNA FO 371/4157.

60. Head of Muhacir Directorate to vilayets and mutesarrifliks, 21 October 1918, *Sevk ve Iskan,* 395, doc. 337; 398, doc. 340; 399, doc. 341; and other documents, *Sevk ve Iskan,* 400–427.

61. Gough-Calthorpe to Curzon, 9 February 1919, UKNA FO 371/4166.

62. Webb to Curzon, 11 September 1919, UKNA FO 371/4159.

63. For Samsun, see Perring to High Commission, 26(?) March 1919, UKNA FO 371/4157.

64. Capt. E. C. Hole to High Commission, 7 May 1919, UKNA FO 371/4157.

65. Lt. C. E. S. Palmer to ?, 9 January 1919, USNA RG 59, 867.00, Roll 7.

66. Palmer to UK high commissioner, 9 January 1919, UKNA FO 371/4157; and "GHQ Intelligence Summary, 5 February 1919," UKNA FO 371/4157.

67. Lt. J. A. Lorimer to General Staff Officer (Naval), Constantinople, 8 February 1919, UKNA FO 371/4173.

68. Dana Getchell, American missionary, Merzifon, to Perring, 16 March 1919, UKNA FO 371/4157.

69. Shaw, *From Empire to Republic,* vol. 2, 887–888.

70. "GHQ Intelligence Summary 5 February 1919," UKNA FO 371/4157.

71. Ralph Chesbrough, "Report on Political, Economic and Commercial Conditions at Samsoun and Surrounding Districts and Possibilities of its Future Commercial Importance," 8 August 1919, USNA RG 59, 867.00, Roll 7.

72. Capt. J. S. Perring, "Erbaa," undated but from July or August 1919; Webb to Curzon, 7 September 1919; Perring to Webb, 23 August 1919; and Suleyman, Public Prosecutor, untitled report, 29 July 1919—all in UKNA FO 371/4158.

73. Perring, "Erbaa," undated but from July or August 1919, UKNA FO 371/4158.

74. Perring to ?, 23 June 1920, UKNA FO 371/5053.

75. Luther Fowle, US High Commission, Constantinople, "Memorandum Concerning Condition of Deported Armenians in Asia-Minor, and Measures for their Relief," undated, but attached to US consul, Saloniki, to Secstate, 26 December 1918, USNA RG 59, 867.4016, Roll 46.

76. Reshid Pasha, quoting commander of the 9th Ottoman Army, to French authorities, 15 February 1919, USNA RG 84, Turkey (Constantinople), Vol. 405. See also Heck to Robert Woods, American Chargé d'Affaires, Paris, 15 February 1919; and Note to British, French and Italian Commissioners, 11 January 1919; both in USNA RG 84, Turkey (Constantinople), Vol. 405.

77. Untitled Armenian Patriarchate report, July 1919, USNA RG 84, Turkey (Constantinople), Vol. 406.

78. Armenian Patriarchate, report of 12 June from Balukessir, USNA RG 84, Turkey (Constantinople), Vol. 406

79. Chambers to Barton, 22 March 1918, Houghton ABC 16.9.5, A467, Reel 669.

80. Reshid Pasha, quoting commander of the 9th Ottoman Army, to French authorities, 15 February 1919, USNA RG 84, Turkey (Constantinople), Vol. 405. See also Heck to Robert Woods, American Chargé d'Affaires, Paris, 15 February 1919; and Note to British, French and Italian Commissioners, 11 January 1919; both in USNA RG 84, Turkey (Constantinople), Vol. 405.

81. Zeidner, *Tricolor over the Taurus,* 95–96.

82. Jackson to SecState, 31 May 1919, USNA RG 84, Turkey (Constantinople), Vol. 405.

83. Gough-Calthorpe to Curzon, 30 July 1919, UKNA FO 371/4158.

84. De Robeck to FO, 23 February 1920, UKNA FO 371/5103.

85. "Minutes of the 33rd Meeting of the A.G.S. and the Armenian and Greek Representatives," 25 February 1920, UKNA FO 371/5087.

86. Webb to Curzon, 11 September 1919, UKNA FO 371/4159.

87. Peet to Bristol, 29 July 1920, and accompanying statistical table, USNA RG 84, Turkey (Constantinople), Vol. 424.

88. Barton, *Story of Near East Relief,* 4.

89. Signature unclear, "Near East Relief," 29 June 1921, USNA RG 59, 860J.4016/50–860J.4016P 81/99, Roll 5.

90. Gates to Bristol, 25 January 1921, USNA RG 84, Turkey (Constantinople), Vol. 444.

91. See, for example, unsigned memo, "Near East Relief Work in the Four Areas Anatolia, Caucasus, Syria, Persia," undated but attached to G. D. White to Howland Shaw, Constantinople, 4 November 1922, USNA RG 84, Turkey (Constantinople), Vol. 465.

92. Reed to Peet, 4 October 1922, USNA RG 84, Turkey (Constantinople), Vol. 464.

93. Webb to Balfour, 24 March 1919, UKNA FO 371/4195.

94. Webb to Balfour, 15 March 1919, UKNA FO 371/4138.

95. Deedes to undersecretary of state, FO, 20 March 1919, UKNA FO 371/4173.

96. Unsigned, "Memorandum on Repatriation Trip to Makrikeuy & District on the 29th March 1919," UKNA FO 371/4157.

97. Webb to Curzon, 11 September 1919, UKNA FO 371/4159.

98. Armenian Patriarchate, report from Yozgat, 2 June 1919 ("The returning Armenians are threatened with death"), and report from Balikessir, 12 June 1919 ("massacres are threatened every day"), USNA RG 59, 860L.00–860J.01/179, Roll 1.

99. Gates to Rumbold, 16 February 1920, and attached statistics, UKNA FO 371/6556.

100. Gough-Calthorpe to Curzon, 27 June 1919, UKNA FO 371/4158, and accompanying table of crimes, "Trebizond and Samsun Districts, Insecurity," undated.

101. Heathcote-Smith, "Black Sea Trip," 30 July 1919, UKNA FO 371/4158.

102. Armenian Patriarchate memorandum, report from Samsun, 27 May 1919, USNA RG 84, Turkey (Constantinople), Vol. 406.

103. Gates to Bristol, 26 May 1919, LC, Bristol Papers 31. Gough-Calthorpe to Curzon, 30 July 1919, UKNA FO 371/4158. The "Turkish boycott" in Amasya caused returnees "great hardships" (unsigned but by British officer, "Amassia," undated but from July 1919, UKNA FO 371/4158).

104. Armenian Patriarchate, report from Everek, 10 July 1919, USNA RG 59, 860J.00–860J.01, Roll 1.

105. Armenian Patriarchate, report from Yozgat (?), 4 June 1919, USNA RG 84, Turkey (Constantinople), Vol. 406, tells of Ghevont Seraidarian and Yervant Apkarian, accused of killing a Turk four years before.

106. Smith (Tiflis) to SecState, 26 March 1919, USNA RG 59, 867.4016, Roll 46.

107. WO to undersecretary of state, FO, 11 August 1919, UKNA FO 371/4192.

108. UK SecState to Civil Commissioner (Baghdad), 2 June 1919, UKNA FO 371/4142.

109. Armenian Patriarchate, untitled and undated memorandum, attached to Gates to Belin, 17 February 1921, USNA RG 84, Turkey (Constantinople), Vol. 439.

110. Hohler's statement, "Summary of the Proceedings of the Allied High Commissioners Conference Held at the British High Commission on the 6th March 1919," UKNA FO 371/4155.

111. Bristol to Smith, 28 June 1919, LC, Bristol Papers 31.

112. Louis Mallet (Paris) to Balfour, 11 April 1919, UKNA FO 371/4188.

113. G.O.C. Mesopotamia to War Office, 21 April 1919, UKNA FO 371/4191.

114. Greek Legation, London, to Curzon, 11 April 1919, UKNA FO 371/4177.

115. "Massacre d'Armeniens a Karabagh," communiqué du Bureau d'Information Armenien de Paris, 9 July 1919, Bodl. MS Lord Bryce Papers 210.

116. Hohler's statement, "Summary of the Proceedings. . . . 6th March 1919," UKNA FO 371/4155.

117. Webb to Curzon, 11 September 1919, UKNA FO 371/4159.

118. "Refugee Camp, Baquba, Monthly Report for the Month of January, 1920," UKNA FO 371/5125.

119. Civil commissioner, Baghdad, to ?, 9 May 1920, UKNA FO 371/5125; and B. B. Cubitt to ?, 30 September 1920, UKNA FO 371/5127.

120. FO to India Office, 30 June 1920, UKNA FO 371/5126; and Edwin Montagu, "The Assyrian and Armenian Refugees in Mesopotamia," 5 July 1920, UKNA FO 371/5126.

121. Montagu, "The Assyrian and Armenian Refugees in Mesopotamia," 4 November 1920, UKNA FO 371/5127.

122. Thomas Owens, US consul, Baghdad, to SecState, 4 December 1920, USNA RG 84, Turkey (Constantinople), Vol. 424.

123. De Robeck to Curzon, 24 November 1919, UKNA FO 371/4160.

124. Perring to de Robeck, 29 October 1919, UKNA FO 371/4160.

125. Perring to de Robeck, 9 February 1920, UKNA FO 371/5213.

126. "Les Bandes Nationalistes turques operant en Cilicie," Bureau d'Information Armenien de Paris, 5 November 1919, Bodl. MS Lord Bryce Papers 210.

127. Bristol to Jackson, 21 June 1920, LC, Bristol Papers 32.

128. Armenian Patriarchate, report from Mersin from 21 September 1920, attached to Bristol to Secstate, 6 November 1920, USNA RG 59, 860J.00–860J.01, Roll 1.

129. Rumbold, "Turkey Annual Report 1920," c. March 1921, Bodl. MS Rumbold Papers 28.

130. League of Nations, "Deported Women and Children in Turkey and Asia Minor, Note by the Secretary General," coopting Jeppe "Interim Report from the Aleppo Section of the Commission of Inquiry," 26 January 1922, UKNA FO 371/7878.

131. The wartime mass murder of Armenian men created a mass of destitute women who no doubt helped fill Constantinople's postwar ranks of Christian prostitutes (see Vice-Admiral A. P. Niblack to chief of naval operations, 10 December 1921, USNA RG 59, 867.00, Roll 10).

132. Unnamed Armenian physician to ?, 25 March 1919, Bodl. MS Lord Bryce Papers 205.

133. Kevorkian, *Armenian Genocide,* 758.

134. Cox to Simla and SecState, 12 April 1917, UKNA FO 371/3050.

135. Capt. F. E. Carver, assistant political officer, to civil commissioner, Baghdad, 24 January 1919, UKNA FO 371/4177.

136. Thomas Mugerditchian, "The Diarbekir Massacres and Kurdish Atrocities," 1919, 57, USNA RG 59, 867.4016, Roll 46.

137. Lt. J. A. Lorimer to General Staff Officer (Naval), Constantinople, 8 February 1919, UKNA FO 371/4173.

138. General Staff Intelligence, "Notes on the Situation in Anatolia," undated but attached to Webb to Balfour, 16 March 1919, UKNA FO 371/4157.

139. Lt. J. A. Lorimer to General Staff Officer (Naval), Constantinople, 8 February 1919, UKNA FO 371/4173.

140. Chambers, Adana, to Case, 14 May 1919, Houghton ABC 16.9.5, A467, Reel 669; and "Copy of Letter from Mrs. T. D. Christie," Tarsus, 22 April 1919, Houghton ABC 16.9.5, A467, Reel 672.

141. Lewis Heck to SecState, 12 February 1919, USNA RG 84, Turkey (Constantinople), Vol. 400.

142. Webb to General Officer Commanding-in-Chief, British Salonica Force, 1 March 1919, UKNA FO 371/4173. By March 1919 1,300 Greek and Armenian women and children had been recovered in Constantinople ("Recovery of Islamised Greeks and Armenians in Constantinople and Suburbs" and "Numbers of Armenian Orphans Collected from Houses and Orphanages in Constantinople," both undated but attached to Gough-Calthorpe, high commissioner, to Balfour, 22 March 1919, UKNA FO 371/4177).

143. Ahmet Izzet, Interior Minister's adjutant, to the mutesarriflik of Kayseri, 5 February 1919, *Sevk ve Iskan*, 447–448, doc. 367; Ahmet Izzet to *all* vilayets, 20 February 1919, *Sevk ve Iskan*, 454, doc. 375; and Ahmet Izzet to Ankara vilayet, 25 February 1919, *Sevk ve Iskan*, 460, doc. 379. See also Shaw, *From Empire to Republic*, vol. 1, 245–253.

144. Kerr, *Lions of Marash*, 43–44.

145. Kevorkian, *Armenian Genocide*, 758.

146. Kevorkian, *Armenian Genocide*, 760.

147. Kerr, *Lions of Marash*, 43–48.

148. League of Nations, "Deportation of Women and Children in Turkey and Neighbouring Countries," 4 September 1922, UKNA FO 371/7881; and League of Nations, "Work of the Commission for the Protection of Women and Children in the Near East," 11 September 1923, UKNA FO 371/9111.

149. Rumbold, "Turkey Annual Report 1920," c. March 1921, Bodl. MS Rumbold Papers 28.

150. Gates to Rumbold, 16 February 1920, and attached Armenian Patriarch memorandum, UKNA FO 371/6556.

151. FO to Robinson, Armenian Red Cross Society, 22 May 1923, UKNA FO 371/9110; and Rendel minute, 26 June 1924, UKNA FO 371/10225.

152. Peet to Barton, 16 March 1921, Houghton ABC 16.9.3, Vol. 52.

153. League of Nations, "Deported Women and Children in Turkey and Asia Minor, Note by the Secretary General," incorporating Jeppe, "Interim Report from the Aleppo Section of the Commission of Inquiry," 26 January 1922, UKNA FO 371/7878.

154. Mehmet Ali, Interior Minister, to valis and mutesarrifs, 10 May 1919, *Sevk ve Iskan*, 485, doc. 395.

155. Armenian Patriarchate, report from Yozgat, 17 July 1919, USNA RG 59, 860J.00–860J.01, Roll 1; and Shaw, *From Empire to Republic*, vol. 1, 253–254.

156. "Information Collected by U.S.S. Cole (Lt. J. W. Gregory U.S.N.) from Turkish Governor [of Samsun], Captain Ferrin, S. Br. Off., A.C.R.N.E. Nurse in Armenian Orphanage, and American Tobacco Man," undated but from 1919, USNA RG 59, 867.00, Roll 7.

157. CO USS *Olympia* to Bristol, 9 September 1919, USNA RG 59, 867.00, Roll 7.

158. Webb to Curzon, 11 September 1919, UKNA FO 371/4159.

159. Eken, *Kapancızade Hamit Bey*, 43–44.

160. Bristol, "Part Three, Report of Operations for the Week Ending 20 July 1919," LC, Bristol Papers, War Diary.

161. Riggs to family, 18 July 1920, Houghton ABC 16.9.7, Vol. 26; Entry for 23 December 1920, LC, Bristol Papers, War Diary; and Riggs to Barton, 28 December 1920, Houghton ABC 16.9.7, Vol. 26.

162. Dr. M. Fremont Smith, "Report on Political Conditions in Sivas," February 1920, attached to J. P. Coombs, NER, to Bristol, 23 February 1920, USNA RG 84, Turkey (Constantinople), Vol. 420.

163. Report by the Armenian Patriarchate transmitted by Bristol to Lambert, 20 May 1920, USNA RG 84, Turkey (Constantinople), Vol. 415.

164. Gough-Calthorpe to Curzon, 30 July 1919, UKNA FO 371/4158; and Webb to Curzon, 11 September 1919, UKNA FO 371/4159.

165. Entry for 19 April 1922, LC, Bristol Papers, War Diary.

166. Rendel minute, 11 June 1924, UKNA FO 371/10225; and Rumbold, "Turkey Annual Report 1920," c. March 1921, Bodl. MS Rumbold Papers 28.

167. Jeppe reported that she had "rescued" 241 "women and girls" between 1 March 1922 and 30 June 1924 ("Report by the Chairman of the League of Nations Commission for the Protection of Women and Children in the Near East from July 1923 to July 1924," 1 September 1924, UKNA FO 371/10225). Rendel doubted that she actually rescued women and children so much as aided "those already recovered" (Rendel minute, 11 June 1924, UKNA FO 371/10225).

168. League of Nations News Bureau press release, undated but from November 1921, USNA RG 59, 860J.4016/50–860J.4016/081/99, Roll 5.

169. Unsigned, "The Situation in Armenia," 27 August 1920, Bodl. MS Lord Bryce Papers 210.

170. Rumbold to Curzon, 12 May 1923, UKNA FO 371/9110.

171. Emily Robinson, Armenian Red Cross & Refugee Fund, to Rumbold, 8 May 1923, UKNA FO 371/9110.

172. See Henderson to Curzon, 9 May 1923, UKNA FO 371/9095, for events in an orphanage in Scutari.

173. Ward to SecState Hughes, 3 May 1922, USNA RG9 867.4016, Roll 48.

174. Akçam, *Shameful Act,* 237.

175. Akçam, *Shameful Act,* 258–259.

176. Akçam, *Shameful Act,* 235.

177. Akçam, *Shameful Act,* 236–237.

178. Gough-Calthorpe to FO, 11 January 1919, UKNA FO 371/4141.

179. "Ermenilerin Tehcir Sebepleri," 19 January 1919, *Sevk ve Iskan,* 428–440, doc. 358.

180. Akcam, *Shameful Act,* 268, 322.

181. Government resolution 490, 11 December 1918, *Sevk ve Iskan,* 407–408, doc. 346; Government resolution 492, 14 December 1918, 408–410, doc. 347.

182. Akçam, *Shameful Act,* 314–327.

183. Akçam, *Shameful Act,* 240; and Kevorkian, *Armenian Genocide,* 735–742.

184. Akçam, *Shameful Act,* 270.

185. Akçam, *Shameful Act,* 239.

186. Gough-Calthorpe to SecState, 21 April 1919, and attached Capt. E. La Fontaine to Capt. Hoyland, General Staff Intelligence, 12 April 1919; minute by Hoyland, 15 April 1919; and La Fontaine to Hoyland, 14 April 1919, all in UKNA FO 371/4173. See also Göçek, *Denial of Violence,* 365–367.

187. Akçam, *Shameful Act,* 328.

188. Armenian Patriarchate, untitled roundup of information, entry for 8 June 1919, Malatia, referring specifically to "the famous slaughterer Mahmoud, son of Hasim Bey," USNA RG 59, 860J.00–860J.01/179, Roll 1.

189. Akçam, *Shameful Act,* 329–330.

190. Webb to Curzon, 11 September 1919, UKNA FO 371/4159.

191. Akçam, *Shameful Act,* 242–243.

192. Kevorkian, *Armenian Genocide,* 796–798.

193. "Révélations et aveux du Général Moustapha Pacha," Communiqué du Bureau de Presse et d'Information Arménien, 13 February 1920, Bodl. MS Lord Bryce Papers 210.

194. Göçek, *Denial of Violence,* 45, 369–371.

195. Theda Phelps to Allan Dulles, State Department, undated but c. July 1922, USNA RG 59, 867.4016, Roll 47.

196. Zeidner, *Tricolor over the Taurus,* 117.

197. H. Bax Ironside, Sofia, to FO, 3 March 1915, and WO to undersecretary of state, FO, 9 March 1915, both in UKNA FO 371/2484; and Armenian National Defense Committee of America to Edward Grey, 23 March 1915, and WO to undersecretary of state, FO, 15 April 1915, both in UKNA FO 371/2485.

198. Macdonogh, DMI, to War Office, 24 August 1916, UKNA FO 371/2769.

199. Zeidner, *Tricolor over the Taurus,* 16–17.

200. Moumdjian, "Armenian Legion."

201. Zeidner, *Tricolor over the Taurus,* 71, 74.

202. Heck, Constantinople, to SecState, 17 January 1919, USNA RG 84, Turkey (Constantinople), Vol. 405. Admiral Gough-Calthorpe (Constantinople) to ?, 18 December 1918, UKNA FO 371/3421.

203. Zeidner, *Tricolor over the Taurus,* 78.

204. GHQ Egyptian Expeditionary Force, to Foreign Secretary, 20 June 1919, UKNA FO 371/4181.

205. Moumdjian, "Armenian Legion."

206. Gates to Lybyer, 12 April 1919, UKNA FO 371/4157.

207. Zeidner, *Triciolor over the Taurus,* 105–109, 131, 134. In Adana, at the end of April 1919, the British conducted house-to-house searches for arms.

208. Allenby to War Office, 21 May 1919, UKNA FO 371/4181.

209. Curzon to Earl of Derby, 8 May 1919, UKNA FO 371/4180.

210. WO to Allenby, 15 May 1919, UKNA FO 371/4181.

211. Kerr, *Lions of Marash,* 53.

212. WO to Allenby, "Military Occupation of Syria and Cilicia," September 1919, UKNA FO 371/4183.

213. Allenby to WO, 23 September 1919, UKNA FO 371/4183.

214. Foreign Office to Lord Derby (Paris), 7 October 1919, UKNA FO 371/4183.

215. Implied in Allenby to Secretary of State for War, 3 January 1920, UKNA FO 371/5032; and Armenian Patriarchate, report from Aleppo (?), 11 October 1919, USNA RG 84, Turkey (Constantinople), Vol. 418. See also Isabel Merrill (Aintab) to Barton, 30 December 1919, Houghton ABC 16.9.5, A467, Reel 671.

216. Meinertzhagen to ?, 17 October 1919, UKNA FO 371/4184.

217. Peet to Barton, 20 April 1920, Houghton ABC 16.9.3, Vol. 52.

218. 13th Cavalry Brigade, "War Diary or Intelligence Summary" for October 1919, UKNA WO 95/4518. See also report, 21 October 1919, BOA, DH. KMS, 56-1, 42.

219. 13th Cavalry Brigade, "War Diary or Intelligence Summary" for November 1919, entries for 1, 4, and 7 November 1919, UKNA WO 95/4518.

220. GHQ Egypt to War Office, 2 November 1919, UKNA FO 371/4184.

221. GHQ Egypt to War Office, 4 November 1919; GHQ to War Office, 6 November 1919, and 23 November 1919—all in UKNA FO 371/4184.

222. Kerr, *Lions of Marash,* 62.

223. GHQ Egypt to WO, 23 November 1919, UKNA FO 371/4184.

224. GHQ Egypt to WO, 7 November 1919, UKNA FO 371/4184.

225. Security Directorate Intelligence Report, 13 November 1919, BOA, DH. EUM. SSM, 39, 27.

226. Security Directorate Intelligence Report, 25 November 1919, BOA, DH. EUM. SSM, 39, 38.

227. Jackson to Bristol, 1 May 1920, USNA RG 84, Turkey (Constantinople), Vol. 421.

228. Jackson to Bristol, 2 February 1920, USNA RG 84, Turkey (Constantinople), Vol. 421.

229. Kelsey to Bristol, 2 August 1920, enclosing Kelsey, "Incidents of the French Occupation of Tarsus," undated; and Bristol to SecState, 4 September 1920; both in USNA RG 84, Turkey (Constantinople), Vol. 421.

230. Reshid Pacha to Defrance, the French high commissioner in Constantinople, 23 December 1919, USNA RG 84, Turkey (Constantinople), Vol. 421.

231. Lt. Commander S. S. Butler, HMS *Sportive,* to de Robeck, 24 February 1920, UKNA FO 371/5033; and Manasseh Sevag to Woodrow Wilson, 3 December 1920, USNA RG 59, 860J.00–860J.01/179, Reel 1. See also Eyres to Rumbold, 26 October 1920, UKNA FO 371/5210.

232. Derby to Curzon, 26 October 1919, UKNA FO 371/4184.

233. Zeidner, *Tricolor over the Taurus,* 122.

234. Allenby to WO, 20 October 1919, UKNA FO 371/4184.

235. Telegrams from Security Directorate and cabinet to valis and *mutasarrıf*s, 29 October to 22 November 1919, BOA, DH. ŞFR, 104, nos. 106, 126, 146, 182, 229, 247, 265.

236. Sublime Porte, Ministry of Foreign Affairs, "Note Verbale" to American High Commission, 18 November 1919, USNA RG 59, 867.00, Roll 8.

237. Rechid (Akif) Pacha, Turkish Foreign Minister, to Defrance, 25 November 1919, USNA RG 84, Turkey (Constantinople), Vol. 421. See also demands for investigation, 9 January 1919, BOA, DH. EUM. 5 Şb, 77 5.

238. Ottoman "aide memoire" to French HC, 30 November 1919, USNA RG 84, Turkey (Constantinople), Vol. 421.

239. Reshid to Defrance, 23 December 1919, USNA RG 84, Turkey (Constantinople), Vol. 421; Bristol to Ellis, 26 February 1920, LC, Bristol Papers 31; and Intelligence report, 10 January 1919, BOA, DH. EUM. 2 Şb, 67/29.

240. Armenian Patriarchate, untitled, undated memorandum, including section based on report from Kilis dated 2 February 1920, attached to Bristol to Secretary of State, 22 April 1920, USNA RG 59, 860J.01/520–860J.4016/49, Roll 4.

241. Jackson to Bristol, 7 June 1920, USNA RG 84, Turkey (Constantinople), Vol. 419.

242. Djelal to Arnold (Adana), 3 January 1920, USNA RG 84, Turkey (Constantinople), Vol. 419.

243. High Commissioner de Robeck to Curzon, 19 November 1919, and text of Kemal circular to high commissions, UKNA FO 371/4185.

244. Harold Buxton, "Cilicia and Northern Syria," 29 February 1920, UKNA FO 371/5042.

245. Aneurin Williams, British Armenia Committee, to Curzon, "Cilicia," 8 June 1920, UKNA FO 371/5049.

246. WO to under-secretary of state, FO, 3 August 1920, enclosing Kemal and Salaheddin, OC 3rd Army Corps, to Kiazim Bey, OC 61st Division at Balikesri, 6 December 1919, UKNA FO 371/5054. Following the meeting Kemal ordered his forces to continue preparing for conflict with the French "but to avoid any armed action until further notice."

247. De Robeck to Curzon, 12 December 1919, UKNA FO 371/4186.

248. Armenian Patriarchate, untitled, undated memorandum, attached to Gates to Belin, 17 February 1921, USNA RG 84, Turkey (Constantinople), Vol. 439.

249. Webb to Curzon, 18 October 1919, UKNA FO 371/4160.

250. Jackson to Bristol, 31 March 1920, USNA RG 59, 867.00, Roll 9.

251. Untitled US intelligence Report sent to US embassy, C'ple, 15 April 1920, USNA RG 59, 867.00, Roll 9.

252. "Journal du siege d'Adana," 17 June–17 August 1920, SHD, GR N7, 4165; and H. C. A. Eyres to Rumbold, 26 October 1920, attached to Rumbold to Curzon, 19 November 1920, UKNA FO 371/5210.

253. Bristol to SecState, 13 September 1920, USNA RG 84, Turkey (Constantinople), Vol. 415.

254. Kevork Vartabed Arslanian, prelate of Adana Armenians, 16 July 1920, USNA RG 59, 860J.01/520–860J.4016/49, Roll 4.

255. List of alleged crimes by Armenian legionnaires attached to letter from chief administrator, OETA (North) to C-in-C, EEF, 24 February 1919, appended to Wavell to high commissioner, 15 April 1919, UKNA FO 371/4165.

256. Ottoman Government, "Aide Memoire," 11 March 1919, UKNA FO 371/4165.

257. See, for example, Irene Gaylord, Konia, to NER managing director, C'ple, 26 June 1920, USNA RG 84, Turkey (Constantinople), Vol. 419.

258. Major E. W. C. Noel, untitled memo, 12 March 1919, UKNA FO 371/4173.

259. "A.J.T.," untitled memorandum, 18 February 1918, UKNA FO 371/3400.

260. Wardrop (Moscow) to FO, 18 July 1918, UKNA FO 371/3402.

261. Rawlinson to Intranscau, Tiflis, undated, UKNA FO 371/4159.

262. GOC in C. Mesopotamia to WO, 10 December 1918, UKNA FO 371/3405.

263. C. Marling (Teheran) to FO, 4 September 1918, UKNA FO 371/3400.

264. Turkish Foreign Ministry, "Memorandum No. 16178," undated, attached to Ravndal to Secstate, 24 June 1919, USNA RG 59, 867.4016, Roll 46.

265. Ottoman "Note to British, French and Italian Commissioners," 11 January 1919, USNA RG 84, Vol. 405.

266. Edib to Bristol, 11 November 1920, USNA RG 84, Turkey (Constantinople), Vol. 439. The Turkish General Kiazim Karabekir Pasha decribed Armenian atrocities around Kars in an undated, untitled report, attached to Bristol to SecState, 19 January 1921, USNA RG 84, Turkey (Constantinople), Vol. 438.

267. Angora Government report, untitled, attached to Halide Edib to Bristol, 4 November 1920, USNA RG 59, 860J.4016/50–860J.4016P81/99, Roll 5.

268. Bristol to SecState, 29 June 1921, USNA RG 84, Turkey (Constantinople), Vol. 438; and Crutcher via USS *Overton*, 26 June 1921, USNA RG 84, Turkey (Constantinople), Vol. 439.

269. Rosalind Toynbee to her mother, Lady Mary Murray, 18 June 1921, Bodl. MS Toynbee 50.

270. The description by Shaw (*From Empire to Republic*, vol. 2, 865–883) of the behavior of the Armenian troops as murderous and of French rule in Cilicia as "harsh" is highly tendentious and exaggerated, echoing Turkish spokesmen. Shaw speaks of the legionnaires "killing, raping, ravaging and robbing everyone and everything in sight," but in effect offers a description (870–871) of French and Armenian behavior as corrupt, discriminatory, and harassing rather than lethal or barbaric.

271. Bristol to W. T. Ellis, 26 February 1920, LC, Bristol Papers 31.

272. Stanley Kerr, "The Story of Marash," undated but probably from July–August 1920, Houghton ABC 16.9.1, Vol. 2; and Kerr, untitled "statement," 22 July 1920, USNA RG 59, 860J.01/520–860J.4016/49, Roll 4.

273. Wooley to FO, 26 December 1918, UKNA FO 371/3400. Kerr, "The Story of Marash," undated but probably from July–August 1920, Houghton ABC 16.9.1, Vol. 2, said that 20,000 had returned.

274. Peet to Barton, 2 March 1920, Houghton ABC 16.9.3, Vol. 52.

275. Shaw, *From Empire to Republic*, vol. 2, 890.

276. Zeidner, *Tricolor over the Taurus*, 168; and Kerr, *Lions of Marash*, 63.

277. Zeidner, *Tricolor over the Taurus*, 169–171.

278. Accounts of the "flag incident" are confused. This description is compiled from information provided in Armenian Women's Association to Bristol, 5 March 1920, enclosing, undated, "The Events of Marash," unsigned, USNA RG 84, Turkey (Constantinople), Vol. 419; and Chambers, "Memorandum Concerning the Marash Disturbances of January 21 to February 10, 1920," undated, enclosed in de Robeck to Curzon, 4 March 1920, UKNA FO 371/5044. According to Zeidner, *Tricolor over the Taurus*, 168n200, Kemal had ordered the locals "not to yield" over the flag. See also report compiled by the Armenian Patriarchate, attached to de Robek to Curzon, 7 April 1920, UKNA FO 371/5047; and Hartunian, *Neither to Laugh nor to Weep*, 128–131.

279. Unsigned, "Copy of a Portion of a letter from Marash to Dr. Lambert, Re: Political Situation," 4 January 1920, USNA RG 59, 867.00, Roll 8.

280. "Sister E." to Armenian Catholic Patriarch, Constantinople, 12 January 1920, USNA RG 59, 867.00.

281. Kerr, *Lions of Marash*, 181.

282. Chambers, "Memorandum Concerning the Marash Disturbances . . . ," UKNA FO 371/5044.

283. Kerr, *Lions of Marash*, 92–94, says the legionnaires were sent out to bring back and guard a supply convoy from Bel Pounar.

284. "Extracts from Diary of YMCA Secretary [C.F.H.] Crathern Concerning the Siege and War in Marash Jan. 20th to Feb. 11th 1920," enclosed in Jackson to Bristol, 4 March 1920, USNA RG 84, Turkey (Constantinople), Vol. 415 (hereafter Crathern, Diary); and Kerr, untitled memorandum, 22 July 1920, USNA RG 59, 860J.01/520–860J.4016/49, Roll 4. See also report compiled by the Armenian Patriarchate, attached to de Robek to Curzon, 7 April 1920, UKNA FO 371/5047.

285. Rechid Pacha to Defrance, 24 January 1920, USNA RG 84, Turkey (Constantinople), Vol. 421.

286. Crathern, Diary, entry for 21 January 1920; and Kerr, "Story of Marash," Houghton ABC 16.9.1, Vol. 2.

287. Admiral D.N.S. in Beirut to the Naval Ministry, Paris, 8 February 1920, SHD, GR N7, 4165.

288. Unsigned, "The Following is the Story Told by Boghos Masseredjian, a Resident of Marash Who left Marash with the French, Walked to Islahie and Went (?) by Train to Aleppo," undated, USNA RG 84, Turkey (Constantinople), Vol. 421.

289. Kerr, *Lions of Marash*, 95–97.

290. Zeidner, *Tricolor over the Taurus*, 206–207.

291. Zeidner, *Tricolor over the Taurus*, 205–206.

292. Zeidner, *Tricolor over the Taurus*, 190n223. Zeidner, however, adds that between early December 1919 and 11 January 1920, Kemal repeatedly "instructed his lieutenants in the South to avoid attacking either the French or the Armenians" (197) and, perhaps confusingly, that "during . . . January through April" Kemal's aides, Kilic Ali and Ali Saip, had "quickly created a general conflagration" (201) in the South.

293. Kerr, *Lions of Marash*, 98–99.

294. Evelyn Trostle, NER Marash, to ?, 22 January 1920, USNA RG 84, Turkey (Constantinople), Vol. 419.

295. "The Following is the Story Told by Boghos Masseredjian . . . ," USNA RG 84, Turkey (Constantinople), Vol. 421; and Armenian National Union of Adana, untitled memorandum, appended to Zaven, the Armenian Patriarch, to Phipps, 24 March 1920, UKNA FO 371/5044.

296. Kerr, "The Story of Marash," Houghton ABC 16.9.1, Vol. 2.

297. Report compiled by the Armenian Patriarchate, attached to de Robeck to Curzon, 7 April 1920, UKNA FO 371/5047.

298. Mrs. M. C. Wilson, "Marash. (Written as a Diary.) Siege of Marash. Fourteenth Day. Feb. 3," USNA RG 84, Turkey (Constantinople), Vol. 419. The Armenians felt that the French were deliberately refraining from protecting them (see W. S. Dodd to managing director, 3 February 1920, Houghton ABC 16.9.3, Vol. 50. The French, he felt, "are careless of whether Armenians are massacred or not").

299. Crathern, Diary, entry for 23 January 1920.

300. Crathern, Diary, entries for 22, 23, and 24 January 1920; "The Following is the Story Told by Boghos Masseredjian . . . ," USNA RG 84, Turkey (Constantinople), Vol. 421; and Chambers, "Memorandum . . . ," UKNA FO 371/5044.

301. Kerr, "The Story of Marash," Houghton ABC 16.9.1, Vol. 2.

302. Kerr, *Lions of Marash*, 101–102.

303. Wilson to Jackson, 1 February 1920, Houghton ABC 16.9.3, Vol. 52.

304. Chambers, "Memorandum . . . ," UKNA FO 371/5044.

305. Crathern, Diary, entry for 24 January 1920.

306. Mrs. Wilson, ". . . Siege of Marash . . . ," 3 February 1920, USNA RG 84, Turkey (Constantinople), Vol. 419.

307. Evelyn Trostle to ?, 22 January 1920, USNA RG 84, Turkey (Constantinople), Vol. 419. The letter was probably sent in February.

308. Crathern, Diary, entry for 24 January 1920.

309. Crathern, Diary, entry for 25 January 1920; and Kerr, "The Story of Marash," Houghton ABC 16.9.1, Vol. 2.

310. Crathern, Diary, entry for 4 February 1920.

311. Crathern, Diary, entry for 26 January 1920.

312. Crathern, Diary, entry for 28 January 1920.

313. Jackson to Bristol, 27 February 1920, USNA RG 84, Turkey (Constantinople), Vol. 415.

314. Crathern, Diary, entries for 25 and 29 January 1920.

315. Crathern, Diary, entry for 5 February 1920. Kerr recalled a meal of "mule roast with mule gravy over our mashed potatoes" (Kerr, "The Story of Marash," Houghton ABC 16.9.1, Vol. 2).

316. Dodd, director of NER Adana, to managing director, Constantinople, 3 February 1920, Houghton ABC 16.9.3, Vol. 50.

317. Armenian Patriarchate, untitled, undated report attached to Bristol to Secretary of State, 22 April 1920, USNA RG 59, 860J.01/520–860J.4016/49, Roll 4.

318. Chief Agent of Lord Mayor of London's Fund for Relief of Armenian Refugees, to ?, 11 February 1920, UKNA FO 371/5041. Following the murders Kemal apparently ordered his forces not to harm missionaries (Kemal to Halide Edili Hamin, 16 February 1920, attached to Halide Edili to Bristol, 1 March 1920, USNA RG 59, 860J.01/520–860J.4016/49, Roll 4).

319. Kemal to Mahmoud, GOC 20th Army Corps (?), 24 January 1920, in General Staff "Intelligence," Army of the Black Sea, Constantinople, "Weekly Report No. 71, for Week Ending 2nd June, 1920," UKNA FO 371/5169.

320. Dr. R. A. Lambert, director NER, Aleppo, to Major Nicol, 11 March 1920, Houghton ABC 16.9.1, Vol. 1.

321. Jackson to Bristol, 27 May 1920, USNA RG 84, Turkey (Constantinople), Vol. 421.

322. A collection of "telegrams" from Turkish committees in dozens of towns, attached to Bristol to Secretary of State, 7 February 1920, USNA RG 59, 867.00, Roll 8.

323. A telegram from Cheih Ziaddin, Abdullah and Hadji Mehmed, of Castamouni, to ?, 1 February 1920, USNA RG 84, Turkey (Constantinople), Vol. 419.

324. G.S.1, GHQ, EEF, "Note on the Situation in Northern Syria and Cilicia, Period Approximately 1st January to 20th February 1920," 23 February 1920, attached to G. H. Bell to DMI, 23 February 1920, UKNA FO 371/5044.

325. De Robeck to Curzon, 4 February 1920, UKNA FO 371/4162.

326. Jackson to Bristol, 13 February 1920, USNA RG 84, Turkey (Constantinople), Vol. 419. See also Report compiled by the Armenian Patriarchate, attached to de Robek to Curzon, 7 April 1920, UKNA FO 371/5047. See also Hartunian, *Neither to Laugh nor to Weep,* 145–146.

327. Kerr, *Lions of Marash,* 155–163, 166.

328. The French subsequently claimed that Querette had misinterpreted his instructions and was recalled to France to "answer for his conduct." Colonel Robert Normand, commander of the column, was "reprimanded" (unsigned but by an American missionary, "Statement Regarding Interview with General Gouraud and His Secretary," undated but c. 12 May 1920, Houghton ABC 16.9.3, Vol. 52).

329. Crathern, Diary, entry for 10 February 1920; and Kerr, "The Story of Marash," Houghton ABC 16.9.1, Vol. 2.

330. Crathern, Diary, entries for 9 and 10 February 1920; and Dr. M. C. Wilson, director NER, Marash, to Major Arnold, 9 February 1920, USNA RG 84, Turkey (Constantinople), Vol. 419.

331. "The Following . . . Boghos Masseredjian . . . ," USNA RG 84, Turkey (Constantinople), Vol. 421.

332. Crathern, Diary, entry for 10 February 1920.

333. Kerr, "The Story of Marash," Houghton ABC 16.9.1, Vol. 2.

334. Hartunian, *Neither to Laugh nor to Weep,* 144.

335. Kerr, "The Story of Marash," Houghton ABC 16.9.1, Vol. 2; L. P. Chambers to Lord Bryce, "The Fighting at Marash, Jan 21–Feb. 10, 1920," 4 March 1920, Bodl. MS Lord Bryce Papers 206; and Bishop Naroyan (Constantinople) to Nubar Pasha, 25 February 1920, UKNA FO 371/5042. The bishop spoke of 3,000 Armenians "massacred" trying to join the retreat and of 16,000 massacred all told. Chambers wrote of 2,000 Armenians who left town on the morning of February 11, but were "cut to pieces. . . . Barely a score reached safety."

336. Constantinople Branch, M.I.1.c., "The Situation in Marash," 3 February 1920, attached to de Robeck to Curzon, 11 February 1920, UKNA FO 371/5043.

337. Crathern, Diary, entry for 12 February 1920.

338. Kerr, *Lions of Marash,* 189.

339. Constantinople Branch, M.I.1.c., "The Situation in Marash," 3 February 1920, attached to de Robeck to Curzon, 11 February 1920, UKNA FO 371/5043; and "The Following . . . Boghos Masseredjian . . . ," USNA RG 84, Turkey (Constantinople), Vol. 421.

340. Kerr, "The Story of Marash," Houghton ABC 16.9.1, Vol. 2.

341. Kerr, *Lions of Marash,* 190.

342. Kerr, "The Story of Marash," Houghton ABC 16.9.1, Vol. 2.

343. Crathern, Diary, entry for 14 February 1920; and "The Following . . . Boghos Masseredjian . . . ," USNA RG 84, Turkey (Constantinople), Vol. 421.

344. "The Following . . . Boghos Masseredjian . . . ," USNA RG 84, Turkey (Constantinople), Vol. 421.

345. Crathern (Mersin) to Major D. G. Arnold, managing director NER, 17 February 1920, USNA RG 84, Turkey (Constantinople), Vol. 419. According to British intelligence, "between 15 and 20,000 Armenians perished" (Rendel, "Turkish Massacres and Persecutions of Minorities Since the Armistice," 20 March 1922, UKNA FO 371/7876).

346. Curzon, "Memorandum," 6 March 1920, UKNA FO 371/5103.

347. Unsigned report sent by French commanding officer, "Turquie d'Asie," 8 March 1920, SHD, GR N7, 4165.

348. R. A. Lambert to Major Nicol, 11 March 1920, Houghton ABC 16.9.1, Vol. 1.

349. Knabenshue (Beirut) to SecState, 20 February 1920, USNA RG 59, 867.00, Roll 8.

350. Bristol to Lambert, 20 May 1920, enclosing report by Armenian Patriarch, USNA RG 84, Turkey (Constantinople), Vol. 415; and Lambert to Major Nicol, 11 March 1920, Houghton ABC 16.9.1, Vol. 1.

351. Arnold to Bristol, 27 February 1920, quoting (extract) Dodd to Arnold, 22 February 1920, USNA RG 84, Turkey (Constantinople), Vol. 419; and Kerr, "The Story of Marash," Houghton ABC 16.9.1, Vol. 2.

352. Lambert to Major Nicol, 11 March 1920, Houghton ABC 16.9.1, Vol. 1.

353. M. C. Wilson to ?, 26 February 1920, Houghton ABC 16.9.1, Vol. 1.

354. Armenian National Union, Aleppo, to Jackson, 11 September 1920, USNA RG 59, 860J.4016P81/600–860J.48/199, Roll 7.

355. Jackson to Bristol, 14 April 1920, USNA RG 84, Turkey (Constantinople), Vol. 418; and Nicol to ?, 14 June 1920, USNA RG 59, 867.00, Roll 9.

356. Kerr, untitled memorandum written on board USS *John D. Edwards,* 22 July 1920, USNA RG 59, 860J.01/520–860J.4016/49, Roll 4.

357. Lyman to Barton, 8 February 1921, USNA RG 59, 860J.4016P81/600–860J.48/199, Roll 7. Kerr, "The Story of Marash," Houghton ABC 16.9.1, Vol. 2.

358. Stanley Kerr to Doolittle, 29 August 1921, USNA RG 84, Turkey (Constantinople), Vol. 438; and entry for 22 June 1922, LC, Bristol Papers, War Diary.

359. De Robeck to Curzon, 2 March 1920, UKNA FO 371/5402.

360. Bristol to Barton, 19 October 1920, LC, Bristol Papers 32.

361. Dr. A. Nakashian, Constantinople, to Miss Wallis, 27 February 1920, Houghton ABC 16.9.1, Vol. 1.

362. Peet to Barton, 2 March 1920, Houghton ABC 16.9.3, Vol. 52.

363. Curzon, "Memorandum," 6 March 1920, UKNA FO 371/5103.

364. De Robeck to Curzon, 16 March 1920, UKNA FO 371/5043.

365. De Robeck to ?, 15 March 1920, UKNA FO 371/5042.

366. "Weekly Summary of Intelligence Reports Issued by M.I.1.c., Constantinople Branch, for Week ending 5th February, 1920," UKNA FO 371/5165.

367. Armenian Patriarchate, untitled, undated report attached to Bristol to Secretary of State, 22 April 1920, USNA RG 59 860J.01/520–860J.4016/49, Roll 4.

368. Constantinople Branch, M.I.1.c., "The Situation at Marash," 3 February 1920, attached to de Robeck to Curzon, 11 February 1920, UKNA FO 371/5043.

369. Kemal, "Message Submitted to H.I.M., the Sultan, by the Great National Assembly," apparently from 1 May 1920, in Weekly Report No. 70, General Staff Intelligence, Army of the Black Sea, 26 May 1920, UKNA FO 371/5168.

370. *Mufti*s of Yozgat, Marash, etc., "Nationalist Fetva," undated, in "Weekly Report No. 71 for Week Ending 2nd June 1920," General Staff Intelligence, Army of the Black Sea, 2 June 1920, UKNA FO 371/5168.

371. Ravndal to SecState, 31 May 1921, enclosing unsigned, "A Senoussi Chief in Anatolia," undated, USNA RG 84, Turkey (Constantinople), Vol. 439. Sinoussi would continue inciting against the Entente forces through 1921–1922. See also A.F.L, Beirut, to War Office, Paris, 23 April 1922, SHD, N7, 4165; and A.F.L, Beirut, 19 May 1922, to War Office, Paris.

372. Pinkney Tuck to Bristol, 29 July 1920, USNA RG 84, Turkey (Constantinople), Vol. 420.

373. Horton to Bristol, 4 August 1922, USNA RG 84, Turkey (Constantinople), Vol. 459. Horton was speaking of Greek rule. It is worth noting that other American diplomats held contrary views: "The Turk is not a religious fanatic; he is not intolerant of other religions . . ." (Robert Imbrie, Ankara, 11 July 1922, USNA RG 84, Turkey (Constantinople), Vol. 459). Ironically Imbrie was murdered two years later by Muslim fanatics in Teheran.

374. Curzon, "The Turkish Situation and the American Government," 6 March 1920, UKNA FO 371/5216.

375. Bristol to William Dodd, 2 March 1920, USNA RG 84, Turkey (Constantinople), Vol. 419. Bristol was severely criticized, at least in private, by most missionaries and some of his subordinates over his attitude toward the ethnic groups in Turkey (see Chambers to Lord Bryce, undated but from 1920, Bodl. MS Lord Bryce Papers 206; and Jackson to Bristol, 1 May 1920, USNA RG 84, Turkey (Constantinople), Vol. 421).

376. Bristol to SecState, 21 February 1920, USNA RG 59, 867.00, Roll 8.

377. Engert (Aleppo) to SecState, 10 March 1920, USNA RG 59, 867.00, Roll 8.

378. Engert (Aleppo) to SecState, 28 February 1920, USNA RG 59, 867.00, Roll 8.

379. Jackson to Bristol, 31 March 1920, USNA RG 84, Turkey (Constantinople), Vol. 421.

380. Dodd to Bristol, 10 March 1920, USNA RG 84, Turkey (Constantinople), Vol. 415; and message from Mersina, 23 March 1920, in Armenian Patriarchate news bulletin, c. March 1920, USNA RG 59, 860J.01 / 520–860J.4016 / 49, Roll 4. See also "Story of Terfunda Sahagian," attached to de Robek to Curzon, 22 March 1920, UKNA FO 371 / 5045.

381. Dodd to Barton, 25 March / 2 April 1920, Houghton ABC 16.9.1, Vol. 1.

382. Dodd to Bristol, 9 April 1920, USNA RG 84, Turkey (Constantinople), Vol. 418.

383. Renseignements (Semaine du 4 au 10 Mai 1920), Armée Française du Levant, UKNA FO 371 / 5048.

384. Bristol had it right: "The French should either send a large force . . . or get out" (Bristol to Engert, 20 March 1920, LC, Bristol Papers 32).

385. De Robek to Curzon, 22 March 1920, and attachments, UKNA FO 371 / 5045.

386. Jackson to Bristol, 23 March and 12 May 1920, both in USNA RG 84, Turkey (Constantinople), Vol. 418.

387. Dr Lorin Shepard (Aintab) to Jackson, 2 February 1920, USNA RG 84, Turkey (Constantinople), Vol. 418; and British Military intelligence, "Note on the Situation in Northern Syria and Cilicia," undated, attached to Bell to DMI, 23 February 1920, UKNA FO 371 / 5044. Shepard, "Statement Concerning Conditions in Aintab," 18 April 1920, attached to Goldsmith to DMI, 8 June 1920, UKNA FO 371 / 5052.

388. Lambert to Nicol, 11 March 1920, Houghton ABC 16.9.1, Vol. 1; Jackson to Bristol, 23 March 1920, USNA RG 84, Turkey (Constantinople), Vol. 418; and Shepard to Jackson, 11 February 1920, USNA RG 84, Turkey (Constantinople), Vol. 418.

389. Jackson to Bristol, 4 February 1920, USNA RG 84, Turkey (Constantinople), Vol. 419.

390. Report about Antep, 12 February 1920, BOA, DH. EUM. AYŞ, 32 16. See also Special Bureau *(Kalem-i mahsus)* to Maraş governor, 15 March 1920, BOA, DH. ŞFR, 108 / 74.

391. Jackson to Bristol, 23 March 1920, USNA RG 84, Turkey (Constantinople), Vol. 418.

392. Knabenshue to Bristol, 26 March 1920, USNA RG 59, 867.00, Roll 8.

393. Jackson to Bristol, 31 March 1920, USNA RG 84, Turkey (Constantinople), Vol. 418.

394. Elizabeth Harris (superintendent of the Boys' Orphanage, Aintab), untitled memorandum, 22 April 1920, Houghton ABC 16.9.1, Vol. 1; John Boyd, NER director Aintab, to Jackson, 21 April 1920, USNA RG 84, Turkey (Constantinople), Vol. 419; Shepard, "Statement . . . ," 18 April 1920, UKNA FO 371 / 5052; and Bristol to SecState, 12 April 1920, quoting Knabenshue to Bristol the same day, USNA RG 59, 867.00, Roll 8. Harris suggests that the Turks had planned to begin the massacre only the following day and that the shot in the marketplace had been an inadvertent trigger. Hence the mass of armed Turks initially responded lackadaisically; hence the paucity of Armenian casualties that day.

395. Shepard, "Statement . . . ," 18 April 1920, UKNA FO 371 / 5052; and M. W. Frearson, British director of girls' orphanage (Aintab), to British High Commissioner, undated, attached to de Robeck to Curzon, 14 June 1920, UKNA FO 371 / 5051.

396. Shepard, "Statement . . . ," 18 April 1920, UKNA FO 271 / 5052.

397. Jackson to Bristol, 9 April 1920, USNA RG 84, Turkey (Constantinople), Vol. 418. Jackson was fed information by Muslim and Jewish travelers from Antep.

398. Nazaretian to Kurkjian, 11 May 1920, USNA RG 59, 867.00, Roll 9.

399. "Condensed Diary of L. A. Shepard April 15–27, 1920," in UKNA FO 371 / 5052; and Boyd to Jackson, 21 April 1920, USNA RG 84, Turkey (Constantinople), Vol. 419.

400. Harris, untitled memorandum, 22 April 1920, Houghton ABC 16.9.1, Vol. 1; Shepard, "Statement . . . ," 18 April 1920, UKNA FO 371 / 5052; and "Condensed Diary of L. A. Shepard, April 15–27, 1920," UKNA FO 371 / 5052.

401. Shepard, "Statement . . . ," 18 April 1920, UKNA FO 371/5052.

402. "[Shepard] Condensed Diary . . . ," UKNA FO 371/5052.

403. Dodd to Peet, 14 April 1920, USNA RG 84, Turkey (Constantinople), Vol. 419.

404. A. C. Wratislaw, UK consul general, Beirut, to Foreign Secretary, 7 May 1920, UKNA FO 371/5048.

405. Salaheddin, OC 2nd Battalion, 176th Regiment, to Bristol (?), 1 May 1920, USNA RG 59, 860J.01/520–860J.4016/49, Roll 4.

406. Merrill, "Statement Regarding Interview with General Gouraud and His Secretary," 13 May 1920, USNA RG 59, 867.00, Roll 9.

407. Wratislaw to Foreign Secretary, 7 May 1920, UKNA FO 371/5048.

408. "Translation of a copy of a letter from Col. Brémond of the French Army of the Orient to the French consul at Larnaca. The document was secured by Dr. Dodd at Adana and sent to Constantinople," 13 June 1920, Houghton ABC 16.9.3, Vol. 50. About transferring orphans to Cyprus, see Gouraud to French government, 11 May 1920, SHD, N7, 4165.

409. Derby to FO, 24 April 1920; and FO to Aneurin Williams, 28 April 1920, both in UKNA FO 371/5047; and Grahame, Paris, to FO, 3 June 1920, UKNA FO 371/5049.

410. "Extract of Armenian Patriarch's Letter dated 7th May, Paris, 1920," UKNA FO 371/5049.

411. Zeidner, *Tricolor over the Taurus,* 247.

412. Bristol to Lambert, 17 June 1920, quoting an Armenian Patriarchate report, USNA RG 84, Turkey (Constantinople), Vol. 421. See also Atatürk, *Speech Delivered by Ghazi Mustapha Kemal,* 390–391.

413. Wratislaw to Foreign Secretary, 7 May 1920, UKNA FO 371/5048.

414. Jackson to Bristol, 19 May 1920, USNA RG 84, Turkey (Constantinople), Vol. 421.

415. Wratislaw (UK Beirut consulate) to FO, 1 May 1920, UKNA FO 371/5047.

416. Hassan, mufti of Urfa, to US high commissioner, 12 February 1920, USNA RG 84, Turkey (Constantinople), Vol. 419.

417. Ali Riza to French high commissioner, 19 April 1920, USNA RG 84, Turkey (Constantinople), Vol. 419; and Garnet Woodward, "The Siege of Ourfa, 8th February 1920, to 10th April 1920," 24 April 1920, attached to Jackson to Bristol, 26 April 1920, USNA RG 84, Turkey (Constantinople), Vol. 419.

418. "Excerpts from the Diary of Mrs. Richard (Beatrice) Mansfield Concerning the Siege of Ourfa, February 6th to April 16th, [19]20," attached to Jackson to Bristol, 8 May 1920, USNA RG 84, Turkey (Constantinople), Vol. 419.

419. Ali Riza to French high commissioner, 19 April 1920, USNA RG 84, Turkey (Constantinople), Vol. 419.

420. Charles Weeden, treasurer, NER Urfa, to Jackson, 12 April 1920, USNA RG 84, Turkey (Constantinople), Vol. 419.

421. Garnet Woodward, "The Evacuation of Ourfa, April 10 1920," attached to British consulate general (Beirut) to Foreign Secretary, 27 April 1920, UKNA FO 371/5047.

422. Mary Caroline Holmes to Jackson, 25 June 1920, USNA RG 84, Turkey (Constantinople), Vol. 421.

423. Charles Weeden Jr., NER Urfa, to Jackson, 12 April 1920, USNA RG 59, 867.00, Roll 9.

424. Woodward, "The Evacuation . . . ," UKNA FO 371/5047.

425. Mary Caroline Holmes (Urfa) to Jackson, 12 April 1920, USNA RG 59, 867.00, Roll 9.

426. Ali Riza to French high commissioner, 19 April 1920, USNA RG 84, Turkey (Constantinople), Vol. 419.

427. Garnet Woodward, "The Siege of Ourfa, 8th February 1920, to 10th April 1920," 24 April 1920, attached to Jackson to Bristol, 26 April 1920, USNA RG 84, Turkey (Constantinople), Vol. 419.

428. Holmes to Jackson, 12 April 1920, USNA RG 59, 867.00, Roll 9; Jackson to Bristol, 22 April 1920, USNA RG 59, 867.00, Roll 9; and Ali Riza to French HC, 19 April 1920, USNA RG 84, Turkey (Constantinople), Vol. 419. The French Army reported 150 survivors, "Syrie d'Asie" daily report, 28 April 1920, SHD, GR N7, 4165.

429. Holmes to Jackson, 25 June 1920, USNA RG 84, Turkey (Constantinople), Vol. 421.

430. A.F.L. in Beirut to War Ministry, 18 May 1922, SHD, GR N7, 4164.

431. "L'evacuation d'Ourfa," memorandum of the Bureau de presse et d'information Armenien, Paris, 28 April 1920, Bodl. MS Lord Bryce Papers 210.

432. Armenian Patriarchate, report from Aleppo, 30 June 1920, USNA RG 59, 860J.01/520–860J.4016/49, Roll 4.

433. Shepard, "Outline of Events at and Around Aintab, April to August 1920," undated but from September 1920, USNA RG 84, Turkey (Constantinople), Vol. 418.

434. "Note du Chef de Forces Nationalistes Turques à la population Armenienne d'Aintabe," 28 April 1920, UKNA FO 371/5048.

435. Jackson to Bristol, 27 May 1920, USNA RG 84, Turkey (Constantinople), Vol. 421; and "Official French Communication Under Date of May 25, 1920," appended to de Robeck to Curzon, 1 July 1920, UKNA FO 371/5053. See also French army report to ?, "Turquie d'Asie," 28 May 1920, SHD, GR N7, 4165. The numbers appear to be exaggerated.

436. Shepard, "Outline of Events at and Around Aintab, April to August 1920," undated but from September 1920, USNA RG 84, Turkey (Constantinople), Vol. 418.

437. Zeidner, *Tricolor over the Taurus,* 215. See also admiral in Beirut to Navy Ministry, Paris, 26 May 1920, SHD, GR N7, 4165.

438. Dodd (Adana) to Managing Director NER, C'ple, 24 May 1920, USNA RG 84, Turkey (Constantinople), Vol. 410.

439. Mustafa Kemal, "Copy of an Agreement Signed by the French and the Kemalists," 28/29 May 1920, Houghton ABC 16.9.3, Vol. 52; and "Erivan," a note attached to de Robeck to FO, 1 July 1920, UKNA FO 371/5053.

440. Grahame (Paris) to Curzon, 4 June 1920, UKNA FO 371/5049.

441. Captain G. M. Crick, "Report on My Recent Visit to Beirut, Haifa, Acre and Jaffa," 6 June 1920, UKNA FO 371/5278.

442. Dodd to Bristol, 5 June 1920, USNA RG 84, Turkey (Constantinople), Vol. 418.

443. Wallace (Paris) to SecState (DC), 29 June 1920, USNA RG 59, 867.00, Roll 9.

444. Faisal to Allenby and/or Curzon, 5 June 1920, UKNA FO 371/5035.

445. Unsigned, "Report of Adana Station for the Month of June 1920," undated, Houghton ABC 16.9.1, Vol. 1; and de Robeck to FO, 16 June 1920, UKNA FO 371/5050. See also "Renseignements, Semaine du 1 au 7 Juin 1920," UKNA FO 371/5052.

446. Wallace (Paris) to SecState, 23 June 1920, USNA RG 59, 867.00, Roll 9.

447. Wratslaw (Beirut) to FO, 25 June 1920, and high commissioner, Cyprus, to FO, 23 June 1920, both in UKNA FO 371/5051. See also Commander of Military Forces, Constantinople, to Navy Ministry, Paris, 21 June 1920, SHD, GR N7, 4165.

448. Chambers to British High Commission, 15 September 1920, UKNA FO 371/5210.

449. Jackson to Knabenshue, 7 June 1920, USNA RG 84, Turkey (Constantinople), Vol. 419.

450. De Robek to Curzon, encl. 2 (Armenian Patriarchate Report), 28 July 1920, UKNA FO 371/5054.

451. Jackson to Bristol, 14 June 1920, USNA RG 84, Turkey (Constantinople), Vol. 418.

452. "Minutes of the 42nd Meeting of the A.G.S. and Armenian and Greek Representatives," 14 July 1920, UKNA FO 371/5214.

453. Shepard, "Outline of Events at and Around Aintab April to August 1920," undated but early September 1920, USNA RG 84, Turkey (Constantinople), Vol. 418. See also de Robek to Curzon, encl. 2 (Armenian Patriarchate Report), 28 July 1920, UKNA FO 371/5054.

454. "Minutes of the 42nd Meeting of the A.G.S. and Armenian and Greek Representatives," 14 July 1920, UKNA FO 371/5214.

455. Zeidner, *Tricolor over the Taurus,* 250.

456. Armenian Patriarchate, report from Adana from 18 July 1920, attached to Bristol to SecState, 23 October 1920, USNA RG 59, 860J.4016/50–860J.4016P81/99.

457. Lieutenant de V. Rolland to Navy Ministry, 25 September 1920, SHD GR N7, 4165.

458. Lieutenant de V. Rolland to Navy Ministry, 25 September 1920, SHD GR N7, 4165.

459. Olin Lee, YMCA, to F. D. Steger, 14 August 1920, USNA RG 84, Turkey (Constantinople), Vol. 419.

460. Armenian Patriarchate, report from Mersin, 21 September 1920, attached to Bristol to SecState, 6 November 1920, USNA RG 59, 860J.00–860J.01, Roll 1.

461. Armenian Patriarchate, report from Aleppo, 18 September 1920, attached to de Robeck to Curzon, 25 October 1920, UKNA FO 371/5210.

462. Chambers to British High Commission, 15 September 1920, UKNA FO 371/5210.

463. Unsigned, from Mersin, "Letter Descriptive of Situation in Adana on September 24, 1920," attached to de Robeck to Curzon, 18 October 1920, UKNA FO 371/5210; and De Robeck to FO, 13 October 1920, UKNA FO 371/5040.

464. Chambers to Peet, 5 November 1921, USNA RG 59, 860J.4016/50–860J.4016P81/99, Roll 5.

465. Armenian Patriarchate, report from Mersin, 27 September 1920, attached to Bristol to SecState, 6 November 1920, USNA RG 59, 860J.00–860J.01, Roll 1.

466. Unsigned, "Letter Descriptive of Situation in Adana on September 24, 1920," UKNA FO 371/5210; and American Committee for Armenian Independence to State Department, 4 November 1920, USNA RG 59, 860J.00–860J.01/179, Roll 1.

467. Armenian Patriarchate report from Mersin, 21 September 1920, attached to Bristol to SecState, 6 November 1920, USNA RG 59, 860J.00–860J.01, Roll 1.

468. Armenian Patriarchate, report from Mersin, 27 September 1920, attached to Bristol to SecState, 6 November 1920, USNA RG 59, 860J.00–860J.01, Roll 1.

469. D. G. Osborne, FO, to Aneurin Williams, 10 December 1920, UKNA FO 371/5211, conveying the gist of a report by Gouraud.

470. Boyd, "General Statement Concerning Conditions in Aintab, June 15th to October 19, 1920," USNA RG 84, Turkey (Constantinople), Vol. 418; and Willson to Bristol, 20 October 1920, USNA RG 84, Turkey (Constantinople), Vol. 418.

471. Boyd to Miss Maubry, 6 September 1920, USNA RG 84, Turkey (Constantinople), Vol. 418.

472. Treasurer, NER Aleppo, to Nicol, 5 August 1920, USNA RG 84, Turkey (Constantinople), Vol. 418; and Boyd to Miss Maubry, 6 September 1920, USNA RG 84, Turkey (Constantinople), Vol. 418.

473. Boyd, "General Statement Concerning Conditions in Aintab, June 15th to October 19, 1920," undated but attached to Willson to Bristol, 21 October 1920, USNA RG 84, Turkey (Constantinople), Vol. 418.

474. Aneurin Williams, British Armenia Committee, "Cilicia," 8 June 1920, UKNA FO 371/5049.

475. Merrill, "Statement Regarding Interview with General Gouraud and His Secretary," 13 May 1920, USNA RG 59, 867.00, Roll 9.

476. Earl of Derby to Curzon, 7 June 1920, UKNA FO 371/5049.

477. Shepard, "Outline . . . ," USNA RG 84, Turkey (Constantinople), Vol. 418.

478. Shepard to ?, 19 September 1920, USNA RG 84, Turkey (Constantinople), Vol. 418.

479. Boyd, Aintab, to NER director, Aleppo, 1 September 1920, USNA RG 84, Turkey (Constantinople), Vol. 418; and Ernest Altanuniyan (?) (Aleppo) to Jackson, 11 September 1920, USNA RG 59, 860J.4016P81/600–860J.48/199, Roll 7.

480. Shepard to ?, 19 September 1920, USNA RG 84, Turkey (Constantinople), Vol. 418.

481. Willson to Bristol, 1 October 1920, USNA RG 84, Turkey (Constantinople), Vol. 421.

482. Boyd to Knudsen, 21 September 1920, USNA RG 84, Turkey (Constantinople), Vol. 418.

483. Zeidner, *Tricolor over the Taurus,* 255.

484. Fontana (Beirut) to Curzon, 15 October 1920, UKNA FO 371/5040.

485. Willson to Bristol, 6 October 1920, USNA RG 84, Turkey (Constantinople), Vol. 418.

486. "Politique Française a l'egard des Armeniens de Syrie-Cilicie," attachment to WO to Under Secretary of State, Foreign Office, 16 November 1920, UKNA FO 371/5210.

487. Willson to Bristol, 24 December 1920, USNA RG 84, Turkey (Constantinople), Vol. 418.

488. Basil Gabriel, Adana YMCA, to Steger, Constantinople, 1 January 1921, attached to Steger to Bristol, 28 January 1921, USNA RG 84, Turkey (Constantinople), Vol. 439.

489. YMCA Adana to Steger, senior secretary YMCA, Constantinople, 1 January 1920, USNA RG 84, Turkey (Constantinople), Vol. 439.

490. Shaw, *From Empire to Republic,* vol. 3, part 2, 1398.

491. Willson to Bristol, 11 February 1920, USNA RG 84, Turkey (Constantinople), Vol. 440.

492. Bristol to SecState, 30 June 1921, USNA RG 84, Turkey (Constantinople), Vol. 444.

493. Nicol to Bristol, 20 September 1920, USNA RG 84, Turkey (Constantinople), Vol. 444.

494. Adana YMCA to Steger, senior secretary YMCA, Constantinople, 1 January 1920, USNA RG 84, Turkey (Constantinople), Vol. 439.

495. "Account by D. T. Eby of the Siege of Hadjin," undated, attached to de Robeck to Curzon, 6 July 1920, UKNA FO 371/5053.

496. Manoogian, "The Annihilation of Hadjin," 15 November 1920, Bodl. MS Lord Bryce Papers 207.

497. Manoogian, "The Annihilation of Hadjin," 15 November 1920, Bodl. MS Lord Bryce Papers 207.

498. Zeidner, *Tricolor over the Taurus,* 208.

499. Edith Cold (Talas) to Bell, 22 June 1920, Houghton ABC 16.9.2, Vol. 5. Kurds were also cited for their protection of Armenians and missionaries in Mamuret-ül-Aziz vilayet (Bessy Bannerman Murdock, "Report of Work Completed at Arabkir Branch of Harput Near East Relief Unit November 1, 1919–April 1, 1922," 14 June 1922, USNA RG 84, Turkey (Constantinople), Vol. 464).

500. Special Bureau *(Kalem-i mahsus)* to mutesarriflik of Maraş, 25 February 1920, BOA, DH. ŞFR, 107/128.

501. Manoogian, "The Annihilation . . . ," 15 November 1920, Bodl. MS Lord Bryce Papers 207.

502. Dodd to Managing Director, NER, Constantinople, 10 March 1920, USNA RG 84, Turkey (Constantinople), Vol. 415.

503. "Account by D. T. Eby . . . ," UKNA FO 371/5053.

504. "Statement by Dr. Kennedy," undated but c. 28 May 1920, Houghton ABC 16.9.3, Vol. 52; and Manoogian, "The Annihilation . . . ," Bodl. MS Lord Bryce Papers 207.

505. Cold to Bell, 22 June 1920, Houghton ABC 16.9.2, Vol. 5. See also Super, *Massacre Averted,* 35–71.

506. Message from Mersin, 23 March 1920, in Armenian Patriarchate news round-up, sent to US high commission c. end of March 1920, USNA RG 59, 860J.01/52–860J.4016/49, Roll 4.

507. Armenian Patriarchate, report from Mersin, 27 September 1920, USNA RG 59, 860J.00–860J.01, Roll 1.

508. Manoogian, "The Annihilation . . . ," 15 November 1920, Bodl. MS Lord Bryce Papers 207.

509. Elizabeth Webb, "The Fall of Hadjin," undated but from early November 1920, Houghton ABC 16.9.1, Vol. 2.

510. Peet, "Memorandum," 10 February 1921, attached to Rumbold to Curzon, 14 February 1921, UKNA FO 371/6556.

511. Manoogian, "The Annihilation . . . ," 15 November 1920, Bodl. MS Lord Bryce Papers 207.

512. Elizabeth Webb, "The Fall of Hadjin," Houghton ABC 16.9.1, Vol. 2.

513. Manoogian, "The Annihilation . . . ," 15 November 1920, Bodl. MS Lord Bryce Papers 207.

514. Manoogian, "The Annihilation . . . ," 15 November 1920, Bodl. MS Lord Bryce Papers 207.

515. Peet, "Memorandum," 10 February 1921, attached to Rumbold to Curzon, 14 February 1921, UKNA FO 371/6556.

516. Bristol in effect denied the massacre; it was all hearsay—though he gave credence to reports of Armenian massacre and rape of Turks in Hacin (entry for 25 July 1921, LC, Bristol Papers, War Diary).

517. CO, USS *John D. Edwards,* to Bristol, 25 July 1920, USNA RG 84, Turkey (Constantinople), Vol. 421.

518. Armenian Patriarchate circular, 18 July 1920, USNA RG 59, 860J.4016/50–860J.4016P81/99, Roll 5.

519. Olin Lee to Steger, 14 August 1920, USNA RG 84, Turkey (Constantinople), Vol. 419.

520. Entry for 24 March 1921, LC, Bristol Papers, War Diary.

521. UK consulate general, Beirut, to Foreign Secretary, 31 January 1921, UKNA FO 371/6565.

522. Ernest Riggs to Barton, 15 January 1921, Houghton ABC 16.9.7, Vol. 26. Riggs was quoting Robert de Caix, the acting French High Commissioner in Syria.

523. Stanley Kerr to Aleppo director, NER, 2 September 1921, USNA RG 84, Turkey (Constantinople), Vol. 438; and Nicol to Bristol, 20 September 1921, USNA RG 84, Turkey (Constantinople), Vol. 444.

524. Yousif Ikaeb to American consul, Baghdad, 4 June 1921; and "Substance of Telegram Received from British High Commissioner at Baghdad," attached to Rattigan to Bristol, 8 July 1921, both in USNA RG 59, 867.00, Roll 10.

525. Rumbold to Curzon, 21 May 1921, UKNA FO 371/6557.

526. For example, 300 Maraş Armenians recruited to the battalions were murdered near Besny in August 1921 (Kerr to Doolittle, 29 August 1921, LC, Bristol Papers 35).

527. Rev. S. W. Gentle-Cackett to Rumbold, 21 July 1921, enclosing Gentle-Cackett, "How Zeitun Fell," undated, UKNA FO 371/6557. See also French report, 20 September 1921, USNA RG 84, Turkey (Constantinople), Vol. 438.

528. Satow to FO, 18 September 1921, UKNA FO 371/6557; Ward to Hughes, "Memorandum to Supplement the Report Made by Mr. F. D. Yowell and Dr. Mark H. Ward on the Conditions in the Interior of Asia Minor, dated May 5, 1922 and Addressed to the Hon. Charles E. Hughes, Secretary of State," undated but from summer 1922, USNA RG 59, 867.4016, Roll 47; and Olive Crawford to Peet, 25 April 1922, UKNA FO 371/7877.

529. Ward to Hughes, "Memorandum to Supplement the Report . . . ," undated but from summer 1922, USNA RG 59, 867.4016, Roll 47.

530. Rumbold to Oliphant, 3 October 1922, UKNA FO 371/7902.

531. Zeidner, *Tricolor over the Taurus,* 5.

532. Zeidner, *Tricolor over the Taurus,* 146. As Zeidner (149) points out, in 1919 the French abetted the escape of five wanted Turkish war criminals and later armed the Nationalists, even as their own forces were engaged against Kemal's troops in Cilicia.

533. "Despatch from His Majesty's Ambassador at Paris Enclosing the Franco-Turkish Agreement signed at Ankara on October 20, 1921"; and Youssouf Kemal to Franklin-Bouillon, 20 October 1921, both

in UKNA FO 371/6479. "Map No. 2" attached to Hardinge to Curzon, 30 October 1921, UKNA FO 371/6475, details the difference between the Sevres and Kemal–Franklin-Bouillon frontiers.

534. Legation of Greece to Vansittart, 5 December 1921, and attached text of the two "protocols," UKNA FO 371/6479; and Senior Naval Officer, Constantinople, to Commander-in-Chief, Mediterranean, "Situation Report," 2 December 1921, UKNA FO 371/7942.

535. Rumbold to Curzon, 31 October 1921, UKNA FO 371/6476.

536. Satow to Curzon, 14 November 1921, UKNA FO 371/6479.

537. CO, USS *Childs,* to Bristol, 5 January 1922, USNA RG 84, Turkey (Constantinople), Vol. 464.

538. W. J. Childs, "Notes of a Conversation with M. Franklin-Bouillon on January 27, 1922," London, 30 January 1922, UKNA FO 371/7854.

539. Mixed Armenian Council (Constantinople) to Bristol, 14 October 1921, USNA RG 84, Turkey (Constantinople), Vol. 439.

540. A.F.L. (Beirut) to War Ministry, 11 November 1921, SHD, GR N7, 4165.

541. Rumbold to Curzon, 8 November 1921, UKNA FO 371/6467.

542. Cyril Haas (Adana) to Peet, 5 November 1921; and Elizabeth Webb (Adana) to Peet, 6 November 1921, both in Houghton ABC 16.9.3, Vol. 52.

543. Chambers to Peet, 5 November 1921, USNA RG 59, 860J.4016/50–860J.4016P81/99, Roll 5.

544. Jackson to General de Lamothe, 17 November 1921, USNA RG 84, Turkey (Constantinople), Vol. 439.

545. Satow to Curzon, 14 November 1921, UKNA FO 371/6479.

546. Report by Lt. Col. Sarrou of meeting with Gen. Mouhieddin Pasha, 20 November 1921, USNA RG 84, Turkey (Constantinople), Vol. 464.

547. Chambers to Peet, 5 November 1921, USNA RG 59, 860J.4016/50–860J.4016P81/99, Roll 5.

548. "Cabinet 88 (21)," 22 November 1921, UKNA FO 371/6478.

549. Rumbold to Harry Lamb, 1 December 1921, Bodl. MS Rumbold Papers 29.

550. Franklin-Bouillon, Hamid Bey (under secretary of state at Ministry of Interior), and General Muhieddin Pasha, "Appeal to the Inhabitants of Cilicia," 22 November 1921, UKNA FO 371/7948.

551. R. S. Stewart to Knabenshue, 19 December 1921, USNA RG 84, Turkey (Constantinople), Vol. 459.

552. Jackson to Bristol, 1 May 1920, USNA RG 84, Turkey (Constantinople), Vol. 421.

553. Vartabed to Armenian Delegation in Paris, 10 April 1920, UKNA FO 371/5045.

554. Dodd to Barton, 25 March/2 April 1920, Houghton ABC 16.9.1, Vol. 1; and Dodd to Bristol, 9 April 1920, USNA RG 84, Turkey (Constantinople), Vol. 418.

555. Horton to SecState, 31 March 1920, USNA RG 59, 860J.01/520–860J.4016/49, Roll 4.

556. Dodd to Bristol, 9 April 1920, USNA RG 84, Turkey (Constantinople), Vol. 418; and Dodd to Peet, 14 April 1920, USNA RG 84, Turkey (Constantinople), Vol. 419.

557. Shaw, *From Empire to Republic,* vol. 2, 886.

558. Chambers (Adana) to Robert Graves (Constantinople), 9 April 1920, UKNA FO 371/5048.

559. Horton (Smyrna) to SecState, 31 March 1920, USNA RG 59, 867.00, Roll 6.

560. Dodd to Bristol, 9 April 1920, USNA RG 84, Turkey (Constantinople), Vol. 418.

561. Dodd to Peet, 14 April 1920, USNA RG 84, Turkey (Constantinople), Vol. 419.

562. Dodd to Barton, 25 March/2 April 1920, Houghton ABC 16.9.1, Vol. 1.

563. Willson to Bristol, 16 September 1920, USNA RG 84, Turkey (Constantinople), Vol. 422; and Willson to Bristol, 18 November 1920, USNA RG 84, Turkey (Constantinople), Vol. 419.

564. Joseph Bliss and Harold Buxton, Lord Mayor's Fund, to Under Secretary of State, Colonial Office, 7 April 1920, UKNA FO 371/5045.

565. High commissioner, Cyprus, to FO, 23 June 1920, UKNA FO 371/5051.

566. Robinson to under secretary of state FO, 11 April 1920, UKNA FO 371/5046.

567. By 1924 there were about 100,000 Armenians in the United States, most of them recent immigrants. Thereafter, Armenian immigration to the United States slowed substantially as a result of that year's Immigration Act (see de Waal, *Great Catastrophe,* 104).

568. Jackson to Bristol, 26 May 1920, USNA RG 84, Turkey (Constantinople), Vol. 421.

569. French report from Aleppo, 14 October 1921, USNA RG 84, Turkey (Constantinople), Vol. 458.

570. Bristol to Bayard Dodge, 14 November 1921, USNA RG 84, Turkey (Constantinople), Vol. 444.

571. Webb to Curzon, 18 April 1920, UKNA FO 371/5046.

572. Armenian Patriarchate, report from Constantinople, 15 October 1920, attached to Bristol to SecState, 6 November 1920, USNA RG 59, 860J.00–860J.01, Roll 1.

573. De Robeck to Curzon, 17 October 1920, UKNA FO 371/5210.

574. Greek Legation, London, to Curzon, 9 November 1921, UKNA FO 371/65558; and entry for 15 November 1921, LC, Bristol Papers, War Diary.

575. For example, see Annie Davies to Miss Wallis, 13 November 1921, UKNA FO 371/6560, for an incident in Adana.

576. "Minutes of 78th [?] Meeting of the A.G.S. and Armenian and Greek Representatives," 21 December 1921, UKNA FO 371/7933.

577. Jackson to General de Lamothe, 17 November 1921, USNA RG 84, Turkey (Constantinople), Vol. 439.

578. Woodsmall, "Report on a Trip to Adana, December 1921," undated, USNA RG 84, Turkey (Constantinople), Vol. 461.

579. For Turkish description of these events, see Eken, *Kapancızade Hamit Bey,* 297–307.

580. Report by G. Mackereth, acting vice-consul, Beirut, 16 December 1921, attached to Satow to Curzon, 17 December 1921, UKNA FO 371/6561. The French estimated that a thousand refugees a day reached Mersin from the interior (Gouraud to War Ministry, 28 November 1921, SHD, GR N7, 4165).

581. Jackson to Bristol, 9 November 1921, USNA RG 84, Turkey (Constantinople), Vol. 440.

582. Pakan Catiacos, Adana, to Pere Haroutune Yosayian, 10 November 1921, LC, Bristol Papers 36.

583. Annie Davies to Miss Wallis, 13 November 1921, UKNA FO 371/6560.

584. Ralph Harlow, Smyrna, to Officers of the ABC, 1 December 1921, Houghton ABC 16.9.3, Vol. 51.

585. "Minutes of the 77th Meeting of the A.G.S. and Armenian and Greek Representatives," 7 December 1921, UKNA FO 371/6549.

586. "Memorandum by Mr. Oliphant," 22 November 1921, UKNA FO 371/6559; and Pere Tavoukdjian to Briand, undated but from November 1921, LC, Bristol Papers 36.

587. Unsigned, "Report for [Aintab Central Turkey] College Year 1921–1922," undated, Houghton ABC 16.9.1, A467, Reel 674; and James Morgan to Curzon, 7 January 1922, UKNA FO 371/7872; and "Latest Aintab News," January 1923, "What Has Happened at Aintab. Complete Evacuation of the City by the Armenians," by John Merrill, Houghton ABC 16.9.1, A467, Reel 674.

588. James Morgan, British Consulate, Aleppo, to Foreign Secretary, 10 December 1921, UKNA FO 371/6561.

589. Armenian National Union, Aleppo, to French High Commissioner for Syria and Lebanon, 2 March 1922, USNA RG 84, Turkey (Constantinople), Vol. 459.

590. Armenian notables to mutesarrif, 27 June 1922, attached to Rumbold to Curzon, 12 August 1922, UKNA FO 371/7874.

591. "Memorandum by Mr. Ryan," undated but attached to Rumbold to Curzon, 12 August 1922, UKNA FO 371/7874; and Morgan to Curzon, 7 January 1922, UKNA FO 371/7872.

592. Ruth Woodsmall, acting executive, YWCA Near East, "Report on a Trip to Adana, December 1921," undated, USNA RG 84, Turkey (Constantinople), Vol. 461. On Dörtyol, see Satow to Curzon, 20 January 1922, UKNA FO 371/7872.

593. Pakan Catiacos, Adana, to Pere Haroutune Yosayian, Aleppo, 10 November 1921, LC, Bristol Papers 36.

594. Rumbold to Curzon, 20 December 1921, UKNA FO 371/6561.

595. Morgan, Aleppo, to Curzon, 8 April 1922, UKNA FO 371/7874.

596. Entry for 15 November 1921, LC, Bristol Papers, War Diary.

597. Lt. Commander J. C. Cunningham, OC USS *Williamson,* to Bristol, "Visit of USS Williamson to Mersina Area," diary, 18 November–11 December 1921, USNA RG 84, Turkey (Constantinople), Vol. 464.

598. Entry for 22 November 1921, LC, Bristol Papers, War Diary.

599. I. H. Mayfield, CO USS *Childs,* diary, entry for 11 December 1921, USNA RG 84, Turkey (Constantinople), Vol. 464.

600. Greek Legation, London, to Curzon, 9 November 1921, UKNA FO 371/6558. The French estimated that a thousand left Mersin per day (Gouraud to War Ministry, 25 October 1921, SHD, GR N7, 4165).

601. J. C. Cunningham, OC USS *Williamson,* to Bristol, "Visit of USS Williamson to Mersina Area," diary entries for 23 November and 1 December 1921, USNA RG 84, Turkey (Constantinople), Vol. 464.

602. Eyre Crowe to Bell, 2 December 1921, UKNA FO 371/6559.

603. Jackson to Bristol, 16 November 1921, USNA RG 84, Turkey (Constantinople), Vol. 444; and "Minutes of 78th [?] Meeting of the A.G.S. and Armenian and Greek Representatives," 21 December 1921, UKNA FO 371/7933. By then, caravans had arrived in Aleppo from Antep, Mersin, Urfa, and Diyarbekir (Gouraud to War Ministry, 29 November 1921, SHD, GR N7, 4165). See also Satow, Beirut, to Foreign Secretary, 25 November 1921, UKNA FO 371/6560.

604. Greek Legation, London, to Curzon, 3 December 1921, UKNA FO 371/6559; and James Morgan, UK consul, Aleppo, to Foreign Secretary, 3 December 1921, UKNA FO 371/6561.

605. Woodsmall, "Report on a Trip to Adana, December 1921," undated, USNA RG 84, Turkey (Constantinople), Vol. 461.

606. Mayfield, CO USS *Childs,* diary, entries for 11 (?) and 13–14 December 1921, USNA RG 84, Turkey (Constantinople), Vol. 464. Bristol suspected that, while pretending to accept his advice, the NER executives were secretly encouraging their field workers to expatriate the orphans (entry for 5 June 1922, Bristol War Diary, USNA RG 59, 867.00, Roll 11).

607. Assistant director NER, Aleppo, L. Hekinian, to managing Director, NER Beirut, 26 June 1923, UKNA FO N371/9098.

608. Consul Charles Allen to Bristol, 6 February 1922, USNA RG 59, 867.4016, Roll 46.

609. John Merrill, "Latest Aintab News," April 1923, Houghton ABC 16.9.6.1, Reel 674.

610. "Extracts from letter from the Rev. S. S. Manoogian," 27 April 1922, UKNA FO 371/7874.

611. Woodsmall, "Report of a Trip to Adana, December 1921," undated, USNA RG 84, Turkey (Constantinople), Vol. 461.

612. Entry for 3 January 1922, LC, Bristol Papers, War Diary.

613. Rumbold to Curzon, 12 August 1922, UKNA FO 371/7874.

614. John Merrill, "The Latest News from Aintab," 18 March 1922, Houghton ABC 16.9.6.1, A467, Reel 674; and R. E. Wilson, Mersina, to Ravndal, 2 January 1921 [sic, should be 1922], USNA RG 59, 867.00, Roll 10.

615. Rumbold to Balfour, 27 June 1922, enclosing text of "Le Loi des Biens Abandonnés," 20 April 1922; and minute by Rendel, 7 July 1922, both in UKNA FO 371/7948.

616. "Extract from letter, Adana, dated February 8th, 1922," UKNA FO 371/7874; and James Morgan, Aleppo, to Curzon, 22 March 1922, UKNA FO 371/7874.

617. Phillips, acting US HC, to SecState, 19 October 1922, USNA RG 84, Turkey (Constantinople), Vol. 464.

618. Maynard B. Barnes, Smyrna, "Evacuation of Christian Population of Western Anatolia," 12 October 1922, USNA RG 84, Turkey (Constantinople), Vol. 464.

619. A.F.L., Beirut, to War Ministry, 29 November 1922, SHD, GR N7, 4165.

620. FO to A. Geddes (Washington), 9 November 1922, UKNA FO 371/7957.

621. Bristol to SecState, 19 November 1922, USNA RG 84, Turkey (Constantinople), Vol. 464.

622. Child, Grew to SecState, 23 November 1922, USNA RG 59, 867.4016, Roll 48.

623. L. Hekimian (or Hekinian), Aleppo, 8 November 1922, UKNA FO 371/9098.

624. H. B. McFee, Managing Director NER, Beirut, to Jaquith, 23 October 1922, USNA RG 84, Turkey (Constantinople), Vol. 465.

625. Entry for 25 October 1922, diary of Commanding Officer (USS *Overton?*), to Bristol, USNA RG 84, Turkey (Constantinople), Vol. 462.

626. Morgan (Aleppo) to Curzon, 15 November 1922, UKNA FO 371/7875.

627. US high commission, "Memorandum," 3 November 1922, USNA RG 84, Turkey (Constantinople), Vol. 464; and Bristol to SecState, 7 November 1922, USNA RG 84, Turkey (Constantinople), Vol. 464.

628. Smart (Aleppo) to Curzon, 17 January 1923, UKNA FO 371/9129.

629. Lorrin Shepard, Aintab, to "Ernest," 6 December 1922, Houghton ABC 16.9.2, Vol. 5.

630. Dr. Caroline Hamilton, Aintab, to Miss Lamson, 6 December 1922, Houghton ABC 16.9.2, Vol. 2.

631. Shepard to Ernest, 6 December 1922, Houghton ABC 16.9.2, Vol. 5.

632. John Merrill, "Latest Aintab News, January 1923. What has Happened at Aintab. Complete Evacuation of the City by the Armenians," Houghton ABC 16.9.1, A467, Reel 674. See also Jackson to Bristol, "Expelling of Christians by Turks," 28 November 1922, USNA RG 84, Turkey (Constantinople), Vol. 459.

633. Kieser, "Introduction," in Kieser, ed., *Turkey beyond Nationalism,* ix.

634. "Enclosure No. 1 with Despatch No. 404," August 1922, USNA RG 84, Turkey (Constantinople), Vol. 461; and Jackson to Bristol, ? November 1922, USNA RG 84, Turkey (Constantinople), Vol. 464.

635. Shepard to Ernest, 6 December 1922, Houghton ABC 16.9.2, Vol. 5; and Merrill, "Latest Aintab News, January 1923. What has Happened at Aintab. Complete Evacuation of the City by the Armenians," Houghton ABC 16.9.1, A467, Reel 674.

636. Hekinian, "Refugee Situation," 11 December 1923, attached to Vaughn-Russell to Foreign Secretary, 14 December 1923, UKNA FO 371/10195.

637. Jackson, "Emigration of Christians from Turkish Territory," 11 December 1922, USNA RG 84, Turkey (Constantinople), Vol. 459, and attached affidavits by Sarkissian, Yeghoyian, and Arakelian.

638. Hekinian, Aleppo, to NER managing director, Beirut, 28 August 1923, UKNA FO 371/9098.

639. Hekinian, "Refugee Situation," undated but attached to Smart, Aleppo, to Foreign Secretary, 29 January 1924, UKNA FO 371/10159.

640. Jackson, "Expelling of Christians by Turks," 28 November 1922, USNA RG 84, Turkey (Constantinople), Vol. 459.

641. Ravndal to Bristol, 3 May 1923, USNA RG 84, Turkey (Constantinople), Vol. 484. The 100,000 figure for Anatolia seems excessive, unless it includes "Islamized" Armenians.

642. Barton to SecState, 18 (?) September 1923, quoting report by the American missionary Rev. J. C. Martin, USNA RG 59, 860J.4016P81/600–860J.48/199, Roll 7.

643. A.F.L. in Beirut to War Ministry, 7 February 1923, SHD, GR N7, 4165.

644. Paul Buhrman, "Political and Economic Conditions, Aleppo District," 19 November 1923, USNA RG 84, Turkey (Constantinople), Vol. 479.

645. Buhrman to SecState, 10 May 1924, USNA RG 59, 867.4016, Roll 48.

646. Dobbs to Colonial Secretary, 29 April 1924, and Hough (Aleppo) to MacDonald, 2 June 1924, both in UKNA FO 371/101095. Russell to Foreign Secretary, 20 February 1924, UKNA FO 371/10195. "So much for the minority provisions of the Treaty of Lausanne," minuted George Rendel, 10 March 1924.

647. Buhrman to SecState, 23 February 1924, USNA RG 59, 867.4016, Roll 48.

648. C. B. Wylie, Standard Oil, "Report on Inspection Trip through Anatolia," 6 August 1924, attached to Scotten to Secstate, 15 August 1924, USNA RG 59, 867.00, Roll 17.

649. Buhrman, US consul, Aleppo, to SecState, 13 February 1924, and Buhrman to SecState, 11 March 1924, both in USNA RG 59, 867.4016, Roll 48.

650. Buhrman to SecState, 11 March 1924, USNA RG 59, 867.4016, Roll 48.

651. Internal report, 9 March 1924, BOA, HR. IM, 239 34. See also 11 March 1924, BOA, HR. IM, 239 37.

652. Buhrman to SecState, 24 March 1924, USNA RG 59, 867.4016, Roll 48.

653. John Randolph, "Economic and Political Information re Turkey: The Mosul Question, etc.," 12 March 1924, USNA RG 59, 867.00, Roll 15.

654. Buhrman to SecState, 11 April 1924, USNA RG 59, 867.4016, Roll 48.

655. Russell to Foreign Secretary, 24 March 1924, UKNA FO 371/10195.

656. *Times* (London), 5 April 1924, and Rendel minute, 7 April 1924, UKNA FO 371/10195. It is possible that the Interior Ministry order pertained not to Anatolian residents but to Armenians living abroad not being allowed to enter this area, but Rendel pointed out that "remaining Christians" within the forbidden zone "are being vigorously expelled from many [of its] districts."

657. George Seldes, "Chaldeans Outraged and Massacred by Turks," datelined 18 October, Mosul, *Los Angeles Times,* 25 October 1925. Seldes interviewed escapees, priests, and British officials.

658. John Randolph, US consul, Baghdad, to SecState, 14 April 1926, and Randolph, "Alleged Turkish Persecution of Minorities Continues in Azakh Village North of Iraq Frontier," 15 March 1927, both in USNA RG 59, 867.4016, Roll 48.

659. De Waal, *Great Catastrophe,* 100.

660. Thomsen, "The Assyrians/Syriacs of Turkey," 3. See also Karimova and Deverell, "Minorities in Turkey," 12.

661. Gaunt, "Ottoman Treatment of the Assyrians," 245.

662. Assyrian-Chaldean delegation, Paris, "The Assyrian-Chaldean Question before the Peace Conference," undated but from 1919, USNA RG 84, Turkey (Constantinople), Vol. 404.

663. Political officer, UK administration Baghdad, to ?, 26 December 1918, UKNA FO 371/3386.

664. Curzon, "Memorandum," 13 November 1919, UKNA FO 371.

665. Kevorkian, *Armenian Genocide,* 94, cites a report indicating that 1,272 Syriac Christians were murdered during the Adana massacres.

666. Gaunt, *Massacres,* 92.

667. Captain G. S. Reed, "Mesopotamia: Assyrian Refugees in Baqubah," 1 July 1919, UKNA FO 371/4192.

668. Gaunt, *Massacres,* 90–92.

669. E. W. McDowell to Allen Dulles, 14 August 1923, and attached untitled memorandum, 14 August 1923, by McDowell, an American missionary, USNA RG 84, Turkey (Constantinople), Vol. 479. Gaunt says the Assyrian tribal "declaration of war" against the Ottomans was issued in May 1915, months after the Turks started butchering them (Gaunt, *Massacres,* 123).

670. Kaiser, *Extermination of Armenians,* 125–126; and Gaunt, *Massacres,* 127.

671. Gaunt, *Massacres,* 123.

672. E. T. Allen, "Outline of Events in the District of Urumia, and the Syrian Connection Therewith, Since the Beginning of the War," undated, *U.S. Official Records,* 603; W. A. Shedd to J. L. Caldwell, US

minister, Teheran "[Report from Persia]," 23 June 1915, *U.S. Official Records,* 479; and Gaunt, *Massacres,* 123.

673. Gaunt, *Massacres,* 137–138.

674. Gaunt, *Massacres,* 128.

675. Gaunt, "Ottoman Treatment of the Assyrians," 247–249; and Gaunt, *Massacres,* 125.

676. Suny, *They Can Live in the Desert,* 234.

677. Gaunt, *Massacres,* 131.

678. Quoted in Gaunt, *Massacres,* 133–134.

679. Gaunt, *Massacres,* 136–137.

680. Gaunt, *Massacres,* 140.

681. "Refugees from the Hakkiari District: Series of Extracts from Letters by Members of the American Mission Board at Urmia," and "Refugees from Hakkiari: Letter, Dated 26th September/9th October, 1915, from a Relative of Mar Shimun, the Patriarch," Bryce and Toynbee, eds., *Treatment of Armenians,* 172–173 and 175–176; and Gaunt, *Massacres,* 145.

682. Hofmann, "Cumulative Genocide," 49.

683. Kevorkian, *Armenian Genocide,* 379–380.

684. Kevorkian, *Armenian Genocide,* 376.

685. Gaunt, "Ottoman Treatment of the Assyrians," 246.

686. Kevorkian, *Armenian Genocide,* 371–374; and Kaiser, *Extermination of Armenians,* 324.

687. Gaunt, "Ottoman Treatment of the Assyrians," 256–257.

688. Kevorkian, *Armenian Genocide,* 340.

689. Morgenthau, *Ambassador Morgenthau's Story,* 307.

690. Kevorkian, *Armenian Genocide,* 379–380.

691. Shedd to Caldwell, 23 June 1915 "[Report from Persia]," *U.S. Official Records,* 479; and Gaunt, *Massacres,* 62–64.

692. "Urmia Statement by the Rev. William A. Shedd, D.D. . . . ." Bryce and Toynbee, eds., *Treatment of Armenians,* 102.

693. "First Exodus from Urmia, January 1915: Report Dated 1st March 1915, from the Reverend Robert M. Labaree, of the American Mission Station at Tabriz; to the Hon. F. Willoughby Smith U.S. Consul at Tiflis; Communicated by the Board of Foreign Missions of the Presbyterian Church in the U.S.A.," Bryce and Toynbee, eds., *Treatment of Armenians,* 108–109.

694. Shedd to Caldwell, 23 June 1915, "[Report from Persia]," *U.S. Official Records,* 478.

695. "Urmia: Narrative of Dr. Jacob Sargis Recorded in a Despatch Dated Petrograd, 12th February, 1916," Bryce and Toynbee, eds., *Treatment of Armenians,* 160.

696. Shedd to Caldwell, 23 June 1915, "[Report from Persia]," *U.S. Official Records,* 482; Kevorkian, *Armenian Genocide,* 227; and Gaunt, *Massacres,* 81–84.

697. Khosroeva, "Assyrian Genocide," 271.

698. Gaunt, "Ottoman Treatment of the Assyrians," 253. Gaunt, *Massacres,* 104–105.

699. "Azerbaijan behind the Russian Front: Extracts from a Series of Letters by the Rev. Robert M. Labaree . . . Letter Dated Tabriz, 12th March, 1915 (to Mr. Labaree's Mother)," Bryce and Toynbee, eds., *Treatment of Armenians,* 110. Khosroeva, "Assyrian Genocide," 271, says the massacre at Gulpashan took place in January 1915.

700. Entry for 20 January 1915, "Urmia during the Turko-Kurdish Occupation: Diary of a Missionary edited by Miss Mary Schauffler Platt," Bryce and Toynbee, eds., *Treatment of Armenians,* 119–120.

701. Both quoted in Gaunt, *Massacres,* 107; see also 110–111.

702. Scheubner-Richter to Bethmann Hollweg, 4 December 1916, *German Foreign Office,* 694; and Gaunt, *Massacres,* 109–110.

703. For a description of the work of these missions and conditions in Urmia town during January–May 1915, see Gaunt, *Massacres,* 112–117.

704. "Urmia: Statement by the Rev. William A. Shedd . . . ," Bryce and Toynbee, eds., *Treatment of Armenians,* 103–104; Gaunt, *Massacres,* 115–116; and Shedd to Caldwell, 23 June 1915, "[Report from Persia]," *U.S. Official Records,* 479–481.

705. Kevorkian, *Armenian Genocide,* 389–390, 394.

706. E. T. Allen, "Outline of Events in the District of Urumia, and the Syrian Connection Therewith, Since the Beginning of the War," undated (but probably from April–June 1917), *U.S. Official Records,* 605.

707. Allen, "Outline of Events . . . ," undated, *U.S. Official Records,* 607–609; and Kevorkian, *Armenian Genocide,* 707–708.

708. J. M. Yonan and Pera Mirza, Assyrian Refugee Committee, "The Assyrian People and their Relations with the Allies in the Present War," undated but attached to Cox to Balfour, 30 December 1918, UKNA FO 371/4177; and Reed, "Mesopotamia: Assyrian Refugees at Baqubah," 1 July 1919, UKNA FO 371/4192.

709. McDowell, memorandum, 14 August 1923, USNA RG 84, Turkey (Constantinople), Vol. 479.

710. Atatürk, *Speech Delivered by Ghazi Mustapha Kemal,* 689.

711. McDowell, memorandum, 14 August 1923, USNA RG 84, Turkey (Constantinople), Vol. 479.

9. Turks and Greeks, 1919–1924

Epigraph: Pallavicini to Austrian Foreign Ministry, 31 November 1915, quoting Abdullah Noury Bey, former secretary general of the Special Organization and, from fall 1915, director of the Sub-Directorate of Deportees, Aleppo, in Kevorkian, *Armenian Genocide,* 627.

1. "Minutes of the 68th [?] Meeting of the Armenian-Greek Section and Armenian and Greek Representatives," 29 March 1922, UKNA FO 371/7933.

2. White, president of Anatolia College, Merzifon, to Warren D. Robbins, US State Department, 18 November 1921, USNA RG 59, 867.4016, Roll 46.

3. See minutes by Toynbee ("AJT"), 6 December 1918, and "ACK (?)," 4 December 1918, on a Pontic Greek memorandum from November 1918, UKNA FO 371/3419. Chrysanthos, archbishop of Trabzon; Constantine-Jason G. Constantinides, president of the Pan-Pontic Congress; and Socrates Oeconomos, president of the National League of the Euxine Pontus at Paris, to Lloyd George, 10 March 1920, UKNA FO 371/5192, gives the figure of 850,000 Greeks in the Pontus from a total population of 1.7 million in the empire. However, included in the figure for the Pontus are a quarter of a million Pontic Greeks exiled in southern Russia and Caucasia who, according to these men, wished to return.

4. Nationalist Government, "Certain Facts with Reference to the Greek Rebellion in the Pontus and the Steps Taken by the Turkish Government," undated but from May 1922, Bodl. MS Toynbee Papers 50.

5. McCarthy, *Death and Exile,* 288–289.

6. Atatürk, *Speech Delivered by Ghazi Mustapha Kemal,* 528.

7. Eken, *Kapancızade Hamit Bey,* 42.

8. Bristol to SecState, 18 November 1921, USNA RG 59, 860J.4016/50–860J.4016P81/99, Roll 5.

9. Heathcote-Smith, "Pontine Republic," 15 July 1919, attached to Gough-Calthorpe to Curzon, 25 July 1919, UKNA FO 371/4158; and Shaw, *From Empire to Republic,* vol. 2, 593.

10. Lt. Col. Ian Smith, General Staff "Intelligence," GHQ Army of the Black Sea, "Report on Situation in Samsun-Amasia district," 13 July 1919, UKNA FO 371/4158.

11. Atatürk, *Speech Delivered by Ghazi Mustapha Kemal,* 9–10.

12. Cebesoy, *Milli Mücadele Hatıraları,* 49.

13. Even Shaw was unable to demonstrate any substantial Ottoman Greek support for Pontic separatism (Shaw, *From Empire to Republic,* vol. 2, 582–585).

14. Rendel, "Turkish Massacres and Persecutions of Minorities since the Armistice," 20 March 1922, UKNA FO 371/7876.

15. White to Robbins, 18 November 1921, USNA RG 59, 867.4016, Roll 46.

16. Ralph Chesbrough, "Report on the Political, Military, Commercial and Economic Situation in Trebizond and the Surrounding Vilayets," 3 August 1919, attached to Ravndal to SecState, 18 August 1919, USNA RG 59, 867.00, Roll 7.

17. Shaw, *From Empire to Republic,* vol. 2, 592–593.

18. The high figure is given by Rendel, "Atrocities in Asia Minor Etc. Protests Received by His Majesty's Government, and Action Taken," 28 December 1921, UKNA FO 371/7875.

19. Eliot (Athens) to FO, 26 July 1915, UKNA FO 371/2487.

20. Morgenthau to wife, 7 December 1915, FDRL, HM Sr. Papers, Letters 473, quoting Tsamados, the Greek ambassador to Constantinople.

21. Unsigned, "Persecution and Annihilation of the Makri and Livissi Communities," undated, but probably from early 1919, attached to Gates to Heck, 4 February 1919, USNA RG 84, Turkey (Constantinople), Vol. 400. Almost all the Christians in the area were Greek.

22. Gough-Calthorpe to Balfour, 3 February 1919, and attached memorandum by "Representatives of Makri and Livissi," L. Eliou, R. Mousseos, and A. Stamatiades, "Persecution and Annihilation of the Makri and Livissi Communities," 27 January 1919, UKNA FO 371/4172.

23. Greek Patriarchate, "Persecution of the Greeks in Turkey, 1914–1918," undated but probably from 1919, Bodl. MS Toynbee Papers 57 (hereafter cited as Greek Patriarchate, "Persecution of the Greeks . . . ,"), 94–96, report from 2 February 1915.

24. Morgenthau to wife, 7 December 1915, FDRL, HM Sr. Papers, Letters 473, quoting Tsamados, the Greek ambassador to Constantinople.

25. Eliot (Athens) to FO, 26 July 1915, UKNA FO 371/2487.

26. Greek Ministry of Foreign Affairs, "Persecutions of the Greek Population in Turkey Since the Beginning of the European War According to Official Reports of Hellenic Diplomatic and Consular Agents," 1918, 11, quoting Greek consul in Konia, dispatch from 7 March 1917, Bodl. MS Toynbee Papers 57 (hereafter cited as Greek Foreign Ministry, "Persecutions of the Greek Population . . ."").

27. Hofmann, "Cumulative Genocide," 92–93.

28. Rendel, "Memorandum by Mr. Rendel on Conversation with Col. Rawlinson on 23rd May 1922," 24 May 1922, UKNA FO 371/7878.

29. Hofmann, Bjornlund, and Meichanetsidis, eds., *Genocide of the Ottoman Greeks,* 1.

30. Einstein, *Inside Constantinople,* entries for 3, 15, 17, and 19 May 1915, pp. 19, 44, 48, and 51–52.

31. Greek Patriarchate, "Persecution of the Greeks . . . ," 63 and 48–49.

32. Entry for 12 July 1915, Morgenthau, *United States Diplomacy on the Bosphorus,* 275; and Einstein, *Inside Constantinople,* entry for 28 July 1915, 202–203.

33. Allen to Ravndal, 5 March 1915, *U.S. Official Records,* 493; and Akçam, *Shameful Act,* 107.

34. Greek Patriarchate, "Persecution of the Greeks . . . ," 42–44.

35. Memorandum, probably by Greek Patriarchate, "Evacuation of the Different Towns and Villages and Violent Manner of Expelling their Inhabitants," undated but attached to Morgenthau to SecState, 10 August 1915, USNA RG 59, 867.4016, Roll 43.

36. Greek Patriarchate, "Persecution of the Greeks . . . ," 19–20.

37. Memorandum, probably by Greek Patriarchate, "Evacuation of the Different Towns and Villages and Violent Manner of Expelling their Inhabitants," undated but attached to Morgenthau to SecState, 10 August 1915, USNA RG 59, 867.4-16, Roll 43.

38. Greek Patriarchate, "Persecution of the Greeks . . . ," 49.

39. Greek Patriarchate, "Persecution of the Greeks . . . ," 83.

40. Greek Patriarchate, "Persecution of the Greeks . . . ," 109.

41. Youssouf Kemal to patriarch, undated but c. June 1915, in Greek Patriarchate, "Persecution of the Greeks . . . ," 142.

42. Henry Morgenthau to family, 22 July 1915, FDRL, HM Sr. Papers, Letters 475.

43. Morgenthau to "Folks," 17 May 1915, FDRL, HM Sr. Papers, Letters 474.

44. Morgenthau to SecState, 10 August 1915, USNA RG 59, 867.4016, Roll 43.

45. Talât to *mutasarrif* of Eskişehir, 9 August 1915, *Sevk ve Iskan,* 208, doc. 150.

46. Report by the Greek Legation, Constantinople, 8 September 1915, in Greek Foreign Ministry, "Persecutions of the Greek Population . . . ," 31; and Greek Patriarchate, "Persecution of the Greeks . . . ," 9–10 and 23.

47. Hofmann, "Cumulative Genocide," 56.

48. Greek Patriarchate, "Persecution of the Greeks . . . ," 33–35.

49. Jackson (Washington DC), untitled memorandum, 4 March 1918, USNA RG 59, 867.4016, Roll 46.

50. An American missionary to "friends," Erzurum, 26 February 1916, Houghton ABC 16.9.7, A467, Reel 716.

51. Greek Foreign Ministry, "Persecutions of the Greek Population . . . ," 33 (report by Greek Legation in Petrograd, 30 August 1916); and Greek Patriarchate, "Persecution of the Greeks . . . ," 110–111.

52. Greek Patriarchate, "Persecution of the Greeks . . . ," 127.

53. Greek Patriarchate, "Persecution of the Greeks . . . ," 100–105, quoting letter of 15 December 1916 from the metropolitan.

54. Hofmann, "Cumulative Genocide," 57–58.

55. Greek Patriarchate, "Persecution of the Greeks . . . ," 112–113, quoting letter from Chrysostomos, 12 October 1918.

56. British intelligence, "Refet Pasha (Ali Refet Pasha)," undated, UKNA FO 371/6501; and Greek Patriarchate, "Persecution of the Greeks . . . ," 120.

57. Lt. Earl Zimmer, USS *Olympia,* to CO, 8 September 1919, USNA RG 59, 867.00, Roll 7.

58. Greek Foreign Ministry, "Persecutions of the Greek Population . . . ," 34–37, quoting Greek Legation in Constantinople reports from 14 and 29 January and 7 and 29 February 1917. For the Amasya and Eliaz-Keuy deportations, see Greek Patriarchate, "Persecution of the Greeks . . . ," 120.

59. Ralph Chesbrough, "Report on Political, Economic and Commercial Conditions at Samsoun and Surrounding Districts and Possibilities of Future Commercial Possibilities," 8 August 1919, USNA RG 59, 867.00, Roll 7.

60. Greek Patriarchate, "Persecution of the Greeks . . . ," 127. Greek Foreign Ministry, "Persecutions of the Greek Population . . . ," 37.

61. Germanos to Mary Graffam, 20 December 1916, and Graffam to Peet, 24 December 1916, both in LC, HM Sr. Papers, Reel 22; and Greek Foreign Ministry, "Persecutions of the Greek Population . . . ," 13; and Greek Patriarchate, "Persecution of the Greeks . . . ," 120–121.

62. Zimmer, USS *Olympia* to CO, 8 September 1919, USNA RG 59, 867.00, Roll 7.

63. Hofmann, "Cumulative Genocide," 58; and Toynbee, *Western Question,* 144.

64. Greek Foreign Ministry, "Persecutions of the Greek population . . . ," 39–40, based on reports from Greek Legation, Constantinople, 24 April and 1 May 1917; and Greek Patriarchate, "Persecution of the Greeks . . . ," based on reports from the priests of the dioceses to patriarchate, 67.

65. Gough-Calthorpe to Balfour, 3 February 1919, and attached memorandum "Persecution and Annihilation of the Makri and Livissi Communities," UKNA FO 371/4172.

66. Greek Patriarchate, "Persecution of the Greeks . . . ," 59–60.

67. Quoted in Hofmann, "Cumulative Genocide," 59.

68. Suny, *They Can Live in the Desert,* 213.

69. A. A. Pallis in "Minutes of the 34th Meeting between the A.G.S. [Armenian-Greek Section] and the Armenian and Greek Representatives," 10 March 1920, UKNA FO 371/5087.

70. De Robeck to Curzon, 29 March 1920, and Pallis, Greek High Commission, Constantinople, balance sheet for 1919, 17 February 1920, both in UKNA FO 371/5087.

71. Hofmann, "Cumulative Genocide," 102–103, gives various figures, but most observers appear to have arrived at this estimate.

72. Horton to Bristol, 23 January 1920, USNA RG 59, 867.00, Roll 8.

73. Horton to Bristol, 10 February 1920, USNA RG 84, Turkey (Constantinople), Vol. 424.

74. FO to Granville, 21 November 1918, and Cecil to Gough-Calthorpe, 15 November 1918, both in UKNA FO 371/3417.

75. Webb to FO, 1 January 1919, UKNA FO 371/4172.

76. Interior Ministry to valis and mutesarrifs, 5 November 1918, *Sevk ve Iskan,* 399–401, doc. 342.

77. Interior Ministry to vali of Hüdavendigâr (Bursa), 24 December 1918, *Sevk ve Iskan,* 411–412, doc. 349; and Interior Ministry memo, 26 December 1918, *Sevk ve Iskan,* 412–417, doc. 350.

78. Webb to Balfour, 13 January 1919, and Heathcote-Smith, "Repatriation of Greeks, Preliminary Specimen Cases Illustrating the Repatriation Problem," undated, both in UKNA FO 371/4172.

79. C. E. Heathcote-Smith, "Report on Ayvali," 23 February 1919, and C. R. Hadkinson to Senior Naval Officer, Smyrna, 13 January 1919, both in UKNA FO 371/4157.

80. Perring to High Commissioner, 5 March 1919, UKNA FO 371/4157.

81. Gough-Calthorpe to Balfour, 8 February 1919, and attached Godfrey Wittall, "Report on the Repatriation of Ottoman Greeks at Pendik, Kartal and Maltepe," 30 January 1919, UKNA FO 371/4177.

82. Webb to Balfour, 14 March 1919, and attached memorandum to[?] Heathcote-Smith, "Repatriation," 23 February 1919, UKNA FO 371/4177. Heathcote-Smith recommended the transfer inland of the muhacirs along the coast. This proposed exchange was never ratified or implemented.

83. P. E. King, apparently of the American Tobacco Company, to Heck, 11 January 1919, and King to Heck, 13 January 1919, both in UKNA FO 371/4157; and Lt. Harty to General Staff Officer, Constantinople, 21 January 1919, USNA RG 84, Turkey (Constantinople), Vol. 408.

84. Eken, *Kapancızade Hamit Bey,* 43.

85. Lt. F. W. P. Slade (RNVR), reports from Castamouni and Eregli, from mid-June 1919, UKNA FO 371/4158; and A. Hadkinson, relief officer, "Report on the Following Places Visited between the 25th April and 20th May 1919, Tchataldja, Chorlu . . . [in] Adrianople [vilayet]," 22 May 1919, UKNA FO 371/4157. See also report on Greek atrocities in Çatalca, 25 November 1919, BOA, DH. EUM. SSM, 39/38.

86. White, NER, to Ravndal, Constantinople, 20 June 1919, USNA RG 59, 867.00, Roll 7.

87. Capt. M. A. B. Johnson, Smyrna, reports on Budrum, Mughla, Scala Nouva, and repatriation, 7 May 1919, UKNA FO 371/4157.

88. A. Hadkinson, relief officer, "Report on the Following Places Visited between the 25th April and 20th May 1919, Tchataldja, Chorlu . . . [in] Adrianople [vilayet]," 22 May 1919, UKNA FO 371/4157. See also Security directorate report on Greek atrocities in Çatalca, 25 November 1919, BOA, DH. EUM. SSM, 39/38.

89. "Copy of Report Dated 1st May [1919] from Intelligence Officer, Sochia," and Greek and Turkish reports on the affair, UKNA FO 371/4157.

90. Ottoman Foreign Ministry to Heck, 27 February 1919, USNA RG 84, Turkey (Constantinople), Vol. 408.

91. Deedes, "Meeting with Hamdi Bey, the Director of Refugee Department, Ministry of Interior, February 14th, 1919," UKNA FO 371/4177.

92. Pallis, "Report on the Greek Central Relief Commission's Balance-Sheet for the Year 1919," 17 February 1920, USNA RG 84, Turkey (Constantinople), Vol. 424; and de Robeck to Curzon, 29 March 1920, UKNA FO 371/5087.

93. Horton to Bristol, 10 February 1920, USNA RG 84, Turkey (Constantinople), Vol. 424.

94. Bristol to Eliot Mears, Trade Commissioner, Dept. of Commerce, DC, 19 November 1920, USNA RG 84, Turkey (Constantinople), Vol. 424.

95. Bristol to Horton, 10 January 1920, USNA RG 84, Turkey (Constantinople), Vol. 408.

96. Horton to Bristol, 17 March 1920, USNA RG 84, Turkey (Constantinople), Vol. 421.

97. Horton to Bristol, 23 April 1920, USNA RG 84, Turkey (Constantinople), Vol. 421.

98. Caffery to ?, c. 25 March 1923, USNA RG 84, Turkey (Constantinople), Vol. 484; and entry for 9 April 1923, Bristol War Diary, USNA RG 59, 867.00, Roll 14.

99. Lt. N. W. Harty, Samsun, 25 January 1919, USNA RG 84, Turkey (Constantinople), Vol. 408.

100. British Control Officer in Uzun Keupru Sector E.R.A.A. Grout to Colonel Samson, 28 March 1919, UKNA FO 371/4157.

101. Capt. E. LaFontaine, Kadikeuy, to Capt. Holand, 1 April 1919, UKNA FO 371/4157.

102. "Anti-Greek Persecutions in Turkey 1908–1921, Statements Submitted to the Third National Assembly in Athens, Sessions 5th, 6th and 8th April, 1921," London 1921, UKNA FO 2371/6535.

103. Rendel, "Turkish Massacres and Persecutions of Minorities since the Armistice," 20 March 1922, quoting a report by Lt. Slade from 11 September 1919, UKNA FO 371/7876.

104. Rendel, "Turkish Massacres and Persecutions of Minorities since the Armistice," 20 March 1922, quoting a report by de Robeck from 11 November 1919, UKNA FO 371/7876.

105. Representatives of 51 communities to high commissioners (?), 7 March 1920, USNA RG 84, Turkey (Constantinople), Vol. 419.

106. Capt. J. S. Perring (Samsun), to ?, 31 March 1920, and attached reports, UKNA FO 371/5047.

107. Perring to ?, 3 June 1920, UKNA FO 371/5050.

108. Unsigned, "Situation at Ordou," undated but attached to Webb to Curzon, 15 May 1920, UKNA FO 371/5048.

109. Pinkney Tuck to SecState, 29 July 1920, USNA RG 59, 867.00, Roll 9.

110. Tuck (Samsun) to Bristol, 9 July 1920, USNA RG 59, 867.00, Roll 10. On developments in the Ankara parliament, see Eken, *Kapancızade Hamit Bey,* 585–586.

111. "Summary of Report from the Bishop of Dercos (Therapia) dated 15th March 1920," UKNA FO 371/5213.

112. Webb to FO (?), 25 April 1920, UKNA FO 371/5047.

113. James Morgan, Smyrna, to High Commissioner, 31 March 1920, UKNA FO 371/5133.

114. Sefal, Turkish Foreign Ministry, to De Robeck, 29 March 1920, UKNA FO 371/5133.

115. The Inter-Allied Report from 1921 is quoted in Rendel, "The Turkish Massacres . . . ," 20 March 1922, UKNA FO 371/7876. See also petition sent to De Robeck by Armenians and Greeks of Adapazarı, 22 July 1920, UKNA FO 371/5054.

116. "Minutes of the 41st Meeting of the A.G.S. and the Armenian and Greek Representatives," 30 June 1920, UKNA FO 371/5214. See also Atatürk, *Speech Delivered by Ghazi Mustapha Kemal,* 371–372.

117. A.G.S., "Memorandum," 20 October 1920, UKNA FO 371/5057.

118. "Minutes of the 37th Meeting of the A.G.S and the Armenian and Greek Representatives," 5 May 1920, UKNA FO 371/5213.

119. "Minutes of the 47th Meeting of the A.G.S. & Armenian and Greek Representatives," 29 September 1920, UKNA FO 371/5214.

120. De Robeck to Curzon, 6 August 1920, UKNA FO 371/5214.

121. Lucien Wolf to undersecretary of state, FO, 27 July 1920; and E. C. Hole, Smyrna, to High Commissioner, 19 October 1920, both in UKNA FO 371/5272. Eventually, the Jews reached Smyrna (Committee of Inhabitants of Aidin, Nazli etc. to Lloyd George, 12 November 1920, UKNA FO 371/5287).

122. Commodore M. Fitzmaurice to C-in-C, Mediterranean Station, 23 July 1920, UKNA FO 371/5136.

123. De Robeck to Curzon, 6 October 1920, UKNA FO 371/5214; de Robeck to Curzon, 10 November 1920, UKNA FO 371/5057; and De Robeck to Curzon, 8 September 1920, UKNA FO 371/5214.

124. Interior Ministry's section of public order (Asayış Kalemi) police reports, 4 August 1920, BOA, DH. EUM. AYŞ, 44/63; ibid., 10 August 1920, DH. EUM. AYŞ, 44/79; and ibid., 20 September 1920, DH. EUM. AYŞ, 56/39.

125. Unsigned, "Summary of Reports on the Operations of the Greek army in Asia Minor and Thrace during June and July 1920, compiled by the British Military Mission, with Greek General Headquarters," undated, UKNA FO 371/5136.

126. HMS *Bryony,* "Smyrna Letter of Proceedings," 10 September 1920, UKNA FO 371/5135.

127. HMS *Bryony,* "Smyrna Letter of Proceedings," 7 August 1920, UKNA FO 371/5135.

128. HMS *Bryony,* "Smyrna Letter of Proceedings," 10 September 1920, UKNA FO 371/5135.

129. "Minutes of the 45th Meeting of the A.G.S. and Armenian and Greek Representatives," 1 September 1920, and "Minutes of the 46th Meeting of the A.G.S. & Armenian and Greek Representatives," 15 September 1920, both in UKNA FO 371/5214; and A.G.S., "Memorandum," 20 October 1920, UKNA FO 371/5057.

130. "Weekly Summary of Intelligence Reports Issued by M.I.1.c., Constantinople Branch, for Week Ending 16th April 1920," UKNA FO 371/5167.

131. De Robeck to Curzon, 25 May 1920, UKNA FO 371/5048.

132. "A Nationalist Proclamation," 24 May 1920, UKNA FO 371/5052.

133. De Robeck to Curzon, 19 June 1920, UKNA FO 371/5052.

134. C-in-C Mediterranean to Admiralty Intelligence, 15 June 1920, UKNA FO 371/5050.

135. C-in-C Mediterranean to Admiralty, 21 June 1920, UKNA FO 371/5050.

136. Armenian Patriarchate, report dated 11 August, Bursa, USNA RG 59, 860J.4016/50–860J.401 6P81/99, Roll 5. See also report by Greek Patriarchate attached to De Robeck to Curzon, 25 August 1920, UKNA FO 371/5054.

137. Edith Parsons to friends, 18 July 1920, Houghton ABC 16.9.3, Vol. 51.

138. "Summary of Intelligence Report Issued by M.I.1.c, Constantinople Branch, for Fortnight Ending 19.8.20," UKNA FO 371/5171. For the destruction that followed, see GHQ General Staff, Intelligence, Constantinople, "Weekly Report No. 79 for Week Ending 28th July 1920," UKNA FO 371/5170.

139. "Extracts from Ironside Forces, Daily Situation Reports . . . Report No. 79, dated 17.7.20," UKNA FO 371/5054.

140. A.G.S., "Memorandum," 20 October 1920, UKNA FO 371/5057.

141. Armenian Patriarchate, reports from Ismid, 22 and 24 July 1920, USNA RG 59, 860J.01/520–860J.4016/49, Roll 4.

142. GOC Army of the Black Sea to British High Commissioner, 4 October 1920, UKNA FO 371/5214.

143. Armenian Patriarchate, report from Constantinople, 30 July 1920, attached to Bristol to SecState, 22 September 1920, USNA RG 59, 860J.01/520–860J.4016/49, Roll 4.

144. Armenian Patriarchate, reports from Ismid, 22 and 24 July 1920, USNA RG 59, 860J.01/520–860J.4016/49, Roll 4; and A.G.S., "Memorandum," UKNA FO 371/5057.

145. FO to G. K. A. Bell, 23 October 1920, UKNA FO 371/5287; and Rendel, "Turkish Massacres and Persecutions of Minorities since the Armistice," 20 March 1922, UKNA FO 371/7876.

146. GHQ, ABS (Army of the Black Sea), "Turkish Atrocities at Isnik," 7 October 1920, UKNA FO 371/5214.

147. "Minutes of the 47th Meeting of the A.G.S. & Armenian and Greek Representatives," 29 September 1920, UKNA FO 371/5214.

148. "Minutes of the 47th Meeting of the A.G.S. & Armenian and Greek Representatives," 29 September 1920, UKNA FO 371/5214.

149. Greek Legation, London, to Curzon, 11 May 1921, and attached "Memorandum" by Greek officers of the Army in Asia Minor, UKNA FO 371/6512.

150. H. Earle Russell to SecState, 21 September 1920, USNA RG 59, 860J.01/520–860J.4016/49, Roll 4.

151. Director, NER, Bursa, to Bristol, 3 December 1920, USNA RG 84, Turkey (Constantinople), Vol. 415; and Greek Ecumenical patriarchate, "A Summary of the Events of Kutahia as Exposed by the Greek Orthodox Community of the Town," undated but from September 1921, USNA RG 84, Turkey (Constantinople), Vol. 438.

152. Committee of Inhabitants Aidin, Nazli, Denizli, etc. to Lloyd George, 12 November 1920, UKNA FO 371/5287.

153. A.G.S., "Memorandum," 20 October 1920, UKNA FO 371/5057.

154. Petition signed by 51 communities in central Anatolia, attached to de Robeck to Curzon, 8 September 1920, UKNA FO 371/5054.

155. Greek Legation, London, to Curzon 11 May 1921, and attached "Memorandum," prepared by Greek army officers, UKNA FO 371/6512.

156. Lt. Commander G. Muirhead Gould, "Intelligence Summary No. 19," October 1920, UKNA FO 371/5287.

157. "Minutes of the 53rd Meeting of the A.G.S. & Armenian & Greek Representatives," 5 January 1921, and "Minutes of the 58th Meeting of the A.G.S. & Armenian and Greek Representatives," 16 March 1920, both in UKNA FO 371/6548; and Greek Legation, London, to Curzon, 31 March 1921, UKNA FO 371/6491.

158. William Hawkes, "Report of Conditions in Sivas," 5 June 1922, USNA RG 59, 867.4016, Roll 47.

159. Armenian Patriarchate report from Zoungouldek, 26 August 1920, USNA RG 59, 867.00, Roll 4.

160. Annie Allen, "Interview with Mustafa Kemal Pasha at Angora," 9 October 1920, LC, Bristol Papers 34.

161. Tuck to SecState, 19 January 1921, USNA RG 84, Turkey (Constantinople), Vol. 440. "Hellenic Greeks" were citizens and subjects of the Kingdom of Greece.

162. Jackson to Bristol, 10 September 1921, USNA RG 84, Turkey (Constantinople), Vol. 438.

163. Rendel, "Turkish Massacres and Persecutions of Minorities since the Armistice," 20 March 1922, UKNA FO 371/7876.

164. War Office, "Turkish Atrocities," 22 May 1922, UKNA FO 371/7878; and "A.1. Turkey. Unrest in Northern Anatolia," containing what purports to be the (intercepted) text of Fethi to Kemal, "14" (or 4) February "1338 [sic, should be 1339]," UKNA FO 371/7876.

165. C. S. Joyce, Diary of USS *Fox,* Samsun, from 12 to 28 May 1921, USNA RG 84, Turkey (Constantinople), Vol. 440.

166. Rendel, "Turkish Massacres and Persecutions of Minorities since the Armistice," 20 March 1922, UKNA FO 371/7876.

167. Unsigned, "Recent Conditions and Events in Northern Anatolia Particularly in Marsovan," undated but from October 1921, UKNA FO 371/6578.

168. Julian Gillespie, US assistant trade commissioner, US High Commission (Ankara) to Bristol, 10 January 1922, USNA RG 59, 867.00, Roll 10. It is unclear whether he was penalized. In any event he was soon back in the saddle, and in August–September 1922 would lead the army that conquered Ionia.

169. "Answers by Mustapha Kemal Pasha (Written by Yussuf Bey, Minister of Foreign Affairs), Memorandum to Lt. R. S. Dunn," 3 July 1921, LC, Bristol Papers 35.

170. For example, White to Robbins, 18 November 1921, USNA RG 59, 867.4016, Roll 46.

171. Hosford, "Recent Conditions and Events in Northern Anatolia Particularly in Marsovan," 6 December 1921, USNA RG 59, 867.4016, Roll 46, and USNA RG 59, 867.00, Roll 10.

172. Toynbee to Charles, 9 June 1921, Bodl. MS Toynbee Papers 51.

173. Allen Dulles (for HC) to SecState, 28 June 1921, USNA RG 84, Turkey (Constantinople), Vol. 438. Shaw, *From Empire to Republic*, vol. 3, part 1, 1297, who devotes dozens of pages to Greek atrocities, covers the massive Turkish massacres and deportations in 1921 in exactly half a sentence: "At the same time . . . most of the Greeks who had evaded Nureddin Pasha's earlier deportation of Pontus sympathizers and supporters were now also deported to Sivas and other places in central Anatolia." There is no description of the deportations or mention of the accompanying massacres. He also writes that a Greek naval shelling on June 8, 1921, "destroy[ed] much of Samsun"—a complete fiction.

174. Commander C. H. Knox-Little, HMS *Sportive*, "Letter of Proceedings in Black Sea from July 27th to August 3rd," 3 August 1921, UKNA FO 371/6498. For the Turkish Security Directorate's Travel and Transportation section *(Seyrüsefer kalemi)* reports on Greek naval activities in the Black Sea, see BOA, DH. EUM. SSM, 46/35, 31 August 1921; and Interior Ministry's Special Section *(Kalem-i Mahsus)* reports, 24 September 1921, DH. KMS, 60-3/19.

175. "Diary of Station Ship at Samsun, USS *Brooks*, from 7 July 1921 till ? July 1921," entry for 14 July 1921, USNA RG 84, Turkey (Constantinople), Vol. 438.

176. Head of the Armenian Protestant Community in Turkey to Bristol, 18 July 1921, USNA RG 84, Turkey (Constantinople), Vol. 438.

177. Bristol to SecState, 18 July 1921, and Bristol to Izzet Pasha, Constantinople's foreign minister, 19 July 1921, both in USNA RG 84, Turkey (Constantinople), Vol. 438. Ankara denied that orders had been issued to deport women and children (see Bristol to SecState, 2 August 1921, USNA RG 84, Turkey (Constantinople), Vol. 438).

178. USS *Overton*, "Samsun Diary," 3 August 1921, USNA RG 84, Turkey (Constantinople), Vol. 440.

179. Donald Hosford, "Brief Memorandum of Recent Conditions and Events in Northern Anatolia, particularly in Marsovan," undated but from October 1921, Houghton ABC 16.9.1, Vol. 2.

180. "Minutes of the 73rd Meeting of the A.G.S. and Armenian and Greek Representatives," 12 October 1921, UKNA FO 371/6549.

181. CO USS *Overton* to Bristol, Diary for May 1921, 7 June 1921, USNA RG 84, Turkey (Constantinople), Vol. 440.

182. Unsigned, "The Tragedy of Baffra in Pontus, by an eye-witness . . . who Escaped the Massacre of Baffra and was rescued with 100 Others on a Sailing Ship to Medea in Thrace," undated but possibly from 5 July 1921, Bodl. MS Toynbee Papers 50.

183. CO USS *Overton* to Bristol, Diary for May 1921, 7 June 1921, USNA RG 84, Turkey (Constantinople), Vol. 440.

184. Greek Patriarchate, "Bulletin," 31 August 1921, USNA RG 84, Turkey (Constantinople), Vol. 438.

185. "Enclosure in Mr. Lindley's Despatch No. 286 of June 3rd 1922," UKNA FO 371/7879.

186. Unsigned, "The Tragedy of Baffra in Pontus, by an eye-witness . . . ," undated, Bodl. MS Toynbee Papers 50.

187. Communiqué from the League of Nations to its member states, 14 November 1921, UKNA FO 371/6536.

188. Rendel, "Turkish Massacres and Persecutions of Minorities since the Armistice," 20 March 1922, UKNA FO 371/7876.

189. Youssouf Kemal to high commissioners, 15 September 1921, USNA RG 59, 860J.4016/50–86 0J.4016P81/99.

190. "Enclosure in Mr. Lindley's Despatch No. 286 of June 3rd 1922," UKNA FO 371/7879.

191. CO USS *Williamson* to Bristol, 28 September 1921, USNA RG 84, Turkey (Constantinople), Vol. 440.

192. CO USS *McFarland* to Bristol, 1 September 1921, and Bristol to SecState, 1 September 1921, both in USNA RG 84, Turkey (Constantinople), Vol. 438; and CO USS *Sturtevant* to Bristol, 20 September 1921, USNA RG 84, Turkey (Constantinople), Vol. 438.

193. CO USS *McFarland* to Bristol, ? October 1921, USNA RG 84, Turkey (Constantinople), Vol. 440.

194. Prof. J. P. Xenides, "The Recent Greek Deportations and Other Atrocities in Asia Minor," undated but from November 1921, USNA RG 59, 867.4016, Roll 46.

195. USS *Overton,* "Samsun Diary," 3 August 1921, USNA RG 84, Turkey (Constantinople), Vol. 440.

196. CO USS *Williamson* to Bristol, 28 September 1921, USNA RG 84, Turkey (Constantinople), Vol. 440.

197. Lt. Commander E. G. Haas, CO USS *Sturtevant,* to Bristol, diary entry for 21 September 1921, USNA RG 84, Turkey (Constantinople), Vol. 440.

198. Lt. Commander E. G. Haas, USS *Sturtevant,* to Bristol, 28 September 1921, diary entry for 21 September 1921, USNA RG 84, Turkey (Constantinople), Vol. 440.

199. "Destruction of Greek Villages above Ordou February 12–16, 1922," attached to Riggs to Bristol, 21 June 1922, USNA RG 59, 867.4016, Roll 47; and Lindley to Balfour, 21 June 1922, and attached unsigned memorandum, "Condition of Greeks of Pontus," undated, UKNA FO 371/7880.

200. USS *Brooks* to Bristol, 8 July 1921, USNA RG 84, Turkey (Constantinople), Vol. 438.

201. "Enclosure in Mr. Lindley's Despatch No. 286 of June 3rd 1922, (Free) Translation of Telegram, Forwarded by Sub-Governor of Tyroleos, Thrace, on the Part of Twenty-One Greeks and Circassian Refugees from Baffra, Pontus," UKNA FO 371/7879. Bafra Circassians saved about 140 Greek neighbors by hiding them in cellars.

202. Gertrude Anthony to Bristol, 1 November 1921, USNA RG 84, Turkey (Constantinople), Vol. 438; and Hofmann, "Cumulative Genocide," 75. Anthony spent 21 March–13 June 1921 in Samsun and 13 June–3 October 1921 in Merzifon.

203. USS *Humphreys* to Bristol, 8 June 1921, and Bristol to SecState, 8 June 1921, both in USNA RG 84, Turkey (Constantinople), Vol. 438.

204. "Minutes of the 70th Meeting of the A.G.S. and Armenian and Greek Representatives," 31 August 1921, UKNA FO 371/6548. See also CO USS *Overton* to Bristol, "Samsoun Diary," 3 August 1921, USNA RG 84, Turkey (Constantinople), Vol. 440.

205. CO USS *McFarland* to Bristol, "Report of Operations October 27, 1921 to November 11, 1921," USNA RG 84, Turkey (Constantinople), Vol. 440.

206. CO USS *St. Louis* to Bristol, 24 September 1921, USNA RG 84, Turkey (Constantinople), Vol. 440.

207. "USS *Overton:* Notes on Samsoun Station after being Relieved by USS *Humphreys,"* entries for 16–17 June 1921, USNA RG 84, Turkey (Constantinople), Vol. 440.

208. USS *Scorpion* to Bristol, 19 June 1921, USNA RG 84, Turkey (Constantinople), Vol. 438.

209. Allen Dulles to SecState, 28 June 1921, USNA RG 84, Turkey (Constantinople), Vol. 438.

210. Unsigned memorandum, Samsun, 10 June 1921, LC, Bristol Papers 35.

211. "Diary of Station Ship at Samsun, USS *Brooks,* from 7 July till ? July 1921," entries for 16 and 17 July 1921, USNA RG 84, Turkey (Constantinople), Vol. 438; and, "Report on Situation . . . Part Two," 24 July 1921, LC, Bristol Papers, War Diary.

212. "Statement of Ethel Thompson of Boston, Mass., concerning her work in the interior of Anatolia from August, 1921–June 11, 1922," 4 August 1922, USNA RG 59, 867.4016, Roll 47.

213. Ralph Harlow, International College, Smyrna, to Officers of the Board (ABC), 1 December 1921, Houghton ABC 16.9.3, Vol. 51.

214. USS *Brooks* to Bristol, 10 July 1921, USNA RG 84, Turkey (Constantinople), Vol. 438.

215. "Minutes of the 76th [should be 77th?] Meeting of the A.G.S. and Armenian and Greek Representatives," 23 November 1921, UKNA FO 371/6549.

216. White to Robbins, State Department, 18 November 1921, Houghton ABC 16.9.3, Vol. 49.

217. Knapp, "Memorandum Regarding Treatment of Americans in Asia Minor," 27 June 1922, USNA RG 59, 867.4016, Roll 47.

218. "Foreign Schools and their Influence," in *Enyud* (?), Ankara area, undated but from late June 1921, Houghton ABC 16.9.2, Vol. 1.

219. "American Institutions in Our Country," undated but possibly from May 1922, in "Extracts from Nationalist Newspapers, Indicating the Attitude of the Official Press towards American Relief Workers," UKNA FO 371/7879.

220. Bristol, draft letter to SecState, 28 July 1921, LC, Bristol Papers 35.

221. Theodore Riggs to friends, 17 April 1921, Houghton ABC 16.9.1, Vol. 2.

222. Bristol (draft letter) to SecState, 28 July 1921, LC, Bristol Papers 35; and White to Robbins, 18 November 1921, Houghton ABC 16.9.3, Vol. 49.

223. The description of the Merzifon massacre is based on D. M. Hosford, "Brief Memorandum of Recent Conditions and Events in Northern Anatolia, Particularly in Marsovan," 6 December 1921, UKNA FO 371/6538; and Gertrude Anthony to Bristol, 1 November 1921, USNA RG 84, Turkey (Constantinople), Vol. 438. The A.G.S. estimated the number killed in the town at 950 ("Deportations and Massacre on Black Sea Littoral, and Massacre at Marsovan," UKNA FO 371/6534). Bristol and Anthony thought the number was around 1,200 (entry for 1 November 1921, LC, Bristol Papers, War Diary).

224. Youssouf Kemal, Minister of Foreign Affairs to High Commissioner, 15 September 1921, USNA RG 84, Turkey (Constantinople), Vol. 438.

225. Julian Gillespie, assistant US trade commissioner, Ankara, to Bristol, 10 January 1922, quoting the Nationalist foreign minister, Youssouf Kemal, USNA RG 59, 867.00, Roll 10.

226. Communiqué from the League of Nations to its member states, 14 November 1921, UKNA FO 371/6536.

227. Untitled memorandum by Theda Phelps to Allen Dulles, July 1922, USNA RG 59, 867.4016, Roll 47.

228. "Minutes of the 61st Meeting of the A.G.S. and Armenian and Greek Representatives," 27 April 1921, UKNA FO 371/6548.

229. Greek Patriarchate, circular 20 August/2 September 1921; and unsigned, untitled, undated memorandum, both in USNA RG 84, Turkey (Constantinople), Vol. 438.

230. "Minutes of the 65th Meeting of the A.G.S. and the Armenian and Greek Representatives," 22 June 1921, UKNA FO 371/6548.

231. Legation of Greece, London, to Curzon, 8 June 1921, UKNA FO 371/6516; and Greek Ecumenical Patriarchate "bulletin," 9 September 1921, USNA RG 84, Turkey (Constantinople), Vol. 438.

232. Committee of Greek Refugees of Konia and Silleh & Surrounding Districts (Smyrna) to Lloyd George, 14 March 1922, UKNA FO 371/7878; and untitled memorandum attached to Rumbold to Curzon, 31 August 1921, UKNA FO 371/6527.

233. Entry for 15 July 1921, LC, Bristol Papers, War Diary.

234. Unsigned (by a missionary), "Report of Adabazar and Ismidt Schools, 1914–1921," undated but probably from summer 1921, Houghton ABC 16.9.1, Vol. 1.

235. Vice-Consul W. L. C. Knight to Earl Granville, 30 June 1921, UKNA FO 371/6523.

236. "Minutes of the 66th Meeting of the A.G.S. and Armenian and Greek Representatives," 6 July 1921, UKNA FO 371/6548.

237. C. Parren and T. Nicolaides to "Madam," 13 April 1922, attached to Barry, Catholic Women's Suffrage Society, to SecState, 11 May 1922, UKNA FO 371/7877.

238. Graves to Toynbee, 27 July 1921, Bodl. MS Toynbee Papers 52. F. J. Baker to Eric Drummond, 9 October 1922, UKNA FO 371/7955.

239. "Diary of . . . USS *Brooks*, from 7 July till ? July 1921," entry for 15 July 1921, USNA RG 84, Turkey (Constantinople), Vol. 438.

240. Dulles, "Memorandum of Conversation with Commander Bristol of the USS *Overton*, regarding the situation of American tobacco interests in Samsoun as Affected by the Nationalists," 6 August 1921, LC, Bristol Papers 35.

241. Dunn (Ankara), "Interview with Youssouf Kemal Bey, Minister of Foreign Affairs," 30 June 1921, LC, Bristol Papers 35.

242. Dunn, "Second Interview with Youssouf Kemal Bey," 5 July 1921, LC, Bristol Papers 35.

243. "Youssuf Kemal et la question Armenienne: Le delegué Kemaliste pretend ne rien savoir," 21 February 1922, *Bosphore.*

244. Rendel, "Memorandum by Mr. Rendel on Conversation with Col. Rawlinson on 23rd May 1922," 24 May 1922, UKNA FO 371/7878.

245. Rendel, "Atrocities in Asia Minor Etc. Protests Received by His Majesty's Government, and Action Taken," 28 December 1921, UKNA FO 371/7875.

246. "Deportations and Atrocities in Samsoun—Service Report," 19 April 1922, quoting from a report by Jackson dated 23 March 1922, USNA RG 84, Turkey (Constantinople), Vol. 466.

247. Armenian-Greek Section of the British High Commission, Constantinople, "Deportations and Massacre on Black Sea Littoral, and Massacre at Marsovan," undated but covering note Rumbold to Curzon, 22 October 1921, UKNA FO 371/6534.

248. Bristol to SecState, 25 July 1921, USNA RG 84, Turkey (Constantinople), Vol. 438.

249. Bristol to SecState, 25 July 1921, USNA RG 84, Turkey (Constantinople), Vol. 438; and Rumbold to Curzon, 2 December 1921, UKNA FO 371/6536.

250. USS *Sands,* "Diary at Samsoun," entries for 28 and 29 November and ? December 1921, USNA RG 84, Turkey (Constantinople), Vol. 440.

251. "Minutes of the 81st Meeting of the A.G.S. and Armenian and Greek Representatives," 1 February 1922, UKNA FO 371/7933.

252. Rendel, minute, "Atrocities File 19," 27 March 1922, UKNA FO 371/7876.

253. CO USS *Sturtevant* to Bristol, 20 January 1922, diary, entry for 31 December 1921, USNA RG 84, Turkey (Constantinople), Vol. 459.

254. "Destruction of Greek Villages above Ordou, February 12–16, 1922," attached to Riggs to Bristol, 21 June 1922, USNA RG 59, 867.4016, Roll 47.

255. Hosford, "Brief Memorandum of Recent Conditions and Events in Northern Anatolia, particularly in Marsovan," undated but from October 1921, Houghton ABC 16.9.1, Vol. 2; and "Minutes of the 74th Meeting of the A.G.S. and Armenian and Greek Representatives," 12 October 1921, UKNA FO

371/6549. A list of those hanged in Amasya was published in the Turkish newspaper *Ehali,* Samsun, on 25 September 1921. Shaw writes that the Samsun Independence Court executed "485" Pontus Greeks and the special Amasya Independence Court executed "several hundred" during August–November 1922 (Shaw, *From Empire to Republic,* vol. 3, part 1, 1016, 1018).

256. Xenides, "The Recent Greek Deportations and Other Atrocities in Asia Minor," undated but from November 1921, USNA RG 59, 867.4016, Roll 46.

257. "Minutes of the 76th Meeting of the A.G.S. and Armenian and Greek Representatives," 9 November 1921, UKNA FO 371/6549.

258. Rumbold to Curzon, 6 October 1921, UKNA FO 371/6531; and "Minutes of the 73rd Meeting of the A.G.S. and Armenian and Greek Representatives," 12 October 1921, UKNA FO 371/6549.

259. Peet to Barton, 9 November 1921, Houghton ABC 16.9.3, Vol. 52; and "Minutes of the 76th [77th?] Meeting of the A.G.S. and Armenian and Greek Representatives," 23 November 1921, UKNA FO 371/6549. "Crucified" in this context usually meant being nailed to a door or wall or board, not necessarily a cross.

260. Greek Patriarchate to President of the Council of the League of Nations, 13/26 November 1921, UKNA FO 371/6537.

261. "Minutes of the 84th Meeting of the A.G.S. and Armenian and Greek Representatives," 15 March 1922, UKNA FO 371/7933.

262. Rumbold to FO, 17 February 1922, UKNA FO 371/7855.

263. USS *Sands,* "Diary at Samsoun," entries for 8 and 12 March 1922, USNA RG 84, Turkey (Constantinople), Vol. 463.

264. CO USS *Fox,* Webb Trammell, to Bristol, "Diary," entry for 10 April 1922, USNA RG 84, Turkey (Constantinople), Vol. 462; and CO USS *Childs* to Bristol, "Diary Samsoun," entry for 18 May 1922, USNA RG 84, Turkey (Constantinople), Vol. 462.

265. E. G. Haas, CO USS *Sturtevant,* to Bristol, 1 May 1922, "Diary," USNA RG 84, Turkey (Constantinople), Vol. 463; and CO USS *Childs* to Bristol, "Diary Samsoun," entry for 18 May 1922, USNA RG 84, Turkey (Constantinople), Vol. 462.

266. Armenian patriarchate report, 25 August 1922, UKNA FO 371/7954.

267. Rumbold to FO (No. 241), 10 May 1922, UKNA FO 371/7876.

268. "Comité des Grecs originaires du Pont-Euxin" in Athens, to British Ambassador, 17 July 1921, UKNA FO 371/6527.

269. Rumbold to FO, 27 May 1922, UKNA FO 371/7878.

270. Rumbold to FO, (No. 242), 10 May 1922, UKNA FO 371/7876.

271. Commander E. G. (?) Haas, USS *Sturtevant,* Samsun, "Diary," entry for 18 April 1922, USNA RG 84, Turkey (Constantinople), Vol. 463.

272. Olive Crawford, Trebizond, to Peet, 2 August 1922, USNA RG 84, Turkey (Constantinople), Vol. 464.

273. "Statement of Ethel Thompson, of Boston, Mass., Concerning Her Work in the Interior of Anatolia from August, 1921–June 11, 1922," 4 August 1922, USNA RG 59, 867.4016, Roll 47.

274. Gibbons, "Trebizond, Asiatic Turkey," 20 May 1922, UKNA FO 371/7878. One of Gibbons' informants was a missionary, Olive N. Crawford. She also, separately, described what she had seen in Trabzon (Crawford to Peet, 2 August 1922, USNA RG 84, Turkey (Constantinople), Vol. 464).

275. Report by J. H. Crutcher, NER director, Trebizond, in CO USS *Fox,* "Diary," 18 June 1922, USNA RG 84, Turkey (Constantinople), Vol. 462.

276. Theda Phelps to the State Department, 2 June 1922, USNA RG Turkey (Constantinople), Vol. 464; and unsigned, "Memorandum," 31 May 1922, attached to Rumbold to Balfour, 2 June 1922, UKNA FO 371/7879.

277. Crawford to Peet, 25 April 1922, UKNA FO 371/7878.

278. Theda Phelps to the State Department, 2 June 1922, USNA RG Turkey (Constantinople), Vol. 464; and unsigned, "Memorandum," 31 May 1922, attached to Rumbold to Balfour, 2 June 1922, UKNA FO 371/7879.

279. "Statement of Ethel Thompson, of Boston, Mass., concerning her work in the interior of Anatolia from August, 1921–June 11, 1921," 4 August 1922, USNA RG 59, 867.4016, Roll 47.

280. Satow (Beirut) to Curzon, 3 April 1922, UKNA FO 371/7876.

281. B. Bannerman Murdoch and J. Herbert Knapp, "Report of Greek and Armenian Deportees who Passed through Arabkir or were Stationed at Arabkir," 14 June 1922, USNA RG 84, Turkey (Constantinople), Vol. 464.

282. Greek Patriarchate, "A Summary of a letter written by a Greek from Samsoun and sent from the mountain of Ayou-tepe," undated, USNA RG 84, Turkey (Constantinople), Vol. 438; and "Minutes of the 71st Meeting of the A.G.S. and Armenian and Greek Representatives," 14 September 1921, UKNA FO 371/6548. See also "Deposition assermentée, de MM. Jacobe Cantoni . . . ," 18 July 1921, appended to Rattigan to Curzon, 27 July 1921, UKNA FO 371/6524.

283. USS *Sands,* "Diary at Samsoun," entry for 30 November 1921, USNA RG 84, Turkey (Constantinople), Vol. 440.

284. Unsigned, "Report Made from Information Given by John Eufremides and George Isaridi, Refugees from Pontus, November 1921," undated, UKNA FO 3721/7876.

285. Hofmann, "Cumulative Genocide," 98.

286. For example, the vali of Diyarbekir allowed NER to temporarily shelter and feed Greek deportees passing through and in October–December 1921 allowed deportees to settle in villages and earn a living. "In the protection of the deportees the Turkish Government helped us by every means in their power," missionary Emily Wade reported in "To whom it may concern," 23 June 1922, USNA RG 84, Turkey (Constantinople), Vol. 465.

287. "Statement of Ethel Thompson, of Boston, Mass., Concerning Her Work in the Interior of Anatolia from August, 1921–June 11, 1922," 4 August 1922, USNA RG 59, 867.4016, Roll 47.

288. Ibid.

289. Henderson, "Turkey Annual Report 1922," c. November 1923, UKNA FO 371/9176.

290. Yowell to Charles Evans Hughes, 2 May 1922, USNA RG 59, 867.4016, Roll 48.

291. Ward to Hughes, undated but c. 5 May 1922, and Ward, "Memorandum of Greek Deportations," undated but from May 1922, both attached to the Yowell-Ward report, UKNA FO 371/7879.

292. Ward to Hughes, undated but c. 5 May 1922, UKNA FO 371/7879.

293. Jaquith to Vickerey, NER, New York, 3 May 1922, USNA RG 59, 867.4016, Roll 46.

294. Yowell and Ward to Jackson, 5 April 1922, USNA RG 59, 867.4016, Roll 46. See also "Killing by Turks has been Renewed," *New York Times,* 6 May 1922.

295. "Extracts from the Diary of Dr. Mark Ward, Mezreh, Mamouret ul Aziz, Anatolia," attached to Bristol to SecState, 12 July 1922, USNA RG 84, Turkey (Constantinople), Vol. 464; and Ward, "Memorandum of Greek Deportations," undated but from May 1922, UKNA FO 371/7879.

296. Ward and Yowell to Jackson, 5 April 1922, USNA RG 59, 867.4016, Roll 46.

297. Xenides, "The Recent Greek Deportations and Other Atrocities in Asia Minor," undated but from November 1921, USNA RG 59, 867.4016, Roll 46.

298. Joseph Beach, Henry Murphy, Lillian Sewny, and Katherine Fletcher, "Report on Conditions in Anatolia Submitted by Members of the Cesarea Unit, Near East Relief, to the United States High Commission, Constantinople," 4 December 1922, USNA RG 59, 867.4016, Roll 48.

299. Secret Intelligence Service (SIS), "The Great National Assembly and Dr. Yowell's Report on Turkish Atrocities," 30 May 1922, UKNA FO 371/7879.

300. Translated text of Kemal's speech attached to Rumbold to Balfour, 27 June 1922, UKNA FO 371/7867.

301. Alleged letter from "Jaquith" to Fethi, 22 June 1922; and W. A. Kennedy to an editor in *The Daily Telegraph,* 29 June 1922, both in UKNA FO 371/7880.

302. Turkish Government, "Certain Facts with Reference to the Greek Rebellion in the Pontus and Steps Taken by the Turkish Government," undated but from May 1922, Bodl. MS Toynbee Papers 50; and "The Explanation of the Ministry of Interior," Ankara, 22 May 1922, in "Explanation Furnished by Anatolian News Agency in Connection with Allegations Made by Major Yowell," UKNA FO 371/7878.

303. Rumbold to FO, 10 May 1922, (No. 241), UKNA FO 371/7876.

304. Ministry of Interior, Ankara, 22 May 1922, in "Explanation Furnished by Anatolian News Agency in Connection with Allegations Made by Major Yowell," UKNA FO 371/7878.

305. Entry for 24 May 1922, LC, Bristol Papers, War Diary.

306. Rumbold to Balfour, 30 May 1922, UKNA FO 371/7878.

307. Hosford, "Brief Memorandum . . . ," 6 December 1921, USNA RG 59, 867.00, Roll 10.

308. SIS, "The Great National Assembly and the Commission of Enquiry into Atrocities," 10 June 1922, UKNA FO 371/7880; and "British Secretary's Notes of a Meeting Held at 10, Downing Street, London, on Monday, June 19, 1922, at 2.45 P.M.," UKNA FO 371/7866.

309. Henderson to Balfour, 18 July 1922, UKNA FO 371/7880.

310. CO USS *Overton* (?) to Bristol, Samsun diary, entry for 25 October 1922, USNA RG 84, Turkey (Constantinople), Vol. 462.

311. B. Bannerman Murdoch and J. Herbert Knapp, "Report of Greek and Armenian Deportees who Passed through Arabkir or were Stationed at Arabkir," 14 June 1922, USNA RG 84, Turkey (Constantinople), Vol. 464.

312. Depositions to Greek Red Cross Committee, from April 1923, by ex-PoWs—Gabriel Scalo Choriti and Gheorgios Sava, both of Mitylene, John Ferounakis and Anesti Dimou from Volo, and Peter Papapetropoulos, from Lehana, attached to Bentinck to Curzon, 27 April 1923, UKNA FO 371/9094.

313. Lt. Leno Melas to ?, 28 May 1923, UKNA FO 371/9096.

314. Bentinck to Curzon, 4 July 1923, UKNA FO 371/9097.

315. *Koran,* 47:4.

316. H. Barfield to ?, 11 March 1921 and accompanying tables, UKNA FO 371/6491. In June 1916 some 300 Armenian families were deported to Damascus (Heck to SecState, 11 March 1919, USNA RG 84, Turkey (Constantinople), Vol. 405)—the only large wartime deportation of Smyrniots.

317. Lt. C. E. S. Palmer, Royal Navy, undated memorandum attached to Webb to Balfour, 11 December 1918, UKNA FO 371/3416.

318. Lt. L. R. Gooding to G.S. "I," GHQ, Constantinople, 5 March 1919, UKNA FO 371/4157; and Lt. Col. Ian Smith, Area Control Officer, Smyrna, untitled report, 7 April 1919, UKNA FO 371/4157.

319. Ford, *Eden to Armageddon,* 402.

320. De Robeck to Curzon, Encl. 1 (Report of Inter-Allied Commission on the Greek Occupation), 11 October 1919, UKNA FO 371/5132.

321. Bristol to Horton, 25 February 1920, USNA RG 84, Turkey (Constantinople), Vol. 424.

322. Horton to US Mission, Paris, 19 July 1919, USNA RG 59, 867.00, Roll 7.

323. Commander C. E. Heathcote-Smith, "Memorandum on Greek Aspirations to Asia Minor Coast Strip," undated, attached to Webb to Balfour, 13 March 1919, UKNA FO 371/4165. See also Horton to US Mission, Paris, 19 July 1919, USNA RG 59, 867.00, Roll 7; and Horton to SecState, "The Near Eastern Question," 26 September 1922, USNA RG 59, 867.4016, Roll 47.

324. Churchill, *World Crisis,* 379.

325. Smith, *Ionian Vision,* 90.

326. Vali of Aydın, "Vilayet of Aidin," undated but from May 1919, and "Resume of the Report of General Ali Hadir Pacha, Commanding the 17th Army Corps of Smyrna," undated, both in USNA RG 84, Turkey (Constantinople), Vol. 405.

327. David Forbes (a licorice manufacturer) to Ravndal, 31 May 1919, USNA RG 84, Turkey (Constantinople), Vol. 405.

328. Toynbee, *Western Question,* 272. The Turks claimed 300–400 were murdered; the Greek estimate was about 50 (Inter-Allied Commission report, 11 October 1919, UKNA FO 371/5132).

329. Bristol, "Part Four (continued), Report of Operations for Week Ending 25 May 1919," undated, LC, Bristol Papers, War Diary.

330. "Private and Confidential Report on the Greek Occupation of Smyrna submitted by Mr. John Langdon," 24 June 1919, USNA RG 84, Turkey (Constantinople), Vol. 405; and Horton to American Mission, Paris, 19 July 1919, USNA RG 59, 867.00, Roll 7.

331. "Report of the Inter-Allied Commission of Enquiry into the Greek Occupation of Smyrna and Surrounding Districts," part 1, 7 October 1919, attached to Webb to Curzon, 18 October 1919, UKNA FO 371/5132.

332. Forbes to Ravndal, 31 May 1919, USNA RG 84, Turkey (Constantinople), Vol. 405.

333. Ministry of Interior, Constantinople, to American High Commission, undated, containing a string of real or fabricated telegrams from local governors (Nazili, Denizli, Menteche, etc.) from June–July 1919, USNA RG 84, Turkey (Constantinople), Vol. 406.

334. Toynbee, *Western Question,* 273.

335. Horton to American Mission, Paris, 11 July 1919, USNA RG 59, 867.00, Roll 7; and Ministry of Interior, Constantinople, to American High Commission, undated, containing a string of telegrams from local governors from June–July 1919, USNA RG 84, Turkey (Constantinople), Vol. 406.

336. "Summary of the Painful Deeds Committed by the Greeks in the Vilayet of Aidin," Military Press, Constantinople, 1919, USNA RG 84, Turkey (Constantinople), Vol. 415.

337. "Report of the Inter-Allied Commission of Enquiry into the Greek Occupation of Smyrna and Surrounding Districts," 7 October 1919, UKNA RG 371/5132.

338. Hofmann, "Cumulative Genocide," 67.

339. Admiral Bristol (US) and generals Bunoust (France), Hare (UK) and Dall'ollio (Italy), "Report of the Inter-Allied Commission of Enquiry into the Greek Occupation of Smyrna and Surrounding Districts," 7, 11, and 13 October 1919, is to be found in full, in French, in UKNA FO 371/5132. Parts 2 and 3 of the report, in English, are in Bodl. MS Toynbee Papers 52. The commission's non-voting Greek "observer," Col. Mazarakis, disputed the findings (Smith, *Ionian Vision,* 111 footnote). Shaw's treatment of the Commission's findings (*From Empire to Republic,* vol. 2, 521–527) is seriously marred by (a) his failure to reference its attribution of atrocities also to the Turks and (b) by his conflation of the commission's findings with those of another committee of inquiry, two years later, relating to events only in Yalova-Guemlik.

340. Bristol, "Part Four (continued), Report of Operations for Week Ending 25 May 1919," undated, LC, Bristol Papers, War Diary; and Bristol to Admiral Philip Andrews, 28 May 1919, LC, Bristol Papers 31.

341. Horton to SecState, 13 October 1919, USNA RG 84, Turkey (Constantinople), Vol. 406. Even Toynbee called Stergiadis "a fine fellow . . . [who] is trying to administer decently—with remarkable success" (Toynbee to Charles, 9 June 1921, Bodl. MS Toynbee Papers 51).

342. Smith, *Ionian Vision,* 100.

343. Horton to Bristol, "Political Conditions in Asia Minor," 4 August 1922, USNA RG 84, Turkey (Constantinople), Vol. 459.

344. "Memorandum by Mr. Hole on Events in Smyrna," 18 September 1922, USNA RG 84, Turkey (Constantinople), Vol. 466.

345. Rumbold to Curzon, 18 September 1922, USNA RG 84, Turkey (Constantinople), Vol. 466.

346. Rumbold to Curzon, 12 September 1922, UKNA FO 371/7889. See also unsigned, "Summary of a Confidential Report on Recent Events at Pergamos, Soma and District," 28 October 1922, attached to Henderson to Oliphant, 4 November 1922, UKNA FO 371/7950.

347. Shaw, *From Empire to Republic*, vol. 2, 504, 507; and Chrysostomos to Meletios, the patriarch in Constantinople, 31 August 1922, q. in Nikolaos Hlamides, "The Smyrna Holocaust," 199.

348. Sarah Jacob to D. A. Davis, a 10-page report in diary form, 14 September 1922, Houghton ABC 16.9.1, Vol. 1.

349. Smith, *Ionian Vision*, 302.

350. Brock, HMS *Iron Duke* to Admiralty, 2 October 1922, UKNA FO 371/7906; and H. E. Knauss, CO USS *Simpson*, Diary, entry for 8 September 1922, USNA RG 84, Turkey (Constantinople), Vol. 463.

351. Smith, *Ionian Vision*, 301–302.

352. Smith, *Ionian Vision*, 304–305.

353. E. M. Yantis, "Report of the Smyrna Fire," undated but from October–November 1922, USNA RG 84, Turkey (Constantinople), Vol. 466.

354. Knauss, CO, USS *Simpson*, Diary, entry for 9 September 1922, USNA RG 84, Turkey (Constantinople), Vol. 463.

355. Jaquith to Bristol, 11 October 1922, USNA RG 84, Turkey (Constantinople), Vol. 466.

356. W. Post, NER, "The Tragedy of Smyrna," 2 October 1922, UKNA FO 371/9108.

357. A. J. Hepburn to Bristol (a 47-page report covering 8–17 September), 25 September 1922, USNA RG 84, Turkey (Constantinople), Vol. 466.

358. Chester Fairwold (?) to Bristol, 29 October 1922, USNA RG 84, Turkey (Constantinople), Vol. 466.

359. "Statement by Dr. Alexander MacLachlan, president of the International College, Paradise, Smyrna, Asia Minor, to Mason Mitchell, American Consul, Malta, Valetta," 21 September 1922, USNA RG 84, Turkey (Constantinople), Vol. 466; and "Report by the Rev. Charles Dobson on Smyrna," undated but from late October 1922, UKNA FO 371/7949. See also Hepburn to Bristol, 25 September 1922, USNA RG 84, Turkey (Constantinople), Vol. 466.

360. "Memorandum by Mr. Hole on Events in Smyrna," 18 September 1922, USNA RG 84, Turkey (Constantinople), Vol. 466.

361. Hlamides, "Smyrna Holocaust," 203.

362. Myrtle Nolan, "Report on Smyrna Disaster to the American High Commission, Constantinople," 7 October 1922, USNA RG 84, Turkey (Constantinople), Vol. 466.

363. Knauss, CO USS *Simpson*, Diary, entry for 9 September 1922, USNA RG 84, Turkey (Constantinople), Vol. 463.

364. Post, "The Tragedy of Smyrna," 2 October 1922, UKNA FO 371/9108.

365. Nolan, "Report on Smyrna Disaster to the American High Commission, Constantinople," 7 October 1922, USNA RG 84, Turkey (Constantinople), Vol. 466.

366. Sarah Jacob to D. A. Davis, 14 September 1922, Houghton ABC 16.9.1, Vol. 1.

367. Knauss, CO USS *Simpson*, Diary, entry for 10 September 1922, USNA RG 84, Turkey (Constantinople), Vol. 463.

368. Post, "The Tragedy of Smyrna," 2 October 1922, UKNA FO 371/9108.

369. Theodore Bartoli, "Some Truths about the Smyrna Catastrophe," undated, attached to Bartoli to SecState, 5 December 1922, USNA RG 59, 867.4016, Roll 48.

370. Dobkin, *Smyrna 1922*, 133–134. See also Mango, *Atatürk*, 345.

371. "Report by Rev. Charles Dobson on Smyrna," undated but from late October 1922, UKNA FO 371/7949; and Bartoli, "Some Truths about the Smyrna Catastrophe," undated but attached to Bartoli to SecState, 5 December 1922, USNA RG 59, 867.4016, Roll 48.

372. Mango, *Atatürk*, 330; and Lt. Col. Ian Smith, untitled report, 7 April 1919, UKNA FO 371/4157.

373. "Memorandum by Mr. Hole on Events in Smyrna," 18 September 1922, USNA RG 84, Turkey (Constantinople), Vol. 466.

374. Rene Puaux, "Translation of Extracts from 'La Morte de Smyrne,'" undated but from November 1922, a pamphlet published in Paris, based on testimony by T. Roy Treloar, USNA RG 59, 867.4016, Roll 47; and Post, "The Tragedy of Smyrna," 2 October 1922, UKNA FO 371/9108.

375. "Memorandum by Mr. Hole on Events in Smyrna," 18 September 1922, USNA RG 84, Turkey (Constantinople), Vol. 466.

376. Hlamides, "Smyrna Holocaust," 206.

377. Dobkin, *Smyrna 1922*, 135.

378. Theodore Bartoli, "Some Truths about the Smyrna Catastrophe," attached to Bartoli to SecState, 5 December 1922, USNA RG 59, 867.4016. The church story may be untrue (see Lt. A. S. Merrill, USS *Litchfield*, Smyrna, Diary, entry for 10 September 1922, USNA RG 84, Turkey (Constantinople), Vol. 466).

379. Peet to Riggs, 20 September 1922, Houghton ABC 16.9.3, Vol. 52.

380. Knauss, CO USS *Simpson*, Diary, entry for 11 September 1922, USNA RG 84, Turkey (Constantinople), Vol. 463.

381. Puaux, "Translation of Extracts from 'La Mort de Smyrne,'" USNA RG 59, 867.4016, Roll 47.

382. Barnes to SecState, "The Occupation of Smyrna by the Turks and the Burning of the City," 18 September 1922, UKNA FO 371/7950.

383. Horton to SecState, 12 September 1922, USNA RG 84, Turkey (Constantinople), Vol. 466. Shaw, *From Empire to Republic*, vol. 4, 1730, devotes almost no space to the events in Smyrna between September 9 and 13, though he describes at length the concurrent Muslim celebrations in Constantinople of the Turkish victory. He sums things up as follows: "The Greeks . . . offered little opposition . . . to the Turkish occupation. . . . On the other hand, the Armenians in the city responded with force, rioting in the Armenian quarter starting on September 11, shooting and throwing bombs at Turks passing through on their way to other parts of the city. A series of fires broke out there . . . starting in the early afternoon of September 13." Not a word is provided about the slaughter or rape of Christians or about the Turkish looting. Without doubt, this is one of the most dishonest exhibitions of the historian's craft we have come across.

384. Hartunian, *Neither to Laugh nor to Weep*, 191. Hartunian was probably unique in having witnessed and undergone all three stages of the Turkish destruction of the Christians—in Severek in 1895, in Maraş in 1915–1916, and in Maraş and Smyrna in 1920–1922.

385. Hepburn to Bristol, 25 September 1922, USNA RG 84, Turkey (Constantinople), Vol. 466.

386. Post, "The Tragedy of Smyrna," 2 October 1922, UKNA FO 371/9108.

387. Hepburn to Bristol, 25 September 1922, USNA RG 84, Turkey (Constantinople), Vol. 466.

388. Davis to Bristol, 11 September 1922, USNA RG 84, Turkey (Constantinople), Vol. 466. Barnes recorded Nureddin as saying that "the Greeks and Armenians must leave Asia Minor" (Barnes, "Evacuation of Christian Population of Western Anatolia," 12 October 1922, USNA RG 84, Turkey (Constantinople), Vol. 464). Another description of the meeting is in A. S. Merrill, Smyrna, Diary, entry for 11 September 1922, USNA RG 84, Turkey (Constantinople), Vol. 466.

389. Dobkin, *Smyrna 1922*, 143–144.

390. Barnes to State Department, "Evacuation of Christian Population of Western Anatolia," 12 October 1922, USNA RG 84, Turkey (Constantinople), Vol. 464.

391. Post, "The Tragedy of Smyrna," 2 October 1922, UKNA FO 371/9108; and Davis to Bristol, 6 November 1922, USNA RG 84, Turkey (Constantinople), Vol. 466. The text of Nureddin's proclamations nos. 5 and 6 from, respectively, 16 and 24 September 1922, are in UKNA FO 371/10177.

392. Mills to Miss Lamson, 20 September 1920, Houghton ABC 16.9.2, Vol. 3.

393. Davis to Bristol, 6 November 1922, USNA RG 84, Turkey (Constantinople), Vol. 466.

394. Jaquith to Bristol, 11 October 1922, USNA RG 84, Turkey (Constantinople), Vol. 466. Jaquith was in Smyrna during 9–16 September.

395. Myrtle Nolan, "Report on Smyrna Disaster to the American High Commission, Constantinople," 7 October 1922, USNA RG 84, Turkey (Constantinople), Vol. 466.

396. Hepburn to Bristol, 25 September 1922, USNA RG 84, Turkey (Constantinople), Vol. 466.

397. "Statement by Dr. Alexander MacLachlan . . . , president of the International College, Paradise, Smyrna, Asia Minor, to Mason Mitchell (?), American Consul, Malta," 21 September 1922, USNA RG 84, Turkey (Constantinople), Vol. 466.

398. MacLachlan, Cass Arthur Reed, S. L. Caldwell, R. H. MacLachlan, M. B. Mills, and Rosalind Reed to Barton, Constantinople, 15 or 16 (unclear) February 1919, USNA RG 84, Turkey (Constantinople), Vol. 405.

399. "Memorandum of Mr. Hole on Events in Smyrna," 18 September 1922, USNA RG 84, Turkey (Constantinople), Vol. 466.

400. Barnes to SecState, "The Occupation of Smyrna by the Turks and the Burning of the City," 18 September 1922, UKNA FO 371/7950.

401. Yantis, "Report of the Smyrna Fire," undated, USNA RG 84, Turkey (Constantinople), Vol. 466.

402. Horton, *Blight of Asia,* 162–164.

403. "Report by the Rev. Charles Dobson on Smyrna," undated but from late October 1922, UKNA FO 371/7949.

404. Rendel, "Notes on Turkish Atrocities from February to September 1922," 10 October 1922, UKNA FO 371/7955. This does not explain the initial, systematic murder of Smyrna's Armenians.

405. Prentiss to *New York Times,* 9 October 1922, USNA RG 84, Turkey (Constantinople), Vol. 466.

406. Kevorkian, *Armenian Genocide,* 257.

407. Vice-consul, Smyrna, to Morgenthau, 14 August 1914, and enclosed letter, unsigned, 14 August 1914, USNA RG 59, 867.00, Roll 5; and vice-consul to Morgenthau, 20 August 1914, USNA RG 59, 867.00, Roll 5. See also Hollis to Morgenthau, 13 August 1914, USNA RG 59, 867.00, Roll 6; GOC Egypt to Secretary for War, 15 November 1914, UKNA FO 371/2141; C. E. Heathcote-Smith, acting UK consul-general, Smyrna, to Mallet, 20 August 1914, UKNA FO 371/2143; and entry for 6 October 1914, Morgenthau, *United States Diplomacy on the Bosphorus,* 107.

408. Mark Prentiss, "The Hitherto Untold Story of the Smyrna Fire Told by Mark O. Prentiss, American Representative of the Near East Relief," January 1923, attached to Prentiss to Bristol, 11 January 1923, LC, Bristol Papers 38.

409. Chester Fairwold to Bristol, 29 October 1922, USNA RG 84, Turkey (Constantinople), Vol. 466.

410. Horton to State Department, 2 September 1922, USNA RG 84, Turkey (Constantinople), Vol. 829.

411. Entry for 8 September 1922, Bristol War Diary, USNA RG 59, 867.00, Roll 11.

412. Merrill to Stanav, 6 September 1922, in "Diary, Smyrna," entry for 6 September 1922, USNA RG 84, Turkey (Constantinople), Vol. 466.

413. Knauss, USS *Simpson,* Diary, entry for 17 September 1922, USNA RG 84, Turkey (Constantinople), Vol. 463.

414. "Memorandum by Mr. Hole on Events in Smyrna," 18 September 1922, USNA RG 84, Turkey (Constantinople), Vol. 466.

415. Post, "The Tragedy of Smyrna," 2 October 1922, UKNA FO 371/9108.

416. Hepburn to Bristol, 25 September 1922, USNA RG 84, Turkey (Constantinople), Vol. 466.

417. Dobkin, *Smyrna 1922,* 170.

418. Barnes to SecState, "The Occupation of Smyrna by the Turks and the Burning of the City," 18 September 1922, UKNA FO 371/7950; and Lindley to FO, 19 September, UKNA FO 371/7890.

419. Post, "The Tragedy of Smyrna," 2 October 1922, UKNA FO 371/9108. Post was in Smyrna from 9 September until about 15 September.

420. Brock to Admiralty, 2 October 1922, UKNA FO 371/7906.

421. Davis to Bristol, 6 November 1922, USNA RG 84, Turkey (Constantinople), Vol. 466.

422. Dobkin, *Smyrna 1922,* 184. On the smell, see also the account by Charles James Howe, a British officer on HMS *Diligence,* q. in Hlamides, "Smyrna Holocaust," 211.

423. "Memorandum by Mr. Hole on Events in Smyrna," 18 September 1922, USNA RG 84, Turkey (Constantinople), Vol. 466.

424. Dobkin, *Smyrna 1922,* 184.

425. Hepburn to Bristol, 25 September 1922, USNA RG 84, Turkey (Constantinople), Vol. 466.

426. US High Commission, Constantinople, to director, Bureau of Foreign and Domestic Commerce, Department of Commerce, Washington DC, "Monthly Report, October," 2 November 1923, USNA RG 84, Turkey (Constantinople), Vol. 479. See also Gouraud to War Ministry, 27 November 1922, SHD, GR N7, 4165.

427. Vickrey to SecState, 29 November 1922, USNA RG 59, 867.4016, Roll 48.

428. Prentiss, "The Hitherto Untold Story of the Smyrna Fire Told by Mark O. Prentiss, American Representative of the NER, Armenians, Not Turks, Set the Fire—Evidence of Smyrna Fire Chief [Grescovich] Revealed," January 1922, attached to Prentiss to Bristol, 11 January 1923, LC, Bristol Papers 38.

429. A. S. Merrill, USS *Litchfield,* Smyrna, Diary, entry for 15 September 1922, USNA RG 84, Turkey (Constantinople), Vol. 466.

430. Entry for 17 October 1922, Bristol War Diary, USNA RG 59, 867.00, Roll 19.

431. Entry for 11 December 1922, Bristol War Diary, USNA RG 59, 867.00, Roll 13.

432. Hepburn to Bristol, 25 September 1922, USNA RG 84, Turkey (Constantinople), Vol. 466.

433. Unsigned, "Report from Anatolia," undated, but attached to DMI, WO, to Eyre Crowe, 30 October 1922, UKNA FO 371/7907.

434. Hartunian, *Neither to Laugh nor to Weep,* 196.

435. Dobkin, *Smyrna 1922,* 155.

436. Mills to Lamson, 20 September 1922, Houghton ABC 16.9.2, Vol. 3.

437. Post, "The Tragedy of Smyrna," 2 October 1922, UKNA FO 371/9108.

438. US High Commission, "Who Burned Smyrna?—Service Report," 29 September 1922, USNA RG 84, Turkey (Constantinople), Vol. 466.

439. "Memorandum by Mr. Hole on Events in Smyrna," 18 September 1922, USNA RG 84, Turkey (Constantinople), Vol. 466.

440. Rumbold to FO, 17 September 1922, UKNA FO 371/7888; Rumbold to Curzon, 18 September 1922, UKNA FO 371/7950 ("It is probably [the Turks'] intention that the future Smyrna should be a purely Turkish town . . ."); and Horton, *Blight of Asia,* 144–154.

441. Post, "The Tragedy of Smyrna," 2 October 1922, UKNA FO 371/9108.

442. Dobkin, *Smyrna 1922,* 156, 230–233. In December 1924 the American Tobacco Company brought suit against the Guardian Assurance Company at the High Court of Justice in London. The insurance company refused to pay, claiming that the fire was a result of "warlike operations" (Dobkin, *Smyrna 1922,* 230–233).

443. Dobkin, *Smyrna 1922,* 157.

444. Davis to Bristol, 6 November 1922, USNA RG 84, Turkey (Constantinople), Vol. 466.

445. Peet to Barton, 20 September 1922, Houghton ABC 16.9.3, Vol. 52.

446. Lindley to FO, 29 September 1922, UKNA FO 371/7896. For the expulsion of "Greek and Armenian men, women and children" from Kırkağaç, northeast of Smyrna, see unsigned, "Summary of a

Confidential Report on Recent Events at Pergamos, Soma and District," 28 October 1922, attached to Henderson to Oliphant, 4 November 1922, UKNA FO 371/7950.

447. Greek Legation, London, to Curzon, 10 October 1922, UKNA FO 371/7955.

448. Rendel, "Notes on Turkish Atrocities from February to September 1922," 10 October 1922, UKNA FO 371/7955.

449. Nansen to high commissioners in Constantinople, 10 October 1922, UKNA FO 371/7956.

450. "Minutes of a Conference held in the British Embassy on Thursday, October 12, 1922, to Discuss the Refugee Problem in Greece and Asia Minor with Dr. Nansen," UKNA FO 371/7956.

451. Post, "The Tragedy of Smyrna," 2 October 1922, UKNA FO 371/9108.

452. Jaquith to Bristol, 11 October 1922, USNA RG 84, Turkey (Constantinople), Vol. 466. See also Knauss, USS *Simpson,* Diary, entry for 18 September 1922, USNA RG 84, Turkey (Constantinople), Vol. 463.

453. Knauss, USS *Simpson,* Diary, entry for 18 September 1922, USNA RG 84, Turkey (Constantinople), Vol. 463.

454. Bristol, "Report of Operations for Week Ending 17 September 1922," LC, Bristol Papers, War Diary.

455. Joseph Beach to State Department, 2 December 1922, USNA RG 84, Turkey (Constantinople), Vol. 464; and Beach, Henry Murphy, Lillian Sewny, and Katharine Fletcher, "Report of Conditions in Anatolia Submitted by Members of the Cesarea Unit, NER, to the US High Commission, Constantinople," 4 December 1922, USNA RG 59, 867.4016, Roll 48.

456. "Part Three, Report of Operations for Week Ending 8 October 1922," LC, Bristol Papers, War Diary.

457. State Dept., Division of Near Eastern Affairs, to Dulles, 16 October 1922, USNA RG 59, 867.4016, Roll 48.

458. Greek Legation, London, to Curzon, 27 October 1922, UKNA FO 371/7957.

459. Bristol to Eugenia S. Bumgardner, 7 December 1922, LC, Bristol Papers 38.

460. Hadkinson to Rumbold, 20 September 1922, UKNA FO 371/7950.

461. Yantis, "Report of the Smyrna Fire," undated but from October–November 1922, USNA RG 84, Turkey (Constantinople), Vol. 466.

462. Dobkin, *Smyrna 1922,* unnumbered footnote on page 201 and page 265 footnote 201, implies that more than 100,000 Christians died in Smyrna and environs, and states that this was Horton's estimate. But it wasn't. Horton, *Blight of Asia,* 173, merely cited estimates by the Reuter news agency and an article in the London *Daily Chronicle.*

463. Hlamides, "Smyrna Holocaust," 223–224.

464. Bristol, "Memorandum," 21 September 1921, USNA RG 84, Turkey (Constantinople), Vol. 466.

465. "Account of Meeting of an Allied Mixed Committee on Refugee Problems [27 May 1922]," undated but attached to Rumbold to Balfour, 6 June 1922, UKNA FO 371/7866; and Rumbold to FO, 9 September 1922, UKNA FO 371/7886.

466. Barnes, "Evacuation of Christian Population of Western Anatolia," Smyrna, 12 October 1922, USNA RG 84, Turkey (Constantinople), Vol. 464.

467. Davis, chairman, Disaster Relief Committee, Constantinople Chapter, American Red Cross, to Bristol, 6 November 1922, USNA RG 84, Turkey (Constantinople), Vol. 466. Davis was in Smyrna from 9 to 22 September.

468. A. S. Merrill, Smyrna, Diary, entry for 11 September 1922, USNA RG 84, Turkey (Constantinople), Vol. 466. See also Emily McCallum (Piraeus) to Kate Samson (Boston), 30 September 1922, Houghton ABC 16.9.2, Vol. 3.

469. Nureddin, "Proclamation," 23 September 1922, UKNA FO 371/7898.

470. Barnes, "Evacuation of Christian Population of Western Anatolia," Smyrna, 12 October 1922, USNA RG 84, Turkey (Constantinople), Vol. 464.

471. Hepburn to Bristol, 25 September 1922, USNA RG 84, Turkey (Constantinople), Vol. 466.

472. Entry for 22 September 1922, LC, Bristol Papers, War Diary.

473. Powell, CO USS *Edsall,* "Situation at Smyrna," 19 September 1922, USNA RG 84, Turkey (Constantinople), Vol. 462; and Rendel, "Assistance Given by His Majesty's Government in Evacuating and Relieving Refugees from Asia Minor," 13 October 1922, UKNA FO 371/7955.

474. Powell, USS *Edsall,* to Bristol, 9 October 1922, USNA RG 84, Turkey (Constantinople), Vol. 462.

475. Powell, USS *Edsall,* Diary—Smyrna, entry for 24 September 1922, USNA RG 59, 867.00, Roll 12.

476. Captain H. C. Buckle, OC HMS *Curacoa,* to Rear Admiral Wilmot Nicholson, 2 October 1922, UKNA FO 371/7958.

477. Fairwold (?) to Bristol, 29 October 1922, USNA RG 84, Turkey (Constantinople), Vol. 466.

478. Powell, USS *Edsall,* Diary, entry for 15 October 1922, USNA RG 84, Turkey, (Constantinople), Vol. 462.

479. Barnes, "Evacuation of Christian Population of Western Anatolia," Smyrna, 12 October 1922, USNA RG 84, Turkey (Constantinople), Vol. 464.

480. Powell, USS *Edsall,* Diary, 1 October 1922, USNA RG 84, Turkey (Constantinople), Vol. 462.

481. McCormick to Bristol, 22 October 1922, USNA RG 84, Turkey (Constantinople), Vol. 464; and USS *King* to Bristol, "Report on Alaya and Adalia, Asia Minor," 5 November 1922, USNA RG 84, Turkey (Constantinople), Vol. 462. See also Powell, USS *Edsall,* 9 October 1922, USNA RG 84, Turkey (Constantinople), Vol. 462; and Barnes, "Evacuation of Christian Population of Western Anatolia," 12 October 1922, USNA RG 84, Turkey (Constantinople), Vol. 464.

482. Clark, *Twice a Stranger,* 24.

483. Üngör, "Turkey for the Turks," 295.

484. E. A. Walleson (?), USS *Lawrence,* to Powell, 10 October 1922, USNA RG 84, Turkey (Constantinople), Vol. 462.

485. Clark, *Twice a Stranger,* 25. See also "Extracts from a [YMCA team] report on the Conditions of Refugees in the Greek Islands," attached to F. O. Lindley to Curzon, 10 November 1922, UKNA FO 371/7960.

486. Howard, *Partition of Turkey,* 272–273.

487. Bristol to US Legation, Athens, 28 October 1922, USNA RG 84, Turkey (Constantinople), Vol. 465; and Bristol to SecState, 23 October 1922, USNA RG 84, Turkey (Constantinople), Vol. 465.

488. Frederic R. Dolbeare, acting US High Commissioner, 29 November 1922, USNA RG 84, Turkey (Constantinople), Vol. 465.

489. Hemingway, *Toronto Daily Star,* 22 October 1922, q. in Clark, *Twice a Stranger,* 48.

490. Charles Wilson, Sofia, to Foreign Minister, 1 April 1923, USNA RG 84, Turkey (Constantinople), Vol. 479.

491. Rumbold to FO, 12 November 1922, UKNA FO 371/7911.

492. CO USS *Simpson,* Beirut, Diary, entry for 11 December 1922, USNA RG 59, 867.00, Roll 13.

493. Powell USS *Edsall,* Diary, entry for 18 October 1922, USNA RG 84, Turkey (Constantinople), Vol. 462.

494. Urquhart to Rumbold, 13 October 1922, UKNA FO 371/7949.

495. Nicholson to C-in-C, Mediterranean Station, 19 October 1922, UKNA FO 371/7950.

496. Rumbold to Curzon, 12 September 1922, UKNA FO 371/7889.

497. Bristol to SecState, 17 October 1922, USNA RG 84, Turkey (Constantinople), Vol. 459.

498. Bristol to Eugenia Bumgardner, 7 December 1922, LC, Bristol Papers 38.

499. Curzon to ?, 22 September 1922, UKNA FO 371/7892.

500. "The Situation in the Near East . . . Conclusions of Cabinet on 23rd September, 1922," UKNA FO 371/7893.

501. Harington to WO, 24 September 1922, UKNA FO 371/7895; and Harington to WO, 26 and 27 September 1922, UKNA FO 371/7896.

502. Gilbert, *Rumbold,* 262.

503. "Draft Minutes of a Conference of Ministers Held at 10, Downing Street. . . . 27th September, 1922 . . . ," UKNA FO 371/7896; "Draft Conclusions of a Conference of Ministers held at 10, Downing Street . . . on 28th September, 1922 . . . ," UKNA FO 371/7896; and "Draft Minutes of a Conference of Ministers held at Lord Curzon's House, No. 1 Carlton House Terrace, London . . . 29th September, 1922 . . . ," UKNA FO 371/7898.

504. Harington to WO, 28 September 1922, UKNA FO 371/7896; and Harington to WO, 30 September 1922, UKNA FO 371/7899.

505. Barton to "Friends," 16 October 1922, Houghton ABC 16.9.2, Vol. 5.

506. Rendel, "Situation in Constantinople and Safety of Christian Minorities," 13 November 1922, with attached "Extracts from Recent telegrams . . . ," UKNA FO 371/7958.

507. Gates to Staub, 2 November 1922, Houghton ABC 16.9.2, Vol. 5.

508. James Morgan (Aleppo) to Curzon, 13 December 1922, UKNA FO 371/7875.

509. Executive Officer, USS *Overton,* to Bristol, "Diary, Samsoun," entries for 1 and 4 November 1922, USNA RG 84, Turkey (Constantinople), Vol. 463.

510. Entry for 13 November 1922, LC, Bristol Papers, War Diary.

511. Bristol, "Memorandum," 16 November 1922, LC, Bristol Papers 38.

512. Henderson to FO, 1 December 1922, UKNA FO 371/7960.

513. Nevile Henderson to FO, 4 December 1922, UKNA FO 371/7960. Henderson was Rumbold's deputy.

514. Entry for 16 November 1922, LC, Bristol Papers, War Diary.

515. Bristol to SecState, 19 November 1922, USNA RG 59, 867.4016, Roll 47.

516. Entry for 4 November 1922, LC, Bristol Papers, War Diary.

517. Entry for 4 November 1922, LC, Bristol Papers, War Diary, giving text of Aide Memoire to Turkish Government.

518. Rumbold to FO, 5 November 1922, UKNA FO 371/7957. Rendel minuted that it was "hard to believe" that there are "over 1 million Christians left in Anatolia. . . . If there really were a million left, then the pre-war estimates were wrong" (6 November 1922).

519. Jackson to SecState, 28 November 1922, USNA RG 59, 867.4016, Roll 48.

520. Morgan (Aleppo) to Curzon, 13 December 1922, UKNA FO 371/7875.

521. Fowle to Vickrey, 14 November 1922, USNA RG 59, 867.4016, Roll 47.

522. Bristol, "Report on Operations for Week Ending 3 December 1922," part 3, LC, Bristol Papers, War Diary.

523. Jackson to SecState, 25 November 1922, USNA RG 59, 867.4016, Roll 47; and Morgan (Aleppo) to Curzon, 22 November 1922, UKNA FO 371/7875.

524. Jackson to SecState, 18 November 1922, USNA RG 59, 867.4016, Roll 47.

525. USS *Overton,* Diary, entry for 23 November 1922, USNA RG 59, 867.00, Roll 13.

526. USS *Overton,* Diary, Samsoun, entries for 3 and 4 November 1922, USNA RG 84, Turkey (Constantinople), Vol. 463.

527. USS *Overton,* Diary, entries for 27, 28, and 30 November 1922, USNA RG 84, Turkey (Constantinople), Vol. 463.

528. Jackson to SecState, 9 December 1922, USNA RG 59, 867.4016, Roll 48; and texts, translations of articles into English appended to Jackson to SecState, 28 November 1922, USNA RG 59, 867.4016, Roll 48.

529. Jackson to SecState, 26 November 1922, USNA RG 59, 867.4016, Roll 47.

530. USS *Overton*, Diary, entry for 1 November 1922, USNA RG 84, Turkey (Constantinople), Vol. 463.

531. Hofmann, "Cumulative Genocide," 83 and 100.

532. Rendel, "Memorandum Regarding Pontic Refugees," 26 February 1923, UKNA FO 371/9092.

533. Quoted in NER, "Report of the Near East Relief for the Year Ending December 31, 1922" (Washington DC, 1923), 15.

534. USS *Barry*, "Samsoun Diary," entry for 25 November 1922, USNA RG 84, Turkey (Constantinople), Vol. 462.

535. CO USS *Simpson* to Bristol, "Diary Samsoun," entry for 1 April 1923, USNA RG 84, Turkey (Constantinople), Vol. 483.

536. C. F. Grant, Samsun Unit, NER, to managing director, NER, 15 March 1923, USNA RG 84, Turkey (Constantinople), Vol. 484.

537. CO USS *Hatfield* to Bristol, "Diary—Mersina," entry for 16 May 1923, USNA RG 84, Turkey (Constantinople), Vol. 483.

538. Jackson to SecState, 4 December 1922, USNA RG 59, 867.4016, Roll 48; and Jackson to SecState, 11 December 1922, USNA RG 59, 867.4016, Roll 48. Jackson feared the Turks intended to conquer Mosul and Aleppo and dreaded another "Smyrna."

539. US Government official, "Report on the Condition of the Asia Minor Refugees in Certain Greek Islands," undated but attached to Bentinck (Athens) to Curzon, 2 December 1922, UKNA FO 371/7961.

540. Crutcher to managing director, NER, Constantinople, 13 April 1923, USNA RG 84, Turkey (Constantinople), Vol. 484.

541. C. W. Fowle, NER director for Syria and Palestine, "Memoranda [sic] Gurumza Massacre," 4 June 1923, attached to Knabenshue to Bristol, 11 June 1923, USNA RG 84, Turkey (Constantinople), Vol. 484; CO USS *Bulmer* to Bristol, "Station Diary," 7 May 1923, USNA RG 84, Turkey (Constantinople), Vol. 483; and Satow to Foreign Secretary, 24 May 1923, UKNA FO 371/9110.

542. USS *McCormick*, Diary, entry for 3 December 1922, USNA RG 59, 867.00, Roll 13.

543. Entry for 18 January 1923, CO USS *Overton*, Diary, USNA RG 84, Turkey (Constantinople), Vol. 483.

544. Lt. Sigler, USS *McFarland*, "Sanitary Report on Mersina," 8 February 1923, USNA RG 84, Turkey (Constantinople), Vol. 483.

545. Ahmed, president of Mersina municipality, to NER Mersina, 10 February 1923, in CO USS *Barry* to Bristol, 19 February 1923, USNA RG 59, 867.00, Roll 14.

546. CO USS *Lawrence* to Bristol, "Diary—Mersina and Alexandretta," entry for 15 March 1923, USNA RG 84, Turkey (Constantinople), Vol. 483; and CO USS *Bulmer* to Bristol, "Station Diary—Mersina," entries for 5 and 6 March 1923, USNA RG 84, Turkey (Constantinople), Vol. 483.

547. Entry for 6 April 1923, R. K. Awtrey, CO USS *Hatfield*, "Station Diary—Mersina and Alexandretta," USNA RG 59, 867.00, Roll 14.

548. Joseph Beach, NER director, Mersina, "Report of Refugee Situation, Mersina, April 8, 1923," USNA RG 84, Turkey (Constantinople), Vol. 485.

549. CO USS *Lawrence* to Bristol, "Diary—Samsun," entry for 20 April 1923, USNA RG 84, Turkey (Constantinople), Vol. 483.

550. Entry for 26 November 1922, USS *Overton* diary, USNA RG 84, Turkey (Constantinople), Vol. 463.

551. USS *Barry*, "Samsoun Diary," entry for 24 November 1922, USNA RG 84, Turkey (Constantinople), Vol. 462.

552. Crutcher to Jaquith, 16 March 1923, USNA RG 84, Turkey (Constantinople), Vol. 484; and USS *Bulmer* to Bristol, 7 January 1923, USNA RG 84, Turkey (Constantinople), Vol. 484.

553. USS *Bulmer* to Bristol, 7 January 1923, USNA RG 84, Turkey (Constantinople), Vol. 484.

554. Entry for 15 February 1923, CO USS *Sturtevant,* "Station Diary Trebizond," to Bristol, USNA RG 84, Turkey (Constantinople), Vol. 483.

555. Crutcher to managing director NER, 1 May 1923, and M. Tsamados, Greek Legation, Washington DC, to Allen Dulles, State Department, 14 May 1923, both in USNA RG 84, Turkey (Constantinople), Vol. 484.

556. CO USS *Bainbridge* to Bristol, diary entry for 25 March 1923, USNA RG 84, Turkey (Constantinople), Vol. 483, for threats by *mutasarrif* of Mersina. But other mutesarrifs told American officers that they would not force Greeks to leave or deport them to the interior (CO USS *Bainbridge,* diary entry for 31 March 1923, in LC, Bristol Papers, War Diary, reporting on conversation with Hamdi Bey, the "sub-governor" at Fatsa).

557. Dolbeare to State Department, 3 January 1923, USNA RG 84, Turkey (Constantinople), Vol. 484.

558. CO USS *Overton* to Bristol, "Diary, Mersina," entries for 16 and 19 March 1923, USNA RG 84, Turkey (Constantinople), Vol. 483.

559. CO USS *McFarland* to Bristol, diary entry (Trebizond) 16 March 1923, USNA RG 59, 867.00, Roll 14; CO USS *Simpson* to Bristol, diary entry (Ordu) 31 March 1923, USNA RG 84, Turkey (Constantinople), Vol. 483; and J. B. Rhodes, CO USS *Litchfield* to Bristol, diary entry (Samsun) 21 March 1923, USNA RG 84, Turkey (Constantinople), Vol. 483.

560. Bristol, "Part Three, Report of Conditions for Week Ending April 1, 1923," LC, Bristol Papers, War Diary.

561. Knapp, USS *Lawrence,* Mersina, to USS *Overton,* 19 March 1923, in OC USS *Overton* to Bristol, "Diary: Alexandretta," entry for 19 March 1923, USNA RG 59, 867.00, Roll 14.

562. Crutcher to Bristol, 7 April 1923, USNA RG 84, Turkey (Constantinople), Vol. 484.

563. Bristol, "Part Three, Report of Conditions for Week Ending April 1, 1923," LC, Bristol Papers, War Diary.

564. "Translation of Order Posted on the Gates of Armenian and Greek Churches in Mersine, March 16, 1923," USNA RG 84, Turkey (Constantinople), Vol. 485.

565. USS *Overton* to Bristol, 22 March 1923, USNA RG 84, Turkey (Constantinople), Vol. 485.

566. Bristol, "Part Four, Report of Operations for Week Ending 25 March, 1923 . . . A General Summery," LC, Bristol Papers, War Diary.

567. Joseph Beach, NER director, Mersina, "Report of Refugee Situation, Mersine, April 8, 1923," USNA RG 84, Turkey (Constantinople), Vol. 485.

568. Entry for 4 April 1923, LC, Bristol Papers, War Diary.

569. Beach, "Report of Refugee Situation, Mersine, April 8, 1923," USNA RG 84, Turkey (Constantinople), Vol. 485.

570. CO USS *McFarland* to Bristol, "Diary—Samsoun," entry for 22 March 1923, USNA RG 84, Turkey (Constantinople), Vol. 483.

571. CO USS *Goff* to Bristol, "Diary—Samsoun," entry for 23 May 1923, USNA RG 84, Turkey (Constantinople), Vol. 483.

572. USS *Sturtevant,* "Station Diary—Mersina," 2 January 1923, USNA RG 84, Turkey (Constantinople), Vol. 463.

573. CO USS *Litchfield* to Bristol, "Diary—Samsoun," "Summary of Refugee Situation," 1 June 1923, USNA RG 59, 867.00, Roll 15.

574. CO USS *Edsall* to Bristol, "Diary—Mersina," entry for 16 April 1923, USNA RG 84, Turkey (Constantinople), Vol. 483.

575. L. L. Jordan, CO USS *Barry,* to Bristol, 6 January 1923, USNA RG 84, Turkey (Constantinople), Vol. 483.

576. CO USS *Edsall* to Bristol, "Diary—Alexandretta," entry for 18 April 1923, USNA RG 84, Turkey (Constantinople), Vol. 483.

577. Arthur Ringland, "Greek Refugee Situation in Constantinople," 7 March 1923, USNA RG 84, Turkey (Constantinople), Vol. 484.

578. Wilfred Post to Ravndal, 4 March 1923, and enclosed memorandum (by Post), "Refugees in Constantinople," USNA RG 84, Turkey (Constantinople), Vol. 484.

579. Jordan, CO USS *Barry,* to Bristol, 6 January 1923, USNA RG 84, Turkey (Constantinople), Vol. 483; and USS *Barry* to Bristol, 7 January 1923, USNA RG 84, Turkey (Constantinople), Vol. 484. The higher figure may have lumped together refugees and permanent residents.

580. Hekinian to managing director NER, Beirut, 28 August 1923, UKNA FO 371/9098.

581. "List of Refugees in Greece," 7/20 December 1922, enclosed in C. H. Bentinck (Athens) to FO, 27 December 1922, UKNA FO 371/9091.

582. "Statistics of Refugees in Greece," "communicated by Major R. de L. Barton, June 5th, 1923," UKNA FO 371/9096.

583. Unsigned, "Report on the Condition of the Asia Minor Refugees in Certain Greek Islands," undated, attached to Bentinck (Athens) to Curzon, 2 December 1922, UKNA FO 371/7961.

584. Rendel, "Memorandum on the Present Situation as Regards Refugees in Greece," 17 November 1922, UKNA FO 371/7959; and Rendel, "Memorandum," 28 November 1922, UKNA FO 371/7960.

585. F.O. Lindley to Curzon, 7 October 1922, and E. H. Mitchell to Lindley, 2 October 1922, both in UKNA FO 371/7955.

586. Dobkin, *Smyrna 1922,* 214.

587. E. H. Mitchell to Lindley, 2 October 1922, attached to Lindley to Curzon, 7 October 1922, UKNA FO 371/7955.

588. "Summary of Intelligence No. 5, October 30th," attached to directorate of All British Appeal for the Relief of the Famine in Russia and Distress in the Near East, to Rendel, 30 October 1922, UKNA FO 371/7957.

589. Entry for 1 February 1923, CO USS *Goff,* diary, USNA RG 84, Turkey (Constantinople), Vol. 483.

590. CO, US naval detachment in Turkish waters, "War Diary—Greece," 22 May 1923, USNA RG 84, Turkey (Constantinople), Vol. 483.

591. Ruth Parmelee to Peet, 23 October 1922, USNA RG 84, Turkey (Constantinople), Vol. 465.

592. C. Claflin Davis to Allen Dulles, 3 March 1921, USNA RG 84, Turkey (Constantinople), Vol. 444.

593. Parmelee to Peet, 23 October 1922, USNA RG 84, Turkey (Constantinople), Vol. 465.

594. Crutcher to assistant managing director, NER, 14 August 1923, USNA RG 84, Turkey (Constantinople), Vol. 484.

595. "Part Three, Report of Operations for Week Ending 19 August 1923," entry for 11 August 1923, LC, Bristol Papers, War Diary.

596. CO USS *Simpson* to Bristol, "Diary—Samsoun," entry for 22 August 1923, USNA RG 84, Turkey (Constantinople), Vol. 483.

597. C. C. Thurber, assistant managing director, NER, Constantinople, to Bristol, 24 August 1923, USNA RG 84, Turkey (Constantinople), Vol. 485.

598. D. C. Hibbard, Michael Melas, and William Rapp, "Second Annual Report of the Athens American Relief Committee on Refugee Conditions in Greece and the Greek Islands," 13 November 1923, USNA RG 84, Turkey (Constantinople), Vol. 484. For an overview of the refugees' absorption, Pentzo-poulos, *Balkan Exchange,* 75–219.

599. N. S. Roberts to Department of Overseas Trade, 30 January 1923, UKNA FO 371/9113.

600. Rendel, *Sword and the Olive,* 54.

601. Quoted in Pentzopoulos, *Balkan Exchange,* 58 and footnote 24.

602. Entry for 30 March 1923, LC, Bristol Papers, War Diary.

603. Smith, *Ionian Vision,* 32–33.

604. Entry for 6 October 1919, LC, Bristol Papers, War Diary; and Venizelos to Lloyd George, 27 October 1919, q. in Smith, *Ionian Vision,* 115.

605. Treaty of Sevres, article 143.

606. Toynbee to the editor, 30 April 1921 (a draft letter), Bodl. MS Toynbee Papers 50.

607. Peet to Barton, 20 September 1922, Houghton ABC 16.9.3, Vol. 52.

608. "Draft Minutes of the Eighth Meeting [of Lausanne's Territorial and Military Commission], December 1, 1922 . . . ," Curzon's opening statement, UKNA FO 371/7967.

609. Rendel, "Memorandum on the Proposed Exchange of Greek and Turkish Minorities," 30 November 1922, UKNA FO 371/7954.

610. Lindley to FO, 21 February 1922, UKNA FO 371/7856. Greece and Bulgaria had signed their population exchange agreement, the "Convention between Greece and Bulgaria," at Neuilly-sur-Seine on November 27, 1919 (see Annex 1 to Rendel, "Memorandum on the Proposed Exchange of Greek and Turkish Minorities," 30 November 1922, UKNA FO 371/7954).

611. Untitled memorandum of conversation by Eyre Crowe, FO, 12 October 1922, UKNA FO 371/7904.

612. Lindley to Curzon, 23 November 1922, UKNA FO 371/7965.

613. Rendel, "Memorandum on the Proposed Exchange of Greek and Turkish Minorities," 30 November 1922, UKNA FO 371/7954. The number for Asia Minor seems inflated.

614. "Minutes of Conference Held in the British Embassy on Sunday, October 15, 1922 at 12 Noon, to Discuss . . . ," attached to Rumbold to Curzon, 17 October 1922, UKNA FO 371/7906.

615. "Minutes of Conference held at the British Embassy on Sunday, October 15, 1922, at 12 Noon, to Discuss . . . ," attached to Rumbold to Curzon, 17 October 1922, UKNA FO 371/7906.

616. Rumbold to FO, 1 November 1922, UKNA FO 371/7957.

617. Lindley (Athens) to FO, 3 November 1922, UKNA FO 371/7957.

618. "Enclosure in No. 1, Report by Dr. Nansen," UKNA FO 371/7954.

619. Rendel, "Memorandum on the Proposed Exchange of Greek and Turkish Minorities," 30 November 1922, UKNA FO 371/7954.

620. "Extracts from Notes of Mrs. Frederick Hasluck," in Bentinck to Curzon, 19 January 1923, UKNA FO 371/9092.

621. E. C. Hole, acting UK consul general, Salonica, to Bentinck, 24 February 1923, UKNA FO 371/9093.

622. J. McG. Dawkins, Canea, Crete, to Bentinck, 2 March 1923, UKNA FO 371/9089.

623. Bentinck to Curzon, 22 January 1923, UKNA FO 371/9092.

624. Bentinck to Curzon, 31 January 1923, UKNA FO 371/9092.

625. "Draft Minutes of the Twenty-Third Meeting, January 27, 1923 [of the Territorial and Military Commission] . . . ," UKNA FO 371/9063.

626. Curzon (Lausanne) to FO, 11 December 1922, UKNA FO 371/7966.

627. Clark, *Twice a Stranger,* 88.

628. Text of "Convention . . . ," UKNA FO 371/9173.

629. Caffery, American Legation, Athens, to Bristol, 18 February 1923, USNA RG 84, Turkey (Constantinople), Vol. 486.

630. Rumbold to Curzon, 8 March 1923, UKNA FO 371/9093.

631. "No. 594," untitled, unsigned memorandum attached to Bentinck to FO, 1 March 1923, and FO to Rumbold, 6 March 1923, both in UKNA FO 371/9092.

632. "Part Three, Reports of Operations for Week Ending 4 March 1923," LC, Bristol Papers, War Diary.

633. Bentinck to FO, 10 March 1923, UKNA FO 371/9092.

634. Entry for 7 July 1923, Bristol War Diary, USNA RG 59, 867.00, Roll 15.

635. Bentinck to Curzon, 10 October 1923, UKNA FO 371/9172.

636. NER, "The Near East Relief and the Exchange of Population," 15 November 1923, USNA RG 84, Turkey (Constantinople), Vol. 486; and Crutcher to Jaquith, 7 November 1923, USNA RG 84, Turkey (Constantinople), Vol. 486.

637. USS *Simpson,* "Simpson Diary—Samsoun," entry for 5 November 1923, USNA RG 59, 867.00, Roll 16.

638. Q. in Clark, *Twice a Stranger,* 160.

639. Ruchdy, "Protest," undated but with covering letter Ismet to secretary general, 8 November 1923, UKNA FO 371/9172.

640. Rendel, minute, 12 November 1923, UKNA FO 371/9176.

641. Edmonds to Lindsay, 27 February 1924, and Edmonds to Henderson, 29 August 1924, both in UKNA FO 371/10184; and "Migrations of the Greeks and Turks," *Manchester Guardian,* 25 March 1924.

642. Henderson to Curzon, 18 September 1923, UKNA FO 371/9132.

643. Bentinck to Ramsay MacDonald, 30 (?) July 1924, UKNA FO 371/10223.

644. L. Patterson, Constantinople, to "Major," 11 November 1923, UKNA FO 371/9174.

645. T. H. Robbins, USS *Scorpion,* "Patrol Activities," 8 October 1923, USNA RG 84, Turkey (Constantinople), Vol. 480; and Henderson to Curzon, 9 October 1923, UKNA FO 371/9174.

646. J. F. R. Vaughan-Russell to Foreign Secretary, 20 February 1924, and Rendel minute, 10 March 1924, UKNA FO 371/10195.

647. Vaughn-Russell, UK consulate Aleppo, to SecState, FO, 24 March 1924, UKNA FO 371/10195. The "conditions," some dating back to *dhimmi* days, were published in a Damascus newspaper, *Al Taqqaddum,* on 22 March 1924.

648. R. C. Lindsay to MacDonald, 2 April 1924, and Lindsay to MacDonald, 16 April 1924, both in UKNA FO 371/10195.

649. Hough, Aleppo, to MacDonald, 2 June 1924, and Dobbs, Baghdad, to Colonial Secretary, 29 April 1924, both in UKNA FO 371/10195.

650. Vaughan-Russell to MacDonald, 4 March 1924, UKNA FO 371/10195.

651. Unsigned but NER, "Field Secretary's Report to Committee ad interim on Anatolian Trip September 1924," undated, Houghton ABC 16.9.2, Vol. 1.

652. R. D. T. Davies to R. E. Wood, commercial secretary, UK High Commission, Constantinople, 23 September 1924, UKNA FO 371/10229.

653. Henderson to MacDonald, 10 September 1924, UKNA FO 371/10184.

654. "Turkish 'round-up' of Greeks," *The Times,* 20 October 1924.

655. R. C. Lindsay, Constantinople, to MacDonald, 28 October 1924, UKNA FO 371/10185.

656. "Enclosure in No. 1," attached to Lindsay to Austin Chamberlain, 24 December 1924, UKNA FO 371/10185.

657. Rendel, "Atrocities in Asia Minor Etc. Protests Received by His Majesty's Government, and Action Taken," 28 December 1921, UKNA FO 371/7875.

658. Rumbold to Curzon, 3 January 1921, UKNA FO 371/6561; Hadji Osmanoghlou Ahmed, etc. to US High Commissioner, Constantinople, undated but received in September 1919, USNA RG 84, Turkey (Constantinople), Vol. 419; and James Morgan, Smyrna, to British High Commission, 31

October 1919, and James Morgan, Smyrna, to British High Commission, 26 March 1920, both in UKNA FO 371/5133, dealing with the murder of a Turk, one Houloussi Effendi, "by eight men in Greek uniform." The letters indicate that such killings were rare. Similarly a Turkish complaint, listing Greek offenses against Turks in and around Smyrna (National Defense Committee, Smyrna, "Report from Smyrna dated January 17th 1920," USNA RG 84, Turkey (Constantinople), Vol. 415), speaks almost exclusively of minor crimes.

659. Horton to Bristol, 23 January 1920, USNA RG 59, 867.00, Roll 8.

660. Commodore M. Fitzmaurice to C-in-C, Mediterranean, 22 April 1920, UKNA FO 371/5133.

661. Toynbee, *Western Question,* 281–282.

662. For example, a bombing of the railway near Odemish resulted in Greek reprisals against nearby Sarikli and Yeni Keui; hundreds of Turks were imprisoned and, in Sarikli, only one house remained standing (General F. Milne, C-in-C Army of the Black Sea, to UK High Commissioner, Constantinople, 13 April 1920, and attached "Extracts from various reports received from Advanced HQ, Smyrna, during the Months of February and March 1920 . . . ," UKNA FO 371/5133).

663. Governor's Office, Bursa Vilayet, "Report of the Troubles at Orkhan-Ghazi and the Surrounding Vicinity," 27 October 1920, USNA RG 84, Turkey (Constantinople), Vol. 418.

664. Servet Bey, mayor of Panderma, etc. to US High Commissioner, Constantinople, 16 November 1920, USNA RG 84, Turkey (Constantinople), Vol. 415.

665. H. Earle Russell, consul-in-charge, Smyrna, to SecState, 20 August 1920, USNA RG 84, Turkey (Constantinople), Vol. 418.

666. Unsigned, "Summary of a Confidential Report on Recent Events at Pergamos, Soma and District," 28 October 1922, UKNA FO 371/7950.

667. Rumbold to Curzon, 3 January 1921, UKNA FO 371/6561.

668. Forbes to Lord Riddell, 30 April 1921, an extract attached to Riddell to Vansittart, 18 May 1921, UKNA FO 371/6492.

669. Horton to Bristol, 19 April 1921, USNA RG 84, Turkey (Constantinople), Vol. 437. Horton says that few Ottoman Christians actually volunteered. But there can be little doubt regarding their revanchist urges. The British consul in Smyrna described one group of recruits tearing off fezzes, insulting Turkish schoolchildren, and then shooting "indiscriminately" from train windows (Lamb to Rumbold, 1 April 1921, UKNA FO 371/6492).

670. Swedish Legation, Constantinople, to US High Commission, 7 March 1921, and enclosed letter of complaint from the Sublime Porte, USNA RG 84, Turkey (Constantinople), Vol. 438.

671. Ahmed Mouhtar, Ankara Government foreign minister, to Allied foreign ministers, 7 April 1921, USNA RG 84, Turkey (Constantinople), Vol. 438.

672. Sublime Porte to ?, 6 April 1921, USNA RG 84, Turkey (Constantinople), Vol. 438.

673. Entry for 2 April 1921, LC, Bristol Papers, War Diary.

674. Hadji Hassan, Rachid Aha, etc., to ?, date unclear, 1921, USNA RG 84, Turkey (Constantinople), Vol. 438; Abdul Vahab, Habib Pacha Zade, etc., to US High Commissioner, 16 April 1921, USNA RG 84, Turkey (Constantinople), Vol. 438; and Ibrahim Oglou Ismail, Hassan Oglou Halil Ibrahim, etc., to the US High Commissioner, 9 May 1921, USNA RG 84, Turkey (Constantinople), Vol. 438.

675. Fevzi, "temporary" foreign minister, Ankara, to high commissioners, 7 June 1921, USNA RG 84, Turkey (Constantinople), Vol. 438.

676. USS *Sands,* "Diary at Samsun," entry for 8 March 1922, USNA RG 84, Turkey (Constantinople), Vol. 463.

677. Smith, *Ionian Vision,* footnote on 218.

678. Constantine to Princess Paola of Saxe-Weimar, 9 August 1921, q. in Smith, *Ionian Vision,* 232.

679. Smith, *Ionian Vision,* 211–212.

680. Rendel, "Atrocities in Asia Minor etc. Protests Received by His Majesty's Government, and Action Taken" (a draft memorandum), 28 December 1921, UKNA FO 371/7875. Rendel noted, "It has been far easier to deal with atrocities committed by the Greeks than with those committed by the Turks." The Greeks allowed Allied officers free access and Greek atrocities were "definitely limited" in time and space. With the Turks, "both the area and the period covered are far greater." See also Charles Walker, Admiralty, to undersecretary of state, UKNA FO 371/6523, 16 July 1921, and attached "Terms of Reference."

681. "Report of the Inter-Allied Commission Instructed to Conduct Enquiries Regarding the Excesses Committed Against the Turkish Population in the Regions of Yalova and Guemlek," 23 May 1921, and "Diary of the Inter-Allied Commission Sent to Enquire into the Incidents in the Regions of Guemlek and Yalova," published, with some passages blacked out, in "Turkey No. 1 (1921), Reports on Atrocities in the Districts of Yalova and Guemlek and in the Ismid Peninsula," Cmd. 1478, 1921, Bodl. MS Toynbee Papers 52.

682. Rumbold to FO, 21 May 1921, UKNA FO 371/6512.

683. Entry for 27 May 1921, LC, Bristol Papers, War Diary.

684. "Commission of Enquiry for the Ismidt Peninsula to Sir H. Rumbold," 18 May 1921, and attached "Schedule," both enclosed in Rumbold to Curzon, 20 May 1920, UKNA FO 371/6514.

685. "Report of the Ismid Commission of Enquiry," 1 June 1921, in "Turkey No. 1 (1921), Reports on Atrocities in the Districts of Yalova and Guemlek and in the Ismid Peninsula," Cmd. 1478, 1921, Bodl. MS Toynbee Papers 52.

686. A. Toynbee to Ryan, 22 June 1921, Bodl. MS Toynbee Papers 52.

687. Gehri, "Mission d'Enquête en Anatolie (12–22 mai 1921)," Bodl. MS Toynbee Papers 52.

688. Rosalind Toynbee, C'ple, to Gilbert Murray, 28 May 1921, Bodl. MS Toynbee Papers 50. Rosalind described Admiral Bristol as "an admirable person . . . fair and moderate and unprejudiced."

689. Rosalind Toynbee to mother, 18 June 1921, Bodl. MS Toynbee Papers 50.

690. G. M. Franks, Gerbaud and de Malso, "Report," 25 June 1921, attached to Frank Rattigan to Curzon, 30 June 1921, UKNA FO 371/6522.

691. Youssouf Kemal to high commissioners, 6 July 1921, USNA RG 59, 860J.4016/50–860J.4016 P81/99, Roll 5. See also Rattigan to FO, 5 July 1921, UKNA FO 371/6521.

692. A. Toynbee to "Mother," 5 July 1921, Bodl. MS Toynbee Papers 50.

693. Rosalind Toynbee to Mary Murray (her mother), 5 July 1921, Bodl. MS Toynbee Papers 50.

694. A. Toynbee to Bristol, 7 August 1921, LC, Bristol Papers 35.

695. Rosalind Toynbee, handwritten untitled memorandum, undated, Bodl. MS Toynbee Papers 52. A typewritten, edited version of this report, titled "Note by Mrs. Arnold Toynbee," dated 20 September 1921, is in Bodl. MS Toynbee Papers 50. See also McNeill, *Arnold J. Toynbee,* 106–108.

696. Arnold Toynbee, Smyrna, to Bristol, 7 August 1921, LC, Bristol Papers 35.

697. Toynbee, *Western Question,* 316.

698. Rendel minute, 14 October 1922, UKNA FO 371/7955.

699. Toynbee's reversal from critic of the Turks to sympathizer may have been driven by moral consideration surrounding what he witnessed in Anatolia. Or, he may have anticipated eventual Turkish triumph and wanted to ingratiate himself with the victors. Another possible factor is the alienation from the British upper class he experienced at the time. Toynbee increasingly opposed what he believed were untenable imperialist projects. In his notes from the period, Toynbee expressed hope that he might "affect the peace with Turkey, and with luck, might even forestall the threatened clash between politically awakened Islamic peoples and the British Empire." See McNeill, *Arnold J. Toynbee,* 80–84, 106–108.

700. Bristol to SecState, 26 May 1921, USNA RG 84, Turkey (Constantinople), Vol. 438.

701. Bristol to SecState, 7 June 1921 (via USS *Scorpion*), USNA RG 84, Turkey (Constantinople), Vol. 438.

702. Entry for 22 July 1921, LC, Bristol Papers, War Diary.

703. Entry for 20 July 1921, LC, Bristol Papers, War Diary.

704. Bristol to Nicol, 12 August 1921, USNA RG 84, Turkey (Constantinople), Vol. 444.

705. Toynbee to Montgomery, undated but c. June 1922, USNA RG 59, 967.4016, Roll 47.

706. Annie Allen and Florence Billings, "Report on Certain Destroyed Villages in the Turkish Zone in Anatolia," undated but from September or October 1921, USNA RG 84, Turkey (Constantinople), Vol. 438.

707. Quoted in Rumbold to FO, 6 March 1922, UKNA FO 371/7876.

708. Edith Parsons, "Enclosure No. 1 with Dispatch No. 472," 21 September 1922, USNA RG 84, Turkey (Constantinople), Vol. 465.

709. William Wright (NER) "Report of Devastated Regions in the Broussa Area," 14 October 1922, USNA RG 84, Turkey (Constantinople), Vol. 464.

710. Untitled memorandum by Perry, *New York Herald* correspondent, undated but from October 1922, LC, Bristol Papers 37. See also "Copy of Report made by a Turkish Interpreter who accompanied Prof. J. K. Biorge on his Visit to Magnesia, Cassaba, Salikli and Alashehir," 8 October 1922, USNA RG 84, Turkey (Constantinople), Vol. 466.

711. Minute by Rendel, 14 October 1922, UKNA FO 371/7955.

712. Dr. A. Tevfik and 'Youssouf,' Committee for the Defence of the Rights of Occidental Thrace, 25 July 1922, and appended "Series of Atrocities Committed by the Greeks in Western Thrace," USNA RG 84, Turkey (Constantinople), Vol. 466.

713. Granville (Athens) to FO, 8 June 1921, UKNA FO 371/6516.

714. "Memorandum by Eyre Crowe Sent to the Prime Minister, 5 pm Nov. 30, 1922," UKNA FO 371/7960. See also Harington to WO, 26 October 1922, UKNA FO 371/7957.

715. Hole to Bentinck, 22 February 1923, UKNA FO 371/9089.

716. J. McG. Dawkins (Canea, Crete) to Bentinck (Athens), 10 February 1923, UKNA FO 371/9089.

717. Dawkins to Bentinck, 2 March 1923, UKNA FO 371/9089.

718. Bentinck to Curzon, 29 (?) April 1923, UKNA FO 371/9094.

Conclusion

1. Suny, *They Can Live in the Desert*, 209. By 2016 Turkey's population, according to official data, was 99.8 percent Muslim, due to lower Christian birthrates and, more importantly, steady Christian emigration, especially after the anti-Greek pogrom in Istanbul in 1955 (see Vryonis, *Mechanism of Catastrophe*).

2. Kevorkian, *Armenian Genocide*, 693.

3. Dündar, *Crime of Numbers*, 150–151.

4. Akçam, *Young Turks' Crime*, 258–261.

5. Dündar, *Crime of Numbers*, 150–151. The number presumably includes converts to Islam.

6. Hofmann, "Cumulative Genocide," 104.

7. Hlamides, "Smyrna Holocaust," 224–225, especially note 120.

8. McCarthy, *Death and Exile*, 292.

9. Bloxham, *Great Game of Genocide*, 98.

10. Rudolph Rummel, an American political scientist and statistician, estimated that the Turks and their helpers killed "from 3,500,000 to over 4,300,000 Armenians, Greeks, Nestorians and other Christians" between 1900 and 1923 (Rummel, *Statistics of Democide*, 78). He did not include in his estimate those murdered before 1900 or in 1924. In any event, his total seems vastly inflated and at odds with the estimates of most historians.

11. Morgenthau, *Morgenthau's Story*, 325.

12. Hovannisian, ed., *The Armenian Genocide: Cultural and Ethical*, 6–7.

13. They were also eager to "Turkify" the state, which accounts for the successive anti-Kurdish campaigns of the CUP and Kemal during World War I and the 1920s and 1930s. These campaigns, though also guided by the lights of social or demographic engineering, fall outside the remit of this book. But, in brief: hard on the heels of the vital Kurdish assistance rendered to the government in destroying the Armenians, the Turks in 1916–1918 deported hundreds of thousands of Kurds from eastern to central and western Anatolia. Turkification was the goal, as defined in the secret statutes or bylaws of the Directorate for the Settlement of Tribes and Refugees, headed by Şükrü Kaya Bey. The directorate orchestrated the deportations. Many Kurdish deportees died on the roads or were slaughtered by Turkish troops and police. But here, unlike with the Armenians, the main aim was to assimilate—Turkify—rather than exterminate, though killing Kurds was also acceptable. As Enver reportedly told a session of the CUP central committee after the loss at Sarıkamış, "Though we are outwardly defeated . . . in actuality we are triumphal because we left the dead bodies of several tens of thousands young Kurds on the roads from the forests of Sarikamish to Erzurum." But the westward transplantation of the Kurds was far more difficult than the destruction of the Armenians, which explains why it was drawn out and only partially successful. Firstly, the Turks didn't enjoy the services of Kurdish helpers, as they had with the Armenians. Secondly, the Kurds were by and large warlike and well-armed (Baibourtian, *The Kurds*, 214–216). Moreover, being largely nomads, the Kurdish tribesmen proved more resilient and were able, in many cases, to make their way back to the Kurdish heartland. See also Üngör, *Making of Modern Turkey*, 107–169.

14. Q. in Dobkin, *Smyrna 1922*, 34.

15. Morgenthau, *Morgenthau's Story*, 342.

16. Q. in Akçam, *Shameful Act*, 123.

17. Cheikh Ziaddin, Abdullah and Hajji Mehmed, to ?, 1 February 1920, USNA RG 84, Turkey (Constantinople), Vol. 419.

18. Horton to SecState, 26 September 1922, USNA RG 59, 867.4016, Roll 47.

19. Q. in Suny, *They Can Live in the Desert*, 215.

20. Q. by Suny, *They Can Live in the Desert*, 134.

21. Q. in Dobkin, *Smyrna 1922*, 46.

22. Morgenthau, *Morgenthau's Story*, 290. See also 276–286.

23. Quoted in Shaw, *Empire to Republic*, vol. 2, 399–400.

24. Kevorkian, *Armenian Genocide*, 1–2 and 810.

25. Suny, *They Can Live in the Desert*, xiv–xv.

26. Suny, *They Can Live in the Desert*, 52, 56–57.

27. See Ihrig, *Atatürk*, especially 81–87, 206–208, 223–225.

28. Lower, *Hitler's Furies*, 37.

29. For a partial comparison between German and Turkish looting policies see Kurt, "Legal and Official Plunder."

Bibliography

Archives

Australian War Memorial

Başbakanlık Osmanlı Arşivi (BOA; Prime Ministry's Ottoman Archives), Istanbul, Turkey

A. MKT. MHM	Sadâret Mektubî Kalemi Mühimme Kalemi (Odası) Belgeler
	(Grand Vizier's Chamber, Important Affairs Office Documents)
DH. EUM.	Dahiliye Nezareti, Emniyet-i Umumiye
	(Interior Ministry, Public Security Directorate)
DH. EUM.	2Şb Dahiliye Nezareti, Emniyet-i Umumiye, 2 şübesi
	(Interior Ministry, Public Security Directorate, 2nd Bureau)
DH. EUM.	AYŞ. Dahiliye Nezareti, Emniyet-i Umumiye, Asayiş Kalemi
	(Interior Ministry, Public Security Directorate, Public Order
	Bureau)
DH. EUM.	MEM Dahiliye Nezareti, Emniyet-i Umumiye, Memurin Kalemi
	Belgeleri
	(Interior Ministry, Public Security Directorate, Officer Chamber
	Documents)
DH. EUM.	SSM Dahiliye Nezareti, Emniyet-i Umumiye, Seyrüsefer Kalemi
	(Interior Ministry, Public Security Directorate, Traffic and
	Passages Chamber)
DH. I. UM	Dahiliye Nezareti İdare-i Umumiye Evraki
	(Interior Ministry, General Directory Papers)
DH. KMS	Dahiliye Nezareti, Kalem-i Mahsus Müdüriyeti
	(Interior Ministry, Directorate of Special Section)
DH. ŞFR.	Dahiliye Nezareti, Şifre Kalemi
	(Interior Ministry, Cypher Section)
HR. SYS.	Hariciye Nezareti, Muhaberat-i Umumiye Dairesi, SIyasi Evrakı
	Kataloğu
	(Foreign Ministry, General Intelligence Section, Political
	Documents)

IAMM	Iskan-i Aşair ve Muhacirin Müdüriyeti
	(Directorate for the Settlement of Tribes and Immigrants)
I. HUS	Irade Hususi (Privy Directives)
Y. A. HUS	Yıldız Saray Sadaret Hususi Maruzat Evrakı
	(Yıldız Palace, Grand Vizier's Office, Requests / Submissions)
Y. A. RES	Yıldız Sadaret Resmi Maruzat Evrakı
	(Yıldız Palace, Grand Vizier's Office, Official Submissions)
Y. EE	Yıldız Esas Evrakı
	(Yıldız Essential Papers)
Y. MTV	Yıldız Mütenevvi Maruzât Evrakı
	(Yıldız Diverse Submissions)
Y. PRK. ASK	Yıldız Perakende Evrakı, Askeri Maruzât
	(Yıldiz Occasional Documents, Military Submissions)
Y. PRK. BŞK	Başkitabet Dairesi Maruzatı
	(Yıldız Occasional Documents, Chief Scribal Department Submissions)
Y. PRK. UM.	Yıldız Perakende Evrakı, Umum Vilayetler Tahriratı
	(Yıldız Occasional Documents, Notes of all vilayets)
Y. PRK. ZB	Yıldız Perakende Evrakı, Zabtiye Nezâreti Maruzâtı
	(Yıldız Occasional Documents, Police Ministry Submissions)

Bodleian Library MS Collections (Bodl. MS), University of Oxford
  Lord Bryce Papers
  Horace Rumbold Papers
  Arnold Toynbee Papers

Deutschland, Politisches Archiv des Auswärtiges, Botschaft-Konsulat (DE / PA-AA / BoKon)
  (Political Archive of the German Foreign Office, Embassy-Consulate)

Franklin Delano Roosevelt Library (FDRL), Hyde Park, New York
  Henry Morgenthau Sr. Papers

Houghton Library, Harvard University
  Papers of the American Board of Commissioners for Foreign Missions (ABC)

Library of Congress (LC), Washington DC
  Mark Bristol Papers
  Henry Morgenthau Sr. Papers, 1795–1941

Ministère des Affaires Etrangères (MAE; Ministry of Foreign Affairs), La Courneuve, Paris
  Turquie: Nouvelle Serie (NS)—Turquie
  Affaires jusqu'à 1896: Affaires Politiques jusqu'en 1896—Turquie

Österreich, Haus- Hof- und Staats Archiv (HHStA; Austrian Habsburg Archives)
Politisches Archiv XII, Türkei 1848–1918 (PA XII; Political Archive, Turkey, 1848–1918)

Service Historique de la Défense (SHD; Ministry of Defense), Vincennes, France
Serie N, 1918–1924

St Antony's College Middle East Centre Archive (SAMECA), University of Oxford
Philip Price Papers

United Kingdom National Archives (UKNA), London
FO 195   Foreign Office: Embassy and Consulates, Turkey, General
                Correspondence
FO 371   Foreign Office: Political Departments: General Correspondence
                from 1906–1966
WO 95   War Office: British Army War Diaries 1914–1922

United States National Archives (USNA), College Park, Maryland, and Washington DC
RG 84   Records of Foreign Service Posts of the Department of State
RG 59   Department of State Central Files
RG 256   Records of the American Commission to Negotiate Peace

Documentary Collections

Gust, Wolfgang, comp. and ed. *The Armenian Genocide: Evidence from the German Foreign Office Archives, 1915–1916.* New York: Berghahn, 2014. (*German Foreign Office*)

Ohandjanian, Artem, comp. and ed. *Österreich-Ungarn und Armenien 1912–1918: Sammlung diplomatischer Aktenstücke* (Austro-Hungary and the Armenians 1912–1918: Collection of Diplomatic Documents). Jerewan: Institut-Museum für Armenischen Genozid, 2005. (*OeUA*)

Osmani Belgelerinde Ermenilerin Sevk ve Iskanı (1878–1920) (Referral and Relocation of Armenians in Ottoman Documents). Comp. Yusuf Sarinay et al. Ankara: T. C. Başbakanlık Devlet Arşivleri Genel Müdürlüğü (General Directorate of State Archives), 2007. (*Sevk ve Iskan*)

Osmanlı Belgelerinde Ermeni-Rus Ilişkileri (1841–1898) (Armenian-Russian Relations in Ottoman Documents). Comp. Yusuf Sarinay et al. Ankara: T. C. Başbakanlık Devlet Arşivleri Genel Müdürlüğü (General Directorate of State Archives), 2006. (*Ermeni-Rus Ilişkileri*)

Osmanlı Belgelerinde Ermeni Isyanları (Armenian Uprising in Ottoman Documents). Ankara: T. C. Başbakanlık Devlet Arşivleri Genel Müdürlüğü (General Directorate of State Archives), 2008. (*Ermeni Isyanları*)
Vol. 1: *1878–1895,* comp. Hüseyin Özdemir et al.
Vol. 2: *1895–1896,* comp. Yusuf Sarinay et al.

Papers Relating to the Foreign Relations of the United States . . . 1895, Part II. Turkey (Documents 479–746). U.S. Department of State. Washington DC: U.S. Government Printing Office, 1896. https://history.state.gov/historicaldocuments/frus1895p2 /comp16. (*FRUS 1895*)

Papers Relating to the Foreign Relations of the United States . . . 1896. Turkey (Documents 788–896). U.S. Department of State. Washington DC: U.S. Government Printing Office, 1897. https://history.state.gov/historicaldocuments/frus1896/comp26. (*FRUS* 1896)

Sarafian, Ara, comp. *United States Official Records on the Armenian Genocide 1915–1917,* Princeton, NJ: Gomidas Institute, 2004. (*U.S. Official Records*)

Şimşir, Bilâl N., ed. *British Documents on Ottoman Armenians,* Vol. 1: *1856–1880.* Ankara: Türk Tarih Kurumu Basımevi, 1982.

UK Blue Books

   Turkey No. 1 (1895) Correspondence Relating to the Asiatic Provinces of Turkey Part 1 Events at Sassoon and Commission of Inquiry at Moush HMSO 1895

   Turkey No. 2 (1896) Correspondence Relative to the Armenian Question and Reports from Her Majesty's Consular Officers in Asiatic Turkey HMSO 1896

   Turkey No. 3 (1896) Correspondence Relating to the Asiatic Provinces of Turkey 1892–1893 HMSO 1896

   Turkey No. 5 (1896) Correspondence Relating to the Asiatic Provinces of Turkey: Reports by Vice-Consul Fitzmaurice from Birejik, Ourfa, Adiasman and Behesni HMSO 1896

   Turkey No. 6 (1896) Correspondence Relating to the Asiatic Provinces of Turkey 1894–1895 HMSO 1896

   Turkey No. 8 (1896) Further Correspondence Relating to the Asiatic Provinces of Turkey HMSO 1896

Secondary Works

Adanır, Fikret. "Non-Muslims in the Ottoman Army and the Ottoman Defeat in the Balkan War of 1912–1913." In Suny, Goçek, and Naimark, *A Question of Genocide,* 113–125.

Ahmad, Feroz. *The Making of Modern Turkey.* London: Routledge, 1994.

——. *The Young Turks: The Committee of Union and Progress in Turkish Politics, 1908–1914.* Oxford: Clarendon Press, 1969.

Akçam, Taner. *From Empire to Republic: Turkish Nationalism and the Armenian Genocide.* London: Zed Books, 2004.

——. *The Genocide of the Armenians and the Silence of the Turks.* London: St. Martin's Press, 1999.

——. "The Ottoman Documents and the Genocidal Policies of the Committee for Union and Progress (*İttihat ve Terakki*) toward the Armenians in 1915." *Genocide Studies and Prevention* 1, no. 2 (2006): 127–148.

———. *A Shameful Act: The Armenian Genocide and the Question of Turkish Responsibility*. London: Constable, 2007.

———. *The Young Turks' Crime against Humanity: The Armenian Genocide and Ethnic Cleansing in the Ottoman Empire*. Princeton, NJ: Princeton University Press, 2012.

———, and Ümit Kurt. *Kanunların Ruhu: Emval-I Metruke Kanunlarında Soykırımın Izini Sürmek*s. Istanbul: Iletişim Yayınları, 2012.

Aktar, Ayhan. "Debating the Armenian Massacres in the Last Ottoman Parliament, November-December 1918." *History Workshop Journal* 64 (2007): 240-270.

Alkan, Necati. "Fighting for the Nuṣayrī Soul: State, Protestant Missionaries and the ʿAlawīs in the Late Ottoman Empire." *Die Welt des Islams* 52 (2012): 23-50.

Anderson, Margaret Lavinia. "Who Still Talked about the Extermination of the Armenians? German Talk and German Silences." In Suny, Goçek, and Naimark, *A Question of Genocide*, 199-220.

Arpee, Leon. "A Century of Armenian Protestantism." *Church History* 5, no. 2 (1936): 150-167.

Artinian, Vartan. *The Armenian Constitutional System in the Ottoman Empire 1839-1863: A Study of Its Historical Development*. Istanbul: private edition, 1988.

Astourian, Stephan H. "The Silence of the Land: Agrarian Relations, Ethnicity and Power." In Suny, Goçek, and Naimark, *A Question of Genocide*, 55-81.

Atatürk, Mustafa Kemal. *A Speech Delivered by Ghazi Mustapha Kemal, President of the Turkish Republic, October 1927* (translation of the *Nutuk* speech). Leipzig: K. F. Koehler, 1929.

Augustinos, Gerasimos. *The Greeks of Asia Minor: Confession, Community, and Ethnicity in the Nineteenth Century*. Kent, OH: Kent State University Press, 1992.

Baibourtian, Vahan. *The Kurds, the Armenian Question, and the History of Armenian-Kurdish Relations*. Trans. Mariam Mesropyan. Ottawa: the author, 2013.

Balakian, Grigoris. *Armenian Golgotha*. New York: Vintage, 2010.

Balakian, Peter. *The Burning Tigris: The Armenian Genocide and America's Response*. New York: Harper Collins, 2003.

Bardakçı, Murat. *Talât Paşanın Evrak-ı Metrukesi*. Istanbul: Everest Yayınları, 2008.

Barton, James L. *Story of Near East Relief*. New York: MacMillan, 1930.

Bartov, Omer and Eric D. Weitz, eds., *Shatterzone of Empires: Coexistence and Violence in the German, Habsburg, Russian and Ottoman Borderlands*. Bloomington, Indiana University Press, 2013.

Başak, Tolga. *İngilterenin Ermeni Politikası, 1830-1923*. Istanbul: IQ Kültür Sanat Yayıncılık, 2008.

Bauer, Yehuda. *Rethinking the Holocaust*. New Haven, CT: Yale University Press, 2001.

Bjornlund, Matthias. "Danish Sources on the Destruction of Ottoman Greeks, 1914-1916." In Hofmann, Bjornlund, and Meichanetsidis, *Genocide of the Ottoman Greeks*, 137-178.

———. "'A Fate Worse than Dying': Sexual Violence during the Armenian Genocide." In *Brutality and Desire: War and Sexuality in Europe's Twentieth Century,* ed. Dagmar Herzog, 16–58. London: Palgrave MacMillan, 2009.

Bloxham, Donald. "The Armenian Genocide of 1915–1916: Cumulative Radicalisation and the Development of a Destruction Policy." *Past and Present* 181, no. 1 (2003): 141–191.

———. *The Great Game of Genocide: Imperialism, Nationalism and the Destruction of the Ottoman Armenians.* Oxford: Oxford University Press, 2005.

Braude, Benjamin. "Foundation Myths of the Millet System." In *Christians and Jews in the Ottoman Empire: The Functioning of a Plural Society,* ed. Benjamin Braude and Bernard Lewis, 2 vols., 1:69–88. New York: Holmes and Meier, 1982.

Bryce, Viscount James. *The Treatment of Armenians in the Ottoman Empire 1915–1916: Documents Presented to Viscount Grey of Falloden by Viscount Bryce,* ed. Arnold Toynbee. London: His Majesty's Stationery Office, 1916.

———, and Arnold Toynbee. *The Treatment of Armenians in the Ottoman Empire 1915–1916,* ed. and intro. Ara Sarafian, uncensored ed. Princeton, NJ: Gomidas Institute, 2000.

Bulut, Hüseyin ve Nurettin Birol. "XIX Yüzyılın sonlarında Sivas vilayetinde Ermenilerin Faaliyetleri ve Alınması düşünülen tedbirler ve Mehmet Ali ibn Abdullah Selim'in Layihası." *Erzincan Eğitim Fakültesi Dergisi* 8, no. 1 (2006): 1–11.

Çaksu, Ali. "Janissary Coffee Houses in Late Eighteenth-Century Istanbul." In *Ottoman Tulips, Ottoman Coffee,* ed. Dana Sajdi. London: Tauris Academic, 2007.

Cebesoy, Ali Fuat. *Milli Mücadele Hatıraları.* Istanbul: Vatan Neşriyat, 1953.

Celal Bey. Memoirs, "The Armenian Affair, Its Reasons and Effects," *Vakit,* 12 December 1918.

Çetin, Fethiye. *My Grandmother.* London: Verso, 2008.

Churchill, Winston. *The World Crisis.* London: Thornton Butterworth, 1923. Reprint, New York: Free Press, 2005.

Clark, Bruce. *Twice a Stranger: How Mass Expulsion Forged Modern Greece and Turkey.* London: Granta, 2006.

Courtois, Sébastien de. *The Forgotten Genocide: Eastern Christians, the Last Arameans.* Trans. Vincent Aurora. London: Gorgias Press, 2004.

Cuthell, David. *The Muhacirin Komisyonu: An Agent in the Transformation of Ottoman Anatolia, 1860–1866.* New York: Columbia University Press, 2005.

Dadrian, Vahakn N. "The Armenian Question and the Wartime Fate of the Armenians as Documented by the Officials of the Ottoman Empire's World War I Allies: Germany and Austria Hungary." *International Journal of Middle East Studies* 34, no. 1 (2002): 59–85.

———. "The Documentation of the World War I Armenian Massacres in the Proceedings of the Turkish Military Tribunal." *International Journal of Middle East Studies* 23, no. 4 (1991): 549–576.

———. *German Responsibility in the Armenian Genocide: A Review of the Historical Evidence of German Complicity.* Watertown, MA: Blue Crane, 1996.

———. *The History of the Armenian Genocide: Ethnic Conflict from the Balkans to Anatolia to the Caucasus,* 6th rev. ed. New York: Berghahn Books, 1996.

———. "The Naim-Andonian Documents on the World War I Destruction of Ottoman Armenians: The Anatomy of a Genocide." *International Journal of Middle East Studies* 18 (1986): 311–360.

———. "The Role of the Special Organization in the Armenian Genocide during the First World War." In *Minorities in Wartime,* ed. Panikos Panayi. Providence, RI: Berg, 1993.

———. "The Role of Turkish Physicians in the World War I Genocide of Ottoman Armenians." *Holocaust and Genocide Studies* 1, no. 2 (1986): 169–192.

———. "The Secret Young-Turk Ittihadist Conference and the Decision for the World War I Genocide of the Armenians." *Holocaust and Genocide Studies* 7, no. 2 (1993): 173–201.

———. *Warrant for Genocide: Key Elements of Turko-Armenian Conflict.* New Brunswick, NJ: Transaction, 1999.

———, and Taner Akçam. *Judgment at Istanbul: The Armenian Genocide Trials.* New York: Berghahn Books, 2010.

Davis, Leslie. *The Slaughterhouse Province: An American Diplomat's Report on the Armenian Genocide, 1915–1917.* New York: Caratzas, 1989.

Davison, Roderick. "Nationalism as an Ottoman Problem and the Ottoman Response." In Haddad and Ochsenwald, *Nationalism in a Non-National State.*

Demirel, Muammer ve Mehmet Takkaç. "Ermeni Tehciri Anilari Uzerine." *A.U. Türkiyat araştırmaları Enstitüsü Dergisi* 33 (Erzurum 2007): 263–276.

Derdarian, Mae. *Vergeen: A Survivor of the Armenian Genocide.* Los Angeles: Atmus Press, 1996.

Deringil, Selim. "'The Armenian Question Is Finally Closed': Mass Conversions of Armenians in Anatolia during the Hamidian Massacres of 1895–1897." *Comparative Studies in Society and History* 51, no. 2 (2009): 344–371.

———. "The Invention of Tradition as Public Image in the Late Ottoman Empire, 1808–1908." *Comparative Studies in Society and History* 35, no. 1 (1993): 3–29.

———. "The Study of the Armenian Crisis of the Late Ottoman Empire, or 'Seizing the Document by the Throat.'" *New Perspectives on Turkey* 27 (Fall 2002): 35–59.

———. "There Is No Compulsion in Religion: On Conversion and Apostasy in the Late Ottoman Empire: 1839–1856." *Comparative Studies in Society and History* 42, no. 3 (2000): 547–575.

———. *The Well-Protected Domains: Ideology and the Legitimation of Power in the Ottoman Empire 1876–1909.* London: I. B. Tauris, 1998.

Der Matossian, Bedross. "From Bloodless Revolution to Bloody Counterrevolution: The Adana Massacres of 1909." *Genocide Studies and Prevention* 6, no. 2 (2011): 152–173.

———. "Ottoman Armenian Kesaria / Kayseri in the Nineteenth Century." In *Armenian Kesaria/Kayseri and Cappadocia,* ed. Richard G. Hovannisian. Costa Mesa, CA: Mazda, 2013.

———. "The Taboo within the Taboo: The Fate of 'Armenian Capital' at the End of the Ottoman Empire." *European Journal of Turkish Studies: Social Sciences on Contemporary Turkey* (2011): 1–19.

De Waal, Thomas. *Great Catastrophe: Armenians and Turks in the Shadow of Genocide.* Oxford: Oxford University Press, 2015.

Diamadis, Panayiotis. "Children and Genocide." In *Genocide Perspectives: Essays on Holocaust and Genocide,* ed. Colin Tatz, vol. 4 (1997; Sydney: Center for Genocide Studies, Macquarie University, 2012; UTS ePress, 2012).

Dobkin, Marjorie Housepian. *Smyrna 1922: The Destruction of a City.* London: Faber, 1972. Reprint, New York: Newmark Press, 1998.

Dontas, Domna. "Greece: The Greek Foreign Ministry." In *The Times Survey of Foreign Ministries of the World,* ed. Zara Steiner, 259–271. London: Times Books, 1982.

Dündar, Fuat. *Crime of Numbers: The Role of Statistics in the Armenian Question, 1878–1918.* New Brunswick, NJ: Transaction, 2010.

———. "Pouring People into the Desert: 'The Definitive Solution' of the Unionists to the Armenian Question." In Suny, Göçek, and Naimark, *A Question of Genocide,* 276–284.

Einstein, Lewis. *Inside Constantinople: A Diplomatist's Diary during the Dardanelles Expedition, April-September, 1915.* London: J. Murray, 1917.

Eken, Halit. *Kapancızade Hamit Bey, Bir Milli Mücadele Valisi ve Anıları.* Istanbul: Yeditepe Yayınevi, 2008.

Erickson, Edward J. "The Armenians and Ottoman Military Policy, 1915." *War in History* 15, no. 2 (2008): 141–167.

———. "Captain Larkin and the Turks: The Strategic Impact of the Operations of HMS Doris in Early 1915." *Middle Eastern Studies* 46, no. 1 (2010): 151–162.

Erol, Emre. *The Ottoman Crisis in Western Anatolia: Turkey's Belle Epoque and the Transition to a Modern Nation State.* London: I. B. Tauris, 2016.

Ford, Roger. *Eden to Armageddon: World War I in the Middle East.* New York: Pegasus Books, 2010.

Fromkin, David. *A Peace to End All Peace: Creating the Modern Middle East, 1914–1922.* New York: Henry Holt, 1989.

Gaunt, David. *Massacres, Resistance, Protectors: Muslim-Christian Relations in Eastern Anatolia during World War I.* London: Gorgias Press, 2006.

———. "The Ottoman Treatment of the Assyrians." In Suny, Göçek, and Naimark, *A Question of Genocide,* 243–259.

Georgelin, Hervé. "Armenian Inter-Community Relations in Late Ottoman Smyrna." In *Armenian Smyrna/Izmir: The Aegean Communities,* ed. Richard G. Hovannisian, 177–190. Costa Mesa, CA: Mazda, 2012.

Gilbert, Martin. *Sir Horace Rumbold: Portrait of a Diplomat.* London: Heinemann, 1973.

Ginio, Eyal. *The Ottoman Culture of Defeat: The Balkan Wars and Their Aftermath.* Oxford: Oxford University Press, 2016.

———. "Paving the Way for Ethnic Cleansing: Eastern Thrace during the Balkan Wars and Their Aftermath." In *Shatterzone of Empires: Coexistence and Violence in the German, Habsburg, Russian and Ottoman Borderlands,* ed. Omer Bartov and Eric D. Weitz, 283–297. Bloomington: Indiana University Press, 2013.

Gladstone, W. E. *Bulgarian Horrors and the Question of the East.* New York: Lovell, Adam, Wesson and Company, 1876.

Göçek, Fatma Müge. *Denial of Violence: Ottoman Past, Turkish Present, and Collective Violence against the Armenians, 1789–2009.* Oxford: Oxford University Press, 2015.

———. "Ethnic Segmentation, Western Education and Political Outcomes: Nineteenth Century Ottoman Society." *Poetics Today* 14, no. 3 (1993): 507–538.

Gondicas, Dimitri, and Charles Issawi. eds. *Ottoman Greeks in the Age of Nationalism.* Princeton, NJ: Darwin Press, 1999.

Güngör, Salâhattin. "Bir Canlı Tarih Konuşuyor" [Living History Speaks]. *Resimli Tarih Mecmuası* 4, no. 43 (1953).

Gürün, Kamuran. *The Armenian File: The Myth of Innocence Exposed.* 1985. Istanbul: Türkiye İş Bankası, 2007.

Hacikyan, Agop J., coordinating ed. *The Heritage of Armenian Literature.* Vol. 3, *From the Eighteenth Century to Modern Times.* Detroit: Wayne State University Press, 2005.

Haddad, "Nationalism in the Ottoman Empire." In Haddad and Ochsenwald, eds., *Nationalism in a Non-National State.*

Haddad, William W., and William Ochsenwald, eds. *Nationalism in a Non-National State: The Dissolution of the Ottoman Empire.* Columbus: Ohio State University Press, 1977.

Hanioğlu, M. Şükrü. *Ataturk: An Intellectual Biography.* Princeton, NJ: Princeton University Press, 2011.

———. *A Brief History of the Late Ottoman Empire.* Princeton, NJ: Princeton University Press, 2008.

Hartunian, Abraham. *Neither to Laugh nor to Weep: A Memoir of the Armenian Genocide.* Cambridge, MA: Armenian Heritage Press, 1986.

Hepworth, George. *Through Armenia on Horseback.* New York: Dutton, 1898.

Herzog, Dagmar, ed. *Brutality and Desire: War and Sexuality in Europe's Twentieth Century.* London: Palgrave Macmillan, 2009.

Hewson, Robert. *Armenia: A Historical Atlas.* Chicago: University of Chicago Press, 2001.

Heyd, Uriel. *Foundations of Turkish Nationalism: The Life and Teachings of Ziya Gokalp.* London: Harvill Press, 1950.

Hlamides, Nikolaos. "The Smyrna Holocaust: The Final Phase of the Greek Genocide." In Hofmann, Bjornlund, and Meichanetsidis, *Genocide of the Ottoman Greeks*, 195–228.

Hofmann, Tessa. "Cumulative Genocide: The Massacres and Deportations of the Greek Population of the Ottoman Empire (1912–1923)." In Hofmann, Bjornlund, and Meichanetsidis, *Genocide of the Ottoman Greeks*, 39–111.

———, Matthias Bjornlund, and Vasileios Meichanetsidis, eds. *The Genocide of the Ottoman Greeks: Studies on the State-Sponsored Campaign of Extermination of the Christians of Asia Minor (1912–1922) and Its Aftermath: History, Law, Memory.* New York: Aristide D. Caratzas, 2011.

Holland, Thomas E., ed. *The European Concert in the Eastern Question: A Collection of Treaties and Other Public Acts.* Oxford: Clarendon Press, 1885.

Horton, George. *The Blight of Asia: An Account of the Systematic Extermination of Christian Populations by Mohammedans and of the Culpability of Certain Great Powers; with the True Story of the Burning of Smyrna.* Indianapolis: Bobbs-Merrill, 1953.

Hovannisian, Richard G., ed. *The Armenian Genocide: Cultural and Ethical Legacies.* New Brunswick, NJ: Transaction, 2007.

———, ed. *The Armenian Genocide: History, Politics, Ethics.* London: Palgrave MacMillan, 1992.

———. "The Ebb and Flow of the Armenian Minority in the Arab Middle East." *Middle East Journal* 28, no. 1 (1974): 19–32.

———. "Simon Vratzian and Armenian Nationalism." *Middle Eastern Studies* 5, no. 3 (1969): 192–220.

Howard, Harry N. *The Partition of Turkey: A Diplomatic History 1913–1923.* New York: Howard Fertig, 1966.

Ihrig, Stefan. *Atatürk in the Nazi Imagination.* Cambridge, MA: Belknap Press of Harvard University Press, 2014.

———. *Justifying Genocide: Germany and the Armenians from Bismarck to Hitler.* Cambridge, MA: Harvard University Press, 2016.

Jacobsen, Maria. *Diaries of a Danish Missionary: Harpoot, 1907–1919,* trans. Kristen Vind, ed. Ara Sarafian. Princeton, NJ: Gomidas Institute Books, 2001.

Kaiser, Hilmar. *The Extermination of Armenians in the Diyarbekir Region.* Istanbul: Bilgi University Press, 2014.

———, ed. *Eberhard Count Wolffskeel von Reichenberg, Zeitoun, Mousa Dagh, Ourfa: Letters on the Armenian Genocide.* Princeton, NJ: Gomidas Institute Books, 2001.

———, with Luther and Nancy Eskijian. *At the Crossroads of Der Zor: Death, Survival and Humanitarian Resistance in Aleppo, 1915–1917.* Princeton, NJ: Gomidas Institute Books, 2002.

Kamouzis, Dimitri. "Elites and the Formation of National Identity: The Case of the Greek Orthodox *millet* (Mid Nineteenth Century to 1922)." In *State National-*

isms in the Ottoman Empire, Greece and Turkey: Orthodox and Muslims 1830–1945, ed. B. C. Fortna, S. Katsikas, D. Kamouzis, and P. Konortas, 13–46. London: Routledge, 2013.

Karimova, Nigar, and Edward Deverell. "Minorities in Turkey." Occasional Papers no. 19, Swedish Institute of International Affairs, Stockholm, February 2001, http://miris .eurac.edu/mugs2/do/blob.pdf?type=pdf&serial=1101210931437.

Kasparian, Alice Odian. "The 1915 Massacres of the Armenians in the State of Angora, Turkey." *Journal of Armenian Studies* 4 (1992): 119–136.

Kerr, Stanley E. *The Lions of Marash: Personal Experiences with American Near East Relief, 1919–1922*. Albany: SUNY Press, 1973.

Kershaw, Ian. *The Nazi Dictatorship: Problems and Perspectives of Interpretation*. Oxford: Oxford University Press, 2000.

Kevorkian, Raymond. *The Armenian Genocide: A Complete History*. London: I. B. Tauris, 2011.

——. L'extermination des déportés Arméniens ottomans dans les camps de concentration de Syrie-Mésopotamie (1915–1916), in "La Deuxième phase du génocide," special issue, *Revue d'Histoire Arménienne Contemporaine* 2 (1998).

Khosroeva, Anahit. "The Assyrian Genocide in the Ottoman Empire and Adjacent Territories." In Hovannisian, *Armenian Genocide: Cultural and Ethical Legacies*, 267–274.

Kieser, Hans-Lukas. "Beatrice Rohner (1876–1947) and the Armenian Genocide." In Kieser, *A Quest for Belonging*, 219–234.

——. "Dr. Mehmet Reshid (1873–1919), A Political Doctor." In Kieser, *A Quest for Belonging*, 179–217.

——, ed. *A Quest for Belonging: Anatolia beyond Empire and Nation*. Istanbul: Isis Press, 2007.

——. *Talaat Pasha: Father of Modern Turkey, Architect of Genocide*. Princeton, NJ: Princeton University Press.

——, ed. *Turkey beyond Nationalism: Towards Post-Nationalist Identities*. London: I. B. Tauris, 2006.

King, Charles. *Midnight at the Pera Palace: The Birth of Modern Istanbul*. New York: Norton, 2014.

Kinross, Lord. *Ataturk: A Biography of Mustafa Kemal, Father of Modern Turkey*. New York: William Morrow, 1965.

Kitromilides, Paschalis M., ed. *Eleftherios Venizelos: The Trials of Statesmanship*. Edinburgh: Edinburgh University Press, 2006.

——. "Greek Irredentism in Asia Minor and Cyprus." *Middle Eastern Studies* 26, no. 1 (1990): 3–17.

——. "'Imagined Communities' and the Origins of the National Question in the Balkans." *European History Quarterly* 19, no. 2 (1989): 149–192.

Klein, Janet. *The Margins of Empire: Kurdish Militias in the Ottoman Tribal Zone.* Stanford, CA: Stanford University Press, 2011.

Knapp, Grace H. *The Tragedy of Bitlis,* New York: Fleming H. Revell, 1919.

Kofos, Evangelos. "Patriarch Joachim III (1878–1884) and the Irredentist Policy of the Greek States." *Journal of Modern Greek Studies* 4, no. 2 (1986): 107–120.

Koliopoulos, John S. "Brigandage and Irredentism in Nineteenth-Century Greece." *European History Quarterly* 19, no. 2 (1989): 193–228.

Künzler, Jakob. *In the Land of Blood and Tears: Experiences in Mesopotamia during the World War (1914–1918),* ed. Ara Ghazarians. Arlington, MA: Armenian Cultural Foundation, 2007.

Kuper, Leo, and Gary Remer. "The Religious Element in Genocide." *Journal of Armenian Studies* 4 (1992): 307–329.

Kurt, Ümit. "The Curious Case of Ali Cenani Bey: The Story of a Génocidaire During and After the 1915 Armenian Genocide." *Patterns of Prejudice* 52, no. 1 (2018): 58–77.

——. "Legal and Official Plunder of Armenian and Jewish Properties in Comparative Perspective: The Armenian Genocide and the Holocaust." *Journal of Genocide Research* 17, no. 3 (2015): 305–326.

Levy-Daphny, Tsameret. "What Will You Leave after You Die? Material Culture, Elite Dynamics and Household among Ottoman Elite in Diyarbakır in the Eighteenth Century" (Ph.D. diss., Tel Aviv University, 2015).

Lewis, Bernard. *The Emergence of Modern Turkey,* 3rd ed. Oxford: Oxford University Press, 2001.

——. *From Babel to Dragomans: Interpreting the Middle East.* Oxford: Oxford University Press, 2005.

Lewy, Guenter. *The Armenian Massacres in Ottoman Turkey: A Disputed Genocide.* Salt Lake City: University of Utah Press, 2005.

Lower, Wendy. *Hitler's Furies: German Women in the Nazi Killing Fields.* Boston: Houghton Mifflin Harcourt, 2013.

Lowry, Heath. *The Story behind Ambassador Morgenthau's Story.* Istanbul: Isis Press, 1990.

MacMillan, Margaret. *Peacemakers: Six Months That Changed the World.* London: John Murray, 2003.

Makdisi, Ussama. "Reclaiming the Land of the Bible: Missionaries, Secularism and Evangelical Modernity." *American Historical Review* 102, no. 3 (1997): 680–713.

Mango, Andrew. *Atatürk.* Woodstock, NY: Overlook Press, 2000.

Mazower, Mark. *Salonica, City of Ghosts: Christians, Muslims and Jews 1430–1950.* 2005. Reprint, New York: Vintage, 2006.

McCarthy, Justin. *Death and Exile: The Ethnic Cleansing of Ottoman Muslims 1821–1922.* Princeton, NJ: Darwin Press, 1995.

McMeekin, Sean. *The Ottoman Endgame: War, Revolution, and the Making of the Modern Middle East, 1908–1923*. London: Penguin Books, 2015.

McNeill, William H. *Arnold J. Toynbee: A Life*. Oxford: Oxford University Press, 1990.

Millman, Richard. "The Bulgarian Massacres Reconsidered." *Slavonic and East European Review* 58, no. 2 (1980): 218–231.

Milton, Giles. *Paradise Lost: Smyrna 1922*. New York: Basic Books, 2008.

Morgenthau, Henry. *Ambassador Morgenthau's Story*. Garden City, NY: Doubleday, Pahe, 1918.

———. *United States Diplomacy on the Bosphorus: The Diaries of Ambassador Morgenthau, 1913–1916,* comp. Ara Sarafian. Princeton, NJ: Gomidas Institute, 2004.

Morley, Bertha. *Marsovan 1915: The Diaries of Bertha Morley*. London: Gomidas Institute, 2000.

Moumdjian, Garabet K. "The Armenian Legion." In "Cilica under French Mandate, 1918–1921." Armenian-History.com, n.d. http://www.armenian-history.com/Nyuter /HISTORY/G_Moumdjian/Armenian_Legion_1918_1921.htm.

Mourelos, John. "The 1914 Persecutions of Greeks in the Ottoman Empire in Thrace and Ionia and the First Attempt at an Exchange of Minorities between Greece and Turkey." In Hofmann, Bjornlund, and Meichanetsidis, *Genocide of the Ottoman Greeks,* 113–136.

Mugreditchian, Thomas K. *The Diyarbekir Massacres and Kurdish Atrocities*. London: Gomidas Institute, 2013.

Mutlu, Servet. "Late Ottoman Population and Its Ethnic Distribution." *Turkish Journal of Population Studies* 25 (2003): 3–38.

Nazim Paşa, Hüseyin. *Ermeni Olayları Tarihi,* 2 vols. Ankara: Başbakanlık Genel Müdürlüğü, 1998.

Nogales, Rafael de. *Four Years beneath the Crescent*. New York: C. Scribner's Sons, 1926.

Nubar, Boghos. *The Pre-War Population of Cilicia*. London: Pettitt, Cox and Bowers, 1920.

Onal, Sami. *Sadettin Paşa'nın Anıları: Ermeni-Kurt Olayları, Van, 1896*. Istanbul: Remzi Kitabevi, 2003.

Orel, Şinasi, and Süreyya Yuca. *The Talat Pasha "Telegrams": Historical Fact or Armenian Fiction?* Nicosia, Cyprus: K. Rustem and Brother, 1983.

Pamuk, Şevket. *A Monetary History of the Ottoman Empire*. Cambridge: Cambridge University Press, 2000.

———. "The Ottoman Empire in the 'Great Depression' of 1873–1896." *Journal of Economic History* 44, no. 1 (1984): 107–118.

Papademetriou, Tom. *Render unto the Sultan: Power, Authority and the Greek Orthodox Church in the Early Ottoman Centuries*. Oxford: Oxford University Press, 2015.

Payaslian, Simon. *The History of Armenia*. New York: Palgrave Macmillan, 2007.

Pentzopoulos, Dimitri. *The Balkan Exchange of Minorities and Its Impact on Greece,* 2nd impression. London: Hurst, 2002.

Quataert, Donald. *The Ottoman Empire 1700–1922.* Cambridge: Cambridge University Press, 2000.

Rawlinson, Alfred. *Adventures in the Near East 1918–1922.* London: Andrew Melrose, 1924.

Rendel, George. *The Sword and the Olive: Recollections of Diplomacy and the Foreign Service 1913–1954.* London: John Murray, 1957.

Reynolds, Michael A. *Shattering Empires: The Clash and Collapse of the Ottoman and Russian Empires, 1908–1918.* Cambridge: Cambridge University Press, 2011.

Riggs, Henry H. *Days of Tragedy in Armenia.* London: Gomidas Institute, 1997.

Rogan, Eugene. *The Fall of the Ottomans: The Great War in the Middle East.* New York: Basic Books, 2015.

Rubin, Avi. *Ottoman Nizamiye Courts: Law and Modernity.* London: Palgrave, 2011.

Rummel, Rudolph. *Statistics of Democide, Genocide and Mass Murder since 1900.* Münster: LIT Verlag, 1998.

Sahara, Tetsuya. "The 1909 Adana Incident (Part 2): The Young Turk Revolution and the Muslim-Armenian Confrontation in Adana." *Meiji University Repository,* 31 March 2011, 41–97, https://m-repo.lib.meiji.ac.jp/dspace/bitstream/10291/14819/1/kyouyoronshu_467_41.pdf.

Şahin, Gürsoy. *Katolik Ermeniler Sivaslı Mihitar ve Mihitaristler.* Istanbul: IQ Kültür Sanat Yayıncılık, 2008.

Salt, Jeremy. *Imperialism, Evangelism and the Ottoman Armenians 1878–1896.* London: Frank Cass, 1993.

———. "The Narrative Gap in Ottoman Armenian History." *Middle Eastern Studies* 39, no. 1 (2003): 19–36.

Sarafian, Ara. *Talât Pasha's Report on the Armenian Genocide.* London: Gomidas Institute, 2011.

Shaw, Stanford. *From Empire to Republic: The Turkish War of National Liberation 1918–1923, A Documentary Study,* 5 vols. Ankara: Tarih Kurumu Basiomevi, 2000.

———. *History of the Ottoman Empire and Modern Turkey,* vol. 2. Cambridge: Cambridge University Press, 1977.

———. *The Jews of the Ottoman Empire and the Turkish Republic.* New York: New York University Press, 1991.

Shipley, Alice Muggerditchian. *We Walked, Then Ran.* Phoenix, AZ: Alice Shipley, 1984.

Shirinian, Lorne, and Alan Whitehorn. *The Armenian Genocide: Resisting the Inertia of Indifference.* Kingston, ON: Blue Heron Press, 2001.

Simşir, Bilal. *Kürtçülük 1787–1923.* Istanbul: Bilgi Yayinevi, 2007.

Smith, Michael Llewellyn. *Ionian Vision: Greece in Asia Minor 1919–1922.* London: Hurst, 1998.

———. "Venizelos' Diplomacy, 1910–23: From Balkan Alliance to Greek-Turkish Settlement." In Kitromilides, *Eleftherios Venizelos,* 134–192.

Somakian, Manoug Joseph. *Empires in Conflict: Armenia and the Great Powers.* London: I. B. Tauris, 1995.

Stamatopoulos, Dimitris. "From Millets to Minorities in the 19th Century Ottoman Empire: An Ambiguous Modernization." In *Citizenship in Historical Perspective,* ed. Steven G. Ellis, Gudmundur Hálfadanarson, and Ann Katherine Isaacs, 253–273. Pisa: Edizione PLUS–Pisa University Press, 2006.

Suny, Ronald. *"They Can Live in the Desert but Nowhere Else": A History of the Armenian Genocide.* Princeton, NJ: Princeton University Press, 2015.

———, Fatma Müge Göçek, and Norman Naimark, eds. *A Question of Genocide: Armenians and Turks at the End of the Ottoman Empire.* Oxford: Oxford University Press, 2011.

Super, Mary. *A Massacre Averted: An Armenian Town, an American Nurse, and the Turkish Army They Resisted,* ed. Nancy Klancher. Princeton, NJ: Markus Wiener, 2011.

Surmelian, Leon Z. *I Ask You, Ladies and Gentlemen.* New York: E. P. Dutton, 1945.

Taylor, A. J. P. *English History 1914–1945.* London: Penguin Books, 1970.

Ternon, Yves. *Bir Soykırım Tarihi: 20 Yıl Sonra "Ermeni Tabusu" Davası.* Istanbul: Belge, 2012.

Thomsen, Jenny. "The Assyrians / Syriacs of Turkey: A Forgotten People" (B.A. thesis, Malmö University, 2008).

Torosyan, Yüzbaşı Sarkis. *Çanakkale'den Filistin Cephesi'ne,* ed. Ayhan Aktar. Istanbul: İletişim Yayınları, 2012.

Toynbee, Arnold. *The Western Question in Greece and Turkey: A Study in the Contact of Civilizations,* 2nd ed. London: Constable, 1923. Reprint, New York: Howard Fertig, 1970.

Travis, Hannibal. "'Native Christians Massacred': The Ottoman Genocide of the Assyrians during World War I." *Genocide Studies and Prevention* 1, no. 3 (2006): 327–372.

"Treaty of Peace with Turkey," Sèvres, 10 August 1920, *Treaty Series* No. 11 (1920). *American Journal of International Law* 15, no. 3, Supplement: Official Documents (July 1921): 179–181.

Üngör, Uğur Ümit. "Center and Periphery in the Armenian Genocide: The Case of Diyarbekir Province." In *The Armenian Genocide, Turkey and Europe,* ed. Hans-Lukas Kieser and Elmar Plozza, 71–88. Hampshire, UK: Chronos, 2006.

———. *The Making of Modern Turkey: Nation and State in Eastern Anatolia, 1913–1950.* Oxford: Oxford University Press, 2011.

———. "Orphans, Converts, and Prostitutes: Social Consequences of War and Persecution in the Ottoman Empire, 1914–1923." *War in History* 19, no. 2 (2012): 173–192.

———. "'Turkey for the Turks': Demographic Engineering in Eastern Anatolia 1914–1945." In Suny, Goçek, and Naimark, *A Question of Genocide*, 287–305.

Ureneck, Lou. *Smyrna September 1922: The American Mission to Rescue Victims of the 20th Century's First Genocide.* New York: Harper Collins, 2015.

Ürer, Levent. *Azınlıklar ve Lozan Tartışmaları.* Istanbul: Derin Yayınları, n.d.

Ussher, Clarence Douglas, and Grace Higley Knapp. *An American Physician in Turkey: A Narrative of Adventures in Peace and War.* Whitefish, MT: Kessinger, 1917.

Verheij, Jelle. "'Les Frères de terre et d'eau': Sur le rôle des Kurdes dans les massacres arméniens de 1894–1896." *Annales de l'autre Islam* 5 (1998): 225–276.

Vryonis, Speros. *The Mechanism of Catastrophe: The Turkish Pogroms of September 6–7, 1955, and the Destruction of the Greek Community in Istanbul.* Istanbul: Greekworks.com, 2005.

Walder, David. *The Chanak Affair.* London: MacMillan, 1969.

Watenpaugh, Keith David. "'Are There Any Children for Sale?' Genocide and the Transfer of Armenian Children (1915–1922)." *Journal of Human Rights* 12 no. 3 (2013): 283–295.

Werfel, Franz. *The Forty Days of Musa Dagh.* 1933. Boston: Verba Mundi, 2012.

Wharton, Alyson. *The Architects of Ottoman Constantinople: The Balyan Family and the History of Ottoman Architecture.* London: I. B. Tauris, 2015.

Whooley, John. "The Armenian Catholic Church: A Study in History and Ecclesiology." *Heythrop Journal* 45, no. 4 (2004): 416–434.

Winter, Jay. "Under the Cover of War: Genocide in the Context of Total War." In *America and the Armenian Genocide of 1915,* ed. Jay Winter, 37–51. Cambridge: Cambridge University Press, 2004.

Zeidner, Robert F. *The Tricolor over the Taurus: The French in Cilicia and Vicinity 1918–1922.* Ankara: Atatürk Supreme Council for Culture, Language and History, 2005.

Zürcher, Erik J. "How Europeans Adopted Anatolia and Created Turkey." *European Review* 13, no. 3 (2005): 379–394.

———. "Ottoman Labour Battalions in World War I." Unpublished manuscript, n.d., http://www.hist.net/kieser/aghet/Essays/EssayZurcher.html.

———. "Renewal and Silence: Postwar Unionist and Kemalist Rhetoric on the Armenian Genocide." In Suny, Göçek, and Naimark, *A Question of Genocide,* 306–316.

———. *Turkey, a Modern History.* London: I. B. Tauris, 1993.

———. *The Young Turk Legacy and Nation Building: From the Ottoman Empire to Atatürk's Turkey.* London: I. B. Tauris, 2010.

Acknowledgments

We would like to thank Roni Blushtein-Livnon for her effective map-making, which has added considerably to the book; David Rees of Munich, for helping with the translation of German documents; and Rabea Kirmani, of Georgetown University, for helping us locate some of the photographs used in this book.

We would also like to warmly thank Beni Kedar and Heleen van den Berg for reading and commenting on sections of this book, and Eli Shaltiel for reading, commenting, and pushing for translation.

The staffs of the Houghton Library at Harvard University; at the U.S. National Archives in College Park; UK National Archives in Kew, London; at the Prime Minister's Ottoman Archives (Başbakanlık Osmanlı Arşivi) in Istanbul; at the Archives of the Ministère des Affaires Etrangères, La Courneuve, Paris; and at the Service Historique de la Défense, Vincennes, Paris, deserve our deep gratitude for helping find the documentation used in this study. We also thank the Library of Congress, Washington, DC, for their assistance and permission to use photographs from their collections.

We would like to thank Simon Waxman, of Harvard University Press, for carefully copyediting the manuscript, and Anne McGuire for her Sisyphean struggle with our endnotes.

Cheers to Aliza Ouzan-Suissa for assisting with those never-ending administrative tasks.

And last but not least, our heartfelt thanks go to Georges Borchardt for representing us, through thick and thin, and landing us on the welcoming shores of Harvard University Press.

Benny

I would like to thank Chenia and Yuval Carmel for their friendship, hospitality, and help during my stints of research and writing in Washington.

I would like to thank Professors Bob Lieber and Charles King, of Georgetown University, for providing me with the conditions that facilitated writing the last parts of this book.

I would like to thank Harvard University and Professor Michael Brenner and the faculty of Ludwig-Maximilians University in Munich for providing me with the space and time in which to work on the material in this book.

Lastly, I would like to thank my wife, Leah, and my kids, Erel, Yagi, and Orian, for their support during the years of labor on this book.

Dror

I would like to thank Nimrod Hurvitz, Ehud Toledano, Bedross Der Matossian, and many dear Turkish friends—who will remain unnamed—for their advice, smart suggestions, and interest in the project.

Lastly, I would like to thank Dana Poless and my kids, David, Lior, and Omer, for their love, support, and encouragement when the task seemed insurmountable.

Illustration Credits

165   Zeytun, photo by Dror Ze'evi, July 2016.

179   Kemah Gorge, photo by Dror Ze'evi, July 2016.

184   Source: Wikimedia commons, https://upload.wikimedia.org/wikipedia/commons /6/66/Waitingformassacref.png; original source: "Waiting for they know not what," in Aurora Mardiganian, *Ravished Armenia: The Story of Aurora Mardiganian, the Christian Girl Who Lived through the Great Massacres* (New York: Kingfield, 1918), opp. p. 158.

191   "Group photograph of 11, including Hamlin, Parsons, Riggs, Bliss, Schnauffler, etc.," Houghton Library, American Board of Commissioners for Foreign Missions Collection, ABC 78.2, Picture Collection, box 17, folder 3, courtesy of Houghton Library, Harvard University.

196   "Syria—Aleppo—Armenian woman kneeling . . . ," n.d., photographic print by Near East Relief, George Grantham Bain Collection, Prints and Photographs Division, Library of Congress, LOT 10898, LCCN 2006679122.

207   Source: Wikimedia commons, https://commons.wikimedia.org/wiki/File:Armenian _Resistance_-_Urfa_-_July_1915.png; original source: "The civilian Armenians of Urfa who defended themselves against the Turks and the Kurds in July, 1915," in G. Pasdermadjian, *Why Armenia Should Be Free,* trans. Aram Torossian (Boston: Hairenik Publishing Company, 1918).

210   "Red Cross," c. 1915, glass negative, Bain News Service, George Grantham Bain Collection, Prints and Photographs Division, Library of Congress, LCCN 2014707367.

233   "Armenian doctors hanged in public at Haleb / Aleppo, 1916," CPA Media, Pictures from History, Granger Historical Picture Archive, New York, all rights reserved, image no. 0617526.

235   "23 Armenian orphans in Aleppo collected from Kurds and Turks by Karen Jeppe," Archive PL / Alamy Stock Photo, image no. PA2A8W.

239   "The corpses of Armenian citizens massacred by Turkish forces during the Armenian Genocide, c. 1915," CPA Media, Pictures from History, Granger Historical Picture Archive, New York, all rights reserved, image no. 0617486.

267   "Types of British Indian troops . . . ," received 10 August 1920, glass negative, American National Red Cross Collection, Prints and Photographs Division, Library of Congress, LCCN 2017677754.

270   "Armenian refugees," received October 1918, glass negative, American National Red Cross Collection, Prints and Photographs Division, Library of Congress, LCCN 2017669468.

287 "This is the delegation of Turks which was sent to Lausanne . . . ," 1923, photographic print, Frank and Frances Carpenter Collection, Prints and Photographs Division, Library of Congress, LOT 11462, LCCN 90715422.

298 "Refugees waiting for work at Marsavan [i.e. Marsovan]," May 1919, photographic print, American National Red Cross Collection, Prints and Photographs Division, Library of Congress, LCCN 2010650524.

304 "Armenian widows, with children, Turkey," April or May 1909, glass negative, George Grantham Bain Collection, Prints and Photographs Division, Library of Congress, LCCN 2014683948.

317 "Near East relief—Armenian orphans boarding barges at Constantinople, bound for Greece," c. 1915, photographic print by Near East Relief, George Grantham Bain Collection, Prints and Photographs Division, Library of Congress, LOT 10898, LCCN 93515692.

330 "The Turks' bag of game . . . ," February 1919, photographic print, American National Red Cross Collection, Prints and Photographs Division, Library of Congress, LCCN 2010650511.

363 (top) "Near East relief—Armenian orphans being enloaded in barges from Constantinople, bound for Greece," between 1915 and 1916, photographic print, George Grantham Bain Collection, Prints and Photographs Division, Library of Congress, LOT 10898, LCCN 2002717995.

363 (bottom) "Like little French Soldiers," 1915 or 1916, photographic print by Near East Relief, George Grantham Bain Collection, Prints and Photographs Division, Library of Congress, LOT 10898, LCCN 91786367.

418 "'There are smiles.' A typical boy-refugee of Greece, snapped on the streets of Salonica . . . ," received 24 October 1919, glass negative, American National Red Cross Collection, Prints and Photographs Division, Library of Congress, LCCN 2017670368.

431 "Greek irregular volunteers on the frontier, Thessaly, Greece," c. 1897, stereograph, Underwood and Underwood, Prints and Photographs Division, Library of Congress, LOT 11678, LCCN 2003681469.

460 "Turkish officials and little 'sole survivor' of a village of 350, Candia, Crete," c. 1897, stereograph, Underwood and Underwood, Prints and Photographs Division, Library of Congress, LOT 11678, LCCN 2003681473.

Index

Page numbers in *italics* indicate photographs, maps, and tables.